OzZnO22k

MW01097004

Information Systems: A Manager's Guide to Harnessing Technology Version 1.4

By

John Gallaugher

MGkwMTlW

zRqwcsIU

ejr9

zR

flatworld KNOWLEDGE

S-945805-BW-2

9 781453 345788

Information Systems: A Manager's Guide to Harnessing Technology
Version 1.4

John Gallaugher

Published by:

Flat World Knowledge, Inc.
One Bridge Street
Irvington, NY 10533

Brief Contents

Contents

About the Author

John Gallaugher is an associate professor of information systems (IS) at Boston College's Carroll School of Management.

As founding faculty for the Boston College TechTrek West and TechTrek East programs and as co-lead to several of the university's international field study courses, Professor Gallaugher has led his students on scores of master-class visits with executives at firms ranging from Amazon to Zynga. Gallaugher is also co-advisor to the Boston College Venture Competition, an organization whose affiliated businesses have gone on to win entrepreneurship awards at MIT and Yale, gain admittance to the elite Y-Combinator accelerator program, launch multiple products, and raise millions in capital.

A dedicated teacher and active researcher, Professor Gallaugher has been recognized for excellence and innovation in teaching by several organizations, including Boston College, *BusinessWeek*, *Entrepreneur Magazine*, and the Decision Sciences Institute. Professor Gallaugher's research has been published in the *Harvard Business Review*, *MIS Quarterly*, and other leading IS journals. Professor Gallaugher has been a featured speaker at Apple Inc's AcademiX educator conference, and was the keynote speaker at AIBUMA (the African International Business and Management Conference) in Nairobi Kenya. He has consulted for and taught executive seminars for several organizations, including Accenture, Alcoa, Duke Corporate Education, ING, Partners Healthcare, Staples, State Street, the University of Ulster, and the U.S. Information Agency. His comments on business and technology have appeared in the *New York Times*, National Public Radio, *BusinessWeek*, the *Boston Globe*, *Wired*, the Associated Press, Chronicle (WCVB-TV), *The Daily Yomiuri* (Japan), and the *Nation* (Thailand), among others.

Professor Gallaugher publishes additional content related to his teaching and research at http://gallaugher.com. He is also active on twitter at @gallaugher.

Acknowledgments

Sincerest thanks to the cofounders of Flat World Knowledge, Jeff Shelstad and Eric Frank, for their leadership and passion in restructuring the textbook industry and for approaching me to be involved with their efforts. Thanks also to Flat World's dynamite team of editorial, marketing, and sales professionals—in particular to Melissa Yu, Jenn Yee, Sharon Koch, Brett Sullivan, and Michael Boezi.

A tremendous thanks to my student research team at Boston College. In particular, the work of Phil Gill, Xin (Steven) Liu, and Kathie Chang sped things along and helped me fill this project with rich, interesting examples.

I am also deeply grateful to my colleagues at Boston College, especially to my former department chair, Jim Gips, and current department chair, Robert Fichman, for their unwavering support of the project; to Jerry Kane for helping shape the social media section; to Sam Ransbotham for guiding me through the minefield of information security; to Mary Cronin, Peter Olivieri, and Jack Spang for suggestions and encouragement; and to the many administrators who have been so supportive of this effort.

Thanks also to the many alumni, parents, and friends of Boston College who have so generously invited me to bring my students to visit with and learn from them. The East and West Coast leadership of the Boston College Technology Council have played a particularly important role in making this happen. From Bangalore to Boston, Seoul to Silicon Valley, you've provided my students with world-class opportunities, enabling us to meet with scores of CEOs, senior executives, partners, and entrepreneurs. My students and I remain deeply grateful for your commitment and support.

And my enduring thanks to my current and former students, who continue to inspire, impress, and teach me more than I thought possible. It's deeply rewarding to see so many former students return to campus as executive speakers and to host visiting students at their own start-ups. Serving as your professor has been my great privilege.

I would also like to thank the following colleagues who so kindly offered their time and comments while reviewing this work:

- Donald Army, Dominican University of California
- David Bloomquist, Georgia State University
- Teuta Cata, Northern Kentucky University
- Chuck Downing, Northern Illinois University
- John Durand, Pepperdine University
- Marvin Golland, Polytechnic Institute of New York University
- Brandi Guidry, University of Louisiana
- Kiku Jones, The University of Tulsa
- Fred Kellinger, Pennsylvania State University–Beaver Campus
- Ram Kumar, University of North Carolina–Charlotte
- Eric Kyper, Lynchburg College
- Alireza Lari, Fayetteville State University
- Mark Lewis, Missouri Western State University
- Eric Malm, Cabrini College
- Roberto Mejias, University of Arizona
- Esmail Mohebbi, University of West Florida
- John Preston, Eastern Michigan University
- Shu Schiller, Wright State University
- Tod Sedbrook, University of Northern Colorado
- Richard Segall, Arkansas State University
- Ahmad Syamil, Arkansas State University
- Sascha Vitzthum, Illinois Wesleyan University

I'm also grateful to the kindness and insight provided by early adopters of this text. Your comments, encouragement, suggestions, and student feedback were extremely helpful in keeping me focused and motivated on advancing the current edition:

- Animesh Animesh, McGill University
- Michel Benaroch, Syracuse University
- Hanyin Cheng, Morgan Stanley
- Barney Corwin, University of Maryland—College Park
- Lauren B. Eder, Rider University

- Rob Fichman, Boston College
- James Gips, Boston College
- Wolfgang Gatterbauer, Carnegie Mellon University
- Roy Jones, University of Rochester
- Jakob Iverson, University of Wisconsin—Oshkosh
- Jerry Kane, Boston College
- Fred Kellinger, Penn State University—Beaver Campus
- Eric Kyper, Lynchburg College
- Ann Majchrzak, University of Southern California
- Eric Malm, Cabrini College
- Michael Martel, Ohio University
- Ido Millet, Pennsylvania State University—Erie Campus
- Ellen Monk, University of Delaware
- Marius (Florin) Niculescu, Georgia Tech
- Sam Ransbotham, Boston College
- Nachiketa Sahoo, Carnegie Mellon University
- Shu Schiller, Wright State University
- Tom Schambach, Illinois State University
- Avi Seidman, University of Rochester
- Jack Spang, Boston College
- Veda Storey, Georgia State University
- Sascha Vitzthum, Illinois Wesleyan University

Boston College students Courtney Scrib and Nate Dyer also pointed me to examples I've used in this edition, as did ACU student Aaron Andrew. Thanks for thinking of me and for sharing your very useful ideas!

I'll continue to share what I hope are useful insights via my blog, The Week In Geek (http://www.gallaugher.com), and Twitter (@gallaugher). Do feel free to offer comments, encouragement, ideas, and examples for future versions. Sincerest thanks to all who continue to share the word about this project with others. Your continued advocacy helps make this model work!

Dedication

For Ian, Maya, Lily, and Kim—zettabytes of love!

Preface

Thanks for using this book. I very much hope that you enjoy it!

I find the space where business and technology meet to be tremendously exciting, but it's been painful to see the anemic national enrollment trends in tech disciplines. The information systems (IS) course should be the most exciting class within any university. No discipline is having a greater impact on restructuring work, disrupting industries, and creating opportunity. And none more prominently features young people as leaders and visionaries. But far too often students resist rather than embrace the study of tech.

My university has had great success restructuring the way we teach our IS core courses, and much of the material used in this approach has made it into this book. The results we've seen include a fourfold increase in IS enrollments in four years, stellar student ratings for the IS core course, a jump in student placement, an increase in the number of employers recruiting on campus for tech-focused jobs, and the launch of several student-initiated start-ups.

Material in this book is used at both the graduate and undergraduate levels. I think it's a mistake to classify books as focused on just grad or undergrad students. After all, we'd expect our students at all levels to be able to leverage articles in the *Wall Street Journal* or *BusinessWeek*. Why can't our textbooks be equally useful?

You'll also find this work to be written in an unconventional style for a textbook, but hey, why be boring? Let's face it, *Fortune* and *Wired* wouldn't sell a single issue if forced to write with the dry-encyclopedic prose used by most textbooks. Many students and faculty have written with kind words for the tone and writing style used in this book, and it's been incredibly rewarding to hear from students who claim they have actually looked forward to assigned readings and have even read ahead or explored unassigned chapters. I hope you find it to be equally engaging.

The mix of chapter and cases is also meant to provide a holistic view of how technology and business interrelate. Don't look for an "international" chapter, an "ethics" chapter, a "mobile" chapter, or a "systems development and deployment" chapter. Instead, you'll see these topics woven throughout many of our cases and within chapter examples. This is how professionals encounter these topics "in the wild," so we ought to study them not in isolation but as integrated parts of real-world examples. Examples are consumer-focused and Internet-heavy for approachability, but the topics themselves are applicable far beyond the context presented.

Also note that many chapters are meant to be covered across multiple classes. For example, the chapter about Google is in three parts, the one about Netflix is in two, and the one on strategy and technology likely covers more than one lecture as well. Faculty should feel free to pick and choose topics most relevant to their classes, but many will also benefit from the breadth of coverage provided throughout the book. I'd prefer our students to be armed with a comprehensive understanding of topics rather than merely a cursory overview of one siloed area.

There's a lot that's different about this approach, but a lot that's worked exceptionally well, too. I hope that you find the material to be as useful as we have. I also look forward to continually improving this work, and I encourage you to share your ideas with me via Twitter (@gallaugher) or the Web (http://www.gallaugher.com). And if you find the material useful, do let others know, as well. I remain extremely grateful for your interest and support!

Best wishes!

Professor John Gallaugher

Carroll School of Management

Boston College

CHAPTER 1

Setting the Stage: Technology and the Modern Enterprise

1. TECH'S TECTONIC SHIFT: RADICALLY CHANGING BUSINESS LANDSCAPES

LEARNING OBJECTIVE

1. **Appreciate how in recent years, technology has helped bring about radical changes across industries and throughout societies.**

This book is written for a world that has changed radically in the most recent years of your lifetime.

At the start of the prior decade, Google barely existed and well-known strategists dismissed Internet advertising models.[1] By decade's end, Google brought in more advertising revenue than any firm, online or off, and had risen to become the most profitable media company on the planet. Today billions in advertising dollars flee old media and are pouring into digital efforts, and this shift is reshaping industries and redefining skills needed to reach today's consumers.

Prior to the introduction of the iPod, Apple was widely considered a tech industry has-been. Within ten years Apple had grown to be the most valuable firm in the United States, selling more music and generating more profits from mobile device sales than any firm in the world.

Moore's Law and other factors that make technology faster and cheaper have thrust computing and telecommunications into the hands of billions in ways that are both empowering the poor and poisoning the planet.

Social media barely warranted a mention a decade ago, but today, Facebook's user base is larger than any nation, save for China and India. Firms are harnessing social media for new product ideas and for millions in sales. But with promise comes peril. When mobile phones are cameras just a short hop from YouTube, Flickr, and Twitter, every ethical lapse can be captured, every customer service flaw graffiti-tagged on the permanent record that is the Internet. The service and ethics bar for today's manager has never been higher. Social media has also emerged as a catalyst for global change, with Facebook and Twitter playing key organizing roles in uprisings worldwide. While a status update alone won't depose a dictator, technology can capture injustice, broadcast it to the world, disseminate ideas, and rally the far-reaching.

Speaking of globalization, China started the prior decade largely as a nation unplugged and offline. But today China has more Internet users than any other country and has spectacularly launched several publicly traded Internet firms including Baidu, Tencent, and Alibaba. By 2009, China Mobile was more valuable than all but two U.S. corporations. Think the United States holds the number one ranking in home broadband access? Not even close—the United States is ranked fifteenth.[2]

The world's second most populous nation, India, has ridden technology to become a global IT powerhouse. In two decades, India's tech sector has grown from "almost nothing" to a $73 billion industry, expanding even during the recent global recession. Technology has enabled the once almost-exclusively-agrarian nation to become a go-to destination for R&D and engineering across sectors as far-flung as aircraft engine design, medical devices, telecom equipment, and microprocessors.[3]

The way we conceive of software and the software industry is also changing radically. IBM, HP, and Oracle are among the firms that collectively pay thousands of programmers to write code that is then given away for free. Today, open source software powers most of the Web sites you visit. And the rise of open source has rewritten the revenue models for the computing industry and lowered computing costs for start-ups to blue chips worldwide.

Cloud computing and software as a service are turning sophisticated, high-powered computing into a utility available to even the smallest businesses and nonprofits.

Many organizations today collect and seek insights from massive datasets, which are often referred to as “Big Data.” Data analytics and business intelligence are driving discovery and innovation, redefining modern marketing, and creating a shifting knife-edge of privacy concerns that can shred corporate reputations if mishandled.

And the pervasiveness of computing has created a set of security and espionage threats unimaginable to the prior generation.

As recent years have shown, tech creates both treasure and tumult. These disruptions aren’t going away and will almost certainly accelerate, impacting organizations, careers, and job functions throughout your lifetime. It’s time to place tech at the center of the managerial playbook.

KEY TAKEAWAYS

- In the prior decade, firms like Google and Facebook have created profound shifts in the way firms advertise and individuals and organizations communicate.
- New technologies have fueled globalization, redefined our concepts of software and computing, crushed costs, fueled data-driven decision making, and raised privacy and security concerns.

QUESTIONS AND EXERCISES

1. Visit a finance Web site such as http://www.google.com/finance. Compare Google’s profits to those of other major media companies. How have Google’s profits changed over the past few years? Why have the profits changed? How do these compare with changes in the firm you chose?
2. How is social media impacting firms, individuals, and society?
3. How do recent changes in computing impact consumers? Are these changes good or bad? Explain. How do they impact businesses?
4. What kinds of skills do today’s managers need that weren’t required a decade ago?
5. Work with your instructor to decide ways in which your class can use social media. For example, you might create a Facebook group where you can share ideas with your classmates, join Twitter and create a hash tag for your class, or create a course wiki. (See Chapter 7 for more on these and other services.)

2. IT’S YOUR REVOLUTION

LEARNING OBJECTIVE

1. **Name firms across hardware, software, and Internet businesses that were founded by people in their twenties (or younger).**

The intersection where technology and business meet is both terrifying and exhilarating. But if you’re under the age of thirty, realize that this is *your* space. While the fortunes of any individual or firm rise and fall over time, it’s abundantly clear that many of the world’s most successful technology firms—organizations that have had tremendous impact on consumers and businesses across industries—were created by young people. Consider just a few:

Bill Gates was an undergraduate when he left college to found Microsoft—a firm that would eventually become the world’s largest software firm and catapult Gates to the top of the *Forbes* list of world’s wealthiest people (enabling him to also become the most generous philanthropist of our time).

FIGURE 1.1

Young Bill Gates appears in a mug shot for a New Mexico traffic violation. Microsoft, now headquartered in Washington State, had its roots in New Mexico when Gates and partner Paul Allen moved there to be near early PC maker Altair.

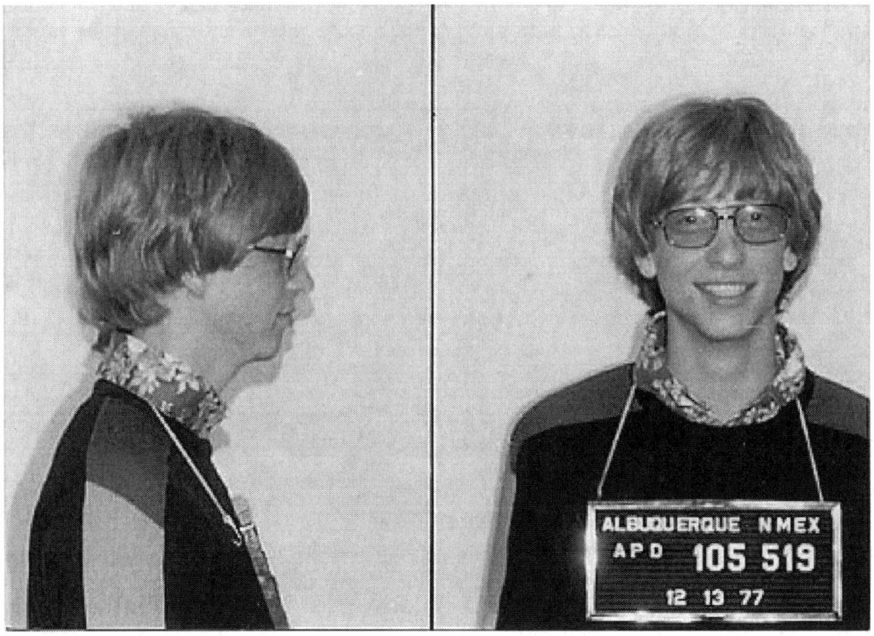

Source: Wikimedia Commons.

Michael Dell was just a sophomore when he began building computers in his dorm room at the University of Texas. His firm would one day claim the top spot among PC manufacturers worldwide.

Mark Zuckerberg founded Facebook as a nineteen-year-old college sophomore.

Steve Jobs was just twenty-one when he founded Apple.

Tony Hsieh proved his entrepreneurial chops when, at twenty-four, he sold LinkExchange to Microsoft for over a quarter of a billion dollars.[4] He'd later serve as CEO of Zappos, eventually selling that firm to Amazon for $900 million.[5]

Sergey Brin and Larry Page were both twenty-something doctoral students at Stanford University when they founded Google. So were Jerry Yang and David Filo of Yahoo! All would become billionaires.

Andrew Mason of Groupon and Steve Chen and Chad Hurley of YouTube were all in their late twenties when they launched their firms. Jeff Bezos hadn't yet reached thirty when he began working on what would eventually become Amazon.

Of course, those folks would seem downright ancient to Catherine Cook, who founded MyYearbook.com, a firm that at one point grew to become the third most popular social network in the United States and eventually sold for $100 million.[6] Cook started the firm when she was a sophomore—in high school.

This trend will almost certainly accelerate. We're in a golden age of tech entrepreneurship where "the cloud" means a startup can rent the computing resources one previously had to buy at great expense; where app stores give code jockeys immediate, nearly zero-cost distribution to a potential market of hundreds of millions of people worldwide; and where social media done right can virally spread awareness of a firm with nary a dime of conventional ad spending. Crafting a breakout hit is tough, but the jackpot can be immense. Kevin Systrom was 26 when he founded the photo-sharing service Instagram. In just 18 months, his 13-person startup garnered 35 million users worldwide, 5 million Android users in just a single week, and sold to Facebook for a cool $1 billion. Systrom's take? $400 million.[7]

But you don't have to build a successful firm to have an impact as a tech revolutionary. Shawn Fanning's Napster, widely criticized as a piracy playground, was written when he was just nineteen. Fanning's code was the first significant salvo in the tech-fueled revolution that brought about an upending of the entire music industry. Finland's Linus Torvals wrote the first version of the Linux operating system when he was just twenty-one. Today Linux has grown to be the most influential component of the open source arsenal, powering everything from cell phones to supercomputers.

TechCrunch crows that Internet entrepreneurs are like pro athletes—"they peak around [age] 25."[8] *BusinessWeek* regularly runs a list of America's Best Young Entrepreneurs—the top twenty-five aged twenty-five and under. *Inc.* magazine's list of the Coolest Young Entrepreneurs is subtitled the "30 under 30." While not exclusively filled with the ranks of tech start-ups, both of these lists are nonetheless dominated with technology entrepreneurs. Whenever you see young people on the cover of a business magazine, it's almost certainly because they've done something groundbreaking with technology. The generals and foot soldiers of the technology revolution are filled with the ranks of the young, some not even old enough to legally have a beer. For the old-timers reading this, all is not lost, but you'd best get cracking with technology, quick. Junior might be on the way to either eat your lunch or be your next boss.

KEY TAKEAWAYS

- Recognize that anyone reading this book has the potential to build an impactful business: Entrepreneurship has no minimum age requirement.
- The ranks of technology revolutionaries are filled with young people, with several leading firms and innovations launched by entrepreneurs who started while roughly the age of the average university student.

QUESTIONS AND EXERCISES

1. Look online for lists of young entrepreneurs. How many of these firms are tech firms or heavily rely on technology? Are there any sectors more heavily represented than tech?
2. Have you ever thought of starting your own tech-enabled business? Brainstorm with some friends. What kinds of ideas do you think might make a good business?
3. How have the costs of entrepreneurship changed over the past decade? What forces are behind these changes? What does this mean for the future of entrepreneurship?
4. Many universities and regions have competitions for entrepreneurs (e.g., business plan competitions, elevator pitch competitions). Does your school have such a program? What are the criteria for participation? If your school doesn't have one, consider forming such a program.
5. Research business accelerator programs such as Y-Combinator, TechStars, and DreamIt. Do you have a program like this in your area? What do entrepreneurs get from participating in these programs? What do they give up? Do you think these programs are worth it? Why or why not? Have you ever used a product or service from a firm that has participated in one of these programs?
6. Explore online for lists of resources for entrepreneurship. Share links to these resources using social media created for class.
7. Have any alumni from your institution founded technology firms or risen to positions of prominence in tech-focused careers? If so, work with your professor to invite them to come speak to your class or to student groups on campus. Your career services, development (alumni giving), alumni association, and LinkedIn searches may be able to help uncover potential speakers.

3. GEEK UP—TECH IS EVERYWHERE AND YOU'LL NEED IT TO THRIVE

LEARNING OBJECTIVES

1. **Appreciate the degree to which technology has permeated every management discipline.**
2. **See that tech careers are varied, richly rewarding, and poised for continued growth.**

Shortly after the start of the prior decade, there was a lot of concern that tech jobs would be outsourced, leading many to conclude that tech skills carried less value and that workers with tech backgrounds had little to offer. Turns out this thinking was stunningly wrong. Tech jobs boomed, and as technology pervades all other management disciplines, tech skills are becoming more important, not less. Today, tech knowledge can be a key differentiator for the job seeker. It's the worker without tech skills that needs to be concerned.

As we'll present in depth in a future chapter, there's a principle called Moore's Law that's behind fast, cheap computing. And as computing gets both faster and cheaper, it gets "baked into" all sorts of products and shows up everywhere: in your pocket, in your vacuum, and on the radio frequency identification (RFID) tags that track your luggage at the airport.

Well, there's also a sort of Moore's Law corollary that's taking place with people, too. As technology becomes faster and cheaper and developments like open source software, cloud computing, software as a service (SaaS), and outsourcing push technology costs even lower, tech skills are being embedded inside more and more job functions. What this means is that even if you're not expecting to become the next Tech Titan, your career will doubtless be shaped by the forces of technology. Make no mistake about it—there isn't a single modern managerial discipline that isn't being deeply and profoundly impacted by tech.

3.1 Finance

Many business school students who study finance aspire to careers in investment banking. Many i-bankers will work on IPOs (initial public stock offerings), in effect helping value companies the first time these firms wish to sell their stock on the public markets. IPO markets need new firms, and the tech industry is a fertile ground that continually sprouts new businesses like no other. Other i-bankers will be involved in valuing merger and acquisition (M&A) deals, and tech firms are active in this space, too. Leading tech firms are flush with cash and constantly on the hunt for new firms to acquire. Over the past five years, Google has bought a whopping 103 firms, IBM has bought sixty-four, Microsoft has bought sixty-three, Cisco has bought fifty-seven, and Intel has bought forty-eight![9] And even in nontech industries, technology impacts nearly every endeavor as an opportunity catalyst or a disruptive wealth destroyer. The aspiring investment banker who doesn't understand the role of technology in firms and industries can't possibly provide an accurate guess at how much a company is worth.

TABLE 1.1 2011 Tech Deals by Sector

Sector	Deals	Value (millions)
Software	93	$40,770
IT Services	51	$19,286
Internet	71	$22,896
Hardware	53	$17,101
Semiconductor	40	$25,059

Source: "US Technology M&A Insights 2012," PwC, March 2012.

TABLE 1.2 Acquisition Deals by Firm

Company	Deals	Value (millions)
Hewlett-Packard Co.	39	$36,841
Oracle Corp.	47	$25,083
Google, Inc.	103	$22,074
Microsoft Corp.	63	$19,864
Cisco Systems, Inc.	57	$17,634
IBM Corp.	64	$12,476
Intel Corp.	48	$10,889
Dell, Inc.	25	$8,665

Source: The Deal, May 7, 2012

Those in other finance careers will be lending to tech firms and evaluating the role of technology in firms in an investment portfolio. Most of you will want to consider tech's role as part of your personal investments. And modern finance simply wouldn't exist without tech. When someone arranges for a bridge to be built in Shanghai, those funds aren't carried over in a suitcase—they're digitally transferred from bank to bank. And forces of technology blasted open the two-hundred-year-old floor trading mechanism of the New York Stock Exchange, in effect forcing the NYSE to sell shares in itself to finance the acquisition of technology-based trading platforms that were threatening to replace it. As another example of the importance of tech in finance, consider that Boston-based Fidelity Investments, one of the nation's largest mutual fund firms, spends roughly $2.8 billion a year on technology. Tech isn't a commodity for finance—it's the discipline's lifeblood.

3.2 Accounting

Sarbanes-Oxley Act

Also known as Sarbox or SOX; U.S. legislation enacted in the wake of the accounting scandals of the early 2000s. The act raises executive and board responsibility and ties criminal penalties to certain accounting and financial violations. Although often criticized, SOX is also seen as raising stakes for mismanagement and misdeeds related to a firm's accounting practices.

If you're an accountant, your career is built on a foundation of technology. The numbers used by accountants are all recorded, stored, and reported by information systems, and the reliability of any audit is inherently tied to the reliability of the underlying technology. Increased regulation, such as the heavy executive penalties tied to the **Sarbanes-Oxley Act** in the United States, have ratcheted up the importance of making sure accountants (and executives) get their numbers right. Negligence could mean jail time. This means the link between accounting and tech have never been tighter, and the stakes for ensuring systems accuracy have never been higher.

Business students might also consider that while accounting firms regularly rank near the top of *BusinessWeek*'s "Best Places to Start Your Career" list, many of the careers at these firms are highly tech-centric. Every major accounting firm has spawned a tech-focused consulting practice, and in many cases, these firms have grown to be larger than the accounting services functions from which they sprang. Today, Deloitte's tech-centric consulting division is larger than the firm's audit, tax, and risk practices. At the time of its spin-off, Accenture was larger than the accounting practice at former parent Arthur Andersen (Accenture executives are also grateful they split before Andersen's collapse in the wake of the prior decade's accounting scandals). Now, many accounting firms that had previously spun off technology practices are once again building up these functions, finding strong similarities between the skills of an auditor and skills needed in emerging disciplines such as information security and privacy.

3.3 Marketing

Technology has thrown a grenade onto the marketing landscape, and as a result, the skill set needed by today's marketers is radically different from what was leveraged by the prior generation. Online channels have provided a way to track and monitor consumer activities, and firms are leveraging this insight to understand how to get the right product to the right customer, through the right channel, with the right message, at the right price, at the right time. The success or failure of a campaign can often be immediately assessed based on online activity such as Web site visit patterns and whether a campaign results in an online purchase.

The ability to track customers, analyze campaign results, and modify tactics has amped up the return on investment of marketing dollars, with firms increasingly shifting spending from tough-to-track media such as print, radio, and television to the Web.[10] And new channels continue to emerge. Firms as diverse as Southwest Airlines, Starbucks, UPS, and Zara have introduced apps for the iPhone, iPad, and iPod touch. In roughly four years, iOS devices are now in the hands, backpacks, purses, and pockets of over 200 million people worldwide, delivering location-based messages and services and even allowing for cashless payment.[11]

The rise of social media is also part of this blown-apart marketing landscape. Now all customers can leverage an enduring and permanent voice, capable of broadcasting word-of-mouth influence in ways that can benefit and harm a firm. Savvy firms are using social media to generate sales, improve their reputations, better serve customers, and innovate. Those who don't understand this landscape risk being embarrassed, blindsided, and out of touch with their customers.

Search engine marketing (SEM), search engine optimization (SEO), customer relationship management (CRM), personalization systems, and a sensitivity to managing the delicate balance between gathering and leveraging data and respecting consumer privacy are all central components of the new marketing toolkit. And there's no looking back—tech's role in marketing will only grow in prominence.

3.4 Operations

A firm's operations management function is focused on producing goods and services, and operations students usually get the point that tech is the key to their future. Quality programs, process redesign, supply chain management, factory automation, and service operations are all tech-centric. These points are underscored in this book as we introduce several examples of how firms have designed fundamentally different ways of conducting business (and even entirely different industries), where value and competitive advantage are created through technology-enabled operations.

3.5 Human Resources

Technology helps firms harness the untapped power of employees. Knowledge management systems are morphing into social media technologies—social networks, wikis, and Twitter-style messaging systems that can accelerate the ability of a firm to quickly organize and leverage teams of experts. And crowdsourcing tools and question-and-answer sites like Quora allow firms to reach out for expertise beyond their organizations. Human resources (HR) directors are using technology for employee training, screening, and evaluation. The accessibility of end-user technology means that every employee can reach the public, creating an imperative for firms to set policy on issues such as firm representation and disclosure and to continually monitor and enforce policies as well as capture and push out best practices. The successful HR manager recognizes that technology continually changes an organization's required skill sets as well as employee expectations.

The hiring and retention practices of the prior generation are also in flux. Recruiting hasn't just moved online; it's now grounded in information systems that scour databases for specific skill sets, allowing recruiters to cast a wider talent net than ever before. Job seekers are writing résumés with keywords in mind, aware that the first cut is likely made by a database search program, not a human being. The rise of professional social networks also puts added pressure on employee satisfaction and retention. Prior HR managers fiercely guarded employee directories for fear that a headhunter or competitive firm might raid top talent. Now the equivalent of a corporate directory can be easily pulled up via LinkedIn, a service complete with discrete messaging capabilities that can allow competitors to rifle-scope target your firm's best and brightest. Thanks to technology, the firm that can't keep employees happy, engaged, and feeling valued has never been more vulnerable.

3.6 The Law

And for those looking for careers in corporate law, many of the hottest areas involve technology. Intellectual property, patents, piracy, and privacy are all areas where activity has escalated dramatically in recent years. The number of U.S. patent applications waiting approval has tripled in the past decade, while China saw a threefold increase in patent applications in just five years.[12] Firms planning to leverage new inventions and business methods need legal teams with the skills to sleuth out whether a firm can legally do what it plans to. Others will need legal expertise to help them protect proprietary methods and content, as well as to help enforce claims in the home country and abroad.

3.7 Information Systems Careers

While the job market goes through ebbs and flows, recent surveys have shown there to be more IT openings than in any field except health care.[13] *Money* magazine ranked tech jobs as two of the top five "Best Jobs in America."[14] Tech jobs make up five of the top 10 "Best Jobs" on the *US News* list.[15] *BusinessWeek* ranks consulting (which heavily hires tech grads) and technology as the second and third highest paying industries for recent college graduates.[16] Technology careers have actually ranked among the safest careers to have during the most recent downturn.[17] And *Fortune*'s ranks of the "Best Companies to Work For" is full of technology firms and has been topped by a tech business for six years straight.[18]

Students studying technology can leverage skills in ways that range from the highly technical to those that emphasize a tech-centric use of other skills. And why be restricted to just the classes taught on campus? Resources like iTunes U., CodeAcademy, Udemy, edX, YouTube, and others provide a smorgasbord of learning where the smart and motivated can geek up. The high demand for scarce technical talent has led many tech firms to offer six-figure starting salaries to graduating seniors from top universities.[19] Opportunities for programmers abound, particularly for those versed in new technologies. But there are also non-programming roles for experts in areas such as user-interface design (who work to make sure systems are easy to use), process design (who leverage technology to make firms more efficient), and strategy (who specialize in technology for competitive advantage). Nearly every large organization has its own information systems department. That group not only ensures that systems get built and keep running but also increasingly takes on strategic roles targeted at proposing solutions for how technology can give the firm a competitive edge. Career paths allow for developing expertise in a particular technology (e.g., business intelligence analyst, database administrator, social media manager), while project management careers leverage skills in taking projects from idea through deployment.

Even in consulting firms, careers range from hard-core programmers who "build stuff" to analysts who do no programming but might work identifying problems and developing a solutions blueprint that is then turned over to another team to code. Careers at tech giants like Apple, Google, and Microsoft don't all involve coding end-user programs either. Each of these firms has their own client-facing staff that works with customers and partners to implement solutions. Field engineers at these firms may work as part of a sales team to show how a given company's software and services can be used. These engineers often put together prototypes that are then turned over to a client's in-house staff for further development. An Apple field engineer might show how a firm can leverage podcasting in its organization, while a Google field engineer can help a firm incorporate search, banner, and video ads into its online efforts. Careers that involve consulting and field engineering are often particularly attractive for those who enjoy working with an ever-changing list of clients and problems across various industries and in many different geographies.

Upper-level career opportunities are also increasingly diverse. Consultants can become partners who work with the most senior executives of client firms, helping identify opportunities for those organizations to become more effective. Within a firm, technology specialists can rise to be chief information officer or chief technology officer—positions focused on overseeing a firm's information systems development and deployment. And many firms are developing so-called *C-level* specialties in emerging areas with a technology focus, such as chief information security officer (CISO), and chief privacy officer (CPO). Senior technology positions may also be a ticket to the chief executive's suite. A recent *Fortune* article pointed out how the prominence of technology provides a training ground for executives to learn the breadth and depth of a firm's operations and an understanding of the ways in which firms are vulnerable to attack and where it can leverage opportunities for growth.[20]

3.8 Your Future

With tech at the center of so much change, realize that you may very well be preparing for careers that don't yet exist. But by studying the intersection of business and technology today, you develop a base to build upon and critical thinking skills that will help you evaluate new, emerging technologies. Think you can afford to wait on tech study then quickly get up to speed? Whom do you expect to have an easier time adapting and leveraging a technology like social media—today's college students who are immersed in technology or their parents who are embarrassingly dipping their toes into the waters of Facebook? Those who put off an understanding of technology risk being left in the dust.

Consider the nontechnologists who have tried to enter the technology space these past few years. News Corp. head Rupert Murdoch piloted his firm to the purchase of MySpace only to see this one-time leader lose share to rivals.[21] Former Warner executive Terry Semel presided over Yahoo!'s[22] malaise as Google blasted past it. Barry Diller, the man widely credited with creating the Fox Network, led InterActive Corp. (IAC) in the acquisition of a slew of tech firms ranging from Expedia to Ask.com, only to break the empire up as it foundered.[23] And Time Warner head Jerry Levin presided over the acquisition of AOL, executing what many consider to be one of the most disastrous mergers in U.S. business history.[24] Contrast these guys against the technology-centric successes of Mark Zuckerberg (Facebook), Steve Jobs (Apple), and Sergey Brin and Larry Page (Google).

While we'll make it abundantly clear that a focus solely on technology is a recipe for disaster, a business perspective that lacks an appreciation for tech's role is also likely to be doomed. At this point in history, technology and business are inexorably linked, and those not trained to evaluate and make decisions in this ever-shifting space risk irrelevance, marginalization, and failure.

KEY TAKEAWAYS

- As technology becomes cheaper and more powerful, it pervades more industries and is becoming increasingly baked into what were once nontech functional areas.
- Technology is impacting every major business discipline, including finance, accounting, marketing, operations, human resources, and the law.
- Tech jobs rank among the best and highest-growth positions, and tech firms rank among the best and highest-paying firms to work for.
- Information systems (IS) jobs are profoundly diverse, ranging from those that require heavy programming skills to those that are focused on design, process, project management, privacy, and strategy.

QUESTIONS AND EXERCISES

1. Look at *Fortune*'s "Best Companies to Work For" list. How many of these firms are technology firms? Which firm would you like to work for? Are they represented on this list?
2. Look at *BusinessWeek*'s "Best Places to Start Your Career" list. Is the firm you mentioned above also on this list?
3. What are you considering studying? What are your short-term and long-term job goals? What role will technology play in that career path? What should you be doing to ensure that you have the skills needed to compete?
4. Which jobs that exist today likely won't exist at the start of the next decade? Based on your best guess on how technology will develop, can you think of jobs and skill sets that will likely emerge as critical five and ten years from now?

4. THE PAGES AHEAD

LEARNING OBJECTIVE

1. **Understand the structure of this text, the issues and examples that will be introduced, and why they are important.**

Hopefully this first chapter has helped get you excited for what's to come. The text is written in a style meant to be as engaging as the material you'll be reading for the rest of your management career—articles in business magazines and newspapers. The introduction of concepts in this text are also example rich, and every concept introduced or technology discussed is always grounded in a real-world example to show why it's important. But also know that while we celebrate successes and expose failures in that space where business and technology come together, we also recognize that firms and circumstances change. Today's winners have no guarantee of sustained dominance. What you should acquire in the pages that follow are a fourfold set of benefits that (1) provide a description of what's happening in industry today, (2) offer an introduction to key business and technology concepts, (3) offer a durable set of concepts and frameworks that can be applied even as technologies and industries change, and (4) develop critical thinking that will serve you well throughout your career as a manager.

Chapters don't have to be read in order, so feel free to bounce around, if you'd like. But here's what you can expect:

Chapter 2 focuses on building big-picture skills to think about how to leverage technology for competitive advantage. Technology alone is rarely the answer, but through a rich set of examples, we'll show how firms can weave technology into their operations in ways that create and reinforce resources that can garner profits while repelling competitors. A mini case examines tech's role at FreshDirect, a firm that has defied the many failures in the online grocery space and devastated traditional rivals. BlueNile, Cisco, Dell, TiVo and Yahoo! are among the many firms providing a rich set of examples illustrating successes and failures in leveraging technology. The chapter will show how firms use technology to create and leverage brand, scale economies, switching costs, data assets, network effects, and distribution channels. We'll introduce how technology relates to two popular management frameworks—the value chain and the five forces model. And we'll provide a solid decision framework for considering the controversial and often misunderstood role that technology plays among firms that seek an early-mover advantage.

In Chapter 3, we see how a tech-fed value chain helped Spanish clothing giant Zara craft a counterintuitive model that seems to defy all conventional wisdom in the fashion industry. We'll show how Zara's model differs radically from that of the firm it displaced to become the world's top clothing retailer: Gap. We'll show how technology impacts product design, product development, marketing, cycle time, inventory management, and customer loyalty and how technology decisions influence broad profitability that goes way beyond the cost-of-goods thinking common among many retailers. We'll also offer a mini case on Fair Factories Clearinghouse, an effort highlighting the positive role of technology in improving ethical business practices. Another mini case shows the difference between thinking about technology versus broad thinking about systems, all through an examination of how high-end fashion house Prada failed to roll out technology that on the surface seemed very similar to Zara's.

Chapter 4 studies Neflix in two parts. The first half of the chapter tramples the notion that dot-com start-up firms can't compete against large, established rivals. We'll show how information systems at Netflix created a set of assets that grew in strength and remains difficult for rivals to match. The economics of pure-play versus brick-and-mortar firms is examined, and we'll introduce managerial thinking on various concepts such as the data asset, personalization systems (recommendation engines and collaborative filtering), the long tail and the implications of technology on selection and inventory, crowdsourcing, using technology for novel revenue models (subscription and revenue-sharing with suppliers), forecasting, and inventory management. The second part of the chapter covers Netflix's uncertain future, where we present how the shift from atoms (physical discs) to bits (streaming and downloads) creates additional challenges. Issues of digital products, licensing and partnerships, revenue models, and delivery platforms are all discussed.

Chapter 5 focuses on understanding the implications of technology change for firms and society. The chapter offers accessible definitions for technologies impacted by Moore's Law, but goes beyond semiconductors and silicon to show how the rate of magnetic storage (e.g., hard drives) and networking create markets filled with uncertainty and opportunity. The chapter will show how tech has enabled the rise of Apple and Amazon, created mobile phone markets that empower the poor worldwide, and has created five waves of disruptive innovation over five decades. We'll also show how Moore's Law, perhaps the greatest economic gravy train in history, will inevitably run out of steam as the three demons of heat, power, and limits on shrinking transistors halt the advancement of current technology. Studying technologies that "extend" Moore's Law, such as multicore semiconductors, helps illustrate both the benefit and limitation of technology options, and in doing so, helps develop skills around recognizing the pros and cons of a given innovation. Supercomputing, grid, and cloud computing are introduced through examples that show how these advances are changing the economics of computing and creating new opportunity. Finally, issues of e-waste are explored in a way that shows that firms not only need to consider the ethics of product sourcing, but also the ethics of disposal.

In Chapter 6, we'll see how technologies, services, and platforms can create nearly insurmountable advantages. Tech firms from Facebook to Intel to Microsoft are dominant because of network effects—the idea that some products and services get more valuable as more people use them. Studying network effects creates better decision makers. The concept is at the heart of technology standards and platform competition, and understanding network effects can help managers choose technologies that are likely to win, hopefully avoiding getting caught with a failed, poorly supported system. Students learn how network effects work and why they're difficult to unseat. The chapter ends with an example-rich discussion of various techniques that one can use to compete in markets where network effects are present.

Peer production and social media have created some of the Internet's most popular destinations and most rapidly growing firms, and they are empowering the voice of the customer as never before. In Chapter 7, students learn about various technologies used in social media and peer production, including blogs, wikis, social networking, Twitter, and more. Prediction markets and crowdsourcing are introduced, along with examples of how firms are leveraging these concepts for insight and innovation. Finally, students are offered guidance on how firms can think SMART by creating a social media awareness and response team. Issues of training, policy, and response are introduced, and technologies for monitoring and managing online reputations are discussed.

Chapter 8 will allow us to study success and failure in IS design and deployment by examining one of the Web's hottest firms. Facebook is one of the most accessible and relevant Internet firms to so many, but it's also a wonderful laboratory to discuss critical managerial concepts. The founding story of Facebook introduces concepts of venture capital, the board of directors, and the role of network effects in entrepreneurial control. Feeds show how information, content, and applications can spread virally, but also introduce privacy concerns. Facebook's strength in switching costs demonstrates how it has been able to envelop additional markets from photos to chat to video and more. The failure of the Beacon system shows how even bright technologists can fail if they ignore the broader procedural and user implications of an information systems rollout. Social networking advertising is contrasted with search, and the perils of advertising alongside social media content are introduced. Issues of predictors and privacy are covered. And the case allows for a broader discussion on firm value and what Facebook might really be worth.

Chapter 9 offers a primer to help managers better understand what software is all about. The chapter offers a brief introduction to software technologies. Students learn about operating systems, application software, and how these relate to each other. Enterprise applications are introduced, and the alphabet soup of these systems (e.g., ERP, CRM, and SCM) is accessibly explained. Various forms of distributed systems (client-server, Web services, messaging) are also covered. The chapter provides a managerial overview of how software is developed, offers insight into the importance of Java and scripting languages, and explains the differences between compiled and interpreted systems. System failures, total cost of ownership, and project risk mitigation are also introduced. The array of concepts covered helps a manager understand the bigger picture and should provide an underlying appreciation for how systems work that will serve even as technologies change and new technologies are introduced.

The software industry is changing radically, and that's the focus of Chapter 10. The issues covered in this chapter are front and center for any firm making technology decisions. We'll cover open source software, software as a service, hardware clouds, and virtualization. Each topic is introduced by discussing advantages, risks, business models, and examples of their effective use. The chapter ends by introducing issues that a manager must consider when making decisions as to whether to purchase technology, contract or outsource an effort, or develop an effort in-house.

In Chapter 11, we'll study data, which is often an organization's most critical asset. Data lies at the heart of every major discipline, including marketing, accounting, finance, operations, forecasting, and planning. We'll help managers understand how data is created, organized, and effectively used. We'll cover limitations in data sourcing, issues in privacy and regulation, and tools for access, including various business intelligence technologies. A mini case on Wal-Mart shows data's use in empowering a firm's entire value chain, while the mini case on Caesars Entertainment (formerly known as Harrah's) shows how data-driven customer relationship management is at the center of creating an industry giant.

Chapter 12 unmasks the mystery of the Internet—it shows how the Internet works and why a manager should care about IP addresses, IP networking, the DNS, peering, and packet versus circuit switching. We'll also cover last-mile technologies and the various strengths and weaknesses of getting a faster Internet to a larger population. The revolution in mobile technologies and the impact on business will also be presented.

Chapter 13 helps managers understand attacks and vulnerabilities and how to keep end users and organizations more secure. The ever-increasing number of megabreaches at firms that now include TJX, Heartland, Epsilon, Sony, and even security firm RSA, plus the increasing vulnerability of end-user systems, have highlighted how information security is now the concern of the entire organization, from senior executives to frontline staff. This chapter explains what's happening with respect to information security—what kinds of attacks are occurring, who is doing them, and what their motivation is. We'll uncover the source of vulnerabilities in systems: human, procedural, and technical. Hacking concepts such as botnets, malware, phishing, and SQL injection are explained using plain, accessible language. Also presented are techniques to improve information security both as an end user and within an organization. The combination of current issues and their relation to a broader framework for security should help you think about vulnerabilities even as technologies and exploits change over time.

Chapter 14 discusses one of the most influential and far-reaching firms in today's business environment. As pointed out earlier, a decade ago Google barely existed, but it now earns more ad revenue and is a more profitable media company than any firm, online or off. Google is a major force in modern marketing, research, and entertainment. In this chapter you'll learn how Google (and Web search in general) works. Issues of search engine ranking, optimization, and search infrastructure are introduced. Students gain an understanding of search advertising and other advertising techniques, ad revenue models such as CPM and CPC, online advertising networks, various methods of customer profiling (e.g., IP addresses, geotargeting, cookies), click fraud, fraud prevention, and issues related to privacy and regulation. The chapter concludes with a broad discussion of how Google is evolving (e.g., Android, Chrome, Apps, YouTube) and how this evolution is bringing it into conflict with several well-funded rivals, including Amazon, Apple, Microsoft, and more.

Nearly every industry and every functional area is increasing its investment in and reliance on information technology. With opportunity comes trade-offs: research has shown that a high level of IT investment is associated with a more frenzied competitive environment.[25] But while the future is uncertain, we don't have the luxury to put on the brakes or dial back the clock—tech's impact is here to stay. Those firms that emerge as winners will treat IT efforts "as opportunities to define and deploy new ways of working, rather than just projects to install, configure, or integrate."[26] The examples, concepts, and frameworks in the pages that follow will help you build the tools and decision-making prowess needed for victory.

KEY TAKEAWAYS

- This text contains a series of chapters and cases that expose durable concepts, technologies, and frameworks, and does so using cutting-edge examples of what's happening in industry today.
- While firms and technologies will change, and success at any given point in time is no guarantee of future victory, the issues illustrated and concepts acquired should help shape a manager's decision making in a way that will endure.

QUESTIONS AND EXERCISES

1. Which firms do you most admire today? How do these firms use technology? Do you think technology gives them an advantage over rivals? Why or why not?
2. What areas covered in this book are most exciting? Most intimidating? Which do you think will be most useful?

ENDNOTES

1. M. Porter, "Strategy and the Internet," *Harvard Business Review* 79, no. 3 (March 2001): 62–78.
2. S. Shankland, "Google to Test Ultrafast Broadband to the Home," *CNET*, February 10, 2010.
3. V. Wadhwa, "Indian Technology's Fourth Wave," *BusinessWeek*, December 8, 2010.
4. M. Chafkin, "The Zappos Way of Managing," *Inc.*, May 1, 2009.
5. S. Lacy, "Amazon Buys Zappos; The Price Is $928m., Not $847m.," *TechCrunch*, July 22, 2009.
6. A. Shontell, "This 21-Year-Old Just Sold Her Startup For $100 Million," *BusinessInsider*, July 20, 2011.
7. J. Guynn, "Insta-Rich: How Instagram Becaome a $1 Billion Compnay in 18 Months," *Los Angeles Times*, April 20, 2012.
8. M. Arrington, "Internet Entrepreneurs Are Like Professional Athletes, They Peak Around 25," *TechCrunch*, April 30, 2011.
9. S. Miller, "The Trouble with Tech M&A," *The Deal*, May 7, 2012.
10. J. Pontin, "But Who's Counting?" *Technology Review*, March/April 2009.
11. D. Coldewey, "iOS Passes 200 Million Devices, 25 Million of Which Are iPads," *TechCrunch*, June 6, 2011.
12. J. Schmid and B. Poston, "Patent Backlog Clogs Recovery," *Milwaukee Journal Sentinel*, August 15, 2009.
13. 2009 figures are from http://www.indeed.com.
14. "Best Jobs in America," *CNNMoney*, 2009, http://money.cnn.com/magazines/moneymag/bestjobs/2009/snapshots/1.html.
15. U.S. News Staff, "The 25 Best Jobs," http://money.usnews.com/careers/best-jobs/rankings/the-25-best-jobs (accessed May 29, 2012).
16. L. Gerdes, "The Best Places to Launch a Career," *BusinessWeek*, September 15, 2008.
17. T. Kaneshige, "Surprise! Tech Is a Safe Career Choice Today," *InfoWorld*, February 4, 2009.
18. See "Best Companies to Work For," *Fortune*, 2007—2010. For 2010 list, see http://money.cnn.com/magazines/fortune/bestcompanies/2010/full_list/index.html.
19. E. Goode, "For Newcomers in Silicon Valley, the Dream of Entrepreneurship Still Lives," *New York Times*, January 24, 2012.
20. J. Fortt, "Tech Execs Get Sexy," *Fortune*, February 12, 2009.
21. O. Malik, "MySpace, R.I.P.," *GigaOM*, February 10, 2010.
22. J. Thaw, "Yahoo's Semel Resigns as Chief amid Google's Gains," *Bloomberg*, June 18, 2007.
23. G. Fabrikant and M. Helft, "Barry Diller Conquered. Now He Tries to Divide," *New York Times*, March 16, 2008.
24. J. Quinn, "Final Farewell to Worst Deal in History—AOL-Time Warner," *Telegraph* (UK), November 21, 2009.
25. E. Brynjolfsson, A. McAfee, M. Sorell, and F. Zhu, "Scale without Mass: Business Process Replication and Industry Dynamics," *SSRN*, September 30, 2008.
26. A. McAfee and E. Brynjolfsson, "Dog Eat Dog," *Sloan Management Review*, April 27, 2007.

CHAPTER 2

Strategy and Technology: Concepts and Frameworks for Understanding What Separates Winners from Losers

1. INTRODUCTION

LEARNING OBJECTIVES

1. **Define operational effectiveness and understand the limitations of technology-based competition leveraging this principle.**
2. **Define strategic positioning and the importance of grounding competitive advantage in this concept.**
3. **Understand the resource-based view of competitive advantage.**
4. **List the four characteristics of a resource that might possibly yield sustainable competitive advantage.**

Managers are confused, and for good reason. Management theorists, consultants, and practitioners often vehemently disagree on how firms should craft tech-enabled strategy, and many widely read articles contradict one another. Headlines such as "Move First or Die" compete with "The First-Mover Disadvantage." A leading former CEO advises, "destroy your business," while others suggest firms focus on their "core competency" and "return to basics." The pages of the *Harvard Business Review* have declared, "IT Doesn't Matter," while a *New York Times* bestseller hails technology as the "steroids" of modern business.

Theorists claiming to have mastered the secrets of strategic management are contentious and confusing. But as a manager, the ability to size up a firm's strategic position and understand its likelihood of sustainability is one of the most valuable and yet most difficult skills to master. Layer on thinking about technology—a key enabler to nearly every modern business strategy, but also a function often thought of as easily "outsourced"—and it's no wonder that so many firms struggle at the intersection where strategy and technology meet. The business landscape is littered with the corpses of firms killed by managers who guessed wrong.

Developing strong strategic thinking skills is a career-long pursuit—a subject that can occupy tomes of text, a roster of courses, and a lifetime of seminars. While this chapter can't address the breadth of strategic thought, it is meant as a primer on developing the skills for strategic thinking about technology. A manager that understands issues presented in this chapter should be able to see through seemingly conflicting assertions about best practices more clearly; be better prepared to recognize opportunities and risks; and be more adept at successfully brainstorming new, tech-centric approaches to markets.

1.1 The Danger of Relying on Technology

sustainable competitive advantage

Financial performance that consistently outperforms industry averages.

Firms strive for sustainable competitive advantage, financial performance that consistently outperforms their industry peers. The goal is easy to state, but hard to achieve. The world is so dynamic, with new products and new competitors rising seemingly overnight, that truly sustainable advantage might seem like an impossibility. New competitors and copycat products create a race to cut costs, cut prices, and increase features that may benefit consumers but erode profits industry-wide. Nowhere is this balance more difficult than when competition involves technology. The fundamental strategic question in the Internet era is, "*How can I possibly compete when everyone can copy my technology and the competition is just a click away?*" Put that way, the pursuit of sustainable competitive advantage seems like a lost cause.

But there are winners—big, consistent winners—empowered through their use of technology. How do they do it? In order to think about how to achieve sustainable advantage, it's useful to start with two concepts defined by Michael Porter. A professor at the Harvard Business School and father of the *value chain* and the *five forces* concepts (see the sections later in this chapter), Porter is justifiably considered one of the leading strategic thinkers of our time.

operational effectiveness

Performing the same tasks better than rivals perform them.

fast follower problem

Exists when savvy rivals watch a pioneer's efforts, learn from their successes and missteps, then enter the market quickly with a comparable or superior product at a lower cost before the first mover can dominate.

According to Porter, the reason so many firms suffer aggressive, margin-eroding competition is because they've defined themselves according to operational effectiveness rather than strategic positioning. Operational effectiveness refers to performing the same tasks better than rivals perform them. Everyone wants to be better, but the danger in operational effectiveness is "sameness." This risk is particularly acute in firms that rely on technology for competitiveness. After all, technology can be easily acquired. Buy the same stuff as your rivals, hire students from the same schools, copy the look and feel of competitor Web sites, reverse engineer their products, and you can match them. The fast follower problem exists when savvy rivals watch a pioneer's efforts, learn from their successes and missteps, then enter the market quickly with a comparable or superior product at a lower cost.

Since tech can be copied so quickly, followers can be fast, indeed. Several years ago while studying the Web portal industry (Yahoo! and its competitors), a colleague and I found that when a firm introduced an innovative feature, at least one of its three major rivals would match that feature in, on average, only one and a half months.[1] Groupon CEO Andrew Mason claimed the daily deal service had spawned 500 imitators within two years of launch.[2] When technology can be matched so quickly, it is rarely a source of competitive advantage. And this phenomenon isn't limited to the Web.

Consider TiVo. At first blush, it looks like this first mover should be a winner since it seems to have established a leading brand; TiVo is now a verb for digitally recording TV broadcasts. But despite this, TiVo has largely been a money loser, going years without posting an annual profit. By the time 1.5 million TiVos had been sold, there were over thirty million digital video recorders (DVRs) in use.[3] Rival devices offered by cable and satellite companies appear the same to consumers and are offered along with pay television subscriptions—a critical distribution channel for reaching customers that TiVo doesn't control.

The Flip video camera is another example of technology alone offering little durable advantage. The pocket-sized video recorders used flash memory instead of magnetic storage. Flip cameras grew so popular that Cisco bought Flip parent Pure Digital, for $590 million. The problem was digital video features were easy to copy, and constantly falling technology costs (see Chapter 5) allowed rivals to embed video into their products. Later that same year Apple (and other firms) began including video capture as a feature in their music players and phones. Why carry a Flip when one pocket device can do everything? The Flip business barely lasted two years, and by spring 2011 Cisco had killed the division, taking a more than half-billion-dollar spanking in the process.[4]

strategic positioning

Performing different tasks than rivals, or the same tasks in a different way.

Operational effectiveness is critical. Firms must invest in techniques to improve quality, lower cost, and design efficient customer experiences. But for the most part, these efforts can be matched. Because of this, operational effectiveness is usually not sufficient enough to yield sustainable dominance over the competition. In contrast to operational effectiveness, strategic positioning refers to performing different activities from those of rivals, or the same activities in a different way. Technology itself is often very easy to replicate, and those assuming advantage lies in technology alone may find themselves in a profit-eroding arms race with rivals able to match their moves step by step. But while technology can be copied, technology can also play a critical role in creating and strengthening strategic *differences*—advantages that rivals will struggle to match.

1.2 Different Is Good: FreshDirect Redefines the NYC Grocery Landscape

For an example of the relationship between technology and strategic positioning, consider FreshDirect. The New York City–based grocery firm focused on the two most pressing problems for Big Apple shoppers: selection is limited and prices are high. Both of these problems are a function of the high cost of real estate in New York. The solution? Use technology to craft an ultraefficient model that makes an end-run around stores.

The firm's "storefront" is a Web site offering one-click menus, semiprepared specials like "meals in four minutes," and the ability to pull up prior grocery lists for fast reorders—all features that appeal to the time-strapped Manhattanites who were the firm's first customers. (The Web's not the only channel to reach customers—the firm's mobile apps are hugely popular, especially for repeat orders.)[5] Next-day deliveries are from a vast warehouse the size of five football fields located in a lower-rent industrial area of Queens. At that size, the firm can offer a fresh goods selection that's over five times larger than local supermarkets. Area shoppers—many of whom don't have cars or are keen to avoid the traffic-snarled streets of the city—were quick to embrace the model. The service is now so popular that apartment buildings in New York have begun to redesign common areas to include secure freezers that can accept FreshDirect deliveries, even when customers aren't there.[6]

FIGURE 2.1 The FreshDirect Web Site and the Firm's Tech-Enabled Warehouse Operation

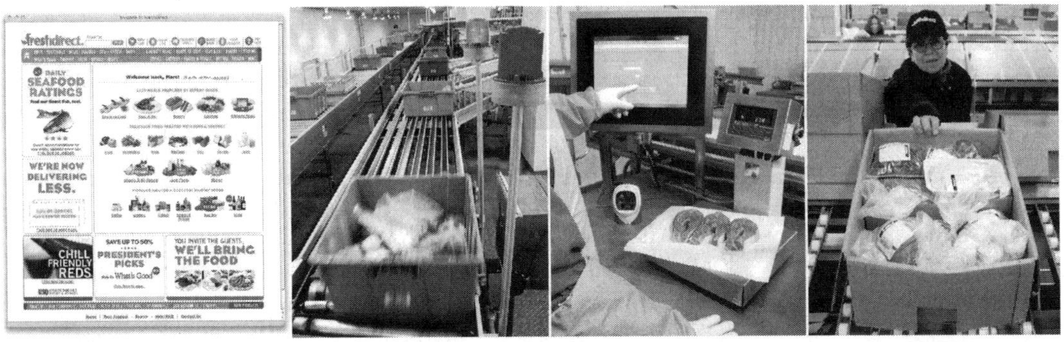

Source: Used with permission from FreshDirect. See the photographic tour at the FreshDirect Web site, http://www.freshdirect.com/about/index.jsp?siteAccessPage=c_aboutus.

The FreshDirect model crushes costs that plague traditional grocers. Worker shifts are highly efficient, avoiding the downtime lulls and busy rush hour spikes of storefronts. The result? Labor costs that are 60 percent lower than at traditional grocers. FreshDirect buys and prepares what it sells, leading to less waste, an advantage that the firm claims is "worth 5 percentage points of total revenue in terms of savings."[7] Overall perishable inventory at FreshDirect turns 197 times a year versus 40 times a year at traditional grocers.[8] **Higher inventory turns** mean the firm is selling product faster, so it collects money quicker than its rivals do. And those goods are fresher since they've been in stock for less time, too. Consider that while the average grocer may have seven to nine days of seafood inventory, FreshDirect's seafood stock turns each day. Stock is typically purchased direct from the docks in order to fulfill orders placed less than twenty-four hours earlier.[9]

inventory turns

Sometimes referred to as inventory turnover, stock turns, or stock turnover. It is the number of times inventory is sold or used during the course of a year. A higher figure means that a firm is selling products quickly.

Artificial intelligence software, coupled with some seven miles of fiber-optic cables linking systems and sensors, supports everything from baking the perfect baguette to verifying orders with 99.9 percent accuracy.[10] Since it lacks the money-sucking open-air refrigerators of the competition, the firm even saves big on energy (instead, staff bundle up for shifts in climate-controlled cold rooms tailored to the specific needs of dairy, deli, and produce). The firm also uses recycled biodiesel fuel to cut down on delivery costs.

FreshDirect buys directly from suppliers, eliminating middlemen wherever possible. The firm also offers suppliers several benefits beyond traditional grocers, all in exchange for more favorable terms. These include offering to carry a greater selection of supplier products while eliminating the "slotting fees" (payments by suppliers for prime shelf space) common in traditional retail, cobranding products to help establish and strengthen supplier brand, paying partners in days rather than weeks, and sharing data to help improve supplier sales and operations. Add all these advantages together and the firm's big, fresh selection is offered at prices that can undercut the competition by as much as 35 percent.[11] And FreshDirect does it all with margins in the range of 20 percent (to as high as 45 percent on many semiprepared meals), easily dwarfing the razor-thin 1 percent margins earned by traditional grocers.[12]

Today, FreshDirect serves a base of some 600,000 paying customers. That's a population roughly the size of metro-Boston, serviced by a single grocer with no physical store. The privately held firm has been solidly profitable for several years. Even in recession-plagued 2009, the firm's CEO described 2009 earnings as "pretty spectacular,"[13] while 2010 revenues were estimated at roughly $300 million.[14]

straddling

Attempts to occupy more than one position, while failing to match the benefits of a more efficient, singularly focused rival.

Technology is critical to the FreshDirect model, but it's the collective impact of the firm's differences when compared to rivals, this tech-enabled strategic positioning, that delivers success. Operating for more than half a decade, the firm has also built up a set of strategic assets that not only address specific needs of a market but are now extremely difficult for any upstart to compete against. Traditional grocers can't fully copy the firm's delivery business because this would leave them **straddling** two markets (low-margin storefront and high-margin delivery), unable to gain optimal benefits from either. Entry costs for would-be competitors are also high (the firm spent over $75 million building infrastructure before it could serve a single customer), and the firm's complex and highly customized software, which handles everything from delivery scheduling to orchestrating the preparation of thousands of recipes, continues to be refined and improved each year.[15] On top of all this comes years of customer data used to further refine processes, speed reorders, and make helpful recommendations. Competing against a firm with such a strong and tough-to-match strategic position can be brutal. Just five years after launch there were one-third fewer supermarkets in New York City than when FreshDirect first opened for business.[16]

1.3 But What Kinds of Differences?

The principles of operational effectiveness and strategic positioning are deceptively simple. But while Porter claims strategy is "fundamentally about being different,"[17] how can you recognize whether your firm's differences are special enough to yield sustainable competitive advantage?

resource-based view of competitive advantage

The strategic thinking approach suggesting that if a firm is to maintain sustainable competitive advantage, it must control an exploitable resource, or set of resources, that have four critical characteristics. These resources must be (1) valuable, (2) rare, (3) imperfectly imitable, and (4) nonsubstitutable.

dense wave division multiplexing (DWDM)

A technology that increases the transmission capacity (and hence speed) of fiber-optic cable. Transmissions using fiber are accomplished by transmitting light inside "glass" cables. In DWDM, the light inside fiber is split into different wavelengths in a way similar to how a prism splits light into different colors.

An approach known as the **resource-based view of competitive advantage** can help. The idea here is that if a firm is to maintain sustainable competitive advantage, it must control a set of exploitable resources that have four critical characteristics. These resources must be (1) *valuable*, (2) *rare*, (3) *imperfectly imitable* (tough to imitate), and (4) *nonsubstitutable*. Having all four characteristics is key. Miss value and no one cares what you've got. Without rareness, you don't have something unique. If others can copy what you have, or others can replace it with a substitute, then any seemingly advantageous differences will be undercut.

Strategy isn't just about recognizing opportunity and meeting demand. Resource-based thinking can help you avoid the trap of carelessly entering markets simply because growth is spotted. The telecommunications industry learned this lesson in a very hard and painful way. With the explosion of the Internet it was easy to see that demand to transport Web pages, e-mails, MP3s, video, and everything else you can turn into ones and zeros, was skyrocketing.

Most of what travels over the Internet is transferred over long-haul fiber-optic cables, so telecom firms began digging up the ground and laying webs of fiberglass to meet the growing demand. Problems resulted because firms laying long-haul fiber didn't fully appreciate that their rivals and new upstart firms were doing the exact same thing. By one estimate there was enough fiber laid to stretch from the Earth to the moon some 280 times![18] On top of that, a technology called **dense wave division multiplexing (DWDM)** enabled existing fiber to carry more transmissions than ever before. The end result—these new assets weren't rare and each day they seemed to be less valuable.

For some firms, the transmission prices they charged on newly laid cable collapsed by over 90 percent. Established firms struggled, upstarts went under, and WorldCom became the biggest bankruptcy in U.S. history. The impact was also felt throughout all industries that supplied the telecom industry. Firms like Sun, Lucent, and Nortel, whose sales growth relied on big sales to telecom carriers, saw their value tumble as orders dried up. Estimates suggest that the telecommunications industry lost nearly $4 trillion in value in just three years,[19] much of it due to executives that placed big bets on resources that weren't strategic.

KEY TAKEAWAYS

- Technology can be easy to copy, and technology alone rarely offers sustainable advantage.
- Firms that leverage technology for strategic positioning use technology to create competitive assets or ways of doing business that are difficult for others to copy.
- True sustainable advantage comes from assets and business models that are simultaneously valuable, rare, difficult to imitate, and for which there are no substitutes.

QUESTIONS AND EXERCISES

1. What is operational effectiveness?
2. What is strategic positioning?
3. Is a firm that competes based on the features of technology engaged in operational effectiveness or strategic positioning? Give an example to back up your claim.
4. What is the "resource-based" view of competitive advantage? What are the characteristics of resources that may yield sustainable competitive advantage?
5. TiVo has a great brand. Why hasn't it profitably dominated the market for digital video recorders?
6. Examine the FreshDirect business model and list reasons for its competitive advantage. Would a similar business work in your neighborhood? Why or why not?
7. What effect did FreshDirect have on traditional grocers operating in New York City? Why?
8. Choose a technology-based company. Discuss its competitive advantage based on the resources it controls.
9. Use the resource-based view of competitive advantage to explain the collapse of many telecommunications firms in the period following the burst of the dot-com bubble.
10. Consider the examples of Barnes and Noble competing with Amazon, and Apple offering iTunes. Are either (or both) of these efforts straddling? Why or why not?

2. POWERFUL RESOURCES

LEARNING OBJECTIVES

1. **Understand that technology is often critical to enabling competitive advantage, and provide examples of firms that have used technology to organize for sustained competitive advantage.**
2. **Understand the value chain concept and be able to examine and compare how various firms organize to bring products and services to market.**
3. **Recognize the role technology can play in crafting an imitation-resistant value chain, as well as when technology choice may render potentially strategic assets less effective.**
4. **Define the following concepts: brand, scale, data and switching cost assets, differentiation, network effects, and distribution channels.**
5. **Understand and provide examples of how technology can be used to create or strengthen the resources mentioned above.**

Management has no magic bullets. There is no exhaustive list of key resources that firms can look to in order to build a sustainable business. And recognizing a resource doesn't mean a firm will be able to acquire it or exploit it forever. But being aware of major sources of competitive advantage can help managers recognize an organization's opportunities and vulnerabilities, and can help them brainstorm winning strategies. And these assets rarely exist in isolation. Oftentimes, a firm with an effective strategic position can create an arsenal of assets that reinforce one another, creating advantages that are particualrly difficult for rivals to successfully challenge.

2.1 Imitation-Resistant Value Chains

While many of the resources below are considered in isolation, the strength of any advantage can be far more significant if firms are able to leverage several of these resources in a way that makes each stronger and makes the firm's way of doing business more difficult for rivals to match. Firms that craft an **imitation-resistant value chain** have developed a way of doing business that others will struggle to replicate, and in nearly every successful effort of this kind, technology plays a key enabling role. The **value chain** is the set of interrelated activities that bring products or services to market (see below). When we compare FreshDirect's value chain to traditional rivals, there are differences across every element. But most importantly, the elements in FreshDirect's value chain work together to create and reinforce competitive advantages that others cannot easily copy. Incumbents trying to copy the firm would be *straddled* across two business models, unable to reap the full advantages of either. And late-moving pure-play rivals will struggle, as FreshDirect's lead time allows the firm to develop brand, scale, data, and other advantages that newcomers lack (see below for more on these resources).

imitation-resistant value chain

A way of doing business that competitors struggle to replicate and that frequently involves technology in a key enabling role.

value chain

The set of activities through which a product or service is created and delivered to customers.

Framework: The Value Chain

alue chain is the "set of activities through which a product or service is created and delivered to custom-[20] There are five primary components of the value chain and four supporting components. The primary omponents are:

- *Inbound logistics*—getting needed materials and other inputs into the firm from suppliers
- *Operations*—turning inputs into products or services
- *Outbound logistics*—delivering products or services to consumers, distribution centers, retailers, or other partners
- *Marketing and sales*—customer engagement, pricing, promotion, and transaction
- *Support*—service, maintenance, and customer support

The secondary components are:

- *Firm infrastructure*—functions that support the whole firm, including general management, planning, IS, and finance
- *Human resource management*—recruiting, hiring, training, and development
- *Technology / research and development*—new product and process design
- *Procurement*—sourcing and purchasing functions

While the value chain is typically depicted as it's displayed in the figure below, goods and information don't necessarily flow in a line from one function to another. For example, an order taken by the marketing function can trigger an inbound logistics function to get components from a supplier, operations functions (to build a product if it's not available), or outbound logistics functions (to ship a product when it's available). Similarly, information from service support can be fed back to advise research and development (R&D) in the design of future products.

The Value Chain

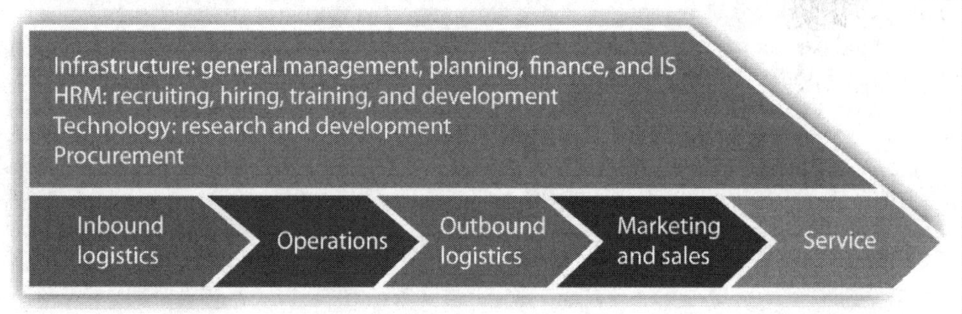

When a firm has an imitation-resistant value chain—one that's tough for rivals to copy in a way that yields similar benefits—then a firm may have a critical competitive asset. From a strategic perspective, managers can use the value chain framework to consider a firm's differences and distinctiveness compared to rivals. If a firm's value chain can't be copied by competitors without engaging in painful trade-offs, or if the firm's value chain helps to create and strengthen other strategic assets over time, it can be a key source for competitive advantage. Many of the examples used in this book, including FreshDirect, Amazon, and Zara, illustrate this point.

An analysis of a firm's value chain can also reveal operational weaknesses, and technology is often of great benefit to improving the speed and quality of execution. Firms can often buy software to improve things, and tools such as *supply chain management* (SCM; linking inbound and outbound logistics with operations), *customer relationship management* (CRM; supporting sales, marketing, and in some cases R&D), and *enterprise resource planning* software (ERP; software implemented in modules to automate the entire value chain), can have a big impact on more efficiently integrating the activities within the firm, as well as with its suppliers and customers. But remember, these software tools can be purchased by competitors, too. While valuable, such software may not yield lasting competitive advantage if it can be easily matched by competitors as well.

There's potential danger here. If a firm adopts software that changes a unique process into a generic one, it may have co-opted a key source of competitive advantage particularly if other firms can buy the same stuff. This isn't a problem with something like accounting software. Accounting processes are standardized and accounting isn't a source of competitive advantage, so most firms buy rather than build their own accounting software. But using packaged, third-party SCM, CRM, and ERP software typically requires adopting a very specific way of doing things, using software and methods that can be purchased and adopted by others. During its period of PC-industry dominance, Dell stopped deployment of the logistics and manufacturing modules of a packaged ERP implementation when it realized that the software would require the firm to make changes to its unique and highly successful operating model and that many of the firm's unique supply chain advantages would change to the point where the firm was doing the same thing using the same software as its competitors. By contrast, Apple had no problem adopting third-party ERP software because the firm competes on product uniqueness rather than operational differences.

Dell's Struggles: Nothing Lasts Forever

Michael Dell enjoyed an extended run that took him from assembling PCs in his dorm room as an undergraduate at the University of Texas at Austin to heading the largest PC firm on the planet. For years Dell's superefficient, vertically integrated manufacturing and direct-to-consumer model combined to help the firm earn seven times more profit on its own systems when compared with comparably configured rival PCs.[21] And since Dell PCs were usually cheaper, too, the firm could often start a price war and still have better overall margins than rivals.

It was a brilliant model that for years proved resistant to imitation. While Dell sold direct to consumers, rivals had to share a cut of sales with the less efficient retail chains responsible for the majority of their sales. Dell's rivals struggled in moving toward direct sales because any retailer sensing its suppliers were competing with it through a direct-sales effort could easily chose another supplier that sold a nearly identical product. It wasn't that HP, IBM, Sony, and so many others didn't see the advantage of Dell's model—these firms were wedded to models that made it difficult for them to imitate their rival without the inefficient burden of straddling two different models of doing business.

But then Dell's killer model, one that had become a staple case study in business schools worldwide, began to lose steam. Nearly two decades of observing Dell had allowed the contract manufacturers serving Dell's rivals to improve manufacturing efficiency.[22] Component suppliers located near contract manufacturers, and assembly times fell dramatically. And as the cost of computing fell, the price advantage Dell enjoyed over rivals also shrank in absolute terms. That meant savings from buying a Dell weren't as big as they once were. On top of that, the direct-to-consumer model also suffered when sales of notebook PCs outpaced the more commoditized desktop market. Notebooks can be considered to be more differentiated than desktops, and customers often want to compare products in person—lift them, type on keyboards, and view screens—before making a purchase decision.

In time, these shifts created an opportunity for rivals to knock Dell from its ranking as the world's number one PC manufacturer. Dell has even abandoned its direct-only business model and now also sells products through third-party brick-and-mortar retailers. Dell's struggles as computers, customers, and the product mix changed all underscore the importance of continually assessing a firm's strategic position among changing market conditions. There is no guarantee that today's winning strategy will dominate forever.

2.2 Brand

A firm's **brand** is the symbolic embodiment of all the information connected with a product or service, and a strong brand can also be an exceptionally powerful resource for competitive advantage. Consumers use brands to *lower search costs*, so having a strong brand is particularly vital for firms hoping to be the first online stop for consumers. Want to buy a book online? Auction a product? Search for information? Which firm would you visit first? Almost certainly Amazon, eBay, or Google. But how do you build a strong brand? It's *not* just about advertising and promotion. First and foremost, customer experience counts. A strong brand *proxies quality* and *inspires trust*, so if consumers can't rely on a firm to deliver as promised, they'll go elsewhere. As an upside, tech can play a critical role in rapidly and cost-effectively strengthening a brand. If a firm performs well, consumers can often be enlisted to promote a product or service (so-called **viral marketing**). Consider that while scores of dot-coms burned through money on Super Bowl ads and other costly promotional efforts, Google, Hotmail, Skype, eBay, Facebook, LinkedIn, Twitter, YouTube, and so many other dominant online properties built multimillion member followings before committing any significant spending to advertising.

brand

The symbolic embodiment of all the information connected with a product or service.

viral marketing

Leveraging consumers to promote a product or service.

FIGURE 2.3

Icons accompanying stories on the *New York Times* Web site enlist customers to spread the word about products and services, user to user, like a virus.

Early customer accolades for a novel service often mean that positive press (a kind of free advertising) will also likely follow.

But show up late and you may end up paying much more to counter an incumbent's place in the consumer psyche. In recent years, Amazon has spent no money on television advertising, while rivals Buy.com and Overstock.com spent millions. Google, another strong brand, has become a verb, and the cost to challenge it is astonishingly high. Yahoo! and Microsoft's Bing each spent $100 million on Google-challenging branding campaigns, but the early results of these efforts seemed to do little to grow share at Google's expense.[23] Branding is difficult, but if done well, even complex tech products can establish themselves as killer brands. Consider that Intel has taken an ingredient product that most people don't understand, the microprocessor, and built a quality-conveying name recognized by computer users worldwide.

2.3 Scale

scale advantages

Advantages related to size.

economies of scale

When costs can be spread across increasing units of production or in serving multiple customers. Businesses that have favorable economies of scale (like many Internet firms) are sometimes referred to as being highly scalable.

Many firms gain advantages as they grow in size. Advantages related to a firm's size are referred to as **scale advantages**. Businesses benefit from **economies of scale** when the cost of an investment can be spread across increasing units of production or in serving a growing customer base. Firms that benefit from scale economies as they grow are sometimes referred to as being *scalable*. Many Internet and tech-leveraging businesses are highly scalable since, as firms grow to serve more customers with their existing infrastructure investment, profit margins improve dramatically.

Consider that in just one year, the Internet firm BlueNile sold as many diamond rings with just 115 employees and one Web site as a traditional jewelry retailer would sell through 116 stores.[24] And with lower operating costs, BlueNile can sell at prices that brick-and-mortar stores can't match, thereby attracting more customers and further fueling its scale advantages. Profit margins improve as the cost to run the firm's single Web site and operate its one warehouse is spread across increasing jewelry sales.

A growing firm may also gain *bargaining power with its suppliers or buyers*. Apple's dominance of smartphone and tablet markets has allowed the firm to lock up 60 percent of the world's supply of advanced touch-screen displays, and to do so with better pricing than would be available to smaller rivals.[25] Similarly, for years eBay could raise auction fees because of the firm's market dominance. Auction sellers who left eBay lost pricing power since fewer bidders on smaller, rival services meant lower prices.

The scale of technology investment required to run a business can also act as a barrier to entry, discouraging new, smaller competitors. Intel's size allows the firm to pioneer cutting-edge manufacturing techniques and invest $7 billion on next-generation plants.[26] And although Google was started by two Stanford students with borrowed computer equipment running in a dorm room, the firm today runs on an estimated 1.4 million servers.[27] The investments being made by Intel and Google would be cost-prohibitive for almost any newcomer to justify.

2.4 Switching Costs and Data

Switching costs exist when consumers incur an expense to move from one product or service to another. Tech firms often benefit from strong switching costs that cement customers to their firms. Users invest their time learning a product, entering data into a system, creating files, and buying supporting programs or manuals. These investments may make them reluctant to switch to a rival's effort.

switching costs

The cost a consumer incurs when moving from one product to another. It can involve actual money spent (e.g., buying a new product) as well as investments in time, any data loss, and so forth.

Similarly, firms that seem dominant but that don't have high switching costs can be rapidly trumped by strong rivals. Netscape once controlled more than 80 percent of the market share in Web browsers, but when Microsoft began bundling Internet Explorer with the Windows operating system and (through an alliance) with America Online (AOL), Netscape's market share plummeted. Customers migrated with a mouse click as part of an upgrade or installation. Learning a new browser was a breeze, and with the Web's open standards, most customers noticed no difference when visiting their favorite Web sites with their new browser.

Sources of Switching Costs

- Learning costs: Switching technologies may require an investment in learning a new interface and commands.
- Information and data: Users may have to reenter data, convert files or databases, or may even lose earlier contributions on incompatible systems.
- Financial commitment: Can include investments in new equipment, the cost to acquire any new software, consulting, or expertise, and the devaluation of any investment in prior technologies no longer used.
- Contractual commitments: Breaking contracts can lead to compensatory damages and harm an organization's reputation as a reliable partner.
- Search costs: Finding and evaluating a new alternative costs time and money.
- Loyalty programs: Switching can cause customers to lose out on program benefits. Think frequent purchaser programs that offer "miles" or "points" (all enabled and driven by software).[28]

It is critical for challengers to realize that in order to win customers away from a rival, a new entrant must not only demonstrate to consumers that an offering provides more value than the incumbent, they have to ensure that their value added exceeds the incumbent's value *plus* any perceived customer switching costs (see Figure 2.4). If it's going to cost you and be inconvenient, there's no way you're going to leave unless the benefits are overwhelming.

Data can be a particularly strong switching cost for firms leveraging technology. A customer who enters her profile into Facebook, movie preferences into Netflix, or grocery list into FreshDirect may be unwilling to try rivals—even if these firms are cheaper or offer more features—if moving to the new firm means she'll lose information feeds, recommendations, and time savings provided by the firms that already know her well. Fueled by scale over time, firms that have more customers and have been in business longer can gather more data, and many can use this data to improve their value chain by offering more accurate demand forecasting or product recommendations.

FIGURE 2.4

In order to win customers from an established incumbent, a late-entering rival must offer a product or service that not only exceeds the value offered by the incumbent but also exceeds the incumbent's value and any customer switching costs.

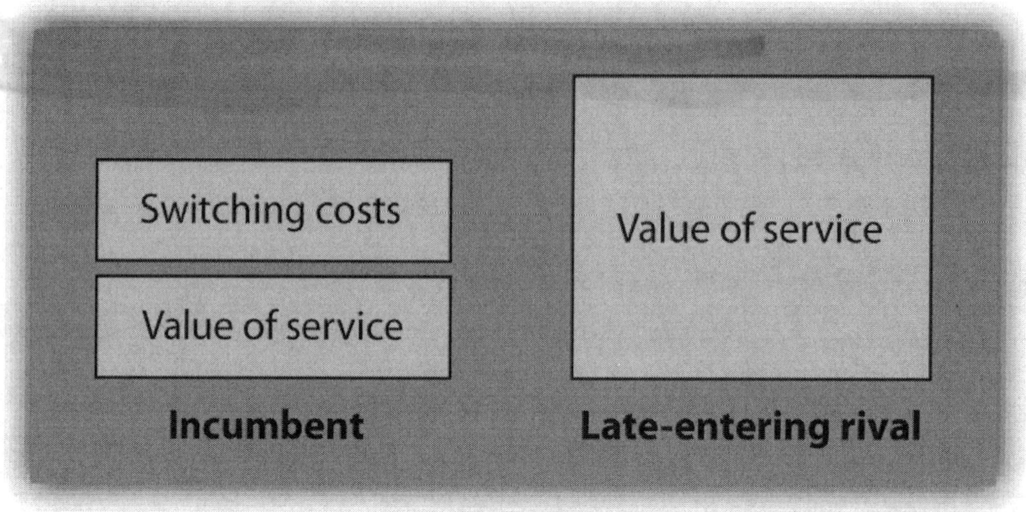

Competing on Tech Alone Is Tough: Gmail versus Rivals

Switching e-mail services can be a real a pain. You've got to convince your contacts to update their address books, hope that any message-forwarding from your old service to your new one remains active and works properly, and regularly check the old service to be sure nothing is caught in junk folder purgatory. Not fun. So when Google entered the market for free e-mail, challenging established rivals Yahoo! and Microsoft Hotmail, it knew it needed to offer an overwhelming advantage to lure away customers who had used these other services for years. Google's offering? A mailbox with vastly more storage than its competitors. With 250 to 500 times the capacity of rivals, Gmail users were liberated from the infamous "mailbox full" error, and could send photos, songs, slideshows, and other rich media files as attachments.

A neat innovation, but one based on technology that incumbents could easily copy. Once Yahoo! and Microsoft saw that customers valued the increased capacity, they quickly increased their own mailbox size, holding on to customers who might otherwise have fled to Google. Four years after Gmail was introduced, the service still had less than half the users of each of its two biggest rivals.

FIGURE 2.5 E-mail Market Share in Millions of Users[29]

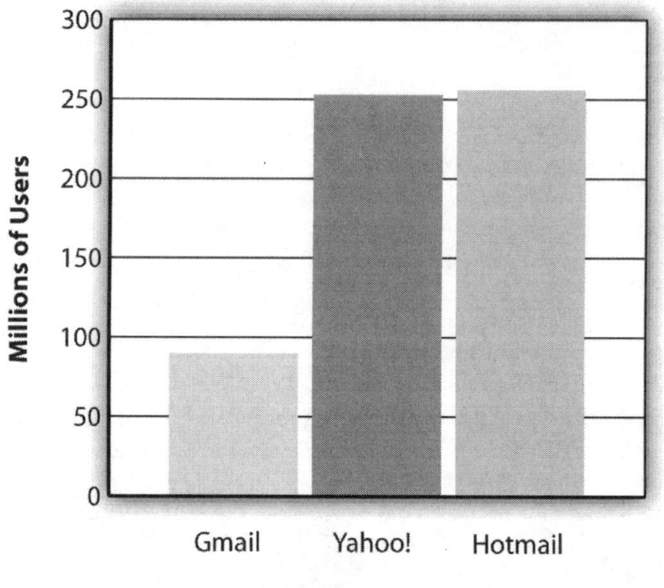

2.5 Differentiation

Commodities are products or services that are nearly identically offered from multiple vendors. Consumers buying commodities are highly price-focused since they have so many similar choices. In order to break the commodity trap, many firms leverage technology to *differentiate* their goods and services. Dell gained attention from customers not only because of its low prices, but also because it was one of the first PC vendors to build computers based on customer choice. Want a bigger hard drive? Don't need the fast graphics card? Dell will oblige.

Data is not only a switching cost, it also plays a critical role in differentiation. Each time a visitor returns to Amazon, the firm uses browsing records, purchase patterns, and product ratings to present a custom home page featuring products that the firm hopes the visitor will like. Customers value the experience they receive at Amazon so much that the firm received the highest score ever recorded on the University of Michigan's American Customer Satisfaction Index (ACSI). The score was not just the highest performance of any online firm, it was the highest ranking that any service firm in any industry had ever received.

Capital One has also used data to differentiate its offerings. The firm mines data and runs experiments to create risk models on potential customers. Because of this, the credit card firm aggressively pursued a set of customers that other lenders considered too risky based on simplistic credit scoring. Technology determined that a subset of underserved customers was not properly identified by conventional techniques and was actually a good bet. Finding profitable new markets that others ignored allowed Capital One to grow its EPS (earnings per share) 20 percent a year for seven years, a feat matched by less than 1 percent of public firms.[30]

2.6 Network Effects

Facebook is by far the most dominant social network worldwide. Microsoft Windows has a 90 percent market share in operating systems. EBay has an 80 percent share of online auctions. Why are these firms so dominant? Largely due to the concept of **network effects** (see Chapter 6). Network effects (sometimes called *network externalities* or *Metcalfe's Law*) exist when a product or service becomes more valuable as more people use it. If you're the first person with a Facebook account, then Facebook isn't very valuable. But with each additional user, there's one more person to communicate with. A firm with a big network of users might also see value added by third parties. Apple's iOS devices (the iPhone, iPod touch, and iPad) and Google's Android dominate rivals from Microsoft and HP in part because Apple and Google have tens of thousands more apps that run on and enhance these devices, and most of these apps are provided by firms other than Apple and Google. Third-party add-on products, books, magazines, or even skilled labor are all attracted to networks of the largest number of users, making dominant products even more valuable.

network effects

Also known as Metcalfe's Law, or network externalities. When the value of a product or service increases as its number of users expands.

Switching costs also play a role in determining the strength of network effects. Tech user investments often go far beyond simply the cost of acquiring a technology. Users spend time learning a product; they buy add-ons, create files, and enter preferences. Because no one wants to be stranded with an abandoned product and lose this additional investment, users may choose a technically inferior product simply because the product has a larger user base and is perceived as having a greater chance of being offered in the future. The virtuous cycle of network effects[31] doesn't apply to all tech products, and it can be a particularly strong asset for firms that can control and leverage a leading standard (think Apple's iPhone and iPad with their closed systems versus the once-dominant but now rarely used Netscape browser, which was almost entirely based on open standards), but in some cases where network effects are significant, they can create winners so dominant that firms with these advantages enjoy a near-monopoly hold on a market.

2.7 Distribution Channels

If no one sees your product, then it won't even get considered by consumers. So **distribution channels**—the path through which products or services get to customers—can be critical to a firm's success. Again, technology opens up opportunities for new ways to reach customers.

distribution channels

The path through which products or services get to customers.

Users can be recruited to create new distribution channels for your products and services (usually for a cut of the take). You may have visited Web sites that promote books sold on Amazon.com. Web site operators do this because Amazon gives them a percentage of all purchases that come in through these links. Amazon now has over 1 million of these "associates" (the term the firm uses for its **affiliates**), yet it only pays them if a promotion gains a sale. Google similarly receives some 30 percent of its ad revenue not from search ads, but from advertisements distributed within third-party sites ranging from lowly blogs to the *New York Times*.[32]

affiliates

Third parties that promote a product or service, typically in exchange for a cut of any sales.

In recent years, Google and Microsoft have engaged in bidding wars, trying to lock up distribution deals that would bundle software tools, advertising, or search capabilities with key partner offerings. Deals with partners such as Dell, Nokia, and Verizon Wireless have been valued at up to $1 billion each.[33]

The ability to distribute products by bundling them with existing offerings is a key Microsoft advantage. But beware—sometimes these distribution channels can provide firms with such an edge that international regulators have stepped in to try to provide a more level playing field. Microsoft was forced by European regulators to unbundle the Windows Media Player, for fear that it provided the firm with too great an advantage when competing with the likes of RealPlayer and Apple's QuickTime (see Chapter 6).

2.8 What about Patents?

Intellectual property protection can be granted in the form of a patent for those innovations deemed to be useful, novel, and nonobvious. In the United States, technology and (more controversially) even business models can be patented, typically for periods of twenty years from the date of patent application. Firms that receive patents have some degree of protection from copycats that try to identically mimic their products and methods.

The patent system is often considered to be unfairly stacked against start-ups. U.S. litigation costs in a single patent case average about $5 million,[34] and a few months of patent litigation can be enough to sink an early stage firm. Large firms can also be victims. So-called patent trolls hold intellectual property not with the goal of bringing novel innovations to market but instead in hopes that they can sue or extort large settlements from others. BlackBerry maker Research in Motion's $612 million settlement with the little-known holding company NTP is often highlighted as an example of the pain trolls can inflict.[35] Litigation threats are pushing rivals to cooperate in patent portfolio acquisition. Apple, EMC, Ericsson, Microsoft, RIM, and Sony pooled resources for a $4.5 billion purchase of some 6,000 patents formally held by the bankrupt telecom equipment firm Nortel.[36]

Even if an innovation is patentable, that doesn't mean that a firm has bulletproof protection. Some patents have been nullified by the courts upon later review (usually because of a successful challenge to the uniqueness of the innovation). Software patents are also widely granted, but notoriously difficult to defend. In many cases, coders at competing firms can write substitute algorithms that aren't the same, but accomplish similar tasks. For example, although Google's PageRank search algorithms are fast and efficient, Microsoft, Yahoo! and others now offer their own noninfringing search that presents results with an accuracy that many would consider on par with PageRank. Patents do protect tech-enabled operations innovations at firms like Netflix and Caesars Entertainment Corporation (formerly known as Harrah's), and design innovations like the iPod click wheel. But in a study of the factors that were critical in enabling firms to profit from their innovations, Carnegie Mellon professor Wes Cohen found that patents were only the fifth most important factor. Secrecy, lead time, sales skills, and manufacturing all ranked higher.[37]

KEY TAKEAWAYS

- Technology can play a key role in creating and reinforcing assets for sustainable advantage by enabling an imitation-resistant value chain; strengthening a firm's brand; collecting useful data and establishing switching costs; creating a network effect; creating or enhancing a firm's scale advantage; enabling product or service differentiation; and offering an opportunity to leverage unique distribution channels.
- The value chain can be used to map a firm's efficiency and to benchmark it against rivals, revealing opportunities to use technology to improve processes and procedures. When a firm is resistant to imitation, a superior value chain may yield sustainable competitive advantage.
- Firms may consider adopting packaged software or outsourcing value chain tasks that are not critical to a firm's competitive advantage. A firm should be wary of adopting software packages or outsourcing portions of its value chain that are proprietary and a source of competitive advantage.
- Patents are not necessarily a sure-fire path to exploiting an innovation. Many technologies and business methods can be copied, so managers should think about creating assets like the ones previously discussed if they wish to create truly sustainable advantage.
- Nothing lasts forever, and shifting technologies and market conditions can render once strong assets as obsolete.

QUESTIONS AND EXERCISES

1. Define and diagram the value chain.
2. Discuss the elements of FreshDirect's value chain and the technologies that FreshDirect uses to give the firm a competitive advantage. Why is FreshDirect resistant to imitation from incumbent firms? What advantages does FreshDirect have that insulate the firm from serious competition from start-ups copying its model?
3. Which firm should adopt third-party software to automate its supply chain—Dell or Apple? Why? Identify another firm that might be at risk if it adopted generic enterprise software. Why do you think this is risky and what would you recommend as an alternative?
4. Identify two firms in the same industry that have different value chains. Why do you think these firms have different value chains? What role do you think technology plays in the way that each firm competes? Do these differences enable strategic positioning? Why or why not?
5. How can information technology help a firm build a brand inexpensively?
6. Describe BlueNile's advantages over a traditional jewelry chain. Can conventional jewelers successfully copy BlueNile? Why or why not?
7. What are switching costs? What role does technology play in strengthening a firm's switching costs?
8. In most markets worldwide, Google dominates search. Why hasn't Google shown similar dominance in e-mail, as well?
9. How can technology be a distribution channel? Name a firm that has tried to leverage its technology as a distribution channel.
10. Do you think it is possible to use information technology to achieve competitive advantage? If so, how? If not, why not?
11. What are network effects? Name a product or service that has been able to leverage network effects to its advantage.
12. For well over a decade, Dell earned above average industry profits. But lately the firm has begun to struggle. What changed?
13. What are the potential sources of switching costs if you decide to switch cell phone service providers? Cell phones? Operating systems? PayTV service?
14. Why is an innovation based on technology alone often subjected to intense competition?
15. Can you think of firms that have successfully created competitive advantage even though other firms provide essentially the same thing? What factors enable this success?
16. What role did network effects play in your choice of an operating system? Of a social network? Of a word processor? Of a mobile phone? Why do so many firms choose to standardize on Microsoft Windows for PCs and laptops?
17. What can a firm do to prepare for the *inevitable* expiration of a patent (patents typically expire after twenty years)? Think in terms of the utilization of other assets and the development of advantages through employment of technology.

3. BARRIERS TO ENTRY, TECHNOLOGY, AND TIMING

LEARNING OBJECTIVES

1. **Understand the relationship between timing, technology, and the creation of resources for competitive advantage.**
2. **Argue effectively when faced with broad generalizations about the importance (or lack of importance) of technology and timing to competitive advantage.**
3. **Recognize the difference between low barriers to entry and the prospects for the sustainability of new entrant's efforts.**

Some have correctly argued that the barriers to entry for many tech-centric businesses are low. This argument is particularly true for the Internet where rivals can put up a competing Web site or deploy a rival app seemingly overnight. But it's absolutely critical to understand that market entry is *not* the same as building a sustainable business and just showing up doesn't guarantee survival.

Platitudes like "follow, don't lead"[38] can put firms dangerously at risk, and statements about low entry barriers ignore the difficulty many firms will have in matching the competitive advantages of successful tech pioneers. Should Blockbuster have waited while Netflix pioneered? In a year where Netflix profits were up sevenfold, Blockbuster lost more than $1 billion, and today Blockbuster is bankrupt.[39]

Should Sotheby's have dismissed seemingly inferior eBay? Sotheby's made $171 million in 2011, but eBay earned over $3.2 billion. Barnes & Noble waited seventeen months to respond to Amazon.com. 2011 was a down year for Amazon due to investments in the Kindle and other new businesses, but the firm still earned $630 million in profits, while Barnes & Noble lost over $73 million. Today Amazon sports a market cap roughly 100 times greater than its one-time rival, and it has expanded far beyond being just a books and media business.[40] During that same year, Borders—once the nation's number two book chain—declared bankruptcy and closed all of its stores. Today's Internet giants are winners because in most cases, they were the first to move with a profitable model and they were able to quickly establish resources for competitive advantage. With few exceptions, established offline firms have failed to catch up to today's Internet leaders.

TABLE 2.1 A Tale of Two Firms

	2007	2008	2009	2010
Amazon	$476 million	$645 million	$902 million	$1,152 million
Barnes & Noble	$150 million	$135 million	$75 million	$36 million

Barnes & Noble saw net income cut in half from 2007 to 2009 then fall half again in 2010. Over the same period Amazon's profits are up nearly threefold—in a recession.

Timing and technology alone will not yield sustainable competitive advantage. Yet both of these can be *enablers* for competitive advantage. Put simply, it's not the time lead or the technology; it's what a firm *does* with its time lead and technology. True strategic positioning means that a firm has created differences that cannot be easily matched by rivals. Moving first pays off when the time lead is used to create critical resources that are valuable, rare, tough to imitate, and lack substitutes. Anything less risks the arms race of operational effectiveness. Build resources like brand, scale, network effects, switching costs, or other key assets and your firm may have a shot. But guess wrong about the market or screw up execution and failure or direct competition awaits. It is true that most tech can be copied—there's little magic in eBay's servers, Intel's processors, Oracle's database software, or Microsoft's operating systems that past rivals have not at one point improved upon. But the lead that each of these tech-enabled firms had was leveraged to create network effects, switching costs, data assets, and helped build solid and well-respected brands.

But Google Arrived Late! Why Incumbents Must Constantly Consider Rivals

Although its share is slowly eroding, Yahoo! has been able to hold onto its lead in e-mail for so long because the firm quickly matched and nullified Gmail's most significant tech-based innovations before Google could inflict real damage. Perhaps Yahoo! had learned from prior errors. The firm's earlier failure to respond to Google's emergence as a credible threat in search advertising gave Sergey Brin and Larry Page the time they needed to build the planet's most profitable Internet firm.

Yahoo! (and many Wall Street analysts) saw search as a commodity—a service the firm had subcontracted out to other firms including Alta Vista and Inktomi. Yahoo! saw no conflict in taking an early investment stake in Google or in using the firm for its search results. But Yahoo! failed to pay attention to Google's advance. As Google's innovations in technology and interface remained unmatched over time, this allowed the firm to build its brand, scale, and advertising network (distribution channel) that grew from network effects because content providers and advertisers attract one another. These are all competitive resources that rivals have never been able to match.

Now Google (and Apple, too) are once again running from this playbook—turning the smartphone software market into what increasingly looks like a two-horse race. Many rivals, including Microsoft, had been trying to create a mobile standard for years, but their technical innovations offered little durable strategic value. It wasn't until app stores flourished, offered with a high-quality user experience, that dominant smartphone platforms emerged. Yes, Google and Apple arrived late, but nothing before them had created defensible strategic assets, and that left an opening.

Google's ability to succeed after being late to the search and mobile party isn't a sign of the power of the late mover; it's a story about the failure of incumbents to monitor their competitive landscape, recognize new rivals, and react to challenging offerings. That doesn't mean that incumbents need to respond to every potential threat. Indeed, figuring out which threats are worthy of response is the real skill here. Video rental chain Hollywood Video wasted over $300 million in an Internet streaming business years before high-speed broadband was available to make the effort work.[41] But while Blockbuster avoided the balance sheet–cratering gaffes of Hollywood Video, the firm also failed to respond to Netflix—a new threat that had timed market entry perfectly (see Chapter 4).

Firms that quickly get to market with the "right" model can dominate, but it's equally critical for leading firms to pay close attention to competition and innovate in ways that customers value. Take your eye off the ball and rivals may use time and technology to create strategic resources. Just look at Friendster—a firm that was once known as the largest social network in the United States but has become virtually irrelevant today.

KEY TAKEAWAYS

- It doesn't matter if it's easy for new firms to enter a market if these newcomers can't create and leverage the assets needed to challenge incumbents.
- Beware of those who say, "IT doesn't matter" or refer to the "myth" of the first mover. This thinking is overly simplistic. It's not a time or technology lead that provides sustainable competitive advantage; it's what a firm does with its time and technology lead. If a firm can use a time and technology lead to create valuable assets that others cannot match, it may be able to sustain its advantage. But if the work done in this time and technology lead can be easily matched, then no advantage can be achieved, and a firm may be threatened by new entrants

QUESTIONS AND EXERCISES

1. Does technology lower barriers to entry or raise them? Do low entry barriers necessarily mean that a firm is threatened?
2. Is there such a thing as the first-mover advantage? Why or why not?
3. Why did Google beat Yahoo! in search?
4. A former editor of the *Harvard Business Review*, Nick Carr, once published an article in that same magazine with the title "IT Doesn't Matter." In the article he also offered firms the advice: "Follow, Don't Lead." What would you tell Carr to help him improve the way he thinks about the relationship between time, technology, and competitive advantage?
5. Name an early mover that has successfully defended its position. Name another that had been superseded by the competition. What factors contributed to its success or failure?
6. You have just written a word processing package far superior in features to Microsoft Word. You now wish to form a company to market it. List and discuss the barriers your start-up faces.
7. What kinds of strategic assets are Google's Android and Apple's iOS seeking to create and exploit? Do you think these firms will be more successful than rivals? Why or why not?

4. KEY FRAMEWORK: THE FIVE FORCES OF INDUSTRY COMPETITIVE ADVANTAGE

LEARNING OBJECTIVES

1. **Diagram the five forces of competitive advantage.**
2. **Apply the framework to an industry, assessing the competitive landscape and the role of technology in influencing the relative power of buyers, suppliers, competitors, and alternatives.**

Professor and strategy consultant Gary Hamel once wrote in a *Fortune* cover story that "the dirty little secret of the strategy industry is that it doesn't have any theory of strategy creation."[42] While there is no silver bullet for strategy creation, strategic frameworks help managers describe the competitive environment a firm is facing. Frameworks can also be used as brainstorming tools to generate new ideas for responding to industry competition. If you have a model for thinking about competition, it's easier to understand what's happening and to think creatively about possible solutions.

Porter's five forces

Also known as Industry and Competitive Analysis. A framework considering the interplay between (1) the intensity of rivalry among existing competitors, (2) the threat of new entrants, (3) the threat of substitute goods or services, (4) the bargaining power of buyers, and (5) the bargaining power of suppliers.

One of the most popular frameworks for examining a firm's competitive environment is **Porter's five forces**, also known as the *Industry and Competitive Analysis*. As Porter puts it, "analyzing [these] forces illuminates an industry's fundamental attractiveness, exposes the underlying drivers of average industry profitability, and provides insight into how profitability will evolve in the future." The five forces this framework considers are (1) the intensity of rivalry among existing competitors, (2) the threat of new entrants, (3) the threat of substitute goods or services, (4) the bargaining power of buyers, and (5) the bargaining power of suppliers (see Figure 2.6).

FIGURE 2.6 The Five Forces of Industry and Competitive Analysis

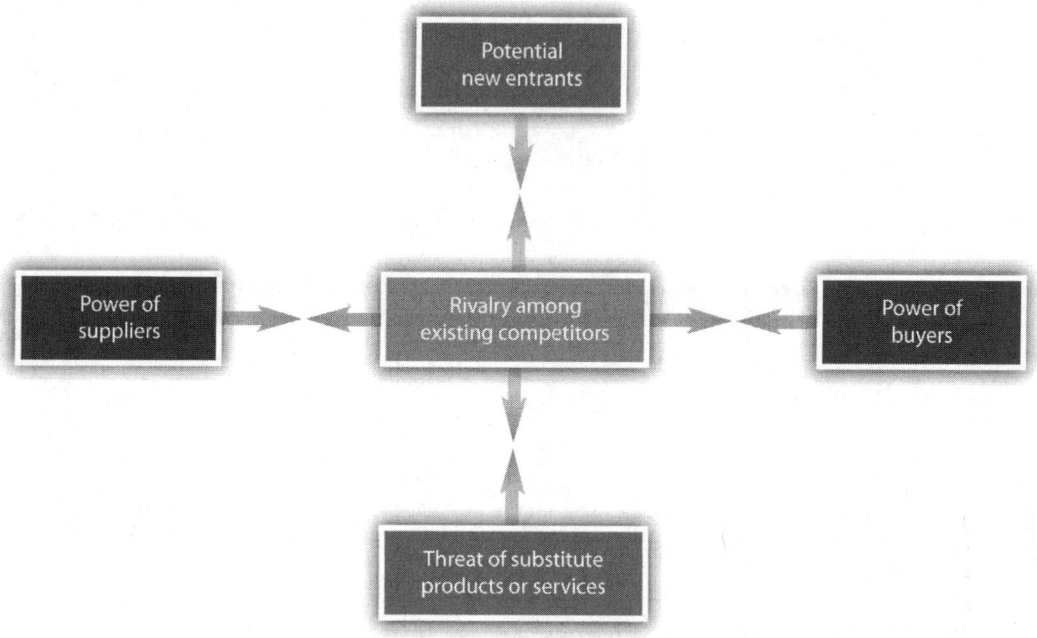

New technologies can create jarring shocks in an industry. Consider how the rise of the Internet has impacted the five forces for music retailers. Traditional music retailers like Tower and Virgin found that customers were seeking music online. These firms scrambled to invest in the new channel out of what is perceived to be a necessity. Their *intensity of rivalry* increases because they not only compete based on the geography of where brick-and-mortar stores are physically located, they now compete online as well. Investments online are expensive and uncertain, prompting some firms to partner with *new entrants* such as Amazon. Free from brick-and-mortar stores, Amazon, the dominant new entrant, has a highly scalable cost structure. And in many ways the online buying experience is superior to what customers saw in stores. Customers can hear samples of almost all tracks, selection is seemingly limitless (the *long tail* phenomenon—see this concept illuminated in Chapter 4), and data is leveraged using *collaborative filtering* software to make product recommendations and assist in music discovery.[43] Tough competition, but it gets worse because CD sales aren't the only way to consume music. The process of buying a plastic disc now faces *substitutes* as digital music files become available on commercial music sites. Who needs the physical atoms of a CD filled with ones and zeros when you can buy the bits one song at a time? Or don't buy anything and subscribe to a limitless library instead.

From a sound quality perspective, the *substitute good* of digital tracks purchased online is almost always inferior to their CD counterparts. To transfer songs quickly and hold more songs on a digital music player, tracks are encoded in a smaller file size than what you'd get on a CD, and this smaller file contains lower playback fidelity. But the additional tech-based market shock brought on by digital music players (particularly the iPod) has changed listening habits. The convenience of carrying thousands of songs trumps what most consider just a slight quality degradation. ITunes is now responsible for selling more music than any other firm, online or off. Apple can't rest on its laurels, either. The constant disruption of tech-enabled substitute goods has created rivals like Spotify and Pandora that don't sell music at all, yet have garnered tens of millions of users across desktop and mobile platforms. Most alarming to the industry is the other widely adopted substitute for CD purchases—theft. Illegal music "sharing" services abound, even after years of record industry crackdowns. And while exact figures on real losses from online piracy are in dispute, the music industry has seen album sales drop by 45 percent in less than a decade.[44] All this choice gives consumers (buyers) *bargaining power*. They demand cheaper prices and greater convenience. The *bargaining power of suppliers*—the music labels and artists—also increases. At the start of the Internet revolution, retailers could pressure labels to limit sales through competing channels. Now, with many of the major music retail chains in bankruptcy, labels have a freer hand to experiment, while bands large and small have new ways to reach fans, sometimes in ways that entirely bypass the traditional music labels.

While it can be useful to look at changes in one industry as a model for potential change in another, it's important to realize that the changes that impact one industry do not necessarily impact other industries in the same way. For example, it is often suggested that the Internet increases bargaining power of buyers and lowers the bargaining power of suppliers. This suggestion is true for some industries like auto sales and jewelry where the products are commodities and the **price transparency** of the Internet counteracts a previous **information asymmetry** where customers often didn't know enough information about a product to bargain effectively. But it's not true across the board.

price transparency

The degree to which complete information is available.

information asymmetry

A decision situation where one party has more or better information than its counterparty.

In cases where network effects are strong or a seller's goods are highly differentiated, the Internet can strengthen supplier bargaining power. The customer base of an antique dealer used to be limited by how many likely purchasers lived within driving distance of a store. Now with eBay, the dealer can take a rare good to a global audience and have a much larger customer base bid up the price. Switching costs also weaken buyer bargaining power. Wells Fargo has found that customers who use online bill pay (where switching costs are high) are 70 percent less likely to leave the bank than those who don't, suggesting that these switching costs help cement customers to the company even when rivals offer more compelling rates or services.

Tech plays a significant role in shaping and reshaping these five forces, but it's not the only significant force that can create an industry shock. Government deregulation or intervention, political shock, and social and demographic changes can all play a role in altering the competitive landscape. Because we live in an age of constant and relentless change, mangers need to continually visit strategic frameworks to consider any market-impacting shifts. Predicting the future is difficult, but ignoring change can be catastrophic.

KEY TAKEAWAYS

- Industry competition and attractiveness can be described by considering the following five forces: (1) the intensity of rivalry among existing competitors, (2) the potential for new entrants to challenge incumbents, (3) the threat posed by substitute products or services, (4) the power of buyers, and (5) the power of suppliers.
- In markets where commodity products are sold, the Internet can increase buyer power by increasing price transparency.
- The more differentiated and valuable an offering, the more the Internet shifts bargaining power to sellers. Highly differentiated sellers that can advertise their products to a wider customer base can demand higher prices.
- A strategist must constantly refer to models that describe events impacting their industry, particularly as new technologies emerge.

QUESTIONS AND EXERCISES

1. What are Porter's "five forces"?
2. Use the five forces model to illustrate competition in the newspaper industry. Are some competitors better positioned to withstand this environment than others? Why or why not? What role do technology and resources for competitive advantage play in shaping industry competition?
3. What is price transparency? What is information asymmetry? How does the Internet relate to these two concepts? How does the Internet shift bargaining power among the five forces?
4. How has the rise of the Internet impacted each of the five forces for music retailers?
5. In what ways is the online music buying experience superior to that of buying in stores?
6. What is the *substitute* for music CDs? What is the comparative sound quality of the substitute? Why would a listener accept an inferior product?
7. Based on Porter's five forces, is this a good time to enter the retail music industry? Why or why not?
8. What is the cost to the music industry of music theft? Cite your source.
9. Discuss the concepts of price transparency and information asymmetry as they apply to the diamond industry as a result of the entry of BlueNile. Name another industry where the Internet has had a similar impact.
10. Under what conditions can the Internet strengthen supplier bargaining power? Give an example.
11. What is the effect of switching costs on buyer bargaining power? Give an example.
12. How does the Internet impact bargaining power for providers of rare or highly differentiated goods? Why?

ENDNOTES

1. J. Gallaugher and C. Downing, "Portal Combat: An Empirical Study of Competition in the Web Portal Industry," *Journal of Information Technology Management* 11, no. 1—2 (2000): 13—24.
2. B. Weiss, "Groupon's $6 Billion Gambler," *The Wall Street Journal*, December 20, 2010.
3. N. DiMeo, "TiVo's Goal with New DVR: Become the Google of TV," *Morning Edition*, National Public Radio, April 7, 2010.
4. E. Rusli, "Cisco Shutters Flip, Two Years After Acquisition," *New York Times*, April 12, 2011.
5. R. M. Schneiderman, "FreshDirect Goes to Greenwich," *Wall Street Journal*, April 6, 2010.
6. L. Croghan, "Food Latest Luxury Lure," *New York Daily News*, March 12, 2006.
7. P. Fox, "Interview with FreshDirect Co-Founder Jason Ackerman," Bloomberg Television, June 17, 2009.
8. E. Schonfeld, "The Big Cheese of Online Grocers Joe Fedele's Inventory-Turning Ideas May Make FreshDirect the First Big Web Supermarket to Find Profits," *Business 2.0*, January 1, 2004.
9. T. Laseter, B. Berg, and M. Turner, "What FreshDirect Learned from Dell," *Strategy+Business*, February 12, 2003.
10. J. Black, "Can FreshDirect Bring Home the Bacon?" *BusinessWeek*, September 24, 2002; S. Sieber and J. Mitchell, "FreshDirect: Online Grocery that Actually Delivers!" *IESE Insight*, 2007.
11. H. Green, "FreshDirect," *BusinessWeek*, November 24, 2003.
12. S. Sieber and J. Mitchell, "FreshDirect: Online Grocery that Actually Delivers!" *IESE Insight*, 2007; D. Kirkpatrick, "The Online Grocer Version 2.0," *Fortune*, November 25, 2002; P. Fox, "Interview with FreshDirect Co-Founder Jason Ackerman," Bloomberg Television, June 17, 2009.
13. P. Fox, "Interview with FreshDirect Co-Founder Jason Ackerman," Bloomberg Television, June 17, 2009.
14. R. M. Schneiderman, "FreshDirect Goes to Greenwich," *Wall Street Journal*, April 6, 2010.
15. C. Valerio, "Interview with FreshDirect Co-Founder Jason Ackerman," *Venture*, Bloomberg Television, September 18, 2009.
16. R. Shulman, "Groceries Grow Elusive for Many in New York City," *Washington Post*, February 19, 2008.
17. M. Porter, "What Is Strategy?" *Harvard Business Review* 74, no. 6 (November–December 1996): 61–78.
18. L. Kahney, "Net Speed Ain't Seen Nothin' Yet," *Wired News*, March 21, 2000.
19. L. Endlich, *Optical Illusions: Lucent and the Crash of Telecom* (New York: Simon & Schuster, 2004).
20. M. Porter, "Strategy and the Internet," *Harvard Business Review* 79, no. 3 (March 2001): 62–78.
21. B. Breen, "Living in Dell Time," *Fast Company*, December 19, 2007, http://www.fastcompany.com/magazine/88/dell.html.
22. T. Friscia, K. O'Marah, D. Hofman, and J. Souza, "The AMR Research Supply Chain Top 25 for 2009," *AMR Research*, May 28, 2009, http://www.amrresearch.com/Content/View.aspx?compURI=tcm:7-43469.
23. J. Edwards, "JWT's $100 Million Campaign for Microsoft's Bing Is Failing," *BNET*, July 16, 2009.
24. T. Mullaney, "Jewelry Heist," *BusinessWeek*, May 10, 2004.
25. S. Yin, "Report: Apple Controls 60% of Touchscreen Supply," *PCMag.com*, February 17, 2011.
26. J. Flatley, "Intel Invests $7 Billion in Stateside 32nm Manufacturing," *Engadget*, February 10, 2009.
27. R. Katz, "Tech Titans Building Boom," *IEEE Spectrum* 46, no. 2 (February 1, 2009): 40–43.
28. Adapted from C. Shapiro and H. Varian, "Locked In, Not Locked Out," *Industry Standard*, November 2–9, 1998.
29. J. Graham, "E-mail Carriers Deliver Gifts of Nifty Features to Lure, Keep Users," *USA Today*, April 16, 2008.
30. T. Davenport and J. Harris, *Competing on Analytics: The New Science of Winning* (Boston: Harvard Business School Press, 2007).
31. A virtuous adoption cycle occurs when network effects exist that make a product or service more attractive (increases benefits, reduces costs) as the adopter base grows.
32. Google Fourth Quarter 2008 Earnings Summary, http://investor.google.com/earnings.html.
33. N. Wingfield, "Microsoft Wins Key Search Deals," *Wall Street Journal*, January 8, 2009; P. Clarke, "Report: Microsoft to Pay Nokia $1 Billion for Support," *EETimes*, March 8, 2011.
34. B. Feld, "Why the Decks Are Stacked against Software Startups in Patent Litigation," *Technology Review*, April 12, 2009.
35. T. Wu, "Weapons of Business Destruction," *Slate*, February 6, 2006; R. Kelley, "BlackBerry Maker, NTP Ink $612 Million Settlement," *CNN Money*, March 3, 2006.
36. E. Mills, "DOJ Clears Apple-Microsoft-RIM Deal to buy Nortel Patents," *CNet*, February 13, 2012.
37. T. Mullaney and S. Ante, "InfoWars," *BusinessWeek*, June 5, 2000.
38. N. Carr, "IT Doesn't Matter," *Harvard Business Review* 81, no. 5 (May 2003): 41—49.
39. "Movies to Go," *Economist*, July 9, 2005.
40. FY 2011 net income and May 30, 2012, market cap figures for both firms.
41. N. Wingfield, "Netflix vs. the Naysayers," *Wall Street Journal*, March 21, 2007.
42. G. Hamel, "Killer Strategies that Make Shareholders Rich," *Fortune*, June 23, 1997.
43. For more on the long tail and collaborative filtering, see Chapter 4.
44. K. Barnes, "Music Sales Boom, but Album Sales Fizzle for '08," *USA Today*, January 4, 2009.

CHAPTER 3
Zara: Fast Fashion from Savvy Systems

1. INTRODUCTION

LEARNING OBJECTIVE

1. **Understand how Zara's parent company Inditex leveraged a technology-enabled strategy to become the world's largest fashion retailer.**

The poor, ship-building town of La Coruña in northern Spain seems an unlikely home to a tech-charged innovator in the decidedly ungeeky fashion industry, but that's where you'll find "The Cube," the gleaming, futuristic central command of the Inditex Corporation (Industrias de Diseño Textil), parent of game-changing clothes giant, Zara. The blend of technology-enabled strategy that Zara has unleashed seems to break all of the rules in the fashion industry. The firm shuns advertising and rarely runs sales. Also, in an industry where nearly every major player outsources manufacturing to low-cost countries, Zara is highly vertically integrated, keeping huge swaths of its production process in-house. These counterintuitive moves are part of a recipe for success that's beating the pants off the competition, and it has turned the founder of Inditex, Amancio Ortega, into Spain's wealthiest man and the world's richest fashion executive.

The firm tripled in size between 1996 and 2000, and then its revenue skyrocketed from $2.43 billion in 2001 to $18.3 billion in 2011. In August 2008, sales edged ahead of Gap, making Inditex the world's largest fashion retailer.[1] Table 3.1 compares the two fashion retailers. While Inditex supports eight brands, Zara is unquestionably the firm's crown jewel and growth engine, accounting for roughly two-thirds of sales.[2]

FIGURE 3.1

Zara's operations are concentrated in Spain, but they have stores around the world like these in Manhattan and Shanghai.

Source: Used with permission from Inditex.

TABLE 3.1 Gap versus Inditex at a Glance

	Gap	Inditex
Revenue	$14.5 billion	$18.3 billion
Net Income	$833 million	$2.56 billion
Number of Stores	3,248	5,527
Number of Countries	31	82
Biggest Brand	Gap	Zara
Number of Other Brands	4	7
Based in	San Francisco, USA	Arteixo (near La Coruña), Spain
First Store Opened	1969	1975

Sources: Year-end 2011 figures from http://www.gapinc.com, http://www.inditex.com, and http://www.bloomberg.com.

1.1 Why Study Zara?

While competitors falter, Zara is undergoing one of the fastest global expansions the fashion world has ever seen, opening one store per day and entering new markets worldwide—seventy-seven countries so far. The chain's profitability is among the highest in the industry.[3] The fashion director for luxury goods maker LVMH calls Zara "the most innovative and devastating retailer in the world."[4]

Zara's duds look like high fashion but are comparatively inexpensive (average item price is $27, although prices vary by country).[5] A Goldman analyst has described the chain as "Armani at moderate prices," while another industry observer suggests that while fashions are more "Banana Republic," prices are more "Old Navy."[6] Legions of fans eagerly await "Z-day," the twice-weekly inventory delivery to each Zara location that brings in the latest clothing lines for women, men, and children.

In order to understand and appreciate just how counterintuitive and successful Zara's strategy is, and how technology makes all of this possible, it's important to first examine the conventional wisdom in apparel retail. To do that we'll look at former industry leader—Gap.

1.2 Gap: An Icon in Crisis

Most fashion retailers place orders for a seasonal collection months before these lines make an appearance in stores. While overseas contract manufacturers may require hefty lead times, trying to guess what customers want months in advance is a tricky business. In retail in general and fashion in particular, there's a saying: inventory equals death. Have too much unwanted product on hand and you'll be forced to mark down or write off items, killing profits. For years, Gap sold most of what it carried in stores. Micky Drexler, a man with a radar-accurate sense of style and the iconic CEO who helped turn Gap's button-down shirts and khakis into America's business casual uniform, led the way. Drexler's team had spot-on tastes throughout the 1990s, but when sales declined in the early part of the following decade, Drexler was left guessing on ways to revitalize the brand, and he guessed wrong—disastrously wrong. Chasing the youth market, Drexler filled Gap stores with miniskirts, low-rise jeans, and even a much-ridiculed line of purple leather pants.[7] The throngs of teenagers he sought to attract never showed up, and the shift in offerings sent Gap's mainstay customers to retailers that easily copied the styles that Gap had made classic.

The inventory hot potato Drexler was left with crushed the firm. Gap's same-store sales declined for twenty-nine months straight. Profits vanished. Gap founder and chairman Dan Fisher lamented, "It took us thirty years to get to $1 billion in profits and two years to get to nothing."[8] The firm's debt was downgraded to junk status. Drexler was out and for its new head the board chose Paul Pressler, a Disney executive who ran theme parks and helped rescue the firm's once ailing retail effort.

Pressler shut down hundreds of stores, but the hemorrhaging continued largely due to bad bets on colors and styles.[9] During one holiday season, Gap's clothes were deemed so off target that the firm scrapped its advertising campaign and wrote off much of the inventory. The marketing model used by Gap to draw customers in via big-budget television promotion had collapsed. Pressler's tenure saw same-store sales decline in eighteen of twenty-four months.[10] A *Fortune* article on Pressler's leadership was titled "Fashion Victim." *BusinessWeek* described his time as CEO as a "Total System Failure,"[11] and Wall Street began referring to him as DMW for Dead Man Walking. In January 2007, Pressler resigned, with Gap hoping its third chief executive of the decade could right the ailing giant.

contract manufacturing

Outsourcing production to third-party firms. Firms that use contract manufacturers don't own the plants or directly employ the workers who produce the requested goods.

Contract Manufacturing: Lower Costs at What Cost?

Conventional wisdom suggests that leveraging cheap **contract manufacturing** in developing countries can keep the cost of goods low. Firms can lower prices and sell more product or maintain higher profit margins—all good for the bottom line. But many firms have also experienced the ugly downside to this practice. Global competition among contract firms has led to race-to-the-bottom cost-cutting measures. Too often, this means that in order to have the low-cost bid, contract firms skimp on safety, ignore environmental concerns, employ child labor, and engage in other ghastly practices.

The apparel industry in particular has been plagued by accusations of employing sweatshop labor to keep costs down. Despite the fact that Gap audits contract manufacturers and has a high standard for partner conduct, the firm has repeatedly been taken to task by watchdog groups, the media, and its consumers, who have exposed unacceptable contract manufacturing conditions that Gap failed to catch. This negative exposure includes the October 2007 video showing Gap clothes made by New Delhi children as young as ten years old in what were described as "slave labor" conditions.[12]

Gap is not alone; Nike, Wal-Mart, and many other apparel firms have been tarnished in similar incidents. Big firms are big targets and those that fail to adequately ensure their products are made under acceptable labor conditions risk a brand-damaging backlash that may turn off customers, repel new hires, and leave current staff feeling betrayed. Today's manager needs to think deeply not only about their own firm's ethical practices, but also those of all of their suppliers and partners.

Tech for Good: The Fair Factories Clearinghouse

The problem of sweatshop labor has plagued the clothing industry for years. Managers often feel the pressure to seek ever-lower costs and all too often end up choosing suppliers with unacceptably poor practices. Even well-meaning firms can find themselves stung by corner-cutting partners that hide practices from auditors or truck products in from unmonitored off-site locations. The results can be tragic for those exploited, and can carry lasting negative effects for the firm. The sweatshop moniker continues to dog Nike years after allegations were uncovered and the firm moved aggressively to deal with its problems.

Nike rival Reebok (now part of Adidas) has always taken working conditions seriously. The firm even has a Vice President of Human Rights and has made human dignity a key platform for its philanthropic efforts. Reebok invested millions in developing an in-house information system to track audits of its hundreds of suppliers along dimensions such as labor, safety, and environmental practices. The goal in part was to identify any bad apples, so that one division, sporting goods, for example, wouldn't use a contractor identified as unacceptable by the sneaker line.

The data was valuable to Reebok, particularly given that the firm has hundreds of contract suppliers. But senior management realized the system would do even more good if the whole industry could share and contribute information. Reebok went on to donate this system and provided critical backing to help create the nonprofit organization Fair Factories Clearinghouse. With management that included former lawyers for Amnesty International, Fair Factories (FairFactories.org) provides systems where apparel and other industries can share audit information on contract manufacturers. Launching the effort wasn't as easy as sharing the technology. The U.S. Department of Justice needed to provide a special exemption and had to be convinced the effort wouldn't be used by buyers to collude and further squeeze prices from competitors (the system is free of pricing data).

Suppliers across industries now recognize that if they behave irresponsibly the Fair Factories system will carry a record of their misdeeds, notifying all members to avoid the firm. As more firms use the system, its database becomes broader and more valuable. To their credit, both Gap and Nike have joined the Fair Factories Clearinghouse.

KEY TAKEAWAYS

- Zara has used technology to dominate the retail fashion industry as measured by sales, profitability, and growth.
- Excess inventory in the retail apparel industry is the kiss of death. Long manufacturing lead times require executives to guess far in advance what customers will want. Guessing wrong can be disastrous, lowering margins through markdowns and write-offs.
- Contract manufacturing can offer firms several advantages, including lower costs and increased profits. But firms have also struggled with the downside of cost-centric contract manufacturing when partners have engaged in sweatshop labor and environmental abuse.
- Firms with products manufactured under acceptable labor conditions face multiple risks, including legal action, brand damage, reduced sales, lower employee morale, and decreased appeal among prospective employees.

QUESTIONS AND EXERCISES

1. Has anyone shopped at Zara? If so, be prepared to share your experiences and observations with your class. What did you like about the store? What didn't you like? How does Zara differ from other clothing retailers in roughly the same price range? If you've visited Zara locations in different countries, what differences did you notice in terms of offerings, price, or other factors?
2. What is the "conventional wisdom" of the fashion industry with respect to design, manufacturing, and advertising?
3. What do you suppose are the factors that helped Gap to at one point rise to be first in sales in the fashion industry?
4. Who ran Gap in the 1990s? How did the executive perform prior to leaving Gap? Describe what happened to sales. Why?
5. Who was the Gap's second CEO of this decade? How did sales fare under him? Why?
6. Where do Gap clothes come from? Who makes them? Why? Are there risks in this approach?
7. Describe the downside of working with a supplier exposed as having used unethical practices. How does this potentially damage a firm? How can technology play a role in helping a firm become more socially responsible with its supply sourcing?
8. Describe the Fair Factories Clearinghouse. Which firm thought of this effort? Why did they give the effort away? Think in terms of strategic resources: what happens as more firms join this effort and share their data?

2. DON'T GUESS, GATHER DATA

LEARNING OBJECTIVE

1. **Contrast Zara's approach with the conventional wisdom in fashion retail, examining how the firm's strategic use of information technology influences design and product offerings, manufacturing, inventory, logistics, marketing, and ultimately profitability.**

personal digital assistants (PDAs)

Handheld computing devices meant largely for mobile use outside an office setting. PDAs were initially (nonphone) handheld computing devices, but sophisticated computing capabilities have now been integrated into other mobile device classes, such as smartphones and tablets.

Having the wrong items in its stores hobbled Gap for nearly a decade. But how do you make sure stores carry the kinds of things customers want to buy? Try asking them. Zara's store managers lead the intelligence-gathering effort that ultimately determines what ends up on each store's racks. Armed with **personal digital assistants (PDAs)**—handheld computing devices meant largely for mobile use outside an office setting—to gather customer input, staff regularly chat up customers to gain feedback on what they'd like to see more of. A Zara manager might casually ask, "What if this skirt were in a longer length?" "Would you like it in a different color?" "What if this V-neck blouse were available in a round neck?" Managers are motivated because they have skin in the game. The firm is keen to reward success—as much as 70 percent of salaries can come from commissions.[13]

Another level of data gathering starts as soon as the doors close. Then the staff turns into a sort of investigation unit in the forensics of trendspotting, looking for evidence in the piles of unsold items that customers tried on but didn't buy. Are there any preferences in cloth, color, or styles offered among the products in stock?[14]

point-of-sale (POS) systems

Transaction processing systems that capture customer purchases. Cash registers and store checkout systems are examples of point-of-sale systems. These systems are critical for capturing sales data and are usually linked to inventory systems to subtract out any sold items.

PDAs are also linked to the store's **point-of-sale (POS) system**—a transaction processing system that captures customer purchase information—showing how garments rank by sales. Using these two systems, managers can quickly and regularly send updates that combine the hard data captured at the cash register with insights on what customers would like to see.[15] All this valuable data allows the firm to plan styles and issue rebuy orders based on feedback rather than hunches and guesswork. The goal is to improve the frequency and quality of decisions made by the design and planning teams.

2.1 Design

Rather than create trends by pushing new lines via catwalk fashion shows, Zara designs follow evidence of customer demand. Data on what sells and what customers want to see goes directly to "The Cube" outside La Coruña, where teams of some three hundred designers crank out an astonishing thirty thousand items a year versus two to four thousand items offered up at big chains like H&M (the world's third largest fashion retailer) and Gap.[16] While H&M has offered lines by star designers like Stella McCartney and Karl Lagerfeld, as well as celebrity collaborations with Madonna and Kylie Minogue, the Zara design staff consists mostly of young, hungry *Project Runway* types fresh from design school. There are no prima donnas in "The Cube." Team members must be humble enough to accept feedback from colleagues and share credit for winning ideas. Individual bonuses are tied to the success of the team, and teams are regularly rotated to cross-pollinate experience and encourage innovation.

2.2 Manufacturing and Logistics

In the fickle world of fashion, even seemingly well-targeted designs could go out of favor in the months it takes to get plans to contract manufacturers, tool up production, then ship items to warehouses and eventually to retail locations. But getting locally targeted designs quickly onto store shelves is where Zara really excels. In one telling example, when Madonna played a set of concerts in Spain, teenage girls arrived to the final show sporting a Zara knockoff of the outfit she wore during her first performance.[17] The average time for a Zara concept to go from idea to appearance in store is fifteen days versus their rivals who receive new styles once or twice a season. Smaller tweaks arrive even faster. If enough customers come in and ask for a round neck instead of a V neck, a new version can be in stores with in just ten days.[18] To put that in perspective, Zara is *twelve times* faster than Gap despite offering roughly *ten times* more unique products![19] At H&M, it takes three to five months to go from creation to delivery—and they're considered one of the best. Other retailers need an average of six months to design a new collection and then another three months to manufacture it. VF Corp (Lee, Wrangler) can take nine months just to design a pair of jeans, while J. Jill needs a year to go from concept to store shelves.[20] At Zara, most of the products you see in stores didn't exist three weeks earlier, not even as sketches.[21]

The firm is able to be so responsive through a competitor-crushing combination of **vertical integration** and technology-orchestrated coordination of suppliers, just-in-time manufacturing, and finely tuned logistics. Vertical integration is when a single firm owns several layers in its **value chain**.[22] While H&M has nine hundred suppliers and no factories, nearly 60 percent of Zara's merchandise is produced in-house, with an eye on leveraging technology in those areas that speed up complex tasks, lower cycle time, and reduce error. Profits from this clothing retailer come from blending math with a data-driven fashion sense. Inventory optimization models help the firm determine how many of which items in which sizes should be delivered to each specific store during twice-weekly shipments, ensuring that each store is stocked with just what it needs.[23] Outside the distribution center in La Coruña, fabric is cut and dyed by robots in twenty-three highly automated factories. Zara is so vertically integrated, the firm makes 40 percent of its own fabric and purchases most of its dyes from its own subsidiary. Roughly half of the cloth arrives undyed so the firm can respond as any midseason fashion shifts occur. And in the face of record-high cotton prices in 2010, Zara was able to retool offerings away from more costly fabrics, preserving margins. By contrast, rival H&M saw profits drop 10 percent largely due to margin pressure.[24] After cutting and dying, many items are stitched together through a network of local cooperatives that have worked with Inditex so long they don't even operate with written contracts. The firm does leverage contract manufacturers (mostly in Turkey and Asia) to produce staple items with longer shelf lives, such as t-shirts and jeans, but such goods account for only about one-eighth of dollar volume.[25]

vertical integration

When a single firm owns several layers in its value chain.

value chain

The set of activities through which a product or service is created and delivered to customers.

All of the items the firm sells end up in a five-million-square-foot distribution center in La Coruña, or a similar facility in Zaragoza in the northeast of Spain. The La Coruña facility is some nine times the size of Amazon's warehouse in Fernley, Nevada, or about the size of ninety football fields.[26] The facilities move about two and a half million items every week, with no item staying in-house for more than seventy-two hours. Ceiling-mounted racks and customized sorting machines patterned on equipment used by overnight parcel services, and leveraging Toyota-designed logistics, whisk items from factories to staging areas for each store. Clothes are ironed in advance and packed on hangers, with security and price tags affixed. This system means that instead of wrestling with inventory during busy periods, employees in Zara stores simply move items from shipping box to store racks, spending most of their time on value-added functions like helping customers find what they want. Efforts like this help store staff regain as much as three hours in prime selling time.[27]

Trucks serve destinations that can be reached overnight, while chartered cargo flights serve farther destinations within forty-eight hours.[28] The firm recently tweaked its shipping models through Air France–KLM Cargo and Emirates Air so flights can coordinate outbound shipment of all Inditex brands with return legs loaded with raw materials and half-finished clothes items from locations outside of Spain. Zara is also a pioneer in going green. In fall 2007, the firm's CEO unveiled an environmental strategy that includes the use of renewable energy systems at **logistics** centers including the introduction of biodiesel for the firm's trucking fleet.

logistics

Coordinating and enabling the flow of goods, people, information, and other resources among locations.

2.3 Stores

Most products are manufactured for a limited production run. While running out of bestsellers might be seen as a disaster at most retailers, at Zara the practice delivers several benefits.

First, limited runs allow the firm to cultivate the exclusivity of its offerings. While a Gap in Los Angeles carries nearly the same product line as one in Milwaukee, each Zara store is stocked with items tailored to the tastes of its local clientele. A Fifth Avenue shopper quips, "At Gap, everything is the same," while a Zara shopper in Madrid says, "You'll never end up looking like someone else."[29] Upon visiting a Zara, the CEO of the National Retail Federation marveled, "It's like you walk into a new store every two weeks."[30]

Second, limited runs encourage customers to buy right away and at full price. Savvy Zara shoppers know the newest items arrive on black plastic hangers, with store staff transferring items to wooden ones later on. Don't bother asking when something will go on sale; if you wait three weeks the item you wanted has almost certainly been sold or moved out to make room for something new. Says one twenty-three-year-old Barcelona shopper, "If you see something and don't buy it, you can forget about coming back for it because it will be gone."[31] A study by consulting firm Bain & Company estimated that the industry average markdown ratio is approximately 50 percent, and until recently, less than 1 percent of JCPenny revenue came from items bought at full price.[32] Contrast this with Zara, where 85 percent of products are sold without a discount.[33]

The constant parade of new, limited-run items also encourages customers to visit often. The average Zara customer visits the store seventeen times per year, compared with only three annual visits made to competitors.[34] Even more impressive—Zara puts up these numbers with almost no advertising. The firm's founder has referred to advertising as a "pointless distraction." The assertion carries particular weight when you consider that during Gap's collapse, the firm increased advertising spending but sales dropped.[35] Fashion retailers spend an average of 3.5 percent of revenue promoting their products, while ad spending at Inditex is just 0.3 percent.[36]

Finally, limited production runs allow the firm to, as Zara's CEO once put it, "reduce to a minimum the risk of making a mistake, and we do make mistakes with our collections."[37] Failed product introductions are reported to be just 1 percent, compared with the industry average of 10 percent.[38] So even though Zara has higher manufacturing costs than rivals, Inditex gross margins are 56.8 percent compared to 37.5 percent at Gap.[39]

While stores provide valuable frontline data, headquarters plays a major role in directing in-store operations. Software is used to schedule staff based on each store's forecasted sales volume, with locations staffing up at peak times such as lunch or early evening. The firm claims these more flexible schedules have shaved staff work hours by 2 percent. This constant refinement of operations throughout the firm's value chain has helped reverse a prior trend of costs rising faster than sales.[40]

Even the store displays are directed from "The Cube," where a basement staging area known as "Fashion Street" houses a Potemkin village of bogus storefronts meant to mimic some of the chain's most exclusive locations throughout the world. It's here that workers test and fine-tune the chain's award-winning window displays, merchandise layout, and even determine the in-store soundtrack. Every two weeks, new store layout marching orders are forwarded to managers at each location.[41]

Technology ≠ Systems. Just Ask Prada

Here's another interesting thing about Zara. Given the sophistication and level of technology integration within the firm's business processes, you'd think that Inditex would far outspend rivals on tech. But as researchers Donald Sull and Stefano Turconi discovered, "Whether measured by IT workers as a percentage of total employees or total spending as a percentage of sales, Zara's IT expenditure is less than one-fourth the fashion industry average."[42] Zara excels by targeting technology investment at the points in its value chain where it will have the most significant impact, making sure that every dollar spent on tech has a payoff.

Contrast this with high-end fashion house Prada's efforts at its flagship Manhattan location. The firm hired the Pritzker Prize—winning hipster architect Rem Koolhaas to design a location Prada would fill with jaw-dropping technology. All items for sale in the store would sport **radio frequency identification (RFID) tags** (small chip-based tags that wirelessly emit a unique identifying code for the item that they are attached to). Walk into a glass dressing room and customers could turn the walls opaque, then into a kind of combination mirror and heads-up display. By wirelessly reading the tags on each garment, dressing rooms would recognize what was brought in and make recommendations of matching accessories as well as similar products that patrons might consider. Customers could check inventory, and staff wielding PDAs could do the same. A dressing room camera would allow clients to see their front and back view side-by-side as they tried on clothes.

radio frequency identification (RFID) tags

Small chip-based tags that wirelessly emit a unique identifying code for the item that they are attached to. Think of RFID systems as a next-generation bar code.

information system (IS)

An integrated solution that combines five components: hardware, software, data, procedures, and the people who interact with and are impacted by the system.

return on investment (ROI)

The amount earned from an expenditure.

It all sounded slick, but execution of the vision was disastrous. Customers didn't understand the foot pedals that controlled the dressing room doors and displays. Reports surfaced of fashionistas disrobing in full view, thinking the walls went opaque when they didn't. Others got stuck in dressing rooms when pedals failed to work, or doors broke, unable to withstand the demands of the high-traffic tourist location. The inventory database was often inaccurate, regularly reporting items as out of stock even though they weren't. As for the PDAs, staff reported that they "don't really use them anymore" and that "we put them away so tourists don't play with them." The investment in Prada's in-store technology was also simply too high, with estimates suggesting the location took in just one-third the sales needed to justify expenses.[43]

The Prada example offers critical lessons for managers. While it's easy to get seduced by technology, an **information system (IS)** is actually made up of more than *hardware* and *software*. An IS also includes *data* used or created by the system, as well as the *procedures* and the *people* who interact with the system.[44] Getting the right mix of these five components is critical to executing a flawless information system rollout. Financial considerations should forecast the **return on investment (ROI)**—the amount earned from an expenditure—of any such effort (i.e., what will we get for our money and how long will it take to receive payback?). And designers need to thoroughly test the system before deployment. At Prada's Manhattan flagship store, the effort looked like tech chosen because it seemed fashionable rather than functional.

KEY TAKEAWAYS

- Zara store management and staff use PDAs and POS systems to gather and analyze customer preference data to plan future designs based on feedback, rather than on hunches and guesswork.
- Zara's combination of vertical integration and technology-orchestrated supplier coordination, just-in-time manufacturing, and logistics allows it to go from design to shelf in days instead of months.
- Advantages accruing to Inditex include fashion exclusivity, fewer markdowns and sales, lower marketing expenses, and more frequent customer visits.
- Zara's IT expenditures are low by fashion industry standards. The spectacular benefits reaped by Zara from the deployment of technology have resulted from targeting technology investment at the points in the value chain where it has the greatest impact, and not from the sheer magnitude of the investment. This is in stark contrast to Prada's experience with in-store technology deployment.
- While information technology is just hardware and software, information systems also include data, people, and procedures. It's critical for managers to think about systems, rather than just technologies, when planning for and deploying technology-enabled solutions.

QUESTIONS AND EXERCISES

1. In what ways is the Zara model counterintuitive? In what ways has Zara's model made the firm a better performer than Gap and other competitors?
2. What factors account for a firm's profit margin? What does Gap focus on? What factors does Zara focus on to ensure a strong profit margin?
3. How is data captured in Zara stores? Using what types or classifications of information systems? How does the firm use this data?
4. What role does technology play in enabling the other elements of Zara's counterintuitive strategy? Could the firm execute its strategy without technology? Why or why not?
5. How does technology spending at Zara compare to that of rivals? Advertising spending? Failed product percentages? Markdowns?
6. What risks are inherent in the conventional practices in the fashion industry? Is Zara susceptible to these risks? Is Zara susceptible to different risks? If so, what are these?
7. Consider the Prada case mentioned in the sidebar "Technology ≠ Systems." What did Prada fail to consider when it rolled out the technology in its flagship location? Could this effort have been improved for better results? If you were put in charge of this kind of effort, what would determine whether you'd go forward with the effort or not? If you did go forward, what factors would you consider and how might you avoid some of the mistakes made by Prada?

3. MOVING FORWARD

LEARNING OBJECTIVES

1. **Detail how Zara's approach counteracts specific factors that Gap has struggled with for over a decade.**
2. **Identify the environmental threats that Zara is likely to face, and consider options available to the firm for addressing these threats.**

The holy grail for the strategist is to craft a sustainable competitive advantage that is difficult for competitors to replicate. And for nearly two decades Zara has delivered the goods. But that's not to say the firm is done facing challenges.

Consider the limitations of Zara's Spain-centric, just-in-time manufacturing model. By moving all of the firm's deliveries through just two locations, both in Spain, the firm remains hostage to anything that could create a disruption in the region. Firms often hedge risks that could shut down operations—think weather, natural disaster, terrorism, labor strife, or political unrest—by spreading facilities throughout the globe. If problems occur in northern Spain, Zara has no such fallback.

operations

The organizational activities that are required to produce goods or services. Operations activities can involve the development, execution, control, maintenance, and improvement of an organization's service and manufacturing procedures.

In addition to the **operations** vulnerabilities above, the model also leaves the firm potentially more susceptible to financial vulnerabilities during periods when the euro strengthens relative to the dollar. Many low-cost manufacturing regions have currencies that are either pegged to the dollar or have otherwise fallen against the euro. This situation means Zara's Spain-centric costs rise at higher rates compared to competitors, presenting a challenge in keeping profit margins in check. Rising transportation costs are another concern. If fuel costs rise, the model of twice-weekly deliveries that has been key to defining the Zara experience becomes more expensive to maintain.

Still, Zara is able to make up for some cost increases by raising prices overseas (in the United States, Zara items can cost 40 percent or more than they do in Spain). Zara reports that all North American stores are profitable, and that it can continue to grow its presence, serving forty to fifty stores with just two U.S. jet flights a week.[45] Management has considered a logistics center in Asia, but expects current capacity will suffice until 2013.[46] Another possibility might be a center in the Maquiladora region of northern Mexico, which could serve the U.S. markets via trucking capacity similar to the firm's Spain-based access to Europe, while also providing a regional center to serve expansion throughout the Western Hemisphere.

Rivals have studied the Zara recipe, and while none have attained the efficiency of Amancio Ortega's firm, many are trying to learn from the master. There is precedent for contract firms closing the cycle time gap with vertically integrated competitors that own their own factories. Dell (a firm that builds its own PCs while nearly all its competitors use contract labor) has seen its manufacturing advantage from vertical integration fall as the partners that supply rivals have mimicked its techniques and have become far more efficient.[47] In terms of the number of new models offered, clothing is actually more complex than computing, suggesting that Zara's value chain may be more difficult to copy. Still, H&M has increased the frequency of new items in stores, Forever 21 and Uniqlo get new looks within six weeks, and Renner, a Brazilian fast fashion rival, rolls out mini collections every two months.[48] Rivals have a keen eye on Inditex, with the CFO of luxury goods firm Burberry claiming the firm is a "fantastic case study" and "we're mindful of their techniques."[49]

Finally, firm financial performance can also be impacted by broader economic conditions. When the economy falters, consumers simply buy less and may move a greater share of their wallet to less-stylish and lower-cost offerings from deep discounters like Wal-Mart. Zara is also particularly susceptible to conditions in Europe since that market accounts for roughly two-thirds of firm sales.[50] Global expansion will provide the firm with a mix of locations that may be better able to endure downturns in any single region. Recent Spanish and European financial difficulties have made clear the need to decrease dependence on sales within one region.

Zara's winning formula can only exist through management's savvy understanding of how information systems can enable winning strategies (many tech initiatives were led by José Maria Castellano, a "technophile" business professor who became Ortega's right-hand man in the 1980s).[51] It is technology that helps Zara identify and manufacture the clothes customers want, get those products to market quickly, and eliminate costs related to advertising, inventory missteps, and markdowns. A strategist must always scan the state of the market as well as the state of the art in technology, looking for new opportunities and remaining aware of impending threats. With systems so highly tuned for success, it may be unwise to bet against "The Cube."

KEY TAKEAWAY

- Zara's value chain is difficult to copy; but it is not invulnerable, nor is future dominance guaranteed. Zara management must be aware of the limitations in its business model, and must continually scan its environment and be prepared to react to new threats and opportunities.

QUESTIONS AND EXERCISES

1. The Zara case shows how information systems can impact every single management discipline. Which management disciplines were mentioned in this case? How does technology impact each?
2. Would a traditional Internet storefront work well with Zara's business model? Why or why not?
3. Zara's just-in-time, vertically integrated model has served the firm well, but an excellent business is not a perfect business. Describe the limitations of Zara's model and list steps that management might consider to minimize these vulnerabilities.
4. Search online to find examples of firms that suffered production problems because they employed just-in-time manufacturing or kept limited inventory on hand. What caused the production problems? List any steps you can think of that the firms might consider to minimize the potential of such problems from occurring in the future. What role might technology play in your solution?

ENDNOTES

1. J. Hall, "Zara Is Now Bigger Than Gap," *Telegraph*, August 18, 2008.
2. R. Murphy, "Expansion Boosts Inditex Net," *Women's Wear Daily*, April 1, 2008.
3. D. Sull and S. Turconi, "Fast Fashion Lessons," *Business Strategy Review*, Summer 2008.
4. J. Surowiecki, "The Most Devastating Retailer in the World," *New Yorker*, September 18, 2000.
5. C. Rohwedder, "Zara Grows as Retail Rivals Struggle," *Wall Street Journal*, March 26, 2009.
6. J. Folpe, "Zara Has a Made-to-Order Plan for Success," *Fortune*, September 4, 2000.
7. J. Boorstein, "Fashion Victim," *Fortune*, April 13, 2006.
8. P. Sellers, "Gap's New Guy Upstairs," *Fortune*, April 14, 2003.
9. L. Lee, "Paul Pressler's Fall from The Gap," *BusinessWeek*, February 26, 2007.
10. J. Boorstein, "Fashion Victim," *Fortune*, April 13, 2006.
11. L. Lee, "Paul Pressler's Fall from the Gap," *BusinessWeek*, February 26, 2007.
12. E. Cho, "Gap: Report of Kids' Sweatshop 'Deeply Disturbing,'" *CNN.com*, October 29, 2007, http://www.cnn.com/2007/WORLD/asiapcf/10/29/gap.labor/index.html#cnnSTCVideo.
13. K. Capell, "Zara Thrives by Breaking All the Rules," *BusinessWeek*, October 9, 2008.
14. D. Sull and S. Turconi, "Fast Fashion Lessons," *Business Strategy Review*, Summer 2008.
15. C. Rohwedder and K. Johnson, "Pace-Setting Zara Seeks More Speed to Fight Its Rising Cheap-Chic Rivals," *Wall Street Journal*, February 20, 2008.
16. M. Pfeifer, "Fast and Furious," *Latin Trade*, September 2007; and "The Future of Fast Fashion," *Economist*, June 18, 2005.
17. "The Future of Fast Fashion," *Economist*, June 18, 2005.
18. J. Tagliabue, "A Rival to Gap That Operates Like Dell," *New York Times*, May 30, 2003.
19. M. Helft, "Fashion Fast Forward," *Business 2.0*, May 2002.
20. L. Sullivan, "Designed to Cut Time," *InformationWeek*, February 28, 2005.
21. J. Surowiecki, "The Most Devastating Retailer in the World," *New Yorker*, September 18, 2000.
22. Definition from the "father" of the value chain, Michael Porter. See M. Porter, "Strategy and the Internet," *Harvard Business Review* 79, no. 3 (March 2001): 62—78, among others.
23. C. Gentry, "European Fashion Stores Edge Past U.S. Counterparts," *Chain Store Age*, December 2007.
24. M. Johnson, "Investors Relieved as Inditex Profit Soars." *Financial Times*. March 21, 2011.
25. N. Tokatli, "Global Sourcing: Insights from the Global Clothing Industry—The Case of Zara, a Fast Fashion Retailer," *Journal of Economic Geography* 8, no. 1 (2008): 21—38.
26. M. Helft, "Fashion Fast Forward," *Business 2.0*, May 2002.
27. C. Rohwedder and K. Johnson, "Pace-Setting Zara Seeks More Speed to Fight Its Rising Cheap-Chic Rivals," *Wall Street Journal*, February 20, 2008; and K. Capell, "Zara Thrives by Breaking All the Rules," *BusinessWeek*, October 9, 2008.
28. K. Capell, "Zara Thrives by Breaking All the Rules," *BusinessWeek*, October 9, 2008.
29. K. Capell, "Fashion Conquistador," *BusinessWeek*, September 4, 2006.
30. M. Helft, "Fashion Fast Forward," *Business 2.0*, May 2002.
31. K. Capell, "Fashion Conquistador," *BusinessWeek*, September 4, 2006.
32. B. Tuttle, "In Major Shakeup, JCPenney Promises no more 'Fake Prices,'" *Fortune*, January 26, 2012.
33. D. Sull and S. Turconi, "Fast Fashion Lessons," *Business Strategy Review*, Summer 2008; and K. Capell, "Fashion Conquistador," *BusinessWeek*, September 4, 2006.
34. N. Kumar and S. Linguri, "Fashion Sense," *Business Strategy Review*, Summer 2006.
35. P. Bhatnagar, "How Do You Ad(dress) the Gap?" *Fortune*, October 11, 2004.
36. "Zara, A Spanish Success Story," *CNN.com*, June 15, 2001, http://edition.cnn.com/BUSINESS/programs/yourbusiness/stories2001/zara.
37. C. Vitzthum, "Zara's Success Lies in Low-Cost Lines and a Rapid Turnover of Collections," *Wall Street Journal*, May 18, 2001.
38. N. Kumar and S. Linguri, "Fashion Sense," *Business Strategy Review*, Summer 2006.
39. C. Rohwedder, "Zara Grows as Retail Rivals Struggle," *Wall Street Journal*, March 26, 2009. For labor cost comparison, K. Capell, "Zara Thrives by Breaking All the Rules," *BusinessWeek*, October 9, 2008, reports that workers in Spain earn an average of $1,650/month versus $206/month in China's Guangdong Province.
40. C. Rohwedder and K. Johnson, "Pace-Setting Zara Seeks More Speed to Fight Its Rising Cheap-Chic Rivals," *Wall Street Journal*, February 20, 2008.
41. C. Rohwedder and K. Johnson, "Pace-Setting Zara Seeks More Speed to Fight Its Rising Cheap-Chic Rivals," *Wall Street Journal*, February 20, 2008.
42. D. Sull and S. Turconi, "Fast Fashion Lessons," *Business Strategy Review*, Summer 2008.
43. G. Lindsay, "Prada's High-Tech Misstep," *Business 2.0*, March 1, 2004.
44. A. Sanchenko, "Foundations of Information Systems in Business" (lecture, October 13, 2007), http://www.scribd.com/doc/396076/Foundations-of-Information-Systems-in-Business.
45. J. Tagliabue, "A Rival to Gap That Operates Like Dell," *New York Times*, May 30, 2003.
46. C. Rohwedder and K. Johnson, "Pace-Setting Zara Seeks More Speed to Fight Its Rising Cheap-Chic Rivals," *Wall Street Journal*, February 20, 2008.
47. T. Friscia, K. O'Marah, D. Hofman, and J. Souza, "The AMR Research Supply Chain Top 25 for 2009," *AMR Research*, May 28, 2009, http://www.amrresearch.com/Content/View.aspx?compURI=tcm:7-43469.
48. M. Pfeifer, "Fast and Furious," *Latin Trade*, September 2007; and C. Rohwedder and K. Johnson, "Pace-Setting Zara Seeks More Speed to Fight Its Rising Cheap-Chic Rivals," *Wall Street Journal*, February 20, 2008.
49. C. Rohwedder and K. Johnson, "Pace-Setting Zara Seeks More Speed to Fight Its Rising Cheap-Chic Rivals," *Wall Street Journal*, February 20, 2008.
50. M. Baigorri, "Inditex 2011 Profits Rise 12% on Asian, Online Expansion," *Bloomberg*, March 21, 2012.
51. C. Rohwedder and K. Johnson, "Pace-Setting Zara Seeks More Speed to Fight Its Rising Cheap-Chic Rivals," *Wall Street Journal*, February 20, 2008.

CHAPTER 4

Netflix in Two Acts: The Making of an E-commerce Giant and the Uncertain Future of Atoms to Bits

1. INTRODUCTION

LEARNING OBJECTIVES

1. **Understand the basics of the two services operating under the Netflix business model.**
2. **Recognize the downside the firm may have experienced from an early IPO.**
3. **Appreciate why other firms found Netflix's market attractive, and why many analysts incorrectly suspected Netflix was doomed.**
4. **Understand the factors that led to customer exodus and stock market collapse, and identify mistakes Netflix made in rebranding the firm and splitting its offerings.**

In 2011 Netflix co-founder and CEO Reed Hastings went from tech industry pinnacle to business press punching bag. For years, Netflix was known for best-in-class service, regularly and repeatedly ranking atop multiple customer satisfaction surveys. Hastings had been appointed to the Board of Directors of two of the tech industry's most influential firms—Microsoft and Facebook. The prior year closed with *Fortune* featuring Hastings on its cover as the "Businessperson of the Year." By July 2011, Netflix's profits, customer base, and stock had each hit an all time high. But a poorly-communicated repricing scheme, followed by a failed attempt to split the firm into two websites, led to an exodus of nearly a million customers in three months, a collapse of the firm's share price, and calls for Hastings' resignation.[1]

The problems in the second half of 2011 were particularly shocking since Netflix had spent several years defying the predictions of naysayers. Analysts had spent years underestimating Netflix, assuming it would be vanquished by larger, deep-pocketed rivals. One analyst referred to the firm's impending competition as "The Last Picture Show" for Netflix,[2] another called the firm a "worthless piece of crap," setting a $3 target on a stock then trading at $11 a share.[3]

Doubters were concerned because Netflix was a dot-com, an Internet pure play without a storefront and with a miniscule customer base when compared with its new competition—Blockbuster and Wal-Mart. Hastings told *Fortune* that if he could change one strategic decision, it would have been to delay the firm's initial public stock offering (IPO), claiming that the financial disclosure required by public companies tipped off others that the firm was on a money-making growth tear. "If we had stayed private for another two to four years, not as many people would have understood how big a business this could be."[4] Once the secret was out, Blockbuster showed up, bringing with it 40 million card-carrying customers, and a promise to link DVD-by-mail with the nation's largest network of video stores. Following close behind was Wal-Mart—not just *a* big *Fortune* 500 company but *the* largest firm in the United States ranked by sales. A price war ensued, Netflix was forced to increase advertising, and the outlook for Hastings' baby seemed bleak.

Fast-forward and we see that the stellar rise of Netflix throughly trounced the doomsday predictions of the naysayers. Within a year of launch Wal-Mart had cut and run, dumping their experiment in DVD-by-mail. Blockbuster spent the next several years hemorrhaging billions of dollars, eventually declaring bankruptcy and selling out to satelite pay-TV provider, Dish Network. And that stock that was predicted to drop to $3 a share? It had instead skyrocketed past $300. Like the triumphant final scene in the movies, the dot-com did it. David knocked off not one, but two Goliaths.

Victory, right? Not so fast. At a time when Hastings seems to have achieved the pinnacle of success, Netflix was sent reeling from a sequence of gaffes that caused a customer exodus and share price collapse. The damage started when the single fee for the $10 base Netflix service was unbundled into two separate $8 plans for DVD-by-mail and streaming over the Internet. The move amounted to a 60 percent price hike for subscribers wanting to continue with both offerings, and customers rebelled. The firm's Facebook page quickly amassed over 44,000 negative comments, "Dear Netflix" complaints became a trending topic on Twitter, and customers began referring to the firm's CEO as "Greed Hastings."[5] Despite the outcry Netflix doubled-down in September 2011, announcing it would further split into two distinct services with two separate websites. The switch reads as a primer on what *not* to do when transitioning a business. The unpopular price hikes were followed by changes that actually made the firm's products harder to use by forcing customers to access two different websites, each with a separate database of offerings. Adding to the pain was the embarrassment of a botched rebranding of the DVD-by-mail service under the new name Qwikster. At the time of the rebranding announcement, Netflix had secured the domain Qwikster.com, but not the Twitter handle @Qwikster. The latter was owned by a guy whose drug referencing, foul-mouthed tweets were accompanied by a profile picture of a pot smoking Elmo from *Sesame Street.* Hastings, who stood at the peak of industry just a few weeks earlier, had become both a target of customer vitriol and an industry laughing stock, the subject of *Saturday Night Live* skits and comedian punch lines. Netflix quickly dropped plans for the Qwikster split, but it chose to hold firm with the price increase that started the slide. Over the course of 90 nightmarish days, Netflix lost over 800,000 customers, its stock tumbled from $304 a share to below $75, and its market value shed over $12 billion, including $2.3 billion in a single day.

When announcing Qwikster, Hastings wrote in a blog post that "...my greatest fear at Netflix has been that we wouldn't make the leap from success in DVDs to success in streaming. Most companies that are great at something—like AOL dialup or Borders bookstores—do not become great at new things people want (streaming for us) because they are afraid to hurt their initial business... Companies rarely die from moving too fast, and they frequently die from moving too slowly." But in this case, the poorly handled transition might just have been too much, too soon. It is true that while the DVD business built Netflix into a sector-dominating powerhouse, digital streaming is where the industry is headed. But this business is radically different from DVD-by-mail in several key ways, including content costs, content availability, revenue opportunities, rivals and their motivation, and more. If, and how, Netflix makes the transition from the certain-to-wither DVD-by-mail business to a profitable and dominant future in streaming remains to be seen.

1.1 Why Study Netflix?

Studying Netflix gives us a chance to examine how technology helps firms craft and reinforce a competitive advantage. In the next section we'll pick apart the components of the firm's DVD-by-mail strategy and learn how technology played a starring role in developing assets such as scale, brand, and switching costs that combined to place the firm atop its industry. This will also give us a chance to introduce concepts such as the long tail, collaborative filtering, crowdsourcing, and the value of the data asset. In the second part of this case, we recognize that while Netflix emerged the victorious underdog at the end of the first show, there will be at least one sequel, with the final scene yet to be determined. Act II looks at the very significant challenges the firm faces as its primary business shifts from competing in shipping the atoms of DVDs to one focused on sending bits over the Internet. We'll see that a highly successful firm can still be challenged by technical shifts, giving us an oportunity to examine issues that include digital goods, licensing, platform competition, and supplier power.

How Netflix Works: A Model in Transition

Here's how it started out: Reed Hastings, a former Peace Corps volunteer with a master's in computer science, got the idea for Netflix when he was late in returning the movie *Apollo 13* to his local video store. The forty-dollar late fee was enough to have bought the video outright with money left over. Hastings felt ripped off, and out of this outrage, Netflix was born. The firm's initial model for success was a DVD-by-mail service that charged a flat-rate monthly subscription rather than a per-disc rental fee. Under this model, customers don't pay a cent in mailing expenses, and there are no late fees. Videos arrive in red Mylar envelopes that are addressed and postage-paid for reuse in disc returns. When done watching videos, consumers just slip the DVD back into the envelope, reseal it with a peel-back sticky strip, and drop the disc in the mail. Users make their video choices in their "request queue" at Netflix.com. If a title isn't available, Netflix simply moves to the next title in the queue. Consumers use the Web site to rate videos they've seen, specify their viewing preferences, get video recommendations, check out title details, and even share their viewing habits and reviews.

The Netflix DVD-by-Mail Model

Source: Graphic from the Netflix PR Kit at http://www.netflix.com. Reproduced by permission of Netflix, Inc. Copyright © 2009, Netflix, Inc. All rights reserved.

This model helped Netflix grow into a giant, but technology continues to radically change the firm. Hastings knew that if his firm was successful it would one day transition from reliance on mailed DVDs and introduce streaming video. Says Hastings, "We named the company Netflix for a reason; we didn't name it DVDs-by-mail."[6] In 2007, the firm added a "Watch Now" button next to those videos that could be automatically streamed over the Internet, and offered unlimited streaming as part of the firm's base subscription price. By 2011, the firm was so focused on digital distribution that it made a streaming-only plan the default option for consumers (the first page at Netflix.com didn't even mention DVDs or discs). The still-popular DVD-by-Mail was no longer offered in the firm's base-price product—the disc subscription service that Netflix built its user-base with had become 'an optional add-on'.

The Netflix Streaming Model

Source: Graphic from the Netflix PR Kit at http://www.netflix.com. Reproduced by permission of Netflix, Inc. Copyright © 2009, Netflix, Inc. All rights reserved.

KEY TAKEAWAYS

- Analysts and managers have struggled to realize that dot-com start-up Netflix could actually create sustainable competitive advantage, beating back challenges from Wal-Mart and Blockbuster, among others.
- Data disclosure required by public companies may have attracted these larger rivals to the firm's market.
- Netflix operates via a DVD subscription and video-streaming model. These started as a single subscription, but are now viewed as two separate services. Although sometimes referred to as "rental," the model is really a substitute good for conventional use-based media rental.
- Fear of clinging to a sure-to-shrink DVD-by-mail business model prompted Netflix management to split and reprice its services. However, the price increase, a poorly handled rebranding effort, and a process that would have made the firm's services more difficult to use all contributed to the firm's first major customer contraction and satisfaction decrease.

QUESTIONS AND EXERCISES

1. Describe the two separate Netflix offerings.
2. Which firms are or have been Netflix's most significant competitors in the DVD-by-mail business? How do their financial results or performance of their efforts compare to Netflix's efforts?
3. What appointments have Reed Hastings accepted in addition to his job as Netflix CEO? Why are these appointments potentially important for Netflix?
4. Why did Wal-Mart and Blockbuster managers, as well as Wall Street analysts, underestimate Netflix? What issues might you advise analysts and managers to consider so that they avoid making these sorts of mistakes in the future?
5. Why did Netflix split its business into two separately billed services, and why did it attempt to split the business in two? What did the firm do wrong?
6. Do you think Netflix is right to try to hasten the transition to streaming? Why or why not? What are the risks in waiting? What are the risks in moving too quickly?

2. ACT I: NETFLIX LEVERAGES TECH AND TIMING TO CREATE KILLER ASSETS IN DVD-BY-MAIL

LEARNING OBJECTIVES

1. **Understand how many firms have confused brand and advertising, why branding is particularly important for online firms, and the factors behind Netflix's exceptional brand strength.**
2. **Understand the *long tail* concept, and how it relates to Netflix's ability to offer the customer a huge (the industry's largest) selection of movies.**
3. **Know what *collaborative filtering* is, how Netflix uses collaborative filtering software to match movie titles with the customer's taste, and in what ways this software helps Netflix garner sustainable competitive advantage.**
4. **List and discuss the several technologies Netflix uses in its operations to reduce costs and deliver customer satisfaction and enhance brand value.**
5. **Understand the role that scale economies play in Netflix's strategies, and how these scale economies pose an entry barrier to potential competitors.**
6. **Understand the role that market entry timing has played in the firm's success.**

To understand Netflix's strengths, it's important to view the firm as its customers see it. And for the most part, up until the summer of 2011 what they saw they liked—a lot! The firm has repeatedly ranked at the top of customer satisfaction surveys. Ratings agency ForeSee has named Netflix the number one e-commerce site in terms of customer satisfaction in eleven out of twelve surveys conducted since 2005 (placing it ahead of Apple and Amazon, among others). Netflix has also been cited as the best at satisfying customers by the American Customer Satisfaction Index (ACSI), Nielsen, and *Fast Company* and was also named the Retail Innovator of the Year by the National Retail Federation.

Building a great brand, especially one online, starts with offering exceptional value to the customer. Don't confuse branding with advertising. During the dot-com era, firms thought brands could be built through Super Bowl ads and expensive television promotion. Advertising can build awareness, but *brands are built through customer experience.* This is a particularly important lesson for online firms. Have a bad experience at a burger joint and you might avoid that location but try another of the firm's outlets a few blocks away. Have a bad experience online and you're turned off by the firm's one and only virtual storefront. If you click over to an online rival, the offending firm may have lost you forever. But if a firm can get you to stay through quality experience, switching costs and data-driven value might keep you there for a long, long time, even when new entrants try to court you away.

If brand is built through customer experience, consider what this means for the Netflix DVD-by-mail subscriber. They expect the firm to offer a huge selection, to be able to find what they want, for it to arrive on time, for all of this to occur with no-brainer ease of use and convenience, and at a fair price. Technology drives all of these capabilities, so tech has been at the very center of the firm's brand-building efforts.

2.1 Selection: The Long Tail in Action

Customers flocked to Netflix in part because of the firm's staggering selection. A traditional video store (and Blockbuster had some 7,800 of them) stocks roughly three thousand DVD titles on its shelves. For comparison, Netflix offers its customers a selection of over 125,000 DVD titles, and rising! At traditional brick-and-mortar retailers, shelf space is the biggest constraint limiting a firm's ability to offer customers what they want when they want it. Just which films, documentaries, concerts, cartoons, TV shows, and other fare make it inside the four walls of a Blockbuster store is dictated by what the average consumer is most likely to be interested in. To put it simply, Blockbuster stocked blockbusters.

Finding the right product mix and store size can be tricky. Offer too many titles in a bigger storefront and there may not be enough paying customers to justify stocking less popular titles (remember, it's not just the cost of the DVD—firms also pay for the real estate of a larger store, the workers, the energy to power the facility, etc.). For a profitable business there should be a breakeven point arrived at by considering the number of customers that can reach a location, along with factors such as store size, store inventory, the payback from that inventory, and the cost to own and operate the store. Anyone who has visited a video store only to find a title out of stock has run up against the limits of the physical store model.

But many online businesses are able to run around these limits of geography and shelf space. Internet firms that ship products can get away with having just a few highly automated warehouses, each stocking just about all the products in a particular category. And for firms that distribute products digitally, the efficiencies are even greater because there's no warehouse or physical product at all (more on that later).

Offer a nearly limitless selection and something interesting happens: there's actually *more money* to be made selling the obscure stuff than the hits. At Amazon.com, roughly 60 percent of books sold are titles that aren't available in even the biggest Borders or Barnes & Noble Superstores.[7] And at Netflix, roughly 75 percent of DVD titles shipped are from back-catalog titles, not new releases (at Blockbuster outlets the equation is nearly flipped, with some 70 percent of business coming from new releases).[8] Consider that Netflix sends out forty-five thousand different titles each day. That's *fifteen times* the selection available at your average video store! Each quarter, roughly 95 percent of titles are viewed—that means that every few weeks Netflix is able to find a customer for nearly *every* DVD title that has *ever* been commercially released.

This phenomenon whereby firms can make money by selling a near-limitless selection of less-popular products is known as the **long tail**. The term was coined by Chris Anderson, an editor at *Wired* magazine, who also wrote a best-selling business book by the same name. The "tail" (see Figure 4.3) refers to the demand for less popular items that aren't offered by traditional brick-and-mortar shops. While most stores make money from the area under the curve from the vertical axis to the dotted line, long tail firms can also sell the less popular stuff. Each item under the right part of the curve may experience less demand than the most popular products, but someone somewhere likely wants it. And as demonstrated from the examples above, the total demand for the obscure stuff is often much larger than what can be profitably sold through traditional stores alone. While some debate the size of the tail (e.g., whether obscure titles collectively are more profitable for most firms), two facts are critical to keep above this debate: (1) selection attracts customers, and (2) the Internet allows large-selection inventory efficiencies that offline firms can't match.

long tail

In this context, refers to an extremely large selection of content or products. The long tail is a phenomenon whereby firms can make money by offering a near-limitless selection.

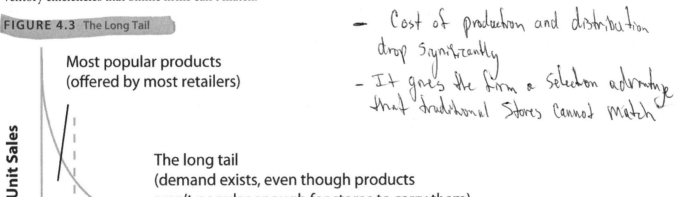

FIGURE 4.3 The Long Tail

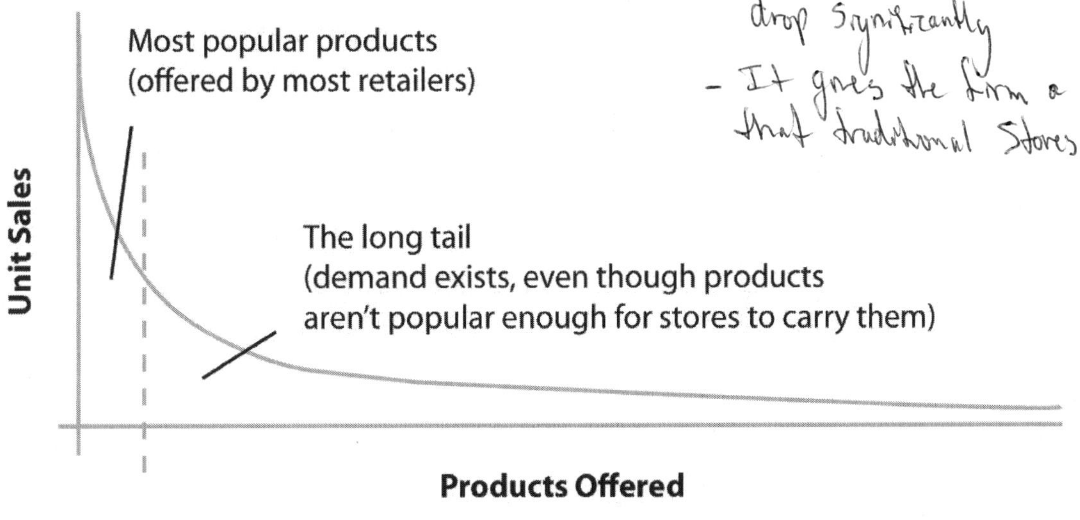

The long tail works because the cost of production and distribution drop to a point where it becomes economically viable to offer a huge selection. For Netflix, the cost to stock and ship an obscure foreign film is the same as sending out the latest Will Smith blockbuster. The long tail gives the firm a selection advantage (or one based on scale) that traditional stores simply cannot match.

For more evidence that there is demand for the obscure stuff, consider Bollywood cinema—a term referring to films produced in India. When ranked by the number of movies produced each year, Bollywood is actually bigger than Hollywood, but in terms of U.S. demand, even the top-grossing Hindi film might open in only one or two American theaters, and few video stores carry many Bollywood DVDs. Again, we see the limits that geography and shelf space impose on traditional stores. As Anderson puts it, when it comes to traditional methods of distribution, "an audience too thinly spread is the same as no audience at all."[9] While there are roughly 1.7 million South Asians living in the United States, Bollywood fans are geographically disbursed, making it difficult to offer content at a physical storefront. Fans of foreign films would often find the biggest selection at an ethnic grocery store, but even then, that wouldn't be much. Enter Netflix. The firm has found the U.S. fans of South Asian cinema, sending out roughly one hundred thousand Bollywood DVDs a month. As geographic constraints go away, untapped markets open up!

For evidence on Netflix's power to make lucrative markets from nonblockbusters, visit the firm's "Top 100 page."[10] You'll see a list loaded with films that were notable for their *lack* of box office success. In one six-year period during Netflix's hyper-growth, the top spot was held not by a first-run megahit but by the independent film *Crash* (an Oscar winner, but box office weakling).[11]

fixed costs

A cost that does not vary according to production volume.

Netflix has used the long tail to its advantage, crafting a business model that creates close ties with film studios. In most cases, studios earn a percentage of the subscription revenue for every disk sent out to a Netflix customer. In exchange, Netflix gets DVDs at a very low cost. The movie business is characterized by large **fixed costs** up front. Studio marketing budgets are concentrated on films when they first appear in theaters and when they're first offered on DVD. After that, studios are done promoting a film, focusing instead on their most current titles. But Netflix is able to find an audience for a film without the studios spending a dime on additional marketing. Since so many of the titles viewed on Netflix are in the long tail, revenue sharing is all gravy for the studios—additional income they would otherwise be unlikely to get. It's a win-win for both ends of the supply chain. These supplier partnerships grant Netflix a sort of soft bargaining power that's distinctly opposite the strong-arm price bullying that giants like Wal-Mart are often accused of.

The VCR, the Real "Killer App"?

Netflix's coziness with movie studios grateful to generate revenue from back-catalog movie titles is particularly noteworthy, given that the film industry has often viewed new technologies with a suspicion bordering on paranoia. In one of the most notorious incidents, Jack Valenti, the former head of the Motion Picture Association of America (MPAA) once lobbied the U.S. Congress to limit the sale of home video recorders, claiming, "the VCR is to the American film producer and the American public as the Boston strangler is to the woman home alone."[12]

Not only was the statement over the top, Jack couldn't have been more wrong. Revenue from the sale of VCR tapes would eventually surpass the take from theater box offices, and today, home video brings in about two times box office earnings.

2.2 Cinematch: Technology Creates a Data Asset That Delivers Profits

Netflix proves there's both demand and money to be made from the vast back catalog of film and TV show content. But for the model to work best, the firm needed to address the biggest inefficiency in the movie industry—"audience finding," that is, matching content with customers. To do this, Netflix leverages some of the industry's most sophisticated technology, a proprietary recommendation system that the firm calls Cinematch.

Each time a customer visits Netflix after sending back a DVD, the service essentially asks "So, how did you like the movie?" With a single click, each film can be rated on a scale of one to five stars. If you're new to Netflix, the service can prompt you with a list of movies (or you can search out and rate titles on your own). Love *Rushmore* but hate *The Life Aquatic*? Netflix wants to know.

The magic of Cinematch happens not by offering a gross average user rating—user tastes are too varied and that data's too coarse to be of significant value. Instead, Cinematch develops a map of user ratings and steers you toward titles preferred by people with tastes that are most like yours. Techies and marketers call this trick **collaborative filtering**. The term refers to a classification of software that monitors trends among customers and uses this data to personalize an individual customer's experience. Input from collaborative filtering software can be used to customize the display of a Web page for each user so that an individual is greeted only with those items the software predicts they'll want most. The kind of data mining done by collaborative filtering isn't just used by Netflix; other sites use similar systems to recommend music, books, even news stories. While other firms also employ collaborative filtering, Netflix has been at this game for years, and is constantly tweaking its efforts. The results are considered the industry gold standard.

collaborative filtering

A classification of software that monitors trends among customers and uses this data to personalize an individual customer's experience.

Collaborative filtering software is powerful stuff, but is it a source of competitive advantage? Ultimately it's just math. Difficult math, to be sure, but nothing prevents other firms from working hard in the lab, running and refining tests, and coming up with software that's as good, or perhaps one day even better than Netflix's offering. But what the software has created for the early-moving Netflix is an enormous data advantage that is valuable, results yielding, and impossible for newcomers to match. Even if Netflix gave Cinematch to its competitors, they'd be without the over five billion ratings that the firm has amassed (according to the firm, users add about a million new ratings to the system each day). More ratings make the system seem smarter, and with more info to go on, Cinematch can make more accurate recommendations than rivals.

FIGURE 4.4 Netflix and Recommendations

Source: Netflix Investor Day presentation, May 2008.

Reproduced by permission of Netflix, Inc. Copyright © 2009, Netflix, Inc. All rights reserved.

Evidence suggests that users trust and value Cinematch. Recommended titles make up over 60 percent of the content users place in their queues—an astonishing penetration rate. Compare that to how often you've received a great recommendation from the sullen teen behind the video store counter. While data and algorithms improve the service and further strengthen the firm's brand, this data is also a switching cost. Drop Netflix for a rival and the average user abandons the two hundred or more films they've rated. Even if one is willing to invest the time in recreating their ratings on another site, the rival will still make less accurate recommendations because there are fewer users and less data to narrow in on similarities across customers.

One way to see how strong these switching costs are is to examine the Netflix **churn rate**. Churn is a marketing term referring to the rate at which customers leave a product or service, and up until the customer rebellion following the 2011 re-pricing and Qwikster debacle, Netflix did a good job at keeping customers. A low churn is usually key to profitability because it costs more to acquire a customer than to keep one. And the longer a customer stays with the firm, the more profitable they become and the less likely they are to leave. If customers weren't completely satisfied with the Netflix experience, many would be willing to churn out and experiment with rivals offering cheaper service. However, the year after Blockbuster and Wal-Mart launched with copycat efforts, the rate at which customers left Netflix actually *fell* below 4 percent. Up until summer 2011, churn rates had remained stable, despite a challenging recession.[13]

churn rate

The rate at which customers leave a product or service.

All of this impacts marketing costs, too. Happy customers refer friends (free marketing from a source consumers trust). During the high growth period for the DVD-by-mail business, 94 percent of Netflix subscribers say they have recommended the service to someone else, and 71 percent of new subscribers say an existing subscriber has encouraged them to sign up.

The Netflix Prize

Netflix isn't content to stand still with its recommendation engine. Recognizing that there may be useful expertise outside its Los Gatos, California headquarters, the firm launched a **crowdsourcing** effort known as The Netflix Prize (for more on crowdsourcing, see Chapter 7).

crowdsourcing

The act of taking a job traditionally performed by a designated agent (usually an employee) and outsourcing it to an undefined generally large group of people in the form of an open call.

The Netflix Prize Leader Board

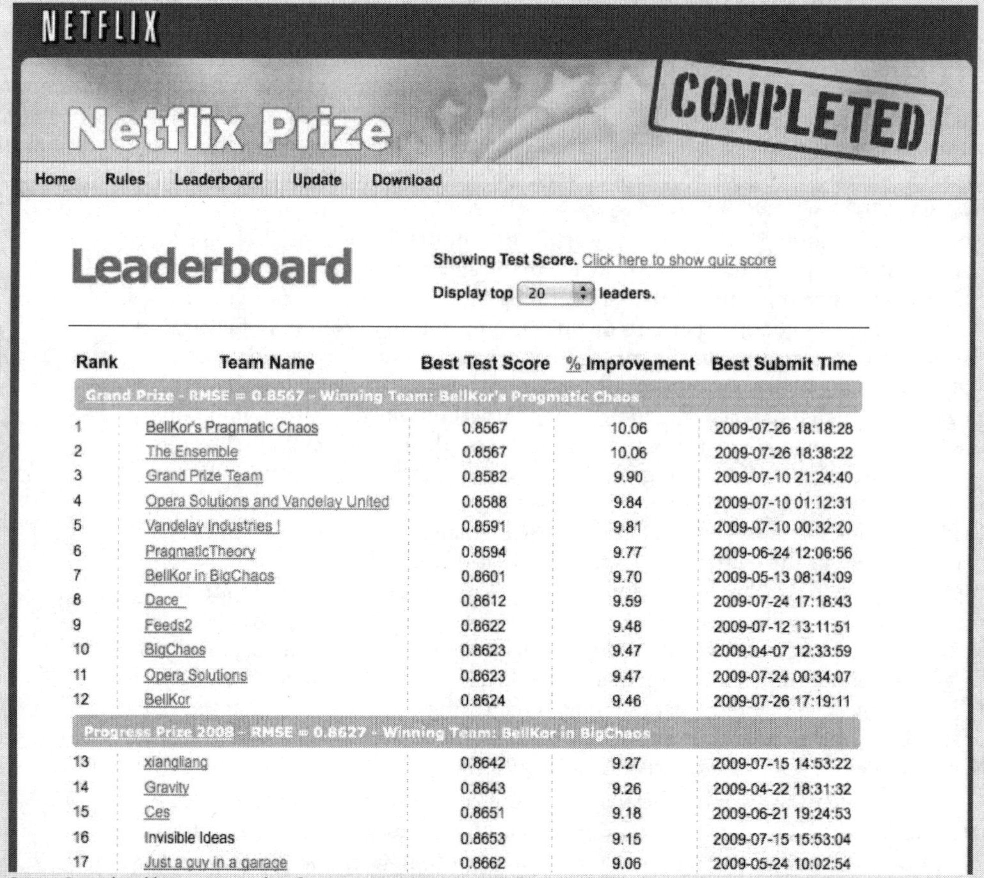

Rank	Team Name	Best Test Score	% Improvement	Best Submit Time
Grand Prize - RMSE = 0.8567 - Winning Team: BellKor's Pragmatic Chaos				
1	BellKor's Pragmatic Chaos	0.8567	10.06	2009-07-26 18:18:28
2	The Ensemble	0.8567	10.06	2009-07-26 18:38:22
3	Grand Prize Team	0.8582	9.90	2009-07-10 21:24:40
4	Opera Solutions and Vandelay United	0.8588	9.84	2009-07-10 01:12:31
5	Vandelay Industries !	0.8591	9.81	2009-07-10 00:32:20
6	PragmaticTheory	0.8594	9.77	2009-06-24 12:06:56
7	BellKor in BigChaos	0.8601	9.70	2009-05-13 08:14:09
8	Dace_	0.8612	9.59	2009-07-24 17:18:43
9	Feeds2	0.8622	9.48	2009-07-12 13:11:51
10	BigChaos	0.8623	9.47	2009-04-07 12:33:59
11	Opera Solutions	0.8623	9.47	2009-07-24 00:34:07
12	BellKor	0.8624	9.46	2009-07-26 17:19:11
Progress Prize 2008 - RMSE = 0.8627 - Winning Team: BellKor in BigChaos				
13	xiangliang	0.8642	9.27	2009-07-15 14:53:22
14	Gravity	0.8643	9.26	2009-04-22 18:31:32
15	Ces	0.8651	9.18	2009-06-21 19:24:53
16	Invisible Ideas	0.8653	9.15	2009-07-15 15:53:04
17	Just a guy in a garage	0.8662	9.06	2009-05-24 10:02:54

Source: Reproduced by permission of Netflix, Inc. Copyright © 2009, Netflix, Inc. All rights reserved.

The goal was simple: Offer $1 million to the first group or individual who can improve Cinematch's ratings accuracy by 10 percent. In order to give developers something to work with, the firm turned over a large ratings database (with customer-identifying information masked, of course). The effort attracted over 30,000 teams from 170 countries. Not bad when you consider that $1 million would otherwise fund just four senior Silicon Valley engineers for about a year. And the effort earned Netflix a huge amount of PR, as newspapers, magazines, and bloggers chatted up the effort.

While Netflix gains access to any of the code submitted as part of the prize, it isn't exclusive access. The Prize underscores the value of the data asset. Even if others incorporate the same technology as Netflix, the firm still has user data (and attendant customer switching costs) that prevent rivals with equal technology from posing any real threat. Results incorporating many innovations offered by contest participants were incorporated into Cinematch, even before the prize was won.

As the contest dragged on, many participants wondered if the 10 percent threshold could ever be reached. While many teams grew within striking distance, a handful of particularly vexing titles thwarted all algorithms, including the notorious *Napoleon Dynamite*. The film is so quirky, and Netflix customers so polarized, that there's little prior indicator to suggest if you're in the "love it" or "hate it" camp. One contestant claimed that single film was responsible for 15 percent of the gap between his team's effort and the million dollars.[14]

The eventual winner turned out to be a coalition of four teams from four countries—prior rivals who sought to pool their noggins and grab fame and glory (even if their individual prize split was less). BellKor's Pragmatic Chaos, the first team to cross the 10 percent threshold, included a pair of coders from Montreal; two U.S. researchers from AT&T Labs; a scientist from Yahoo! Research, Israel; and a couple of Austrian college students turned consultants.[15] It's safe to say that without the Netflix Prize, these folks would likely never have met, let alone collaborated.

Patron Saint of the Independent Film Crowd

Many critically acclaimed films that failed to be box office hits have gained a second life on Netflix, netting significant revenue for the studios, with no additional studio marketing. *Babel*, *The Queen*, and *The Last King of Scotland* are among the films that failed to crack the top twenty in the box office, but ranked among the most requested titles on Netflix during the year after their release. Netflix actually delivered more revenue to Fox from *The Last King of Scotland* than it did from the final X-Men film.[16]

In the true spirit of the long tail, Netflix has occasionally acquired small market titles for exclusive distribution. One of its first efforts involved the Oscar-nominated PBS documentary, *Daughters from Danang*. PBS hadn't planned to distribute the disc after the Academy Awards; it was simply too costly to justify producing a run of DVDs that almost no retailer would carry. But in a deal with PBS, Netflix assumed all production costs in exchange for exclusive distribution rights. For months after, the film repeatedly ranked in the Top 15 most requested titles in the documentary category. Cost to PBS—nothing.[17]

2.3 A Look at Operations

Tech also lies at the heart of the warehouse operations that deliver customer satisfaction and enhance brand value. As mentioned earlier, brand is built through customer experience, and a critical component of customer experience is for subscribers to get their DVDs as quickly as possible. In order to do this, Netflix has blanketed the country with a network of fifty-eight ultra high-tech distribution centers that collectively handle in excess of 1.8 million DVDs a day. These distribution centers are purposely located within driving distance of over 100 U.S. Postal Service (USPS) processing and distribution facilities.

By 4:00 a.m. each weekday, Netflix trucks collect the day's DVD shipments from these USPS hubs and returns the DVDs to the nearest Netflix center. DVDs are fed into custom-built sorters that handle disc volume on the way in and the way out. That same machine fires off an e-mail as soon as it detects your DVD was safely returned (now rate it via Cinematch). Most DVDs never hit the restocking shelves. Scanners pick out incoming titles that are destined for other users and place these titles into a sorted outbound pile with a new, appropriately addressed red envelope. Netflix not only helps out the postal service by picking up and dropping off the DVDs at its hubs, it presorts all outgoing mail for faster delivery. This extra effort has a payoff—Netflix gets the lowest possible postal rates for first-class mail delivery. And despite the high level of automation, 100 percent of all discs are inspected by hand so that cracked ones can be replaced, and dirty ones can be given a wipe down.[18] Total in and out turnaround time for a typical Netflix DVD is just eight hours![19]

First-class mail takes only one day to be delivered within a fifty-mile radius, so the warehouse network allows Netflix to service over 97 percent of its customer base within a two-day window—one day is allotted for receipt; early the next morning the next item in their queue is processed; and the new title arrives at the customer's address by that afternoon.

FIGURE 4.6 A Proprietary Netflix Sorting Machine

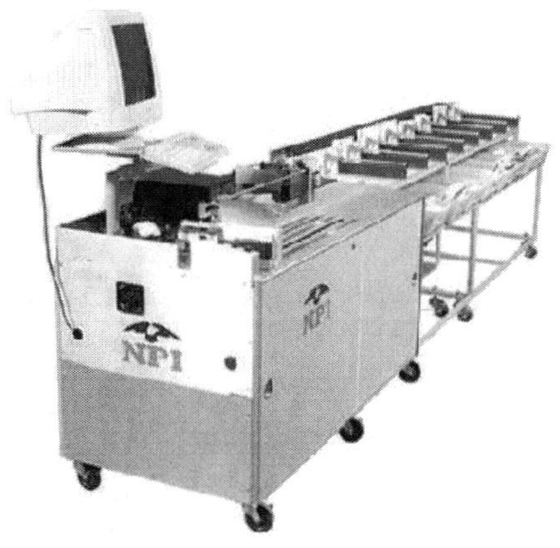

Source: Netflix Investor Day presentation, May 2008.

FIGURE 4.7 USPS Hubs Serviced by the Netflix Distribution Center Network

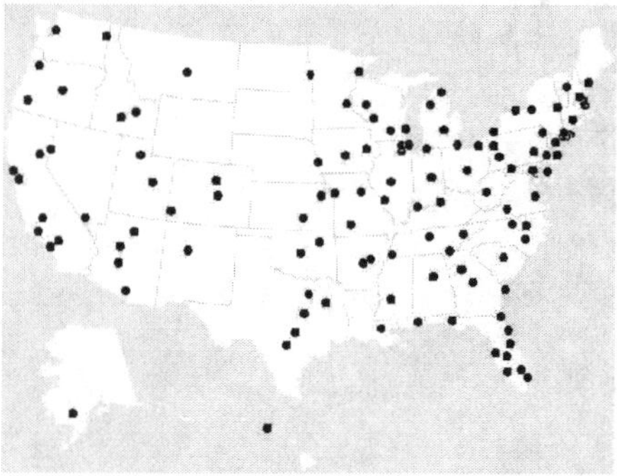

Source: Netflix Investor Day presentation, May 2008.

Warehouse processes don't exist in a vacuum; they are linked to Cinematch to offer the firm additional operational advantages. The software recommends movies that are likely to be in stock so users aren't frustrated by a wait.

Everyone on staff is expected to have an eye on improving the firm's processes. Every warehouse worker gets a Netflix subscription so that they understand the service from the customer's perspective and can provide suggestions for improvement. Quality management features are built into systems supporting nearly every process at the firm, allowing Netflix to monitor and record the circumstances surrounding any failures. When an error occurs, a tiger team of quality improvement personnel swoops in to figure out how to prevent any problems from recurring. Each customer complaint that the firm must field is a cost, not a revenue enhancement, and each error increases the chance that a dissatisfied customer will bolt for a rival.

By paying attention to process improvements and designing technology to smooth operations, Netflix has slashed the number of customer representatives even as subscriptions ballooned. In the early days, when the firm had one hundred and fifteen thousand customers, Netflix had one-hundred phone support reps. By the time the customer base had grown thirtyfold, errors had been reduced to the point where only forty-three reps were needed.[20] Even more impressive, because of the firm's effective use of technology to drive the firm's operations, fulfillment costs as a percentage of revenue have actually dropped even though postal rates have increased and Netflix has cut prices.

2.4 Killer Asset Recap: Understanding Scale

Netflix executives are quite frank that the technology and procedures that make up their model can be copied, but they also realize the challenges that any copycat rival faces. Says the firm's VP of Operations, "Anyone can replicate the Netflix operations if they wish. It's not going to be easy. It's going to take a lot of time and a lot of money."[21]

While Netflix might have seemed like David battling the Goliaths of Wal-Mart and Blockbuster, within the DVD-by-mail segment Netflix is now the biggest player by far, and this size gives the firm significant scale advantages. The yearly cost to run a Netflix-comparable nationwide delivery infrastructure is about $300 million.[22] Think about how this relates to economies of scale. In Chapter 2, we said that firms enjoy *scale economies* when they are able to leverage the cost of an investment across increasing units of production. Even if rivals have identical infrastructures, the more profitable firm will be the one with more customers (see Figure 4.8). And the firm with better scale economies is in a position to lower prices, as well as to spend more on customer acquisition, new features, or other efforts. Smaller rivals have an uphill fight, while established firms that try to challenge Netflix with a copycat effort are in a position where they're straddling markets, unable to gain full efficiencies from their efforts.

FIGURE 4.8

Running a nationwide sales network costs an estimated $400 million a year. But Netflix has several times more subscribers than Blockbuster. Which firm has economies of scale?[23]

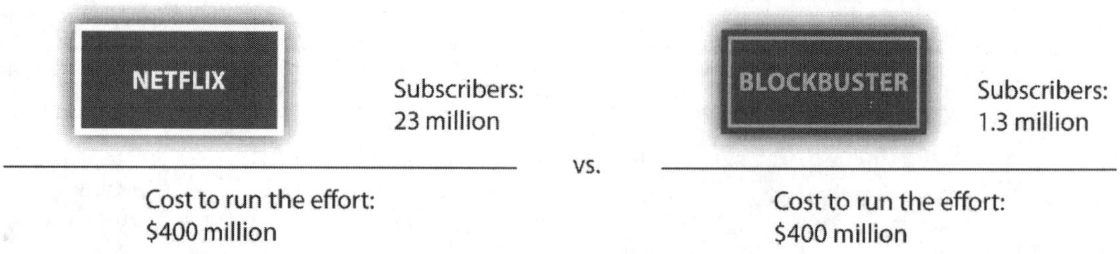

For Blockbuster, the arrival of Netflix plays out like a horror film where it is the victim. Netflix pressure forced Blockbuster to drop late fees, costing the firm about $400 million a year.[24] The Blockbuster store network once had the advantage of scale, but eventually its many locations were seen as an inefficient and bloated liability. During a three-year period that included the launch of its Total Access DVD-by-mail effort, Blockbuster lost over $4 billion and closed hundreds of stores.[25] The firm tried to outspend Netflix on advertising—even running Super Bowl ads for Total Access—but a money loser can't outspend its more profitable rival for long, and Blockbuster was eventually forced to cut back on promotion. Blockbuster also couldn't sustain subscription rates below Netflix's, so it has given up its price advantage. A Viacom executive said about the firm, "Blockbuster will certainly not survive and it will not be missed."[26] This assessment had to sting, given that Viacom was once Blockbuster's parent (the firm was spun off in 2004). In September 2010, Blockbuster declared bankruptcy, and in April 2011 the firm was purchased by Dish Network at a bankruptcy auction.[27]

For Netflix, what delivered the triple scale advantage of the largest selection, the largest network of distribution centers, and the largest customer base and the firm's industry-leading strength in brand and data assets? Moving first. Timing and technology don't always yield sustainable competitive advantage, but in this case, Netflix leveraged both to craft an extraordinarily valuable pool of assets.

But as we'll see in the next section, while technology shifts helped Netflix attack Blockbuster's once-dominant position, even newer technology shifts may threaten Netflix. As they like to say in the mutual fund industry "Past results aren't a guarantee of future returns."

KEY TAKEAWAYS

- Durable brands are built through customer experience, and technology lies at the center of the Netflix top satisfaction ratings and hence the firm's best-in-class brand strength.
- Physical retailers are limited by shelf space and geography. This limitation means that expansion requires building, stocking, and staffing operations in a new location.
- Internet retailers serve a larger geographic area with comparably smaller infrastructure and staff. This fact suggests that Internet businesses are more scalable. Firms providing digital products and services are potentially far more scalable, since physical inventory costs go away.
- The ability to serve large geographic areas through lower-cost inventory means Internet firms can provide access to the long tail of products, potentially earning profits from less popular titles that are unprofitable for physical retailers to offer.
- Netflix technology revitalizes latent studio assets. Revenue sharing allows Netflix to provide studios with a costless opportunity to earn money from back catalog titles: content that would otherwise not justify further marketing expense or retailer shelf space.
- The strategically aligned use of technology by this early mover has allowed Netflix to gain competitive advantage through the powerful resources of brand, data and switching costs, and scale.
- Collaborative filtering technology has been continually refined, but even if this technology is copied, the true exploitable resource created and leveraged through this technology is the data asset.
- Technology leveraged across the firm's extensive distribution network offers an operational advantage that allows the firm to reach nearly all of its customers with one-day turnaround.

QUESTIONS AND EXERCISES

1. What are Netflix's sources of competitive advantage?
2. Does Netflix have a strong brand? Offer evidence demonstrating why the firm's brand is or isn't strong. How is a strong brand built?
3. Scale advantages are advantages related to size. In what key ways is Netflix "bigger" than the two major competitors who tried to enter the DVD-by-mail market?
4. What is the long tail? How "long" is the Netflix tail compared to traditional video stores?
5. What "class" of software does Netflix use to make movie recommendations? Think about Chapter 2: Which key competitive resource does this software "create"? What kinds of benefits does this provide to the firm? What benefits does it provide to Netflix's suppliers?
6. Could a new competitor match Netflix's recommendation software? If it did, would this create a threat to Netflix? Why or why not?
7. What is the Netflix churn rate and what are the reasons behind this rate?
8. Netflix uses technology to coordinate the process of sorting and dropping off DVDs for the U.S. Postal Service. This application of technology speeds delivery. What other advantage does it give the firm?
9. How has Netflix improved its customer service operation? Describe the results and impact of this improvement.

3. ACT II: NETFLIX AND THE SHIFT FROM MAILING ATOMS TO STREAMING BITS

LEARNING OBJECTIVES

1. **Understand the shift from atoms to bits, and how this is impacting a wide range of industries.**
2. **Recognize the various key issues holding back streaming video models.**
3. **Know the methods that Netflix is using to attempt to counteract these challenges.**

atoms to bits

The idea that many media products are sold in containers (physical products, or atoms) for bits (the ones and zeros that make up a video file, song, or layout of a book). As the Internet offers fast wireless delivery to TVs, music players, book readers, and other devices, the "atoms" of the container aren't necessary. Physical inventory is eliminated, offering great cost savings.

Nicholas Negroponte, the former head of MIT's Media Lab and founder of the One Laptop per Child effort, wrote a now-classic essay on the shift from **atoms to bits**. Negroponte pointed out that most media products are created as bits—digital files of ones and zeros that begin their life on a computer. Music, movies, books, and newspapers are all created using digital technology. When we buy a CD, DVD, or even a "dead tree" book or newspaper, we're buying physical atoms that are simply a container for the bits that were created in software—a sound mixer, a video editor, or a word processor.

The shift from atoms to bits is realigning nearly every media industry. Newspapers struggle as readership migrates online and once-lucrative classified ads and job listings shift to the bits-based businesses of Craigslist, Monster.com, and LinkedIn. Apple dominates music sales, selling not a single "atom" of physical CDs, while most of the atom-selling "record store" chains of a decade ago are bankrupt. Amazon jumped into the atoms-to-bits shift when it developed the Kindle digital reader. Who needs to kill a tree, spill ink, fill a warehouse, and roll a gas-guzzling truck to get you a book? Kindle can slurp your purchases through the air and display them on a device lighter than any college textbook. When the Kindle was released, many thought it to be an expensive, niche product for gadget lovers, but in less than four years, the firm was selling more electronic books than print titles,[28] and in both unit sales and total revenue, the Kindle had become the best-selling product ever sold on Amazon.com.[29]

There's a clear potential upside to the Netflix model as it shifts from mailing atoms to streaming bits: it will eliminate a huge chunk of costs associated with shipping and handling. Postage represents about one-third of the firm's expenses. A round-trip DVD mailing, even at the deep discounts Netflix receives from the U.S. Postal Service, runs about eighty cents, while the bandwidth and handling costs to send bits to a TV set are around a nickel.[30] Netflix is such a large customer of the U.S. postal service that it represents some 20 percent of first-class "flats."[31] The U.S. Postal Service is also a potentially troubling long-term partner; with the agency's budget woes threatening price hikes, service slowdowns, and the cancellation of Saturday delivery.

Netflix built a profit-machine finely tuned to get DVDs to consumers within a day. But when the DVD dies, the high-tech shipping and handling infrastructure that Netflix has relentlessly built will be rendered worthless. Just about everything in the streaming business is different: content availability, content acquisition costs, potential opportunities for revenue and expansion, potential partners, competitors and their motivation. The question is, can Hastings pull off yet another victory and recast Netflix for the day that DVDs disappear, or will the atoms-to-bits shift decimate his firm's hard-earned competitive advantage and render his firm as irrelevant as Blockbuster?

fixed costs

Costs that do not vary according to production volume.

marginal costs

The costs associated with each additional unit produced.

Digital Products and Marginal Costs

Imagine you're an auto manufacturer. Before you can begin producing any vehicles you'll need to make some investments to get started. These **fixed costs** might include buying land and building a manufacturing plant. There are also costs associated with each individual unit produced. These are the **marginal costs** and would include things like the parts, materials, labor, and energy used to produce each additional car.

It's often argued that the marginal cost of digital goods is effectively zero. That's because computers can make limitless duplicates of digital content—no material required—and the Internet can be used to almost instantly distribute content to customers. In practice there are some costs associated with digital distribution. These might include the costs that a firm must pay to telecommunications providers that connect them to the Internet (the more a firm transmits, the more it typically has to pay), or the cost of running programs on the servers of other companies (see the cloud computing discussion in the chapter "Software in Flux"). For example, to deliver streaming video, Netflix actually uses computers provided by the cloud computing services of Amazon (making Amazon and Netflix both partners and competitors, a phenomenon often referred to as coopetition, or *frenemies*[32]). License fees can also add to the marginal costs of Netflix streaming. While computing costs might total just a nickel for each video streamed, if content providers charge Netflix a per-unit basis for streamed content, then this also gets added to marginal costs.

3.1 Access to Content

First the content. Three years after the launch of Netflix streaming option (enabled via a "Watch Now" button next to movies that can be viewed online), only about 17 percent of the firm's DVD catalog was available via streaming, and it wasn't the best 17 percent. While the number of titles available for streaming by Netflix has steadily increased, acquiring content has been a significant challenge. The DVD side of the business benefits from a Supreme Court ruling known as the "First Sale Doctrine." The ruling allows a firm to loan out physical copies of purchased products, so if studios sell their DVDs retail, they can't prevent Netflix, or anyone else, from buying DVDs at full price and sending purchased discs to subscribers. But "First Sale Doctrine" applies to the physical disc, not to streaming, so Netflix can't offer Internet streaming without separate licenses for this content.[33] It's not just studio reluctance or fear of piracy. There are often complicated legal issues involved in securing the digital distribution rights for all of the content that makes up a movie. Music, archival footage, and performer rights may all hold up a title from being available under "Watch Now." The 2007 Writers Guild strike occurred largely due to negotiations over digital distribution, showing just how troublesome these issues can be.

Add to that the exclusivity contracts negotiated by key channels, in particular the so-called *premium* television networks. Film studios release their work in a system called **windowing**. Content is available to a given distribution channel (in theaters, through hospitality channels like hotels and airlines, on DVD, via pay-per-view, via pay cable, then broadcast commercial TV) for a specified time window, usually under a different revenue model (ticket sales, disc sales, license fees for broadcast). Windows controlled by pay television channels can be particularly challenging, since many have negotiated exclusive access to content as they strive to differentiate themselves from one another. This exclusivity means that even when a title becomes available for streaming by Netflix, it may disappear when a pay TV window opens up. If HBO or Showtime has exclusive rights to broadcast a film, it's pulled from the Netflix streaming service until the exclusive pay TV time window closes. Partnerships with cable networks Starz and Epix initially helped provide access to some content locked up inside pay television windows, and deals with individual networks and studios allow for streaming of current-season shows.[34] However even these can get caught up in licensing details. For example, Sony titles were pulled from Netflix when a contract cap specifying the maximum number of subscribers that can stream Sony content was exceeded.[35] Netflix still has a long way to go before its streaming offerings catch up to the long tail of the firm's disc inventory.

windowing

Industry practice whereby content (usually a motion picture) is available to a given distribution channel for a specified time period or "window," usually under a different revenue model (e.g., ticket sale, purchase, license fee).

Even those studios that embrace the audience-finding and revenue-sharing advantages of Netflix don't want to undercut higher-revenue early windows. Fox, Universal, and Warner have all demanded that Netflix delay sending DVDs to customers until twenty-eight days after titles go on sale. In exchange, Netflix has received guarantees that these studios will offer more content for digital streaming.

FIGURE 4.9 Film Release Windows

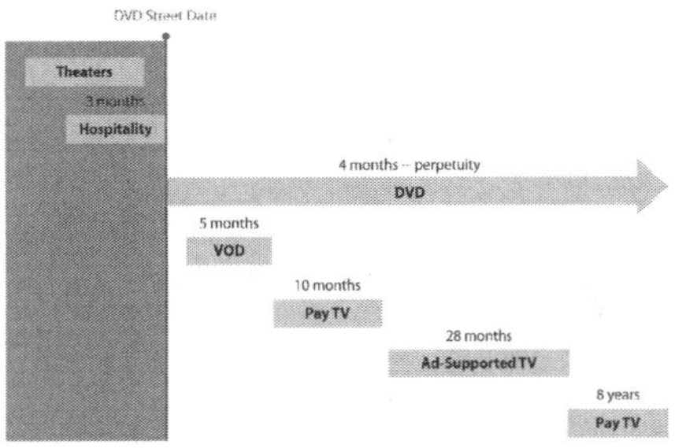

Source: Reproduced by permission of Netflix, Inc. Copyright © 2009, Netflix, Inc. All rights reserved.

There's also the influence of the king of DVD sales: Wal-Mart. The firm accounts for about 40 percent of DVD sales—a scale that delivers a lot of the bargaining power it has used to "encourage" studios to hold content from competing windows or to limit offering digital titles at competitive pricing during the peak new release period.[36] Apparently, Wal-Mart isn't ready to yield ground in the shifts from atoms to bits, either. The retail giant spent an estimated $100 million to buy the little-known video streaming outfit VUDU.[37] Wal-Mart's negotiating power with studios may help it gain special treatment for VUDU. As an example, VUDU was granted exclusive high-definition streaming rights for the hit movie *Avatar*, offering the title online the same day the DVD appeared for sale.[38]

Studios may also be wary of the increasing power Netflix has over product distribution, and as such, they may be motivated to keep rivals around. Studios have granted Blockbuster more favorable distribution terms than Netflix. While the bankrupt firm was bought out by Dish Network and remains a shadow of its former self, in many cases, Blockbuster can now distribute DVDs the day of release instead of waiting nearly a month, as Netflix does.[39] Studios are likely concerned that Netflix may be getting so big that it will one day have Wal-Mart-like negotiating leverage.

Controlling rising licensing costs presents a further challenge. Unlike DVD costs, which largely remain fixed (buy a DVD and you own it for life), streaming costs are usually licensed for a limited time period and costs often rise when licenses are renewed. Netflix financials indicate the firm's cost of acquiring streaming content has steadily risen, from $48 million in 2008 to $64 million in 2009, then to a whopping $406 million in 2010.

Streaming licensing deals also complicate a firm's cost estimates because rates vary widely even when titles are available. Studios might offer titles via a flat rate for unlimited streams, a rate according to a service's overall subscribers, a per-stream rate, a rate for a given number of streams, a premium for exclusive content, and various permutations in between. Some vendors have been asking as much as four dollars per stream for more valuable content—a fee that would quickly erase subscriber profits, making any such titles too costly to add to the firm's library. And some firms may require separate licenses to stream to international markets.

Another problem—some firms steadfastly refuse to offer Netflix streaming rights. Time Warner's HBO has thus far tried to keep streaming a perk limited to its own paying subscribers. It offers video-on-demand and *HBO Go* app access for its cable customers, but refuses to offer current content for streaming via Netflix. And while the Starz network initially licensed its content to Netflix for $30 million, it turned down ten times that amount to renew the deal in 2011.[40] HBO and Starz fear that a Netflix with broad content offerings might prompt cable subscribers to become *cord cutters* (eliminating cable all together) or *cord shavers* (who drop premium cable channels). Why pay $15 for a package of premium cable channels if Netflix could offer the same content and more for just $8.

One way Netflix can counter rivals with exclusive content is to offer exclusive content of its own. The firm has secured exclusive streaming rights for several popular shows, including the AMC series *Mad Men*. Netflix also paid $100 million for the initial twenty-six-episode exclusive for the series *House of Cards*, beating out HBO and AMC in a bidding war for a brand-new series featuring Oscar-winner Kevin Spacey and which will be produced by David Fincher (director of *The Social Network*). It's a risky move—unlike most of Netflix's other content, *House of Cards* hasn't been produced, so no one knows if it'll be a hit. And it's unknown if the prospect of exclusive content bidding wars will prompt more firms to share their content instead of fighting over it. But Netflix's growing audience size is now comparable to that of the largest cable firms, with some suggesting Netflix is a quasi-network (Netflix now has more subscribers than Showtime and Comcast and is closing in on HBO[41]). Hastings says he anticipates that Netflix will do more exclusive deals for new content, stating, "We're willing to do that if we have to, but we think it makes more economic sense for us and pay television [providers like HBO] to share windows."[42]

Supplier Power and Atoms to Bits

The winner-take-all, winner-take-most dynamics of digital distribution can put suppliers at a disadvantage. If firms rely on one channel partner for a large portion of sales, that partner has an upper hand in negotiations. For years, record labels and movie studios complained that Apple's dominance of iTunes allowed them little negotiating room in price setting. A boycott where NBC temporarily lifted TV shows from iTunes is credited with loosening Apple's pricing policies. Similarly, when Amazon's Kindle dominated the e-book reader market, Amazon enforced a $9.99 price on electronic editions, even as publishers lobbied for higher rates. It wasn't until Apple arrived with a creditable e-book rival in the iPad that Amazon's leverage was weakened to the point where publishers were allowed to set their own e-book prices.[43]

Taken together, all these content acquisition factors make it clear that attempts to profitably shift the long tail from atoms to bits will be significantly more difficult than buying DVDs and stacking them in a remote warehouse. Netflix has to be selective in the deals it'll cut because licensing costs could crater earnings. Unlike the DVD business, streaming content acquisition can't be about acquiring nearly every available title. Instead it's about having *enough* compelling content to attract paying subscribers, all while controlling costs to ensure profitability.

3.2 But How Does It Get to the TV?

The other major problem lies in getting content to the place where most consumers want to watch it: the living room TV. Netflix's "Watch Now" button first worked only on Windows PCs. The months before Netflix launced streaming were fueled with speculation that the firm would partner with TiVo, but when the settop box firm announced its first streaming partner it was Amazon. At that point Netflix found itself up against a host of rivals that all had a path to the television: Apple had its own hardware solution in Apple TV (not to mention the iPod and iPhone for portable viewing), the cable companies delivered OnDemand through their set-top boxes, and now Amazon had TiVo.

An internal team at Netflix developed a prototype set-top box that Hastings himself supported offering. But most customers aren't enthusiastic about purchasing yet another box for their set top, the consumer electronics business is brutally competitive, and selling hardware would introduce an entirely new set of inventory, engineering, marketing, distribution, and competitive complexities.

The solution Netflix eventually settled on was to think beyond one hardware alternative and instead recruit others to provide a wealth of choice. The firm developed a software platform and makes this available to manufacturers seeking to include Netflix access in their devices. Today, Netflix streaming is baked into over two hundred consumer electronics products, including televisions and DVD players from LG, Panasonic, Samsung, Sony, Toshiba, and Vizio. The migration to Blu-ray has also helped the firm piggyback its way into the living room. Buy one of the increasing number of Blu-ray players that has partnered with Hastings's firm and for just eight bucks a month you can get a ticket to the all-you-can-eat Netflix buffet. Netflix streaming is also available on all major video game consoles, the iOS and Android mobile platforms, and on the Kindle Fire and Barnes & Noble Nook. Even TiVo now streams Netflix. And that internally developed Netflix set-top box? The group was spun out to form Roku, an independent firm that launched their own $99 Netflix streamer. By developing an ecosystem of streaming providers, Netflix has expanded from a network of over 50 warehouses that distribute DVDs to one that can also enlist millions of devices to instantly deliver its content.

By working with consumer electronics firms, offering Netflix streaming as a feature or an app, Hastings's firm has ended up with more television access than either Amazon or Apple, despite the fact that both of these firms got their digital content to the TV set first. Partnerships have helped create distribution breadth, giving Hastings an enviable base through which to grow the video streaming business.

Disintermediation and Digital Distribution

The purchase of NBC/Universal by Comcast, the largest cable television provider in the United States, has consolidated content and distribution in a single firm. The move can be described as both vertical integration (when an organization owns more than one layer of its value chain) and **disintermediation** (removing an organization from a firm's distribution channel).[44] Disintermediation in the video industry offers two potentially big benefits. First, studios don't need to share revenue with third parties; they can keep all the money generated through new windows. Also critically important, studios keep the interface with their customers. Remember, in the digital age data is valuable; if another firm sits between a supplier and its customers, the supplier loses out on a key resource for competitive advantage. For more on the value of the data asset in maintaining and strengthening customer relationships, see Chapter 11.

disintermediation

Removing an organization from a firm's distribution channel. Disintermediation collapses the path between supplier and customer.

Who's going to win the race for delivering bits to the television is still very much an uncertain bet. The models all vary significantly. Netflix pioneered unlimited subscription streaming, but Dish Network's Blockbuster and Wal-Mart's VUDU also offer Netflix-like subscriptions and have copied Hastings's lead, partnering with consumer electronics makers to bring their services to TV sets. Apple's iTunes offers video purchases and "rentals" that can also play across PCs and Macs, as well as the firm's iPod, iPhone, iPad, and Apple TV products. Microsoft also offers an online rental and purchase service via Xbox. Amazon has expanded its Internet video purchase and rental business with the addition of free streaming for thousands of titles as a perk to those customers paying for its Amazon Prime shipping service. Amazon's consumer electronics partnerships have also expanded (those vendors are quite promiscuous) and many of the same firms partnering with Netflix also stream Amazon content. And Amazon is getting into the disc-by-mail act, too, acquiring LoveFilm (often described as the "Netflix of Europe"), for some $200 million in early 2011.[45] YouTube now offers thousands of television shows and movies via both ad-supported and rental models, and the firm's parent has launched Google TV to make television access easier. Facebook has begun to experiment with video streaming, working with Warner Brothers to stream *The Dark Knight* for a fee of thirty Facebook credits. With Netflix offering apps on so many of these competing platforms, the firm's frenemies list is a long one.

Networks and content providers also have their own offerings: many stream content on their own Web sites; Comcast and Verizon have apps that stream content to phones, PCs, and tablets; and Hulu is a joint venture backed by NBC, Fox, and other networks. Hulu offers a basic ad-supported PC streaming service as well as Hulu Plus, a subscription service that offers more content as well as streaming to certain consumer electronics devices. Whether all these efforts are individually sustainable remains to be seen. Many are efforts offered by deep-pocketed rivals that can subsidize experimentation through profits from their primary businesses, so even if efforts are slow to gain traction, a shakeout may take time.

A bits-based business can also be risky if the infrastructure is unreliable. If a store or warehouse has a problem, a firm can try to service customers from another location. But if the technology that supports your services breaks, then your entire business is brought to its knees. Netflix has suffered a series of such outages in the past, and any repeated reliability concerns risks prompting customers to seek alternatives.[46]

bandwidth caps

A limit, imposed by the Internet service provider (e.g., a cable or telephone company) on the total amount of traffic that a given subscriber can consume (usually per each billing period).

Then there's the issue of unhappy consumer Internet service providers. Netflix streaming has become the single largest source of North American Internet traffic, making up nearly 30 percent of data flowing into homes (a figure that grew 44 percent in just six months).[47] Many Internet service providers aren't pleased by the growth of Netflix streaming, viewing Netflix as a rapidly-expanding, network-clogging traffic hog. Netflix pays its own Internet service providers to connect the firm to the Internet and to support its heavy volume of outbound traffic. But Netflix offers no such payment to the ISPs used by consumers (e.g., your local cable and telephone companies). Several ISPs, including Comcast (which also owns content through its purchase of NBC/Universal), AT&T, and Charter, have experimented with **bandwidth caps** that place a ceiling on a customer's total monthly consumption (users can usually bump up the ceiling, but they have to pay to do it). Today few U.S. users are running into the ceiling, but that may change as more family members sport tablets, smartphones, and other streaming devices and as new, traffic-heavy technologies like Apple's FaceTime and Microsoft's Skype become more widely used. In Canada, Netflix has already lowered stream quality to deal with that nation's more restrictive traffic consumption limits. Netflix hasn't been shy about sharing its concern on bandwidth caps with the FCC, arguing that caps are really a much higher markup than the incremental cost of Internet transmission and claiming that if caps restrict users then this could stifle innovation.[48] If U.S. bandwidth caps start to limit consumer access to streaming, Netflix could suffer.

3.3 No Turning Back

While one day the firm will lose the investment in its warehouse infrastructure, nearly all assets have a limited lifespan. That's why corporations depreciate assets, writing their value down over time. The reality is that the shift from atoms to bits isn't flicking on like a light switch; it is a hybrid transition taking place over several years. Try to make the transition to streaming-only too quickly, and as the Qwikster debacle showed, customers may leave. But move too slowly and rivals can gain ground. If the firm can grab compelling content at manageable costs, broaden distribution options, grow its customer base, and lock them in with the switching costs created by Cinematch (all big "ifs"), it just might cement its position as a key player in a bits-only world. Even with the controversy over the price increase, *PC World* pointed out that Netflix still represented a far greater value than any of the available alternatives.[49]

Yes, streaming has challenges, but it also presents Netflix with a wide array of opportunities. Building out warehouse networks worldwide is impractical, but streaming will be the only option offered as Netflix rapidly expands, rolling its service out to an additional 43 countries worldwide.[50] Also remember that while Netflix built its business on a single monthly subscription fee, there's nothing that says this is the only model the firm will adhere to in the future. Netflix could also offer services such as pay-per-view content, higher-priced plans for premium offerings, and more. The firm's rich experience in matching content to customer preference might also provide the foundation for an ad-supported offering. Imagine getting content for lower prices, or even for free, if you allow Netflix to profile your viewing habits and serve up ads that it thinks you'll like. Streaming on-demand content with targeted ads could be a goldmine combination that radically undercuts the one-commercial-for-all model of current broadcast television.

Is the hybrid atoms and bits strategy a dangerous straddling gambit or a clever expansion that will keep the firm dominant? Netflix really doesn't have a choice but to try. Hastings already has a long history as one of the savviest strategic thinkers in tech. As the networks say, stay tuned!

TABLE 4.1 Netflix DVD-by-Mail versus Streaming

	Netflix DVD-by-Mail	Netflix Streaming	Notes
Content Acquistion Costs	Fixed.	Variable and increasing. No consistency in licensing parameters (variants include per subscriber, per use, per stream, duration of deal, exclusivity).	Starz turned down a Netflix 10x offer to renew licensing just 3 years after first pact. U.S. "first sale doctrine" means Netflix can buy and send out DVDs, but this ruling doesn't apply to streaming/broadcast.
Competitors	Mostly vanquished (bankrupt, inefficient Blockbuster bought by Dish). Indirect competition from Redbox kiosks but rival selection is small without delivery convenience.	Numerous with different models.	Digital video content available from Amazon, Apple, Dish/Blockbuster, Google/YouTube, Hulu, Walmart/Vudu, Cable providers (OnDemand), Pay channels (e.g. HBO Go).
Competitor Motivation	Market has little appeal for new entrants.	Maturing tech firms see streaming as a growth market, and revenue models/goals vary (subscription/PPV/Download-to-own, advertising, to fuel hardware purchases). Cable channels and cable providers fear subscriber loss.	Many rivals are highly profitable in other industries/have resources for expansion and to sustain prolonged competition. Pay channels fear their content will be devalued if Netflix is both cheaper and has a greater selection. Cable providers/channels fear chord cutting/shaving customers.
Plans	Fixed price per month based on number of DVDs at a time. High volume customers that frequently return DVDs are unprofitable.	Unlimited monthly subscription to all content.	Rival plans vary and include: subscription, free/commercial-supported, rental, pay-per-view, download to own.
Innovation	Very limited since DVD content is fixed by the studios and burned onto a disc.	Opportunities for new content and revenue models.	Streaming offers Netflix and rivals a chance to experiment with mixed revenue streams (premium priced 'windows,' ad-supported offerings with ability to gather/leverage high-value customer data), and the ability to launch new content/services DVDs can't match (social, interactive premium content).
Availability	Any DVD that can be purchased (125,000 title long tail).	Limited to what studios will license (20,000 title shorter tail, fewer new/hit titles).	Content is licensed from studios (content owners) or cable channels (if channels have the right to re-license broadcast/streaming rights to others). HBO and others won't share. Pay channels get exclusives in 'window' that may require content to be pulled from streaming.
Delivery Infrastructure	Tough to duplicate (58 warehouses). Staffed and maintained—require steady/increasing subscribers to keep margins high.	Currently uses public cloud (Amazon), but with proprietary technology.	Postal costs to increase while service may decrease (Saturday eliminated, delivery speed slowed). Public cloud use means rivals have access to similar delivery infrastructure assets. ISPs threaten end-user bandwidth caps that may lower streaming appeal.
Delivery To	Any device with a DVD player. Selected on web, delivery in about a day.	Any network-connected screen (TV, PC, mobile) w/a Netflix client. Instantly browse, preview, watch, and rate content.	Blu-ray likely the last physical standard. The future is streaming and Netflix has the largest partner platform, integrating in game consoles, TVs, DVD players, mobile devices, and more. Device partnerships are not exclusive to Netflix and rivals are expanding streaming reach w/similar integration.

	Netflix DVD-by-Mail	Netflix Streaming	Notes
Global Expansion	Expensive to replicate infrastructure regionally.	Can be served from the cloud, but reliant on local backbone and last-mile broadband.	DVD-by-mail needs cheap/fast local postal networks. Streaming costs are mostly dropping worldwide, but availability limited in some areas, quality varies, and bandwidth caps may limit appeal.
Market Outlook/ Challenges	U.S. DVD-by-mail is mature and likely to decrease. Profit margins associated with running a nationwide warehouse network will go down if subscribers drop/ shift to streaming.	A growing but highly unpredictable business in terms of future costs, content availability, rival intensity, appeal vs. alternatives, and more. Key is in creating strategic assets that others can't match, but what are they? Brand, scale advantages, and data drove DVD-by-mail dominance.	Uncertain if Netflix will gain streaming subscribers ahead of rivals. Wildcard: Netflix CEO Reed Hastings sits on the board of both Microsoft and Facebook—allies with potential for even stronger partnerships, but which are also potential competitors.

KEY TAKEAWAYS

- The shift from atoms to bits is impacting all media industries, particularly those relying on print, video, and music content. Content creators, middlemen, retailers, consumers, and consumer electronics firms are all impacted.
- Netflix's shift to a streaming model (from atoms to bits) is limited by access to content and in methods to get this content to televisions.
- While the "First Sale Doctrine" allows Netflix to send out physical DVDs to subscribers, this law doesn't apply to streaming.
- Windowing, exclusives, and other licensing issues limit available content, and inconsistencies in licensing rates make profitable content acquisitions a challenge. Although the marginal cost for digital goods is zero, this benefit doesn't apply to licensees.
- Netflix makes its streaming technology available to hardware firms, and it has developed streaming apps for a host of consumer electronics devices. As a result, Netflix streaming is available on more devices than any competing rival service.
- Netflix competitors in streaming are large, deep pocketed, and may have different motivations for offering streaming content (such as generating ad revenue, pay-per-view content sales, or as an incentive to make existing hardware platforms more attractive).
- The streaming business also offers Netflix opportunities to explore new revenue models, and it allows for rapid expansion into international markets.

QUESTIONS AND EXERCISES

1. Contrast Netflix's two businesses: DVD-by-mail and streaming. How do costs differ? How are these costs likely to change over time? How is subscriber interest in these services likely to change over time? What factors influence the reliability of each service? What threats are each of these businesses likely to face?
2. Who are the rivals to Netflix's "Watch Now" effort? Do any of these firms have advantages that Netflix lacks? What are these advantages?
3. Why would a manufacturer of DVD players be motivated to offer the Netflix "Watch Now" feature in its products?
4. Describe various revenue models available as video content shifts from atoms to bits. What are the advantages and disadvantages to each—for consumers, for studios, for middlemen like television networks and Netflix?
5. Make a chart of the various firms offering video-streaming services. List the pros and cons of each, along with its revenue model. Which efforts do you think will survive a shakeout? Why?
6. Wal-Mart backed out of the DVD-by-mail industry. Why does the firm continue to have so much influence with the major film studios? What strategic asset is Wal-Mart leveraging?
7. Investigate the firm Red Box. Do you think they are a legitimate threat to Netflix? Why or why not?
8. Is Netflix a friend or foe to the studios? Make a list of reasons why they would "like" Netflix, and why studios might be fearful of the firm. What is disintermediation, and what incentives do studios have to try to disintermediate Netflix?
9. Why didn't Netflix vertically integrate and offer its own set-top box for content distribution?
10. What has been the impact of Netflix summer 2011 move from single plan pricing to separate pricing for streaming and DVD-by-mail? What factors motivated this move? Do you think splitting the service into separate plans was a wise move? Why or why not?
11. Investigate the current status of bandwidth caps. Do you think bandwidth caps are fair? Why or why not?
12. Investigate Netflix stock price. One of the measures of whether a stock is "expensive" or not is the price-earnings ratio (share price divided by earnings per share). P/Es vary widely, but historic P/Es are about fifteen. What is the current P/E of Netflix? Do you think the stock is fairly valued based on prospects for future growth, earnings, and market dominance? Why or why not? How does the P/E of Netflix compare with that of other well-known firms, both in and out of the technology sector? Arrive in class with examples you are ready to discuss.
13. Netflix has begun to invest in securing the rights to original, previously unaired programming. What are the benefits and risks of such efforts?

ENDNOTES

1. J. Poggi, "3 Reasons Netflix Reed Hastings Shouldn't Be Fired... Yet," TheStreet.com, Oct. 24, 2011.
2. M. Conlin, "Netflix: Flex to the Max," BusinessWeek, September 24, 2007.
3. M. Copeland, "Reed Hastings: The Leader of the Pack," Fortune, Nov. 18, 2010.
4. M. Boyle, "Questions for...Reed Hastings," Fortune, May 23, 2007.
5. D. Pogue, "Why Netflix Raised Prices," The New York Times, July 14, 2011. E. Mack, "'Dear Netflix': Price hike ignites social-media fire," CNet, July 12, 2011. And G. Sandoval, "Don't call Netflix's CEO 'Greed' Hastings just yet," CNet, July 25, 2011.
6. M. Boyle, "Questions for...Reed Hastings," *Fortune*, May 23, 2007.
7. C. Anderson, "The Long Tail," *Wired* 12, no. 10 (October 2004), http://www.wired.com/wired/archive/12.10/tail.html.
8. B. McCarthy, "Netflix, Inc." (remarks, J. P. Morgan Global Technology, Media, and Telecom Conference, Boston, May 18, 2009).
9. C. Anderson, "The Long Tail," *Wired* 12, no. 10 (October 2004), http://www.wired.com/wired/archive/12.10/tail.html.
10. http://www.netflix.com/Top100.
11. R. Elder, "'Crash' Remains Top DVD Rental," *Chicago Tribune*, April 14, 2009.
12. J. Bates, "Formidable Force for Hollywood," *Los Angeles Times*, April 27, 2007.
13. "Final Transcript: NFLX—Q1 2011 Netflix Inc. Earnings Conference Call," Thompson StreetEvents, April 25, 2011.
14. C. Thompson, "If You Liked This, You're Sure to Love That," *New York Times*, November 21, 2008.
15. B. Patterson, "Netflix Prize Competitors Join Forces, Cross Magic 10-Percent Mark," *Yahoo! Tech*, June 29, 2009.
16. Netflix Investor Day presentation, May 2008, accessed via http://ir.netflix.com/events.cfm.
17. C. Anderson, "The Long Tail," *Wired* 12, no. 10 (October 2004), http://www.wired.com/wired/archive/12.10/tail.html.
18. B. McCarthy, "Netflix, Inc." (remarks, J. P. Morgan Global Technology, Media, and Telecom Conference, Boston, May 18, 2009).
19. N. Kenny, "Special Report: Inside Netflix," WMC TV, July 7, 2009.
20. J. McGregor, "High Tech Achiever," *Fast Company*, October 2005.
21. Netflix Investor Day presentation, 2008, accessed via http://ir.netflix.com/events.cfm.
22. S. Reda and D. Schulz, "Concepts that Clicked," *Stores*, May 2008.
23. M. Hoffman, "Netflix Tops 23 Million Subscribers," *Inc.*, April 25, 2011; T. Hals and L. Baker, "Dish Expands Scope with Blockbuster Win," *Reuters*, April 6, 2011; infrastructure cost estimates from S. Reda and D. Schulz, "Concepts That Clicked," *Stores*, May 2008.
24. T. Mullaney, "Netflix: The Mail-Order House That Clobbered Blockbuster," *BusinessWeek*, May 25, 2006.
25. N. MacDonald, "Blockbuster Proves It's Not Dead Yet," *Maclean's*, March 12, 2008.
26. E. Epstein, "Hollywood's New Zombie: The Last Days of Blockbuster," *Slate*, January 9, 2006, http://www.slate.com/id/2133995.
27. T. Hals and L. Baker, "Dish Expands Scope with Blockbuster Win," Reuters, April 6, 2011.
28. M. Hamblen, "Amazon: E-Books Now Outsell Print Books," *ComputerWorld*, May 19, 2011.
29. A. Golsalves, "Amazon Says Kindle Best Selling Product Ever," *InformationWeek*, December 27, 2010.
30. B. McCarthy, "Netflix, Inc." (remarks, J. P. Morgan Global Technology, Media, and Telecom Conference, Boston, MA, May 18, 2009).
31. D. Primack, "Netflix to U.S. Post: Drop Dead," Fortune, July 12, 2011.
32. A. Brandenberger and B. Nalebuff, Co-opetition: A Revolution Mindset that Combines Competition and Cooperation: The Game Theory Strategy That's Changing the Game of Business (New York: Broadway Business, 1997); and S. Johnson, "The Frenemy Business Relationship," Fast Company, November 25, 2008.
33. D. Roth, "Netflix Everywhere: Sorry Cable, You're History," *Wired*, September 21, 2009.
34. S. Portnoy, "Netflix News: Starz Catalog Added to Online Service, Streaming to PS3, Xbox 360 through PlayOn Beta Software," *ZDNet*, October 2, 2008, http://blogs.zdnet.com/home-theater/?p=120.
35. J. Pepitone, "Netflix's vanished Sony films are an ominous sign," Fortune, July 11, 2011.
36. R. Grover, "Wal-Mart and Apple Battle for Turf," *BusinessWeek*, August 31, 2006.
37. B. Stone, "Wal-Mart Adds Clout to Streaming," *New York Times*, February 22, 2010.
38. J. Jacobson, "VUDU/Wal-Mart Gets Avatar HD Streaming Exclusive," *Electronic House*, April 22, 2010.
39. J. Birchall, "Blockbuster Strikes Deal to Ensure DVD Supply," *Financial Times*, April 8, 2010.
40. W. Donckles, "Netflix and Starz Can't Strike a Deal Over Streaming," Technorati, Sept. 7, 2011.
41. B. Evangelista, "Netflix Growth Moves It into No. 2 behind HBO," *San Francisco Chronicle*, April 26, 2011.
42. L. Rose, "Netflix Will Distribute David Fincher's 'House of Cards'—It's Official," *Hollywood Reporter*, March 18, 2011.
43. M. Rich and B. Stone, "Publisher Wins Fight with Amazon over E-Books," *New York Times*, January 31, 2010.
44. J. Gallaugher, "E-Commerce and the Undulating Distribution Channel," *Communications of the ACM*, July 2002.
45. C. Byrne, "Amazon Acquires LoveFilm, Europe's Netflix, for Approximately $200 Million," *VentureBeat*, January 20, 2011.
46. L. Whitney, "Netflix Streaming Service Hit by Outage," CNet, July 18, 2011.
47. R. Lawler, "Netflix Traffic Now Bigger Than BitTorrent. Has Hollywood Won?," GigaOm, May 17, 2011.
48. R. Lawler, "Netflix Traffic Now Bigger Than BitTorrent. Has Hollywood Won?," *GigaOM*, May 17, 2011.
49. P. Suarez, "Netflix Alternatives: Other Places You Can Get Streaming Media, DVD Rentals," PC World, July 12, 2011.
50. J. Pepitone, "Netflix Expands to 43 New Countries," Fortune, July 5, 2011.

CHAPTER 5
Moore's Law: Fast, Cheap Computing and What It Means for the Manager

1. INTRODUCTION

LEARNING OBJECTIVES

1. **Define Moore's Law and understand the approximate rate of advancement for other technologies, including magnetic storage (disk drives) and telecommunications (fiber-optic transmission).**
2. **Understand how the price elasticity associated with faster and cheaper technologies opens new markets, creates new opportunities for firms and society, and can catalyze industry disruption.**
3. **Recognize and define various terms for measuring data capacity.**
4. **Consider the managerial implication of faster and cheaper computing on areas such as strategic planning, inventory, and accounting.**

Faster and cheaper—those two words have driven the computer industry for decades, and the rest of the economy has been along for the ride. Today it's tough to imagine a single industry not impacted by more powerful, less expensive computing. Faster and cheaper puts mobile phones in the hands of peasant farmers, puts a free video game in your Happy Meal, and drives the drug discovery that may very well extend your life.

1.1 Some Definitions

This phenomenon of "faster, cheaper" computing is often referred to as **Moore's Law**, after Intel cofounder, Gordon Moore. Moore didn't show up one day, stance wide, hands on hips, and declare "behold my law," but he did write a four-page paper for *Electronics Magazine* in which he described how the process of chip making enabled more powerful chips to be manufactured at cheaper prices.[1]

Moore's Law

Chip performance per dollar doubles every eighteen months.

Moore's friend, legendary chip entrepreneur and CalTech professor Carver Mead, later coined the "Moore's Law" moniker. That name sounded snappy, plus as one of the founders of Intel, Moore had enough geek cred for the name to stick. Moore's original paper offered language only a chip designer would love, so we'll rely on the more popular definition: *chip performance per dollar doubles every eighteen months.* (Moore's original paper stated transistors per chip, a proxy for power, would double every two years, but many sources today refer to the *eighteen*-month figure, so we'll stick with that—either way, we're still talking about ridiculously accelerating power and plummeting costs.)

Moore's Law applies to chips—broadly speaking, to *processors*, or the electronics stuff that's made out of silicon.[2] The **microprocessor** is the brain of a computing device. It's the part of the computer that executes the instructions of a computer program, allowing it to run a Web browser, word processor, video game, or virus. For processors, Moore's Law means that next generation chips should be twice as fast in *eighteen* months, but cost the same as today's models (or from another perspective, in a year and a half, chips that are same speed as today's models should be available for half the price).

microprocessor

The part of the computer that executes the instructions of a computer program.

random-access memory (RAM)

The fast, chip-based volatile storage in a computing device.

volatile memory

Storage (such as RAM chips) that is wiped clean when power is cut off from a device.

nonvolatile memory

Storage that retains data even when powered down (such as flash memory, hard disk, or DVD storage).

flash memory

Nonvolatile, chip-based storage, often used in mobile phones, cameras, and MP3 players. Sometimes called flash RAM, flash memory is slower than conventional RAM, but holds its charge even when the power goes out.

solid state electronics

Semiconductor-based devices. Solid state components often suffer fewer failures and require less energy than mechanical counterparts because they have no moving parts. RAM, flash memory and microprocessors are solid state devices. Hard drives are not.

semiconductor

A substance such as silicon dioxide used inside most computer chips that is capable of enabling as well as inhibiting the flow of electricity. From a managerial perspective, when someone refers to semiconductors, they are talking about computer chips, and the semiconductor industry is the chip business.

optical fiber line

A high-speed glass or plastic-lined networking cable used in telecommunications.

Random-access memory (RAM) is chip-based memory. The RAM inside your personal computer is **volatile memory**, meaning that when the power goes out, all is lost that wasn't saved to **nonvolatile memory** (i.e., a more permanent storage media like a hard disk or flash memory). Think of RAM as temporary storage that provides fast access for executing computer programs and files. When you "load" or "launch" a program, it usually moves from your hard drive to those RAM chips, where it can be more quickly executed by the processor.

Cameras, MP3 players, USB drives, and mobile phones often use **flash memory** (sometimes called *flash RAM*). It's not as fast as the RAM used in most traditional PCs, but holds data even when the power is off (so flash memory is also nonvolatile memory). You can think of flash memory as the chip-based equivalent of a hard drive. In fact, flash memory prices are falling so rapidly that several manufactures including Apple and the One Laptop per Child initiative (see the "Tech for the Poor" sidebar later in this section) have begun offering chip-based, nonvolatile memory as an alternative to laptop hard drives. The big advantage? Chips are **solid state electronics** (meaning no moving parts), so they're less likely to fail, and they draw less power. The solid state advantage also means that chip-based MP3 players like the iPod nano make better jogging companions than hard drive players, which can skip if jostled. For RAM chips and flash memory, Moore's Law means that in *eighteen* months you'll pay the same price as today for twice as much storage.

Computer chips are sometimes also referred to as **semiconductors** (a substance such as silicon dioxide used inside most computer chips that is capable of enabling as well as inhibiting the flow of electricity). So if someone refers to the *semiconductor industry*, they're talking about the chip business.[3]

Strictly speaking, Moore's Law does not apply to other technology components. But other computing components are also seeing their price versus performance curves skyrocket exponentially. Data storage doubles every twelve months. Networking speed is on a tear, too. With an equipment change at the ends of the cables, the amount of data that can be squirted over an **optical fiber line** can double every nine months.[4] These numbers should be taken as rough approximations and shouldn't be expected to be strictly precise over time. However, they are useful as rough guides regarding future computing price/performance trends. Despite any fluctuation, it's clear that the price/performance curve for many technologies is exponential, offering astonishing improvement over time.

FIGURE 5.1 Advancing Rates of Technology (Silicon, Storage, Telecom)

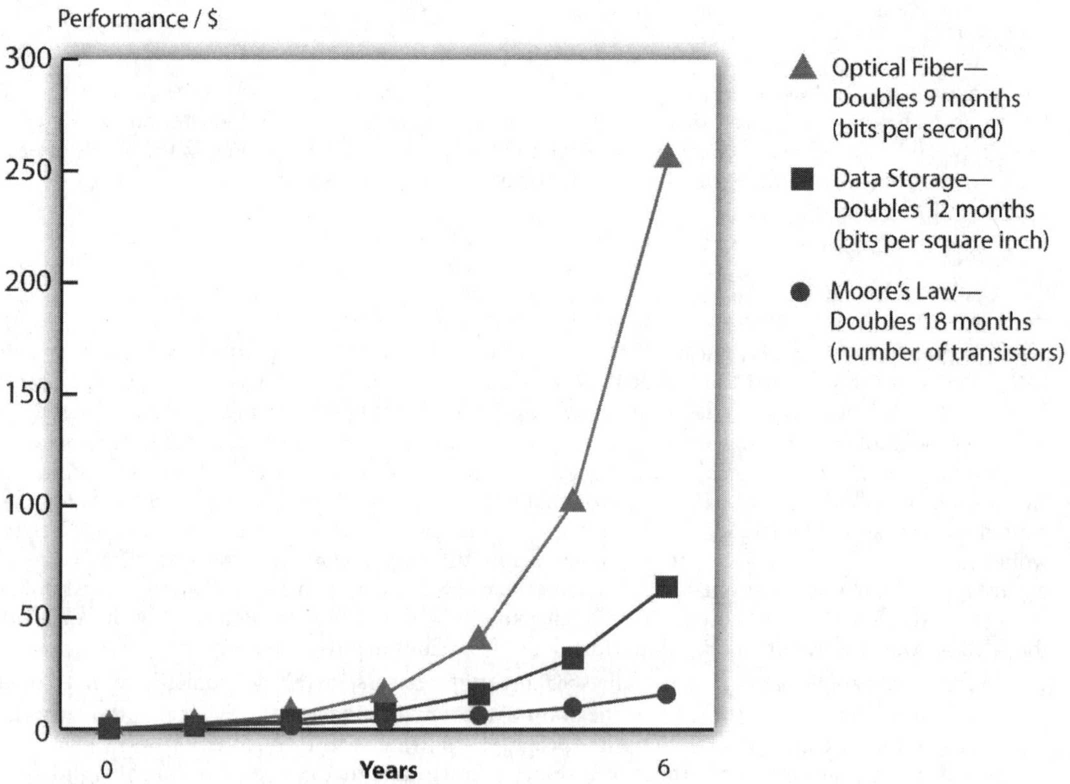

Source: Adopted from Shareholder Presentation by Jeff Bezos, Amazon.com, 2006.

1.2 Get Out Your Crystal Ball

Faster and cheaper makes possible the once impossible. As a manager, your job will be about predicting the future. First, consider how the economics of Moore's Law opens new markets. When technology gets cheap, **price elasticity** kicks in. Tech products are highly *price elastic*, meaning consumers buy more products as they become cheaper.[5] And it's not just that existing customers load up on more tech; entire *new markets* open up as firms find new uses for these new chips.

price elasticity

The rate at which the demand for a product or service fluctuates with price change. Goods and services that are highly price elastic (e.g., most consumer electronics) see demand spike as prices drop, whereas goods and services that are less price elastic are less responsive to price change (think heart surgery).

Just look at the *five waves of computing* we've seen over the previous five decades.[6] In the *first wave* in the 1960s, computing was limited to large, room-sized mainframe computers that only governments and big corporations could afford. Moore's Law kicked in during the 1970s for the *second wave*, and minicomputers were a hit. These were refrigerator-sized computers that were as speedy as or speedier than the prior generation of mainframes, yet were affordable by work groups, factories, and smaller organizations. The 1980s brought *wave three* in the form of PCs, and by the end of the decade nearly every white-collar worker in America had a fast and cheap computer on their desk. In the 1990s *wave four* came in the form of Internet computing—cheap servers and networks made it possible to scatter data around the world, and with more power, personal computers displayed graphical interfaces that replaced complex commands with easy-to-understand menus accessible by a mouse click. At the close of the last century, the majority of the population in many developed countries had home PCs, as did most libraries and schools.

Now we're in *wave five*, where computers are so fast and so inexpensive that they have become ubiquitous—woven into products in ways few imagined years before. Silicon is everywhere! It provides the smarts in the world's billion-plus mobile phones. It's in the throwaway radio frequency identification (RFID) tags that track your luggage at the airport. It's the brains inside robot vacuum cleaners, next generation Legos, and the table lamps that change color when the stock market moves up or down. These digital shifts can rearrange entire industries. Consider that today the firm that sells more cameras than any other is Nokia, a firm that offers increasingly sophisticated chip-based digital cameras as a giveaway as part of its primary product, mobile phones. This shift has occurred with such sweeping impact that former photography giants Kodak and the now-merged Konica-Minolta have exited the camera business.

Ambient Devices and the Fifth Wave

Pritesh Gandhi almost never gets caught in the rain without his umbrella. That's because Gandhi's umbrella regularly and wirelessly checks weather reports on its own. If the umbrella gets word it will rain in the next few hours, the handle blinks with increasing urgency, warning its owner with a signal that seems to declare, "You will soon require my services." Gandhi is CEO of "fifth wave" firm Ambient Devices, a Massachusetts start-up that's embedding computing and communications technology into everyday devices in an attempt to make them "smarter" and more useful (the weather-sensing umbrella was developed while he helmed the firm).

Ambient's ability to pull off this little miracle is evidence of how quickly innovative thinkers are able to take advantage of new opportunities and pioneer new markets enabled by Moore's Law. The firm's first product, the Orb, is a lamp that can be set up to change color in real time in reaction to factors such as the performance of your stock portfolio or the intensity of the local pollen count. In just six months, the ten refugees from MIT's Media Lab that founded Ambient Devices took the idea for the Orb, designed the device and its software, and licensed wireless spectrum from a pager firm that had both excess capacity and a footprint to cover over 90 percent of the United States.[7]

Ambient has since expanded the product line to several low-cost appliances designed to provide information at a glance. These include the Ambient Umbrella, as well as useful little devices that grab and display data ranging from sports scores to fluctuating energy prices (so you'll put off running the dishwasher until evening during a daytime price spike). The firm even partnered with LG on a refrigerator that can remind you of an upcoming anniversary as you reach for the milk.

Products developed by "fifth wave" firm Ambient Devices include the weather-reading Ambient Umbrella, the Energy Joule, a seven-day forecaster, and the Orb lamp.

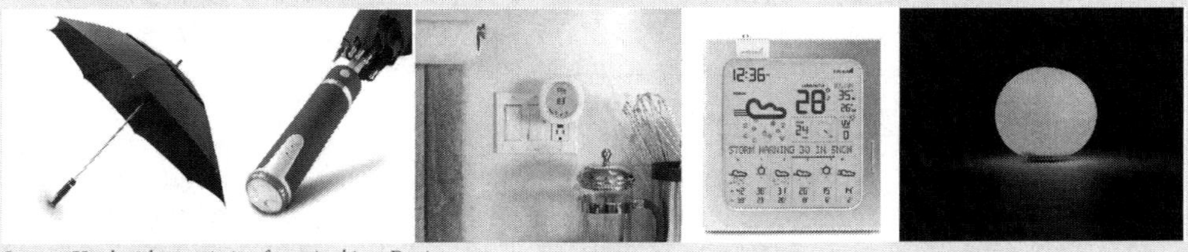

Source: Used with permission from Ambient Devices.

Moore's Law inside Your Medicine Cabinet

Moore's Law is about to hit your medicine cabinet, and several early-stage efforts show the potential for fifth-wave computing to improve healthcare quality while lowering costs. The GlowCap from Vitality, Inc., is a "smart" pill bottle that will flash when you're supposed to take your medicine. It will play a little tune if you're an hour late for your dose and will also squirt a signal to a night-light that flashes as a reminder (in case you're out of view of the cap). GlowCaps can also be set to call or send a text if you haven't responded past a set period of time. And the device will send a report to you, your doc, or whomever else you approve. The GlowCap can even alert your pharmacy when it's time for refills. The bottles sell for as little as $10 but in some cases are likely to be free. The business case for that? The World Health Organization estimates drug adherence at just 50 percent, and analysts estimate that up to $290 billion in increased medical costs are due to patients missing their meds. Vitality CEO David Rose (who incidentally also cofounded Ambient Devices) recently cited a test in which GlowCap users reported a 98 percent medication adherence rate.[8]

The GlowCap from Vitality, Inc., will flash, beep, call, and text you if you've skipped your meds. It can also send reports to you, your doctor, and your loved ones and even notify your pharmacy when it's time for a refill.

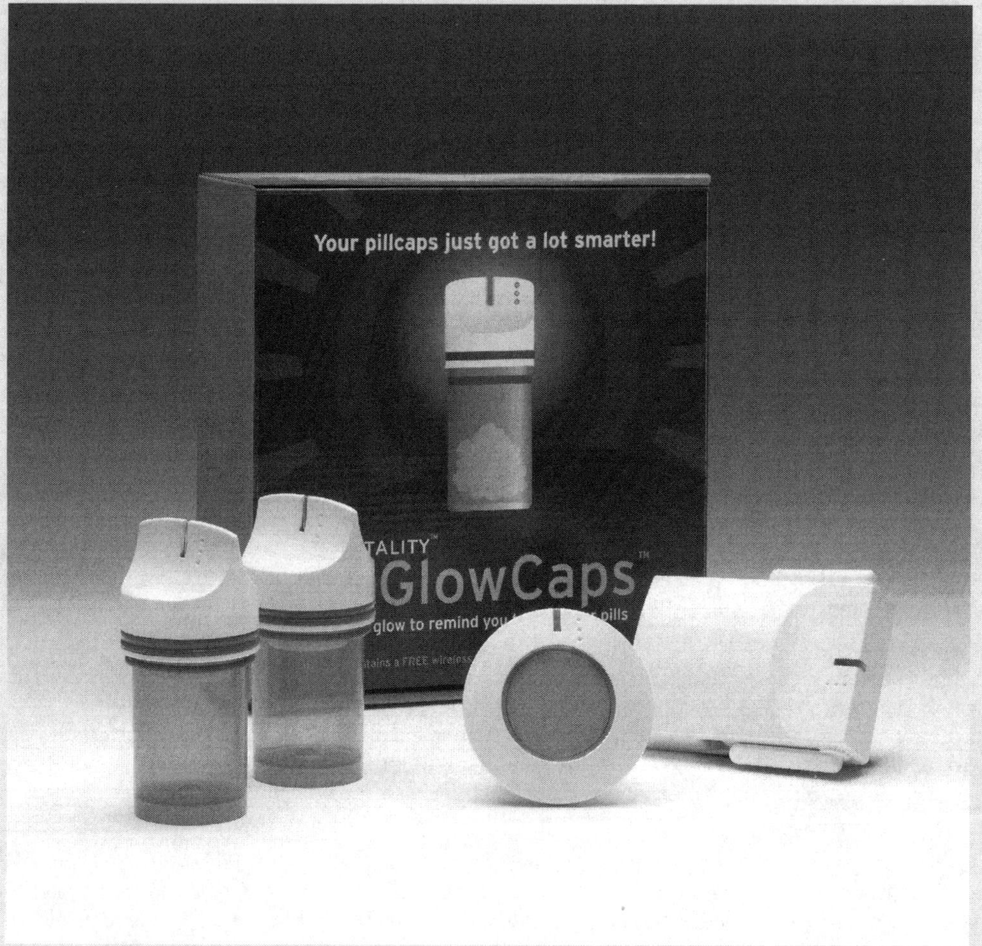

Source: Used with permission from Vitality, Inc.

And there might also be a chip inside the pills, too! Proteus, a Novartis-backed venture, has developed a sensor made of food and vitamin materials that can be swallowed in medicine. The sensor is activated and powered by the body's digestive acids (think of your stomach as a battery). Once inside you, the chip sends out a signal with vitals such as heart rate, body angle, temperature, sleep, and more. A waterproof skin patch picks up the signal and can wirelessly relay the pill's findings when the patient walks within twenty feet of their phone. Proteus will then compile a report from the data and send it to their mobile device or e-mail account. The gizmo's already in clinical trials for heart disease, hypertension, and tuberculosis and for monitoring psychiatric illnesses.[9] And a pill with built-in smarts can identify itself to help guard against taking counterfeit drugs, a serious worldwide concern. Pills that chat with mobile phones could help promote telemedicine, bringing health care to hard-to-reach rural populations. And games and social apps based on this information can provide motivating, fun ways to nudge patients into healthy habits. The CEO of Proteus Health says that soon you may be able to think of your body as "the ultimate game controller."[10]

One of the most agile surfers of this *fifth wave* is Apple, Inc.—a firm with a product line that is now so broad that in January 2007, it dropped the word "Computer" from its name. Apple's keen insight on where trends in computing power and performance are headed is captured in this quotation by the firm's co-founder, the late Steve Jobs: "There's an old Wayne Gretzky quote that I love. 'I skate to where the puck is going to be, not where it has been.' And we've always tried to do that at Apple. Since the very very beginning. And we always will."[11] The curves above aren't perfect, but they can help managers see where the puck is headed, helping the savvy manager predict the future, plan for the impossible to become possible, and act as the disruptor rather than the disrupted.

Apple's breakout resurgence owes a great deal to the iPod. At launch, the original iPod sported a 5 GB hard drive that Steve Jobs declared would "put 1,000 songs in your pocket." Cost? $399. Less than six years later, Apple's highest-capacity iPod sold for fifty dollars less than the original, yet held *forty times* the songs. By that time the firm had sold over one hundred fifty million iPods—an adoption rate faster than the original Sony Walkman. Apple's high-end models have morphed into Internet browsing devices capable of showing maps, playing videos, and gulping down songs from Starbucks' Wi-Fi while waiting in line for a latte.

The original iPod has also become the jumping-off point for new business lines including the iPhone, Apple TV, iPad, and iTunes. As an online store, iTunes is always open. ITunes regularly sells tens of millions of songs on Christmas Day alone, a date when virtually all of its offline competition is closed for the holiday. In a short five years after its introduction, iTunes has sold over 4 billion songs and has vaulted past retail giants Wal-Mart, Best Buy, and Target to become the number one music retailer in the world. Today's iTunes is a digital media powerhouse, selling movies, TV shows, games, and other applications. And with podcasting, Apple's iTunes University even lets students at participating schools put their professors' lectures on their gym playlist for free. Surfing the fifth wave has increased the value of Apple stock sixteenfold six years after the iPod's launch. Ride these waves to riches, but miss the power and promise of Moore's Law and you risk getting swept away in its riptide. Apple's rise occurred while Sony, a firm once synonymous with portable music, sat on the sidelines unwilling to get on the surfboard. Sony's stock stagnated, barely moving in six years. The firm has laid off thousands of workers while ceding leadership in digital music (and video) to Apple.

TABLE 5.1 Top U.S. Music Retailers

1992	2005	2006	2008
1. Musicland	1. Wal-Mart	1. Wal-Mart	1. **iTunes**
2. The Handleman	2. Best Buy	2. Best Buy	2. Wal-Mart
3. Tower Records	3. Target	3. Target	3. Best Buy
4. Trans World Music	. . . 7. **iTunes**	4. **iTunes**, Amazon tie	4. Amazon, Target tie
Moore's Law restructures industries. The firms that dominated music sales when you were born are now bankrupt, while one that had never sold a physical music CD now sells more than anyone else.			

Source: Michelle Quinn and Dawn C. Chmielewski, "Top Music Seller's Store Has No Door," Los Angeles Times, April 4, 2008.

TABLE 5.2 Tech's Price/Performance Trends in Action: Amazon Kindle and Apple Music Storage

Amazon Kindle		Apple	
First Generation	Fourth Generation	iPod	iCloud
250 MB	2 GB	5 GB	5 GB
November 2007	September 2011	October 2001	October 2011
$399	$79	$399	Free

Amazon's first Kindle sold for nearly $400. Less than four years later, Amazon was selling an updated version of the Kindle for one-fifth that price. Similarly, Apple offered 5 GB of music storage in the original iPod (also priced at roughly $400). By the iPod's tenth birthday, Apple was giving away 5 GB of storage (for music or other media) for free via its iCloud service. Other factors influence price drops, such as being able to produce products and their components at scale, but Moore's Law and related price/performance trends are clearly behind the price decreases we see across a wide variety of tech products and services.

While the change in hard drive prices isn't directly part of Moore's Law (hard drives are magnetic storage, not silicon chips), as noted earlier, the faster and cheaper phenomenon applies to storage, too. Look to Amazon as another example of jumping onto a once-impossible opportunity courtesy of the price/performance curve. When Amazon.com was founded in 1995, the largest corporate database was one terabyte, or TB (see "Bits and Bytes") in size. In 2003, the firm offered its "Search Inside the Book" feature, digitizing the images and text from thousands of books in its catalog. "Search Inside the Book" lets customers peer into a book's contents in a way that's both faster and more accurate than browsing a physical bookstore. Most importantly for Amazon and its suppliers, titles featured in "Search Inside the Book" enjoyed a 7 percent sales increase over nonsearchable books. When "Search Inside the Book" launched, the database to support this effort was 20 TB in size. In just eight years, the firm found that it made good business sense to launch an effort that was a full *twenty times* larger than anything used by *any* firm less than a decade earlier. And of course, all of these capacities seem laughably small by today's standards. (See Chapter 11.) For Amazon, the impossible had not just become possible; it became good business. By 2009, digital books weren't just for search; they were for sale. Amazon's Kindle reader (a Moore's Law marvel sporting a microprocessor and flash storage) became the firm's top-selling product in terms of both unit sales and dollar volume. The real business opportunity for Amazon isn't Kindle as a consumer electronics device but as an ever-present, never-closing store, which also provides the firm with a migration path from atoms to bits. (For more on that topic, see Chapter 4.) By 2011, Amazon (by then the largest book retailer in North America) reported that it was selling more electronic books than print ones.[12] Apple's introduction of the iPad, complete with an iBook store, shows how Moore's Law rewrites the boundaries of competition—bringing a firm that started as a computer retailer and a firm that started as an online bookstore in direct competition with one another.

Bits and Bytes

Computers express data as bits that are either one or zero. Eight bits form a byte (think of a byte as being a single character you can type from a keyboard). A kilobyte refers to roughly a thousand bytes, or a thousand characters, megabyte = 1 million, gigabyte = 1 billion, terabyte = 1 trillion, petabyte = 1 quadrillion, and exabyte = 1 quintillion bytes.

While storage is most often listed in bytes, telecommunication capacity (bandwidth) is often listed in bits per second (bps). The same prefixes apply (Kbps = kilobits, or one thousand bits, per second, Mbps = megabits per second, Gbps = gigabits per second, and Tbps = terabits per second).

These are managerial definitions, but technically, a kilobyte is 2^{10} or 1,024 bytes, mega = 2^{20}, giga = 2^{30}, tera = 2^{40}, peta = 2^{50}, and exa = 2^{60}. To get a sense for how much data we're talking about, see the table below.[13]

Bytes Defined

	Managerial Definition	Exact Amount	To Put It in Perspective
1 Byte	One keyboard character	8 bits	1 letter or number = 1 byte
1 Kilobyte (KB)	One thousand bytes	2^{10} bytes	1 typewritten page = 2 KB
			1 digital book (Kindle) = approx. 500—800 KB
1 Megabyte (MB)	One million bytes	2^{20} bytes	1 digital photo (7 megapixels) = 1.3 MB
			1 MP3 song = approx. 3 MB
			1 CD = approx. 700 MB
1 Gigabyte (GB)	One billion bytes	2^{30} bytes	1 DVD movie = approx. 4.7 GB
			1 Blu-ray movie = approx. 25 GB
1 Terabyte (TB)	One trillion bytes	2^{40} bytes	Printed collection of the Library of Congress = 20 TB
1 Petabyte (PB)	One quadrillion bytes	2^{50} bytes	eBay data warehouse (2010) = 10 PB[14]
1 Exabyte (EB)	One quintillion bytes	2^{60} bytes	
1 Zettabyte (ZB)	One sextillion bytes	2^{70} bytes	Amount of data consumed by U.S. households in 2008 = 3.6 ZB

Here's another key implication—if you are producing products with a significant chip-based component, the chips inside that product rapidly fall in value. That's great when it makes your product cheaper and opens up new markets for your firm, but it can be deadly if you overproduce and have excess inventory sitting on shelves for long periods of time. Dell claims its inventory depreciates as much as a single percentage point in value each week.[15] That's a big incentive to carry as little inventory as possible, and to unload it, fast!

While the strategic side of tech may be the most glamorous, Moore's Law impacts mundane management tasks, as well. From an accounting and budgeting perspective, as a manager you'll need to consider a number of questions: How long will your computing equipment remain useful? If you keep upgrading computing and software, what does this mean for your capital expense budget? Your training budget? Your ability to make well-reasoned predictions regarding tech's direction will be key to answering these questions.

Tech for the Poor

Nicholas Negroponte, the former head of MIT's Media Lab, is on a mission. His OLPC (One Laptop per Child) project aims to deliver education to children in the world's poorest communities via ultralow-cost computing devices that the firm has developed. The first offering, the XO laptop, cost less than $200, although a sub-$100 tablet is in the works. The XO sports a rubberized keyboard and entirely solid-state design (flash RAM rather than hard drive) that helps make the machine durable. The XO's ultrabright screen is readable in daylight and can be flipped to convert into an e-book reader. And a host of open source software and wiki tools for courseware development all aim to keep the costs low. Mesh networking allows laptops within a hundred feet or so to communicate with each other, relaying a single Internet connection for use by all. And since the XO is targeted at the world's poorest kids in communities where power generation is unreliable or nonexistent, several battery-charging power generation schemes are offered, including a hand crank and foldout flexible solar panels. The OLPC Foundation delivered over 2.4 million laptops to children in twenty-four countries.[16] The XO is a product made possible by the rapidly falling price of computing.

The XO PC

Source: Used with permission from fuseproject.

While the success of the OLPC effort will reveal itself over time, another tech product containing a microprocessor is already transforming the lives of some of the world's most desperate poor—the cell phone. There are three billion people worldwide that don't yet have a phone, but they will, soon. In the ultimate play of Moore's Law opening up new markets, mobiles from Vodafone and Indian telecom provider Spice sell for $25 or less. While it took roughly twenty years to sell a billion mobile phones worldwide, the second billion sold in four years, and the third billion took just two years. Today, some 80 percent of the world's population lives within cellular network range (double the 2000 level), and the vast majority of mobile subscriptions are in developing countries.[17]

Why such demand? Mobiles change lives for the better. According to Columbia economist Jeffrey Sachs, "The cell phone is the single most transformative technology for world economic development."[18] Think about the farmer who can verify prices and locate buyers before harvesting and transporting perishable crops to market; the laborer who was mostly unemployed but with a mobile is now reachable by those who have day-to-day work; the mother who can find out if a doctor is in and has medicine before taking off work to make the costly trek to a remote clinic with her sick child; or the immigrant laborer serving as a housekeeper who was "more or less an indentured servant until she got a cell phone" enabling new customers to call and book her services.[19]

As an example of impact, look to poor fishermen in the Indian state of Kerala. By using mobile phones to find the best local marketplace prices for sardines, these fishermen were able to increase their profits by an average of 8 percent even though consumer prices for fish *dropped* 4 percent. The trends benefiting both buyer and seller occurred because the fishermen no longer had to throw away unsold catch previously lost by sailing into a port after all the buyers had left. The phone-equipped fleet now see more consistent pricing, spreading their catch more evenly whereas previous fisherman often inefficiently clustered in one market, overserving one population while underserving another. A London Business School study found that for every ten mobile phones per one hundred people, a country's GDP bumps up 0.5 percent.[20]

Bangladeshi economist Mohammed Yunus won the Nobel Peace Prize based on his work in the microfinance movement, an effort that provides very small loans to the world's poorest entrepreneurs. Microfinance loans grew the market for Grameen Phone Ltd., a firm that has empowered over two hundred and fifty thousand Bangladeshi "phone ladies" to start businesses that helped their communities become more productive. Phone ladies bought a phone and special antenna on microcredit, allowing them to become a sort of village operator and charge a small commission for sending and receiving calls. Through phone ladies, the power of the mobile reaches even those too poor to afford buying one outright. Grameen Phone grew, reaching revenues of over $1 billion, and became Bangladesh's largest telecom provider.

In another ingenious scheme, phone minutes become a proxy for currency. The *New York Times* reports that a person "working in Kampala, for instance, who wishes to send the equivalent of five dollars back to his mother in a village will buy a five-dollar prepaid airtime card, but rather than entering the code into his own phone, he will call the village phone operator and read the code to her. [The operator] then uses the airtime for her phone and completes the transaction by giving the man's mother the money, minus a small commission."[21]

When phones can be used as currency for purchases or payments, who needs Visa or, for that matter, a wallet and cash? The M-PESA mobile banking service run by Kenya's Safaricom, allows customers to transfer cash using text messages. The majority of Kenyan adults have M-PESA accounts, paying for everything from groceries to cab rides to school tuition. The service can also allow family members to quickly and securely send cash across the country. Only 4 million Kenyans have traditional bank accounts, but 17 million use M-PESA, and upwards of 11 percent of Kenya's GDP flows through the service.[22] M-PESA is spreading to other regions and is even used in Afghanistan, while similar schemes are offered by firms such as WIZZIT in South Africa and GCASH in the Philippines. The "mobile phone as bank" may bring banking to a billion unserved customers in a few years.

KEY TAKEAWAYS

- Moore's Law applies to the semiconductor industry. The widely accepted managerial interpretation of Moore's Law states that for the same money, roughly eighteen months from now you should be able to purchase computer chips that are twice as fast or store twice as much information. Or over that same time period, chips with the speed or storage of today's chips should cost half as much as they do now.
- Nonchip-based technology also advances rapidly. Disk drive storage doubles roughly every twelve months, while equipment to speed transmissions over fiber-optic lines has doubled every nine months. While these numbers are rough approximations, the price/performance curve of these technologies continues to advance exponentially.
- These trends influence inventory value, depreciation accounting, employee training, and other managerial functions. They also help improve productivity and keep interest rates low.
- From a strategic perspective, these trends suggest that what is impossible from a cost or performance perspective today may be possible in the future. This fact provides an opportunity to those who recognize and can capitalize on the capabilities of new technology. As technology advances, new industries, business models, and products are created, while established firms and ways of doing business can be destroyed.
- Managers must regularly study trends and trajectory in technology to recognize opportunity and avoid disruption.

QUESTIONS AND EXERCISES

1. What is Moore's Law? What does it apply to?
2. Are other aspects of computing advancing as well? At what rates?
3. What is a microprocessor? What devices do you or your family own that contain microprocessors (and hence are impacted by Moore's Law)?
4. What is a semiconductor? What is the substance from which most semiconductors are made?
5. How does flash memory differ from the memory in a PC? Are both solid state?
6. Which of the following are solid state devices: an iPod shuffle, a TiVo DVR, a typical laptop PC?
7. Why is Moore's Law important for managers? How does it influence managerial thinking?
8. What is price elasticity? How does Moore's Law relate to this concept? What's special about falling chip prices compared to price drops for products like clothing or food?
9. Give examples of firms that have effectively leveraged the advancement of processing, storage, and networking technology.
10. What are the five waves of computing? Give examples of firms and industries impacted by the fifth wave.
11. As Moore's Law advances, technology becomes increasingly accessible to the poor. Give examples of how tech has benefited those who likely would not have been able to afford the technology of a prior generation.
12. How have cheaper, faster chips impacted the camera industry? Give an example of the leadership shifts that have occurred in this industry.
13. What has been the impact of "faster, cheaper" on Apple's business lines?
14. How did Amazon utilize the steep decline in magnetic storage costs to its advantage?
15. How does Moore's Law impact production and inventory decisions?

2. THE DEATH OF MOORE'S LAW?

LEARNING OBJECTIVES

1. **Describe why Moore's Law continues to advance and discuss the physical limitations of this advancement.**
2. **Name and describe various technologies that may extend the life of Moore's Law.**
3. **Discuss the limitations of each of these approaches.**

Moore simply observed that we're getting better over time at squeezing more stuff into tinier spaces. Moore's Law is possible because the distance between the pathways inside silicon chips gets smaller with each successive generation. While chip plants (semiconductor fabrication facilities, or **fabs**) are incredibly expensive to build, each new generation of fabs can crank out more chips per **silicon wafer**. And since the pathways are closer together, electrons travel shorter distances. If electronics now travel half the distance to make a calculation, that means the chip is twice as fast.

fabs

Semiconductor fabrication facilities; the multibillion dollar plants used to manufacture semiconductors.

silicon wafer

A thin, circular slice of material used to create semiconductor devices. Hundreds of chips may be etched on a single wafer, where they are eventually cut out for individual packaging.

But the shrinking can't go on forever, and we're already starting to see three interrelated forces—*size*, *heat*, and *power*—threatening to slow down Moore's Law's advance. When you make processors smaller, the more tightly packed electrons will heat up a chip—so much so that unless today's most powerful chips are cooled down, they will melt inside their packaging. To keep the fastest computers cool, many PCs, laptops, and video game consoles need fans, and most corporate data centers have elaborate and expensive air conditioning and venting systems to prevent a meltdown. A trip through the Facebook data center during its recent rise would show that the firm was a "hot" start-up in more ways than one. The firm's servers ran so hot that the Plexiglas sides of the firm's server racks were warped and melting![23] The need to cool modern data centers draws a lot of power and that costs a lot of money.

The chief eco officer at Sun Microsystems has claimed that computers draw 4 to 5 percent of the world's power. Google's chief technology officer has said that the firm spends more to power its servers than the cost of the servers themselves.[24] Apple, Facebook, Microsoft, Yahoo! and Google have all built massive data centers in the Pacific Northwest, away from their corporate headquarters, specifically choosing these locations for access to cheap hydroelectric power. Google's location in The Dalles, Oregon, is charged a cost per kilowatt hour of two cents by the local power provider, less than one-fifth of the eleven-cent rate the firm pays in Silicon Valley.[25] This difference means big savings for a firm that runs more than a million servers.

And while these powerful shrinking chips are getting hotter and more costly to cool, it's also important to realize that chips can't get smaller forever. At some point Moore's Law will run into the unyielding laws of nature. While we're not certain where these limits are, chip pathways certainly can't be shorter than a single molecule, and the actual physical limit is likely larger than that. Get too small and a phenomenon known as quantum tunneling kicks in, and electrons start to slide off their paths. Yikes!

2.1 Buying Time

multicore microprocessors

Microprocessors with two or more (typically lower power) calculating processor cores on the same piece of silicon.

One way to overcome this problem is with **multicore microprocessors**, made by putting two or more lower power processor cores (think of a core as the calculating part of a microprocessor) on a single chip. Philip Emma, IBM's Manager of Systems Technology and Microarchitecture, offers an analogy. Think of the traditional fast, hot, single-core processors as a three hundred-pound lineman, and a dual-core processor as two 160-pound guys. Says Emma, "A 300-pound lineman can generate a lot of power, but two 160-pound guys can do the same work with less overall effort."[26] For many applications, the multicore chips will outperform a single speedy chip, while running cooler and drawing less power. Multicore processors are now mainstream.

Today, most smartphones, PCs, and laptops sold have at least a two-core (dual-core) processor. The Microsoft Xbox 360 has three cores. The PlayStation 3 includes the so-called *cell processor* developed by Sony, IBM, and Toshiba that runs nine cores. Intel has even demonstrated chips with upwards of fifty cores.

Multicore processors can run older software written for single-brain chips. But they usually do this by using only one core at a time. To reuse the metaphor above, this is like having one of our 160-pound workers lift away, while the other one stands around watching. Multicore operating systems can help achieve some performance gains. Versions of Windows or the Mac OS that are aware of multicore processors can assign one program to run on one core, while a second application is assigned to the next core. But in order to take full advantage of multicore chips, applications need to be rewritten to split up tasks so that smaller portions of a problem are executed simultaneously inside each core.

Writing code for this "divide and conquer" approach is not trivial. In fact, developing software for multicore systems is described by Shahrokh Daijavad, software lead for next-generation computing systems at IBM, as "one of the hardest things you learn in computer science."[27] Microsoft's chief research and strategy officer has called coding for these chips "the most conceptually different [change] in the history of modern computing."[28] Despite this challenge, some of the most aggressive adaptors of multicore chips have been video game console manufacturers. Video game applications are particularly well-suited for multiple cores since, for example, one core might be used to render the background, another to draw objects, another for the "physics engine" that moves the objects around, and yet another to handle Internet communications for multiplayer games.

Another approach that's breathing more life into Moore's Law moves chips from being paper-flat devices to built-up 3-D affairs. By building up as well as out, firms are radically boosting speed and efficiency of chips. Intel has flipped upward the basic component of chips—the transistor. Transistors are the supertiny on-off switches in a chip that work collectively to calculate or store things in memory (a high-end microprocessor might include over two billion transistors). While you won't notice that chips are much thicker, Intel says that on the miniscule scale of modern chip manufacturing, the new designs will be 37 percent faster and half as power hungry as conventional chips.[29]

New Materials & Quantum Leaps? Thinking Beyond Moore's Law-Constraining Silicon

Think about it—the triple threat of size, heat, and power means that Moore's Law, perhaps the greatest economic gravy train in history, will likely come to a grinding halt in your lifetime. Multicore and 3-D transistors are here today, but what else is happening to help stave off the death of Moore's Law?

Every once in a while a material breakthrough comes along that improves chip performance. A few years back researchers discovered that replacing a chip's aluminum components with copper could increase speeds up to 30 percent. Now scientists are concentrating on improving the very semiconductor material that chips are made of. While the silicon used in chips is wonderfully abundant (it has pretty much the same chemistry found in sand), researchers are investigating other materials that might allow for chips with even tighter component densities. New processors made with hafnium-based high-k components can pack circuits tighter, leading to faster chips that require less wattage than traditional silicon alone—and even more efficient materials may be on the horizon.[30] Hyperefficient chips of the future may also be made out of carbon nanotubes, once the technology to assemble the tiny structures becomes commercially viable.

Other designs move away from electricity over silicon. Optical computing, where signals are sent via light rather than electricity, promises to be faster than conventional chips, if lasers can be mass produced in miniature (silicon laser experiments show promise). Others are experimenting by crafting computing components using biological material (think a DNA-based storage device).

One yet-to-be-proven technology that could blow the lid off what's possible today is quantum computing. Conventional computing stores data as a combination of bits, where a bit is either a one or a zero. Quantum computers, leveraging principles of quantum physics, employ qubits that can be both one *and* zero at the same time. Add a bit to a conventional computer's memory and you double its capacity. Add a bit to a quantum computer and its capacity increases exponentially. For comparison, consider that a computer model of serotonin, a molecule vital to regulating the human central nervous system, would require 10^{94} bytes of information. Unfortunately there's not enough matter in the universe to build a computer that big. But modeling a serotonin molecule using quantum computing would take just 424 qubits.[31]

Some speculate that quantum computers could one day allow pharmaceutical companies to create hyperdetailed representations of the human body that reveal drug side effects before they're even tested on humans. Quantum computing might also accurately predict the weather months in advance or offer unbreakable computer security. Ever have trouble placing a name with a face? A quantum computer linked to a camera (in your sunglasses, for example) could recognize the faces of anyone you've met and give you a heads-up to their name and background.[32] Opportunities abound. Of course, before quantum computing can be commercialized, researchers need to harness the freaky properties of quantum physics wherein your answer may reside in another universe, or could disappear if observed (Einstein himself referred to certain behaviors in quantum physics as "spooky action at a distance").

Pioneers in quantum computing include IBM, HP, NEC, and a Canadian start-up named D-Wave. If or when quantum computing becomes a reality is still unknown, but the promise exists that while Moore's Law may run into limits imposed by Mother Nature, a new way of computing may blow past anything we can do with silicon, continuing to make possible the once impossible.

KEY TAKEAWAYS

- As chips get smaller and more powerful, they get hotter and present power-management challenges. And at some, point Moore's Law will stop because we will no longer be able to shrink the spaces between components on a chip.
- Multicore chips use two or more low-power calculating "cores" to work together in unison, but to take optimal advantage of multicore chips, software must be rewritten to "divide" a task among multiple cores.
- 3-D transistors are also helping extend Moore's Law by producing chips that require less power and run faster.
- New materials may extend the life of Moore's Law, allowing chips to get smaller, still. Entirely new methods for calculating, such as quantum computing, may also dramatically increase computing capabilities far beyond what is available today.

QUESTIONS AND EXERCISES

1. What three interrelated forces threaten to slow the advancement of Moore's Law?
2. Which commercial solutions, described in the section above, are currently being used to counteract the forces mentioned above? How do these solutions work? What are the limitations of each?
3. Will multicore chips run software designed for single-core processors?
4. As chips grow smaller they generate increasing amounts of heat that needs to be dissipated. Why is keeping systems cool such a challenge? What are the implications for a firm like Yahoo! or Google? For a firm like Apple or Dell?
5. What are some of the materials that may replace the silicon that current chips are made of?
6. What kinds of problems might be solved if the promise of quantum computing is achieved? How might individuals and organizations leverage quantum computing? What sorts of challenges could arise from the widespread availability of such powerful computing technology?

3. BRINGING BRAINS TOGETHER: SUPERCOMPUTING, GRID COMPUTING, AND PUTTING SMARTS IN THE CLOUD

LEARNING OBJECTIVES

1. **Give examples of the business use of supercomputing, grid computing, and cloud computing.**
2. **Describe grid computing and discuss how grids transform the economics of supercomputing.**
3. **Understand the characteristics of problems that are and are not well suited for parallel processing found in modern supercomputing and grid computing efforts as well as multi-core processors.**

supercomputers

Computers that are among the fastest of any in the world at the time of their introduction.

As Moore's Law makes possible the once impossible, businesses have begun to demand access to the world's most powerful computing technology. **Supercomputers** are computers that are among the fastest of any in the world at the time of their introduction.[33] Supercomputing was once the domain of governments and high-end research labs, performing tasks such as simulating the explosion of nuclear devices, or analyzing large-scale weather and climate phenomena. But it turns out with a bit of tweaking, the algorithms used in this work are profoundly useful to business. Consider perhaps the world's most well-known supercomputer, IBM's Deep Blue, the machine that rather controversially beat chess champion Garry Kasparov. While there is not a burning need for chess-playing computers in the world's corporations, it turns out that the computing algorithms to choose the best among multiple chess moves are similar to the math behind choosing the best combination of airline flights.

Paging Doctor Watson

In spring 2011, the world was introduced to another IBM supercomputer—the Jeopardy-playing Watson. Built to quickly answer questions posed in natural language, by the end of a televised three-day tournament Watson had put the hurt on prior Jeopardy champs Ken Jennings and Brad Rutter, trouncing the human rivals and winning one million dollars (donated to a children's charity). Watson's accomplishment represented a four-year project that involved some twenty-five people across eight IBM research labs, creating algorithms, in a system with ninety servers, "many, many" processors, terabytes of storage, and "tens of millions of dollars" in investment.[34] Winning Jeopardy makes for a few nights of interesting TV, but what else can it do? Well, the "Deep QA" technology behind Watson might end up in your doctor's office, and docs could likely use that kind of "exobrain." On average "primary care physicians spend less than twenty minutes face-to-face with each patient per visit, and average little more than an hour each week reading medical journals."[35] Now imagine a physician assistant Watson that could leverage massive diagnosis databases while scanning hundreds of pages in a person's medical history, surfacing a best guess at what docs should be paying attention to. A *JAMA* study suggested that medical errors may be the third leading cause of death in the United States,[36] so there's apparently an enormous and mighty troubling opportunity in health care alone. IBM is partnering with Massachusetts voice-rec leader Nuance Communications (the Dragon people) to bring Watson to the doc's office. Med schools at Columbia and the University of Maryland will help with the research effort. Of course, you wouldn't want to completely trust a Watson recommendation. While Watson was good enough to be tournament champ, IBM's baby missed a final Jeopardy answer of "Chicago" because it answered that Toronto was a U.S. city.

Source: http://www.ibm.com/press.

One of the first customers of Deep Blue technologies was United Airlines, which gained an ability to examine three hundred and fifty thousand flight path combinations for its scheduling systems—a figure well ahead of the previous limit of three thousand. Estimated savings through better yield management? Over $50 million! Finance found uses, too. An early adopter was CIBC (the Canadian Imperial Bank of Commerce), one of the largest banks in North America. Each morning CIBC uses a supercomputer to run its portfolio through Monte Carlo simulations that aren't all that different from the math used to simulate nuclear explosions. An early adopter of the technology, at the time of deployment, CIBC was the only bank that international regulators allowed to calculate its own capital needs rather than use boilerplate ratios. That cut capital on hand by hundreds of millions of dollars, a substantial percentage of the bank's capital, saving millions a year in funding costs. Also noteworthy: the supercomputer-enabled, risk-savvy CIBC was relatively unscathed by the subprime crisis.

Modern supercomputing is typically done via a technique called **massively parallel** processing (computers designed with many microprocessors that work together, simultaneously, to solve problems). The fastest of these supercomputers are built using hundreds of microprocessors, all programmed to work in unison as one big brain. While supercomputers use special electronics and software to handle the massive load, the processors themselves are often of the off-the-shelf variety that you'd find in a typical PC. Virginia Tech created what at the time was the world's third-fastest supercomputer by using chips from 1,100 Macintosh computers lashed together with off-the-shelf networking components. The total cost of the system was just $5.2 million, far less than the typical cost for such burly hardware. The Air Force recently issued a request-for-proposal to purchase 2,200 PlayStation 3 systems in hopes of crafting a supercheap, superpowerful machine using off-the-shelf parts.

massively parallel

Computers designed with many microprocessors that work together, simultaneously, to solve problems.

Another technology, known as **grid computing**, is further transforming the economics of supercomputing. With grid computing, firms place special software on its existing PCs or servers that enables these computers to work together on a common problem. Large organizations may have thousands of PCs, but they're not necessarily being used all the time, or at full capacity. With grid software installed on them, these idle devices can be marshaled to attack portions of a complex task as if they collectively were one massively parallel supercomputer. This technique radically changes the economics of high-performance computing. *BusinessWeek* reports that while a middle-of-the-road supercomputer could run as much as $30 million, grid computing software and services to perform comparable tasks can cost as little as twenty-five thousand dollars, assuming an organization already has PCs and servers in place.

grid computing

A type of computing that uses special software to enable several computers to work together on a common problem as if they were a massively parallel supercomputer.

An early pioneer in grid computing is the biotech firm Monsanto. Monsanto enlists computers to explore ways to manipulate genes to create crop strains that are resistant to cold, drought, bugs, pesticides, or that are more nutritious. Previously with even the largest computer Monsanto had in-house, gene analysis was taking six weeks and the firm was able to analyze only ten to fifty genes a year. But by leveraging grid computing, Monsanto has reduced gene analysis to less than a day. The fiftyfold time savings now lets the firm consider thousands of genetic combinations in a year.[37] Lower R&D time means faster time to market—critical to both the firm and its customers.

Grids are now everywhere. Movie studios use them to create special effects and animated films. Proctor & Gamble has used grids to redesign the manufacturing process for Pringles potato chips. GM and Ford use grids to simulate crash tests, saving millions in junked cars and speeding time to market. Pratt and Whitney test aircraft engine designs on a grid. And biotech firms including Aventis, GlaxoSmithKline, and Pfizer push their research through a quicker pipeline by harnessing grid power. JP Morgan Chase even launched a grid effort that mimics CIBC's supercomputer, but at a fraction of the latter's cost. By the second year of operation, the JPMorgan Chase grid was saving the firm $5 million per year.

You can join a grid, too. SETI@Home turns your computer screen saver into a method to help "search for extraterrestrial intelligence," analyzing data from the Arecibo radio telescope system in Puerto Rico (no E.T. spotted yet). FightAids@Home will enlist your PC to explore AIDS treatments. And Folding@Home is an effort by Stanford researchers to understanding the science of protein-folding within diseases such as Alzheimer's, cancer, and cystic fibrosis. A version of Folding@Home software for the PlayStation 3 had enlisted over half a million consoles within months of release. Having access to these free resources is an enormous advantage for researchers. Says the director of Folding@Home, "Even if we were given all of the NSF supercomputing centers combined for a couple of months, that is still fewer resources than we have now."[38]

Multicore, massively parallel, and grid computing are all related in that each attempts to lash together multiple computing devices so that they can work together to solve problems. Think of multicore chips as having several processors in a single chip. Think of massively parallel supercomputers as having several chips in one computer, and think of grid computing as using existing computers to work together on a single task (essentially a computer made up of multiple computers). While these technologies offer great promise, they're all subject to the same limitation: software must be written to divide existing problems into smaller pieces that can be handled by each core, processor, or computer, respectively. Some problems, such as simulations, are easy to split up, but for problems that are linear (where, for example, step two can't be started until the results from step one are known), the multiple-brain approach doesn't offer much help.

Massive clusters of computers running software that allows them to operate as a unified service also enable new service-based computing models, such as **software as a service (SaaS)** and **cloud computing**. In these models, organizations replace traditional software and hardware that they would run in-house with services that are delivered online. Google, Microsoft, Salesforce.com, and Amazon are among the firms that have sunk billions into these Moore's Law–enabled **server farms**, creating entirely new businesses that promise to radically redraw the software and hardware landscape while bringing gargantuan computing power to the little guy. (See Chapter 10.) Moving 'brains' to the cloud can help increase calculating performance even when we can't pack more processing brawn into our devices, but the cloud requires a long-distance connection that's a lot slower and perhaps less reliable than the quick hop from storage to processor that occurs inside most consumer electronics.

Moore's Law will likely hit its physical limit in your lifetime, but no one really knows if this "Moore's Wall" is a decade away or more. What lies ahead is anyone's guess. Some technologies, such as still-experimental quantum computing, could make computers that are more powerful than all the world's conventional computers combined. Think strategically—new waves of innovation might soon be shouting "surf's up!"

software as a service (SaaS)

A form of cloud computing where a firm subscribes to a third-party software and receives a service that is delivered online.

cloud computing

Replacing computing resources—either an organization's or individual's hardware or software—with services provided over the Internet.

server farm

A massive network of computer servers running software to coordinate their collective use. Server farms provide the infrastructure backbone to SaaS and hardware cloud efforts, as well as many large-scale Internet services.

KEY TAKEAWAYS

- Most modern supercomputers use massive sets of microprocessors working in parallel.
- The microprocessors used in most modern supercomputers are often the same commodity chips that can be found in conventional PCs and servers.
- Moore's Law means that businesses as diverse as financial services firms, industrial manufacturers, consumer goods firms, and film studios can now afford access to supercomputers.
- Grid computing software uses existing computer hardware to work together and mimic a massively parallel supercomputer. Using existing hardware for a grid can save a firm the millions of dollars it might otherwise cost to buy a conventional supercomputer, further bringing massive computing capabilities to organizations that would otherwise never benefit from this kind of power.
- Massively parallel computing also enables the vast server farms that power online businesses like Google and Facebook, and which create new computing models, like software as a service (SaaS) and cloud computing.
- The characteristics of problems best suited for solving via multicore systems, parallel supercomputers, or grid computers are those that can be divided up so that multiple calculating components can simultaneously work on a portion of the problem. Problems that are linear—where one part must be solved before moving to the next and the next—may have difficulty benefiting from these kinds of "divide and conquer" computing. Fortunately many problems such as financial risk modeling, animation, manufacturing simulation, and gene analysis are all suited for parallel systems.

QUESTIONS AND EXERCISES

1. What is the difference between supercomputing and grid computing? How is each phenomenon empowered by Moore's Law?
2. How does grid computing change the economics of supercomputing?
3. Which businesses are using supercomputing and grid computing? Describe these uses and the advantages they offer their adopting firms. Are they a source of competitive advantage? Why or why not?
4. What are the characteristics of problems that are most easily solved using the types of parallel computing found in grids and modern day supercomputers? What are the characteristics of the sorts of problems not well suited for this type of computing?
5. Visit the SETI@Home Web site (http://setiathome.ssl.berkeley.edu/). What is the purpose of the SETI@Home project? How do you participate? Is there any possible danger to your computer if you choose to participate? (Read their rules and policies.)
6. Search online to identify the five fastest supercomputers currently in operation. Who sponsors these machines? What are they used for? How many processors do they have?
7. What is "Moore's Wall"?
8. What is the advantage of using grid computing to simulate an automobile crash test as opposed to actually staging a crash?

4. E-WASTE: THE DARK SIDE OF MOORE'S LAW

LEARNING OBJECTIVES

1. **Understand the magnitude of the environmental issues caused by rapidly obsolete, faster and cheaper computing.**
2. **Explain the limitations of approaches attempting to tackle e-waste.**
3. **Understand the risks firms are exposed to when not fully considering the lifecycle of the products they sell or consume.**
4. **Ask questions that expose concerning ethical issues in a firm or partner's products and processes, and that help the manager behave more responsibly.**

We should celebrate the great bounty Moore's Law and the tech industry bestow on our lives. Costs fall, workers become more productive, innovations flourish, and we gorge at a buffet of digital entertainment that includes music, movies, and games. But there is a dark side to this faster and cheaper advancement. A PC has an expected lifetime of three to five years. A cell phone? Two years or less. Rapid obsolescence means the creation of ever-growing mountains of discarded tech junk, known as

e-waste

Discarded, often obsolete technology; also known as electronic waste.

electronic waste or **e-waste**. According to the U.S. Environmental Protection Agency (EPA), in 2007 the United States alone generated over 2.5 million tons of e-waste,[39] and the results aren't pretty. Consumer electronics and computing equipment can be a toxic cocktail that includes cadmium, mercury, lead, and other hazardous materials. Once called the "effluent of the affluent," e-waste will only increase with the rise of living standards worldwide.

The quick answer would be to recycle this stuff. Not only does e-waste contain mainstream recyclable materials we're all familiar with, like plastics and aluminum, it also contains small bits of increasingly valuable metals such as silver, platinum, and copper. In fact, there's more gold in one pound of discarded tech equipment than in one pound of mined ore.[40] But as the sordid record of e-waste management shows, there's often a disconnect between consumers and managers who *want* to do good and those efforts that are *actually* doing good. The complexities of the modern value chain, the vagaries of international law, and the nefarious actions of those willing to put profits above principle show how difficult addressing this problem will be.

The process of separating out the densely packed materials inside tech products so that the value in e-waste can be effectively harvested is extremely labor intensive, more akin to reverse manufacturing than any sort of curbside recycling efforts. Sending e-waste abroad can be ten times cheaper than dealing with it at home,[41] so it's not surprising that up to 80 percent of the material dropped off for recycling is eventually exported.[42] Much of this waste ends up in China, South Asia, or sub-Saharan Africa, where it is processed in dreadful conditions.

Consider the example of Guiyu, China, a region whose poisoning has been extensively chronicled by organizations such as the Silicon Valley Toxics Coalition, the Basel Action Network (BAN), and Greenpeace. Workers in and around Guiyu toil without protective equipment, breathing clouds of toxins generated as they burn the plastic skins off of wires to get at the copper inside. Others use buckets, pots, or wok-like pans (in many cases the same implements used for cooking) to sluice components in acid baths to release precious metals—recovery processes that create even more toxins. Waste sludge and the carcasses of what's left over are most often dumped in nearby fields and streams. Water samples taken in the region showed lead and heavy metal contamination levels some four hundred to six hundred times greater than what international standards deem safe.[43] The area is so polluted that drinking water must be trucked in from eighteen miles away. Pregnancies are six times more likely to end in miscarriage, and 70 percent of the kids in the region have too much lead in their blood.[44]

FIGURE 5.5 Photos from Guiyu, China[45]

Source: © 2006 Basel Action Network (BAN).

China cares about its environment. The nation has banned the importing of e-waste since 2000.[46] But corruption ensures that e-waste continues to flow into the country. According to one exporter, all that's required to get e-waste past customs authorities is to tape a one-hundred-dollar bill on the side of the container.[47] Well-meaning U.S. recyclers, as well as those attempting to collect technology for reuse in poorer countries, are often in the dark as to where their products end up.

The trade is often brokered by middlemen who mask the eventual destination and fate of the products purchased. BAN investigators in Lagos, Nigeria, documented mountains of e-waste with labels from schools, U.S. government agencies, and even some of the world's largest corporations. And despite Europe's prohibition on exporting e-waste, many products originally labeled for repair and reuse end up in toxic recycling efforts. Even among those products that gain a second or third life in developing nations, the inevitable is simply postponed, with e-waste almost certain to end up in landfills that lack the protective groundwater barriers and environmental engineering of their industrialized counterparts. The reality is that e-waste management is extraordinarily difficult to monitor and track, and loopholes are rampant.

Thinking deeply about the ethical consequences of a firm's business is an imperative for the modern manager. A slip up (intentional or not) can, in seconds, be captured by someone with a cell phone, uploaded to YouTube, or offered in a blog posting for the world to see. When Dell was caught using Chinese prison labor as part of its recycling efforts, one blogger chastised the firm with a tweak of its marketing tagline, posting "Dude, you're getting a cell."[48] The worst cases expose firms to legal action and can tarnish a brand for years. Big firms are big targets, and environmentalists have been quick to push the best-known tech firms and retailers to take back their products for responsible recycling and to eliminate the worst toxins from their offerings.

Consider that even Apple (where Al Gore sits on the firm's Board of Directors), has been pushed by a coalition of environmental groups on all of these fronts. Critics have shot back that signaling out Apple is unfair. The firm was one of the first computer companies to eliminate lead-lined glass monitors from its product line, and has been a pioneer of reduced-sized packaging that leverage recyclable materials. And Apple eventually claimed the top in Greenpeace's "Greener Electronics" rankings.[49] But if the firm that counts Al Gore among its advisors can get tripped up on green issues, all firms are vulnerable.

Environmentalists see this pressure to deal with e-waste as yielding results: Apple and most other tech firms have continually moved to eliminate major toxins from their manufacturing processes. All this demonstrates that today's business leaders have to be far more attuned to the impact not only of their own actions, but also to those of their suppliers and partners. How were products manufactured? Using which materials? Under what conditions? What happens to items when they're discarded? Who provides collection and disposal? It also shows the futility of legislative efforts that don't fully consider and address the problems they are meant to target.

Finding Responsible E-waste Disposers

A recent sting operation led by the U.S. Government Accountability Office (U.S. GAO) found that forty-three American recyclers were willing to sell e-waste illegally to foreign countries, without gaining EPA or foreign country approval. Appallingly, at least three of them held Earth Day electronics-recycling events.[50]

So how can firms and individuals choose proper disposal partners? Several certification mechanisms can help shed light on whether the partner you're dealing with is a responsible player. The Basel Action Network e-Stewards program certifies firms via a third-party audit, with compliant participants committing to eliminating e-waste export, land dumping, incineration, and toxic recycling via prison labor. The International Association of Electronics Recyclers (IAER) also offers audited electronics recycler certification. And firms certified as ISO 9001 and ISO 14001 compliant attest to quality management and environmental processes. Standards, techniques, and auditing practices are constantly in flux, so consult these organizations for the latest partner lists, guidelines, and audit practices.[51]

Which brings us back to Gordon Moore. To his credit, Moore is not just the founder of the world's largest microprocessor firm and first to identify the properties we've come to know as Moore's Law, he has also emerged as one of the world's leading supporters of environmental causes. The generosity of the Gordon and Betty Moore foundation includes, among other major contributions, the largest single gift to a private conservation organization. Indeed, Silicon Valley, while being the birthplace of products that become e-waste, also promises to be at the forefront of finding solutions to modern environmental challenges. The Valley's leading venture capitalists, including Sequoia and Kleiner Perkins (where Al Gore is now a partner), have started multimillion-dollar green investment funds, targeted at funding the next generation of sustainable, environmental initiatives.

KEY TAKEAWAYS

- E-waste may be particularly toxic since many components contain harmful materials such as lead, cadmium, and mercury.
- Managers must consider and plan for the waste created by their products, services, and technology used by the organization. Consumers and governments are increasingly demanding that firms offer responsible methods for the disposal of their manufactured goods and the technology used in their operations.
- Managers must audit disposal and recycling partners with the same vigor as their suppliers and other corporate partners. If not, an organization's equipment may end up in environmentally harmful disposal operations.

QUESTIONS AND EXERCISES

1. What is e-waste? What is so dangerous about e-waste?
2. What sorts of materials might be harvested from e-waste recycling?
3. Many well-meaning individuals thought that recycling was the answer to the e-waste problem. But why hasn't e-waste recycling yielded the results hoped for?
4. What lessons do the challenges of e-waste offer the manager? What issues will your firm need to consider as it consumes or offers products that contain computing components?
5. Why is it difficult to recycle e-waste?
6. Why is e-waste exported abroad for recycling rather than processed domestically?
7. What part does corruption play in the recycling and disposal of e-waste?
8. What part might product design and production engineering play in the reduction of the impact of technology waste on the environment?
9. What are the possible consequences should a U.S. firm be deemed "environmentally irresponsible"?
10. Name two companies that have incurred the wrath of environmental advocates. What might these firms have done to avoid such criticism?

ENDNOTES

1. G. Moore, "Cramming More Components onto Integrated Circuits," *Electronics Magazine*, April 19, 1965.
2. Although other materials besides silicon are increasingly being used.
3. Semiconductor materials, like the silicon dioxide used inside most computer chips, are capable of enabling as well as inhibiting the flow of electricity. These properties enable chips to perform math or store data.
4. Fiber-optic lines are glass or plastic data transmission cables that carry light. These cables offer higher transmission speeds over longer distances than copper cables that transmit electricity.
5. As opposed to goods and services that are *price inelastic* (like health care and housing), which consumers will try their best to buy even if prices go up.

6. M. Copeland, "How to Ride the Fifth Wave," *Business 2.0*, July 1, 2005.
7. M. Copeland, "How to Ride the Fifth Wave," *Business 2.0*, July 1, 2005; and J. Miller, "Goodbye G.U.I? Ambient Orb a Computer 'Mood Ring,'" *Mass High Tech*, February 10, 2003.
8. D. Rose, presentation as part of "From Disruption to Innovation" at the MIT Enterprise Forum, Cambridge, MA, June 23, 2010.
9. E. Landau, "Tattletale Pills, Bottles Remind You to Take Your Meds," *CNN*, February 2, 2010.
10. K. Rozendal, "The Democratic, Digital Future of Healthcare," *Scope*, May 13, 2011.
11. H. Mittchell, "Steve Jobs Used Wayne Gretzky as Inspiration," *Los Angeles Times*, October 6, 2011.
12. M. Hamblen, "Amazon: E-Books Now Outsell Print Books," *ComputerWorld*, May 19, 2011.
13. E. Schuman, "At Wal-Mart, World's Largest Retail Data Warehouse Gets Even Larger," *eWeek*, October 13, 2004; and J. Huggins, "How Much Data Is That?" *Refrigerator Door*, August 19, 2008.
14. C. Monash, "eBay Followup—Greenplum Out, Teradata > 10 Petabytes, Hadoop Has Some Value, and More," October 6, 2010. Note eBay plans to increase this value 2.5 times by the end of 2011.
15. B. Breen, "Living in Dell Time," *Fast Company*, November 24, 2004.
16. C. Lawton, "The X.O. Laptop Two Years Later," *Wired*, June 19, 2009, http://laptop.org/map.
17. S. Corbett, "Can the Cellphone Help End Global Poverty?" *New York Times Magazine*, April 13, 2008.
18. J. Ewing, "Upwardly Mobile in Africa," *BusinessWeek*, September 24, 2007, 64–71.
19. S. Corbett, "Can the Cellphone Help End Global Poverty?" *New York Times Magazine*, April 13, 2008.
20. J. Ewing, "Upwardly Mobile in Africa," *BusinessWeek*, September 24, 2007, 64–71.
21. S. Corbett, "Can the Cellphone Help End Global Poverty?" *New York Times Magazine*, April 13, 2008.
22. B. Greeley and E. Ombok, "In Kenya, Security Cash on a Cell Phone," *BusinessWeek*, September 8, 2011.
23. E. McGirt, "Hacker, Dropout, C.E.O.," *Fast Company*, May 2007.
24. D. Kirkpatrick, "The Greenest Computer Company under the Sun," April 13, 2007.
25. S. Mehta, "Behold the Server Farm," *Fortune*, August 1, 2006. Also see Chapter 10 in this book.
26. A. Ashton, "More Life for Moore's Law," *BusinessWeek*, June 20, 2005.
27. A. Ashton, "More Life for Moore's Law," *BusinessWeek*, June 20, 2005.
28. M. Copeland, "A Chip Too Far?" *Fortune*, September 1, 2008.
29. K. Bourzac, "How Three-Dimensional Transistors Went from Lab to Fab," *Technology Review*, May 6, 2011.
30. Y. L. Chen, J. G. Analytis, J.-H. Chu, Z. K. Liu, S.-K. Mo, X. L. Qi, H. J. Zhang, et al., "Experimental Realization of a Three-Dimensional Topological Insulator, Bi_2Te_3," *Science* 325, no. 5937 (July 10, 2009): 178—81; K. Greene, "Intel Looks Beyond Silicon," *Technology Review*, December 11, 2007; and I. Thomson, "AMD: New Trinity Laptop Chips Out-Juice Intel Graphics," *The Register*, May 15, 2012.
31. P. Kaihla, "Quantum Leap," *Business 2.0*, August 1, 2004.
32. P. Schwartz, C. Taylor, and R. Koselka, "The Future of Computing: Quantum Leap," *Fortune*, August 2, 2006.
33. A list of the current supercomputer performance champs can be found at http://www.top500.org.
34. L. Sumagaysay, "After Man vs. Machine on 'Jeopardy,' What's Next for IBM's Watson?" *Good Morning Silicon Valley*, February 17, 2011.
35. C. Nickisch, "IBM to Roll Out Watson, M.D.," *WBUR*, February 18, 2011.
36. B. Starfield, "Is U.S. Health Really the Best in the World?" *Journal of the American Medical Association*, July 26, 2000.
37. P. Schwartz, C. Taylor, and R. Koselka, "The Future of Computing: Quantum Leap," *Fortune*, August 2, 2006.
38. G. Johnson, "Supercomputing '@Home' Is Paying Off," *New York Times*, April 23, 2002.
39. U.S. Environmental Protection Agency, *General Information on E-waste*, February 5, 2009.
40. P. Kovessy, "How to Trash Toxic Tech," *Ottawa Business Journal*, May 12, 2008.
41. C. Bodeen, "In 'E-waste' Heartland, a Toxic China," *International Herald Tribune*, November 18, 2007.
42. E. Royte, "E-waste@Large," *New York Times*, January 27, 2006.
43. E. Grossman, "Where Computers Go to Die—and Kill," *Salon.com*, April 10, 2006, http://www.salon.com/news/feature/2006/04/10/ewaste.
44. *60 Minutes*, "Following the Trail of Toxic E-waste," November 9, 2008.
45. J. Biggs, "Guiyu, the E-waste Capital of China," *CrunchGear*, April 4, 2008.
46. E. Grossman, "Where Computers Go to Die—and Kill," *Salon.com*, April 10, 2006.
47. C. Bodeen, "In 'E-waste' Heartland, a Toxic China," *International Herald Tribune*, November 18, 2007.
48. J. Russell, "Dell under Attack over Using Prison Labour," *Inquirer*, January 10, 2003. See also http://laughingmeme.org/2003/03/23/dell-recycling-a-ways-to-go-still.
49. J. Dalrymple, "Apple Ranks Highest among Greenpeace's Top Tech Companies," *The Loop*, January 7, 2010.
50. U.S. Government Accountability Office (U.S. GAO), *Report to the Chairman: Committee on Foreign Affairs, House of Representatives: Electronic Waste*, August 2008.
51. Basal Action Network e-Stewards program accessed via http://www.e-stewards.org/esteward_certification.html; International Standards Organization accessed via http://www.iso.org/iso/home.htm; the IAER accessed via http://www.iaer.org/search; and G. MacDonald, "Don't Recycle 'E-waste' with Haste, Activists Warn," *USA Today*, July 6, 2008.

CHAPTER 6
Understanding Network Effects

1. INTRODUCTION

LEARNING OBJECTIVES

1. **Define network effects.**
2. **Recognize products and services that are subject to network effects.**
3. **Understand the factors that add value to products and services subject to network effects.**

Network effects

Also known as Metcalfe's Law, or network externalities. When the value of a product or service increases as its number of users expands.

Network effects are sometimes referred to as "Metcalfe's Law" or "network externalities." But don't let the dull names fool you—this concept is rocket fuel for technology firms. Bill Gates leveraged network effects to turn Windows and Office into virtual monopolies and in the process became the wealthiest man in America. Mark Zuckerberg of Facebook, Sergey Brin and Larry Page of Google, Pierre Omidyar of eBay, Andrew Mason of Groupon, Evan Williams and Biz Stone of Twitter, Nik Zennström and Janus Friis of Skype, Steve Chen and Chad Hurley of YouTube, all these entrepreneurs have built massive user bases by leveraging the concept. When network effects are present, *the value of a product or service increases as the number of users grows.* Simply, more users = more value. Of course, most products aren't subject to network effects—you probably don't care if someone wears the same socks, uses the same pancake syrup, or buys the same trash bags as you. But when network effects are present they're among *the most important* reasons you'll pick one product or service over another. You may care very much, for example, if others are part of your social network, if your video game console is popular, and if the Wikipedia article you're referencing has had prior readers. And all those folks who bought HD DVD players sure were bummed when the rest of the world declared Blu-ray the winner. In each of these examples, network effects are at work.

Not *That* Kind of Network

The term "network" sometimes stumps people when first learning about network effects. In this context, a network doesn't refer to the physical wires or wireless systems that connect pieces of electronics. It just refers to a common user base that is able to communicate and share with one another. So Facebook users make up a network. So do owners of Blu-ray players, traders that buy and sell stock over the NASDAQ, or the sum total of hardware and outlets that support the BS 1363 electrical standard.

KEY TAKEAWAY

- Network effects are among the most powerful strategic resources that can be created by technology-based innovation. Many category-dominating organizations and technologies, including Microsoft, Apple, NASDAQ, eBay, Facebook, and Visa, owe their success to network effects. Network effects are also behind the establishment of most standards, including Blu-ray, Wi-Fi, and Bluetooth.

QUESTIONS AND EXERCISES

1. What are network effects? What are the other names for this concept?
2. List several products or services subject to network effects. What factors do you believe helped each of these efforts achieve dominance?
3. Which firm do you suspect has stronger end-user network effects: Google's online search tool or Microsoft's Windows operating system? Why?
4. Network effects are often associated with technology, but tech isn't a prerequisite for the existence of network effects. Name a product, service, or phenomenon that is not related to information technology that still dominates due to network effects.

2. WHERE'S ALL THAT VALUE COME FROM?

LEARNING OBJECTIVES

1. **Identify the three primary sources of value for network effects.**
2. **Recognize factors that contribute to the staying power and complementary benefits of a product or service subject to network effects.**
3. **Understand how firms like Microsoft and Apple each benefit from strong network effects.**

The value derived from network effects comes from three sources: exchange, staying power, and complementary benefits.

2.1 Exchange

Facebook for one person isn't much fun, and the first guy in the world with a fax machine didn't have much more than a paperweight. But as each new Facebook friend or fax user comes online, a network becomes more valuable because its users can potentially communicate with more people. These examples show the importance of *exchange* in creating value. Every product or service subject to network effects fosters some kind of exchange. For firms leveraging technology, this might include anything you can represent in the ones and zeros of digital storage, such as movies, music, money, video games, and computer programs. And just about any standard that allows things to plug into one another, interconnect, or otherwise communicate will live or die based on its ability to snare network effects.

Exercise: Graph It

Some people refer to network effects by the name Metcalfe's Law. It got this name when, toward the start of the dot-com boom, Bob Metcalfe (the inventor of the Ethernet networking standard) wrote a column in *InfoWorld* magazine stating that the value of a network equals its number of users squared. What do you think of this formula? Graph the law with the vertical axis labeled "value" and the horizontal axis labeled "users." Do you think the graph is an accurate representation of what's happening in network effects? If so, why? If not, what do you think the graph really looks like?

2.2 Staying Power

staying power

The long-term viability of a product or service.

Users don't want to buy a product or sign up for a service that's likely to go away, and a number of factors can halt the availability of an effort: a firm could bankrupt or fail to attract a critical mass of user support, or a rival may successfully invade its market and draw away current customers. Networks with greater numbers of users suggest a stronger **staying power**. The staying power, or long-term viability, of a product or service is particularly important for consumers of technology products. Consider that when someone buys a personal computer and makes a choice of Windows, Mac OS, or Linux, their investment over time usually greatly exceeds the initial price paid for the operating system. A user invests in learning how to use a system, buying and installing software, entering preferences or other data, creating files—all of which mean that if a product isn't supported anymore, much of this investment is lost.

The concept of staying power (and the fear of being stranded in an unsupported product or service) is directly related to **switching costs** (the cost a consumer incurs when moving from one product to another) and switching costs can strengthen the value of network effects as a strategic asset. The higher the value of the user's overall investment, the more they're likely to consider the staying power of any offering before choosing to adopt it. Similarly, the more a user has invested in a product, the less likely he or she is to leave.

Switching costs also go by other names. You might hear the business press refer to products (particularly Web sites) as being "sticky" or creating "friction." Others may refer to the concept of "lock-in." And the elite Boston Consulting Group is really talking about a firm's switching costs when it refers to how well a company can create customers who are "barnacles" (that are tightly anchored to the firm) and not "butterflies" (that flutter away to rivals). The more friction available to prevent users from migrating to a rival, the greater the switching costs. And in a competitive market where rivals with new innovations show up all the time, that can be a very good thing!

switching costs

The cost a consumer incurs when moving from one product to another. It can involve actual money spent (e.g., buying a new product) as well as investments in time, any data loss, and so forth.

How Important Are Switching Costs to Microsoft?

"It is this switching cost that has given our customers the patience to stick with Windows through all our mistakes, our buggy drivers, our high **TCO [total cost of ownership]**, *our lack of a sexy vision at times, and many other difficulties [...] Customers constantly evaluate other desktop platforms, [but] it would be so much work to move over that they hope we just improve Windows rather than force them to move. [...] In short, without this exclusive franchise [meaning Windows] we would have been dead a long time ago."*

- Comments from a Microsoft General Manager in a memo to Bill Gates[1]

total cost of ownership (TCO)

An economic measure of the full cost of owning a product (typically computing hardware and/or software). TCO includes direct costs such as purchase price, plus indirect costs such as training, support, and maintenance.

2.3 Complementary Benefits

Complementary benefits are those products or services that add additional value to the network. These products might include "how-to" books, software, and feature add-ons, even labor. You'll find more books on auctioning that focus on eBay, more video cameras that upload to YouTube, and more accountants that know Excel than those tareted at any of their rivals. Why? Book authors, camera manufacturers, and accountants invest their time and resources where they're likely to reach the biggest market and get the greatest benefit. In auctions, video, and spreadsheet software, eBay, YouTube, and Excel each dwarf their respective competition.

Products and services that encourage others to offer complementary goods are sometimes called **platforms.**[2] Allowing other firms to contribute to your platform can be a brilliant strategy because those firms will spend *their* time and money to enhance *your* offerings. Consider the billion-dollar hardware ecosystem that Apple has cultivated around the iPod and that it's now extending to other iOS products. There are over ninety brands selling some 280 models of iPod speaker systems.[3] Thirty-four auto manufacturers now trumpet their cars as being iPod-ready, many with in-car docking stations and steering wheel music navigation systems. Each add-on enhances the value of choosing an iPod over a rival like the Microsoft Zune. And now with the App Store for the iPhone, iPod touch, and iPad, Apple is doing the same thing with software add-ons. Software-based ecosystems can grow very quickly. In less than a year after its introduction, the iTunes App Store boasted over fifty thousand applications, collectively downloaded over one billion times. Less than two years later, downloaded apps topped ten billion.

These three value-adding sources—*exchange*, *staying power*, and *complementary benefits*—often work together to reinforce one another in a way that makes the network effect even stronger. When users *exchanging* information attract more users, they can also attract firms offering *complementary* products. When developers of complementary products invest time writing software—and users install, learn, and customize these products—switching costs are created that enhance the *staying power* of a given network. From a strategist's perspective this can be great news for dominant firms in markets where network effects exist. The larger your network, the more difficult it becomes for rivals to challenge your leadership position.

complementary benefits

Products or services that add additional value to the primary product or service that makes up a network.

platforms

Products and services that allow for the development and integration of software products and other complementary goods. Windows, the iPhone, the Wii, and the standards that allow users to create Facebook apps are all platforms.

KEY TAKEAWAYS

- Products and services subject to network effects get their value from exchange, perceived staying power, and complementary products and services. Tech firms and services that gain the lead in these categories often dominate all rivals.
- Many firms attempt to enhance their network effects by creating a platform for the development of third-party products and services that enhance the primary offering.

QUESTIONS AND EXERCISES

1. What are the factors that contribute to the value created by network effects?
2. Why is staying power particularly important to many technology products and services?
3. Think about the kinds of technology products that you own that are subject to network effects. What sorts of exchange do these products leverage (e.g., information, money, software, or other media)?
4. Think about the kinds of technology projects you own. What sorts of switching costs are inherent in each of these? Are these strong switching costs or weak switching costs? What would it take for you to leave one of these services and use a rival? How might a competitor try to lessen these switching costs to persuade you to adopt their product?
5. Which other terms are sometimes used to describe the phenomenon of switching costs?
6. Think about the kinds of technology products that you own that are subject to network effects. What sorts of complementary benefits are available for these products? Are complementary benefits strong or weak (meaning, do people choose the product primarily based on these benefits, or for some other reason)?
7. Identify firms that you believe have built a strong platform. Can you think of firms that have tried to develop a platform, but have been less successful? Why do you suppose they have struggled?

3. ONE-SIDED OR TWO-SIDED MARKETS?

LEARNING OBJECTIVES

1. **Recognize and distinguish between one-sided and two-sided markets.**
2. **Understand same-side and cross-side exchange benefits.**

3.1 Understanding Network Structure

To understand the key sources of network value, it's important to recognize the structure of the network. Some networks derive most of their value from a single class of users. An example of this kind of network is instant messaging (IM). While there might be some add-ons for the most popular IM tools, they don't influence most users' choice of an IM system. You pretty much choose one IM tool over another based on how many of your contacts you can reach. Economists would call IM a **one-sided market** (a market that derives most of its value from a single class of users), and the network effects derived from IM users attracting more IM users as being **same-side exchange benefits** (benefits derived by interaction among members of a single class of participant).

one-sided market

A market that derives most of its value from a single class of users (e.g., instant messaging).

same-side exchange benefits

Benefits derived by interaction among members of a single class of participant (e.g., the exchange value when increasing numbers of IM users gain the ability to message each other).

But some markets are comprised of two distinct categories of network participant. Consider video games. People buy a video game console largely based on the number of really great games available for the system. Software developers write games based on their ability to reach the greatest number of paying customers, so they're most likely to write for the most popular consoles first. Economists would call this kind of network a **two-sided market** (network markets comprised of two distinct categories of participant, both of which that are needed to deliver value for the network to work). When an increase in the number of users on one side of the market (console owners, for example) creates a rise in the other side (software developers), that's called a **cross-side exchange benefit**.

two-sided market

Network markets comprised of two distinct categories of participant, both of which that are needed to deliver value for the network to work (e.g., video game console owners and developers of video games).

cross-side exchange benefit

When an increase in the number of users on one side of the market (console owners, for example) creates a rise in the other side (software developers).

The Positive Feedback Loop of Network Effects

IM is considered a one-sided market (or one-sided network), where the value-creating, positive-feedback loop of network effects comes mostly from same-side benefits from a single group (IM members who attract other IM members who want to communicate with them). Discount deal sites like Groupon, however, are considered to be two-sided markets, where significant benefits come from two distinct classes of users that add value by attracting each other. In Groupon's case, the more people that subscribe to receive the firm's daily deal messages, the stronger the magnet that attracts potential advertisers who offer more deals, who in turn attract more subscribers (and so on). This dynamic has produced freak-show growth for the Chicago-based firm. Less than two years after Groupon was founded, *Forbes* declared the firm to be the *fastest growing company in history*.[4] While the site has literally hundreds of competitors, few of the upstarts are formidable. The highly profitable Groupon ended 2010 with *ten times* the traffic of its nearest competitor.[5] Groupon isn't out of the clear yet. Firms like Facebook and Google—each with an established ad sales force and already strong relationships with advertisers—are launching their own daily deal efforts, gunning for Groupon's growth. But as for the me-too wannabe upstarts—they've got nothing.

It's also possible that a network may have both same-side and cross-side benefits, too. Xbox 360 benefits from cross-side benefits in that more users of that console attract more developers writing more software titles and vice versa. However, the Xbox Live network that allows users to play against each other has same-side benefits. If your buddies use Xbox Live and you want to play against them, you're more likely to buy an Xbox.

KEY TAKEAWAYS

- In one-sided markets, users gain benefits from interacting with a similar category of users (think instant messaging, where everyone can send and receive messages to one another).
- In two-sided markets, users gain benefits from interacting with a separate, complementary class of users (e.g., in Groupon's daily-deal business, deal subscribers are attracted to the platform because there are more vendors offering deals, while vendors are attracted to Groupon because it has the most customers to receive the deals).

QUESTIONS AND EXERCISES

1. What is the difference between same-side exchange benefits and cross-side exchange benefits?
2. What is the difference between a one-sided market and a two-sided market?
3. Give examples of one-sided and two-sided markets.
4. Identify examples of two-sided markets where both sides pay for a product or service. Identify examples where only one side pays. What factors determine who should pay? Does paying have implications for the establishment and growth of a network effect? What might a firm do to encourage early network growth?
5. The Apple iPhone Developer Program provides developers access to the App Store where they can distribute their free or commercial applications to millions of iPhone and iPod touch customers. Would the iPhone market be considered a one or two-sided market?

4. HOW ARE THESE MARKETS DIFFERENT?

LEARNING OBJECTIVES

1. **Understand how competition in markets where network effects are present differ from competition in traditional markets.**
2. **Understand the reasons why it is so difficult for late-moving, incompatible rivals to compete in markets where a dominant, proprietary standard is present.**

When network effects play a starring role, competition in an industry can be fundamentally different than in conventional, nonnetwork industries.

First, network markets experience *early, fierce competition*. The positive-feedback loop inherent in network effects—where the biggest networks become even bigger—causes this. Firms are very aggressive in the early stages of these industries because once a leader becomes clear, *bandwagons* form, and new adopters begin to overwhelmingly favor the leading product over rivals, tipping the market in favor of one dominant firm or standard. This tipping can be remarkably swift. Once the majority of major studios and retailers began to back Blu-ray over HD DVD, the latter effort folded within weeks.

monopoly

A market where there are many buyers but only one dominant seller.

oligopoly

A market dominated by a small number of powerful sellers.

These markets are also often winner-take-all or winner-take-most, *exhibiting monopolistic tendencies* where one firm dominates all rivals. Look at all of the examples listed so far—in nearly every case the dominant player has a market share well ahead of all competitors. When, during the U.S. Microsoft antitrust trial, Judge Thomas Penfield Jackson declared Microsoft to be a **monopoly** (a market where there are many buyers but only one dominant seller), the collective response should have been "of course." Why? The *natural state* of a market where network effects are present (and this includes operating systems and Office software) is for there to be one major player. Since bigger networks offer more value, they can charge customers more. Firms with a commanding network effects advantage may also enjoy substantial bargaining power over partners. For example, Apple, which controls over 75 percent of digital music sales, for years was able to dictate song pricing, despite the tremendous protests of the record labels.[6] In fact, Apple's stranglehold was so strong that it leveraged bargaining power even though the "Big Four" record labels (Universal, Sony, EMI, and Warner) were themselves an **oligopoly** (a market dominated by a small number of powerful sellers) that together provide over 85 percent of music sold in the United States.

Finally, it's important to note that the best product or service doesn't always win. PlayStation 2 dominated the original Xbox in a prior generation's game console war, despite the fact that nearly every review claimed the Xbox was hands-down a more technically superior machine. Why were users willing to choose an inferior product (PS2) over a superior one (Xbox)? The power of network effects! PS2 had more users, which attracted more developers offering more games.

FIGURE 6.1

Battling a leader with network effects is tough.[7]

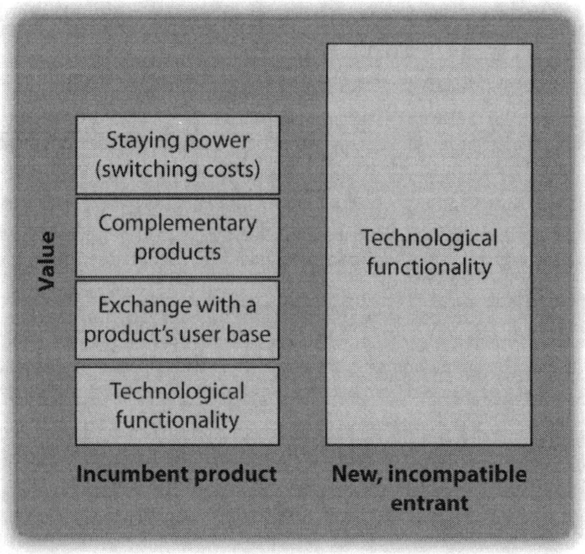

This last note is a critical point to any newcomer wishing to attack an established rival. Winning customers away from a dominant player in a network industry isn't as easy as offering a product or service that is better. Any product that is incompatible with the dominant network has to exceed the value of the technical features of the leading player, plus (since the newcomer likely starts without any users or third-party product complements) the value of the incumbent's exchange, switching cost, and complementary product benefit (see Figure 6.1). And the incumbent must not be able to easily copy any of the newcomer's valuable new innovations; otherwise the dominant firm will quickly match any valuable improvements made by rivals. As such, **technological leapfrogging**, or competing by offering a superior generation of technology, can be really tough.[8]

technological leapfrogging

Competing by offering a new technology that is so superior to existing offerings that the value overcomes the total resistance that older technologies might enjoy via exchange, switching cost, and complementary benefits.

Is This Good for Innovation?

Critics of firms that leverage proprietary standards for market dominance often complain that network effects are bad for innovation. But this statement isn't entirely true. While network effects limit competition *against* the dominant standard, innovation *within* a standard may actually blossom. Consider Windows. Microsoft has a huge advantage in the desktop operating system market, so few rivals try to compete with it. Apple's Mac OS and the open source Linux operating system are the firm's only credible rivals, and both have tiny market shares. But the dominance of Windows is a magnet for developers to innovate within the standard. Programmers with novel ideas are willing to make the investment in learning to write software for Windows because they're sure that a Windows version can be used by the overwhelming majority of computer users.

By contrast, look at the mess we initially had in the mobile phone market. With so many different handsets containing differing computing hardware, offering different screen sizes, running different software, having different key layouts, and working on different carrier networks, writing a game that's accessible by the majority of users is nearly impossible. Glu Mobile, a maker of online games, launched fifty-six reengineered builds of Monopoly to satisfy the diverse requirements of just one telecom carrier.[9] As a result, entrepreneurs with great software ideas for the mobile market were deterred because writing, marketing, and maintaining multiple product versions is both costly and risky. It wasn't until Apple's iPhone arrived, offering developers both a huge market and a consistent set of development standards, that third-party software development for mobile phones really took off.

KEY TAKEAWAYS

- Unseating a firm that dominates with network effects can be extremely difficult, especially if the newcomer is not compatible with the established leader. Newcomers will find their technology will need to be so good that it must leapfrog not only the value of the established firm's tech, but also the perceived stability of the dominant firm, the exchange benefits provided by the existing user base, and the benefits from any product complements. For evidence, just look at how difficult it's been for rivals to unseat the dominance of Windows.
- Because of this, network effects might limit the number of rivals that challenge a dominant firm. But the establishment of a dominant standard may actually encourage innovation within the standard, since firms producing complements for the leader have faith the leader will have staying power in the market.

QUESTIONS AND EXERCISES

1. How is competition in markets where network effects are present different from competition in traditional markets?
2. What are the reasons it is so difficult for late-moving, incompatible rivals to compete in markets where a dominant, proprietary standard is present? What is technological leapfrogging and why is it so difficult to accomplish?
3. Does it make sense to try to prevent monopolies in markets where network effects exist?
4. Are network effects good or bad for innovation? Explain.
5. What is the relationship between network effects and the bargaining power of participants in a network effects "ecosystem"?
6. Cite examples where the best technology did not dominate a network effects-driven market.

5. COMPETING WHEN NETWORK EFFECTS MATTER

LEARNING OBJECTIVES

1. **Plot strategies for competing in markets where network effects are present, both from the perspective of the incumbent firm and the new market entrant.**
2. **Give examples of how firms have leveraged these strategies to compete effectively.**

Why do you care whether networks are one-sided, two-sided, or some sort of hybrid? Well, when crafting your plan for market dominance, it's critical to know if network effects exist, how strong they might be, where they come from, and how they might be harnessed to your benefit. Here's a quick rundown of the tools at your disposal when competing in the presence of network effects.

Strategies for Competing in Markets with Network Effects (Examples in Parentheses)

- Move early (Yahoo! Auctions in Japan)
- Subsidize product adoption (PayPal)
- Leverage viral promotion (Skype; Facebook feeds)
- Expand by redefining the market to bring in new categories of users (Nintendo Wii) or through convergence (iPhone).
- Form alliances and partnerships (NYCE vs. Citibank)
- Establish distribution channels (Java with Netscape; Microsoft bundling Media Player with Windows)
- Seed the market with complements (Blu-ray; Nintendo)
- Encourage the development of complementary goods—this can include offering resources, subsidies, reduced fees, market research, development kits, venture capital (Facebook fbFund).
- Maintain backward compatibility (Apple's Mac OS X Rosetta translation software for PowerPC to Intel)
- For rivals, be compatible with larger networks (Apple's move to Intel; Live Search Maps)
- For incumbents, constantly innovate to create a moving target and block rival efforts to access your network (Apple's efforts to block access to its own systems)
- For large firms with well-known followers, make preannouncements (Microsoft)

5.1 Move Early

In the world of network effects, this is a biggie. Being first allows your firm to start the network effects snowball rolling in your direction. In Japan, worldwide auction leader eBay showed up just five months after Yahoo! launched its Japanese auction service. But eBay was never able to mount a credible threat and ended up pulling out of the market. Being just five months late cost eBay billions in lost sales, and the firm eventually retreated, acknowledging it could never unseat Yahoo!'s network effects lead.

Another key lesson from the loss of eBay Japan? Exchange depends on the ability to communicate! EBay's huge network effects in the United States and elsewhere didn't translate to Japan because most Japanese aren't comfortable with English, and most English speakers don't know Japanese. The language barrier made Japan a "greenfield" market with no dominant player, and Yahoo!'s early move provided the catalyst for victory.

Timing is often critical in the video game console wars, too. Sony's PlayStation 2 enjoyed an eighteen-month lead over the technically superior Xbox (as well as Nintendo's GameCube). That time lead helped to create what for years was the single most profitable division at Sony. By contrast, the technically superior PS3 showed up months after Xbox 360 and at roughly the same time as the Nintendo Wii, and has struggled in its early years, racking up multibillion-dollar losses for Sony.[10]

What If Microsoft Threw a Party and No One Showed Up?

Microsoft launched the Zune media player with features that should be subject to network effects—the ability to share photos and music by wirelessly "squirting" content to other Zune users. The firm even promoted Zune with the tagline "Welcome to the Social." Problem was the Zune Social was a party no one wanted to attend. The late-arriving Zune garnered a market share of just 3 percent, and users remained hard pressed to find buddies to leverage these neat social features.[11] A cool idea does not make a network effect happen.

5.2 Subsidize Adoption

Starting a network effect can be tough—there's little incentive to join a network if there's no one in the system to communicate with. In one admittedly risky strategy, firms may offer to subsidize initial adoption in hopes that network effects might kick in shortly after. Subsidies to adopters might include a price reduction, rebate, or other giveaways. PayPal, a service that allows users to pay one another using credit cards, gave users a modest rebate as a sign-up incentive to encourage adoption of its new effort (in one early promotion, users got back fifteen dollars when spending their first thirty dollars). This brief subsidy paid to early adopters paid off handsomely. EBay later tried to enter the market with a rival effort, but as a late mover its effort was never able to overcome PayPal's momentum. PayPal was eventually purchased by eBay for $1.5 billion, and the business unit is now considered one of eBay's key drivers of growth and profit.

Gilt Groupe, a high-end fashion flash deals site, used subsidies to increase adoption of the firm's mobile app "Gilt on the Go"—fueling the growth of a new and vital distribution channel. Gilt knew that getting its app into the purses and pockets of more of its users would increase the chance that a customer would view more deals and act on them. To encourage mobile owners to download the Gilt app, the company offered instant membership (as opposed to its normal invitation-only model) and a ten-dollar credit to the first ten thousand new subscribers. Awareness of Gilt on the Go spread virally, and apps grew in a flash, accounting for 15 percent of the firm's revenue within months.[12] Some of the best approaches to competing in network markets will simultaneously leverage several of the strategies we're outlining here, and in the case of Gilt, the *subsidy* helped create *viral* promotion that in turn helped establish a new *distribution channel.*

FIGURE 6.2 Gilt Groupe iPad App

Gilt's ten-dollar iPad subsidy and instant membership offer helped fuel adoption of the iPad app. Mobile apps now account for 15 percent of the high-end fashion site's sales.

When Even Free Isn't Good Enough

Subsidizing adoption after a rival has achieved dominance can be an uphill battle, and sometimes even offering a service for free isn't enough to combat the dominant firm. When Yahoo! introduced a U.S. auction service to compete with eBay, it initially didn't charge sellers at all (sellers typically pay eBay a small percentage of each completed auction). The hope was that with the elimination of seller fees, enough sellers would jump from eBay to Yahoo! helping the late-mover catch up in the network effect game.

But eBay sellers were reluctant to leave for two reasons. First, there weren't enough buyers on Yahoo! to match the high bids they earned on much-larger eBay. Some savvy sellers played an arbitrage game where they'd buy items on Yahoo!'s auction service at lower prices and resell them on eBay, where more users bid prices higher.

Second, any established seller leaving eBay would give up their valuable "seller ratings," and would need to build their Yahoo! reputation from scratch. Seller ratings represent a critical switching cost, as many users view a high rating as a method for reducing the risk of getting scammed or receiving lower-quality goods.

Auctions work best for differentiated goods. While Amazon has had some success in peeling away eBay sellers who provide commodity products (a real danger as eBay increasingly relies on fixed-price sales), eBay's dominant share of the online auction market still towers over all rivals.[13] While there's no magic in the servers used to create eBay, the early use of technology allowed the firm to create both network effects and switching costs—a dual strategic advantage that has given it a hammerlock on auctions even as others have attempted to mimic its service and undercut its pricing model.

5.3 Leverage Viral Promotion

Since all products and services foster some sort of exchange, it's often possible to leverage a firm's customers to promote the product or service. Internet calling service Skype (now owned by Microsoft) has over six hundred million registered users yet has spent almost nothing on advertising. Most Skype users were recruited by others who shared the word on free and low-cost Internet calls. And rise of social media has made viral promotion a tool that many firms can exploit. Facebook and Twitter act as a catalyst for friends to share deals, spread a good word, sign up for services, and load applications.

5.4 Expand by Redefining the Market

If a big market attracts more users (and in two-sided markets, more complements), why not redefine the space to bring in more users? Nintendo did this when launching the Wii. While Sony and Microsoft focused on the graphics and raw processing power favored by hard-core male gamers, Nintendo chose to develop a machine to appeal to families, women, and age groups that normally shunned alien shoot-'em ups. By going after a bigger, redefined market, Nintendo was able to rack up sales that exceeded the Xbox 360, even though it followed the system by twelve months.[14]

blue ocean strategy

An approach where firms seek to create and compete in uncontested "blue ocean" market spaces, rather than competing in spaces and ways that have attracted many, similar rivals.

Seeking the Blue Ocean? Better Think Strategically

Reggie Fils-Aimé, the President of Nintendo of America, describes the Wii Strategy as a Blue Ocean effort.[15] The concept of **blue ocean strategy** was popularized by European Institute of Business Administration (INSEAD) professors W. Chan Kim and Renée Mauborgne (authors of a book with the same title).[16] The idea—instead of competing in *blood-red* waters where the sharks of highly competitive firms vie for every available market scrap, firms should seek the *blue waters* of uncontested, new market spaces.

For Nintendo, the granny gamers, moms, and partygoers who flocked to the Wii represented an undiscovered feast in the Blue Ocean. Talk about new markets! Consider that the best-selling video game at the start of 2009 was Wii Fit—a genre-busting title that comes with a scale so you can weigh yourself each time you play. That's a far cry from Grand Theft Auto IV, the title ranking fifth in 2008 sales, and trailing four Wii-only exclusives.

Blue ocean strategy often works best when combined with strategic positioning described in Chapter 2. If an early mover into a blue ocean can use this lead to create defensible assets for sustainable advantage, late moving rivals may find markets unresponsive to their presence. Of course, if your firm's claim in the blue ocean is based on easily imitated resources (like technology features), then holding off rivals will be tougher. For holiday season 2010, Microsoft showed up with its own motion-gaming controller, the Kinect video camera system. Kinect was such a hit with generation Wii that it became the fastest-selling consumer electronics product in history, pumping up Xbox 360 console sales and goosing Microsoft's entertainment division from zero to a billion dollars in profits in just two years.[17]

convergence

When two or more markets, once considered distinctly separate, begin to offer features and capabilities. As an example: the markets for mobile phones and media players are converging.

envelopment

When one market attempts to conquer a new market by making it a subset, component, or feature of its primary offering.

Market expansion sometimes puts rivals who previously did not compete on a collision course as markets undergo **convergence** (when two or more markets, once considered distinctly separate, begin to offer similar features and capabilities). Consider the market for portable electronic devices. Separate product categories for media players, cameras, gaming devices, phones, and global positioning systems (GPS) are all starting to merge. Rather than cede its dominance as a media player, Apple leveraged a strategy known as **envelopment**, where a firm seeks to make an existing market a subset of its product offering. Apple deftly morphed the iPod into the iPhone, a device that captures all of these product categories in one device. But the firm went further; the iPhone is Wi-Fi capable, offers browsing, e-mail, and an application platform based on a scaled-down version of the same OS X operating system used in Macintosh computers. As a "Pocket Mac," the appeal of the device broadened beyond just the phone or music player markets, and within two quarters of launch, iPhone become the second-leading smartphone in North America—outpacing Palm, Microsoft, Motorola and every other rival, except RIM's BlackBerry.[18]

5.5 Alliances and Partnerships

Firms can also use partnerships to grow market share for a network. Sometimes these efforts bring rivals together to take out a leader. In a classic example, consider ATM networks. Citibank was the first major bank in New York City to offer a large ATM network. But the Citi network was initially proprietary, meaning customers of other banks couldn't take advantage of Citi ATMs. Citi's innovation was wildly popular and being a pioneer in rolling out cash machines helped the firm grow deposits fourfold in just a few years. Competitors responded with a partnership. Instead of each rival bank offering another incompatible network destined to trail Citi's lead, competing banks agreed to share their ATM operations through NYCE (New York Cash Exchange). While Citi's network was initially the biggest, after the NYCE launch a Chase bank customer could use ATMs at a host of other banks that covered a geography far greater than Citi offered alone. Network effects in ATMs shifted to the rival bank alliance, Citi eventually joined NYCE and today, nearly every ATM in the United States carries a NYCE sticker.

Google has often pushed an approach to encourage rivals to cooperate to challenge a leader. Its Open Social standard for social networking (endorsed by MySpace, LinkedIn, Bebo, Yahoo! and others) is targeted at offering a larger alternative to Facebook's more closed efforts (see Chapter 8), while its Android open source mobile phone operating system has gained commitments from many handset makers that collectively compete with Apple's iPhone.

Share or Stay Proprietary?

Defensive moves like the ones above are often meant to diffuse the threat of a proprietary rival. Sometimes firms decide from the start to band together to create a new, more open standard, realizing that collective support is more likely to jumpstart a network than if one firm tried to act with a closed, proprietary offering. Examples of this include the coalitions of firms that have worked together to advance standards like Bluetooth and Wi-Fi. While no single member firm gains a direct profit from the sale of devices using these standards, the standard's backers benefit when the market for devices expands as products become more useful because they are more interoperable.

5.6 Leverage Distribution Channels

Firms can also think about novel ways to distribute a product or service to consumers. Sun faced a challenge when launching the Java programming language—no computers could run it. In order for Java to work, computers need a little interpreter program called the Java Virtual Machine (JVM). Most users weren't willing to download the JVM if there were no applications written in Java, and no developers were willing to write in Java if no one could run their code. Sun broke the logjam when it *bundled* the JVM with Netscape's browser. When millions of users downloaded Netscape, Sun's software snuck in, almost instantly creating a platform of millions for would-be Java developers. Today, even though Netscape has failed, Sun's Java remains one of the world's most popular programming languages. Indeed, Java was cited as one of the main reasons for Oracle's 2009 acquisition of Sun, with Oracle's CEO saying the language represented "the single most important software asset we have ever acquired."[19]

And when you don't have distribution channels, create them. That's what Apple did when it launched the Apple retail stores a little over a decade ago. At the time of launch, nearly every pundit expected the effort to fail. But it turns out, the attractive, high-service storefronts were the perfect platform to promote the uniqueness of Apple products. Apple's 300+ stores worldwide now bring in about ten billion dollars in revenue and are among the world's most successful retail outlets on a sales-per-square-foot basis.[20]

FIGURE 6.3 Apple's Retail Stores

Most pundits expected Apple retail to fail. Instead the stores provided a wildly successful channel to reach customers, explain products, and make sales. The Apple Store on Fifth Avenue in Manhattan was recently named the most photographed landmark in New York City.

Source: Photo courtesy of Samantha Marx, http://www.flickr.com/photos/spam/4414006602/.

As mentioned in Chapter 2, Microsoft is in a particularly strong position to leverage this approach. The firm often bundles its new products into its operating systems, Office suite, Internet Explorer browser, and other offerings. The firm used this tactic to transform once market-leader Real Networks into an also-ran in streaming audio. Within a few years of bundling Windows Media Player (WMP) with its other products, WMP grabbed the majority of the market, while Real's share had fallen to below 10 percent.[21]

Caution is advised, however. Regional antitrust authorities may consider product bundling by dominant firms to be anticompetitive. European regulators have forced Microsoft to unbundle Windows Media Player from its operating system and to provide a choice of browsers alongside Internet Explorer.

Antitrust: Real Versus Microsoft

From October 2001 to March 2003, Microsoft's bundling of Windows Media Player in versions of its operating system ensured that the software came preinstalled on nearly all of the estimated 207 million new PCs shipped during that period. By contrast, Real Networks' digital media player was preinstalled on less than 2 percent of PCs. But here's the kicker that got to regulators (and Real): Microsoft's standard contract with PC manufacturers "prevented them not only from removing the Windows Media Player, but even [from] providing a desktop icon for Real Networks."[22] While network effects create monopolies, governments may balk at allowing a firm to leverage its advantages in ways that are designed to deliberately keep rivals from the market.

5.7 Seed the Market

When Sony launched the PS3, it subsidized each console by selling at a price estimated at three hundred dollars below unit cost.[23] Subsidizing consoles is a common practice in the video game industry—game player manufacturers usually make most of their money through royalties paid by game developers. But Sony's subsidy had an additional benefit for the firm—it helped sneak a Blu-ray player into every home buying a PS3 (Sony was backing the Blu-ray standard over the rival HD DVD effort). PS3 has struggled with fierce competition, but initially seeding the market with low-cost Blu-ray players at a time when that hardware sold at a very high price gave eventual winner Blu-ray some extra momentum. Since Sony is also a movie studio and manufacturer of DVD players and other consumer electronics, it had a particularly strong set of assets to leverage to encourage the adoption of Blu-ray over rival HD DVD.

Giving away products for half of a two-sided market is an extreme example of this kind of behavior, but it's often used. In two-sided markets, you charge the one who will pay. Adobe gives away the Acrobat reader to build a market for the sale of software that creates Acrobat files. Firms with Yellow Page directories give away countless copies of their products, delivered straight to your home, in order to create a market for selling advertising. And Google does much the same by providing free, ad-supported search.

5.8 Encourage the Development of Complementary Goods

There are several ways to motivate others to create complementary goods for your network. These efforts often involve some form of developer subsidy or other free or discounted service. A firm may charge lower royalties or offer a period of royalty-free licensing. It can also offer free software development kits (SDKs), training programs, co-marketing dollars, or even start-up capital to potential suppliers. Microsoft and Apple both allow developers to sell their products online through Xbox LIVE Marketplace and iTunes, respectively. This channel lowers developer expenses by eliminating costs associated with selling physical inventory in brick-and-mortar stores and can provide a free way to reach millions of potential consumers without significant promotional spending.

Venture funds can also prompt firms to create complementary goods. Facebook announced it would spur development for the site in part by administering the fbFund, which initially pledged $10 million in start-up funding (in allotments of up to $250,000 each) to firms writing applications for its platform.

5.9 Leverage Backward Compatibility

Those firms that control a standard would also be wise to ensure that new products have **backward compatibility** with earlier offerings. If not, they reenter a market at installed-base zero and give up a major source of advantage—the switching costs built up by prior customers. For example, when Nintendo introduced its 16-bit Super Nintendo system, it was incompatible with the firm's highly successful prior generation 8-bit model. Rival Sega, which had entered the 16-bit market two years prior to Nintendo, had already built up a large library of 16-bit games for its system. Nintendo entered with only its debut titles, and no ability to play games owned by customers of its previous system, so there was little incentive for existing Nintendo fans to stick with the firm.[24]

backward compatibility

The ability to take advantage of complementary products developed for a prior generation of technology.

Backward compatibility was the centerpiece of Apple's strategy to revitalize the Macintosh through its move to the Intel microprocessor. Intel chips aren't compatible with the instruction set used by the PowerPC processor used in earlier Mac models. Think of this as two entirely different languages—Intel speaks French, PowerPC speaks Urdu. To ease the transition, Apple included a free software-based **adaptor**, called Rosetta, that automatically emulated the functionality of the old chip on all new Macs (a sort of Urdu to French translator). By doing so, all new Intel Macs could use the base of existing software written for the old chip; owners of PowerPC Macs were able to upgrade while preserving their investment in old software; and software firms could still sell older programs while they rewrote applications for new Intel-based Macs.

adaptor

A product that allows a firm to tap into the complementary products, data, or user base of another product or service.

Even more significant, since Intel is the same standard used by Windows, Apple developed a free software adaptor called Boot Camp that allowed Windows to be installed on Macs. Boot Camp (and similar solutions by other vendors) dramatically lowered the cost for Windows users to switch to Macs. Within two years of making the switch, Mac sales skyrocketed to record levels. Apple now boasts a commanding lead in notebook sales to the education market,[25] and a survey by Yankee Group found that 87 percent of corporations were using at least some Macintosh computers, up from 48 percent at the end of the PowerPC era two years earlier.[26]

5.10 Rivals: Be Compatible with the Leading Network

Companies will want to consider making new products compatible with the leading standard. Microsoft's Live Maps and Virtual Earth 3D arrived late to the Internet mapping game. Users had already put in countless hours building resources that meshed with Google Maps and Google Earth. But by adopting the same keyhole markup language (KML) standard used by Google, Microsoft could, as *TechCrunch* put it, "drink from Google's milkshake." Any work done by users for Google in KML could be used by Microsoft. Voilà, an instant base of add-on content!

5.11 Incumbents: Close Off Rival Access and Constantly Innovate

Oftentimes firms that control dominant networks will make compatibility difficult for rivals who try to connect with their systems. For example, while many firms offer video conferencing and Internet calling, the clear leader is Skype, a product that for years had been closed to unauthorized Skype clients.

Firms that constantly innovate make it particularly difficult for competitors to become compatible. Again, we can look to Apple as an example of these concepts in action. While Macs run Windows, Windows computers can't run Mac programs. Apple has embedded key software in Mac hardware, making it tough for rivals to write a software emulator like Boot Camp that would let Windows PCs drink from the Mac milkshake. And if any firm gets close to cloning Mac hardware, Apple sues. The firm also modifies software on other products like the iPhone and iTunes each time wily hackers tap into closed aspects of its systems. And Apple has regularly moved to block third-party hardware, such as Palm's mobile phones, from plugging into iTunes. Even if firms create adaptors that emulate a standard, a firm that constantly innovates creates a moving target that's tough for others to keep up with.

Apple has been far more aggressive than Microsoft in introducing new versions of its software. Since the firm never stays still, would-be cloners never get enough time to create a reliable emulator that runs the latest Apple software.

5.12 Large, Well-Known Followers: Preannouncements

Large firms that find new markets attractive but don't yet have products ready for delivery might *preannounce* efforts in order to cause potential adaptors to sit on the fence, delaying a purchasing decision until the new effort rolls out. Preannouncements only work if a firm is large enough to pose a credible threat to current market participants. Microsoft, for example, can cause potential customers to hold off on selecting a rival because users see that the firm has the resources to beat most players (suggesting staying power). Statements from start-ups, however, often lack credibility to delay user purchases. The tech industry acronym for the impact firms try to impart on markets through preannouncements is *FUD* for fear, uncertainty, and doubt.

The Osborne Effect

When a firm preannounces a forthcoming product or service and experiences a sharp and detrimental drop in sales of current offerings as users wait for the new item.

The Osborne Effect

Preannouncers, beware. Announce an effort too early and a firm may fall victim to what's known as "**The Osborne Effect**." It's been suggested that portable computer manufacturer Osborne Computer announced new models too early. Customers opted to wait for the new models, so sales of the firm's current offerings plummeted. While evidence suggests that Osborne's decline had more to do with rivals offering better products, the negative impact of preannouncements has hurt a host of other firms.[27] Among these, Sega, which exited the video game console market entirely after preannouncements of a next-generation system killed enthusiasm for its Saturn console.[28]

congestion effects

When increasing numbers of users lower the value of a product or service.

Too Much of a Good Thing?

When network effects are present, more users attract more users. That's a good thing as long as a firm can earn money from this virtuous cycle. But sometimes a network effect attracts too many users and a service can be so overwhelmed it becomes unusable. These so-called **congestion effects** occur when increasing numbers of users lower the value of a product or service. This most often happens when a key resource becomes increasingly scarce. Users of the game Ultima were disappointed in an early online version that launched without enough monsters to fight or server power to handle the crush of fans. Twitter's early infrastructure was often unable to handle the demands of a service in hypergrowth (leading to the frequent appearance of a not-in-service graphic known in the Twitter community as the "fail whale"). Facebook users with a large number of friends may also find their attention is a limited resource, as feeds push so much content that it becomes difficult to separate interesting information from the noise of friend actions.

And while network effects can attract positive complementary products, a dominant standard may also be the first place where virus writers and malicious hackers choose to strike.

The Twitter Fail Whale

Source: Rob Friedman / playerx / @px (http://px.ns1.net).

Feel confident! Now you've got a solid grounding in network effects, the key resource leveraged by some of the most dominant firms in technology. And these concepts apply beyond the realm of tech, too. Network effects can explain phenomena ranging from why some stock markets are more popular than others to why English is so widely spoken, even among groups of nonnative speakers. On top of that, the strategies explored in the last half of the chapter show how to use these principles to sniff out, create, and protect this key strategic asset. Go forth, tech pioneer—opportunity awaits!

KEY TAKEAWAYS

- Moving early matters in network markets—firms that move early can often use that time to establish a lead in users, switching costs, and complementary products that can be difficult for rivals to match.
- Additional factors that can help a firm establish a network effects lead include subsidizing adoption; leveraging viral marketing, creating alliances to promote a product or to increase a service's user base; redefining the market to appeal to more users; leveraging unique distribution channels to reach new customers; seeding the market with complements; encouraging the development of complements; and maintaining backward compatibility.
- Established firms may try to make it difficult for rivals to gain compatibility with their users, standards, or product complements. Large firms may also create uncertainty among those considering adoption of a rival by preannouncing competing products.

QUESTIONS AND EXERCISES

1. Is market entry timing important for network effects markets? Explain and offer an example to back up your point.
2. How might a firm subsidize adoption? Give an example.
3. Give an example of a partnership or alliance targeted at increasing network effects.
4. Is it ever advantageous for firms to give up control of a network and share it with others? Why or why not? Give examples to back up your point.
5. Do firms that dominate their markets with network effects risk government intervention? Why or why not? Explain through an example.
6. How did Sony seed the market for Blu-ray players?
7. What does backward compatibility mean and why is this important? What happens if a firm is not backward compatible?
8. What tactic did Apple use to increase the acceptability of the Mac platform to a broader population of potential users?
9. How has Apple kept clones at bay?
10. What are preannouncements? What is the danger in announcing a product too early? What is the term for negative impacts from premature product announcements?
11. How did PayPal subsidize adoption?
12. Name two companies that leveraged viral promotion to compete.
13. Name a product that is the result of the *convergence* of media players, cameras, and phones.
14. What is bundling? What are the upsides and downsides of bundling?
15. Why does Adobe allow the *free* download of Acrobat Reader?
16. What tactic might an established firm employ to make it impossible, or at least difficult, for a competitor to gain access to, or become compatible with, their product or service?
17. How do Apple, Microsoft, and Facebook encourage the development of complementary products?
18. What is the "congestion effect"? Give an example.
19. Do network effects apply in nontech areas? Give examples.

ENDNOTES

1. M. Parsons, "Microsoft: 'We'd Have Been Dead a Long Time Ago without Windows APIs," *ZDNet UK*, April 22, 2004, http://news.zdnet.co.uk/software/0,1000000121,39152686,00.htm.
2. T. Eisenmann, G. Parker, and M. Van Alstyne, "Strategies for Two-Sided Markets," *Harvard Business Review*, October 2006.
3. S. Hansell, "The iPod Economy and C.E.S.," *New York Times*, January 7, 2008.
4. C. Steiner, "Meet the Fastest Growing Company in History," *Forbes*, August 8, 2010.
5. J. O'Dell, "By Traffic, Groupon Is Ten Times Bigger Than Its Nearest Competitor," *Mashable*, December 2, 2010.
6. B. Barnes, "NBC Will Not Renew iTunes Contract," *New York Times*, August 31, 2007.
7. Adapted from J. Gallaugher and Y. Wang, "Linux vs. Windows in the Middle Kingdom: A Strategic Valuation Model for Platform Competition" (paper, Proceedings of the 2008 Meeting of Americas Conference on Information Systems, Toronto, CA, August 2008), extending M. Schilling, "Technological Leapfrogging: Lessons from the U.S. Video Game Console Industry," *California Management Review*, Spring 2003.
8. M. Schilling, "Technological Leapfrogging: Lessons from the U.S. Video Game Console Industry," *California Management Review*, Spring 2003.
9. N. Hutheesing, "Answer Your Phone, a Videogame Is Calling," *Forbes*, August 8, 2006.
10. C. Null, "Sony's Losses on PS3: $3 Billion and Counting," *Yahoo! Today in Tech*, June 27, 2008, http://tech.yahoo.com/blogs/null/96355.
11. R. Walker, "AntiPod," *New York Times*, August 8, 2008.
12. B. Gutman, "Gilt Groupe Reveals Its Success with Mobile and Social," *Forbes*, May 17, 2011.
13. B. Stone, "Amid the Gloom, an E-commerce War," *New York Times*, October 12, 2008.
14. M. Sanchanta, "Nintendo's Wii Takes Console Lead," *Financial Times*, September 12, 2007.
15. R. Fils-Aimé (presentation and discussion, Carroll School of Management, Boston College, Chestnut Hill, MA, April 6, 2009).
16. W. C. Kim and R. Mauborgne, *Blue Ocean Strategy: How to Create Uncontested Market Space and Make Competition Irrelevant* (Cambridge, MA: Harvard Business Press, 2005). See http://www.blueoceanstrategy.com.
17. S. Kessler, "Microsoft Kinect Sales Top 10 Million, Set New Guinness World Record," *Mashable*, March 9, 2011; D. Goldman, "Microsoft Profit Soars 31% on Strong Office and Kinect Sales," *CNNMoney*, April 28, 2011.
18. R. Kim, "iPhone No. 2 Smartphone Platform in North America," *The Tech Chronicles—The San Francisco Chronicle*, December 17, 2007.
19. A. Ricadela, "Oracle's Bold Java Plans," *BusinessWeek*, June 2, 2009.
20. C. Jade, "The Apple Store at 10: Past, Present, and Future," *GigaOM*, May 19, 2011; B. Molina, "Apple Store Most Photographed Location in New York City," *USA Today*, June 1, 2011.
21. *BusinessWire*, "Media Player Format Share for 2006 Confirms Windows Media Remains Dominant with a 50.8% Share of Video Streams Served, Followed by Flash at 21.9%—'CDN Growth and Market Share Shifts: 2002–2006,'" December 18, 2006; and T. Eisenmann, G. Parker, and M. Van Alstyne, "Strategies for Two-Sided Markets," *Harvard Business Review*, October 2006.
22. E. Hansen and D. Becker, "Real Hits Microsoft with $1 Billion Antitrust Suit," *CNET*, December 18, 2003, http://news.cnet.com/Real-hits-Microsoft-with-1-billion-antitrust-suit/2100-1025_3-5129316.html; and T. Eisenmann, G. Parker, and M. Van Alstyne, "Strategies for Two-Sided Markets," *Harvard Business Review*, October 2006.
23. C. Null, "Sony's Losses on PS3: $3 Billion and Counting," *Yahoo! Today in Tech*, June 27, 2008, http://tech.yahoo.com/blogs/null/96355.
24. M. Schilling, "Technological Leapfrogging: Lessons from the U.S. Video Game Console Industry," *California Management Review*, Spring 2003.
25. P. Seitz, "An Apple for Teacher, Students: Mac Maker Surges in Education," *Investor's Business Daily*, August 8, 2008.
26. P. Burrows, "The Mac in the Gray Flannel Suit," *BusinessWeek*, May 1, 2008.
27. A. Orlowski, "Taking Osborne out of the Osborne Effect," *The Register*, June 20, 2005.
28. M. Schilling, "Technological Leapfrogging: Lessons from the U.S. Video Game Console Industry," *California Management Review*, Spring 2003.

CHAPTER 7
Social Media, Peer Production, and Web 2.0

1. INTRODUCTION

LEARNING OBJECTIVES

1. **Recognize the unexpected rise and impact of social media and peer production systems, and understand how these services differ from prior generation tools.**
2. **List the major classifications of social media services.**

Over the past few years, a fundamentally different class of Internet services has attracted users, made headlines, and increasingly garnered breathtaking market valuations. Often referred to under the poorly defined umbrella term "Web 2.0," these new services are targeted at harnessing the power of the Internet to empower users to collaborate, create resources, and share information in a distinctly different way than the static Web sites and transaction-focused storefronts that characterized so many failures in the dot-com bubble. Techies often joust over the precise definition of Web 2.0, but these arguments aren't really all that important. What is significant is how quickly the Web 2.0 revolution came about, how unexpected it was, and how deeply impactful these efforts have become for individuals, businesses, and society. Consider the following:

Web 2.0

A term broadly referring to Internet services that foster collaboration and information sharing; characteristics that distinctly set "Web 2.0" efforts apart from the static, transaction-oriented Web sites of "Web 1.0." The term is often applied to Web sites and Internet services that foster social media or other sorts of peer production.

- Six of the world's top ten most heavily trafficked Internet sites are social: Facebook, YouTube, Blogger.com (considered separately from parent Google), Wikipedia, Twitter, and QQ.com (China).[1] Via Alexa.com, June 1, 2011. U.S. users now spend more time with social media than on any other category of Internet use.[2]
- It took just three years for the number of social sites in the top ten to grow from one to six. However, the list is volatile, and half of the top social sites from three years ago (MySpace, Hi5, Orkut) are no longer ranked in the top ten.[3] Morgan Stanley, *Internet Trends Report*, March 2008.
- With only seven full-time employees and an operating budget of less than $1 million, Wikipedia has become the fifth most visited site on the Internet.[4] G. Kane and R. Fichman, "The Shoemaker's Children: Using Wikis for Information Systems Teaching, Research, and Publication," *MIS Quarterly*, March 2009. The site boasts well over eighteen million articles in over 260 different languages, all of them contributed, edited, and fact-checked by volunteers.
- Just twenty months after its founding, YouTube was purchased by Google for $1.65 billion. While Google struggles to figure out how to make profitable what is currently a money-losing resource hog (over forty-eight hours of video are uploaded to YouTube each minute),[5] J. Roettgers, "YouTube Users Upload 48 Hours of Video Every Minute," *GigaOM*, May 25, 2011. the site has emerged as the Web's leading destination for video, hosting everything from apologies from CEOs for service gaffes to questions submitted as part of presidential debates. Fifty percent of YouTube's roughly three hundred million users visit the site at least once a week,[6] and the site serves over three billion videos each day,[7] with an increasing number watching from non-PC devices, including mobile phones and televisions.
- The population of Facebook users is now so large that it could be considered the third largest "nation" in the world. Half the site's users log in at least once a day, spending an average of fifty-five minutes a day on the site.[8] "Facebook Facts and Figures (History and Statistics)," *Website Monitoring Blog*, March 17, 2010. Facebook is solidly profitable and revenues have been growing

with astonishing speed (estimated at over $4 billion in 2011, doubling from the prior year).[9] By spring 2011 some suggested that the value of the privately held firm may have reached $100 billion.[10]

- Facebook and Twitter have become activist tools and have played vital roles in supporting protest movements worldwide. China and Iran are among the governments so threatened by the power of these services that each has, at times, blocked Facebook and Twitter access within their borders.
- Twitter has emerged as a major force that can break news and shape public opinion. By the time Twitter was a five-year-old, the service boasted a population of over two hundred million users that were collectively posting more than a billion tweets (Twitter messages) each week.[11] P. Kafka, "Twitter CEO Dick Costolo Talks about His New Photo Service, but Not about Profits," *AllThingsD*, June 1, 2011. In another nod to the service's significance, the U.S. Library of Congress announced plans to archive every tweet ever sent.[12]
- Services such as Twitter, Yelp, and the highly profitable TripAdvisor have unleashed the voice of the customer so that gripes, praise, and ratings are now often captured and broadcast immediately at the point of service. Reviews are now incorporated into search results and maps, making them the first thing many customers see when encountering a brand online. TripAdvisor, with just five hundred employees, brings in over $500 million in revenue (at roughly 45 percent margins),[13] B. Wash, "Double Duty," *Colby Magazine*, Winter 2009; S. Morrison, "Expedia to Spin Off TripAdvisor," *Wall Street Journal*, April 8, 2011. while Yelp has reportedly turned down acquisition offers valuing it at $700 million.[14]

The Web 2.0 moniker is a murky one because like so many popular technology terms there's not a precise definition. We'll add some precision to our discussion by focusing on social media efforts—technologies that support the creation of *user-generated content*, as well as content editing, commenting, curation, and sharing. Social media efforts include blogs, wikis, social networks, Twitter, and photo and video sharing sites. The rise of social media has also coincided with the rise of mobile computing—meaning the worldwide Internet conversation is always in your pocket. Mobile and social also work together to create entirely new services, like the location-based game / discovery engine / deals platform, Foursquare.

peer production

When users collaboratively work to create content, products, and services. Includes social media sites, open source software, and peer-produced services, such as Skype and BitTorrent, where the participation of users provide the infrastructure and computational resources that enable the service.

The **peer production** leveraged by collaborating users isn't only used to create social media; it can be used to create *services*, too, and these are also considered to be part of Web 2.0. Skype and BitTorrent leverage users' computers instead of a central IT resource to forward phone calls and video. This ability saves their sponsors the substantial cost of servers, storage, and bandwidth. Peer production is also leveraged to create much of the open source software that supports many of the Web 2.0 efforts described above. Techniques such as crowdsourcing, where initially undefined groups of users band together to solve problems, create code, and develop services, are also a type of peer production. These efforts often seek to leverage the so-called wisdom of crowds, the idea that a large, diverse group often has more collective insight than a single or small group of trained professionals.

Table 7.1 lists several examples typically considered to fall under the Web 2.0 classification (a term coined by publisher and pundit Tim O'Reilly), and each is offered alongside its first-generation Internet counterpart.[15]

TABLE 7.1 Web 1.0 versus Web 2.0

Web 1.0		Web 2.0
domain name speculation	→	search engine optimization, fans, and followers
page views	→	cost per click
screen scraping	→	Web services
publishing	→	participation
content management systems	→	wikis
directories (taxonomy)	→	tagging ("folksonomy")
Britannica Online	→	Wikipedia
personal Web sites	→	blogging, status updates, and link sharing
Ofoto	→	Flickr, Facebook, and Twitter
instant messaging	→	Twitter and Facebook
Monster.com	→	LinkedIn
RealNetworks	→	YouTube
YellowPages.com	→	Yelp
Travelocity	→	TripAdvisor
Vonage	→	Skype

Millions of users, billions of dollars, huge social impact, and most of these efforts grew to influence millions in less time than it takes the average freshman to complete college. When technology moves that quickly, even some of the world's most preeminent thought leaders can be sideswiped.

Consider that when management guru Michael Porter wrote a piece titled "Strategy and the Internet" at the end of the dot-com bubble, he lamented the high cost of building brand online, questioned the power of network effects, and cast a skeptical eye on ad-supported revenue models. Well, it turns out Web 2.0 efforts challenged *all* of these concerns. Among the efforts above, all built brand on the cheap with little conventional advertising, and each owes their hypergrowth and high valuation to their ability to harness the network effect.

This chapter can be considered in two parts. The first explains many technologies behind the social media / peer production / Web 2.0 movement, and we provide several examples of their use and impact. The final part of this chapter describes how firms should organize to engage with and take advantage of social media—specifically detailing how to "Get SMART" (with a social media awareness and response team). After going through both sections you should have a solid overview of major social technologies, how businesses are leveraging them, and how firms can organize for effective use while avoiding pitfalls.

TABLE 7.2 Major Social Media Tools

	Description	Features	Technology Providers
Blogs	Short for "Web log"—an online publication that keeps a running chronology of entries. Readers can comment on posts. Can connect to other blogs through blog rolls or trackbacks. **Key uses:** Share ideas, obtain feedback, mobilize a community.	■ Immediate publication and distribution ■ Reverse chronology ■ Comment threads ■ Persistence ■ Searchability ■ Tags ■ Trackbacks	■ Blogger (Google) ■ WordPress ■ Tumblr ■ Posterous
Wikis	A Web site that anyone can edit directly from within the browser. **Key uses:** Collaborate on common tasks or to create a common knowledge base.	■ Collaborative content creation ■ All changes are attributed ■ Revision history, with the ability to roll back changes and revert to earlier versions ■ Automatic notification of updates ■ Searchability ■ Tags ■ Monitoring	■ Socialtext ■ PBWorks ■ Google Sites ■ Atlassian ■ Jive ■ Microsoft (SharePoint) ■ Apple OS X Server
Electronic Social Network	Online community that allows users to establish a personal profile, link to other profiles (i.e., friends), share content, and communicate with members via messaging, posts. Most personal relationships are reciprocal (i.e., both parties agree to be "friends"). **Key Uses:** Discover and reinforce affiliations; identify experts; message individuals or groups; virally share media.	■ Detailed personal profiles using multimedia ■ Affiliations with groups, organizations, and individuals ■ Messaging and public discussions ■ Media sharing ■ "Feeds" of recent activity among members	Open/Public ■ Facebook ■ LinkedIn Private Platforms ■ Ning ■ Lithium ■ SelectMinds ■ LiveWorld ■ IBM/Lotus Connections ■ Salesforce.com ■ Socialtext

	Description	Features	Technology Providers
Microblogging	Short, asynchronous messaging system. Users send messages to "followers" who aren't required to follow back. **Key Uses:** distribute time-sensitive information, share opinions, virally spread ideas, run contests and promotions, solicit feedback, provide customer support, track commentary on firms/products/issues, organize protests.	▪ 140-character messages sent and received from mobile device ▪ Ability to respond publicly or privately ▪ Can specify tags to classify discussion topics for easy searching and building comment threads ▪ Follower lists	Open/Public ▪ Twitter Private Platforms ▪ Socialtext Signals ▪ Yammer ▪ Salesforce.com (Chatter)

KEY TAKEAWAYS

- A new generation of Internet applications is enabling consumers to participate in creating content and services online. Examples include Web 2.0 efforts such as social networks, blogs, Twitter, and wikis, as well as efforts such as Skype and BitTorrent, which leverage the collective hardware of their user communities to provide a service.
- These efforts have grown rapidly, most with remarkably little investment in promotion. Nearly all of these new efforts leverage network effects to add value and establish their dominance and viral marketing to build awareness and attract users.
- Experts often argue whether Web 2.0 is something new or merely an extension of existing technologies, but it's more important to appreciate the magnitude of the impact of the current generation of services.
- Peer production and social media fall under the Web 2.0 umbrella. Social media refers to content that is peer produced and shared online. But peer production also includes services that are enabled when users collaborate (examples include Skype and BitTorrent).
- Many Web 2.0 services often leverage the wisdom of crowds to provide insight, products, or ideas that can be far more accurate or valuable than those provided by a smaller group of professionals.
- Network effects play a leading role in enabling Web 2.0 firms. Many of these services also rely on ad-supported revenue models and open source software.

QUESTIONS AND EXERCISES

1. What distinguishes Web 2.0 technologies and services from the prior generation of Internet sites?
2. Several examples of rapidly rising Web 2.0 efforts are listed in this section. Make your own list of Web 1.0 and Web 2.0 services and technologies. Would you invest in them? Why or why not? Are there cautionary tales of efforts that may not have lived up to their initial hype or promise? Why do you suppose they failed?
3. In what ways do Web 2.0 efforts challenge the assumptions that Michael Porter made regarding Strategy and the Internet?
4. Trends in computing platforms and Internet services change quickly. How have the firms profiled in the bullet points above fared? Has each increased in use, value, and impact or shrunk? Are there other efforts or updates that you think are worthy of making the list in the next edition of this book?

2. BLOGS

LEARNING OBJECTIVES

1. **Know what blogs are and how corporations, executives, individuals, and the media use them.**
2. **Understand the benefits and risks of blogging.**
3. **Appreciate the growth in the number of blogs, their influence, and their capacity to generate revenue.**

Blogs

Online journal entries, usually made in a reverse chronological order. Blogs typically provide comment mechanisms where users can post feedback for authors and other readers.

long tail

In this context, refers to an extremely large selection of content or products. The long tail is a phenomenon whereby firms can make money by offering a near-limitless selection.

Trackbacks

Links in a blog post that refer eaders back to cited sources. Trackbacks allow a blogger to see which and how many other bloggers are referring to their content. A "trackback" field is supported by most blog software and while it's not required to enter a trackback when citing another post, it's considered good "netiquette" to do so.

blog rolls

A list of a blogger's favorite blogs. While not all blogs include blog rolls, those that do are often displayed on the right or left column of a blog's main page.

Blogs (short for Web logs) first emerged almost a decade ago as a medium for posting online diaries. (In a perhaps apocryphal story, *Wired* magazine claimed the term "Web log" was coined by Jorn Barger, a sometimes homeless, yet profoundly prolific, Internet poster.) From humble beginnings, the blogging phenomenon has grown to a point where the number of public blogs tracked by BlogPulse has surpassed 160 million.[16] This is clearly a **long tail** phenomenon, loaded with niche content that remains "discoverable" through search engines and that is often shared via other types of social media like Facebook and Twitter. **Trackbacks** (citation links back to original blog post) and **blog rolls** (a list of a blogger's favorite sites—a sort of shout-out to blogging peers) also help distinguish and reinforce the reputation of widely read blogs.

Most blogs offer a two-way dialogue, allowing users to comment (a sort of "letters to the editor" section for each post). The running dialogue can read like an electronic bulletin board and can be an effective way to gather opinion, brainstorm, and vet ideas. Comments also help keep a blogger honest—a vigorous community of commenters will quickly expose a blogger's errors of fact or logic.

Blogging can have significant appeal for an organization looking to be heard. Corporations that blog can enjoy *immediate* and *unfiltered* distribution of their ideas, with no limits on page size, word count, or publication deadline. And they can gather immediate *feedback* from readers via comments. Corporate blogs can be published directly to the public, skipping what bloggers call the mainstream media (MSM) and presenting their words without a journalist filtering their comments or an editor cutting out key points they'd hoped to make. That appeal has attracted some of the most senior executives to blogging. Hotel chief Bill Marriott, Zappos' Tony Hsieh, Timberland's Jeff Swartz, and Forrester Research's George Colony are among those CEOs who use their blogs for purposes that include a combination of marketing, sharing ideas, gathering feedback, press response, image shaping, and reaching consumers directly.

Given the advantages of blogs over traditional broadcast and "dead tree" print publication, it's not surprising that most mainstream news outlets also supplement their content with blogs that offer greater depth, more detail, and deadline-free timeliness. But they've got competition, and many of the most popular blogs have transformed into robust media enterprises. The political/news blog *The Huffington Post* grew to be more popular than all but eight newspaper sites and was acquired in 2011 by AOL for $315 million, a valuation significantly higher than many publicly traded papers.[17] Keep in mind that this is a site that lacks much of the sports, local news, weather, and other content offered by the locals.

Ratings like this are hard to achieve—most bloggers can't make a living off their musings. But among the elite ranks, killer subscriber numbers are a magnet for advertisers. Top blogs operating on shoestring budgets can snare several hundred thousand dollars a month in ad revenue.[18] Most start with ad networks like Google AdSense, but the most elite engage advertisers directly for high-value deals and extended sponsorships.

Blogs

While the feature set of a particular blog depends on the underlying platform and the preferences of the blogger, several key features are common to most blogs:

- *Immediate and unfiltered publication.* The ability to reach the public without limits on publication size and without having posts filtered, edited, or cut by the mainstream media.
- *Ease of use.* Creating a new post usually involves clicking a single button.
- *Comment threads.* Readers can offer comments on posts.
- *Reverse chronology.* Posts are listed in reverse order of creation, making it easy to see the most recent content.
- *Persistence.* Posts are maintained indefinitely at locations accessible by permanent links.
- *Searchability.* Current and archived posts are easily searchable.

- *Tags.* Posts are often classified under an organized tagging scheme.
- *Trackbacks.* Allows an author to acknowledge the source of an item in their post, which allows bloggers to follow the popularity of their posts among other bloggers.

Despite this increased popularity, blogging has its downside. Blog comments can be a hothouse for spam and the disgruntled. Ham-handed corporate efforts (such as poor response to public criticism or bogus "praise posts") have been ridiculed. Employee blogging can be difficult to control and public postings can "live" forever in the bowels of an Internet search engine or as content pasted on other Web sites. Bloggers, beware—there are dozens of examples of workers who have been fired for what employers viewed as inappropriate posts. The voice of the blogosphere can also wield significant influence. While not all blogosphere commentary deserves a response, firms ignore social media at their own peril (see sidebar below)! Tips on how firms should organize for social media engagement, issues to consider when developing corporate social media policy, and examples of effective and poor social media use are covered in Section 9.

The Power of the Blogosphere

Organized bloggers have often banded together as a powerful voice for change, leading the charge, for example, for news anchor Dan Rather's resignation. Others have helped an otherwise silent market voice be heard, such as when bloggers prompted the design of new insulin pumps. While not all blogosphere commentary deserves a response, firms ignore social media at their own peril! For an example of this, consider the flare-up Ingersoll Rand faced when the blogging community exposed a design flaw in its Kryptonite bike lock. Online posts and a video demonstrated that the thick metal lock could be broken with a simple ball-point pen. When Ingersoll Rand failed to react, the blogosphere erupted with criticism. Just days after online reports appeared, the mainstream media picked up the story. The *New York Times* ran a piece titled "The Pen Is Mightier Than the Lock" that included a series of photos demonstrating the ball-point Kryptonite lock pick. The event tarnished the once-strong brand and eventually resulted in a loss of over $10 million.

Like any Web page, blogs can be public, tucked behind a corporate firewall, or password protected. Third-party blogging services include Google Blogger, WordPress, Tumblr, and Posterous, with most offering a combination of free and premium features. The most popular platform for organizations choosing to host their own blog server is the open source WordPress system. Firms often choose this option to gain more control over security and formatting.

In the end, the value of any particular blog derives from a combination of technical and social features. The technical features make it easy for a blogger and his or her community to reach out for an ongoing conversation on some topic of shared interest. But the social side means that unless a reader base discovers a blog and is engaged, an effort will have little impact.

KEY TAKEAWAYS

- Blogs provide a rapid way to distribute ideas and information from one writer to many readers.
- Search engines, social media sharing, and trackbacks allow a blogger's community of readers to spread the word on interesting posts and help distinguish and reinforce the reputations of widely read blogs.
- The comments section in blogs can create a conversation to gather opinion, vet ideas, and brainstorm. Public commentary can also apply pressure to correct inaccuracies and keep a blogger honest.
- Well-known blogs can be powerfully influential, acting as flashpoints on public opinion.
- Firms ignore influential bloggers at their peril, but organizations should also be cautious about how they use and engage blogs and avoid flagrantly promotional or biased efforts.
- Top blogs have gained popularity, valuations, and profits that far exceed those of many leading traditional newspapers, and leading blogs have begun to attract well-known journalists away from print media.
- Senior executives from several industries use blogs for business purposes, including marketing, sharing ideas, gathering feedback, press response, image shaping, and reaching consumers directly without press filtering.

QUESTIONS AND EXERCISES

1. Search online to find out which blogs are currently the most popular. Why do you suppose the leaders are so popular?
2. How are popular blogs discovered? How is their popularity reinforced?
3. Are blog comment fields useful? If so, to whom or how? What is the risk associated with allowing users to comment on blog posts? How should a blogger deal with comments that they don't agree with?
4. Why would a corporation, an executive, a news outlet, or a college student want to blog? What are the benefits? What are the concerns?
5. Identify firms and executives that are blogging online. Bring examples to class and be prepared to offer your critique of their efforts.
6. How do bloggers make money? Do all bloggers have to make money? Do you think the profit motive influences their content?
7. Investigate current U.S. Federal Trade Commission laws (or the laws in your home country) that govern bloggers and other social media use. How do these restrictions impact how firms interact with bloggers? What are the penalties and implications if such rules aren't followed? Are there unwritten rules of good practice that firms and bloggers should consider as well? What might those be?
8. Investigate blogs online and share your list of favorites with your professor. Why do you like the blogs on your list? Are there blogs that are particularly useful for students of this course? Which ones?
9. What advantage do blogs have over the MSM? What advantage does the MSM have over the most popular blogs?
10. Start a blog using Tumblr, Blogger.com, WordPress.com, or some other blogging service. Post a comment to another blog. Look for the trackback field when making a post—if it's available, be sure to enter the trackback for any content you cite in your blog.

3. WIKIS

LEARNING OBJECTIVES

1. **Know what wikis are and how they are used by corporations and the public at large.**
2. **Understand the technical and social features that drive effective and useful wikis.**
3. **Suggest opportunities where wikis would be useful and consider under what circumstances their use may present risks.**
4. **Recognize how social media such as wikis and blogs can influence a firm's customers and brand.**

wiki

A Web site that can be modified by anyone, from directly within a Web browser (provided that user is granted edit access).

A **wiki** is a Web site anyone can edit directly within a Web browser (provided the site grants the user edit access). Wikis derive their name from the Hawaiian word for "quick." Ward Cunningham, the "wiki father" christened this new class of software with the moniker in honor of the wiki-wiki shuttle bus at the Honolulu airport. Wikis can be one of the speediest ways to collaboratively create content online.

Many popular online wikis serve as a shared knowledge repository in some domain. The largest and most popular wiki is Wikipedia, but there are hundreds of publicly accessible wikis that anyone can participate in, with examples ranging from Wine Wiki for oenophiles to Wookieepedia, the Star Wars wiki. Wikis can also be used for any collaborative effort—from meeting planning to project management. And in addition to the hundreds of public wikis, there are many thousand more that are hidden away behind firewalls, used as proprietary internal tools for organizational collaboration. Many wikis also serve as knowledge management systems that act as a sort of collective corporate memory that's vital for sharing skills, learning, and preserving expertise even when employees leave the firm.

Want to add to or edit a wiki entry? On most sites you just click the "Edit" link. Wikis support **what you see is what you get (WYSIWYG)** editing that, while not as robust as traditional word processors, is still easy enough for most users to grasp without training or knowledge of arcane code or markup language. Users can make changes to existing content and can easily create new pages or articles and link them to other pages in the wiki. Wikis also provide a version history. Click the "History" link on Wikipedia, for example, and you can see when edits were made and by whom. This feature allows the community to **roll back** a wiki to a prior page, in the event that someone accidentally deletes key info, or intentionally defaces a page.

Wikis are available both as software (commercial as well as open source varieties) that firms can install on their own computers and as hosted online services (subscription or ad-supported) where software and content are housed by third parties that run the technology for wiki users. Since wikis can be started without the oversight or involvement of a firm's IT department, their appearance in organizations often comes from grassroots user initiative.

what you see is what you get (WYSIWYG)

A phrase used to describe graphical editing tools, such as those found in a wiki, page layout program, or other design tool.

roll back

The ability to revert a wiki page to a prior version. This is useful for restoring earlier work in the event of a posting error, inaccuracy, or vandalism.

Wikis

As with blogs, a wiki's features set varies depending on the specific wiki tool chosen, as well as administrator design, but most wikis support the following key features:

- All changes are *attributed*, so others can see who made a given edit.
- A complete *revision history* is maintained so changes can be compared against prior versions and rolled back as needed.
- There is automatic *notification* and *monitoring* of updates; users subscribe to wiki content and can receive updates via e-mail or RSS feed when pages have been changed or new content has been added.
- All the pages in a wiki are *searchable*.
- Specific wiki pages can be classified under an organized *tagging* scheme.

Jump-starting a wiki can be a challenge, and an underused wiki can be a ghost town of orphan, out-of-date, and inaccurate content. Fortunately, once users see the value of wikis, use and effectiveness often snowballs. The unstructured nature of wikis are also both a strength and weakness. Some organizations employ **wikimasters** to "garden" community content: "prune" excessive posts, "transplant" commentary to the best location, and "weed" as necessary. Wikipatterns.com offers a guide to the stages of wiki adoption and a collection of community-building and content-building strategies.

The larger and more active a wiki community, the more likely it is that content will be up to date and that errors or vandalism will be quickly corrected (again, we see the influence of network effects, where products and services with larger user bases become more valuable). At Wikipedia, for example, **griefers** and partisans regularly alter pages (in one noteworthy stretch, the page of former U.S. President Jimmy Carter was regularly replaced with a photo of a "scruffy, random unshaven man with his left index finger shoved firmly up his nose.")[19] But the Wikipedia community is so large and attentive that such changes are often recognized in seconds and rolled back, and mischief makers soon give up and move on. Several studies have shown that large community wiki entries are as or more accurate than professional publication counterparts.[20]

wikimasters

Individuals often employed by organizations to review community content in order to delete excessive posts, move commentary to the best location, and edit as necessary.

griefer

Internet vandal and mischief maker; also sometimes referred to as a troll.

Examples of Wiki-Wise Organizations

Wikis can be vital tools for collecting and leveraging knowledge that would otherwise be scattered throughout an organization; reducing geographic distance; removing boundaries between functional areas; and flattening preexisting hierarchies. Companies have used wikis in a number of ways:

- At Pixar, wikis go after that great corporate productivity killer—the poorly planned meeting. All Pixar product meetings have an associated wiki. An online agenda ensures that all attendees arrive knowing the topics and issues to be covered. Anyone attending the meeting (and even those who can't make it) can update the agenda, post supporting materials, and make comments, helping ensure everyone has access to materials for preparation and can arrive with clear expectations and goals to focus on.
- At European investment bank Dresdner Kleinwort Wasserstein, employees use wikis for everything from setting meeting agendas to building multimedia training for new hires. Six months after launch, wiki use had surpassed activity on the firm's established intranet. Wikis are also credited with helping to reduce Dresdner e-mail traffic by 75 percent.[21]

- Sony's PlayStation team uses wikis to regularly maintain one-page overviews on the status of various projects. In this way, legal, marketing, and finance staff can get quick, up-to-date status reports on relevant projects, including the latest projected deadlines, action items, and benchmark progress. Strong security measures are enforced that limit access to only those who must be in the know, since the overviews often discuss products that have not been released.
- Employees at investment-advisory firm Manning and Napier use a wiki to collaboratively track news in areas of critical interest. Providing central repositories for employees to share articles and update evolving summaries on topics such as health care legislation, enables the firm to collect and focus what would otherwise be fragmented findings and insight. Now all employees can refer to central pages that each serve as a lightning rod attracting the latest and most relevant findings.
- Intellipedia is a secure wiki built on Intelink, a U.S. government system connecting sixteen spy agencies, military organizations, and the Department of State. The wiki is a "magnum opus of espionage," handling some one hundred thousand user accounts and five thousand page edits a day. Access is classified in tiers as "unclassified," "secret," and "top secret" (the latter hosting hundreds of thousands of pages and tens of thousands of user accounts). A page on the Mumbai terror attacks was up within minutes of the event, while a set of field instructions relating to the use of chlorine-based terror bombs in Iraq was posted and refined within two days of material identification—with the document edited by twenty-three users at eighteen locations.[22]

When brought outside the firewall, corporate wikis can also be a sort of value-generation greenhouse, allowing organizations to leverage input from their customers and partners:

- Intuit has created a "community wiki" that encourages the sharing of experience and knowledge not just regarding Intuit products, such as QuickBooks, but also across broader topics its customers may be interested in, such as industry-specific issues (e.g., architecture, nonprofit) or small business tips (e.g., hiring and training employees). The TurboTax maker has also sponsored TaxAlmanac.org, a wiki-based tax resource and research community.
- Microsoft leveraged its customer base to supplement documentation for its Visual Studio software development tool. The firm was able to enter the Brazilian market with Visual Studio in part because users had created product documentation in Portuguese.[23]

neutral point of view (NPOV)

An editorial style that is free of bias and opinion. Wikipedia norms dictate that all articles must be written in NPOV.

Don't Underestimate the Power of Wikipedia

Not only is the nonprofit Wikipedia, with its enthusiastic army of unpaid experts and editors, replacing the three-hundred-year reference reign of *Encyclopedia Britannica*, Wikipedia entries can impact nearly all large-sized organizations. Wikipedia is the go-to, first-choice reference site for a generation of "netizens," and Wikipedia entries are invariably one of the top links, often the first link, to appear in Internet search results.

This position means that anyone from top executives to political candidates to any firm large enough to warrant an entry has to contend with the very public record of Wikipedia. In the same way that firms monitor their online reputations in blog posts and Twitter tweets, they've also got to keep an eye on wikis.

But firms that overreach and try to influence an entry outside of Wikipedia's mandated **neutral point of view (NPOV)**, risk a backlash and public exposure. Version tracking means the wiki sees all. Users on computers at right-leaning Fox News were embarrassingly caught editing the wiki page of the lefty pundit and politician Al Franken (a nemesis of Fox's Bill O'Reilly);[24] Sony staffers were flagged as editing the entry for the Xbox game Halo 3;[25] and none other than Wikipedia founder Jimmy Wales was criticized for editing his own Wikipedia biography[26]—acts that some consider bad online form at best, and dishonest at worst.

One last point on using Wikipedia for research. Remember that according to its own stated policies, Wikipedia isn't an original information source; rather, it's a clearinghouse for verified information. So citing Wikipedia as a reference usually isn't considered good form. Instead, seek out original (and verifiable) sources, such as those presented via the links at the bottom of Wikipedia entries.

KEY TAKEAWAYS

- Wikis can be powerful tools for many-to-many content collaboration, and can be ideal for creating resources that benefit from the input of many such as encyclopedia entries, meeting agendas, and project status documents.
- The greater the number of wiki users, the more likely the information contained in the wiki will be accurate and grow in value.
- Wikis can be public or private.
- The availability of free or low-cost wiki tools can create a knowledge clearinghouse on topics, firms, products, and even individuals. Organizations can seek to harness the collective intelligence (wisdom of crowds) of online communities. The openness of wikis also acts as a mechanism for promoting organizational transparency and accountability.

QUESTIONS AND EXERCISES

1. Visit a wiki, either an established site like Wikipedia, or a wiki service like Socialtext. Make an edit to a wiki entry or use a wiki service to create a new wiki for your own use (e.g., for a class team to use in managing a group project). Be prepared to share your experience with the class.
2. What factors determine the value of a wiki? Which key concept, first introduced in Chapter 2, drives a wiki's success?
3. If anyone can edit a wiki, why aren't more sites crippled by vandalism or by inaccurate or inappropriate content? Are there technical reasons not to be concerned? Are there "social" reasons that can alleviate concern?
4. Give examples of corporate wiki use, as well as examples where firms used wikis to engage their customers or partners. What is the potential payoff of these efforts? Are there risks associated with these efforts?
5. Do you feel that you can trust content in wikis? Do you feel this content is more or less reliable than content in print encyclopedias? Than the content in newspaper articles? Why?
6. Have you ever run across an error in a wiki entry? Describe the situation.
7. Is it ethical for a firm or individual to edit their own Wikipedia entry? Under what circumstances would editing a Wikipedia entry seem unethical to you? Why? What are the risks a firm or individual is exposed to when making edits to public wiki entries? How do you suppose individuals and organizations are identified when making wiki edits?
8. Would you cite Wikipedia as a reference when writing a paper? Why or why not?

4. SOCIAL NETWORKS

LEARNING OBJECTIVES

1. **Know what social networks are, be able to list key features, and understand how they are used by individuals, groups, and corporations.**
2. **Understand the difference between major social networks MySpace, Facebook, and LinkedIn.**
3. **Recognize the benefits and risks of using social networks.**
4. **Be aware of trends that may influence the evolution of social networks.**

Social networks have garnered increasing attention as established networks grow and innovate, new networks emerge, and value is demonstrated. The two most dominant public social networks are Facebook and LinkedIn, sites often described as the personal and professional networks, respectively. But there are also a host of third-party networks where firms can "roll their own" private networks. Such services include Ning, Lithium, and SelectMinds.

social network

An online community that allows users to establish a personal profile and communicate with others. Large public social networks include MySpace, Facebook, LinkedIn, and Google's Orkut.

Social networks allow you to set up a profile, share content, comment on what others have shared, and follow the updates of particular users, groups, firms, and brands that may also be part of those networks. Many also are platforms for the deployment of third-party applications (not surprisingly, social games dominate).

Hundreds of firms have established pages on Facebook and communities on LinkedIn, and these are now legitimate customer- and client-engagement platforms. If a customer has decided to press the "like" button of a firm's Facebook page, corporate posts can appear in their news feed, gaining more user attention than the often-ignored ads that run on the sides of social networks. These posts, and much of the other activity that takes place on social networks, spread via feed (or news feed). Pioneered by Facebook but now adopted by most services, feeds provide a timely list of the activities of and public messages from people, groups, and organizations that an individual has an association with.

viral

In this context, information or applications that spread rapidly between users.

Feeds are inherently **viral**. By seeing what others are doing on a social network, and by leveraging the power of others to act as word-of-mouth evangelists, feeds can rapidly mobilize populations, prompt activism, and offer low-cost promotion and awareness of a firm's efforts. Many firms now see a Facebook presence and social engagement strategy as vital. Facebook's massive size and the viral power of spreading the word through feeds, plus the opportunity to invite commentary and engage consumers in a dialogue, rather than a continual barrage of promotion, is changing the way that firms and customers interact (indeed, you'll hear many successful social media professionals declare that social media is more about conversations with customers than about advertising-style promotion).

Feeds are also controversial. Many users have reacted negatively to a public broadcast of their online activity, and feed mismanagement can create accusation of spamming, public relations snafus, and user discontent and can potentially open up a site to legal action. Facebook initially dealt with a massive user outcry at the launch of feeds, and the site also faced a subsequent backlash when its Beacon service broadcast user purchases without first explicitly asking their permission and during attempts to rework its privacy policy and make Facebook data more public and accessible. (See Chapter 8 for more details.)

Social Networks

The foundation of a social network is the user profile, but utility goes beyond the sort of listing found in a corporate information directory. Typical features of a social network include support for the following:

- Detailed *personal profiles*
- Affiliations with *groups* (e.g., alumni, employers, hobbies, fans, health conditions, causes); with *individuals* (e.g., specific "friends"); and with *products*, *firms*, and other *organizations*
- Private *messaging* and public *discussions*
- Media *sharing* (text, photos, video)
- Discovery-fueling feeds of recent activity among members (e.g., status changes, new postings, photos, applications installed)
- The ability to install and use third-party applications tailored to the service (games, media viewers, survey tools, etc.), many of which are also social and allow others to interact

While a Facebook presence has become a must-have for firms (see Chapter 8), LinkedIn has become a vital tool for many businesses and professionals. LinkedIn boasted a nearly $9 billion valuation after its spring 2011 IPO (some say that price is a sign of a tech bubble and is far too high for a firm with less than $16 million in profits the previous year).[27] Regardless of the valuation, the site's growth has been spectacular, and its influence is threatening recruiting sites like Monster.com and CareerBuilder.[28]

LinkedIn was conceived from the start as a social network for business users. On LinkedIn, members post profiles and contact information, list their work history, and can be "endorsed" by others on the network. It's sort of like having your résumé and letters of recommendation in a single location. Users can pose questions to members of their network, engage in group discussions, and ask for introductions through mutual contacts. The site has also introduced a variety of additional services, including messaging, information sharing, and news and content curation—yes, LinkedIn will help you find stuff you're likely to be most interested in (wasn't that Google's job?). The firm makes money from online ads, premium subscriptions, and hiring tools for recruiters.

Active members find the site invaluable for maintaining professional contacts, seeking peer advice, networking, and even recruiting. Starbucks manager of enterprise staffing has stated that LinkedIn is "one of the best things for finding midlevel executives."[29] Such networks are also putting increasing pressure on firms to work particularly hard to retain top talent. While once HR managers fiercely guarded employee directories for fear that a list of talent may fall into the hands of rivals, today's social networks make it easy for anyone to gain a list of a firm's staff, complete with contact information and a private messaging channel.

4.1 Corporate Use of Social Networks

Social networks have also become organizational productivity tools. Employees have organized thousands of groups using publicly available social networking sites because similar tools are not offered by their firms.[30] Assuming a large fraction of these groups are focused on internal projects, this demonstrates a clear pent-up demand for corporate-centric social networks (and creates issues as work dialogue moves outside firm-supported services).

Many firms are choosing to meet this demand by implementing internal social network platforms that are secure and tailored to firm needs. At the most basic level, these networks have supplanted the traditional employee directory. Social network listings are easy to update and expand, and employees are encouraged to add their own photos, interests, and expertise to create a living digital identity.

Firms such as Deloitte, Dow Chemical, and Goldman Sachs have created social networks for "alumni" who have left the firm or retired. These networks can be useful in maintaining contacts for future business leads, rehiring former employees (20 percent of Deloitte's experienced hires are so-called *boomerangs*, or returning employees), or recruiting retired staff to serve as contractors when labor is tight.[31] Maintaining such networks will be critical in industries like IT and health care that are likely to be plagued by worker shortages for years to come.

Social networking can also be important for organizations like IBM, where some 42 percent of employees regularly work from home or client locations. IBM's social network makes it easier to locate employee expertise within the firm, organize virtual work groups, and communicate across large distances.[32] As a dialogue catalyst, a social network transforms the public directory into a font of knowledge sharing that promotes organization flattening and value-adding expertise sharing.

While IBM has developed their own social network platforms, firms are increasingly turning to third-party vendors like SelectMinds (adopted by Deloitte, Dow Chemical, and Goldman Sachs) and LiveWorld (adopted by Intuit, eBay, the NBA, and Scientific American). Ning allows anyone to create a social network and currently hosts over 2.3 million separate online communities.[33] However, with robust corporate tools now offered by LinkedIn, we might see proprietary, in-house efforts start to migrate there over time.

A Little Too Public?

As with any type of social media, content flows in social networks are difficult to control. Embarrassing disclosures can emerge from public systems or insecure internal networks. Employees embracing a culture of digital sharing may err and release confidential or proprietary information. Networks could serve as a focal point for the disgruntled (imagine the activity on a corporate social network after a painful layoff). Publicly declared affiliations, political or religious views, excessive contact, declined participation, and other factors might lead to awkward or strained employee relationships. Users may not want to add a coworker as a friend on a public network if it means they'll expose their activities, lives, persona, photos, sense of humor, and friends as they exist outside of work. And many firms fear wasted time as employees surf the musings and photos of their peers.

All are advised to be cautious in their social media sharing. Employers are trawling the Internet, mining Facebook, and scouring YouTube for any tip-off that a would-be hire should be passed over. A word to the wise: those Facebook party pics, YouTube videos of open mic performances, or blog postings from a particularly militant period might not age well and may haunt you forever in a Google search. Think twice before clicking the upload button! As *Socialnomics* author Erik Qualman puts it, "What happens in Vegas stays on YouTube (and Flickr, Twitter, Facebook…)."

Firms have also created their own online communities to foster brainstorming and customer engagement. Dell's IdeaStorm.com forum collects user feedback and is credited with prompting line offerings, such as the firm's introduction of a Linux-based laptop.[34] At MyStarbucksIdea.com, the coffee giant has leveraged user input to launch a series of innovations ranging from splash sticks that prevent spills in to-go cups, to new menu items. Both IdeaStorm and MyStarbucksIdea run on a platform offered by Salesforce.com that not only hosts these sites but also provides integration into Facebook and other services. Starbucks (the corporate brand with the most Facebook "fans") has extensively leveraged the site, using Facebook as a linchpin in the "Free Pastry Day" promotion (credited with generating one million in-store visits in a single day) and promotion of the firm's AIDS-related (Starbucks) RED campaign, which garnered an astonishing three hundred ninety million "viral impressions" through feeds, wall posts, and other messaging.[35]

Social Networks and Health Care

Dr. Daniel Palestrant often shows a gruesome slide that provides a powerful anecdote for Sermo, the social network for physicians that he cofounded and where he serves as CEO. The image is of an eight-inch saw blade poking through both sides of the bloodied thumb of a construction worker who'd recently arrived in a hospital emergency room. A photo of the incident was posted to Sermo, along with an inquiry on how to remove the blade without damaging tissue or risking a severed nerve. Within minutes replies started coming back. While many replies advised to get a hand surgeon, one novel approach suggested cutting a straw lengthwise, inserting it under the teeth of the blade, and sliding the protected blade out while minimizing further tissue tears.[36] The example illustrates how doctors using tools like Sermo can tap into the wisdom of crowds to save thumbs and a whole lot more.

Sermo is a godsend to remote physicians looking to gain peer opinion on confounding cases or other medical questions. The American Medical Association endorsed the site early on (although they failed to renew during a raucous debate on health care reform),[37] and the *Nature* scientific journals experimented with a "Discuss on Sermo" button alongside the online versions of their medical articles. Doctors are screened and verified to maintain the integrity of participants. Members leverage the site both to share information with each other and to engage in learning opportunities provided by pharmaceutical companies and other firms. Institutional investors also pay for special access to poll Sermo doctors on key questions, such as opinions on pending FDA drug approval. Sermo posts can send valuable warning signals on issues such as disease outbreaks or unseen drug side effects. And doctors have also used the service to rally against insurance company policy changes.

These are some of the rich health monitoring and sharing tools available on PatientsLikeMe. Note that treatments, symptoms, and quality-of-life measures can be tracked over time.

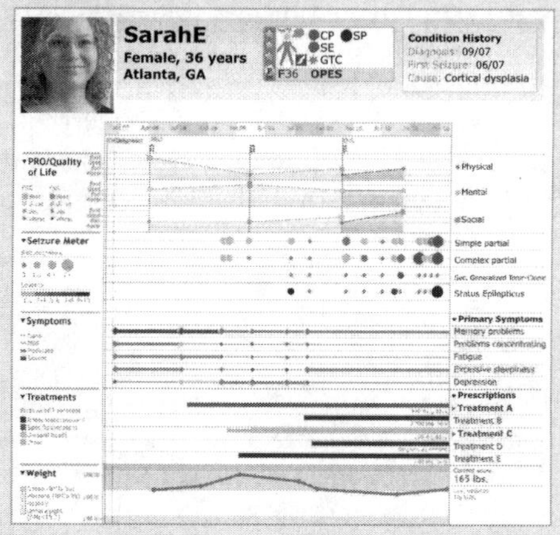

Source: PatientsLikeMe, 2011.

While Sermo focuses on the provider side of the health care equation, a short walk from the firm's Cambridge, Massachusetts, headquarters will bring one to PatientsLikeMe (PLM), a social network empowering chronically ill patients across a wide variety of disease states. The firm's "openness policy" is in contrast to privacy rules posted on many sites and encourages patients to publicly track and post conditions, treatments, and symptom variation over time, using the site's sophisticated graphing and charting tools. The goal is to help others improve the quality of their own care by harnessing the wisdom of crowds.

Todd Small, a multiple sclerosis sufferer, used the member charts and data on PLM to discover that his physician had been undermedicating him. After sharing site data with his doctor, his physician verified the problem and upped the dose. Small reports that the finding changed his life, helping him walk better than he had in a decade and a half and eliminating a feeling that he described as being trapped in "quicksand."[38] In another example of PLM's people power, the site ran its own clinical trial—like experiment to rapidly investigate promising claims that the drug Lithium could improve conditions for ALS (amyotrophic lateral sclerosis) patients. While community efforts did not support these initial claims, a decision was arrived at in months, whereas previous efforts to marshal researchers and resources to focus on the relatively rare disease would have taken many years, even if funding could be found.[39]

Both Sermo and PatientsLikeMe are start-ups that are still exploring the best way to fund their efforts for growth and impact. Regardless of where these firms end up, it should be clear from these examples that social media will remain a powerful force on the health care landscape.

KEY TAKEAWAYS

- Electronic social networks help individuals maintain contacts, discover and engage people with common interests, share updates, and organize as groups.
- Modern social networks are major messaging services, supporting private one-to-one notes, public postings, and broadcast updates or "feeds."
- Social networks also raise some of the strongest privacy concerns, as status updates, past messages, photos, and other content linger, even as a user's online behavior and network of contacts changes.
- Network effects and cultural differences result in one social network being favored over others in a particular culture or region.
- Information spreads virally via news feeds. Feeds can rapidly mobilize populations, and dramatically spread the adoption of applications. The flow of content in social networks is also difficult to control and sometimes results in embarrassing public disclosures.
- Feeds have a downside and there have been instances where feed mismanagement has caused user discontent, public relations problems, and the possibility of legal action.
- The use of public social networks within private organizations is growing, and many organizations are implementing their own, private, social networks.
- Firms are also setting up social networks for customer engagement and mining these sites for customer ideas, innovation, and feedback.

QUESTIONS AND EXERCISES

1. Visit the major social networks (MySpace, Facebook, LinkedIn). What distinguishes one from the other? Are you a member of any of these services? Why or why not?
2. How are organizations like Deloitte, Goldman Sachs, and IBM using social networks? What advantages do they gain from these systems?
3. What factors might cause an individual, employee, or firm to be cautious in their use of social networks?
4. How do you feel about the feed feature common in social networks like Facebook? What risks does a firm expose itself to if it leverages feeds? How might a firm mitigate these kinds of risks?
5. What sorts of restrictions or guidelines should firms place on the use of social networks or the other Web 2.0 tools discussed in this chapter? Are these tools a threat to security? Can they tarnish a firm's reputation? Can they enhance a firm's reputation? How so?
6. Why do information and applications spread so quickly within networks like Facebook? What feature enables this? What key promotional concept (described in Chapter 2) does this feature foster?
7. Why are some social networks more popular in some nations than others?
8. Investigate social networks on your own. Look for examples of their use for fostering political and social movements; for their use in health care, among doctors, patients, and physicians; and for their use among other professional groups or enthusiasts. Identify how these networks might be used effectively, and also look for any potential risks or downside. How are these efforts supported? Is there a clear revenue model, and do you find these methods appropriate or potentially controversial? Be prepared to share your findings with your class.

5. TWITTER AND THE RISE OF MICROBLOGGING

LEARNING OBJECTIVES

1. **Appreciate the rapid rise of Twitter—its scale, scope, and broad appeal.**
2. **Understand how Twitter is being used by individuals, organizations, and political movements.**
3. **Contrast Twitter and microblogging with Facebook, conventional blogs, and other Web 2.0 efforts.**
4. **Consider the commercial viability of the effort, its competitive environment, and concerns regarding limited revenue.**

Spawned in 2006 as a side project at the now-failed podcasting start-up Odeo (an effort backed by Blogger.com founder Evan Williams), Twitter has been on a rocket ride. The site's user numbers have blasted past both mainstream and new media sites, dwarfing the *New York Times* and LinkedIn, among others. Reports surfaced of rebuffed buyout offers as high as $500 million.[40] By its fifth birthday the firm's 500 employees were supporting a global phenomenon embraced by over two hundred million users worldwide,[41] including some 13 percent of U.S. adults.[42] In fact, by 2011 Twitter's reach was so broad that the stealth raid that led to the killing of Osama Bin Laden was inadvertently live-tweeted by an IT-savvy neighbor, commenting on the ruckus in the neighborhood.

FIGURE 7.2 Bin Laden's Neighbor Accidentally Tweets the U.S. Raid

Tweets (topmost is most recent) by Abbottabad, Pakistan—based IT consultant Sohaib Athar (Twitter handle @ReallyVirtal), who had no idea (1) that Osama Bin Laden was his neighbor and (2) that his tweets about the neighborhood disturbance were actually a live account of a U.S. raid.[43]

microblogging

A type of short-message blogging, often made via mobile device. Microblogs are designed to provide rapid notification to their readership (e.g., a news flash, an update on one's activities), rather than detailed or in-depth comments. Twitter is the most popular microblogging service.

tweet

A Twitter post, limited to 140 characters.

SMS

A text messaging standard used by many mobile phones.

hash tags

A method for organizing tweets where keywords are preceeded by the # character.

Twitter is a **microblogging** service that allows users to post 140-character messages (**tweets**) via the Web, **SMS**, or a variety of third-party desktop and smartphone applications. The microblog moniker is a bit of a misnomer. The service actually has more in common with Facebook's status updates and news feeds than it does with traditional blogs. But unlike Facebook, where most users must approve "friends" before they can see status updates, Twitter's default setting allows for asymmetrical following (although it is possible to set up private Twitter accounts and to block followers).

Sure, there's a lot of inane "tweeting" going on—lots of meaningless updates that read, "I'm having a sandwich" or "in line at the airport." But while not every user may have something worthwhile to tweet, many find that Twitter makes for invaluable reading, offering a sense of what friends, customers, thought leaders, and newsmakers are thinking. Twitter leadership has described the service as communicating "The Pulse of the Planet."[44] For many, Twitter is a discovery engine, a taste-making machine, a critical source of market intelligence, a source of breaking news, and an instantaneous way to plug into the moment's zeitgeist.

Many also find Twitter to be an effective tool for quickly blasting queries to friends, colleagues, or strangers who might offer potentially valuable input. Says futurist Paul Saffo, "Instead of creating the group you want, you send it and the group self-assembles."[45] Users can classify comments on a given topic using **hash tags** (keywords preceded by the "#" or "hash" symbol), allowing others to quickly find related tweets (e.g., #iranelection, #mumbai, #swineflu, #sxsw). Any user can create a hash tag—just type it into your tweet (you may want to search Twitter first to make sure that the tag is not in use by an unrelated topic and that if it is in use, it appropriately describes how you want your tweet classified).

Twitter users have broken news during disasters, terror attacks, and other major events. Dictators fear the people power Twitter enables, and totalitarian governments worldwide have moved to block citizen access to the service (prompting Twitter to work on censor-evading technology). During the 2009 Iranian election protests, the U.S. State Department even asked Twitter to postpone maintenance to ensure the service would continue to be available to support the voice and activism of Iran's democracy advocates.[46]

Twitter is also emerging as a legitimate business tool. Consider the following commercial examples:

- Starbucks uses Twitter in a variety of ways. It has run Twitter-based contests and used the service to spread free samples of new products, such as its VIA instant coffee line. Twitter has also been a way for the company to engage customers in its cause-based marketing efforts, such as (Starbucks) RED, which supports (Product) RED. Starbucks has even recruited staff via Twitter and was one of the first firms to participate in Twitter's advertising model featuring "promoted tweets."
- Dell used Twitter to uncover an early warning sign indicating poor design of the keyboard on one of its portable computers. After a series of tweets from early adopters indicated that the apostrophe and return keys were positioned too closely together, the firm dispatched design change orders quickly enough to correct the problem when the next version of the product was launched just three months later. Dell also claims to have netted millions in outlet store sales referred via the Twitter account @DellOutlet (more than 1.5 million followers).[47]
- Brooklyn Museum patrons can pay an additional $20 a year for access to the private, members-only "1stFans" Twitter feed that shares information on special events and exclusive access to artist content.
- Twitter is credited with having raised millions via Text-to-Donate and other fundraising as part of global disaster relief.
- Twitter can be a boon for sharing time-sensitive information. The True Massage and Wellness Spa in San Francisco tweets last-minute cancellations to tell customers of an unexpected schedule opening. With Twitter, appointments remain booked solid. Gourmet food trucks, popular in many American cities, are also using Twitter to share location and create hipster buzz. Los Angeles's Kogi Korean Taco Truck now has over eighty-five thousand followers and uses Twitter to reveal where it's parked, ensuring long lines of BBQ-craving foodies. Of the firm's success, owner Roy Choi says, "I have to give all the credit to Twitter."[48]
- Electronics retailer Best Buy has recruited over 2,300 Blue Shirt and Geek Squad staffers to crowdsource Twitter-driven inquiries via @Twelpforce, the firm's customer service Twitter account. Best Buy staffers register their personal Twitter accounts on a separate Best Buy—run site. Then any registered employees tweeting using the #twelpforce, will automatically have those posts echoed through @Twelpforce, with the employee's account credited at the end of the tweet. As of November 2009, Twelpforce had provided answers to over 19,500 customer inquiries.[49]

FIGURE 7.3 A Sampling of Tweets Filtered through Best Buy's @Twelpforce Twitter Account

@SanDiegoShorty The Internet IP address provided to your cable modem occasionally changes & is updated automatically. via @Agent3012
about 6 hours ago via Twelpforce
@visualmadness Unfortunately future stock is not something we can comment on. Best to check with your local store's came... via @ApplExpert50
about 7 hours ago via Twelpforce
@KurtWerstein You could do that you can also call the store and have them hold the product. It will depend on the coupo... via @MichaelASander
about 11 hours ago via Twelpforce
@MardeeT Yes. Best Buy was running that sale with the purchase of any iPad and the signup of a two year contract with... via @joshtotherescue
about 12 hours ago via Twelpforce
@LtColPANair I would say that good service and product is the best marketing. via @MichaelASander
about 13 hours ago via Twelpforce
@MS_Valentina You won't have to reinstall anything, ram doesn't contain data when your computer is turned off. via @MichaelASander
about 13 hours ago via Twelpforce

Surgeons and residents at Henry Ford Hospital have even tweeted during brain surgery (the teaching hospital sees the service as an educational tool). Some tweets are from those so young they've got "negative age." Twitter.com/kickbee is an experimental fetal monitor band that sends tweets when motion is detected: "I kicked Mommy at 08:52." And savvy hackers are embedding "tweeting" sensors into all sorts of devices. Botanicalls, for example, offers an electronic flowerpot stick that detects when plants need care and sends Twitter status updates to owners (sample post: "URGENT! Water me!").

Organizations are well advised to monitor Twitter activity related to the firm, as it can act as a sort of canary-in-a-coal mine uncovering emerging events. Users are increasingly using the service as a way to form flash protest crowds. Amazon.com, for example, was caught off guard over a holiday weekend when thousands used Twitter to rapidly protest the firm's reclassification of gay and lesbian books (hash tag #amazonfail). Others use the platform for shame and ridicule. BP has endured withering ridicule from the satire account @BPGlobalPR (followed by roughly 200,000 people two months after the spill).

For all the excitement, many wonder if Twitter is overhyped. Some reports suggest that many Twitter users are curious experimenters who drop the service shortly after signing up.[50] This raises the question of whether Twitter is a durable phenomenon or just a fad.

Pundits also wonder if revenues will ever justify its initially high valuation (by 2009 the firm was said to have been worth $1 billion; by 2011 shares trading on private secondary markets suggested a $10 billion valuation).[51] Others wonder if rivals could usurp Twitter's efforts with similar features. Thus far, Twitter has been following a "grow-first-harvest-later" approach.[52] The site's rapid rise has allowed it to attract enough start-up capital to enable it to approach revenue gradually and with caution, in the hopes that it won't alienate users with too much advertising (an approach not unlike Google's efforts to nurture YouTube). MIT's *Technology Review* reports that data sharing deals with Google and Bing may have brought in enough money to make the service profitable in 2009, but that amount was modest (just $25 million).[53] Twitter's advertising platform is expected to be far more lucrative, but the firm has thus far struggled to find the right model. Reflecting Twitter's "deliberately cautious" approach to revenue development, the ad model featuring sponsored "promoted tweets" rolled out first as part of the search, with distribution to individual Twitter feeds progressing as the firm experiments and learns what works best for users and advertisers.

Another issue—as the service grew, many Twitter users rarely visited the firm's Web site. Instead, most active users would post and read tweets using one of many—often free—applications provided by third parties, such as Seesmic, TweetDeck, and Twhirl. This happened because Twitter made its data available for free to other developers via **API (application programming interface)**. Exposing data can be a good move as it spawned an ecosystem of over one hundred thousand complementary third-party products and services that enhance Twitter's reach and usefulness (generating *network effects* from complementary offerings similar to other "platforms" like Windows, iPhone, and Facebook). But there are potential downsides to such openness. If users don't visit Twitter.com, that makes it difficult to count users, serve profiling technologies such as tracking cookies (see Chapter 14), collect additional data on service use, and make money by serving ads or offering promotions on the Web site. All this creates what is known as the "**free rider problem**," where others benefit from a service while offering no value in exchange. Encouraging software and service partners to accept ads for a percentage of the cut could lessen the free rider problem.[54]

application programming interfaces (APIs)

Programming hooks, or guidelines, published by firms that tell other programs how to get a service to perform a task such as send or receive data. For example, Amazon.com provides APIs to let developers write their own applications and Websites that can send the firm orders.

free rider problem

When others take advantage of a user or service without providing any sort of reciprocal benefit.

When users don't visit a service, it makes it difficult to spread awareness of new products and features. It can also create branding challenges and customer frustration. Twitter execs lamented that customers were often confused when they searched for "Twitter" in the iPhone App Store and were presented with scores of offerings but none from Twitter itself.[55] Twitter's purchase of the iPhone app Tweetie (subsequently turned into the free "Twitter for iPhone" app), its acquisition of TweetDeck, and the launch of its own URL-shortening service (limiting opportunities for bit.ly and others) signal that Twitter is willing to move into product and service niches and compete with third parties that are reliant on the Twitter ecosystem.

Twitter also got a boost when Apple deeply embedded Twitter into iOS 5. Users of the more than two hundred million Apple mobile devices gain a new one-button option to tweet photos, Web links, videos, map locations, and more. And the iOS will make Twitter easy to embed in other apps, too. Users can link a Twitter account used on their iOS devices to other apps, which means no need to log in or manually add an account each time you add an app that you'll want to tweet from. While not directly tied to Twitter revenue, these features have the potential to encourage Twitter adoption and decrease friction for embedding a tweet button into even more applications, offering a key alliance that broadens Twitter's distribution and utility and making it even harder for rivals to displace.

Microblogging does appear to be here to stay, and the impact of Twitter has been deep, broad, stunningly swift, and at times humbling in the power that it wields. But whether Twitter will be a durable, profit-gushing powerhouse remains to be seen. Speculation on Twitter's future hasn't prevented many firms from commercializing new microblogging services, and a host of companies have targeted these tools for internal corporate use. Salesforce.com's Chatter, Socialtext Signals, and Yammer are all services that have been billed as "Twitter for the Enterprise." Such efforts allow for Twitter-style microblogging that is restricted for participation and viewing by firm-approved accounts.

KEY TAKEAWAYS

- While many public and private microblogging services exist, Twitter remains by far the dominant service.
- Unlike status updates found on services like Facebook and LinkedIn, Twitter's default supports asymmetric communication, where someone can follow updates without first getting their approval. This function makes Twitter a good choice for anyone cultivating a following—authors, celebrities, organizations, and brand promoters.
- You don't need to tweet to get value. Many Twitter users follow friends, firms, celebrities, and thought leaders, quickly gaining access to trending topics.
- Twitter hash tags (keywords preceded by the # character) are used to organize "tweets" on a given topic. Users can search on hash tags, and many third-party applications allow for tweets to be organized and displayed by tag.
- Firms are leveraging Twitter in a variety of ways, including promotion, customer response, gathering feedback, and time-sensitive communication.
- Like other forms of social media, Twitter can serve as a hothouse that attracts opinion and forces organizational transparency and accountability.
- Activists have leveraged the service worldwide, and it has also served as an early warning mechanism in disasters, terror, and other events.
- Despite its rapid growth and impact, significant questions remain regarding the firm's durability, revenue prospects, and enduring appeal to initial users.
- Sites like Twitter have made data available to third parties via an API (application programming interface). The API has helped a rich ecosystem of over seventy thousand Twitter-supporting products and services emerge. But by making data available to third parties, firms may suffer from the free rider problem where others firms benefit from a service without providing much benefit back to the sponsor itself. Twitter's acquisitions (particularly of popular third-party clients that had used its API) have switched the firm from a platform sponsor to one that has begun to compete with other players in its ecosystem.

QUESTIONS AND EXERCISES

1. If you don't already have one, set up a Twitter account and "follow" several others. Follow a diverse group—corporations, executives, pundits, or other organizations. Do you trust these account holders are who they say they are? Why? Which examples do you think use the service most effectively? Which provide the weaker examples of effective Twitter use? Why? Have you encountered Twitter "spam" or unwanted followers? What can you do to limit such experiences? Be prepared to discuss your experiences with your class.
2. If you haven't done so, install a popular Twitter application such as TweetDeck, Seesmic, or a Twitter client for your mobile device. Why did you select the product you chose? What advantages does your choice offer over simply using Twitter's Web page? What challenges do these clients offer Twitter? Does the client you chose have a clear revenue model? Is it backed by a viable business?
3. Visit search.twitter.com. Which Twitter hash tags are most active at this time? Are there other "trending topics" that aren't associated with hash tags? What do you think of the activity in these areas? Is there legitimate, productive activity happening? Search Twitter on topics, firms, brand names, and issues of interest to you. What do you think of the quality of the information you've uncovered on Twitter? Who might find this to be useful?
4. Why would someone choose to use Twitter over Facebook's status update or other services? Which (if either) do you prefer and why?
5. What do you think of Twitter's revenue prospects? Is the firm a viable independent service or simply a feature to be incorporated into other social media activity? Advocate where you think the service will be in two years, five, ten. Would you invest in Twitter? Would you suggest that other firms do so? Why?
6. Assume the role of a manager for your firm. Advocate how the organization should leverage Twitter and other forms of social media. Provide examples of effective use, and cautionary tales, to back up your recommendation.
7. Some instructors have mandated Twitter for classroom use. Do you think this is productive? Would your professor advocate tweeting during lectures? What are the pros and cons of such use? Work with your instructor to discuss a set of common guidelines for in-class and course use of social media.
8. As of this writing, Twitter was just rolling out advertising via "promoted tweets." Perform some additional research. How have Twitter's attempts to grow revenues fared? How has user growth been trending? Has the firm's estimated value increased or decreased from the offer figures cited in this chapter? Why?
9. What do you think of Twitter's use of the API? What are the benefits of offering an API? What are the downsides? Would you create a company to take advantage of the Twitter API? Why or why not?
10. Twitter's revenue models are constantly evolving. Has the firm introduced new ways to make money since this chapter was written? Investigate its current revenue streams and estimated income, and be prepared to share and discuss with your class.
11. Follow this book's author at http://twitter.com/gallaugher. Tweet him if you run across interesting examples that you think would be appropriate for the next version of the book.

6. OTHER KEY WEB 2.0 TERMS AND CONCEPTS

LEARNING OBJECTIVES

1. **Know key terms related to social media, peer production, and Web 2.0, including RSS, folksonomies, mash-ups, location-based services, virtual worlds, and rich media.**
2. **Provide examples of the effective business use of these terms and technologies.**

6.1 RSS

RSS (an acronym that stands for both "really simple syndication" and "rich site summary") enables busy users to scan the headlines of newly available content and click on an item's title to view items of interest, thus sparing them from having to continually visit sites to find out what's new. Users begin by subscribing to an RSS feed for a Web site, blog, podcast, or other data source. The title or headline of any new content will then show up in an RSS reader. Subscribe to the *New York Times* Technology news feed, for example, and you will regularly receive headlines of tech news from the *Times*. Viewing an article of interest is as easy as clicking the title you like. Subscribing is often as easy as clicking on the RSS icon appearing on the home page of a Web site of interest.

Many firms use RSS feeds as a way to mange information overload, opting to distribute content via feed rather than e-mail. Some even distribute corporate reports via RSS. RSS readers are offered by third-party Web sites such as Google and Yahoo! and they have been incorporated into all popular browsers and most e-mail programs. Most blogging platforms provide a mechanism for bloggers to automatically publish a feed when each new post becomes available. Google's FeedBurner is the largest publisher of RSS blog feeds, and offers features to distribute content via e-mail as well.

RSS

A method for sending/broadcasting data to users who subscribe to a service's "RSS feed." Many Web sites and blogs forward headlines to users who subscribe to their "feed," making it easy to scan headlines and click to access relevant news and information.

RSS reader

A tool for subscribing to and accessing RSS feeds. Most e-mail programs and Web browsers can also act as RSS readers. There are also many Web sites (including Google Reader) that allow users to subscribe to and read RSS feeds.

FIGURE 7.4

RSS readers like Google Reader can be an easy way to scan blog headlines and click through to follow interesting stories.

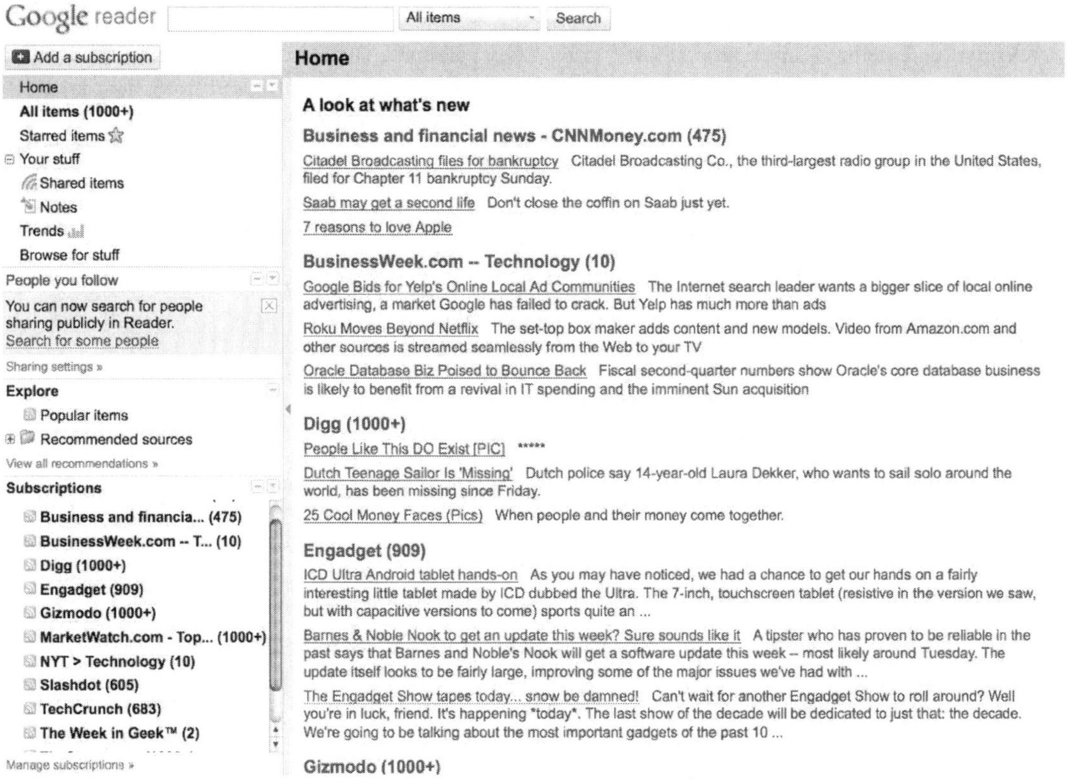

FIGURE 7.5

Web sites that support RSS feeds will have an icon in the address bar. Click it to subscribe.

6.2 Folksonomies

folksonomies

Keyword-based classification systems created by user communities (also known as social tagging).

Folksonomies (sometimes referred to as social tagging) are keyword-based classification systems created by user communities as they generate and review content. (The label is meant to refer to a people-powered taxonomy.) Bookmarking site Del.icio.us, photo-sharing site Flickr (both owned by Yahoo!), and Twitter's hash tags all make heavy use of folksonomies.

With this approach, classification schemes emerge from the people most likely to understand them—the users. By leveraging the collective power of the community to identify and classify content, objects on the Internet become easier to locate, and content carries a degree of recommendation and endorsement.

Flickr cofounder Stewart Butterfield describes the spirit of folksonomies, saying, "The job of tags isn't to organize all the world's information into tidy categories, it's to add value to the giant piles of data that are already out there."[56] The Guggenheim Museum in New York City and the San Francisco Museum of Modern Art, among other museums, are taking a folksonomic approach to their online collections, allowing user-generated categories to supplement the specialized lexicon of curators. Amazon.com has introduced a system that allows readers to classify books, and most blog posts and wiki pages allow for social tagging, oftentimes with hot topics indexed and accessible via a "tag cloud" in the page's sidebar.

6.3 Mash-up

mash-up

The combination of two or more technologies or data feeds into a single, integrated tool.

Mash-ups are combinations of two or more technologies or data feeds into a single, integrated tool. Some of the best known mash-ups leverage Google's mapping tools. Mapnificent.net combines transit agency data with Google Maps to let users find locations that are close to public transportation. HousingMaps.com combines Craigslist.org listings with Google Maps for a map-based display for apartment hunters. IBM linked together job feeds and Google Maps to create a job-seeker service for victims of Hurricane Katrina. SimplyHired links job listings with Google Maps, LinkedIn listings, and salary data from PayScale.com. And Salesforce.com has tools that allow data from its customer relationship management (CRM) system to be combined with data feeds and maps from third parties.

Mash-ups are made easy by a tagging system called **XML** (for extensible markup language). Site owners publish the parameters of XML data feeds that a service can accept or offer (e.g., an address, price, product descriptions, images). Other developers are free to leverage these public feeds using application programming interfaces (APIs), published instructions on how to make programs call one another, to share data, or to perform tasks. Using APIs and XML, mash-up authors smoosh together seemingly unrelated data sources and services in new and novel ways. Lightweight, browser-friendly software technologies like Ajax and HTML5 can often make a Web site interface as rich as a desktop application, and rapid deployment frameworks like Ruby on Rails will enable and accelerate mash-up creation and deployment.

6.4 Location-Based Services

Computing devices increasingly know where you are—and this is creating all sorts of new opportunities for social media. Twitter, Facebook, and Google Buzz are among the many social services that have added location-based options, allowing you to tweet or post a status update attached with a physical location as determined by your phone's **global positioning system (GPS)**, triangulation from nearby cell phone towers, or proximity to neighboring Wi-Fi hotspots. This introduces a whole new way to gather and share information. In a new part of town and curious what folks are saying about the spot? Search for tweets tagged as being posted around that location.

Augmented-reality apps can overlay real data on top of images from a GPS and compass-equipped smartphone. Swivel your iPhone around with Stella Artois's Bar Finder app open, and it'll point you to the nearest Stella-equipped watering hole (it'll also let you text your friends to join you for a drink and call a cab for a safe ride home). Wikitude overlays images appearing through your phone's camera lens with geotagged data from Wikipedia. Point your Yelp app down the street and activate the monocle feature to see starred reviews hover over the top of establishments that appear on screen.

Boston-based SCVNGR (pronounced "scavenger"), a gaming app, has allowed over one thousand clients, including Princeton, MetLife, and Boston's Museum of Fine Arts, to create their own mobile phone–based scavenger hunts. The profitable firm has an 80 percent client return rate and had attracted funding from Google Ventures and Highland Capital Partners all before founder Seth Priebatsch turned twenty-one.[57] SCVNGR has also run promotions that encourage repeat purchases and return visits with a diverse client base that has included American Express, Coca-Cola, and Buffalo Wild Wings. The firm also offers the mobile app LevelUp, which rewards users with Groupon-style deals and includes some rewards if you bring friends (making buying social).

Perhaps the best known among the location-based pure plays is Foursquare. The service allows players to "check in" at different locations, allowing players to earn "badges" displayed in the app for completing specific achievements ("gym rat" for exercise buffs, "school night" for weeknight bar hoppers). Check into a location more than anyone else and you become that spot's "mayor." Foursquare users can follow public location postings from their friends, discovering when a buddy is close by. Users submit tips, and a recommendations button offers suggestions on nearby places to explore. Foursquare grew to over one million users roughly one year after the service debuted at the 2009 South by Southwest conference, and now, roughly two years later, those numbers have grown to ten million.[58] Firms are now using Foursquare for promotions and to support loyalty programs—offering "mayor specials" or other incentives when users are nearby. Starbucks, the Bravo television channel, frozen yogurt chain Tasti D-Lite, and the Milwaukee-based burger chain AJ Bombers are among the diverse clients leveraging the service.

XML

Abbreviation of Extensible Markup Language. A tagging language that can be used to identify data fields made available for use by other applications. For example, programmers may wrap XML tags around elements in an address data stream (e.g., ⟨business name⟩, ⟨street address⟩, ⟨city⟩, ⟨state⟩) to allow other programs to recognize and use these data items.

global positioning system (GPS)

A network of satellites and supporting technologies used to identify a device's physical location.

augmented-reality

Computer applications that overlay real-world images with computer-generated imagery and data.

FIGURE 7.6 A Sampling of Location-Aware Apps

Wikitude shows Wikipedia overlays on top of images appearing through the viewfinder. Stella Artois's Le Bar will point you to establishments offering the brew, and Foursquare offers nearby vendor promotions and discounts.

Of course, all this public location sharing raises privacy concerns. The Web site PleaseRobMe.com was created to draw attention to the potentially dangerous issues around real-time location sharing. After a brief demonstration period, the site stopped its real-time aggregation of publicly accessible user-location data and now serves as an awareness site warning of the "stalkerish" side of location-based apps. In most cases, though, users remain firmly in control—determining if they want to keep a visit private or release their locale to verified "app friends" or to the broader online space.

6.5 Virtual Worlds

virtual world

A computer-generated environment where users present themselves in the form of an *avatar*, or animated character.

avatar

An online identity expressed by an animated or cartoon figure.

In **virtual worlds**, users appear in a computer-generated environment in the form of an **avatar**, or animated character. Users can customize the look of their avatar, interact with others by typing or voice chat, and can travel about the virtual world by flying, teleporting, or more conventional means.

The most popular general-purpose virtual world is Second Life by Linden Labs, although many others exist. Most are free, although game-oriented worlds, such as World of Warcarft (with ten million active subscribers), charge a fee. Many corporations and organizations have established virtual outposts by purchasing "land" in the world of Second Life, while still others have contracted with networks to create their own, independent virtual worlds.

Most organizations have struggled to commercialize these Second Life forays, but activity has been wide-ranging in its experimentation. Reuters temporarily "stationed" a reporter in Second Life, presidential candidates have made appearances in the virtual world, corporations have set up virtual storefronts, and there's a significant amount of virtual mayhem. Second Life "terrorists" have "bombed" virtual outposts run by several organizations, including ABC News, American Apparel, and Reebok.

Even grade schoolers are heavy virtual world users. Many elementary school students get their first taste of the Web through Webkinz, an online world that allows for an animated accompaniment with each of the firm's plush toys. Webkinz's parent company, privately held Ganz, doesn't release financial figures. But according to Compete.com, by the end of 2008 Webkinz.com had roughly the same number of unique visitors as FoxNews.com. The kiddie set virtual world market is considered so lucrative that Disney acquired ClubPenguin for $350 million with agreements to pay another potential three hundred fifty million if the effort hits growth incentives.[59]

6.6 YouTube, Podcasting, and Rich Media

Podcasts

Digital audio or video files served as a series of programs or a multimedia blog.

Blogs, wikis, and social networks not only enable sharing text and photos, they also allow for the creation and distribution of audio and video. **Podcasts** are digital audio files (some also incorporate video), provided as a series of programs. Podcasts range from a sort of media blog, archives of traditional radio and television programs, and regular offerings of original online content. While the term podcast derives from Apple's wildly successful iPod, podcasts can be recorded in audio formats such as MP3 that can be played on most portable media players. (In perhaps the ultimate concession to the market leader, even the iPod rival Microsoft Zune referred to serialized audio files as podcasts on its navigation menu.)

There are many podcast directories, but Apple's iTunes is by far the largest. Anyone who wants to make a podcast available on iTunes can do so for free. A podcast publisher simply records an audio file, uploads the file to a blog or other hosting server, then sends the RSS feed to Apple (copyrighted material cannot be used without permission, with violators risking banishment from iTunes). Files are discovered in the search feature of the iTunes music store, and listings seamlessly connect the user with the server hosting the podcast. This path creates the illusion that Apple serves the file even though it resides on a publisher's servers.

While blogs have made stars of some unknowns, the most popular podcasts are from mainstream media outlets. A recent visit to the podcasting section of iTunes showed that eight of the top ten most popular podcasts were high-quality productions of mainstream media programs, including offerings from CBS, Comedy Central, NPR, and PBS. Podcasts are also revolutionizing education, with scores of universities "open sourcing" their classrooms and offering lectures for public consumption via Apple's iTunesU.

In contrast to iTunes, YouTube actually hosts video on its own servers, so all you need to do is shoot a video and upload it to the site. YouTube is a bastion of amateur video, with most clips shot and uploaded by nonprofessionals. It's also become a protest site (e.g., "A Comcast Technician Sleeping on my Couch"). However, YouTube has also become a go-to distribution platform for professional content such as ad clips, customer support guides, music videos, TV shows, movies, and more. Much of this **rich media** content can be distributed or streamed within another Web site, blog, or social network profile.

rich media

Content that is more complex than simple text. The term can refer to images, animation, audio, and video.

KEY TAKEAWAYS

- RSS fosters the rapid sharing and scanning of information, including updates from Web 2.0 services such as blogs, wikis, and social networks. RSS feeds can be received via Web browsers, e-mail, cell phones, and special RSS readers.
- Folksonomies allow users to collaboratively tag and curate online media, making it easy for others to find useful content. Since folksonomies are created by users themselves, they are often more easily understood and embraced than classification schemes imposed by site owners.
- Mash-ups promote the useful combination of different Web services, such as maps and other information feeds. Mash-up authors leverage technologies such as APIs and XML to combine seemingly unrelated data sources and services in new and novel ways.
- Location-based services are increasingly combining geolocated data with social media. Users can now quickly see related social media surrounding an area, even overlaying this data on top of maps and images through a phone's camera lens. Sites like Foursquare are morphing into loyalty and customer-rewards programs. While users are largely in control of sharing location data, some fear privacy and security issues from oversharing.
- Virtual worlds allow users to interact with and within a computer-generated alternate reality.
- Internet media is increasingly becoming "richer," leveraging audio, video, and animation. Organizations and users are creating and distributing rich media online, with interesting content spreading virally.

QUESTIONS AND EXERCISES

1. What is RSS and an RSS reader? Why would an individual use one? Why would a firm use RSS?
2. Use an RSS reader like Google Reader, or the features built into your e-mail program or browser, and subscribe to RSS feeds. Discuss your experience with the class. Which feeds did you subscribe to? What did you like or not like about using an RSS reader?
3. If you have a smartphone, download Foursquare or other location-based app. Is this service popular in your community? Research how firms are leveraging these tools for real business value.
4. Investigate SCVNGR. Many schools are using the tool for orientation programs. Is your school using this? If so, participate in a SCVNGR game on campus. If not, build a case for considering SCVNGR (or similar service) and share this with your student government or student orientation office.
5. Are privacy concerns from location-based apps valid? What can users do to be safe even while using location-based apps?
6. Visit Second Life or another virtual world. Create an avatar and look for examples of corporate/commercial involvement. Be prepared to discuss your experience—both positive and negative.
7. Investigate some of the many virtual worlds targeted at children, including Webkinz, Club Penguin, and Whyville. What are the revenue models for these efforts? How do these sites ensure they are safe for children? Assume the role of a parent—what are the pros and cons of these sites? Which (if any) would you allow your children to participate in? Why? Would you invest in any of these efforts or advise corporations to enter the kid-focused virtual world space? Why or why not?
8. If you don't already own it, download iTunes for free, go to the iTunes music store, and explore the free podcast section. Alternatively, find podcasts from another service. Which podcasts seem to be the most popular? Why? Do you use podcasts or other rich media? Why or why not?
9. Visit YouTube. Identify examples of corporations using the service. Identify examples of customer use. Be prepared to discuss your findings with the class. Do you think Google is making much money with YouTube? Why or why not?
10. Which firm do you think spends more on the technology infrastructure that powers its service—Apple with iTunes podcasts or Google with YouTube? Explain your answer.
11. Why would a firm make its data available via XML to use as a mash-up? What can it gain? Are there any risks involved in providing programming hooks that allow the creation of mash-ups?
12. Give examples of efforts that take advantage of folksonomies. Why are folksonomies considered to be useful?
13. Do you spend time in rich media Web sites? Which ones? How much time do you or your friends spend on these sites? How would you describe the quality of rich media content found online?
14. How might a firm use rich media online? What concerns does a firm or individual face with respect to rich media?
15. Why do you suppose that the most popular podcasts come from established media firms (e.g., Comedy Central, NPR) rather than amateurs, while the top bloggers emerged outside the professional journalist/writer community?

7. PREDICTION MARKETS AND THE WISDOM OF CROWDS

LEARNING OBJECTIVES

1. **Understand the concept of the wisdom of crowds as it applies to social networking.**
2. **List the criteria necessary for a crowd to be smart.**

wisdom of crowds

The idea that a group of individuals (the crowd), often consisting of untrained amateurs, will collectively have more insight than a single or small group of trained professionals.

Many social software efforts leverage what has come to be known as the **wisdom of crowds**. In this concept, a group of individuals (the crowd often consists mostly of untrained amateurs), collectively has more insight than a single or small group of trained professionals. Made popular by author James Surowiecki (whose best-selling book was named after the phenomenon), the idea of crowd wisdom is at the heart of wikis, folksonomy tagging systems, and many other online efforts. An article in the journal *Nature* positively comparing Wikipedia to *Encyclopedia Britannica* lent credence to social software's use in harnessing and distilling crowd wisdom.[60]

The crowd isn't always right, but in many cases where topics are complex, problems are large, and outcomes are uncertain, a large, diverse group may bring collective insight to problem solving that one smart guy or a professional committee lacks. One technique for leveraging the wisdom of crowds is a **prediction market**, where a diverse crowd is polled and opinions aggregated to form a forecast of an eventual outcome. The concept is not new. The stock market is arguably a prediction market, with a stock price representing collective assessment of the discounted value of a firm's future earnings. But Internet technologies are allowing companies to set up prediction markets for exploring all sorts of problems.

prediction market

Polling a diverse crowd and aggregating opinions in order to form a forecast of an eventual outcome.

Consider Best Buy, where employees are encouraged to leverage the firm's TagTrade prediction market to make forecasts, and are offered small gifts as incentives for participation. The idea behind this incentive program is simple: the "blue shirts" (Best Buy employees) are closest to customers. They see traffic patterns and buying cycles, can witness customer reactions first hand, and often have a degree of field insight not available to senior managers at the company's Minneapolis headquarters. Harness this collective input and you've got a group brain where, as wisdom of crowds proponents often put it, "the we is greater than the me." When Best Buy asked its employees to predict gift card sales, the "crowd's" collective average answer was 99.5 percent accurate; experts paid to make the prediction were off by 5 percent. Another experiment predicting holiday sales was off by only 1/10 of 1 percent. The experts? Off by 7 percent![61]

In an article in the *McKinsey Quarterly*, Surowiecki outlined several criteria necessary for a crowd to be "smart."[62] The crowd must

- be *diverse*, so that participants are bringing different pieces of information to the table,
- be *decentralized*, so that no one at the top is dictating the crowd's answer,
- offer *a collective verdict* that summarizes participant opinions,
- be *independent*, so that each focuses on information rather than the opinions of others.

Google, which runs several predictive markets, underscored these principles when it found that predictions were less accurate when users were geographically proximate, meaning folks in the same work group who sat near one another typically thought too much alike.[63] Poorer predictive outcomes likely resulted because these relatively homogeneous clusters of users brought the same information to the table (yet another reason why organizations should hire and cultivate diverse teams).

Many firms run predictive markets to aid in key forecasts, and with the potential for real financial payoff. But University of Chicago law professor Todd Henderson warns predictive markets may also hold legal and ethical challenges. The Securities and Exchange Commission may look askance at an employee who gets a heads-up in a predictive market that says a certain drug is going to be approved or fail clinical trials. If she trades on this information is she an insider, subject to prosecution for exploiting proprietary data? Disclosure issues are unclear. Gambling laws are also murky, with Henderson uncertain as to whether certain predictive markets will be viewed as an unregulated form of betting.[64]

Publicly accessible prediction markets are diverse in their focus. The Iowa Electronic Market attempts to guess the outcome of political campaigns, with mixed results. Farecast (now part of Microsoft's Bing knowledge engine) claims a 75 percent accuracy rate for forecasting the future price of airline tickets.[65] The Hollywood Stock Exchange allows participants to buy and sell prediction shares of movies, actors, directors, and film-related options. The exchange, now owned by investment firm Cantor Fitzgerald, has picked Oscar winners with 90 percent accuracy.[66] And at HedgeStreet.com, participants can make microbets, wagering as little as ten dollars on the outcome of economic events, including predictions on the prices of homes, gold, foreign currencies, oil, and even the economic impact of hurricanes and tropical storms. HedgeStreet is considered a market and is subject to oversight by the Commodity Futures Trading Commission.[67]

KEY TAKEAWAYS

- Many Web 2.0 efforts allow firms to tap the wisdom of crowds, identifying collective intelligence.
- Prediction markets tap crowd opinion with results that are often more accurate than the most accurate expert forecasts and estimates.
- Prediction markets are most accurate when tapping the wisdom of a diverse and variously skilled and experienced group, and are least accurate when participants are highly similar.

QUESTIONS AND EXERCISES

1. What makes for a "wise" crowd? When might a crowd not be so wise?
2. Find a prediction market online and participate in the effort. Be prepared to share your experience with your class, including any statistics of predictive accuracy, participant incentives, business model of the effort, and your general assessment of the appeal and usefulness of the effort.
3. Brainstorm on the kinds of organizations that might deploy prediction markets. Why might you think the efforts you suggest and advocate would be successful?
4. In what ways are legal issues of concern to prediction market operators?

8. CROWDSOURCING

LEARNING OBJECTIVES

1. **Understand the value of crowdsourcing.**
2. **Identify firms that have used crowdsourcing successfully.**

crowdsourcing

The act of taking a job traditionally performed by a designated agent (usually an employee) and outsourcing it to an undefined generally large group of people in the form of an open call.

The power of Web 2.0 also offers several examples of the democratization of production and innovation. Need a problem solved? Offer it up to the crowd and see if any of their wisdom offers a decent result. This phenomenon, known as **crowdsourcing**, has been defined by Jeff Howe, founder of the blog crowdsourcing.com and an associate editor at *Wired*, as "the act of taking a job traditionally performed by a designated agent (usually an employee) and outsourcing it to an undefined, generally large group of people in the form of an open call."[68]

Can the crowd really do better than experts inside a firm? At least one company has literally struck gold using crowdsourcing. As told by Don Tapscott and Anthony Williams in their book *Wikinomics*, mining firm Goldcorp was struggling to gain a return from its 55,000-acre Canadian property holdings. Executives were convinced there was gold "in them thar hills," but despite years of efforts, the firm struggled to strike any new pay dirt. CEO Rob McEwen, a former mutual fund manager without geology experience who unexpectedly ended up running Goldcorp after a takeover battle then made what seemed like a Hail Mary pass—he offered up all the firm's data, on the company's Web site. Along with the data, McEwen ponied up $575,000 from the firm as prize money for the Goldcorp Challenge to anyone who came up with the best methods and estimates for reaping golden riches. Releasing data was seen as sacrilege in the intensely secretive mining industry, but it brought in ideas the firm had never considered. Taking the challenge was a wildly diverse group of "graduate students, consultants, mathematicians, and military officers." Eighty percent of the new targets identified by entrants yielded "substantial quantities of gold." The financial payoff? In just a few years a $100 million firm grew into a $9 billion titan. For Goldcorp, the crowd coughed up serious coin.

Netflix followed Goldcorp's lead, offering anonymous data to any takers, along with a one-million-dollar prize to the first team that could improve the accuracy of movie recommendations by 10 percent. Top performers among the over thirty thousand entrants included research scientists from AT&T Labs, researchers from the University of Toronto, a team of Princeton undergrads, and the proverbial "guy in a garage" (and yes, that was his team name). Frustrated for nearly three years, it took a coalition of four teams from Austria, Canada, Israel, and the United States to finally cross the 10 percent threshold. The winning team represented an astonishing brain trust that Netflix would never have been able to harness on its own.[69]

Other crowdsourcers include Threadless.com, which produces limited run t-shirts with designs users submit and vote on. Marketocracy runs stock market games and has created a mutual fund based on picks from the 100 top-performing portfolios. Just under seven years into the effort, the firm's m100 Index reports a 75 percent return versus 35 percent for the S&P 500. The St. Louis Cardinals baseball team is even crowdsourcing. The club's One for the Birds contest calls for the fans to submit scouting reports on promising players, as the team hopes to broaden its recruiting radar beyond its classic recruiting pool of Division I colleges.

There are several public markets for leveraging crowdsourcing for innovation, or as an alternative to standard means of production. Waltham, Massachusetts—based InnoCentive allows "seekers" to offer cash prizes ranging from ten to one hundred thousand dollars. Over 120,000 "solvers" have registered to seek solutions for tasks put forward by seekers that include Dow Chemical, Eli Lilly, and Procter & Gamble. Among the findings offered by the InnoCentive crowd are a biomarker that measures progression of ALS. Amazon.com has even created an online marketplace for crowdsourcing called Mechanical Turk. Anyone with a task to be completed or problem to be solved can put it up for Amazon, setting their price for completion or solution. For its role, Amazon takes a small cut of the transaction. And alpha geeks looking to prove their code chops can turn to TopCoder, a firm that stages coding competitions that deliver real results for commercial clients, such as ESPN. TopCoder contests have attracted roughly 300,000 participants from 200 countries.[70]

Not all crowdsourcers are financially motivated. Some benefit by helping to create a better service. Facebook leveraged crowd wisdom to develop versions of its site localized in various languages. Facebook engineers designated each of the site's English words or phrases as a separate translatable object. Members were then invited to translate the English into other languages, and rated the translations to determine which was best. Using this form of crowdsourcing, fifteen hundred volunteers cranked out Spanish Facebook in a month. It took two weeks for two thousand German speakers to draft Deutsch Facebook. How does the Facebook concept of "poke" translate around the world? The Spaniards decided on "dar un toque," Germans settled on "anklopfen," and the French went with "envoyer un poke."[71] Vive le crowd!

KEY TAKEAWAYS

- Crowdsourcing tackles challenges through an open call to a broader community of potential problem solvers. Examples include Goldcorp's discovering of optimal mining locations in land it already held, Facebook's leverage of its users to create translations of the site for various international markets, and Netflix's solicitation of improvements to its movie recommendation software.
- Several firms run third-party crowdsourcing forums, among them InnoCentive for scientific R&D, TopCoder for programming tasks, and Amazon's Mechanical Turk for general work.

QUESTIONS AND EXERCISES

1. What is crowdsourcing? Give examples of organizations that are taking advantage of crowdsourcing and be prepared to describe these efforts.
2. What ethical issues should firms be aware of when considering crowdsourcing? Are there other concerns firms may have when leveraging this technique?
3. Assume the role of a manager or consultant. Recommend a firm and a task that would be appropriate for crowdsourcing. Justify your choice, citing factors such as cost, breadth of innovation, time, constrained resources, or other factors. How would you recommend the firm conduct this crowdsourcing effort?

9. GET SMART: THE SOCIAL MEDIA AWARENESS AND RESPONSE TEAM

LEARNING OBJECTIVES

1. **Illustrate several examples of effective and poor social media use.**
2. **Recognize the skills and issues involved in creating and staffing an effective social media awareness and response team (SMART).**
3. **List and describe key components that should be included in any firm's social media policy.**
4. **Understand the implications of ethical issues in social media such as "sock puppetry" and "astroturfing" and provide examples and outcomes of firms and managers who used social media as a vehicle for dishonesty.**
5. **List and describe tools for monitoring social media activity relating to a firm, its brands, and staff.**
6. **Understand issues involved in establishing a social media presence, including the embassy approach, openness, and staffing.**
7. **Discuss how firms can engage and respond through social media, and how companies should plan for potential issues and crises.**

For an example of how outrage can go viral, consider Dave Carroll.[72] The Canadian singer-songwriter was traveling with his band Sons of Maxwell on a United Airlines flight from Nova Scotia to Nebraska when, during a layover at Chicago's O'Hare International Airport, Carroll saw baggage handlers roughly tossing his guitar case. The musician's $3,500 Taylor guitar was in pieces by the time it arrived in Omaha. In the midst of a busy tour schedule, Carroll didn't have time to follow up on the incident until after United's twenty-four-hour period for filing a complaint for restitution had expired. When United refused to compensate him for the damage, Carroll penned the four-minute country ditty "United Breaks Guitars," performed it in a video, and uploaded the clip to YouTube (sample lyrics: "I should have gone with someone else or gone by car…'cuz United breaks guitars"). Carroll even called out the unyielding United rep by name. Take that, Ms. Irlwig! (Note to customer service reps everywhere: you're always on.)

The clip went viral, receiving 150,000 views its first day and five million more by the next month. Well into the next year, "United Breaks Guitars" remained the top result on YouTube when searching the term "United." No other topic mentioning that word—not "United States," "United Nations," or "Manchester United"—ranked ahead of this one customer's outrage.

Video

Dave Carroll's ode to his bad airline experience, "United Breaks Guitars," went viral, garnering millions of views.

View the video online at: http://www.youtube.com/v/5YGc4zOqozo

Scarring social media posts don't just come from outside the firm. Earlier that same year employees of Domino's Pizza outlet in Conover, North Carolina, created what they thought would be a funny gross-out video for their friends. Posted to YouTube, the resulting footage of the firm's brand alongside vile acts of food prep was seen by over one million viewers before it was removed. Over 4.3 million references to the incident can be found on Google, and many of the leading print and broadcast outlets covered the story. The perpetrators were arrested, the Domino's storefront where the incident occurred was closed, and the firm's president made a painful apology (on YouTube, of course).

Not all firms choose to aggressively engage social media. As of this writing some major brands still lack a notable social media presence (Apple comes immediately to mind). But your customers are there and they're talking about your organization, its products, and its competitors. Your employees are there, too, and without guidance, they can step on a social grenade with your firm left to pick out the shrapnel. Soon, nearly everyone will carry the Internet in their pocket. Phones and MP3 players are armed with video cameras capable of recording every customer outrage, corporate blunder, ethical lapse, and rogue employee. Social media posts can linger forever online, like a graffiti tag attached to your firm's reputation. Get used to it—that genie isn't going back in the bottle.

As the "United Breaks Guitars" and "Domino's Gross Out" incidents show, social media will impact a firm whether it chooses to engage online or not. An awareness of the power of social media can shape customer support engagement and crisis response, and strong corporate policies on social media use might have given the clueless Domino's pranksters a heads-up that their planned video would get them fired and arrested. Given the power of social media, it's time for all firms to get **SMART**, creating a social media awareness and response team. While one size doesn't fit all, this section details key issues behind SMART capabilities, including creating the social media team, establishing firmwide policies, monitoring activity inside and outside the firm, establishing the social media presence, and managing social media engagement and response.

SMART

The social media awareness and response team. A group tasked with creating policies and providing support, training, guidance, and development expertise for and monitoring of a firm's social media efforts.

9.1 Creating the Team

Firms need to treat social media engagement as a key corporate function with clear and recognizable leadership within the organization. Social media is no longer an ad hoc side job or a task delegated to an intern. When McDonald's named its first social media chief, the company announced that it was important to have someone "dedicated 100% of the time, rather than someone who's got a day job on top of a day job."[73] Firms without social media baked into employee job functions often find that their online efforts are started with enthusiasm, only to suffer under a lack of oversight and follow-through. One hotel operator found franchisees were quick to create Facebook pages, but many rarely monitored them. Customers later notified the firm that unmonitored hotel Facebook pages contained offensive messages—a racist rant on one, paternity claims against an employee on another.

Organizations with a clearly established leadership role for social media can help create consistency in firm dialogue; develop and communicate policy; create and share institutional knowledge; provide training, guidance, and suggestions; offer a place to escalate issues in the event of a crisis or opportunity; and catch conflicts that might arise if different divisions engage without coordination.

While firms are building social media responsibility into job descriptions, also recognize that social media is a team sport that requires input from staffers throughout an organization. The social media team needs support from public relations, marketing, customer support, HR, legal, IT, and other groups, all while acknowledging that what's happening in the social media space is distinct from traditional roles in these disciplines. The team will hone unique skills in technology, analytics, and design, as well as skills for using social media for online conversations, listening, trust building, outreach, engagement, and response. As an example of the interdisciplinary nature of social media practice, consider that the social media team at Starbucks (regarded by some as the best in the business) is organized under the interdisciplinary "vice president of brand, content, and online."[74]

Also note that while organizations with SMARTs (social media teams) provide leadership, support, and guidance, they don't necessarily drive all efforts. GM's social media team includes representatives from all the major brands. The idea is that employees in the divisions are still the best to engage online once they've been trained and given operational guardrails. Says GM's social media chief, "I can't go in to Chevrolet and tell them 'I know your story better than you do, let me tell it on the Web.'"[75] Similarly, the roughly fifty Starbucks "Idea Partners" who participate in MyStarbucksIdea are specialists. Part of their job is to manage the company's social media. In this way, conversations about the Starbucks Card are handled by card team experts, and merchandise dialogue has a product specialist who knows that business best. Many firms find that the social media team is key for coordination and supervision (e.g., ensuring that different divisions don't overload consumers with too much or inconsistent contact), but the dynamics of specific engagement still belong with the folks who know products, services, and customers best.

9.2 Responsibilities and Policy Setting

In an age where a generation has grown up posting shoot-from-the-hip status updates and YouTube is seen as a fame vehicle for those willing to perform sensational acts, establishing corporate policies and setting employee expectations are imperative for all organizations. The employees who don't understand the impact of social media on the firm can do serious damage to their employers and their careers (look to Domino's for an example of what can go wrong).

Many experts suggest that a good social media policy needs to be three things: "short, simple, and clear."[76] Fortunately, most firms don't have to reinvent the wheel. Several firms, including Best Buy, IBM, Intel, The American Red Cross, and Australian telecom giant Telstra, have made their social media policies public.

Most guidelines emphasize the "three Rs": representation, responsibility, and respect.

- *Representation.* Employees need clear and explicit guidelines on expectations for social media engagement. Are they empowered to speak on behalf of the firm? If they do, it is critical that employees transparently disclose this to avoid legal action. U.S. Federal Trade Commission rules require disclosure of relationships that may influence online testimonial or endorsement. On top of this, many industries have additional compliance requirements (e.g., governing privacy in the health and insurance fields, retention of correspondence and disclosure for financial services firms). Firms may also want to provide guidelines on initiating and conducting dialogue, when to respond online, and how to escalate issues within the organization.
- *Responsibility.* Employees need to take responsibility for their online actions. Firms must set explicit expectations for disclosure, confidentiality and security, and provide examples of engagement done right, as well as what is unacceptable. An effective social voice is based on trust, so accuracy, transparency, and accountability must be emphasized. Consequences for violations should be clear.
- *Respect.* Best Buy's policy for its Twelpforce explicitly states participants must "honor our differences" and "act ethically and responsibly." Many employees can use the reminder. Sure customer service is a tough task and every rep has a story about an unreasonable client. But there's a difference between letting off steam around the water cooler and venting online. Virgin

Atlantic fired thirteen of the airline's staffers after they posted passenger insults and inappropriate inside jokes on Facebook.[77]

Policies also need to have teeth. Remember, a fourth "R" is at stake—reputation (both the firm's and the employee's). Violators should know the consequences of breaking firm rules and policies should be backed by action. Best Buy's policy simply states, "Just in case you are forgetful or ignore the guidelines above, here's what could happen. You could get fired (and it's embarrassing to lose your job for something that's so easily avoided)."

Despite these concerns, trying to micromanage employee social media use is probably not the answer. At IBM, rules for online behavior are surprisingly open. The firm's code of conduct reminds employees to remember privacy, respect, and confidentiality in all electronic communications. Anonymity is not permitted on IBM's systems, making everyone accountable for their actions. As for external postings, the firm insists that employees not disparage competitors or reveal customers' names without permission and asks that any employee posts from IBM accounts or that mention the firm also include disclosures indicating that opinions and thoughts shared publicly are the individual's and not Big Blue's.

Some firms have more complex social media management challenges. Consider hotels and restaurants where outlets are owned and operated by franchisees rather than the firm. McDonald's social media team provides additional guidance so that regional operations can create, for example, a Twitter handle (e.g., @mcdonalds_cincy) that handle a promotion in Cincinnati that might not run in other regions.[78] A social media team can provide coordination while giving up the necessary control. Without this kind of coordination, customer communication can quickly become a mess.

Training is also a critical part of the SMART mandate. GM offers an intranet-delivered video course introducing newbies to the basics of social media and to firm policies and expectations. GM also trains employees to become "social media proselytizers and teachers." GM hopes this approach enables experts to interact directly with customers and partners, allowing the firm to offer authentic and knowledgeable voices online.

Tweets from the Untrained

Followers of fashion label Kenneth Cole know when the firm's eponymous founder, chairman, and chief creative officer has tweeted via the corporate account—he signs these tweets with his initials KC. But it looks like KC could have used a bit of SMART training when he offered up a meant-to-be-light-hearted quip comparing Egypt's historic Mubarak-ousting protests (where several citizens were killed and injured) to enthusiasm for his firm's "new spring collection." Although the tweet was quickly deleted, screenshots (see below) linger forever, and the media widely reported on the big brand's insensitive gaffe.

KC
KennethCole Kenneth Cole
Re Egypt tweet: we weren't intending to make light of a serious situation. We understand the sensitivity of this historic moment -KC
1 hour ago
KC
KennethCole Kenneth Cole
Millions are in uproar in #Cairo. Rumor is they heard our new spring collection is now available online at http://bit.ly/KCairo -KC
3 hours ago

Training should also cover information security and potential threats. Social media has become a magnet for phishing, virus distribution, and other nefarious online activity. Over one-third of social networking users claim to have been sent malware via social networking sites (see Chapter 13). The social media team will need to monitor threats and spread the word on how employees can surf safe and surf smart.

Since social media is so public, it's easy to amass examples of what works and what doesn't, adding these to the firm's training materials. The social media team provides a catch point for institutional knowledge and industry best practice; and the team can update programs over time as new issues, guidelines, technologies, and legislation emerge.

The social media space introduces a tension between allowing expression (among employees and by the broader community) and protecting the brand. Firms will fall closer to one end or the other of this continuum depending on compliance requirements, comfort level, and goals. Expect the organization's position to move. Firms will be cautious as negative issues erupt, others will jump in as new technologies become hot and early movers generate buzz and demonstrate results. But it's the SMART responsibility to avoid knee-jerk reaction and to shepherd firm efforts with the professionalism and discipline of other management domains.

Astroturfing and Sock Puppets

Social media can be a cruel space. Sharp-tongued comments can shred a firm's reputation and staff might be tempted to make anonymous posts defending or promoting the firm. Don't do it! Not only is it a violation of FTC rules, IP addresses and other online breadcrumbs often leave a trail that exposes deceit.

Whole Foods CEO John Mackey fell victim to this kind of temptation, but his actions were eventually, and quite embarrassingly, uncovered. For years, Mackey used a pseudonym to contribute to online message boards, talking up Whole Foods stock and disparaging competitors. When Mackey was unmasked, years of comments were publicly attributed to him. The *New York Times* cited one particularly cringe-worthy post where Mackey used the pseudonym to complement his own good looks, writing, "I like Mackey's haircut. I think he looks cute!"[79]

Fake personas set up to sing your own praises are known as **sock puppets** among the digerati, and the practice of lining comment and feedback forums with positive feedback is known as **astroturfing**. Do it and it could cost you. The firm behind the cosmetic procedure known as the Lifestyle Lift was fined $300,000 in civil penalties after the New York Attorney General's office discovered that the firm's employees had posed as plastic surgery patients and wrote glowing reviews of the procedure.[80]

Review sites themselves will also take action. TripAdvisor penalizes firms if it's discovered that customers are offered some sort of incentive for posting positive reviews. The firm also employs a series of sophisticated automated techniques as well as manual staff review to uncover suspicious activity. Violators risk penalties that include being banned from the service.

Your customers will also use social media keep you honest. Several ski resorts have been embarrassed when tweets and other social media posts exposed them as overstating snowfall results. There's even an iPhone app skiers can use to expose inaccurate claims.[81]

So keep that ethical bar high—you never know when technology will get sophisticated enough to reveal wrongdoings.

sock puppet

A fake online persona created to promote a particular point of view, often in praise of a firm, product, or individual. Be aware that the use of undisclosed relationships in endorsements is a violation of U.S. Federal Trade Comission rules.

astroturfing

Engineering the posting of positive comments and reviews of a firm's product and services (or negative ones of a firm's competitors). Many ratings sites will penalize firms that offer incentives for positive feedback posts.

9.3 Monitoring

Concern over managing a firm's online image has led to the rise of an industry known as **online reputation management**. Firms specializing in this field will track a client firm's name, brand, executives' names, or other keywords, reporting online activity and whether sentiment trends toward the positive or negative.

But social media monitoring is about more than about managing one's reputation; it also provides critical competitive intelligence, it can surface customer support issues, and it can uncover opportunities for innovation and improvement. Firms that are quick to lament the very public conversations about their brands happening online need to embrace social media as an opportunity to learn more.

Resources for monitoring social media are improving all the time, and a number of tools are available for free. All firms can take advantage of Google Alerts, which flag blog posts, new Web pages, and other publicly accessible content, regularly delivering a summary of new links to your mailbox (for more on using Google for intelligence gathering, see Chapter 14). Twitter search and Twitter clients like TweetDeck can display all mentions of a particular term. And more advanced commercial tools, such as Radian9, HubSpot, and CoTweet, monitor a wide variety of social media mentions, provide metrics for ongoing campaigns and practices, and gauge sentiment and spot opportunities for sales leads or customer service.

online reputation management

The process of tracking and responding to online mentions of a product, organization, or individual. Services supporting online reputation management range from free Google Alerts to more sophisticated services that blend computer-based and human monitoring of multiple media channels.

FIGURE 7.7

Tools, such as those provided by HubSpot (depicted here), track social media mentions by key word or phrase. Savvy organizations can mine comments for competitive intelligence, insight, and product ideas or to coordinate follow-up and thoughtful customer service.

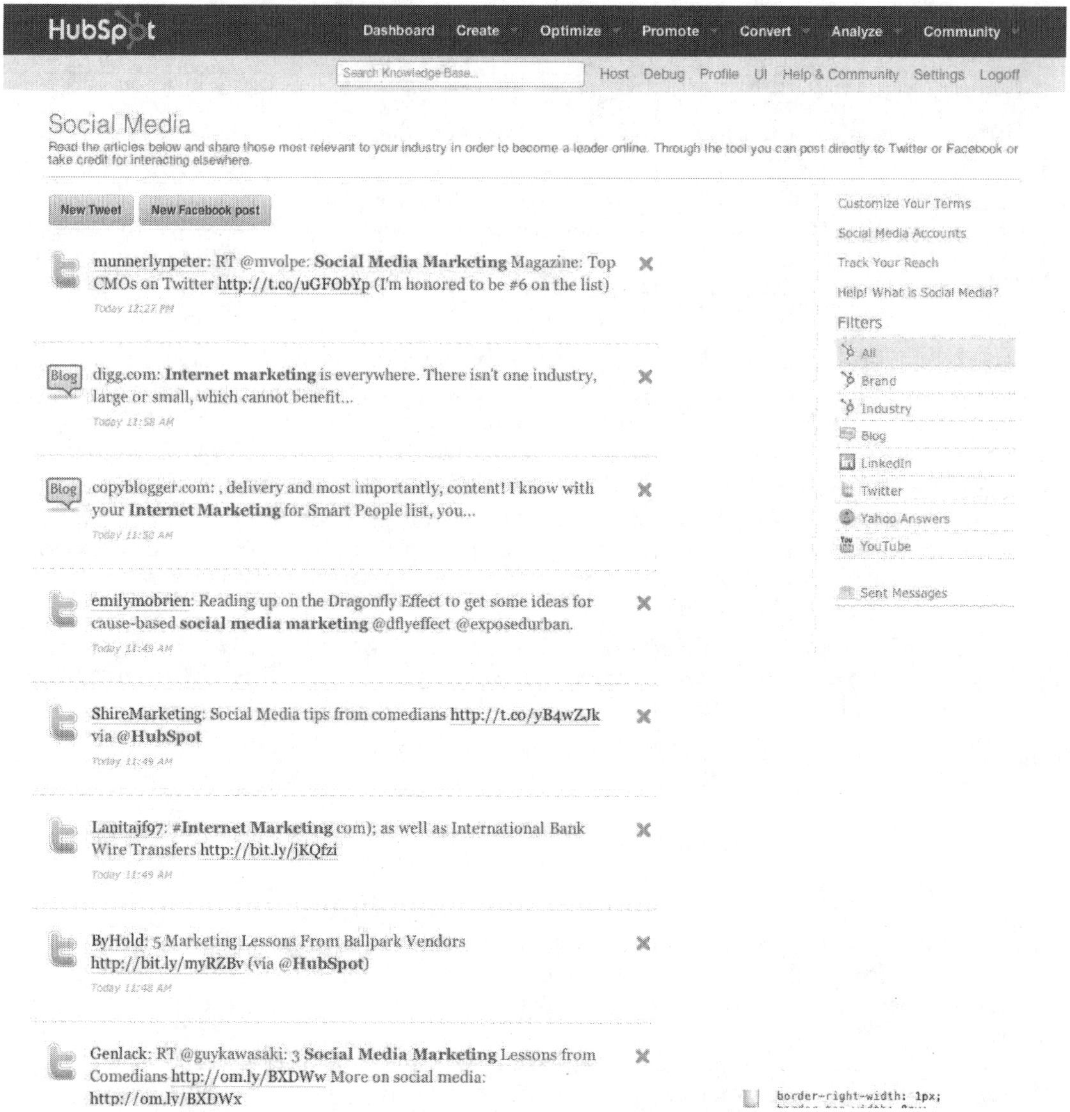

Facebook provides a summary of page activity to administrators (including stats on visits, new fans, wall posts, etc.), while Facebook's Insights tool measures user exposure, actions, and response behavior relating to a firm's Facebook pages and ads.

Bit.ly and many other URL-shortening services allow firms to track Twitter references to a particular page. Since bit.ly applies the same shortened URL to all tweets pointing to a page, it allows firms to follow not only if a campaign has been spread through "retweeting" but also if new tweets were generated outside of a campaign. Graphs plot click-throughs over time, and a list of original tweets can be pulled up to examine what commentary accompanied a particular link.

Location-based services like Foursquare have also rolled out robust tools for monitoring how customers engage with firms in the brick-and-mortar world. Foursquare's analytics and dashboard present firms with a variety of statistics, such as who has "checked in" and when, a venue's male-to-female ratio, and which times of day are more active for certain customers. "Business owners will also be able to offer instant promotions to try to engage new customers and keep current ones."[82] Managers can use the tools to notice if a once-loyal patron has dropped off the map, potentially creating a special promotion to lure her back.

Monitoring should also not be limited to customers and competitors. Firms are leveraging social media both inside their firms and via external services (e.g., corporate groups on Facebook and LinkedIn), and these spaces should also be on the SMART radar. This kind of monitoring can help firms keep pace with employee sentiment and insights, flag discussions that may involve proprietary information or other inappropriate topics, and provide guidance for those who want to leverage social media for the firm's staff—that is, anything from using online tools to help organize the firm's softball league to creating a wiki for a project group. Social media are end-user services that are particularly easy to deploy but that can also be used disastrously and inappropriately, so it's vital for IT experts and other staffers on the social media team to be visible and available, offering support and resources for those who want to take a dip into social media's waters.

9.4 Establishing a Presence

Firms hoping to get in on the online conversation should make it easy for their customers to find them. Many firms take an **embassy** approach to social media, establishing presence at various services with a consistent name. Think facebook.com/starbucks, twitter.com/starbucks, youtube.com/starbucks, flickr.com/starbucks, and so on. Corporate e-mail and Web sites can include icons linking to these services in a header or footer. The firm's social media embassies can also be highlighted in physical space such as in print, on bags and packaging, and on store signage. Firms should try to ensure that all embassies carry consistent design elements, so users see familiar visual cues that underscore they are now at a destination associated with the organization.

embassy

In the context of social media, an established online presence where customers can reach and interact with the firm. An effective embassy approach uses a consistent firm name in all its social media properties.

As mentioned earlier, some firms establish their own communities for customer engagement. Examples include Dell's IdeaStorm and MyStarbucksIdea. Not every firm has a customer base that is large and engaged enough to support hosting its own community. But for larger firms, these communities can create a nexus for feedback, customer-driven innovation, and engagement.

Customers expect an open dialogue, so firms engaging online should be prepared to deal with feedback that's not all positive. Firms are entirely within their right to screen out offensive and inappropriate comments. Noting this, firms might think twice before turning on YouTube comments (described as "the gutter of the Internet" by one leading social media manager).[83] Such comments could expose employees or customers profiled in clips to withering, snarky ridicule. However, firms engaged in curating their forums to present only positive messages should be prepared for the community to rebel and for embarrassing cries of censorship to be disclosed. Firms that believe in the integrity of their work and the substance of their message shouldn't be afraid. While a big brand like Starbucks is often a target of criticism, social media also provides organizations with an opportunity to respond fairly to that criticism and post video and photos of the firm's efforts. In Starbucks' case, the firm shares its work investing in poor coffee-growing communities as well as efforts to support AIDS relief. A social media presence allows a firm to share these works without waiting for conventional public relations (PR) to yield results or for journalists to pick up and interpret the firm's story. Starbucks executives have described the majority of comments the company receives through social media as "a love letter to the firm." By contrast, if your firm isn't prepared to be open or if your products and services are notoriously subpar and your firm is inattentive to customer feedback, then establishing a brand-tarring social media beachhead might not make sense. A word to the self-reflective: Customer conversations will happen online even if you don't have any social media embassies. Users can form their own groups, hash tags, and forums. A reluctance to participate may signal that the firm is facing deeper issues around its product and service.

While firms can learn a lot from social media consultants and tool providers, it's considered bad practice to outsource the management of a social media presence to a third-party agency. The voice of the firm should come *from* the firm. In fact, it should come from employees who can provide authentic expertise. Starbucks' primary Twitter feed is managed by Brad Nelson, a former barista, while the firm's director of environmental affairs, Jim Hanna, tweets and engages across social media channels on the firm's green efforts.

9.5 Engage and Respond

Having an effective social media presence offers "four Ms" of engagement: it's a *megaphone* allowing for outbound communication; it's a *magnet* drawing communities inward for conversation; and it allows for *monitoring* and *mediation* of existing conversations.[84] This dialogue can happen privately (private messaging is supported on most services) or can occur very publicly (with the intention to reach a wide audience). Understanding when, where, and how to engage and respond online requires a deft and experienced hand.

Many firms will selectively and occasionally retweet praise posts, underscoring the firm's commitment to customer service. Highlighting service heroes also reinforces exemplar behavior to employees who may be following the firm online, too. Users are often delighted when a major brand retweets their comments, posts a comment on their blog, or otherwise acknowledges them online—just be sure to do a quick public profile investigation to make sure your shout-outs are directed at customers you want associated with your firm. Escalation procedures should also include methods to flag noteworthy posts, good ideas, and opportunities that the social media team should be paying attention to. The customer base is often filled with heartwarming stories of positive customer experiences and rich with insight on making good things even better.

Many will also offer an unsolicited apology if the firm's name or products comes up in a disgruntled post. You may not be able to respond to all online complaints, but selective acknowledgement of the customer's voice (and attempts to address any emergent trends) is a sign of a firm that's focused on customer care. Getting the frequency, tone, and cadence for this kind of dialogue is more art than science, and managers are advised to regularly monitor other firms with similar characteristics for examples of what works and what doesn't.

Many incidents can be responded to immediately and with clear rules of engagement. For example, Starbuck issues corrective replies to the often-tweeted urban legend that the firm does not send coffee to the U.S. military because of a corporate position against the war. A typical response might read, "Not true, get the facts here" with a link to a Web page that sets the record straight.

Reaching out to key influencers can also be extremely valuable. Prominent bloggers and other respected social media participants can provide keen guidance and insight. The goal isn't to create a mouthpiece, but to solicit input, gain advice, gauge reaction, and be sure your message is properly interpreted. Influencers can also help spread accurate information and demonstrate a firm's commitment to listening and learning. In the wake of the Domino's gross-out, executives reached out to the prominent blog The Consumerist.[85] Facebook has solicited advice and feedback from MoveOn.org months before launching new features.[86] Meanwhile, Kaiser Permanente leveraged advice from well-known health care bloggers in crafting its approach to social media.[87]

However, it's also important to recognize that not every mention is worthy of a response. The Internet is filled with PR seekers, the unsatisfiably disgruntled, axe grinders seeking to trap firms, dishonest competitors, and inappropriate groups of mischief makers commonly referred to as *trolls*. One such group hijacked *Time* Magazine's user poll of the World's Most Influential People, voting their twenty-one-year-old leader to the top of the list ahead of Barack Obama, Vladimir Putin, and the pope. Prank voting was so finely calibrated among the group that the rankings list was engineered to spell out a vulgar term using the first letter of each nominee's name.[88]

To prepare, firms should "war game" possible crises, ensuring that everyone knows their role, and that experts are on call. A firm's social media policy should also make it clear how employees who spot a crisis might "pull the alarm" and mobilize the crisis response team. Having all employees aware of how to respond gives the firm an expanded institutional radar that can lower the chances of being blindsided. This can be especially important as many conversations take place in the so-called dark Web beyond the reach of conventional search engines and monitoring tools (e.g., within membership communities or sites, such as Facebook, where only "friends" have access).

In the event of an incident, silence can be deadly. Consumers expect a response to major events, even if it's just "we're listening, we're aware, and we intend to fix things." When director Kevin Smith was asked to leave a Southwest Airline flight because he was too large for a single seat, Smith went ballistic on Twitter, berating Southwest's service to his thousands of online followers. Southwest responded that same evening via Twitter, posting, "I've read the tweets all night from @ThatKevinSmith—He'll be getting a call at home from our Customer Relations VP tonight."

In the event of a major crisis, firms can leverage online media outside the social sphere. In the days following the Domino's incident, the gross-out video consistently appeared near the top of Google searches about the firm. When appropriate, companies can buy ads to run alongside keywords explaining their position and, if appropriate, offering an apology.[89] Homeopathic cold remedy Zicam countered blog posts citing inaccurate product information by running Google ads adjacent to these links, containing tag lines such as "Zicam: Get the Facts."[90]

Review sites such as Yelp and TripAdvisor also provide opportunities for firms to respond to negative reviews. This can send a message that a firm recognizes missteps and is making an attempt to address the issue (follow-through is critical, or expect an even harsher backlash). Sometimes a private response is most effective. When a customer of Farmstead Cheeses and Wines in the San Francisco Bay area posted a Yelp complaint that a cashier was rude, the firm's owner sent a private reply to the poster pointing out that the employee in question was actually hard of hearing. The complaint was subsequently withdrawn and the critic eventually joined the firm's Wine Club.[91] Private responses may be most appropriate if a firm is reimbursing clients or dealing with issues where public dialogue doesn't help the situation. One doesn't want to train members of the community that public griping gets reward. For similar reasons, in some cases store credit rather than reimbursement may be appropriate compensation.

Who Should Speak for Your Firm? The Case of the Cisco Fatty

Using the Twitter handle "TheConnor," a graduating college student recently offered full-time employment by the highly regarded networking giant Cisco posted this tweet: "Cisco just offered me a job! Now I have to weigh the utility of a fatty paycheck against the daily commute to San Jose and hating the work." Bad idea. Her tweet was public and a Cisco employee saw the post, responding, "Who is the hiring manager. I'm sure they would love to know that you will hate the work. We here at Cisco are versed in the web." Snap!

But this is also where the story underscores the subtleties of social media engagement. Cisco employees are right to be stung by this kind of criticism. The firm regularly ranks at the top of *Fortune*'s list of "Best Firms to Work for in America." Many Cisco employees take great pride in their work, and all have an interest in maintaining the firm's rep so that the company can hire the best and brightest and continue to compete at the top of its market. But when an employee went after a college student so publicly, the incident escalated. The media picked up on the post, and it began to look like an old guy picking on a clueless young woman who made a stupid mistake that should have been addressed in private. There was also an online pile-on attacking TheConnor. Someone uncovered the woman's true identity and posted hurtful and disparaging messages about her. Someone else set up a Web site at CiscoFatty.com. Even Oprah got involved, asking both parties to appear on her show (the offer was declined). A clearer social media policy highlighting the kinds of issues to respond to and offering a reporting hierarchy to catch and escalate such incidents might have headed off the embarrassment and helped both Cisco and TheConnor resolve the issue with a little less public attention.[92]

It's time to take social media seriously. We're now deep into a revolution that has rewritten the rules of customer-firm communication. There are emerging technologies and skills to acquire, a shifting landscape of laws and expectations, a minefield of dangers, and a wealth of unexploited opportunities. Organizations that professionalize their approach to social media and other Web 2.0 technologies are ready to exploit the upside—potentially stronger brands, increased sales, sharper customer service, improved innovation, and more. Those that ignore the new landscape risk catastrophe and perhaps even irrelevance.

KEY TAKEAWAYS

- Customer conversations are happening and employees are using social media. Even firms that aren't planning on creating a social media presence need to professionalize the social media function in their firm (consider this a social media awareness and response team, or SMART).
- Social media is an interdisciplinary practice, and the team should include professionals experienced in technology, marketing, PR, customer service, legal, and human resources.
- While the social media team provides guidance, training, and oversight, and structures crisis response, it's important to ensure that authentic experts engage on behalf of the firm. Social media is a conversation, and this isn't a job for the standard PR-style corporate spokesperson.
- Social media policies revolve around "three Rs": representation, responsibility, and respect. Many firms have posted their policies online so it can be easy for a firm to assemble examples of best practice.
- Firms must train employees and update their knowledge as technologies, effective use, and threats emerge. Security training is a vital component of establishing social media policy. Penalties for violation should be clear and backed by enforcement.
- While tempting, creating sock puppets to astroturf social media with praise posts violates FTC rules and can result in prosecution. Many users who thought their efforts were anonymous have been embarrassingly exposed and penalized. Customers are also using social media to expose firm dishonesty.
- Many tools exist for monitoring social media mentions of an organization, brands, competitors, and executives. Google Alerts, Twitter search, TweetDeck, Twitrratr, bit.ly, Facebook, and Foursquare all provide free tools that firms can leverage. For-fee tools and services are available as part of the online reputation management industry (and consultants in this space can also provide advice on improving a firm's online image and engagement).
- Social media are easy to adopt and potentially easy to abuse. The social media team can provide monitoring and support for firm-focused efforts inside the company and running on third-party networks, both to improve efforts and prevent unwanted disclosure, compliance, and privacy violations.
- The embassy approach to social media has firms establish their online presence through consistently named areas within popular services (e.g., facebook.com/starbucks, twitter.com/starbucks, youtube.com/starbucks). Firms can also create their own branded social media sites using tools such as Salesforce.com's "Ideas" platform.
- Social media provides "four Ms" of engagement: the megaphone to send out messages from the firm, the magnet to attract inbound communication, and monitoring and mediation—paying attention to what's happening online and selectively engage conversations when appropriate. Engagement can be public or private.
- Engagement is often more art than science, and managers can learn a lot by paying attention to the experiences of others. Firms should have clear rules for engagement and escalation when positive or negative issues are worthy of attention.

QUESTIONS AND EXERCISES

1. The "United Breaks Guitars" and "Domino's Gross Out" incidents are powerful reminders of how customers and employees can embarrass a firm. Find other examples of customer-and-employee social media incidents that reflected negatively on an organization. What happened? What was the result? How might these incidents have been prevented or better dealt with?
2. Hunt for examples of social media excellence. List an example of an organization that got it right. What happened, and what benefits were received?
3. Social media critics often lament a lack of ROI (return on investment) for these sorts of efforts. What kind of return should firms expect from social media? Does the return justify the investment? Why or why not?
4. What kinds of firms should aggressively pursue social media? Which ones might consider avoiding these practices? If a firm is concerned about online conversations, what might this also tell management?
5. List the skills that are needed by today's social media professionals. What topics should you study to prepare you for a career in this space?
6. Search online to find examples of corporate social media policies. Share your findings with your instructor. What points do these policies have in common? Are there aspects of any of these policies that you think are especially strong that other firms might adopt? Are there things in these policies that concern you?
7. Should firms monitor employee social media use? Should they block external social media sites at work? Why or why not? Why might the answer differ by industry?
8. Use the monitoring tools mentioned in the reading to search your own name. How would a prospective employer evaluate what they've found? How should you curate your online profiles and social media presence to be the most "corporate friendly"?
9. Investigate incidents where employees were fired for social media use. Prepare to discuss examples in class. Could the employer have avoided these incidents?
10. Use the monitoring tools mentioned in the reading to search for a favorite firm or brand. What trends do you discover? Is the online dialogue fair? How might the firm use these findings?
11. Consider the case of the Cisco Fatty. Who was wrong? Advise how a firm might best handle this kind of online commentary.

ENDNOTES

1. Via Alexa.com, June 1, 2011.
2. "What Americans Do Online: Social Media and Games Dominate Activity," *NielsenWire*, August 2, 2010.
3. Morgan Stanley, *Internet Trends Report*, March 2008.
4. G. Kane and R. Fichman, "The Shoemaker's Children: Using Wikis for Information Systems Teaching, Research, and Publication," *MIS Quarterly*, March 2009.
5. J. Roettgers, "YouTube Users Upload 48 Hours of Video Every Minute," *GigaOM*, May 25, 2011.
6. Morgan Stanley, *Internet Trends Report*, March 2008.
7. B. Erlich, "YouTube: Two Days' Worth of Video Uploaded Every Minute," *Mashable*, May 25, 2011.
8. "Facebook Facts and Figures (History and Statistics)," *Website Monitoring Blog*, March 17, 2010.
9. P. Kafka, "Facebook Isn't Eating Google's Lunch Yet, but It's Getting Hungry…," *AllThingsD*, March 13, 2011.
10. G. Fowler and A. Das, "Facebook Numbers Feed IPO Outlook," *Wall Street Journal*, May 1, 2011.
11. P. Kafka, "Twitter CEO Dick Costolo Talks about His New Photo Service, but Not about Profits," *AllThingsD*, June 1, 2011.
12. N. Bolton, "Chirp, Twitter's First Developer Conference, Opens Its Doors," *New York Times*, April 14, 2010; M. Shaer, "Google Launches Archive Search for Twitter," *Christian Science Monitor*, April 15, 2010.
13. B. Wash, "Double Duty," *Colby Magazine*, Winter 2009; S. Morrison, "Expedia to Spin Off TripAdvisor," *Wall Street Journal*, April 8, 2011.
14. P. Burrows, "Hot Tech Companies Like Yelp Are Bypassing IPOs," *BusinessWeek*, February 4, 2010.
15. Adapted and modified from the original list presented in T. O'Reilly, "What Is Web 2.0?" *O'Reilly*, September 30, 2005.
16. BlogPulse.com stats, June 1, 2011.
17. E. Alterman, "Out of Print, the Death and Life of the American Newspaper," *New Yorker*, March 31, 2008; and M. Learmonth, "Huffington Post More Valuable Than Some Newspaper Cos.," *DigitalNext*, December 1, 2008; V. Kopytoff, "AOL's Bet on Another Makeover," *New York Times*, February 7, 2011.
18. S. Zuckerman, "Yes, Some Blogs Are Profitable—Very Profitable," *San Francisco Chronicle*, October 21, 2007.
19. D. Pink, "The Book Stops Here," *Wired*, March 2005.
20. S. Robert Lichter, *Are Chemicals Killing Us?* Statistical Assessment Service, May 21, 2009; J. Kane, R. Fichman, J. Gallaugher, and J. Glaser, "Community Relations 2.0," *Harvard Business Review*, November 2009.
21. D. Carlin, "Corporate Wikis Go Viral," *BusinessWeek*, March 12, 2007.
22. M. Calabrese, "Wikipedia for Spies: The CIA Discovers Web 2.0," *Time*, April 8, 2009.
23. R. King, "No Rest for the Wiki," *BusinessWeek*, March 12, 2007.
24. A. Bergman, "Wikipedia Is Only as Anonymous as your I.P.," *O'Reilly Radar*, August 14, 2007.
25. I. Williams, "Sony Caught Editing Halo 3 Wikipedia Entry," *Vnunet.com*, September 5, 2007.
26. E. Hansen, "Wikipedia Founder Edits Own Bio," *Wired*, December 19, 2005.
27. S. Woo, L. Cowan, and P. Tam, "LinkedIn IPO Soars, Feeding Web Boom," *Wall Street Journal*, May 20, 2011.
28. M. Boyle, "Recruiting: Enough to Make a Monster Tremble," *BusinessWeek*, June 25, 2009.
29. R. King, "No Rest for the Wiki," *BusinessWeek*, March 12, 2007.
30. E. Frauenheim, "Social Revolution," *Workforce Management*, October 2007.
31. R. King, "Social Networks: Execs Use Them Too," *BusinessWeek*, November 11, 2006.
32. W. Bulkley, "Playing Well with Others," *Wall Street Journal*, June 18, 2007.
33. K. Swisher, "Ning CEO Gina Bianchini to Step Down—Becomes an EIR at Andreessen Horowitz," *AllThingsD*, March 15, 2010.
34. D. Greenfield, "How Companies Are Using I.T. to Spot Innovative Ideas," *InformationWeek*, November 8, 2008.
35. J. Gallaugher and S. Ransbotham, "Social Media and Customer Dialog Management at Starbucks," *MIS Quarterly Executive* 9, no. 4 (December 2010): 197—212.
36. M. Schulder, "50on50: Saw Blade through Thumb. What Would You Do?" *CNN*, November 4, 2009.
37. The AMA and Sermo have since broken ties; see B. Comer, "Sermo and AMA Break Ties," *Medical Marketing and Media*, July 9, 2009.
38. T. Goetz, "Practicing Patients," *New York Times Magazine*, March 23, 2008.
39. J. Kane, R. Fichman, J. Gallaugher, and J. Glaser, "Community Relations 2.0," *Harvard Business Review*, November 2009.
40. S. Ante, "Facebook's Thiel Explains Failed Twitter Takeover," *BusinessWeek*, March 1, 2009.
41. P. Kafka, "Twitter CEO Dick Costolo Talks about His New Photo Service, but Not about Profits," *AllThingsD*, June 1, 2011.
42. B. Womack and B. Pulley, "Twitter Use Climbs to 13% of U.S. Adults Online Boosted by Older Americans," *Bloomberg*, June 1, 2011.
43. J. O'Dell, "One Twitter User Reports Live from Osama Bin Laden Raid," *Mashable*, May 2, 2011.
44. E. Schonfeld, "Twitter's Internal Strategy Laid Bare: To Be 'The Pulse of The Planet,'" *TechCrunch*, July 19, 2009.
45. C. Miller, "Putting Twitter's World to Use," *New York Times*, April 13, 2009.
46. C. Ruffini, "State Dept. Asked Twitter to Delay Maintenance," *CBS News*, June 16, 2009.
47. K. Eaton, "Twitter Really Works: Makes $6.5 Million in Sales for Dell," *Fast Company*, December 8, 2009; J. Abel, "Dude—Dell's Making Money off Twitter!" *Wired News*, June 12, 2009.
48. A. Romano, "Now 4 Restaurant 2.0," *Newsweek*, February 28, 2009.
49. Twitter.com, "Case Study: Best Buy Twelpforce," Twitter 101, https://twitter.com/#!/BESTBUY.
50. D. Martin, "Update: Return of the Twitter Quitters," *Nielsen Wire*, April 30, 2009.
51. D. Rushe, "Twitter Valued at $10bn as Google and Facebook Reportedly Vie to Buy It," *Guardian*, February 10, 2011.
52. J. Murrell, "Twitter Treads Gently into Advertising Minefield," *San Jose Mercury News*, April 13, 2010.
53. D. Talbot, "Can Twitter Make Money?" *Technology Review*, March/April 2010.
54. P. Kafka, "Twitter's Ad Plan: Copy Google," *AllThingsD*, February 25, 2010.
55. D. Goldman, "Twitter Grows Up: Take a Peek Inside," *CNN*, April 16, 2010.
56. D. Terdiman, "Folksonomies Tap People Power," *Wired*, February 1, 2005.
57. J. Kincaid, "SCVNGR Raises $4 Million from Google Ventures," *TechCrunch*, December 24, 2009; R. Kim, "What Makes SCVNGR So Sticky (Hot Sauce Not Included), *GigaOM*, February 17, 2011.
58. R. Kim, "Foursquare Found as Featured Location Service for INQ Facebook Phone," *GigaOM*, May 23, 2011.
59. B. Barnes, "Disney Acquires Web Site for Children," *New York Times*, August 2, 2007.
60. J. Giles, "Special Report: Internet Encyclopedias Go Head to Head," *Nature* 438, no. 15 (December 14, 2005): 900–901.
61. P. Dvorak, "Best Buy Taps 'Prediction Market,'" *Wall Street Journal*, September 16, 2008; and Renée Dye, "The Promise of Prediction Markets: A Roundtable," *McKinsey Quarterly* (2008): 83–93.
62. R. Dye, "The Promise of Prediction Markets: A Roundtable," *McKinsey Quarterly* (2008): 83–93.
63. B. Cowgill, J. Wolfers, and E. Zitzewitz, "Using Prediction Markets to Track Information Flows: Evidence from Google," working paper accessed November 30, 2009, via http://bocowgill.com/GooglePredictionMarketPaper.pdf.
64. R. Dye, "The Promise of Prediction Markets: A Roundtable," *McKinsey Quarterly* 2 (2008): 83–93.
65. "Audit Reveals Farecast Predictive Accuracy at 74.5 percent," *farecast.live.com*, May 18, 2007, http://www.prnewswire.com/news-releases/farecast-launches-new-tools-to-help-savvy-travelers-catch-elusive-airfare-price-drops-this-summer-58165652.html.
66. J. Surowiecki, "Crowdsourcing the Crystal Ball," *Forbes*, October 15, 2007.
67. E. Lambert, "Hedging for Dummies," *Forbes*, March 13, 2006, 70–72.
68. J. Howe, "The Rise of Crowdsourcing," *Wired*, June 2006.
69. S. Lohr, "And the Winner of the $1 Million Netflix Prize (Probably) Is…" *New York Times*, June 26, 2009.
70. M. Brandel, "Should Your Company 'Crowdsource' Its Next Project?" *Computerworld*, December 6, 2007; M. Brandel, "Crowdsourcing: Are You Ready to Ask the World for Answers?" *Computerworld*, March 3, 2008; and TopCoder, 2011, http://topcoder.com/home.
71. D. Kirkpatrick, "Help Wanted: Adults on Facebook," *Fortune*, March 21, 2008.
72. The concepts in this section are based on work by J. Kane, R. Fichman, J. Gallaugher, and J. Glasser, many of which are covered in the article "Community Relations 2.0," *Harvard Business Review*, November 2009.
73. E. York, "McDonald's Names First Social-Media Chief," *Chicago Business*, April 13, 2010.
74. Starbucks was named the best firm for social media engagement in a study by Altimeter Group and WetPaint. See the 2009 ENGAGEMENTdb report at http://engagementdb.com.
75. C. Barger, talk at the Social Media Club of Detroit, November 18, 2009. Also available via UStream and DigitalMarketingZen.com.
76. J. Soat, "7 Questions Key to Social Networking Success," *InformationWeek*, January 16, 2010.
77. L. Conway, "Virgin Atlantic Sacks 13 Staff for Calling Its Flyers 'Chavs,'" *The Independent*, November 1, 2008.
78. E. York, "McDonald's Names First Social-Media Chief," *Chicago Business*, April 13, 2010.
79. A. Martin, "Whole Foods Executive Used Alias," *New York Times*, July 12, 2007.

80. C. Cain Miller, "Company Settles Case of Reviews It Faked," July 14, 2009.

81. L. Rathke, "Report: Ski Resorts Exaggerate Snowfall Totals," *USA Today*, January 29, 2010.

82. N. Bolton, "Foursquare Introduces New Tools for Businesses," March 9, 2010.

83. Brad Nelson, presentation at the Social Media Conference NW, Mount Vernon, WA, March 25, 2010.

84. J. Gallaugher and S. Ransbotham, "Social Media and Dialog Management at Starbucks" (presented at the MISQE Social Media Workshop, Phoenix, AZ, December 2009).

85. A. Jacques, "Domino's Delivers during Crisis: The Company's Step-by-Step Response after a Vulgar Video Goes Viral," *The Public Relations Strategist*, October 24, 2009.

86. B. Stone, "Facebook Aims to Extend Its Reach across the Web," *New York Times*, December 2, 2008.

87. J. Kane, R. Fichman, J. Gallaugher, and J. Glaser, "Community Relations 2.0," *Harvard Business Review*, November 2009.

88. E. Schonfeld, "Time Magazine Throws Up Its Hands As It Gets Pawned by 4Chan," *TechCrunch*, April 27, 2009.

89. S. Gregory, "Domino's YouTube Crisis: 5 Ways to Fight Back," *Time*, April 18, 2009.

90. Zicam had regularly been the victim of urban legends claiming negative side effects from use; see Snopes.com, "Zicam Warning," http://www.snopes.com/medical/drugs/zicam.asp. However, the firm subsequently was cited in an unrelated FDA warning on the usage of its product; see S. Young, "FDA Warns against Using 3 Popular Zicam Cold Meds," *CNN.com*, June 16, 2009.

91. K. Paterson, "Managing an Online Reputation," *New York Times*, July 29, 2009.

92. H. Popkin, "Twitter Gets You Fired in 140 Characters or Less," *MSNBC*, March 23, 2009.

CHAPTER 8

Facebook: Building a Business from the Social Graph

1. INTRODUCTION

LEARNING OBJECTIVES

1. **Be familiar with Facebook's origins and rapid rise.**
2. **Understand how Facebook's rapid rise has impacted the firm's ability to raise venture funding and its founder's ability to maintain a controlling interest in the firm.**

It's hard not to be awed by what Mark Zuckerberg has created. An effort launched from his college dorm is now a species-level phenomenon.[1] Roughly one in every eight people on the planet has a Facebook account—an amazing track record given that Facebook is technically banned in China (taking about 20 percent of the world population off the table).[2] Want to connect to customers? Facebook is increasingly the place to be. The firm has ranked as the most visited site in the United States[3] and is tops in display advertising.[4] Global growth is on a tear, with an excess of 80 percent of Facebook users outside the United States.[5] Facebook is solidly profitable; in 2011 the firm earned about $1 billion on some $3.7 billion in revenues. And Facebook has accomplished all that with fewer employees than Google has job openings.[6]

1.1 The Rise of Facebook

Facebook founder Mark Zuckerberg looked like a social media pioneer from the start. Consider this: During the weeks he spent working on Facebook as a Harvard sophomore, he didn't have time to study for a course he was taking, "Art in the Time of Augustus," so he built a Web site containing all of the artwork in class and pinged his classmates to contribute to a communal study guide. Within hours, the wisdom of crowds produced a sort of custom CliffsNotes for the course, and after reviewing the Web-based crib sheet, he aced the test. Turns out he didn't need to take that exam, anyway. Zuck (that's what the cool kids call him)[7] dropped out of Harvard later that year.

Zuckerberg is known as both a shy, geeky, introvert who eschews parties, and as a brash Silicon Valley bad boy. After Facebook's incorporation, Zuckerberg's job description was listed as "Founder, Master and Commander [and] Enemy of the State."[8] An early business card read "I'm CEO…Bitch."[9] And let's not forget that Facebook came out of drunken experiments in his dorm room, one of which was a system for comparing classmates to farm animals (Zuckerberg, threatened with expulsion, later apologized). For one meeting with Sequoia Capital, the venerable Menlo Park venture capital firm that backed Google and YouTube, Zuckerberg showed up in his pajamas.[10]

By the age of twenty-three, Mark Zuckerberg had graced the cover of *Newsweek*, been profiled on *60 Minutes*, and was discussed in the tech world with a reverence previously reserved only for Steve Jobs and the Google guys, Sergey Brin and Larry Page. But Mark Zuckerberg's star rose much faster than any of his predecessors. Just two weeks after Facebook launched, the firm had four thousand users. Ten months later it was up to one million. The growth continued, and the business world took notice. In 2006, Viacom (parent of MTV) saw that its core demographic was spending a ton of time on

Facebook and offered to buy the firm for three quarters of a billion dollars. Zuckerberg passed.[11] Yahoo! offered up a cool billion (twice). Zuck passed again, both times.

As growth skyrocketed, Facebook built on its stranglehold of the college market, opening up first to high schoolers, then to everyone. Web hipsters started selling shirts emblazoned with "I Facebooked your Mom!" Even Microsoft wanted some of Facebook's magic. In 2006, the firm temporarily locked up the right to broker all banner ad sales that run on the U.S. version of Facebook, guaranteeing Zuckerberg's firm $100 million a year through 2011. In 2007, Microsoft came back, buying 1.6 percent of the firm for $240 million.[12] The investment was a shocker. A firm that at the time had only five hundred employees, $150 million in revenues, and was helmed by a twenty-three-year-old college dropout in his first "real job" was valued at $15 billion—making it more valuable than General Motors. It wasn't a bad bet on Microsoft's part—the investment increased in value nearly sevenfold in five years.

Rupert Murdoch, whose News Corporation owned rival MySpace, once referred to Facebook as "the flavor of the month."[13] But Murdoch, the media titan who stood atop an empire that includes the *Wall Street Journal* and Fox, was utterly schooled by "the kid." Six years after acquiring MySpace for $580 million, Newscorp sold the firm for $35 million, less than one sixteenth of the purchase price.[14] Zuckerberg went on to be named *Time*'s "Person of the Year," while a (mostly fictionalized) account of Facebook's founding[15] was a box-office smash, nominated for a Best Picture Academy Award. The firm's controversial 2012 public offering valued the firm at over $100 billion, and the $16 billion raised in the offering made it the biggest tech IPO in history and the third biggest IPO ever.[16]

Zuckerberg Rules!

Many entrepreneurs accept start-up capital from venture capitalists (VCs), investor groups that provide funding in exchange for a stake in the firm and often (especially in early-stage investments), a degree of managerial control (this may be in the form of a voting seat or seats on the firm's board of directors). Typically, the earlier a firm accepts VC money, the more control these investors can exert (earlier investments are riskier, so VCs can demand more favorable terms). VCs usually have deep entrepreneurial experience and a wealth of contacts, and can often offer important guidance and advice, but strong investor groups can oust a firm's founder and other executives if they're dissatisfied with the firm's performance.

At Facebook, however, the firm's extraordinary growth left potential investors salivating to back a firm perceived as being less risky but carrying the potential of a huge upside. Early backers ceded control—at a time when Facebook's board had only five directors, Zuckerberg appointed three of them. When Facebook filed to go public, Zuckerberg's ownership stake stood at twenty-eight percent, but Facebook created two classes of shares, ensuring that Zuckerberg maintains a majority of voting rights in the public company and virtually guaranteeing that his control of the firm continues, regardless of what investors say. Maintaining this kind of control is unusual (although not unprecedented—Google's founders have a similar ownership and voting structure).[17] Zuckerberg's influence is a testament to the speed with which Facebook expanded. When investors' demand to get in on 'the next big thing' remains high, a firm's owner can extract extraordinary terms for the privilege of coming along for the ride. As *Slate* puts it, Facebook is "conducting an experiment in corporate dictatorship nearly without precedent for such a large and high-profile company." All hail Emperor Zuckerberg![18]

1.2 Why Study Facebook?

Looking at the "flavor of the month" and trying to distinguish the reality from the hype is a critical managerial skill. In Facebook's case, there are a lot of folks with a vested interest in figuring out where the firm is headed. If you want to work there, are you signing on to a firm where your *stock options* and *401k* contributions are going to be worth something or worthless? If you're an investor, should you **short** the firm or increase your holdings? Would you invest in or avoid firms that rely on Facebook's business? Should your firm rush to partner with the firm? Would you extend the firm credit? Offer it better terms to secure its growing business, or worse terms because you think it's a risky bet? Is this firm the next Google (underestimated at first, and now wildly profitable and influential), the next GeoCities (Yahoo! paid $3 billion for it—no one goes to the site today), or the next Skype (deeply impactful with over half a billion accounts worldwide, but so far, not much of a profit generator)? The jury is still out on all this, but let's look at the fundamentals with an eye to applying what we've learned. No one has a crystal ball, but we do have some key concepts that can guide our analysis. There are a lot of broadly applicable managerial lessons that can be gleaned by examining Facebook's successes and missteps. Studying the firm provides a context for examining nework effects, platforms, partnerships, issues in the rollout of new technologies, privacy, ad models, the business value of social media, and more.

short

Short selling is an attempt to profit from a falling stock price. Short sellers sell shares they don't own with an obligation of later repayment. They do so in the hope that the price of sold shares will fall. They then repay share debt with shares purchased at a lower price and pocket the difference (spread) between initial share price and repayment price.

Facebook's Copilot

Don't let Zuck get all the credit. While Facebook's founder is considered the firm's visionary, chief operating officer Sheryl Sandberg is often depicted as the person who runs the place: the coach, the seasoned mentor, the drill sergeant, and the lead "adult" in a workforce that skews remarkably young despite its vast, global influence.

Regularly named to *Fortune* magazine's "Most Powerful Women in Business" list, Sandberg came to Facebook from Google (before that she was chief of staff to U.S. Treasury secretary Larry Summers). In just three years, she's helped steer Facebook to almost unimaginable heights. Users increased tenfold, she's helped devise an advertising platform that has attracted the world's largest brands, she's developed a sales organization that can serve a customer base ranging from the *Fortune* 100 to mom-and-pop stores, and she's helped the firm through several crises, all while turning a profit and pushing revenue higher.

Sandberg, a Harvard grad, left the school with a geeky legacy akin to Zuckerberg's. When she was a student conducting economics research she ran so much data on Harvard's network that she choked the system. Zuckerberg would have much the same impact more than a decade later.[19]

Sheryl Sandberg is a powerful speaker and a leading advocate for increasing the ranks of women in senior management.

View the video online at: http://www.youtube.com/v/18uDutylDa4

KEY TAKEAWAYS

- Facebook was founded by a nineteen-year-old college sophomore and eventual dropout.
- It is currently the largest social network in the world, boasting more than nine hundred million members and usage rates that would be the envy of most media companies.
- The firm's rapid growth and high user engagement allowed Facebook's founder to demand and receive an exceptionally high degree of control over the firm—even as the firm went public.

QUESTIONS AND EXERCISES

1. Who started Facebook? How old was he then? Now? How much control does the founding CEO have over his firm? Why?
2. Which firms have tried to acquire Facebook? Why? What were their motivations and why did Facebook seem attractive? Do you think these bids are justified? Do you think the firm should have accepted any of the buyout offers? Why or why not?
3. Firms' values fluctuate over time. How much is Facebook "worth" today? Has the firm's value gone up or down since its IPO? Why? Was investing in Facebook at IPO a move that paid off or that has resulted in losses?
4. Why was Zuckerberg able to demand and receive control of Facebook, even as the firm went public? What strategic factors were at work in Facebook's rise that gave the founder such leverage?
5. Why study Facebook? Who cares if it succeeds?

2. DOES FACEBOOK WANT TO EAT YOUR FIRM'S LUNCH? ENVELOPING MARKETS ACROSS THE INTERNET

LEARNING OBJECTIVES

1. **Recognize that Facebook's power is allowing it to encroach on and envelop other Internet businesses.**
2. **Understand the concept of the "dark Web" and why some feel this may one day give Facebook a source of advantage vis-à-vis Google.**
3. **Describe why a "walled garden" may be threatening to other firms and the public good.**
4. **Understand the basics of Facebook's infrastructure, and the costs required to power the effort.**

Facebook isn't just a collection of personal home pages and a place to declare your allegiance to your friends. Facebook is gradually turning on features that allow it to leverage its massive user base to encroach on a wide swath of Internet businesses. Consider photos. Google, Yahoo!, and MySpace all spent millions to acquire photo sharing sites (Picasa, Flickr, and Photobucket, respectively). But to become the web's leading photo sharing service, Facebook didn't acquire anyone. The site simply turned on a substandard photo-sharing feature and quickly became the biggest photo-sharing site on the Web. Facebook users now post over three billion photos each month.[20]

Video is also on the rise. YouTube will get you famous, but Facebook is the place most go to share clips they only want friends to see.[21] Facebook users share video at a rate ten times greater than those on Twitter,[22] and services like Viddy are bringing in tens of millions of new users who capture and share video via their mobile devices.[23] And with all those eyeballs turning to Facebook for video, why not become a destination to watch movies and TV shows, too? Facebook has worked with major studios to stream "rentals" of blockbusters that include *The Dark Knight*, the *Harry Potter* films, and *Inception*. Netflix integrates so tightly with Facebook that the firm's CEO sits on Facebook's board.

Facebook has become the *first-choice* communication service for this generation, and with Facebook's unified messaging feature, the site will prioritize e-mail, text messages, and chat in a single inbox, bubbling your friends ahead of the spam. It'll even give you a facebook.com e-mail address.[24] Look out Gmail, Hotmail, and Yahoo!—if users check mail within Facebook, they may visit the big e-mail players less often (meaning less ad revenue for the e-mail firms).

Facebook is a kingmaker, opinion catalyst, and traffic driver, so media outlets want to be friends. Games firms, music services, video sites, daily deal services, media outlets, and more, all integrate into Facebook's Ticker, each hoping that a quick post of activity to Facebook will help spread their services virally. While in the prior decade news stories would carry a notice saying, "Copyright, do not distribute without permission," major news outlets today display Facebook icons alongside every copyrighted story, encouraging users to "share" the content on their profile pages. Great for Facebook, but a sharp elbow to Digg.com and Del.icio.us, which have both seen their link sharing appeal free-fall, even though they showed up first.[25] And despite all the buzz about Twitter, Facebook drives far more traffic to newspaper sites.[26]

Facebook Office? Facebook rolled out the document collaboration and sharing service Docs.com in partnership with Microsoft. Music? Payments? Facebook is hard at work on that, too.[27]

FIGURE 8.1 Is Facebook Coming after Your Business?

Facebook has turned on features and engaged in partnerships that compete with offerings from a wide variety of firms. In this example, Warner Bros. has partnered with Facebook to offer streaming video rental.

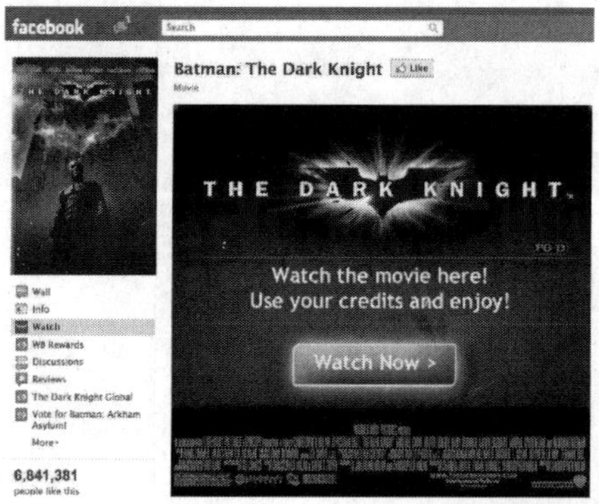

Source: Used by permission of Facebook.

Instagram: Did Zuckerberg Blink?

Facebook's dominance in photo sharing came largely from success over the web, but photo sharing and many other activities are going mobile. By Spring 2012, Instagram, an eighteen-month-old firm with thirteen employees, had fifty million users and was adding new ones at a rate of roughly five million a week.[28] Users loved the beautiful, artistic images Instagram's filters created, and photos were being shared not only on Instagram but also on Facebook's rival Twitter and other services. Analysts suggest mobile could have been Facebook's Achilles heel—allowing a mobile-only photo network to open up and become a platform (Insta-music? Insta-links? Insta-status updates?). Facebook's own IPO filings acknowledged mobile as a potential risk area. Figures showed that Instagram was winning over millions of Facebook users, and Instagram the potential rival had just accepted a new $50 million round of venture funding, valuing the firm at $500 million. Within two days of that deal, Zuckerberg called the firm with an offer it couldn't refuse. Facebook bought Instagram for a cool $1 billion.[29]

As for search, Facebook's tinkering there, as well. Google indexes some Facebook content, but since much of Facebook is private, accessible only among friends, this represents a massive blind spot for Google search. Sites that can't be indexed by Google and other search engines are referred to as the **dark Web**. But while Google lacks access to Facebook's portion of the dark Web, Facebook has repeatedly expanded its partnership with Microsoft's Bing, linking private Facebook content with search. Content that Facebook users have "liked" can influence the ranking of Bing search results. A new social sidebar in Bing that lets you see and respond to Facebook friend updates allows users to ask friends questions and even surfaces friends who may be knowledgeable on a topic.[30] If Facebook can tie together standard Internet search with its dark Web content, this just might be enough for some to break the Google habit.

Facebook's increasing dominance, long reach, and widening ambition have a lot of people worried, including the creator of the World Wide Web. Sir Tim Berners-Lee recently warned that the Web may be endangered by Facebook's colossal **walled garden**.[31] The fear is that if increasingly large parts of the Web reside inside a single (and for the most part closed) service, innovation, competition, and exchange may suffer.

dark Web

Internet content that can't be indexed by Google and other search engines.

walled garden

A closed network or single set of services controlled by one dominant firm.

So What's It Take to Run This Thing?

The Facebook **cloud** (the big group of connected servers that power the site) is scattered across multiple facilities, including server farms in San Francisco, Santa Clara, northern Virginia, Oregon, and North Carolina.[32] The innards that make up the bulk of the system aren't that different from what you'd find on a high-end commodity workstation. Standard hard drives and multicore Intel or AMD processors—just a whole lot of them lashed together through networking and software.

Much of what powers the site is **open source software (OSS)**. The service runs on the Linux operating system and Apache web server software. A good portion of Facebook is written in PHP (a scripting language particularly well-suited for Web site development), while the databases are in MySQL (a popular open source database). Facebook also developed Cassandra, a non-SQL database project for large-scale systems that the firm has since turned over to the open source Apache Software Foundation. The object cache that holds Facebook's frequently accessed objects is in chip-based RAM instead of on slower hard drives and is managed via an open source product called Memcache.

Other code components are written in a variety of languages, including C++, Java, Python, and Ruby, with access between these components managed by a code layer the firm calls Thrift (developed at Facebook, which was also turned over to the Apache Software Foundation). Facebook also developed its own media serving solution, called Haystack. Haystack coughs up photos 50 percent faster than more expensive, proprietary solutions, and since it's done in-house, it saves Facebook costs that other online outlets spend on third-party **content delivery networks (CDN)** like Akamai. Facebook receives some fifty million requests per second,[33] yet 95 percent of data queries can be served from a huge, distributed server cache that lives in over fifteen terabytes of RAM (objects like video and photos are stored on hard drives).[34]

All this technology is expensive, and a big chunk of the capital that Facebook has raised from investors has been targeted at expanding the firm's server network to keep up with the crush of growth. This includes one $100 million investment round "used entirely for servers."[35] Facebook will be buying servers by the thousands for years to come. And it'll pay a pretty penny just to keep things humming. Estimates suggest the firm spends one million dollars a month on electricity, another half million a month on telecommunications bandwidth, and at least fifteen million dollars a year in office and data center rental payments.[36]

Want to build your own server farm like Facebook? The firm will tell you how to do it. In an unprecedented move that coincided with the opening of its Prineville, Oregon, facility, Facebook made public the detailed specifications of its homegrown servers (including custom power supplies, chassis, and battery backup), plus plans used in the Prineville site's building design and electrical and cooling systems. You can find details, photos, and video at opencompute.org. Facebook claims its redesigned servers are 38 percent more efficient and 24 percent cheaper than those sold by major manufacturers. Why give away the low-cost secrets? Says the firm's director of hardware, "Facebook is successful because of the great social product, not [because] we can

cloud

A collection of resources available for access over the Internet.

open source software (OSS)

Software that is free and whose code can be accessed and potentially modified by anyone.

content delivery networks (CDN)

Systems distributed throughout the Internet (or other network) that help to improve the delivery (and hence loading) speeds of Web pages and other media, typically by spreading access across multiple sites located closer to users. Akamai is the largest CDN, helping firms like CNN and MTV quickly deliver photos, video, and other media worldwide.

build low-cost infrastructure. There's no reason we shouldn't help others out with this."[37] One of the firms considering using Facebook designs is Zynga, a firm that itself pays Facebook millions a month in advertising and for using the Facebook Credits payments system. Sharing will be good for Facebook if a more efficient Zynga grows faster and returns more money back to its partner along the way.

KEY TAKEAWAYS

- Facebook's position as the digital center of its members' online social lives has allowed the firm to envelop related businesses such as photo and video sharing, messaging, bookmarking, and link sharing. Facebook has opportunities to expand into other areas as well.
- Much of the site's content is in the dark Web, unable to be indexed by Google or other search engines. Some suggest this may create an opportunity for Facebook to challenge Google in search.
- Some fear that Facebook may be an all-too-powerful walled garden that may stifle innovation, limit competition, and restrict the free flow of information.
- Facebook's growth requires a continued and massive infrastructure investment. The site is powered largely on commodity hardware, open source software, and proprietary code tailored to the specific needs of the service.

QUESTIONS AND EXERCISES

1. What is Facebook? How do people use the site? What do they "do" on Facebook?
2. What markets has Facebook entered? What factors have allowed the firm to gain share in these markets at the expense of established firms? In what ways does it enjoy advantages that a traditional new entrant in such markets would not?
3. What is the "dark Web" and why is it potentially an asset to Facebook? Why is Google threatened by Facebook's dark Web? What firms might consider an investment in the firm, if it provided access to this asset? Do you think the dark Web is enough to draw users to a Facebook search product over Google? Why or why not?
4. As Facebook grows, what kinds of investments continue to be necessary? What are the trends in these costs over time? Do you think Facebook should wait in making these investments? Why or why not?
5. Investments in servers and other capital expenses typically must be depreciated over time. What does this imply about how the firm's profitability is calculated?
6. How have media attitudes toward their copyrighted content changed over the past decade? Why is Facebook a potentially significant partner for firms like the *New York Times*? What does the *Times* stand to gain by encouraging "sharing" its content? What do newspapers and others sites really mean when they encourage sites to "share?" What actually is being passed back and forth? Do you think this ultimately helps or undermines the *Times* and other newspaper and magazine sites? Why?
7. What is a walled garden? Facebook has been called a walled garden—name other firms that might also be described using this term. In your opinion is Facebook a walled garden? Why or why not? What might be the consequences if the firm is widely viewed as being more powerful and less open?

3. THE SOCIAL GRAPH

LEARNING OBJECTIVES

1. **Explain the concept of the "social graph," and explain how Facebook created a social graph stronger than its rivals'.**
2. **Recognize the two strategic resources that are most critical to Facebook's competitive advantage and why Facebook was able to create these resources while MySpace has fallen short.**
3. **Appreciate that while Facebook's technology can be easily copied, barriers to sustain any new entrant are extraordinarily high, and the likelihood that a firm will win significant share from Facebook by doing the same thing is considerably remote.**

At the heart of Facebook's appeal is a concept Zuckerberg calls the **social graph**, which refers to Facebook's ability to collect, express, and leverage the connections between the site's users, or as some describe it, "the global mapping of everyone and how they're related."[38] Think of all the stuff that's on Facebook as a node or endpoint that's connected to other stuff. You're connected to other users (your friends), photos about you are tagged, comments you've posted carry your name, you're a member of groups, you're connected to applications you've installed—Facebook links them all.[39]

social graph

The global mapping of users and organizations, and how they are connected.

Facebook was established in the relatively safe cocoon of American undergraduate life and was conceived as a place where you could *reinforce* contacts among those who, for the most part, you already knew. The site was one of the first social networks where users actually identified themselves using their real names. If you wanted to establish that you worked for a certain firm or were a student of a particular university, you had to verify that you were legitimate via an e-mail address issued by that organization. It was this "realness" that became Facebook's distinguishing feature—bringing along with it a degree of safety and comfort that enabled Facebook to become a true social utility and build out a solid social graph consisting of verified relationships. Since "friending" (which is a link between nodes in the social graph) required both users to approve the relationship, the network fostered an incredible amount of trust. Today, many Facebook users post their cell phone numbers and their birthdays, offer personal photos, and otherwise share information they'd never do outside their circle of friends. Because of trust, Facebook's social graph is incredibly strong.

There is also a strong **network effect** to Facebook (see Chapter 6). People are attracted to the service because others they care about are more likely to be there than anywhere else online. And that large user base has also attracted all sorts of firms and organizations looking to connect with Facebook's masses. Without the network effect Facebook wouldn't exist. And it's because of the network effect that another smart kid in a dorm can't rip off Zuckerberg in any market where Facebook is the biggest fish. Even an exact copy of Facebook would be a virtual ghost town with no social graph (see "It's Not the Technology" below).

network effects

Also known as Metcalfe's Law, or network externalities. When the value of a product or service increases as its number of users expands.

The **switching costs** for Facebook are also extremely powerful. A move to another service means recreating your entire social graph. The more time you spend on the service, the more you've invested in your graph and the less likely you are to move to a rival.

switching costs

The cost a consumer incurs when moving from one product to another. It can involve actual money spent (e.g., buying a new product) as well as investments in time, any data loss, and so forth.

It's Not the Technology

Does your firm have Facebook envy? KickApps, an eighty-person start-up in Manhattan, will give you the technology to power your own social network. All KickApps wants is a cut of the ads placed around your content. In its first two years, the site has provided the infrastructure for twenty thousand "mini Facebooks," registering three hundred million page views a month.[40] NPR, ABC, AutoByTel, Harley-Davidson, and Kraft all use the service (social networks for Cheez Whiz?).

There's also Ning, which has enabled users to create over 2.3 million mini networks organized on all sorts of topics as diverse as church groups, radio personalities, vegans, diabetes sufferers, and networks limited to just family members.

Or how about the offering from Agriya Infoway, based in Chennai, India? The firm will sell you Kootali, a software package that lets developers replicate Facebook's design and features, complete with friend networks, photos, and mini-feeds. They haven't stolen any code, but they have copied the company's look and feel. Those with Zuckerberg ambitions can shell out the four hundred bucks for Kootali. Sites with names like Faceclub.com and Umicity.com have done just that—and gone nowhere.

Mini networks that extend the conversation (NPR) or make it easier to find other rabidly loyal product fans (Harley-Davidson) may hold a niche for some firms. And Ning is a neat way for specialized groups to quickly form in a secure environment that's all their own (it's just us, no "creepy friends" from the other networks). While every market has a place for its niches, none of these will grow to compete with the dominant social networks. Even Google, which has tremendous assets in search capability, Gmail, and other potential distribution channels to leverage in its Google+ effort, hasn't come close to matching Facebook's lead. The value isn't in the technology; it's in what the technology has created over time. For Facebook, it's a huge user base that (for now at least) is not going anywhere else.

KEY TAKEAWAYS

- The social graph expresses the connections between individuals and organizations.
- Trust created through user verification and friend approval requiring both parties to consent encouraged Facebook users to share more and helped the firm establish a stronger social graph than other social networking rivals.
- Facebook's key resources for competitive advantage are network effects and switching costs. These resources make it extremely difficult for copycat firms to steal market share from Facebook.

QUESTIONS AND EXERCISES

1. What is the social graph? Why is Facebook's social graph considered to be stronger than the social graph created by the sites of its early competitors?
2. Does Facebook have to worry about copycat firms from the United States? In overseas markets? Why or why not? If Facebook has a source (or sources) of competitive advantage, explain these. If it has no advantage, discuss why.

4. FACEBOOK FEEDS—EBOLA FOR DATA FLOWS

LEARNING OBJECTIVES

1. **Understand the concept of feeds, why users rebelled against Facebook feeds, and why users eventually embraced this feature.**
2. **Recognize the role of feeds in viral promotions, catalyzing innovation, and supporting rapid organizing.**

While the authenticity and trust offered by Facebook was critical, offering News Feeds concentrated and released value from the social graph. With feeds, each time a user performs an activity in Facebook—makes a friend, uploads a picture, joins a group—the feed blasts this information to all of your friends in a reverse chronological list that shows up right when they next log on. An individual user's activities are also listed on their profile. Get a new job, move to a new city, read a great article, have a pithy quote—post it to Facebook—the feed picks it up, and the world of your Facebook friends will get an update. Corporations love feeds, too! "Like" a firm on Facebook and the firm can post messages to your news feed, where you can "Like" new messages they send out, comment on them, and share the messages virally.

Feeds are perhaps the linchpin of Facebook's ability to strengthen and deliver user value from the social graph, but for a brief period of time it looked like feeds would kill the company. News Feeds were launched on September 5, 2006, just as many of the nation's undergrads were arriving on campus. Feeds reflecting any Facebook activity (including changes to the relationship status) became a sort of gossip page splashed right when your friends logged in. To many, feeds were first seen as a viral blast of digital nosiness—a release of information they hadn't consented to distribute widely.

And in a remarkable irony, user disgust over the News Feed ambush offered a whip-crack demonstration of the power and speed of the feed virus. Facebook protest groups were formed on Facebook itself, and every student who, for example, joined a group named Students Against Facebook News Feed, had this fact blasted to their friends (along with a quick link where friends, too, could click to join the group). Hundreds of thousands of users mobilized against the firm in just twenty-four hours. It looked like Zuckerberg's creation had turned on him, Frankenstein style.

The first official Facebook blog post on the controversy came off as a bit condescending (never a good tone to use when your customers feel that you've wronged them). "Calm down. Breathe. We hear you," wrote Zuckerberg on the evening of September 5. The next post, three days after the News Feed launch, was much more contrite ("We really messed this one up," he wrote). In an open letter, Zuckerberg apologized for the surprise, explaining how users could opt out of feeds. The tactic worked, and the controversy blew over.[41] The ability to stop personal information from flowing into the feed stream was just enough to stifle critics, and as it turns out, a lot of people really liked the feeds and found them useful. It soon became clear that if you wanted to use the Web to keep track of your social life and contacts, Facebook was the place to be. Not only did feeds not push users away, by the start of the next semester subscribers had nearly doubled! Facebook continues to refine feeds in several ways, including refining sharing into categories that include "Top Stories" that the site thinks you'll be most interested in, "Recent News," a "Ticker" for lighter content (e.g. music, games, location updates), and a "Timeline" that offers a sort of digital scrapbook of content that a user has shared online.

KEY TAKEAWAYS

- Facebook feeds foster the viral spread of information and activity.
- Feeds were initially unwanted by many Facebook users. Feeds themselves helped fuel online protests against the feed feature.
- Today feeds are considered one of the most vital, value-adding features on Facebook, and the concept has been widely copied by other social networking sites.
- Users often misperceive technology and have difficulty in recognizing an effort's value (as well as its risks). They have every right to be concerned and protective of their privacy. It is the responsibility of firms to engage users on new initiatives and to protect user privacy. Failure to do so risks backlash.

QUESTIONS AND EXERCISES

1. What is the "linchpin" of Facebook's ability to strengthen and deliver user-value from the social graph?
2. How did users first react to feeds? What could Facebook have done to better manage the launch?
3. How do you feel about Facebook feeds? Have you ever been disturbed by information about you or someone else that has appeared in the feed? Did this prompt action? Why or why not?
4. Visit Facebook and experiment with privacy settings. What kinds of control do you have over feeds and data sharing? Is this enough to set your mind at ease? Did you know these settings existed before being prompted to investigate features?
5. What other Web sites are leveraging features that mimic Facebook feeds? Do you think these efforts are successful or not? Why?

5. FACEBOOK AS A PLATFORM

LEARNING OBJECTIVES

1. **Understand how Facebook created a platform and the potential value this offers the firm.**
2. **Recognize that running a platform also presents a host of challenges to the platform operator.**

application programming interfaces (APIs)

Programming hooks, or guidelines, published by firms that tell other programs how to get a service to perform a task such as send or receive data. For example, Amazon.com provides APIs to let developers write their own applications and Websites that can send the firm orders.

In May 2007, Facebook followed News Feeds with another initiative that set it head and shoulders above its competition. At the firm's first f8 developers conference, Mark Zuckerberg stood on stage and announced that he was opening up the screen real estate on Facebook to other application developers. Facebook published a set of **application programming interfaces (APIs)** that specified how programs could be written to run within and interact with Facebook. Now any programmer could write an application that would live inside a user's profile. Geeks of the world, Facebook's user base could be yours! Just write something good.

Developers could charge for their wares, offer them for free, and even run ads. And Facebook let developers keep what they made (Facebook does revenue share with app vendors for some services, such as the Facebook Credits payment service, mentioned later). This was a key distinction; MySpace (a larger firm at the time) initially restricted developer revenue on the few products designed to run on their site, at times even blocking some applications. The choice was clear: Facebook had rolled out the welcome mat and developers flocked to the site.

To promote the new apps, Facebook would run an Applications area on the site where users could browse offerings. Even better, News Feed was a viral injection that spread the word each time an application was installed. Your best friend just played a game? Maybe you'll check it out, too. The predictions of $1 billion in social network ad spending were geek catnip, and legions of programmers came calling. Apps could be cobbled together on the quick, feeds made them spread like wildfire, and the early movers offered adoption rates never before seen by small groups of software developers. People began speaking of the Facebook Economy. Facebook was considered a platform. Some compared it to the next Windows, Zuckerberg the next Gates (hey, they both dropped out of Harvard, right?).

And each application potentially added more value and features to the site without Facebook lifting a finger. The initial event launched with sixty-five developer partners and eighty-five applications. There were some missteps along the way. Some applications were accused of spamming friends with invites to install them (Facebook eventually put limits on viral communication from apps). There were also security concerns, privacy leaks, and apps that violated the intellectual property of other firms (see the "Errant Apps" sidebar below), but Facebook worked to quickly remove misbehaving apps, correct errors, improve the system, and encourage developers. Just one year in, Facebook had marshaled the efforts of some four hundred thousand developers and entrepreneurs, twenty-four thousand applications had been built for the platform, 140 new apps were being added each day, and 95 percent of Facebook members had installed at least one Facebook application. As Sarah Lacy, author of *Once You're Lucky, Twice You're Good*, put it, "with one masterstroke, Zuck had mobilized all of Silicon Valley to innovate for him."

FIGURE 8.2 Gaming on Facebook's Platform Is a Colossal Business

Zynga, maker of MafiaWars, FarmVille, and CityVille, is estimated to be the second most valuable firm in the video game industry, generating north of $600 million in annual profits through the sale of virtual goods and by running advertising and promotions.

Source: Zynga.

With feeds to spread the word, Facebook was starting to look like the first place to go to launch an online innovation. Skip the Web; if you want to get social, bring it to Zuckerberg's site first (you can almost feel Tim Berners-Lee shuddering). A programmer named Mark Pincus wrote a Texas hold 'em game at his kitchen table.[42] Today his social gaming firm, Zynga, is one of the world's most valuable video game firms, a publicly-traded, multi-billion dollar powerhouse that has launched over three dozen apps and attracted over 230 million users worldwide.[43] Zynga games include MafiaWars, FarmVille (which boasts some twenty times the number of actual farms in the United States),[44] and CityVille. Playfish, the U.K. social gaming firm behind the Facebook hits Pet Society and Restaurant City, was snapped up by Electronic Arts for $300 million plus. And Disney bought Sorority Life maker Playdom for over three quarters of a billion dollars.[45] Lee Lorenzen, founder of Altura Ventures, an investment firm exclusively targeting firms creating Facebook apps, said, "Facebook is God's gift to developers. Never has the path from a good idea to millions of users been shorter."[46]

I Majored in Facebook

Once Facebook became a platform, Stanford professor BJ Fogg thought it would be a great environment for a programming class. In ten weeks his seventy-five students built a series of applications that collectively received over sixteen million installs. By the final week of class, several applications developed by students, including KissMe, Send Hotness, and Perfect Match, had received millions of users, and class apps collectively generated roughly a million dollars in ad revenue. At least three companies were formed from the course.[47]

But legitimate questions remain. Are Facebook apps really a big deal? Just how important will apps be to adding sustained value within Facebook? And how will firms leverage the Facebook framework to extract their own value? A chart from FlowingData showed the top category, Just for Fun, was larger than the next four categories combined. That suggests that a lot of applications are faddish time wasters. Yes, there is experimentation beyond virtual Zombie Bites. Visa has created a small business network on Facebook (Facebook had some eighty thousand small businesses online at the time of Visa's launch). Educational software firm Blackboard offered an application that will post data to Facebook pages as soon as there are updates to someone's Blackboard account (new courses, whether assignments or grades have been posted, etc.). We're still a long way from Facebook as a Windows rival, but the platform helped push Facebook to number one, and it continues to deliver quirky fun (and then some) supplied by thousands of developers off its payroll.

Errant Apps and the Challenges of Running a Platform

Rajat and Jayant Agarwalla, two brothers in Kolkata, India, who ran a modest software development company, decided to write a Scrabble clone as a Facebook application. The app, named Scrabulous, was social—users could invite friends to play, or they could search for new players looking for an opponent. Their application was a smash, snagging three million registered users and seven hundred thousand players a day after just a few months. Scrabulous was featured in *PC World*'s 100 best products of the year, received coverage in the *New York Times*, *Newsweek*, and *Wired*, and was pulling in about twenty-five thousand dollars a month from online advertising. Way to go, little guys![48]

There is only one problem: the Agarwalla brothers didn't have the legal rights to Scrabble, and it was apparent to anyone that from the name to the tiles to the scoring—this was a direct rip-off of the well-known board game. Hasbro owns the copyright to Scrabble in the United States and Canada; Mattel owns it everywhere else. Thousands of fans joined Facebook groups with names like "Save Scrabulous" and "Please God, I Have So Little: Don't Take Scrabulous, Too." Users in some protest groups pledged never to buy Hasbro games if Scrabulous was stopped. Even if the firms wanted to succumb to pressure and let the Agarwalla brothers continue, they couldn't. Both Electronic Arts and RealNetworks have contracted with the firms to create online versions of the game.

While the Facebook Scrabulous app is long gone, the tale serves to illustrate some of the challenges faced when creating a platform. In addition to copyright violations, app makers have crafted apps that annoy, purvey pornography, step over the boundaries of good taste, and raise privacy and security concerns. In fall 2010, the *Wall Street Journal* reported that unscrupulous partners had scraped personal information from the profiles of Facebook users and then sold the information to third parties—a violation of Facebook's terms of service that created a firestorm in the media.[49] Zynga also ran into trouble and was skewered in the press when some of its partners were accused of scamming users into signing up for subscriptions or installing unwanted software in exchange for game credits (Zynga has since taken steps to screen partners and improve transparency).[50]

Firms from Facebook to Apple (through its iTunes Store) have struggled to find the right mix of monitoring, protection, and approval while avoiding cries of censorship and draconian control. Platform owners beware, developers can help you grow quickly and can deliver gobs of value, but misbehaving partners can create financial loss and brand damage and can sow mistrust.

KEY TAKEAWAYS

- Facebook's platform allows the firm to further leverage the network effect. Developers creating applications create complementary benefits that have the potential to add value to Facebook beyond what the firm itself provides to its users.
- There is no revenue-sharing mandate among platform partners—whatever an application makes can be kept by its developers (although Facebook does provide some services via revenue sharing, such as Facebook Credits).
- Most Facebook applications are focused on entertainment. The true, durable, long-term value of Facebook's platform remains to be seen.
- Despite this, top app developers have found Facebook to be extraordinarily lucrative. Zynga is a multibillion-dollar firm, while Playfish and Playdom were acquired for hundreds of millions of dollars each.
- Running a platform can be challenging. Copyright, security, appropriateness, free speech tensions, efforts that tarnish platform operator brands, privacy, and the potential for competition with partners, all can make platform management more complex than simply creating a set of standards and releasing this to the public.

QUESTIONS AND EXERCISES

1. Why did more developers prefer to write apps for Facebook than for MySpace?
2. What competitive asset does the application platform initiative help Facebook strengthen? For example, how do apps make Facebook stronger when compared to rivals?
3. What's Scrabulous? Did the developers make money? What happened to the firm and why?
4. Have you used Facebook apps? Which are your favorites? What makes them successful?
5. Leverage your experience or conduct additional research—are there developers who you feel have abused the Facebook app network? Why? What is Facebook's responsibility (if any) to control such abuse?
6. How do most app developers make money? Have you ever helped a Facebook app developer earn money? How or why not?
7. How do Facebook app revenue opportunities differ from those leveraged by a large portion of iTunes Store apps?

6. ADVERTISING AND SOCIAL NETWORKS: A WORK IN PROGRESS

LEARNING OBJECTIVES

1. **Describe the differences in the Facebook and Google ad models.**
2. **Explain the hunt versus hike metaphor, contrast the relative success of ad performance on search compared to social networks, and understand the factors behind the latter's struggles.**
3. **Recognize how firms are leveraging social networks, including efforts such as Facebook engagement ads and deals, for brand building, product engagement, and driving purchase traffic.**

If Facebook is going to continue to give away its services for free, it needs to make money somehow. Right now the bulk of revenue comes from advertising. Fortunately for the firm, online advertising is hot. For years, online advertising has been the only major media category that has seen an increase in spending (see Chapter 14). Firms spend more advertising online than they do on radio, magazine, cable television, or newspaper ads.[51] But not all Internet advertising is created equal. There are both signs that social networking sites are struggling to find the right ad model and trends suggesting that advertising on social networks could be a money-gushing bonanza.

Google founder Sergey Brin sums up early frustration with social media advertising, saying, "I don't think we have the killer best way to advertise and monetize social networks yet," that social networking ad inventory as a whole was proving problematic and that the "monetization work we were doing [in social media] didn't pan out as well as we had hoped."[52] GM pulled a $10 million account from Facebook just days before the social network's IPO, claiming that paid advertising on the network was simply not effective.[53]

Why has advertising on social networking sites been such a tough nut for some to crack? Firms face two key challenges: **content adjacency** and user attention. The *content adjacency* problem refers to concern over where a firm's advertisements will run. Consider all of the questionable titles in social networking news groups. Do advertisers really want their ads running alongside conversations that are racy, offensive, illegal, or that may even mock their products? This potential juxtaposition is a major problem with any site offering ads adjacent to free-form social media. Summing up industry wariness, one Procter & Gamble manager said, "What in heaven's name made you think you could monetize the real estate in which somebody is breaking up with their girlfriend?"[54] An IDC report suggests that it's because of content adjacency that "brand advertisers largely consider user-generated content as low-quality, brand-unsafe inventory" for running ads.[55]

Now let's look at the user attention problem.

content adjacency

Concern that an advertisement will run near offensive material, embarrassing an advertiser and/or degrading their products or brands.

6.1 Attention Challenges: The Hunt Versus The Hike

In terms of revenue model, Facebook is radically different from Google and the high-value category of search advertising. Users of Google and other search sites are on a *hunt*—a task-oriented expedition to collect information that will drive a specific action. Search users want to learn something, buy something, research a problem, or get a question answered. To the extent that the hunt overlaps with ads, it works. Just searched on a medical term? Google will show you an ad from a drug company. Looking for a toy? You'll see Google ads from eBay sellers and other online shops. Type in a vacation destination and you get a long list of ads from travel providers aggressively courting your spending. Even better, Google only charges text advertisers when a user clicks through. No clicks? The ad runs at no cost to the advertiser. From a return on investment perspective, this is extraordinarily efficient. How often do users click on Google ads? Enough for this to be the single most profitable activity among *any* Internet firm. In 2011, Google revenue came in at nearly $38 billion. Profits exceeded $9.7 billion, almost all of this from pay-per-click ads (see Chapter 14 for more details).

While users go to Google to hunt, they go to Facebook as if they were going on a *hike*—they have a rough idea of what they'll encounter, but they're there to explore and look around and enjoy the sights (or site). They've usually allocated time for fun, and they don't want to leave the terrain when they're having conversations, looking at photos or videos, and checking out updates from friends.

These usage patterns are reflected in click-through rates. Google users click on ads around 2 percent of the time (and at a much higher rate when searching for product information). At Facebook, click-throughs are about 0.04 percent.[56]

Most banner ads don't charge per click but rather **CPM** (cost per thousand) **impressions** (each time an ad appears on someone's screen). But Facebook banner ads performed so poorly that the firm pulled them in early 2010.[57] Lookery, a one-time ad network that bought ad space on Facebook in bulk, had been reselling inventory at a CPM of 7.5 cents (note that Facebook does offer advertisers pay-per-click as well as impression-based, or CPM, options).[58] By contrast, information and news-oriented sites do much better, particularly if these sites draw in a valuable and highly targeted audience. The social networking blog *Mashable* has CPM rates ranging between seven and thirty-three dollars. *Technology Review* magazine boasts a CPM of seventy dollars. *TechTarget*, a Web publisher focusing on technology professionals, has been able to command CPM rates of one hundred dollars and above, fueling that firm's IPO.

CPM

Cost per thousand impressions (the M representing the roman numeral for one thousand).

impression

Each time an ad is served to a user for viewing.

6.2 Getting Creative with Promotions: Does It Work?

Facebook and other social networks are still learning what works, and Facebook, app firms, and advertisers have begun experimenting with all sorts of models. Many feel that Facebook has a unique opportunity to get consumers to engage with their brand, and some initial experiments point where this may be heading.

Many firms have been leveraging so-called **engagement ads** by making their products part of the Facebook fun. Using an engagement ad, a firm can set up a promotion where a user can do things such as "Like" or become a fan of a brand, RSVP to an event and invite others, watch and comment on a video and see what your friends have to say, send a "virtual gift" with a personal message, or answer a question in a poll. The viral nature of Facebook allows actions to flow back into the news feed and spread among friends.

COO Sheryl Sandberg discussed Ben & Jerry's promotion for the ice cream chain's free cone day event. To promote the upcoming event, Ben & Jerry's initially contracted to make two hundred and fifty thousand "gift cones" available to Facebook users; they could click on little icons that would gift a cone icon to a friend, and that would show up in their profile. Within a couple of hours, customers had sent all two hundred and fifty thousand virtual cones. Delighted, Ben & Jerry's bought another two

engagement ads

Promotion technique popular with social media that attempts to get consumers to interact with an ad, then shares that action with friends.

hundred and fifty thousand cones. Within eleven hours, half a million people had sent cones, many making plans with Facebook friends to attend the real free cone day. The day of the Facebook promotion, Ben & Jerry's Web site registered fifty-three million impressions, as users searched for store locations and wrote about their favorite flavors.[59] The campaign dovetailed with everything Facebook was good at: it was viral, generating enthusiasm for a promotional event and even prompting scheduling.

In other promotions, Honda gave away three quarters of a million hearts during a Valentine's Day promo,[60] and the Dr. Pepper Snapple Group offered two hundred and fifty thousand virtual Sunkist sodas, which earned the firm one hundred thirty million brand impressions in twenty-two hours. Says Sunkist's brand manager, "A Super Bowl ad, if you compare it, would have generated somewhere between six to seven million."[61]

Facebook, Help Get Me a Job!

The news is filled with stories about employers scouring Facebook to screen potential hires. But one creative job seeker turned the tables and used Facebook to make it easier for firms to find him. Recent MBA graduate Eric Barker, a talented former screenwriter with experience in the film and gaming industry, bought ads promoting himself on Facebook, setting them up to run only on the screens of users identified as coming from firms he'd like to work for. In this way, someone Facebook identified as being from Microsoft would see an ad from Eric declaring "I Want to Be at Microsoft" along with an offer to click and learn more. The cost to run the ads was usually less than $5 a day. Said Barker, "I could control my bid price and set a cap on my daily spend. Starbucks put a bigger dent in my wallet than promoting myself online." The ads got tens of thousands of impressions, hundreds of clicks, and dozens of people called offering assistance. Today, Eric Barker is gainfully employed at a "dream job" in the video game industry.[62]

Eric Barker used Facebook to advertise himself to prospective employers.

I want to be at Microsoft
Hi, my name is Eric and my dream is to work for Microsoft. I'm a MBA/MFA with a strong media background. Can you help me? Please click!

Of course, even with this business, Facebook may find that it competes with widget makers. Unlike Apple's App Store (where much of developer-earned revenue comes from selling apps), the vast majority of Facebook apps are free and supported by ads. That means Facebook and its app providers are both running at a finite pot of advertising dollars.

While these efforts might be innovative, are they even effective? Some of these programs are considered successes; others, not so much. Jupiter Research surveyed marketers trying to create a viral impact online and found that only about 15 percent of these efforts actually caught on with consumers.[63] Brands seeking to deploy their own applications in Facebook have also struggled. *New Media Age* reported that applications rolled out by top brands such as MTV, Warner Bros., and Woolworths were found to have as little as five daily users. Congestion may be setting in for all but the most innovative applications, as standing out in a crowd of over 550,000 applications becomes increasingly difficult.[64]

Consumer products giant Procter & Gamble (P&G) has been relentlessly experimenting with leveraging social networks for brand engagement, but the results show what a tough slog this can be. The firm did garner fourteen thousand Facebook "fans" for its Crest Whitestrips product, but those fans were earned while giving away free movie tickets and other promos. The *New York Times* quipped that with those kinds of incentives, "a hemorrhoid cream" could have attracted a similar group of "fans." When the giveaways stopped, thousands promptly "unfanned" Whitestrips. Results for Procter & Gamble's "2X Ultra Tide" fan page were also pretty grim. P&G tried offbeat appeals for customer-brand bonding, including asking Facebookers to post "their favorite places to enjoy stain-making moments." But a check eleven months after launch had garnered just eighteen submissions, two from

P&G, two from staffers at spoof news site *The Onion*, and a bunch of short posts such as "Tidealicious!"[65]

Efforts around engagement opportunities like events (Ben & Jerry's) or products consumers are anxious to identify themselves with (a band or a movie) may have more success than trying to promote consumer goods that otherwise offer little allegiance, but efforts are so new that metrics are scarce, impact is tough to gauge, and best practices are still unclear.

6.3 Facebook Ads: Massive Upside and Huge Growth

Concerns over Facebook's ad model were underscored when growth slowed in the two quarters prior to the firm's IPO.[66] For all these challenges and limitations, however, Facebook advertising had grown at a rate strikingly similar to Google's early ad growth trajectory.[67] There are several reasons for this spectacular growth.

First is the advertising appeal of *precise targeting*. Large advertising networks have tried to meticulously track users to develop a profile of their demographics, likes, and interests. At Facebook, the site knows all about you because you've told it the details—your age, the things you're enthusiastic about, where you live, your relationship status. This opens up all sorts of targeting opportunities to even the smallest of advertisers. In one example, a wedding photography studio targeted ads at women aged 24 to 30 whose relationship status was engaged—that's like sticking a flier in front of precisely everyone you want to reach and not wasting a dime on anyone else. The firm, CM Photographics, reports that just $600 in Facebook ads resulted in nearly $40,000 in revenue.[68]

Another key comes from leveraging *social engagement* in the ads themselves. Adding a "like" button to an ad allows firms to turn their advertising message into a trusted referral from users' friends. Making ads more social allows advertisers to engage consumers to comment on content, RSVP to an event, and more. Many of these ads are designed to allow interaction within the ad that keeps them on the page so that users aren't faced with a choice to deviate from their "hike." And while user "Likes" and other updates might be lost in the constant scroll of the news feed, Facebook also lets advertisers pay to create sponsored stories, allowing advertisers to turn a member's Facebook actions (status updates, check-ins, "likes") into an ad on the right-side of the screen.

Facebook Engagement Ads and Sponsored Stories

These videos show how both engagement ads and sponsored stories work.

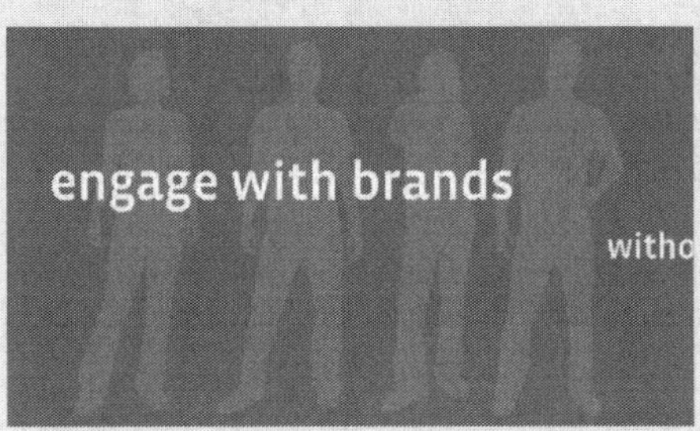

Source: Used by permission of Facebook.

Click to watch: https://www.facebook.com/video/video.php?v=10100328087082670

View the video online at: http://www.youtube.com/v/ce3P79ktpTk

While Facebook's overall click-through rates are low, Facebook execs argue that people remember ads better and are more likely to make purchases when their friends endorse products. Says one ad exec, "If you're an advertiser, there's nothing better than converting customers into unpaid endorsers."[69] Perhaps most critical—if someone "likes" your firm's page, you've got 'em. You can now post status updates that show up in a user's feed, allowing your message to appear in the same stream as postings from friends and to further spread virally. Users, of course, can turn off firm messages if they "unlike" a firm, and users are in control of their social ad participation through Facebook's privacy settings, but this ability to connect to customers in a way that enables continued messaging and promotion is a huge draw for advertisers and gives Facebook ads a unique appeal that none of its rivals can match.

While Facebook doesn't sell banner advertisements, the products described above are considered *display ads*. Facebook serves three times more display ads than anyone else online.[70] As for the increased spending by advertisers on Facebook, only time will tell if GM's experience is an anomaly or a troubling trend and if Facebook can create new promotional mechanisms to further fuel growth.[71]

KEY TAKEAWAYS

- Issues of content adjacency and user attention can make social networking ads less attractive than ads running alongside search and professionally produced content sites.
- Google enjoys significantly higher click-through rates than Facebook. Rates are lower since users of social sites are there to engage friends, not to hunt for products. They are less likely to be drawn away by clicks.
- Display ads are often charged based on impression. Social networks also offer lower CPM rates than many other, more targeted Web sites.
- Many firms have begun to experiment with engagement ads. While there have been some successes, engagement campaigns often haven't yielded significant results
- Despite concern, Facebook ads have grown at a tremendous rate and are highly profitable.
- Facebook ads offer advantages of improved targeting and social engagement. Ads allow customers to endorse a firm's offerings and to virally share a message with others. Facebook can leverage customer engagement in its own ads. And Facebook allows firms to continue to send messages to the news feeds of users who have "liked" their presence on Facebook.

QUESTIONS AND EXERCISES

1. How are most display ads billed? What acronym is used to describe pricing of most display ads?
2. How are most text ads on Google billed? What's the appeal for advertisers?
3. Contrast Facebook and Google click-through rates. Contrast Facebook CPMs with CPMs at professional content sites. Why the discrepancy?
4. What is the content adjacency problem? Search for examples of firms that have experienced embarassment due to content adjacency—describe them, why they occurred, and if site operators could have done something to reduce the likelihood these issues could have occurred.
5. What kinds of Web sites are most susceptible to content adjacency? Are news sites? Why or why not? What sorts of technical features might act as breeding grounds for content adjacency problems?
6. If a firm removed user content because it was offensive to an advertiser, what kinds of problems might this create? When (if ever) should a firm remove or take down user content?
7. How are firms attempting to leverage social networks for brand and product engagement? What advantages do ads on Facebook offer advertisers that they can't necessarily get from competing online ad alternatives?
8. Describe an innovative marketing campaign that has leveraged Facebook or other social networking sites. What factors made this campaign work? Are all firms likely to have this sort of success? Why or why not?
9. Have advertisers ever targeted you when displaying ads on Facebook? How were you targeted? What did you think of the effort?

7. PRIVACY PERIL, BEACON, AND THE TOS DEBACLE: WHAT FACEBOOK'S FAILURES CAN TEACH MANAGERS ABOUT TECHNOLOGY PLANNING AND DEPLOYMENT

LEARNING OBJECTIVES

1. **Understand the difference between opt-in and opt-out efforts.**
2. **Recognize how user issues and procedural implementation can derail even well-intentioned information systems efforts.**
3. **Recognize the risks in being a pioneer associated with new media efforts, and understand how missteps led to Facebook and its partners being embarrassed (and in some cases sued) as a result of system design and deployment issues.**

Conventional advertising may grow into a great business for Facebook, but the firm was clearly sitting on something that was unconventional compared to prior generations of Web services. Could the energy and virulent nature of social networks be harnessed to offer truly useful consumer information to its users? Word of mouth is considered the most persuasive (and valuable) form of marketing,[72] and Facebook was a giant word of mouth machine. What if the firm worked with vendors and grabbed consumer activity at the point of purchase to put it into the news feed and post it to a user's profile? If you rented a video, bought a cool product, or dropped something in your wish list, your buddies could get a heads-up, and they might ask you about it. The person being asked feels like an expert, the person with the question gets a frank opinion, and the vendor providing the data just might get another sale. It looked like a home run.

This effort was named Beacon. Some forty e-commerce sites signed up, including Blockbuster, Fandango, eBay, Travelocity, Zappos, and the *New York Times*. Zuckerberg was so confident of the effort that he stood before a group of Madison Avenue ad executives and declared that Beacon would represent a "once-in-a-hundred-years" fundamental change in the way media works.

Like News Feeds, user reaction was swift and brutal. The commercial activity of Facebook users began showing up without their consent. The biggest problem with Beacon was that it was "opt-out" instead of "opt-in." Facebook (and its partners) assumed users would agree to sharing data in their feeds. A pop-up box did appear briefly on most sites supporting Beacon, but it disappeared after a few seconds.[73] Many users, blind to these sorts of alerts, either clicked through or ignored the warnings. And well…there are some purchases you might not want to broadcast to the world.

"Facebook Ruins Christmas for Everyone!" screamed one headline from MSNBC.com. Another from *U.S. News and World Report* read "How Facebook Stole Christmas." The *Washington Post* ran the story of Sean Lane, a twenty-eight-year-old tech support worker from Waltham, Massachusetts, who got a message from his wife just two hours after he bought a ring on Overstock.com. "Who is this ring for?" she wanted to know. Facebook had not only posted a feed that her husband had bought the ring, but also that he got it for a 51 percent discount! Overstock quickly announced that it was halting participation in Beacon until Facebook changed its practice to opt in.[74]

MoveOn.org started a Facebook group and online petition protesting Beacon. The Center for Digital Democracy and the U.S. Public Interest Research Group asked the Federal Trade Commission to investigate Facebook's advertising programs. And a Dallas woman sued Blockbuster for violating the Video Privacy Protection Act (a 1998 U.S. law prohibiting unauthorized access to video store rental records).

To Facebook's credit, the firm acted swiftly. Beacon was switched to an opt-in system, where user consent must be given before partner data is sent to the feed. Zuckerberg would later say regarding Beacon: "We've made a lot of mistakes building this feature, but we've made even more with how we've handled them. We simply did a bad job with this release, and I apologize for it."[75] Beacon was eventually shut down and $9.5 million was donated to various privacy groups as part of its legal settlement.[76] Despite the Beacon fiasco, new users continued to flock to the site, and loyal users stuck with Zuck. Perhaps a bigger problem was that many of those forty A-list e-commerce sites that took a gamble with Facebook now had their names associated with a privacy screw-up that made headlines worldwide. Not a good thing for one's career. A manager so burned isn't likely to sign up first for the next round of experimentation.

From the Prada example in Chapter 3 we learned that savvy managers look beyond technology and consider complete information systems—not just the hardware and software of technology but also the interactions among the data, people, and procedures that make up (and are impacted by) information systems. Beacon's failure is a cautionary tale of what can go wrong if users fail to broadly consider the impact and implications of an information system on all those it can touch. Technology's reach is often farther, wider, and more significantly impactful than we originally expect.

Predators and Privacy

While spoiling Christmas is bad, sexual predators are far worse. Officials from the New York State Attorney General's office had posed as teenagers on Facebook and received sexual advances. Complaints to the service from investigators posing as parents were also not immediately addressed. These were troubling developments for a firm that prided itself on trust and authenticity.

In an agreement with forty-nine states, Facebook offered a series of aggressive steps. Facebook agreed to respond to complaints about inappropriate content within twenty-four hours and to allow an independent examiner to monitor how it handles complaints. The firm imposed age-locking restrictions on profiles, reviewing any attempt by someone under the age of eighteen to change their date of birth. Profiles of minors were no longer searchable. The site agreed to automatically send a warning message when a child is at risk of revealing personal information to an unknown adult. And links to explicit material, the most offensive Facebook groups, and any material related to cyberbullying were banned.

7.1 Reputation Damage, Increased Scrutiny, and Recovery—Learning from the Facebook TOS Debacle

Facebook also suffered damage to its reputation, brand, and credibility, further reinforcing perceptions that the company acts brazenly, without considering user needs, and is fast and loose on privacy and user notification. Facebook worked through the feeds outrage, eventually convincing users of the benefits of feeds. But Beacon was a fiasco. And now users, the media, and watchdogs were on the alert.

When the firm modified its terms of service (TOS) policy in spring 2009, the uproar was immediate. As a cover story in *New York* magazine summed it up, Facebook's new TOS appeared to state, "We can do anything we want with your content, forever," even if a user deletes their account and leaves the service.[77] Yet *another* privacy backlash!

Activists organized; the press crafted juicy, attention-grabbing headlines; and the firm was forced once again to backtrack. But here's where others can learn from Facebook's missteps and response. The firm was contrite and reached out to explain and engage users. The old TOS were reinstated, and the firm posted a proposed new version that gave the firm broad latitude in leveraging user content without claiming ownership. And the firm renounced the right to use this content if a user closed their Facebook account. This new TOS was offered in a way that solicited user comments, and it was submitted to a community vote, considered binding if 30 percent of Facebook users participated. Zuckerberg's move appeared to have turned Facebook into a democracy and helped empower users to determine the firm's next step.

Despite the uproar, only about 1 percent of Facebook users eventually voted on the measure, but the 74 percent to 26 percent ruling in favor of the change gave Facebook some cover to move forward.[78] This event also demonstrates that a tempest can be generated by a relatively small number of passionate users. Firms ignore the vocal and influential at their own peril!

In Facebook's defense, the broad TOS was probably more a form of legal protection than any nefarious attempt to exploit all user posts ad infinitum. The U.S. legal environment does require that explicit terms be defined and communicated to users, even if these are tough for laypeople to understand. But a "trust us" attitude toward user data doesn't work, particularly for a firm considered to have committed ham-handed gaffes in the past. Managers must learn from the freewheeling Facebook community. In the era of social media, your actions are now subject to immediate and sustained review. Violate the public trust, and expect the equivalent of a high-powered investigative microscope examining your every move and a very public airing of the findings.

For Facebook, that microscope will be in place for at least the next two decades. In a late 2011 deal with the U.S. Federal Trade Commission, Facebook settled a series of governmental inquiries related to issues such as the ones outlined above—events that Zuckerberg admits added up to "a bunch of mistakes" made by the firm. Facebook agreed to undergo twenty years of regular third-party privacy audits, and to a host of additional restrictions that include getting users' consent before making privacy changes, and making content from deleted profiles unavailable after 30 days. If Facebook fails to comply with these terms, it will face fines of $16,000 per violation per day.[79]

KEY TAKEAWAYS

- Word of mouth is the most powerful method for promoting products and services, and Beacon was conceived as a giant word-of-mouth machine with win-win benefits for firms, recommenders, recommendation recipients, and Facebook.
- Beacon failed because it was an opt-out system that was not thoroughly tested beforehand and because user behavior, expectations, and system procedures were not completely taken into account.
- Partners associated with the rapidly rolled out, poorly conceived, and untested effort were embarrassed. Several faced legal action.
- Facebook also reinforced negative perceptions regarding the firm's attitudes toward users, notifications, and their privacy. This attitude only served to focus a continued spotlight on the firm's efforts, and users became even less forgiving.
- Activists and the media were merciless in criticizing the firm's terms of service changes. Facebook's democratizing efforts demonstrate lessons other organizations can learn from, regarding user scrutiny, public reaction, and stakeholder engagement.
- A combination of firm policies, computerized and human monitoring, aggressive reporting and follow-up, and engagement with authorities can reduce online predator risks. Firms that fail to fully engage this threat put users and communities at risk and may experience irreparable damage to firms and reputations.

QUESTIONS AND EXERCISES

1. What was Beacon? Why was it initially thought to be a good idea? What were the benefits to firm partners, recommenders, recommendation recipients, and Facebook? Who were Beacon's partners, and what did they seek to gain through the effort?
2. Describe "the biggest problem with Beacon"? Would you use Beacon? Why or why not?
3. How might Facebook and its partners have avoided the problems with Beacon? Could the effort be restructured while still delivering on its initial promise? Why or why not?
4. Beacon shows the risk in being a pioneer—are there risks in being too cautious and not pioneering with innovative, ground-floor marketing efforts? What kinds of benefits might a firm miss out on? Is there a disadvantage in being late to the party with these efforts as well? Why or why not?
5. Why do you think Facebook changed its terms of service? Did these changes concern you? Were users right to rebel? What could Facebook have done to avoid the problem? Did Facebook do a good job in follow-up? How would you advise Facebook to apply lessons learned form the TOS controversy?
6. Investigate the current policies regarding underage users on Facebook. Do you think the firm adequately protects its users? Why or why not?
7. What age is appropriate for users to begin using social networks? Which services are appropriate at which ages? Are there social networks targeted at very young children? Do you think that these are safe places? Why or why not?

8. ONE GRAPH TO RULE THEM ALL: FACEBOOK REACHES ACROSS THE WEB WITH OPEN GRAPH

LEARNING OBJECTIVES

1. **Describe Facebook's efforts to integrate its service with other Web sites and the potential strategic benefit for Facebook and its partners.**
2. **List and discuss the potential benefits and risks of engaging in the kinds of intersite sharing and collaboration efforts described in this section.**

Facebook's Open Graph offers the world a glimpse of the breadth and depth of Mark Zuckerberg's vision. The initiative places the company directly at the center of identity, sharing, and personalization—not just on Facebook but also across the Web.

With just a few lines of HTML code, any developer could add a Facebook "Like" button to their site and take advantage of the social network's power of viral distribution. A user clicking that page's "Like" button automatically would then send a link to that page to their news feed, where it has the potential to be seen by all of their friends. No additional sign-in is necessary as long as you logged into

Facebook first (reinforcing Facebook's importance as the first stop in your Internet surfing itinerary). The effort was adopted with stunning speed. Facebook's "Like" button served up more than one billion times across the Web in the first twenty-four hours, and over fifty thousand Web sites signed up to add the "Like" button to their content within the first week. (Facebook now includes several new verb options beyond "like.")[80]

Facebook also offered a system where Web site operators can choose to accept a user's Facebook credentials for logging in. Users like this because they can access content without the hurdle of creating a new account. Web sites like it because with the burden of signing up out of the way, Facebook becomes an experimentation lubricant: "Oh, I can use my Facebook ID to sign in? Then let me try this out."

Other efforts allow firms to leverage Facebook data to make their sites more personalized. Firms around the Web can now show if a visitor's friends have "Liked" items on the site, posted comments, or performed other actions. Using this feature, Facebook users logging into Yelp can see a list of restaurants recommended by trusted friends instead of just the reviews posted by a bunch of strangers. Users of the music-streaming site Pandora can have the service customized based on music tastes pulled from their Facebook profile page. They can share stations with friends and have data flow back to update the music preferences listed in their Facebook profile pages. Visit CNN and the site can pull together a list of stories recommended by friends.[81] Think about how this strengthens the social graph. While items in the news feed might quickly scroll away and disappear, that data can now be pulled up within a Web site, providing insight from friends when and where you're likely to want it most.

Taken together, these features enlist Web sites to serve as vassal states in the Facebook empire. Each of these ties makes Facebook membership more valuable by enhancing network effects, strengthening switching costs, and creating larger sets of highly personalized data to leverage.

Facebook: The Bank of the Web?

Those with an eye for business disruption are watching the evolution of Facebook Credits. Credits can be used to pay for items, such as features and enhancements in video games or virtual gifts. Facebook shares Credits revenue with application developers, taking a sizeable 30 percent off the top for acting as banker and transaction clearing house. That's a steep price to pay, but a unified standard may also prompt innovation since users are far more likely to trust Facebook with their credit card than to register their card on multiple services run by little-known app developers. As of July 2011, Facebook Credits are the mandatory in-game currency for all developers on the service.

There are real bucks to be made from digital make-believe. Analysts estimate that in 2011, virtual goods racked up an estimated $2.3 billion in U.S. transactions and $9 billion worldwide.[82] Zynga alone forks over tens of millions each month for Facebook via virtual goods sales.[83] There are also an increasing number of ways to pay for Credits. Facebook's App2Credits effort lets firms offer Credits in ways that don't involve a credit card, including getting Credits as part of a card loyalty program, converting unwanted real-world gift cards into Facebook Credits, or earning Credits for shopping or performing other online tasks.[84]

Credits were rolled out supporting fifteen international currencies and multiple credit cards. Transaction support is provided through a partnership with PayPal, and a deal with mobile payments start-up Zong allows users to bill credits to their phone.[85] Credits can also be redeemed for vouchers that can be used to buy real-world products and services.[86]

All this banking activity leaves some wondering if Facebook might not have grander ambitions. The *Financial Times* has referred to Facebook as being on the path to becoming "The Bank of the Web."[87] Could Facebook morph into an actual real-currency bank? A site that knows how to reach your friends might offer an easy way to, say, settle a dinner tab or hound buddies for their Final Four pool money. This might also be a solid base for even deeper banking links between users and all those firms Facebook has begun to leverage in deeper data-sharing partnerships. This may be something to think about, or perhaps, to bank on!

8.1 Open Graph and Privacy Controversy

The decision to launch many of the new Open Graph features as "opt-out" instead of "opt-in" immediately drew the concern of lawmakers. Given the Beacon debacle, the TOS controversy, and Google's problems with Buzz (see Chapter 14), you'd think Facebook would have known better. But within a week of Open Graph's launch, four U.S. senators contacted the firm, asking why it was so difficult to opt out of the information-sharing platform.[88] Amid a crush of negative publicity, the firm was forced to quickly roll out simplified privacy management controls.

Facebook's struggles show the tension faced by any firm that wants to collect data to improve the user experience (and hopefully make money along the way). Opt-out guarantees the largest possible audience and that's key to realizing the benefits of network effects, data, and scale. Making efforts opt-in creates the very real risk that not enough users will sign up and that the reach and impact of these kinds of initiatives will be limited.[89] *Fast Company* calls this the *paradox of privacy*, saying, "We want some semblance of control over our personal data, even if we likely can't be bothered to manage it."[90] Evidence suggests that most people are accepting some degree of data sharing as long as they know that they can easily turn it off if they want to. For example, when Google rolled out ads that tracked users across the network of Web sites running Google ads, the service also provided a link in each ad where users could visit an "ad preferences manager" to learn how they were being profiled, to change settings, and to opt out (see Chapter 14). It turns out only one in fifteen visitors to the ad preferences manager ended up opting out completely.[91] Managers seeking to leverage data should learn from the examples of Facebook and Google and be certain to offer clear controls that empower user choice.

Busted on Facebook

Chapter 7 warned that your digital life will linger forever and that employers are increasingly plumbing the depths of virtual communities in order to get a sense of job candidates. And it's not just employers. Sleuths at universities and police departments have begun looking to Facebook for evidence of malfeasance. Oxford University fined graduating students more than £10,000 for their postexam celebrations, evidence of which was picked up from Facebook. Police throughout the United States have made underage drinking busts and issued graffiti warnings based on Facebook photos, too. Beware—the Web knows!

8.2 Open Graph and Strategic Concerns: Asset Strength, Free Riders, and Security

Facebook also allows third-party developers to create all sorts of apps to access Facebook data. Facebook feeds are now streaming through devices that include Samsung, Vizio, and Sony televisions; Xbox 360 and Wii game consoles; Verizon's FiOS pay television service; and the Amazon Kindle. While Facebook might never have the time or resources to create apps that put its service on every gadget on the market, they don't need to. Developers using Facebook's access tools will gladly pick up the slack.

But there are major challenges with a more open approach, most notably a weakening of strategic assets, revenue sharing, and security. First, let's discuss weakened assets. Mark Zuckerberg's geeks have worked hard to make their site the top choice for most of the world's social networkers and social network application developers. Right now, everyone goes to Facebook because everyone else is on Facebook. But as Facebook opens up access to users and content, it risks supporting efforts that undermine the firm's two most compelling sources of competitive advantage: network effects and switching costs. Any effort that makes it easier to pack up your "social self" and move it elsewhere risks undermining vital competitive resources advantages (it still remains more difficult to export contacts, e-mails, photos, and video from Facebook than it does from sites supporting OpenSocial, a rival platform backed by Google and supported by many of Facebook's competitors).[92] This situation also puts more pressure on Facebook to behave. Lower those switching costs at a time when users are disgusted with firm behavior, and it's not inconceivable that a sizable chunk of the population could bolt for a new rival (to Facebook's credit, the site also reached out to prior critics like MoveOn.org, showing Facebook's data-sharing features and soliciting input months before their official release).

Along with asset weakening comes the issue of revenue sharing. As mentioned earlier, hosting content (especially photos and rich media) is a very expensive proposition. What incentive does a site have to store data if it will just be sent to a third-party site that will run ads around this content and not share the take? Too much data portability presents a **free rider problem** where firms mooch off Facebook's infrastructure without offering much in return. Consider services like TweetDeck (now owned by Twitter). The free application allows users to access their Facebook feeds and post status updates—alongside Twitter updates and more—all from one interface. Cool for the user, but bad for Facebook, since each TweetDeck use means Facebook users are "off-site," not looking at ads, and hence not helping Zuckerberg & Co. earn revenue. It's as if the site has encouraged the equivalent of an ad blocker, yet Facebook's openness lets this happen!

free rider problem

When others take advantage of a user or service without providing any sort of reciprocal benefit.

Finally, consider security. Allowing data streams that contain potentially private posts and photographs to squirt across the Internet and land where you want them raises all sorts of concerns. What's to say an errant line of code doesn't provide a back door to your address book or friends list? To your messaging account? To let others see photos you'd hoped to only share with family? Security breaches can occur on any site, but once the data is allowed to flow freely, every site with access is, for hackers, the equivalent of a potential door to open or a window to crawl through.

crowdsourcing

The act of taking a job traditionally performed by a designated agent (usually an employee) and outsourcing it to an undefined generally large group of people in the form of an open call.

localization

Adapting products and services for different languages and regional differences.

Social Networking Goes Global

Facebook will eventually see stellar growth start to slow as the law of large numbers sets in. The shift from growth business to mature one can be painful, and for online firms it can occur relatively quickly. That doesn't mean these firms will become unprofitable, but to sustain growth (particularly important for keeping up the stock price of a publicly traded company), firms often look to expand abroad.

Facebook's **crowdsourcing localization** effort, where users were asked to look at Facebook phrases and offer translation suggestions for their local language (see Chapter 7), helped the firm rapidly deploy versions in dozens of markets, blasting the firm past MySpace in global reach. But network effects are both quick and powerful, and late market entry can doom a business reliant on the positive feedback loop of a growing user base.

And global competition is out there. Worldwide, Facebook wannabes include Vkontakte ("in contact"), Russia's most popular social networking site; Google's Orkut (which is tops in Brazil, although Facebook's gaining there, too); and Renren (formerly Xiaonei), which is said to have registered 90 percent of China's college students.

China is proving a particularly difficult market for foreign Internet firms. Google, eBay, Yahoo! and MySpace have all struggled there. And don't be surprised to see some of these well-capitalized overseas innovators making a move on U.S. markets too.

While global growth can seem like a good thing, acquiring global users isn't the same as making money from them. Free sites with large amounts of users from developing nations face real cost/revenue challenges. As the *New York Times* points out, there are 1.6 billion Internet users worldwide, but fewer than half of them have disposable incomes high enough to interest major advertisers, meaning that in terms of average revenue per user (ARPU), these new social networking recruits are likely to be far less lucrative in the near future than the firm's current users.[93] Worse still, telecommunications costs in these markets are also often higher, too. Bandwidth costs and dim revenue options caused video site Veoh to block access coming from Africa, Eastern Europe, Latin America, and some parts of Asia. MySpace already offers a stripped-down Lite option as its default in India. And execs at YouTube and Facebook haven't ruled out lowering the quality of streaming media, file size, or other options, discriminating by region or even by user.

Making money in the face of this so-called "International Paradox" requires an awareness of "fast and cheap" tech trends highlighted in Chapter 5, as well as an ability to make accurate predictions regarding regional macroeconomic trends. Ignore a market that's unprofitable today and a rival could swoop in and establish network effects and other assets that are unbeatable tomorrow. But move too early and losses could drag you down.

Concerns aren't just financial; they're also political and ethical. Facebook is officially banned in China (although many Chinese have used technical work-arounds to access the site), and Zuckerberg is clearly interested in the Chinese market. He spends an hour each day learning Chinese and has made several trips to China, as well.[94] Facebook has discussed a partnership with China's dominant search site, Baidu, but moving forward with an effort that complies with China's filtering requirements leaves executives conflicted. Some say even a censored Facebook would be a catalyst for Chinese democratic reform, while others see this as a compromise of the firm's belief in the power of exchange and promoting the free flow of information. Says the firm's COO Sheryl Sandberg, "There are compromises on not being in China, and there are compromises on being in China. It's not clear to me which one is bigger."[95]

KEY TAKEAWAYS

- Facebook has extended its reach by allowing other Web sites to leverage the site. Facebook partners can add the "Like" button to encourage viral sharing of content, leverage Facebook user IDs for log-in, and tap a user's friend and feed data to personalize and customize a user's experience.
- These efforts come with risks, including enabling free riders that might exploit the firm's content without compensation, and the potential for privacy and security risks.
- Facebook Credits are a currency for use for virtual gifts and games. The service accepts multiple currencies and payment methods; and while virtual goods have the potential to be a big business, some speculate that Facebook may one day be able to develop a payments and banking business from this base.
- Global growth is highly appealing to firms, but expensive bandwidth costs and low prospects for ad revenue create challenges akin to the free rider problem.

QUESTIONS AND EXERCISES

1. Cite effective examples you've seen of Facebook features on other Web sites (or if you haven't seen any, do some background research to uncover such efforts). Why do the efforts you've highlighted "work"? How do they benefit various parties? Does everyone benefit? Is anyone at risk? If so, explain the risks.
2. Should Facebook be as open as it is? In what ways might this benefit the firm? In what ways is it a risk?
3. How can Facebook limit criticism of its data-sharing features? Do you think it made mistakes during rollout?
4. What is TweetDeck? Why is a product like this a potential threat to Facebook?
5. Research OpenSocial online. What is this effort? What challenges does it face in attempting to become a dominant standard?
6. Facebook has global competitors. What determines the success of a social network within a given country? Why do network effects for social networks often fail to translate across national borders?
7. How did Facebook localize its site so quickly for various different regions of the world?
8. What factors encourage firms to grow an international user base as quickly as possible? Why is this a risk, and what is the so-called "International Paradox"? What sorts of firms are at more risk than others?
9. List the pros, cons, and unknowns if Facebook were to seek a way for the Chinese government to allow its expansion into China. What are the risks if the firm remains out of the country? What do you think the firm should do?

9. IS FACEBOOK WORTH IT?

LEARNING OBJECTIVES

1. **Discuss the factors related to Facebook's valuation.**
2. **Compare Facebook's performance at IPO to that of Google, and offer insightful commentary on Facebook's future prospects.**
3. **Highlight areas of concern regarding Facebook's future prospects and areas where Facebook may be able to increase revenues and profits.**

It has often been said that the first phase of the Internet was about putting information online and giving people a way to find it. The second phase of the Web is about connecting people with one another. The Web 2.0 movement is big and impactful, but how much money is in it?

Now that Facebook is a publicly traded company, we can get real numbers on revenue, profitability, and growth, and we can use these numbers to compare Facebook against its rivals. In the quarter prior to its IPO, Facebook's rate of revenue growth was 45 percent, down from 55 percent the prior quarter, which was down again from triple-digit growth the quarter before that.[96] Usually at IPO time, markets like to see accelerating, not decelerating, growth. Facebook went public at a nosebleed rate of 65 times 2013 EPS (earnings per share). For comparison, still-growing Google traded at 13 times 2013 EPS at the time of Facebook's IPO. At IPO, Facebook's market cap was about half of Google's, but if we compare the business in which Facebook and Google most closely compete, display advertising, both are roughly the same size (Facebook at 14 percent of the US market and Google at 13.8 percent), but Google's display business is growing faster.[97] Google also had more cash than Facebook had revenue, and Facebook's free cash flow is actually negative. This can be blamed on the cost to build data centers to support services users get for free (e.g., storage costs for the upwards of 300 million photos uploaded to Facebook each day).[98] Table 8.1 shows a comparison of Facebook and Google at comparable stages.

TABLE 8.1 Comparing Facebook and Google at Comparable Periods in Time

	Facebook (5 years)	Pre-IPO Facebook (8 years)	Pre-IPO Google (5 years)	Post-IPO Google (8 years)
Revenue	$272 million	$3.7 billion	$1.5 billion	$10.6 billion
Net Income	–$56 million	$1 billion	$106 million	$3.5 billion
Market Cap	-	$104 billion	$23 billion	$150 billion+

Facebook went public as an 8-year-old, while Google went public after five years. Facebook's revenues at IPO were $3.7 billion—about 2.5 times Google's $1.5 billion revenues when it went public. Facebook's $1 billion in profits the year before it went public equate to about ten times Google's pre-IPO annual profit of $106 million. And Facebook's market cap at IPO was about $104 billion, over four times Google's post-IPO value of $23 billion. But the comparison isn't Apples-to-Apples (no pun intended). Roll the clock back and 5-year-old Facebook (roughly the age of Google at IPO) actually lost $56 million on revenues of just $272 million. Google as an 8-year-old brought in $10.6 billion in revenue and $3.5 billion in profits, and it sported a market cap of over $150 billion. The 8-year-old comparison also isn't quite a fair one since capital rose during Google's IPO (and secondary offering where it sold still more stock), helping to fuel the firm's growth over those three years. Still, 8-year-old Google made about as much *profit* as 8-year-old Facebook did in *revenue*. As TechCrunch points out, the five-year compound annual growth rate for each firm's revenue during comparable periods (2002–2006 for Google and 2007–2011 for Facebook) was almost exactly the same: 89 percent a year.

FIGURE 8.4 Revenue of Google and Facebook in Billions of Dollars

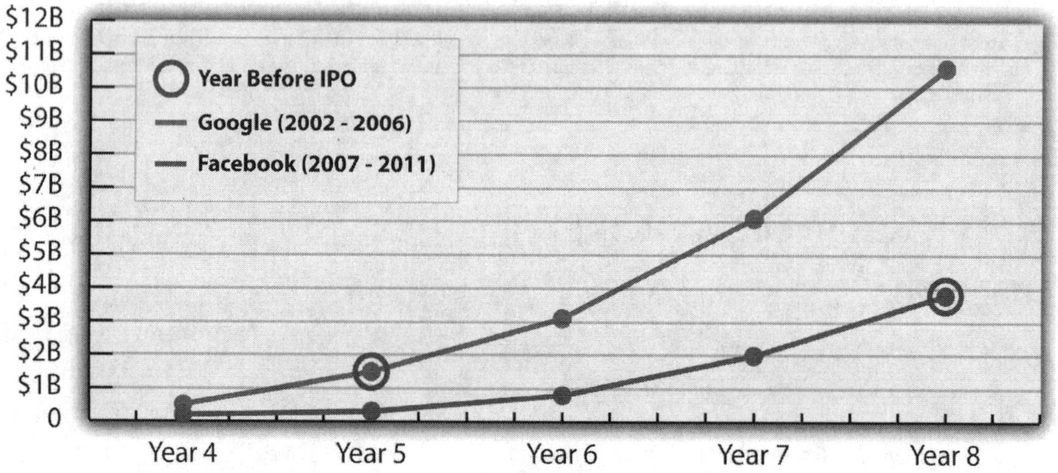

FIGURE 8.5 Revenue per User (2011)

While Facebook has, at times, been the Web's most visited destination, its user base generates far less cash on a per-person basis than many rivals do, including only about one-sixth of Google's per-user figure.[99]

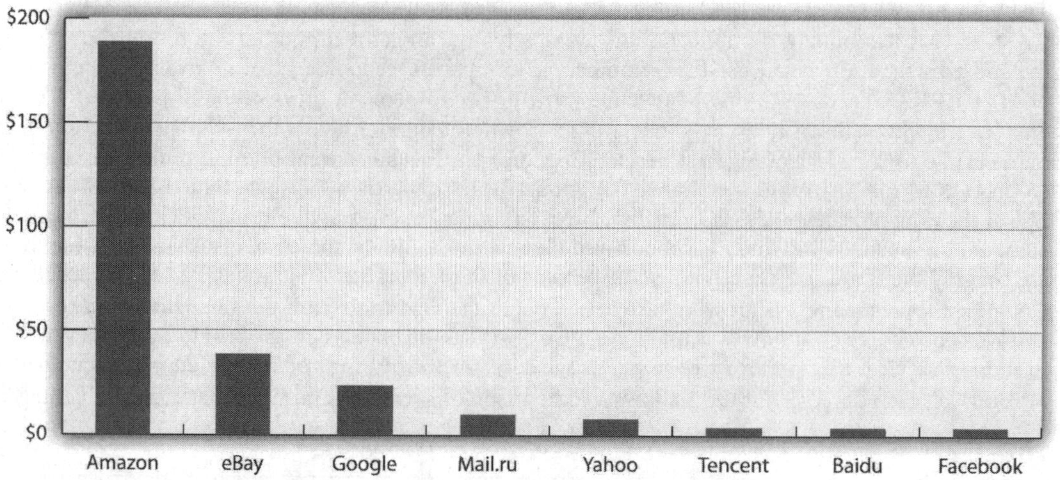

When considering a firm's value, it's also important to realize that just because the market is willing to pay a high price for a firm's stock, it doesn't mean that the firm is actually worth it. A firm's stock price is supposed to reflect the net present value of a firm's future earnings, and unrealistic expectations can distort value. Facebook's stock plummeted following its IPO, losing about a third of its value in a little over two weeks. Much remains to be demonstrated for any high Facebook valuation to hold over the long term. As the chart in Figure 8.5 shows, Facebook still lags well behind many of its rivals in terms of revenue per user; all that time spent on Facebook simply isn't worth as much on a per-user basis as time spent on Google or many other services. Also consider the uncertainty as the firm tries to leverage the social graph. According to Facebook's own research, "an average Facebook user with 500 friends actively follows the news on only forty of them, communicates with twenty, and keeps in close touch with about ten. Those with smaller networks follow even fewer."[100] That might not be enough critical mass to offer real, differentiable value to paying advertisers, and interest in deepening connections among users with "value-shallow" social graphs may in part have motivated Facebook's mishandled attempts to encourage more public data sharing. The advantages of leveraging the friend network hinge on increased sharing and trust, a challenge for a firm that has had so many high-profile privacy stumbles.

Facebook does have a lot of potential in terms of upside earnings. First, Facebook ads run only inside Facebook.com, but Google earns about 30 percent of its revenue from ads it runs on third-party sites (referred to as the Google ad network). Next time you search the web, look for advertisements labeled "Ads by Google." Google serves up these ads and splits the take with Web site operators. If Facebook creates its own ad network, it might be able to offer ad targeting that performs *better* than Google's so-called AdSense product. Google targets ads on other Web sites based largely on keywords found on those sites, also using details it can glean from tracking a person's web browsing history (see Chapter 14 for details). Facebook can do all this, but it could also add in all sorts of data from the dark web that Google can't see: data from a user's social activity, their highly-accurate personal profile, and more. Turning on such an ad network would be simple from a technical perspective. The tough part, however, would be creating an ad network sales force and rolling it out in a way that doesn't cause a privacy debacle or lead to a deluge of scare headlines.

Over a longer term, what about Facebook TV? Facebook almost certainly wants to play a starring role in your living room, making the TV a platform for social activity: video chat, serving targeted ads, social entertainment recommendations, games, and all sorts of commerce. It will be tough to navigate the tensions of bandwidth-capping cable guys, channel owners, and hardware firms keen to build their own platform, but Zuckerberg has Reed Hastings on his board—and as much as the Netflix CEO has been derided following the Qwikster debacle, no one has built a further-reaching platform with consumer electronics firms than Hastings.

Steve Rubel wrote the following on his Micro Persuasion blog: "The Internet amber is littered with fossilized communities that once dominated. These former stalwarts include AOL, Angelfire, theGlobe.com, GeoCities, and Tripod." Network effects and switching cost advantages can be strong, but not necessarily insurmountable if value is seen elsewhere and if an effort becomes more fad than "must have." Time will tell if Facebook's competitive assets and constant innovation are enough to help it avoid the fate of those that have gone before them.

KEY TAKEAWAYS

- Facebook was a profitable and growing company at IPO, and its offering was the largest ever in the technology industry.
- Several metrics suggest that Facebook may have been overvalued at IPO.
- Decelerating growth, lower ARPU than rivals, uncertainty about the ROI of Facebook advertising, and increasing infrastructure costs are all among areas of concern.
- Despite concern, Facebook has significant growth prospects, including the potential to create new products such as a third-party ad network and (longer term) a platform for potentially lucrative social television services.

QUESTIONS AND EXERCISES

1. Circumstances change over time. Research the current state of Facebook's financials—what is the firm's market capitalization? How has the stock performed since IPO? How have revenues performed? What are trends in net income? What are the reasons behind these trends? Do you think that markets are accurate in setting the firm's value at IPO? Why or why not?
2. Do you think Facebook's social graph data is large enough to be leveraged as a source of revenue in ways that are notably different than conventional pay-per-click or CPM-based advertising? Would you be excited about certain possibilities? Creeped out by some? Explain possible scenarios that might work or might fail. Justify your interpretation of these scenarios.
3. So you've had a chance to learn about Facebook, its model, growth, outlook, strategic assets, and competitive environment. How much do you think the firm is worth? Which firms do you think it should compare with in terms of value, influence, and impact? Would you invest in Facebook?
4. Which firms might make good merger partners with Facebook? Would these deals ever go through? Why or why not?

ENDNOTES

1. L. Grossman, "Person of the Year: Mark Zuckerberg," *Time*, December 15, 2010.
2. J. Cassidy, "Facebook: The Ultimate Dot-Com," *New Yorker*, May 16, 2012.
3. L. Sumagaysay, "Facebooking More Than Googling," *Good Morning Silicon Valley*, December 30, 2010.
4. M. Walsh, "Facebook Drives 31% of Display Ads in Q1," *MediaPost*, May 4, 2011.
5. D. Kerr, "Facebook to Inaugurate New Office in Dubai," *CNet*, May 23, 2012.
6. J. Evans, "Can Anything Stop the Facebook Juggernaut?" *TechCrunch*, November 25, 2010.
7. For an insider account of Silicon Valley Web 2.0 start-ups, see Sarah Lacy, *Once You're Lucky, Twice You're Good: The Rebirth of Silicon Valley and the Rise of Web 2.0*. (New York: Gotham Books, 2008).
8. T. McGinn, "Online Facebooks Duel over Tangled Web of Authorship," *Harvard Crimson*, May 28, 2004.
9. C. Hoffman, "The Battle for Facebook," *Rolling Stone*, June 26, 2008, 9.
10. C. Hoffman, "The Battle for Facebook," *Rolling Stone*, June 26, 2008.
11. S. Rosenbush, "Facebook's on the Block," *BusinessWeek*, March 28, 2006.
12. While Microsoft had cut deals to run banner ads worldwide, Facebook dropped banner ads for poor performance in early 2010; see C. McCarthy, "More Social, Please: Facebook Nixes Banner Ads," *CNET*, February 5, 2010.
13. B. Morrissey, "Murdoch: Facebook Is 'Flavor of the Month,'" *Media Week*, June 20, 2008.
14. C. Hoffman, "The Battle for Facebook," *Rolling Stone*, June 26, 2008.
15. L. Grossman, "Person of the Year: Mark Zuckerberg," *Time*, December 15, 2010.
16. J. Pepitone, "Facebook Trading Sets Record IPO Volume," *Fortune*, May 18, 2012.
17. S. Denning, "Is Google's Share-Split Evil?" *Forbes*, April 13, 2012.
18. M. Yglesias, "All Hail, Emperor Zuckerberg," *Slate*, Feb. 3, 2012.
19. B. Stone, "Why Facebook Needs Sheryl Sandberg," *BusinessWeek*, May 16, 2011.
20. J. Kincaid, "Facebook Users Uploaded a Record 750 Million Photos over New Year's," *TechCrunch*, January 3, 2011.
21. F. Vogelstein, "Mark Zuckerberg: The Wired Interview," *Wired*, June 29, 2009.
22. P. Sawers, "Facebook Drives 10 Times More Video Shares Than Twitter as Online TV Viewing Rises Sharply," *The Next Web*, Febraury 15, 2012.
23. L. Segall, "Video Apps Battle to be the Next Instagram," *CNN Money*, May 11, 2012
24. M. Helft, "Facebook Offers New Messaging Tool," *New York Times*, November 15, 2010.
25. D. Lyons, "Digg This: A Cautionary Tale for Web 2.0 Companies," *Newsweek*, October 24, 2010; M. Arrington, "Yahoo Sells Delicious to YouTube Founders," *TechCrunch*, April 27, 2011.
26. S. Kessler, "For Top News Sites, Facebook Drives More Traffic Than Twitter," *Mashable*, May 9, 2011.
27. J. Kincaid, "What Is This Mysterious Facebook Music App?" *TechCrunch*, February 2, 2010; R. Maher, "Facebook's New Payment System Off to Great Start, Could Boost Revenue by $250 Million in 2010," *TBI Research*, February 1, 2010.
28. C. Taylor, "Instagram Passes 50 Million Users, Adds Five Million a Week," *Mashable*, May 1, 2012.
29. N. Carlson, "Here's the Chart that Scared Zuckerberg Into Spending $1 Billion on Instagram," *BusinessInsider*, April 14, 2012; and K. Teare, "It's Not About Instagram—It's About Mobile," *TechCrunch*, April 18, 2012.
30. R. Metz, "With New Look, Bing Gets More Organized, Social," *Technology Review*, May 10, 2012.
31. J. Evans, "Can Anything Stop the Facebook Juggernaut?" *TechCrunch*, November 25, 2010.
32. A. Zeichick, "How Facebook Works," *Technology Review*, July/August 2008; J. Packzkowski, "Superpoke! Facebook Chooses N.C. for $450M Data Center," *AllThingsD*, November 11, 2010: T. Simonite, "Facebook Opens Up Its Hardware Secrets," *Technology Review*, April 7, 2011.
33. S. Gaudin, "Facebook Rolls Out Storage System to Wrangle Massive Photo Stores," *Computerworld*, April 1, 2009, http://www.computerworld.com/s/article/9130959/Facebook_rolls_out_storage_system_to_wrangle_massive_photo_stores.
34. A. Zeichick, "How Facebook Works," *Technology Review*, July/August 2008.
35. S. Ante, "Facebook: Friends with Money," *BusinessWeek*, May 9, 2008.
36. A. Arrington, "Facebook Completes Rollout of Haystack to Stem Losses from Massive Photo Uploads," *TechCrunch*, April 6, 2009.
37. T. Simonite, "Facebook Opens Up Its Hardware Secrets," *Technology Review*, April 7, 2011.
38. A. Iskold, "Social Graph: Concepts and Issues," *ReadWriteWeb*, September 12, 2007.
39. A. Zeichick, "How Facebook Works," *Technology Review*, July/August 2008.
40. B. Urstadt, "The Business of Social Networks," *Technology Review*, July/August 2008.
41. F. Vogelstein, "How Mark Zuckerberg Turned Facebook into the Web's Hottest Platform," *Wired*, September 6, 2007.
42. J. Guynn, "A Software Industry @ Facebook," *Los Angeles Times*, September 10, 2007.
43. D. MacMillan, "Zynga Enlarges Its War Chest," *BusinessWeek*, December 17, 2009.
44. D. MacMillan, P. Burrows, and S. Ante, "Inside the App Economy," *BusinessWeek*, November 2, 2009.
45. B. Barnes and C. Cain Miller, "Disney Buys Playdom in $763 Million Deal, Becoming Hollywood Leader in Social Games," *New York Times*, July 27, 2010.
46. J. Guynn, "A Software Industry @ Facebook," *Los Angeles Times*, September 10, 2007.
47. M. Helft, "The Class That Built Apps, and Fortunes," *New York Times*, May 7, 2011.
48. H. Timmons, "Online Scrabble Craze Leaves Game Sellers at Loss for Words," *New York Times*, March 2, 2008.
49. J. Cheng, "Facebook Punishes App Developers Found Selling User Data," *ArsTechnica*, November 1, 2010.
50. M. Arrington, "Zynga Takes Steps to Remove Scams from Games," *TechCrunch*, November 2, 2009.
51. D. Takahashi, "Internet Ads Finally Surpass Newspapers," *VentureBeat*, April 14, 2011.
52. "Everywhere and Nowhere," *Economist*, March 19, 2008.
53. J. Muller, "GM Says Facebook Ads Don't Work, Pulls $10 Million Ad Account," *Forbes*, May 15, 2012.
54. B. Stone, "Facebook Aims to Extends Its Reach across Web," *New York Times*, December 1, 2008.
55. R. Stross, "Advertisers Face Hurdles on Social Networking Sites," *New York Times*, December 14, 2008.
56. B. Urstadt, "The Business of Social Networks," *Technology Review*, July/August 2008. Rates quoted in this piece seem high, but a large discrepancy between site rates holds across reported data.
57. C. McCarthy, "More Social, Please: Facebook Nixes Banner Ads," *CNET*, February 5, 2010.
58. B. Urstadt, "The Business of Social Networks," *Technology Review*, July/August 2008; J. Hempel, "Finding Cracks in Facebook," *Fortune*, May 13, 2008; and E. Schonfeld, "Are Facebook Ads Going to Zero? Lookery Lowers Its Guarantee to 7.5-cent CMPs," *TechCrunch*, July 22, 2008.
59. Q. Hardy, "Facebook Thinks Outside Boxes," *Forbes*, May 28, 2008.
60. S. Sandberg, "Sheryl Sandberg on Facebook's Future," *BusinessWeek*, April 8, 2009.
61. E. Wong, "Ben & Jerry's, Sunkist, Indy Jones Unwrap Facebook's 'Gift of Gab,'" *Brandweek*, June 1, 2008.
62. Eric is a former student of mine. His story has been covered by many publications, including J. Zappe, "MBA Grad Seeks Job with Microsoft; Posts Ad on Facebook," *ERE.net*, May 27, 2009; G. Sentementes, "'Hire Me' Nation: Using the Web & Social Media to Get a Job," *Baltimore Sun*, July 15, 2009; and E. Liebert, *Facebook Fairytales* (New York: Skyhorse, 2010).
63. M. Cowan, "Marketers Struggle to Get Social," *Reuters*, June 19, 2008, http://www.reuters.com/news/video?videoId=84894.
64. Facebook Press Room, Statistics, April 29, 2010, http://www.facebook.com/press/info.php?statistics.
65. R. Stross, "Advertisers Face Hurdles on Social Networking Sites," *New York Times*, December 14, 2008.
66. H. Blodget, "Well, Now that Everyone Has Sobered Up, Let's Figure Out What Facebook is Actually Worth…" *Business Insider*, May 21, 2012.
67. Eric is a former student of mine. His story has been covered by many publications, including J. Zappe, "MBA Grad Seeks Job with Microsoft; Posts Ad on Facebook," *ERE.net*, May 27, 2009; G. Sentementes, "'Hire Me' Nation: Using the Web & Social Media to Get a Job," *Baltimore Sun*, July 15, 2009; and E. Liebert, *Facebook Fairytales* (New York: Skyhorse, 2010).
68. M. D'Onofrio, "Social Networking Sites Using New Advertising," *BrandingIron*, November 18, 2010.
69. B. Stone, "Why Facebook Needs Sheryl Sandberg," *BusinessWeek*, May 16, 2011.
70. M. Walsh, "Facebook Drives 31% of Display Ads in Q1," *MediaPost*, May 4, 2011.
71. P. Kafka, "Facebook Isn't Eating Google's Lunch Yet, but It's Getting Hungry…," *AllThingsD*, March 13, 2011.
72. V. Kumar, J. Andrew Petersen, and Robert Leone, "How Valuable Is Word of Mouth?" *Harvard Business Review* 85, no. 10 (October 2007): 139—46.
73. E. Nakashima, "Feeling Betrayed, Facebook Users Force Site to Honor Their Privacy," *Washington Post*, November 30, 2007.
74. E. Nakashima, "Feeling Betrayed, Facebook Users Force Site to Honor Their Privacy," *Washington Post*, November 30, 2007.
75. C. McCarthy, "Facebook's Zuckerberg: 'We Simply Did a Bad Job' Handling Beacon," *CNET*, December 5, 2007.
76. J. Brodkin, "Facebook Shuts Down Beacon Program, Donates $9.5 Million to Settle Lawsuit," *NetworkWorld*, December 8, 2009.
77. V. Grigoriadis, "Do You Own Facebook? Or Does Facebook Own You?" *New York*, April 5, 2009.
78. J. Smith, "Facebook TOS Voting Concludes, Users Vote for New Revised Documents," *Inside Facebook*, April 23, 2009.

79. L. Gannes, "Facebook Settles with the FTC for 20 Years of Privacy Audits," *AllThingsD*, November 29, 2011.

80. J. Brodkin, "Facebook Shuts Down Beacon Program, Donates $9.5 Million to Settle Lawsuit," *NetworkWorld*, December 8, 2009; and N. Devore, "Facebook Moves Beyond the "Like" Button, Introduces New Verbs to Timeline," *OBI*, "Jan. 25, 2012.

81. J. Valentino-DeVries, "Facebook CEO Zuckerberg on Plans to Dominate the Web," *Wall Street Journal*, April 21, 2010.

82. *Zacks Equity Research*, "EA's Command and Conquer MMO Goes Live," May 25, 2012; and M. Walsh, "Virtual Goods Sales Hit $2.3 Billion in 2011," *Online Media Daily*, Feb. 29, 2012.

83. J. Kincaid, "Facebook to Make 'Facebook Credits' Mandatory for Game Developers (Confirmed)," *TechCrunch*, January 24, 2011.

84. J. Kincaid, "A Look at the Future of Facebook Credits," *TechCrunch*, April 21, 2010.

85. C. McCarthy, "Facebook to Developers: Get Ready for Credits," *CNET*, February 25, 2010.

86. M. Ingram, "Facebook's Two Deal Weapons: The Social Graph and Credits," *GigaOM*, April 26, 2011.

87. C. Nuttall, "Facebook Credits Bank of the Web," *Financial Times*, April 23, 2010.

88. F. Lardinois, "Is It Time for Facebook to Make Opt-In the Default?" *Read Write Web*, April 27, 2010.

89. F. Lardinois, "Is It Time for Facebook to Make Opt-In the Default?" *Read Write Web*, April 27, 2010.

90. F. Manjoo, "Does Privacy on Facebook, Google, and Twitter Even Matter?" *Fast Company*, May 1, 2010.

91. F. Manjoo, "Does Privacy on Facebook, Google, and Twitter Even Matter?" *Fast Company*, May 1, 2010.

92. F. Vogelstein, "The Great Wall of Facebook," *Wired*, July 2009.

93. B. Stone and M. Helft, "In Developing Countries, Web Grows without Profit," *New York Times*, April 27, 2009.

94. L. Horn, "Facebook's Mark Zuckerberg Visits China's Top Search Engine," *PC Magazine*, December 20, 2010.

95. B. Stone, "Why Facebook Needs Sheryl Sandberg," *BusinessWeek*, May 16, 2011.

96. H. Blodget, "Well, Now that Everyone Has Sobered Up, Let's Figure Out What Facebook is Actually Worth…" *Business Insider*, May 21, 2012.

97. C. Boulton, "Google to Pass Facebook in Display Ads in 2013," *eWeek*, February 26, 2012.

98. J. Cassidy, "Facebook: The Ultimate Dot-Com," *New Yorker*, May 16, 2012.

99. J. Yarrow, "Here's How Much a Unique Visitor Is Worth," *BusinessInsider*, January 5, 2011.

100. S. Baker, "Learning and Profiting from Online Friendships," *BusinessWeek*, May 21, 2009.

CHAPTER 9

Understanding Software: A Primer for Managers

1. INTRODUCTION

LEARNING OBJECTIVES

1. **Recognize the importance of software and its implications for the firm and strategic decision making.**
2. **Understand that software is everywhere; not just in computers, but also cell phones, cars, cameras, and many other technologies.**
3. **Know what software is and be able to differentiate it from hardware.**
4. **List the major classifications of software and give examples of each.**

We know **computing hardware** is getting faster and cheaper, creating all sorts of exciting and disruptive opportunities for the savvy manager. But what's really going on inside the box? It's **software** that makes the magic of computing happen. Without software, your PC would be a heap of silicon wrapped in wires encased in plastic and metal. But it's the instructions—the software code—that enable a computer to do something wonderful, driving the limitless possibilities of information technology.

Software is everywhere. An inexpensive cell phone has about one million lines of code.[1] Ford automobiles actually have more lines of code than Twitter and Facebook combined.[2] In this chapter we'll take a peek inside the chips to understand what software is. A lot of terms are associated with software: operating systems, applications, enterprise software, distributed systems, and more. We'll define these terms up front, and put them in a managerial context. A follow-up chapter, Chapter 10, will focus on changes impacting the software business, including open source software, software as a service (SaaS), and cloud computing. These changes are creating an environment radically different from the software industry that existed in prior decades—confronting managers with a whole new set of opportunities and challenges.

Managers who understand software can better understand the possibilities and impact of technology. They can make better decisions regarding the strategic value of IT and the potential for technology-driven savings. They can appreciate the challenges, costs, security vulnerabilities, legal and compliance issues, and limitations involved in developing and deploying technology solutions. In the next two chapters we will closely examine the software industry and discuss trends, developments and economics—all of which influence decisions managers make about products to select, firms to partner with, and firms to invest in.

computer hardware

The physical components of information technology, which can include the computer itself plus peripherals such as storage devices, input devices like the mouse and keyboard, output devices like monitors and printers, networking equipment, and so on.

software

A computer program or a collection of programs. It is a precise set of instructions that tells hardware what to do.

1.1 What Is Software?

When we refer to computer hardware (sometimes just hardware), we're talking about the physical components of information technology—the equipment that you can physically touch, including computers, storage devices, networking equipment, and other peripherals.

Software refers to a computer program or collection of programs—sets of instructions that tell the hardware what to do. Software gets your computer to behave like a Web browser or word processor, makes your iPod play music and video, and enables your bank's ATM to spit out cash.

It's when we start to talk about the categories of software that most people's eyes glaze over. To most folks, software is a big, incomprehensible alphabet soup of acronyms and geeky phrases: OS, VB, SAP, SQL, to name just a few.

operating system

The software that controls the computer hardware and establishes standards for developing and executing applications.

applications

Includes desktop applications, enterprise software, utilities, and other programs that perform specific tasks for users and organizations.

Don't be intimidated. The basics are actually pretty easy to understand. But it's not soup; it's more of a layer cake. Think about computer hardware as being at the bottom of the layer cake. The next layer is the **operating system**, the collection of programs that control the hardware. Windows, Mac OS X, iOS, and Linux are operating systems. On top of that layer are **applications**—a range of which include end-user programs like those in Office, apps that run on smartphones, and the complex set of programs that manage a business's inventory, payroll, and accounting. At the top of the cake are users.

FIGURE 9.1 The Hardware/Software Layer Cake

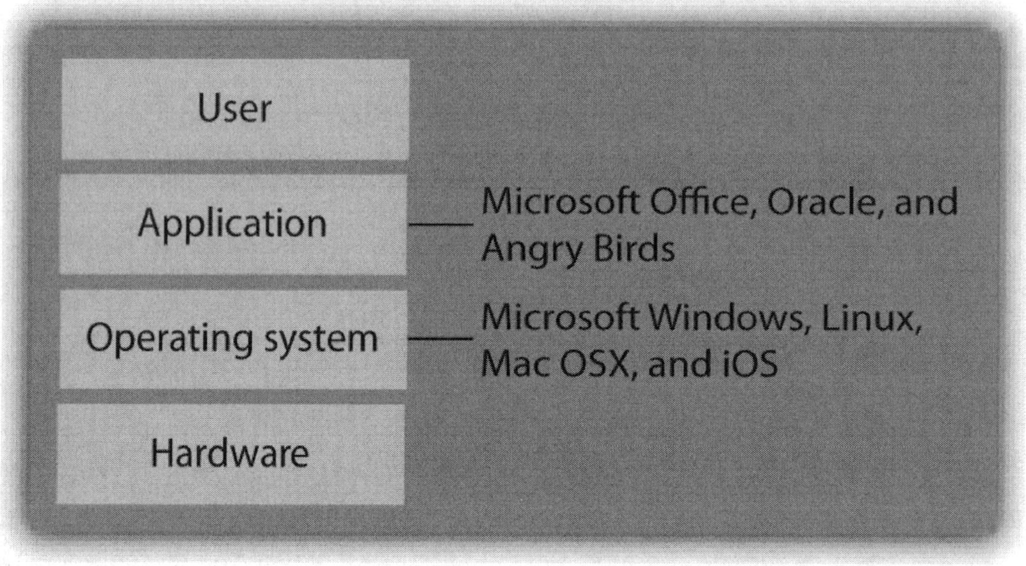

The flexibility of these layers gives computers the customization options that managers and businesses demand. Understanding how the layers relate to each other helps you make better decisions on what options are important to your unique business needs, can influence what you buy, and may have implications for everything from competitiveness to cost overruns to security breaches. What follows is a manager's guide to the main software categories with an emphasis on why each is important.

KEY TAKEAWAYS

- Software refers to a computer program or collection of programs. It enables computing devices to perform tasks.
- You can think of software as being part of a layer cake, with hardware at the bottom; the operating system controlling the hardware and establishing standards, the applications executing one layer up, and the users at the top.
- How these layers relate to one another has managerial implications in many areas, including the flexibility in meeting business demand, costs, legal issues and security.
- Software is everywhere—not just in computers, but also in cell phones, cars, cameras, and many other technologies.

QUESTIONS AND EXERCISES

1. Explain the difference between hardware and software.
2. Why should a manager care about software and how software works? What critical organizational and competitive factors can software influence?
3. What role has software played in your decision to select certain products? Has this influenced why you favored one product or service over another?
4. Find the *Fortune* 500 list online. Which firm is the highest ranked software firm? While the *Fortune* 500 ranks firms according to revenue, what's this firm's profitability rank? What does this discrepancy tell you about the economics of software development? Why is the software business so attractive to entrepreneurs?
5. Refer to earlier chapters (and particularly to Chapter 2): Which resources for competitive advantage might top software firms be able to leverage to ensure their continued dominance? Give examples of firms that have leveraged these assets, and why they are so strong.

2. OPERATING SYSTEMS

LEARNING OBJECTIVES

1. **Understand what an operating system is and why computing devices require operating systems.**
2. **Appreciate how embedded systems extend Moore's Law, allowing firms to create "smarter" products and services**

Computing hardware needs to be controlled, and that's the role of the operating system. The operating system (sometimes called the "OS") provides a common set of controls for managing computer hardware, making it easier for users to interact with computers and for programmers to write application software. Just about every computing device has an operating system—desktops and laptops, enterprise-class server computers, your mobile phone. Even specialty devices like iPods, video game consoles, and television set top boxes run some form of OS.

Some firms, like Apple and Nintendo, develop their own proprietary OS for their own hardware. Microsoft sells operating systems to everyone from Dell to the ATM manufacturer Diebold (listen for the familiar Windows error beep on some cash machines). And there are a host of specialty firms, such as Wind River (purchased by Intel), that help firms develop operating systems for all sorts of devices that don't necessarily look like a PC, including cars, video editing systems, and fighter jet control panels.

Anyone who has used both a PC and a Mac and has noticed differences across these platforms can get a sense of the breadth of what an operating system does. Even for programs that are otherwise identical for these two systems (like the Firefox browser), subtitle differences are visible. Screen elements like menus, scroll bars, and window borders look different on the Mac than they do in Windows. So do the dialogue boxes that show up when you print or save.

These items look and behave differently because each of these functions touches the hardware, and the team that developed Microsoft Windows created a system distinctly different from their Macintosh counterparts at Apple. Graphical **user interface (UI)** items like scroll bars and menus are displayed on the hardware of the computer display. Files are saved to the hardware of a hard drive or other storage device. Most operating systems also include control panels, desktop file management, and other support programs to work directly with hardware elements like storage devices, displays, printers, and networking equipment. The Macintosh Finder and the Windows Explorer are examples of components of these operating systems. The consistent look, feel, and functionality that operating systems enforce across various programs help make it easier for users to learn new software, which reduces training costs and operator error. See Figure 9.2 for similarities and differences.

user interface (UI)

The mechanism through which users interact with a computing device. The UI includes elements of the graphical user interface (or GUI, pronounced *"gooey"*), such as windows, scroll bars, buttons, menus, and dialogue boxes; and can also include other forms of interaction, such as touch screens, motion sensing controllers, or tactile devices used by the visually impaired.

FIGURE 9.2

Differences between the Windows and Mac operating systems are evident throughout the user interface, particularly when a program interacts with hardware.

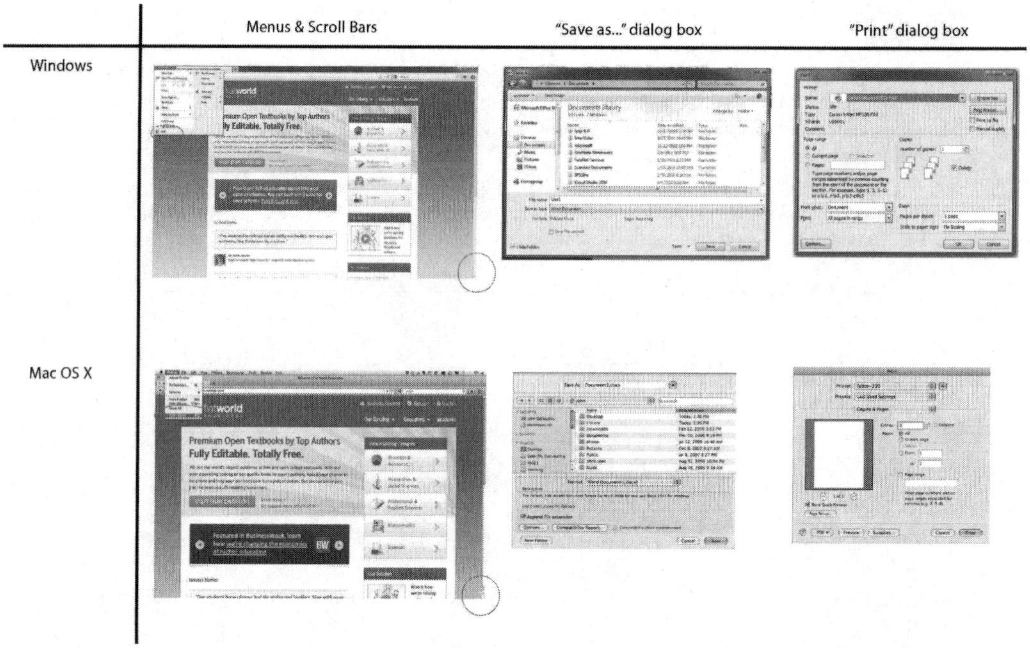

Operating systems are also designed to give programmers a common set of commands to consistently interact with the hardware. These commands make a programmer's job easier by reducing program complexity and making it faster to write software while minimizing the possibility of errors in code. Consider what an OS does for the Wii game developer. Nintendo's Wii OS provides Wii programmers with a set of common standards to use to access the Wiimote, play sounds, draw graphics, save files, and more. Without this, games would be a lot more difficult to write, they'd likely look differently, be less reliable, would cost more, and there would be fewer titles available.

Similarly, when Apple provided developers with a common set of robust, easy-to-use standards for the iPhone and (via the App Store) an easy way for users to install these applications on top of the iPhone/iPod touch/iPad's operating system (iOS), software development boomed, and Apple became hands-down the most versatile mobile computing device available.[3] In Apple's case some *fifty thousand apps* became available through the App Store in less than a year. A good OS and software development platform can catalyze network effects (see Chapter 6). While the OS seems geeky, its effective design has very strategic business implications!

FIGURE 9.3 Operating System Market Share for Desktop, Server, and Mobile Phones

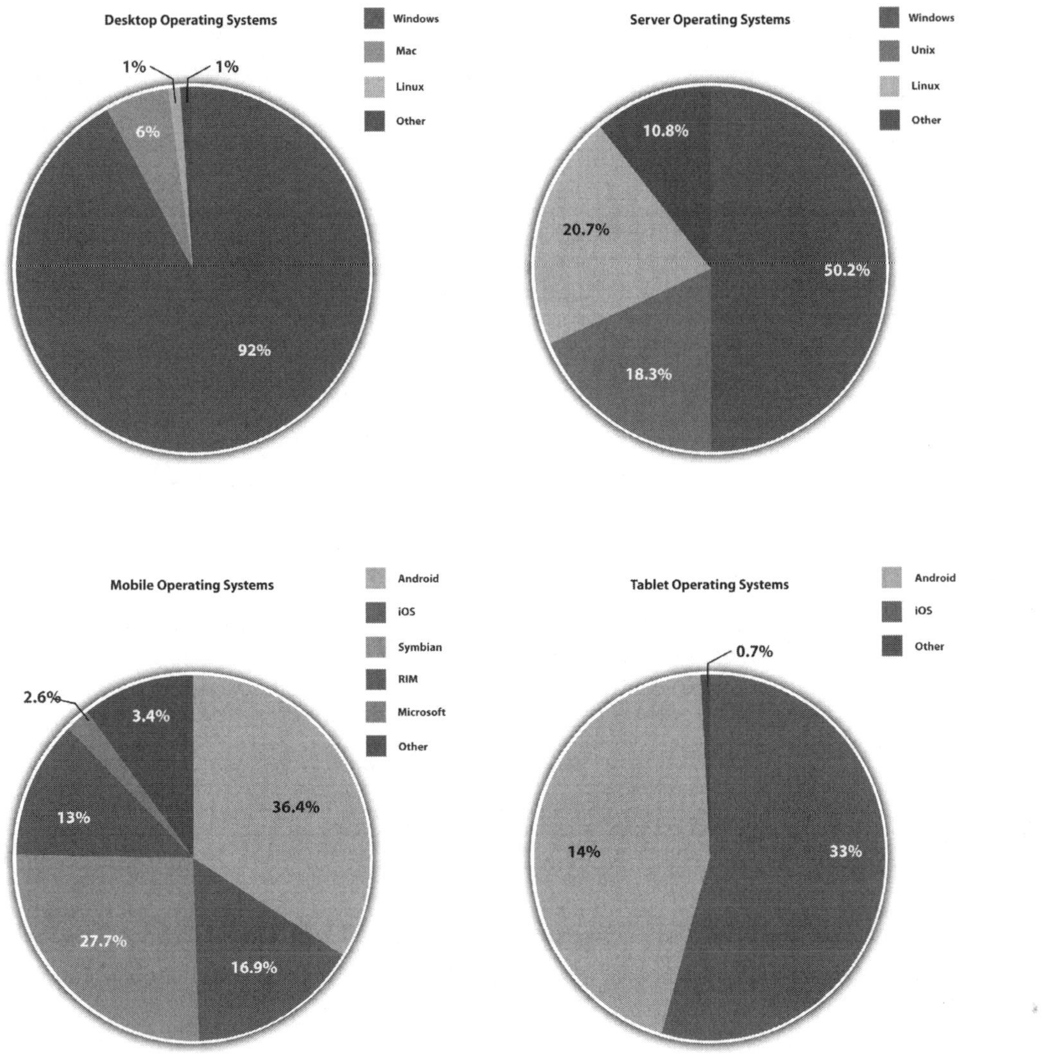

Source: HitsLink (desktop, May 2012), IDC (server, Q1 2012), Gartner (mobile, May 2012), and IDC (March 2012). Note that Android tablet figure includes Kindle Fire.

firmware

Software stored on nonvolatile memory chips (as opposed to being stored on devices such as hard drives or removable discs). Despite the seemingly permanent nature of firmware, many products allow for firmware to be upgraded online or by connecting to another device.

embedded systems

Special-purpose software designed and included inside physical products (often on firmware). Embedded systems help make devices "smarter," sharing usage information, helping diagnose problems, indicating maintenance schedules, providing alerts, or enabling devices to take orders from other systems.

Firmware and Embedded Systems

Most personal computers have an operating system installed on their hard drives. This system allows the OS to be replaced or upgraded easily. But many smaller, special-purpose computing devices have their operating systems installed on nonvolatile memory, often on read-only memory (ROM) chips. Control programs stored on chips are sometimes referred to as **firmware**. The OS in an iPod, mobile phone, or your TV's set-top box is most likely stored as firmware. Your PC also has a tiny bit of firmware that allows it to do very basic functions like start-up (boot) and begin loading its operating system from disk.

Another term you might hear is **embedded systems**. As computing gets cheaper, special-purpose technology is increasingly becoming embedded into all sorts of devices like cars, picture frames, aircraft engines, photocopiers, and heating and air conditioning systems. The software programs that make up embedded systems are often stored as firmware too.

Moore's Law (see Chapter 5) enables embedded systems, and these systems can create real strategic value. The Otis Elevator Company, a division of United Technologies, uses embedded systems in its products to warn its service centers when the firm's elevators, escalators, and moving walkways need maintenance or repair. This warning provides Otis with several key benefits:

1. Since products automatically contact Otis when they need attention, these systems generate a lucrative service business for the firm and make it more difficult for third parties to offer a competing business servicing Otis products.
2. Products contact service technicians to perform maintenance based on exact needs (e.g., lubricant is low, or a part has been used enough to be replaced) rather than guessed schedules, which makes service more cost-effective, products less likely to break down, and customers happier.
3. Any product failures are immediately detected, with embedded systems typically dispatching technicians before a client's phone call.
4. The data is fed back to Otis's R&D group, providing information on reliability and failure so that engineers can use this info to design better products.

Collectively, software embedded on tiny chips yields very big benefits, for years helping Otis remain at the top of its industry.

KEY TAKEAWAYS

- The operating system (OS) controls a computer's hardware and provides a common set of commands for writing programs.
- Most computing devices (enterprise-class server computers, PCs, phones, set-top boxes, video games, cars, the Mars Rover) have an operating system.
- Some products use operating systems provided by commercial firms, while others develop their own operating system. Others may leverage open source alternatives (see Chapter 10).
- Embedded systems are special-purpose computer systems designed to perform one or a few dedicated functions, and are frequently built into conventional products like cars, air conditioners, and elevators.
- Embedded systems can make products and services more efficient, more reliable, more functional, and can enable entire new businesses and create or reinforce resources for competitive advantage.

QUESTIONS AND EXERCISES

1. What does an operating system do? Why do you need an operating system? How do operating systems make a programmer's job easier? How do operating systems make life easier for end users?
2. How has the market for desktop, server, and mobile operating systems changed in recent years? Do certain products seem to be gaining traction? Why do you think this is the case?
3. What kinds of operating systems are used in the devices that you own? On your personal computer? Your mobile phone? The set-top box on top of your television? Are there other operating systems that you come into contact with? If you can't tell which operating system is in each of these devices, see if you can search the Internet to find out.
4. For your list in the prior question (and to the extent that you can), diagram the hardware/software "layer cake" for these devices.
5. For this same list, do you think each device's manufacturer wrote all of the software that you use on these devices? Can you add or modify software to all of these devices? Why or why not? What would the implications be for cost, security, complexity, reliability, updates and upgrades, and the appeal of each device?
6. Some ATM machines use Windows. Why would an ATM manufacturer choose to build its systems owing Windows? Why might it want to avoid this? Are there other non-PC devices you've encountered that were running some form of Windows?
7. What are embedded systems? When might firms want to install software on chips instead of on a hard drive?
8. It's important to understand how technology impacts a firm's strategy and competitive environment. Consider the description of Otis elevator's use of embedded systems. Which parts of the value chain does this impact? How? Consider the "five forces": How does the system impact the firm's competitive environment? Are these systems a source of competitive advantage? If not, explain why not? If they are, what kinds of resources for competitive advantage can these kinds of embedded systems create?
9. Can you think of other firms that can or do leverage embedded systems? Provide examples and list the kinds of benefits these might offer firms and consumers.
10. Research the Americans with Disabilities Act of 1990 (or investigate if your nation has a similar law), and the implications of this legislation for software developers and Web site operators. Have firms been successfully sued when their software or Web sites could not be accessed by users with physical challenges? What sorts of issues should developers consider when making their products more accessible? What practices might they avoid?

3. APPLICATION SOFTWARE

LEARNING OBJECTIVES

1. **Appreciate the difference between desktop and enterprise software.**
2. **List the categories of enterprise software.**
3. **Understand what an ERP (enterprise resource planning) software package is.**
4. **Recognize the relationship of the DBMS (database system) to the other enterprise software systems.**
5. **Recognize both the risks and rewards of installing packaged enterprise systems.**

Operating systems are designed to create a **platform** so that programmers can write additional applications, allowing the computer to do even more useful things. While operating systems control the hardware, *application software* (sometimes referred to as *software applications*, *applications*, or even just *apps*) perform the work that users and firms are directly interested in accomplishing. Think of applications as the place where the users or organization's real work gets done. As we learned in Chapter 6, the more application software that is available for a platform (the more games for a video game console, the more apps for your phone), the more valuable it potentially becomes.

platform

Products and services that allow for the development and integration of software products and other complementary goods. Windows, the iPhone, the Wii, and the standards that allow users to create Facebook apps are all platforms.

desktop software

Applications installed on a personal computer, typically supporting tasks performed by a single user.

enterprise software

Applications that address the needs of multiple users throughout an organization or work group.

software package

A software product offered commercially by a third party.

enterprise resource planning (ERP)

A software package that integrates the many functions (accounting, finance, inventory management, human resources, etc.) of a business.

Desktop software refers to applications installed on a personal computer—your browser, your Office suite (e.g., word processor, spreadsheet, presentation software), photo editors, and computer games are all desktop software. **Enterprise software** refers to applications that address the needs of multiple, simultaneous users in an organization or work group. Most companies run various forms of enterprise software programs to keep track of their inventory, record sales, manage payments to suppliers, cut employee paychecks, and handle other functions.

Some firms write their own enterprise software from scratch, but this can be time consuming and costly. Since many firms have similar procedures for accounting, finance, inventory management, and human resource functions, it often makes sense to buy a **software package** (a software product offered commercially by a third party) to support some of these functions. So-called **enterprise resource planning (ERP)** software packages serve precisely this purpose. In the way that Microsoft can sell you a suite of desktop software programs that work together, many companies sell ERP software that coordinates and integrates many of the functions of a business. The leading ERP vendors include the firm's SAP and Oracle, although there are many firms that sell ERP software. A company doesn't have to install all of the modules of an ERP suite, but it might add functions over time—for example, to plug in an accounting program that is able to read data from the firm's previously installed inventory management system. And although a bit more of a challenge to integrate, a firm can also mix and match components, linking software the firm has written with modules purchased from different enterprise software vendors.

FIGURE 9.4 ERP in Action[4]

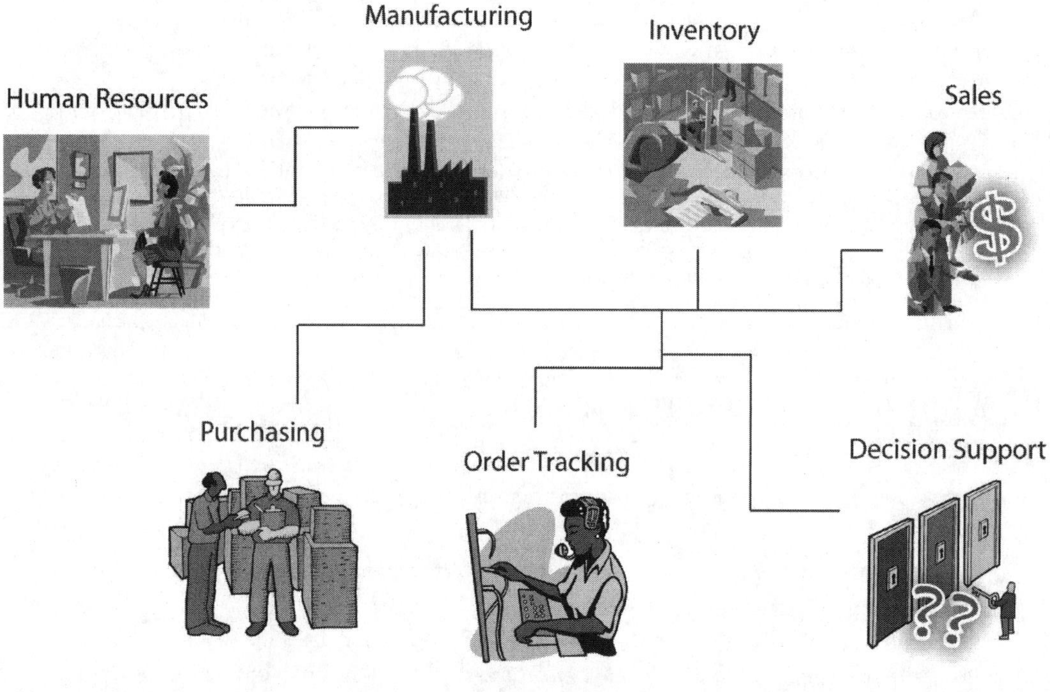

An ERP system with multiple modules installed can touch many functions of the business:

- *Sales*—A sales rep from Vermont-based SnowboardCo. takes an order for five thousand boards from a French sporting goods chain. The system can verify credit history, apply discounts, calculate price (in euros), and print the order in French.
- *Inventory*—While the sales rep is on the phone with his French customer, the system immediately checks product availability, signaling that one thousand boards are ready to be shipped from the firm's Burlington warehouse, the other four thousand need to be manufactured and can be delivered in two weeks from the firm's manufacturing facility in Guangzhou.
- *Manufacturing*—When the customer confirms the order, the system notifies the Guangzhou factory to ramp up production for the model ordered.
- *Human Resources*—High demand across this week's orders triggers a notice to the Guangzhou hiring manager, notifying her that the firm's products are a hit and that the flood of orders coming in globally mean her factory will have to hire more workers to keep up.

- *Purchasing*—The system keeps track of raw material inventories, too. New orders trigger an automatic order with SnowboardCo.'s suppliers, so that raw materials are on hand to meet demand.
- *Order Tracking*—The French customer can log in to track her SnowboardCo. order. The system shows her other products that are available, using this as an opportunity to cross-sell additional products.
- *Decision Support*—Management sees the firm's European business is booming and plans a marketing blitz for the continent, targeting board models and styles that seem to sell better for the Alps crowd than in the U.S. market.

Other categories of enterprise software that managers are likely to encounter include the following:

- **customer relationship management (CRM)** systems used to support customer-related sales and marketing activities
- **supply chain management (SCM)** systems that can help a firm manage aspects of its value chain, from the flow of raw materials into the firm through delivery of finished products and services at the point-of-consumption
- **business intelligence (BI) systems**, which use data created by other systems to provide reporting and analysis for organizational decision making

Major ERP vendors are now providing products that extend into these and other categories of enterprise application software, as well.

Most enterprise software works in conjunction with a **database management system (DBMS)**, sometimes referred to as a "database system." The database system stores and retrieves the data that an application creates and uses. Think of this as another additional layer in our cake analogy. Although the DBMS is itself considered an application, it's often useful to think of a firm's database systems as sitting above the operating system, but under the enterprise applications. Many ERP systems and enterprise software programs are configured to share the same database system so that an organization's different programs can use a common, shared set of data. This system can be hugely valuable for a company's efficiency. For example, this could allow a separate set of programs that manage an inventory and point-of-sale system to update a single set of data that tells how many products a firm has to sell and how many it has already sold—information that would also be used by the firm's accounting and finance systems to create reports showing the firm's sales and profits.

Firms that don't have common database systems with consistent formats across their enterprise often struggle to efficiently manage their value chain. Common procedures and data formats created by packaged ERP systems and other categories of enterprise software also make it easier for firms to use software to coordinate programs between organizations. This coordination can lead to even more value chain efficiencies. Sell a product? Deduct it from your inventory. When inventory levels get too low, have your computer systems send a message to your supplier's systems so that they can automatically build and ship replacement product to your firm. In many cases these messages are sent without any human interaction, reducing time and errors. And common database systems also facilitate the use of BI systems that provide critical operational and competitive knowledge and empower decision making. For more on CRM and BI systems, and the empowering role of data, see Chapter 11.

customer relationship management (CRM)

Systems used to support customer-related sales and marketing activities.

supply chain management (SCM)

Systems that can help a firm manage aspects of its value chain, from the flow of raw materials into the firm, through delivery of finished products and services at the point-of-consumption.

business intelligence (BI) systems

Systems that use data created by other systems to provide reporting and analysis for organizational decision making.

database management system (DBMS)

Sometimes referred to as database software; software for creating, maintaining, and manipulating data.

FIGURE 9.5

An organization's database management system can be set up to work with several applications both within and outside the firm.

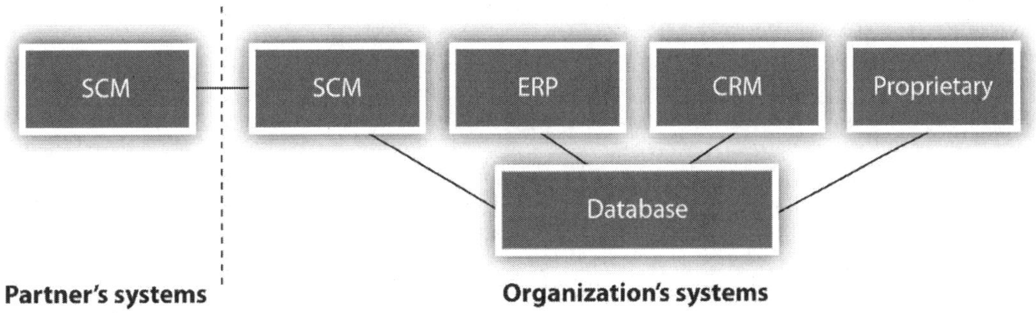

The Rewards and Risks of Packaged Enterprise Systems

When set up properly, enterprise systems can save millions of dollars and turbocharge organizations. For example, the CIO of office equipment maker Steelcase credited the firm's ERP with an eighty-million-dollar reduction in operating expenses saved from eliminating redundant processes and making data more usable. The CIO of Colgate Palmolive also praised their ERP, saying, "The day we turned the switch on, we dropped two days out of our order-to-delivery cycle."[5] Packaged enterprise systems can streamline processes, make data more usable, and ease the linking of systems with software across the firm and with key business partners. Plus, the software that makes up these systems is often debugged, tested, and documented with an industrial rigor that may be difficult to match with proprietary software developed in-house.

But for all the promise of packaged solutions for standard business functions, enterprise software installations have proven difficult. Standardizing business processes in software that others can buy means that those functions are easy for competitors to match, and the vision of a single monolithic system that delivers up wondrous efficiencies has been difficult for many to achieve. The average large company spends roughly $15 million on ERP software, with some installations running into the hundreds of millions of dollars.[6] And many of these efforts have failed disastrously.

FoxMeyer was once a six-billion-dollar drug distributor, but a failed ERP installation led to a series of losses that bankrupted the firm. The collapse was so rapid and so complete that just a year after launching the system, the carcass of what remained of the firm was sold to a rival for less than $80 million. Hershey Foods blamed a $466 million revenue shortfall on glitches in the firm's ERP rollout. Among the problems, the botched implementation prevented the candy maker from getting product to stores during the critical period before Halloween. Nike's first SCM and ERP implementation was labeled a "disaster"; their systems were blamed for over $100 million in lost sales.[7] Even tech firms aren't immune to software implementation blunders. HP once blamed a $160 million loss on problems with its ERP systems.[8] Manager beware—there are no silver bullets. For insight on the causes of massive software failures, and methods to improve the likelihood of success, see Section 6.

KEY TAKEAWAYS

- Application software focuses on the work of a user or an organization.
- Desktop applications are typically designed for a single user. Enterprise software supports multiple users in an organization or work group.
- Popular categories of enterprise software include ERP (enterprise resource planning), SCM (supply chain management), CRM (customer relationship management), and BI (business intelligence) software, among many others.
- These systems are used in conjunction with database management systems, programs that help firms organize, store, retrieve, and maintain data.
- ERP and other packaged enterprise systems can be challenging and costly to implement, but can help firms create a standard set of procedures and data that can ultimately lower costs and streamline operations.
- The more application software that is available for a platform, the more valuable that platform becomes.
- The DBMS stores and retrieves the data used by the other enterprise applications. Different enterprise systems can be configured to share the same database system in order share common data.
- Firms that don't have common database systems with consistent formats across their enterprise often struggle to efficiently manage their value chain, and often lack the flexibility to introduce new ways of doing business. Firms with common database systems and standards often benefit from increased organizational insight and decision-making capabilities.
- Enterprise systems can cost millions of dollars in software, hardware, development, and consulting fees, and many firms have failed when attempting large-scale enterprise system integration. Simply buying a system does not guarantee its effective deployment and use.
- When set up properly, enterprise systems can save millions of dollars and turbocharge organizations by streamlining processes, making data more usable, and easing the linking of systems with software across the firm and with key business partners.

QUESTIONS AND EXERCISES

1. What is the difference between desktop and enterprise software?
2. Who are the two leading ERP vendors?
3. List the functions of a business that might be impacted by an ERP.
4. What do the acronyms ERP, CRM, SCM, and BI stand for? Briefly describe what each of these enterprise systems does.
5. Where in the "layer cake" analogy does the DBMS lie.
6. Name two companies that have realized multimillion-dollar benefits as result of installing enterprise systems.
7. Name two companies that have suffered multimillion-dollar disasters as result of failed enterprise system installations.
8. How much does the average large company spend annually on ERP software?

4. DISTRIBUTED COMPUTING

LEARNING OBJECTIVES

1. **Understand the concept of distributed computing and its benefits.**
2. **Understand the client-server model of distributed computing.**
3. **Know what Web services are and the benefits that Web services bring to firms.**
4. **Appreciate the importance of messaging standards and understand how sending messages between machines can speed processes, cut costs, reduce errors, and enable new ways of doing business.**

When computers in different locations can communicate with one another, this is often referred to as **distributed computing**. Distributed computing can yield enormous efficiencies in speed, error reduction, and cost savings and can create entirely new ways of doing business. Designing systems architecture for distributed systems involves many advanced technical topics. Rather than provide an exhaustive decomposition of distributed computing, the examples that follow are meant to help managers understand the bigger ideas behind some of the terms that they are likely to encounter.

distributed computing

A form of computing where systems in different locations communicate and collaborate to complete a task.

Let's start with the term **server**. This is a tricky one because it's frequently used in two ways: (1) in a hardware context a server is a computer that has been configured to support requests from other computers (e.g., Dell sells servers) and (2) in a software context a server is a program that fulfills requests (e.g., the Apache open source Web server). Most of the time, server *software* resides on server-class *hardware*, but you can also set up a PC, laptop, or other small computer to run server software, albeit less powerfully. And you can use mainframe or super-computer-class machines as servers, too. Also note that many firms chose not to own some of their applications or any of their own server hardware at all. Instead, they pay third-party firms to host their software "in the cloud." This option is particularly attractive for smaller firms that can't or don't want to invest in the expense and expertise associated with owning and operating hardware, for firms looking for extra computing capacity, and for firms that want public servers (e.g., Web sites) to be in fast, reliable locations outside of a company's own private network.

server

A program that fulfills the requests of a client.

The World Wide Web, like many other distributed computing services, is what geeks call a *client-server* system. Client-server refers to two pieces of software, a **client** that makes a request, and a server that receives and attempts to fulfill the request. In our WWW scenario, the client is the browser (e.g., Internet Explorer, Chrome, Firefox, Safari). When you type a Web site's address into the location field of your browser, you're telling the client to "go find the Web server software at the address provided, and tell the server to return the Web site requested."

client

A software program that makes requests of a server program.

application server

Software that houses and serves business logic for use (and reuse) by multiple applications.

Web services

Small pieces of code that are accessed via the application server which permit interoperable machine-to-machine interaction over a network.

It is possible to link simple scripting languages to a Web server for performing calculations, accessing databases, or customizing Web sites. But more advanced distributed environments may use a category of software called an **application server**. The application server (or app server) houses business logic for a distributed system. Individual **Web services** served up by the app server are programmed to perform different tasks: returning a calculation ("sales tax for your order will be $11.58"), accessing a database program ("here are the results you searched for"), or even making a request to another server in another organization ("Visa, please verify this customer's credit card number for me").

FIGURE 9.6

In this multitiered distributed system, client browsers on various machines (desktop, laptop, mobile) access the system through the Web server. The cash register doesn't use a Web browser, so instead the cash register logic is programmed to directly access the services it needs from the app server. Web services accessed from the app server may be asked to do a variety of functions, including perform calculations, access corporate databases, or even make requests from servers at other firms (for example, to verify a customer's credit card).

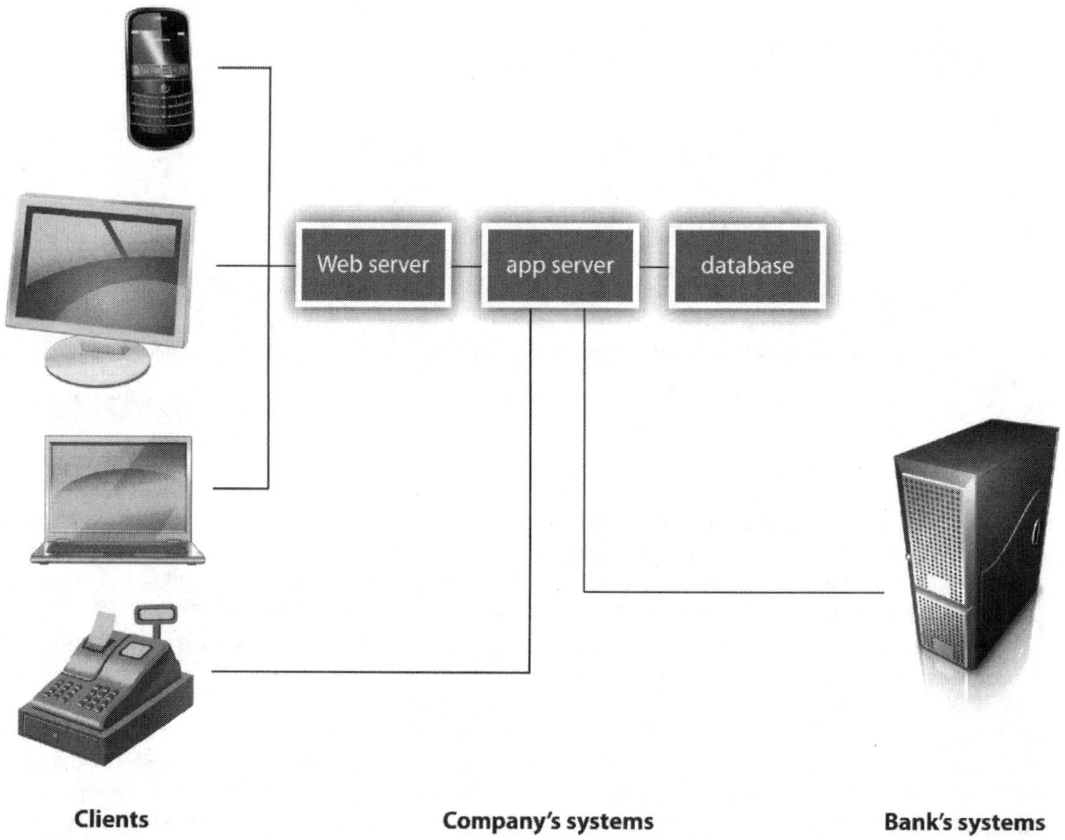

application programming interfaces (APIs)

Programming hooks, or guidelines, published by firms that tell other programs how to get a service to perform a task such as send or receive data. For example, Amazon.com provides APIs to let developers write their own applications and Websites that can send the firm orders.

Those little chunks of code that are accessed via the application server are sometimes referred to as Web services. The World Wide Web consortium defines *Web services* as software systems designed to support interoperable machine-to-machine interaction over a network.[9] And when computers can talk together (instead of people), this often results in fewer errors, time savings, cost reductions, and can even create whole new ways of doing business! Each Web service defines the standard method for other programs to request it to perform a task and defines the kind of response the calling client can expect back. These standards are referred to as **application programming interfaces (APIs)**.

Look at the advantages that Web services bring a firm like Amazon. Using Web services, the firm can allow the same order entry logic to be used by Web browsers, mobile phone applications, or even by third parties who want to access Amazon product information and place orders with the firm (there's an incentive to funnel sales to Amazon—the firm will give you a cut of any sales that you send Amazon's way). Google offers many APIs, including hooks that other developers use to leverage Google Maps. And Facebook and Twitter have APIs that, among other things, allow programmers to write apps that can post status updates and tweets. Organizations that have created a robust set of Web services around their processes and procedures are said to have a **service-oriented architecture (SOA)**. Organizing systems like this, with separate applications in charge of client presentation, business logic, and database, makes systems more flexible. Code can be reused, and each layer can be separately maintained, upgraded, or migrated to new hardware—all with little impact on the others.

service-oriented architecture (SOA)

A robust set of Web services built around an organizations processes and procedures.

Web services sound geeky, but here's a concrete example illustrating their power. Southwest Airlines had a Web site where customers could book flights, but many customers also wanted to rent a car or book a hotel, too. To keep customers on Southwest.com, the firm and its hotel and rental car partners created a set of Web services and shared the APIs. Now customers visiting Southwest.com can book a hotel stay and rental car on the same page where they make their flight reservation. This process transforms Southwest.com into a full service travel destination and allows the site to compete head-to-head with the likes of Expedia, Travelocity, and Orbitz.[10]

Think about why Web services are important from a strategic perspective. By adding hotel and rental car services, Southwest is now able to eliminate the travel agent, along with any fees they might share with the agent. This shortcut allows the firm to capture more profits or pass on savings to customers, securing its position as the first place customers go for low-cost travel. And perhaps most importantly, Southwest can capture key data from visitor travel searches and bookings (something it likely couldn't do if customers went to a site like Expedia or Travelocity). Data is a hugely valuable asset, and this kind of customer data can be used by Southwest to send out custom e-mail messages and other marketing campaigns to bring customers back to the airline. As geeky as they might at first seem, Web services can be very strategic!

FIGURE 9.7

Southwest.com uses Web services to allow car rental and hotel firms to book services through Southwest. This process transforms Southwest.com into a full-service online travel agent.

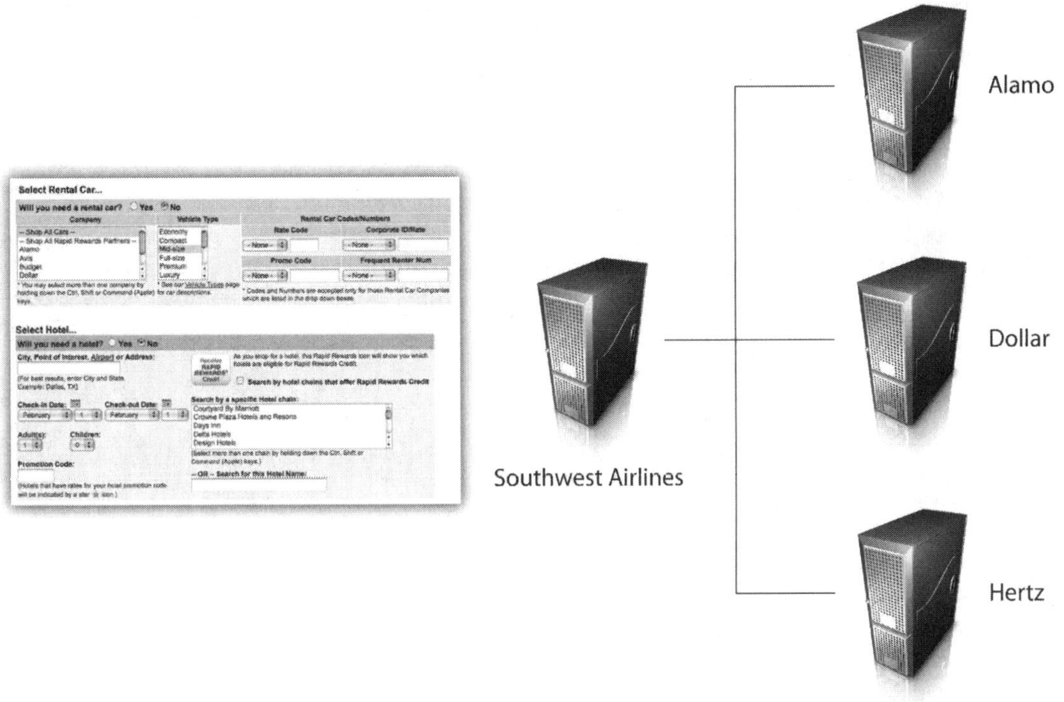

4.1 Formats to Facilitate Sharing Data

EDI (electronic data interchange)

A set of standards for exchanging messages containing formatted data between computer applications.

extensible markup language (XML)

A tagging language that can be used to identify data fields made available for use by other applications. Most APIs and Web services send messages where the data exchanged is wrapped in identifying XML tags.

Two additional terms you might hear within the context of distributed computing are EDI and XML. **EDI (electronic data interchange)** is a set of standards for exchanging information between computer applications. EDI is most often used as a way to send the electronic equivalent of structured documents between different organizations. Using EDI, each element in the electronic document, such as a firm name, address, or customer number, is coded so that it can be recognized by the receiving computer program. Eliminating paper documents makes businesses faster and lowers data entry and error costs. One study showed that firms that used EDI decreased their error rates by 82 percent, and their cost of producing each document fell by up to 96 percent.[11]

EDI is a very old standard, with roots stretching back to the 1948 Berlin Air Lift. While still in use, a new generation of more-flexible technologies for specifying data standards are taking its place. Chief among the technologies replacing EDI is **extensible markup language (XML)**. XML has lots of uses, but in the context of distributed systems, it allows software developers to create a set of standards for common data elements that, like EDI messages, can be sent between different kinds of computers, different applications, and different organizations. XML is often thought of as easier to code than EDI, and it's more robust because it can be extended—organizations can create formats to represent any kind of data (e.g., a common part number, photos, the complaint field collected by customer support personnel). In fact, most messages sent between Web services are coded in XML (the technology is a key enabler in mash-ups, discussed in Chapter 7). Many computer programs also use XML as a way to export and import data in a common format that can be used regardless of the kind of computer hardware, operating system, or application program used. And if you design Web sites, you might encounter XML as part of the coding behind the cascading style sheets (CSS) that help maintain a consistent look and feel to the various Web pages in a given Web site.

Rearden Commerce: A Business Built on Web Services

Web services, APIs, and open standards not only transform businesses, they can create entire new firms that change how we get things done. For a look at the mashed-up, integrated, hyperautomated possibilities that Web services make possible, check out Rearden Commerce, a Foster City, California, firm that is using this technology to become what AMR's Chief Research Office referred to as "Travelocity on Steroids."

Using Rearden, firms can offer their busy employees a sort of Web-based concierge/personal assistant. Rearden offers firms a one-stop shop where employees can not only make the flight, car, and hotel bookings they might do from a travel agent, they can also book dinner reservations, sports and theatre tickets, and arrange for business services like conference calls and package shipping. Rearden doesn't supply the goods and services it sells. Instead it acts as the middleman between transactions. A set of open APIs to its Web services allows Rearden's one hundred and sixty thousand suppliers to send product and service data to Rearden, and to receive booking and sales data from the site.

In this ultimate business mash-up, a mobile Rearden user could use her phone to book a flight into a client city, see restaurants within a certain distance of her client's office, have these locations pop up on a Google map, have listings accompanied by Zagat ratings and cuisine type, book restaurant reservations through Open Table, arrange for a car and driver to meet her at her client's office at a specific time, and sync up these reservations with her firm's corporate calendaring systems. If something unexpected comes up, like a flight delay, Rearden will be sure she gets the message. The system will keep track of any cancelled reservation credits, and also records travel reward programs, so Rearden can be used to spend those points in the future.

In order to pull off this effort, the Rearden maestros are not only skilled at technical orchestration, but also in coordinating customer and supplier requirements. As *TechCrunch*'s Erick Schonfeld put it, "The hard part is not only the technology—which is all about integrating an unruly mess of APIs and Web services—[it also involves] signing commercially binding service level agreements with [now over 160,000] merchants across the world." For its efforts, Rearden gets to keep between 6 percent and 25 percent of every nontravel dollar spent, depending on the service. The firm also makes money from subscriptions, and distribution deals.

The firm's first customers were large businesses and included ConAgra, GlaxoSmithKline, and Motorola. Rearden's customers can configure the system around special parameters unique to each firm: to favor a specific airline, benefit from a corporate discount, or to restrict some offerings for approved employees only. Rearden investors include JPMorgan Chase and American Express—both of whom offer Rearden to their employees and customers. Even before the consumer version was available, Rearden had over four thousand corporate customers and two million total users, a user base larger than better-known firms like Salesforce.com.[12] For all the pizzazz we recognize that, as a start-up, the future of Rearden Commerce remains uncertain; however, the firm's effective use of Web services illustrates the business possibilities as technologies allow firms to connect with greater ease and efficiency.

Connectivity has made our systems more productive and enables entire new strategies and business models. But these wonderful benefits come at the price of increased risk. When systems are more interconnected, opportunities for infiltration and abuse also increase. Think of it this way—each "connection" opportunity is like adding another door to a building. The more doors that have to be defended, the more difficult security becomes. It should be no surprise that the rise of the Internet and distributed computing has led to an explosion in security losses by organizations worldwide.

KEY TAKEAWAYS

- Client-server computing is a method of distributed computing where one program (a client) makes a request to be fulfilled by another program (a server).
- Server is a tricky term and is sometimes used to refer to hardware. While server-class hardware refers to more powerful computers designed to support multiple users, just about any PC or notebook can be configured to run server software. Many firms chose to have their server software hosted "in the cloud" on the computers of third-party firms.
- Web servers serve up Web sites and can perform some scripting.
- Most firms serve complex business logic from an application server.
- Isolating a system's logic in three or more layers (presentation or user interface, business logic, and database) can allow a firm flexibility in maintenance, reusability, and in handling upgrades.
- Web services allow different applications to communicate with one another. APIs define the method to call a Web service (e.g., to get it to do something), and the kind of response the calling program can expect back.
- Web services make it easier to link applications as distributed systems, and can make it easier for firms to link their systems across organizations.
- Popular messaging standards include EDI (older) and XML. Sending messages between machines instead of physical documents can speed processes, drastically cut the cost of transactions, and reduce errors.
- Distributed computing can yield enormous efficiencies in speed, error reduction, and cost savings and can create entirely new ways of doing business.
- When computers can communicate with each other (instead of people), this often results in fewer errors, time savings, cost reductions, and can even create whole new ways of doing business.
- Web services, APIs, and open standards not only transform businesses, they can create entire new firms that change how we get things done.

QUESTIONS AND EXERCISES

1. Differentiate the term "server" used in a hardware context, from "server" used in a software context.
2. Describe the "client-server" model of distributed computing. What products that you use would classify as leveraging client-server computing?
3. List the advantages that Web services have brought to Amazon.
4. How has Southwest Airlines utilized Web services to its competitive advantage?
5. What is Rearden Commerce and which technologies does it employ? Describe Rearden Technology's revenue model. Who were Rearden Technology's first customers? Who were among their first investors?
6. What are the security risks associated with connectivity, the Internet, and distributed processing?

5. WRITING SOFTWARE

LEARNING OBJECTIVES

1. Understand, at a managerial level, what programming languages are and how software is developed.
2. Recognize that an operating system and microprocessor constrain the platform upon which most compiled application software will run.
3. Understand what Java is and why it is significant.
4. Know what scripting languages are.

programming language

Provides the standards, syntax, statements, and instructions for writing computer software.

So you've got a great idea that you want to express in software—how do you go about creating a program? Programmers write software in a **programming language**. While each language has its strengths and weaknesses, most commercial software is written in a variant of the C programming language such as C++ (pronounced "see plus plus"), C# (pronounced "see sharp"), or Objective C (popular for iOS app development). Visual Basic (from Microsoft) and Java (from Sun) are also among the more popular of the dozens of programming languages available. Web developers may favor specialty languages like Ruby and Python, while languages like SQL are used in databases.

integrated development environment (IDE)

An application that includes an editor (a sort of programmer's word processor), debugger, and compiler, among other tools.

compile

Step in which program code written in a language that humans can more easily understand, is then converted into a form (expressed in patterns of ones and zeros) that can be understood and executed by a microprocessor. Programmers using conventional programming languages must compile their software before making it available for execution.

Most professional programmers use an **integrated development environment** (IDE) to write their code. The IDE includes a text editor, a debugger for sleuthing out errors, and other useful programming tools. The most popular IDE for Windows is Visual Studio, while Apple offers the Xcode IDE. Most IDEs can support several different programming languages. The IDE will also **compile** a programmer's code, turning the higher-level lines of instructions that are readable by humans into lower-level instructions expressed as the patterns of ones and zeros that are readable by a computer's microprocessor.

FIGURE 9.8

Microsoft's Visual Studio IDE supports desktop, server, mobile, and cloud computing software development.

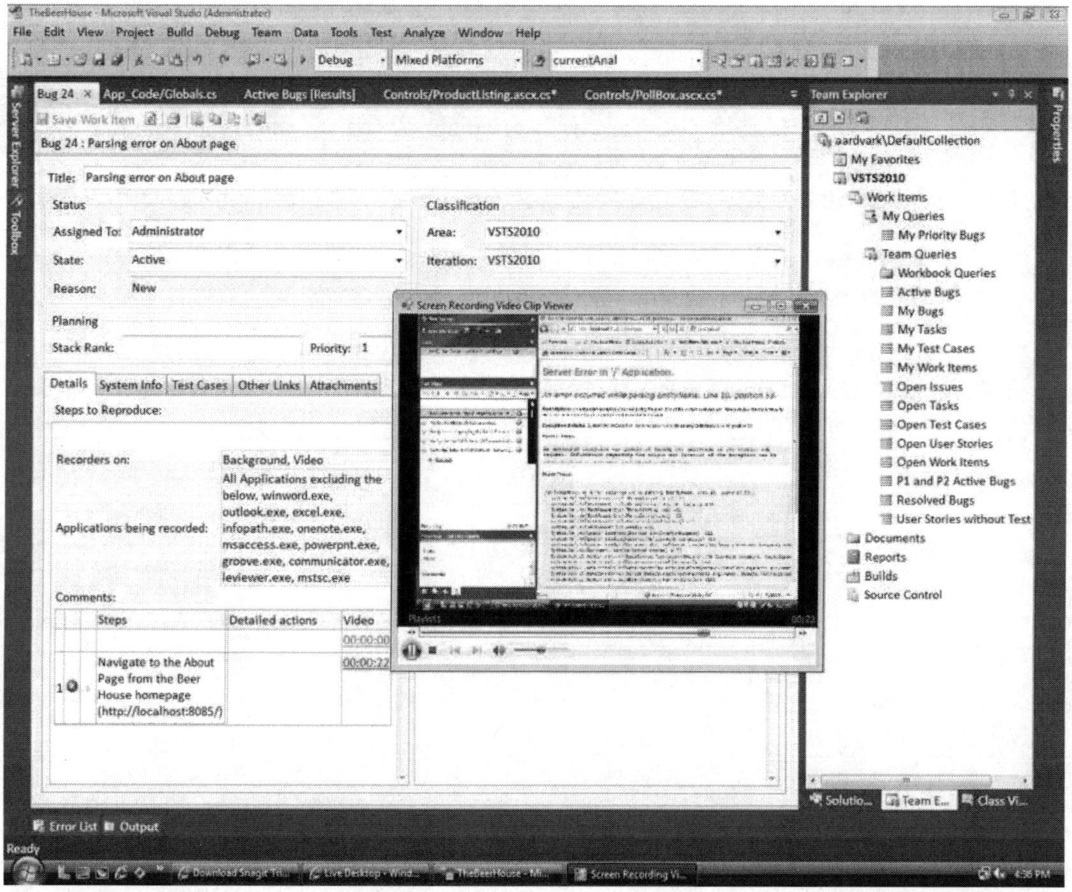

Look at the side of a box of commercial software and you're likely to see system requirements that specify the operating system and processor that the software is designed for (e.g., "this software works on computers with Windows 7 and Intel-compatible processors"). Wouldn't it be great if software could be written once and run everywhere? That's the idea behind **Java**—a programming language developed by Sun Microsystems.

Java programmers don't write code with specific operating system commands (say for Windows, Mac OS X, or Linux), instead they use special Java commands to control their user interface or interact with the display and other hardware. Java programs can run on any computer that has a Java Virtual Machine (JVM), a software layer that interprets Java code so that it can be understood by the operating system and processor of a given computer. Java's platform independence—the ability for developers to "write once, run everywhere"—is its biggest selling point. Many Web sites execute Java applets to run the animation you might see in advertisements or games. Java has also been deployed on over six billion mobile phones worldwide, and is popular among enterprise programmers who want to be sure their programs can scale from smaller hardware up to high-end supercomputers. As long as the machine receiving the Java code has a JVM, then the Java application should run. However, Java has not been popular for desktop applications. Since Java isn't optimized to take advantage of interface elements specific to the Mac or Windows, most Java desktop applications look clunky and unnatural. Java code that runs through the JVM interpreter is also slower than code compiled for the native OS and processor that make up a platform.[13]

Scripting languages are the final category of programming tool that we'll cover. **Scripting languages** typically execute within an application. Microsoft offers a scripting language called VB Script (a derivative of Visual Basic) to automate functions in Office. And most browsers and Web servers support JavaScript, a language that helps make the Web more interactive (despite its name, JavaScript is unrelated to Java). Scripting languages are **interpreted** within their applications, rather than compiled to run directly by a microprocessor. This distinction makes them slower than the kinds of development efforts found in most commercial software. But most scripting languages are usually easy to use, and are often used both by professional programmers and power users.

Java

A programming language, initially developed by Sun Microsystems, designed to provide true platform independence ("write once, run anywhere") for application developers. In most cases, Java apps are developed to be executed by a Java Virtual Machine—an interpreting layer that translates code as it executes, into the format required by the operating system and microprocessor. Without Java, application developers have to write and compile software to execute natively by a specific operating system / microprocessor combination (e.g., Windows/Intel, Linux PowerPC, Mac/Intel, Linux/Intel).

scripting languages

Programming tool that executes within an application. Scripting languages are interpreted within their applications, rather than compiled to run directly by a microprocessor.

interpreted

Languages where each line of written code is converted (by a software program, called an "interpreter") for execution at run-time. Most scripting languages are interpreted languages. Many programmers also write Java applications to be interpreted by the Java Virtual Machine.

KEY TAKEAWAYS

- Programs are often written in a tool called an IDE, an application that includes an editor (a sort of programmer's word processor), debugger, and compiler, among other tools.
- Compiling takes code from the high-level language that humans can understand and converts them into the sets of ones and zeros in patterns representing instructions that microprocessors understand.
- Popular programming languages include C++, C#, Visual Basic, and Java.
- Most software is written for a platform—a combination of an operating system and microprocessor.
- Java is designed to be platform independent. Computers running Java have a separate layer called a Java Virtual Machine that translates (interprets) Java code so that it can be executed on an operating system/processor combination. In theory, Java is "write once, run everywhere," as opposed to conventional applications that are written for an operating system and compiled for an OS/processor combination.
- Java is popular on mobile phones, enterprise computing, and to make Web sites more interactive. Java has never been a successful replacement for desktop applications, largely because user interface differences among the various operating systems are too great to be easily standardized.
- Scripting languages are interpreted languages, such as VB Script or Java Script. Many scripting languages execute within an application (like the Office programs, a Web browser, or to support the functions of a Web server). They are usually easier to program, but are less powerful and execute more slowly than compiled languages.

QUESTIONS AND EXERCISES

1. List popular programming languages.
2. What's an IDE? Why do programmers use IDEs? Name IDEs popular for Windows and Mac users.
3. What is the difference between a compiled programming language and an interpreted programming language?
4. Name one advantage and one disadvantage of scripting languages.
5. In addition to computers, on what other technology has Java been deployed? Why do you suppose Java is particularly attractive for these kinds of applications?
6. What's a JVM? Why do you need it?
7. What if a programmer wrote perfect Java code, but there was a bug on the JVM installed on a given computer? What might happen?
8. Why would developers choose to write applications in Java? Why might they skip Java and choose another programming language?
9. Why isn't Java popular for desktop applications?
10. Go to http://www.java.com. Click on "Do I have Java?" Is Java running on your computer? Which version?

6. UNDERSTANDING TECHNOLOGY BEYOND THE PRICE TAG: TOTAL COST OF OWNERSHIP (TCO) AND THE COST OF TECH FAILURE

LEARNING OBJECTIVES

1. **List the different cost categories that comprise total cost of ownership.**
2. **Understand that once a system is implemented, the costs of maintaining and supporting the system continue.**
3. **List the reasons that technology development projects fail and the measures that can be taken to increase the probability of success.**

Managers should recognize that there are a whole host of costs that are associated with creating and supporting an organization's information systems. Of course, there are programming costs for custom software as well as purchase, configuration, and licensing costs for packaged software, but there's much, much more.

There are costs associated with design and documentation (both for programmers and for users). There are also testing costs. New programs should be tested thoroughly across the various types of hardware the firm uses, and in conjunction with existing software and systems, *before* being deployed throughout the organization. Any errors that aren't caught can slow down a business or lead to costly mistakes that could ripple throughout an organization and its partners. Studies have shown that errors not caught before deployment could be one hundred times more costly to correct than if they were detected and corrected beforehand.[14]

Once a system is "turned on," the work doesn't end there. Firms need to constantly engage in a host of activities to support the system that may also include the following:

compliance

Ensuring that an organization's systems operate within required legal constraints, and industry and organizational obligations

- providing training and end user support
- collecting and relaying comments for system improvements
- auditing systems to ensure compliance (i.e., that the system operates within the firm's legal constraints and industry obligations)
- providing regular backup of critical data
- planning for redundancy and disaster recovery in case of an outage
- vigilantly managing the moving target of computer security issues

With so much to do, it's no wonder that firms spend 70 to 80 percent of their information systems (IS) budgets just to keep their systems running.[15] The price tag and complexity of these tasks can push some managers to think of technology as being a cost sink rather than a strategic resource. These tasks are often collectively referred to as the **total cost of ownership (TCO)** of an information system. Understanding TCO is critical when making technology investment decisions. TCO is also a major driving force behind the massive tech industry changes discussed in Chapter 10.

total cost of ownership (TCO)

All of the costs associated with the design, development, testing, implementation, documentation, training and maintenance of a software system.

6.1 Why Do Technology Projects Fail?

Even though information systems represent the largest portion of capital spending at most firms, an astonishing one in three technology development projects fail to be successfully deployed.[16] Imagine if a firm lost its investment in one out of every three land purchases, or when building one in three factories. These statistics are dismal! Writing in *IEEE Spectrum*, risk consultant Robert Charette provides a sobering assessment of the cost of software failures, stating, "The yearly tab for failed and troubled software conservatively runs somewhere from $60 to $70 billion in the United States alone. For that money, you could launch the space shuttle one hundred times, build and deploy the entire 24-satellite Global Positioning System, and develop the Boeing 777 from scratch—and still have a few billion left over."[17]

Why such a bad track record? Sometimes technology itself is to blame, other times it's a failure to test systems adequately, and sometimes it's a breakdown of process and procedures used to set specifications and manage projects. In one example, a multimillion-dollar loss on the NASA Mars Observer was traced back to a laughably simple oversight—Lockheed Martin contractors using English measurements, while the folks at NASA used the metric system.[18] Yes, a $125 million taxpayer investment was lost because a bunch of rocket scientists failed to pay attention to third grade math. When it comes to the success or failure of technical projects, the devil really is in the details.

Projects rarely fail for just one reason. Project post-mortems often point to a combination of technical, project management, and business decision blunders. The most common factors include the following:[19]

- Unrealistic or unclear project goals
- Poor project leadership and weak executive commitment
- Inaccurate estimates of needed resources
- Badly defined system requirements and allowing "feature creep" during development
- Poor reporting of the project's status
- Poor communication among customers, developers, and users
- Use of immature technology
- Unmanaged risks
- Inability to handle the project's complexity
- Sloppy development and testing practices
- Poor project management
- Stakeholder politics
- Commercial pressures (e.g., leaving inadequate time or encouraging corner-cutting)

Managers need to understand the complexity involved in their technology investments, and that achieving success rarely lies with the strength of the technology alone.

But there is hope. Information systems organizations can work to implement procedures to improve the overall quality of their development practices. Mechanisms for quality improvement include **capability maturity model integration (CMMI)**, which gauge an organization's process maturity and capability in areas critical to developing and deploying technology projects, and provides a carefully chosen set of best practices and guidelines to assist quality and process improvement.[20]

capability maturity model integration (CMMI)

A process-improvement approach (useful for but not limited to software engineering projects) that can assist in assessing the maturity, quality, and development of certain organizational business processes, and suggest steps for their improvement.

Firms are also well served to leverage established project planning and software development methodologies that outline critical businesses processes and stages when executing large-scale software development projects. The idea behind these methodologies is straightforward—why reinvent the wheel when there is an opportunity to learn from and follow blueprints used by those who have executed successful efforts. When methodologies are applied to projects that are framed with clear business goals and business metrics, and that engage committed executive leadership, success rates can improve dramatically.[21]

While software development methodologies are the topic of more advanced technology courses, the savvy manager knows enough to inquire about the development methodologies and quality programs used to support large scale development projects, and can use these investigations as further input when evaluating whether those overseeing large scale efforts have what it takes to get the job done.

KEY TAKEAWAYS

- The care and feeding of information systems can be complex and expensive. The total cost of ownership of systems can include software development and documentation, or the purchase price and ongoing license and support fees, plus configuration, testing, deployment, maintenance, support, training, compliance auditing, security, backup, and provisions for disaster recovery. These costs are collectively referred to as TCO, or a system's total cost of ownership.
- Information systems development projects fail at a startlingly high rate. Failure reasons can stem from any combination of technical, process, and managerial decisions.
- IS organizations can leverage software development methodologies to improve their systems development procedures, and firms can strive to improve the overall level of procedures used in the organization through models like CMMI. However, it's also critical to engage committed executive leadership in projects, and to frame projects using business metrics and outcomes to improve the chance of success.
- System errors that aren't caught before deployment can slow down a business or lead to costly mistakes that could ripple throughout an organization. Studies have shown that errors not caught before deployment could be 100 times more costly to correct than if they were detected and corrected beforehand.
- Firms spend 70 to 80 percent of their IS budgets just to keep their systems running.
- IS organizations can employ project planning and software development methodologies to implement procedures to improve the overall quality of their development practices.

QUESTIONS AND EXERCISES

1. List the types of total ownership costs associated with creating and supporting an organization's information systems.
2. On average, what percent of firms' IS budgets is spent to keep their systems running?
3. What are the possible effects of not detecting and fixing major system errors before deployment?
4. List some of the reasons for the failure of technology development projects.
5. What is the estimated yearly cost of failed technology development projects?
6. What was the reason attributed to the failure of the NASA Mars Observer project?
7. What is capability maturity model integration (CMMI) and how is it used to improve the overall quality of a firm's development practices?
8. Perform an Internet search for "IBM Rational Portfolio Manager." How might IBM's Rational Portfolio Manager software help companies realize more benefit from their IT systems development project expenditures? What competing versions of this product offered by other organizations?

ENDNOTES

1. R. Charette, "Why Software Fails," *IEEE Spectrum*, September 2005.
2. S. Lacy, "Is Atlassian the Next Big Enterprise Software IPO?" *Pando Daily*, February 22, 2012.
3. The iPhone and iPod touch OS is derived from Apple's Mac OS X operating system.
4. Adapted from G. Edmondson, "Silicon Valley on the Rhine," *BusinessWeek International*, November 3, 1997.
5. A. Robinson and D. Dilts, "OR and ERP," *ORMS Today*, June 1999.
6. C. Rettig, "The Trouble with Enterprise Software," *MIT Sloan Management Review* 49, no. 1 (2007): 21–27.
7. C. Koch, "Nike Rebounds: How (and Why) Nike Recovered from Its Supply Chain Disaster," *CIO*, June 15, 2004.
8. R. Charette, "Why Software Fails," *IEEE Spectrum*, September 2005.
9. W3C, "Web Services Architecture," *W3C Working Group Note*, February 11, 2004.
10. J. McCarthy, "The Standards Body Politic," *InfoWorld*, May 17, 2002.
11. "Petroleum Industry Continues to Explore EDI," *National Petroleum News* 90, no. 12 (November 1998).
12. M. Arrington, "Rearden Commerce: Time for the Adults to Come In and Clean House," *TechCrunch*, April 5, 2007; E. Schonfeld, "At Rearden Commerce, Addiction Is Job One," *TechCrunch*, May 6, 2008; and M. Arrington, "2008: Rearden Commerce Has a Heck of a Year," *TechCrunch*, January 13, 2009.
13. Some offerings have attempted to overcome the speed issues associated with interpreting Java code. Just-in-time compilation stores code in native processor-executable form after each segment is initially interpreted, further helping to speed execution. Other environments allow for Java to be compiled ahead of time so that it can be directly executed by a microprocessor. However, this process eliminates code portability—Java's key selling point. And developers preparing their code for the JVM actually precompile code into something called Java bytecode, a format that's less human friendly but more quickly interpreted by JVM software.
14. R. Charette, "Why Software Fails," *IEEE Spectrum*, September 2005.
15. C. Rettig, "The Trouble with Enterprise Software," *MIT Sloan Management Review* 49, no. 1 (2007): 21—27.
16. L. Dignan, "Survey: One in 3 IT Projects Fail; Management OK with It," *ZDNet*, December 11, 2007.
17. R. Charette, "Why Software Fails," *IEEE Spectrum*, September 2005.
18. R. Lloyd, "Metric Mishap Caused Loss of NASA Orbiter," *CNN*, September 20, 1999.
19. List largely based on R. Charette, "Why Software Fails," *IEEE Spectrum*, September 2005.
20. R. Kay, "QuickStudy: Capability Maturity Model Integration (CMMI)," *Computerworld*, January 24, 2005; and Carnegie Mellon Software Engineering Institute, *Welcome to CMMI*, 2009, http://www.sei.cmu.edu/cmmi.
21. A. Shenhar and D. Dvir, *Reinventing Project Management: The Diamond Approach to Successful Growth and Innovation* (Boston: Harvard Business School Press, 2007).

CHAPTER 10

Software in Flux: Partly Cloudy and Sometimes Free

1. INTRODUCTION

LEARNING OBJECTIVES

1. **Understand how low marginal costs, network effects, and switching costs have combined to help create a huge and important industry.**
2. **Recognize that the software industry is undergoing significant and broadly impactful change brought about by several increasingly adopted technologies including open source software, cloud computing, and software as a service.**

For many, software has been a magnificent business. It is the two-hundred-billion-dollar-per-year juggernaut[1] that placed Microsoft's Bill Gates and Oracle's Larry Ellison among the wealthiest people in the world. Once a successful software product has been written, the economics for a category-leading offering are among the best you'll find in any industry. Unlike physical products assembled from raw materials, the **marginal cost** to produce an additional copy of a software product is effectively zero. Just duplicate, no additional input required. That quality leads to businesses that can gush cash. Microsoft generates one and a half billion dollars a month from Windows and Office alone.[2] Network effects and switching cost can also offer a leading software firm a degree of customer preference and lock in that can establish a firm as a standard, and in many cases creates winner-take-all (or at least winner-take-most) markets.

marginal cost

The cost of producing one more unit of a product.

But as great as the business has been, the fundamental model powering the software industry is under assault. **Open source software (OSS)** offerings—free alternatives where anyone can look at and potentially modify a program's code—pose a direct challenge to the assets and advantages cultivated by market leaders. Giants shudder—"How can we compete with free," while others wonder, "How can we make money and fuel innovation on free?" And if free software wasn't enough of a shock, the way firms and users think about software is also changing. A set of services referred to as **cloud computing** is making it more common for a firm to move software out of its own IS shop so that it is run on someone else's hardware. In one variant of this approach known as **software as a service (SaaS)**, users access a *vendor's software* over the Internet, usually by simply starting up a Web browser. With SaaS, you don't need to own the program or install it on your own computer. Hardware clouds can let firms take *their software* and run it on someone else's hardware—freeing them from the burden of buying, managing, and maintaining the physical computing that programs need. Another software technology called **virtualization** can make a single computer behave like many separate machines. This function helps consolidate computing resources and creates additional savings and efficiencies.

These transitions are important. They mean that smaller firms have access to the kinds of burly, sophisticated computing power than only giants had access to in the past. Start-ups can scale quickly and get up and running with less investment capital. Existing firms can leverage these technologies to reduce costs. Got tech firms in your investment portfolio? Understanding what's at work here can inform decisions you make on which stocks to buy or sell. If you make tech decisions for your firm or make recommendations for others, these trends may point to which firms have strong growth and sustainability ahead, or which may be facing troubled times.

open source software (OSS)

Software that is free and where anyone can look at and potentially modify the code.

cloud computing

Replacing computing resources—either an organization's or individual's hardware or software—with services provided over the Internet.

software as a service (SaaS)

A form of cloud computing where a firm subscribes to a third-party software and receives a service that is delivered online.

virtualization

A type of software that allows a single computer (or cluster of connected computers) to function as if it were several different computers, each running its own operating system and software. Virtualization software underpins most cloud computing efforts, and can make computing more efficient, cost-effective, and scalable.

KEY TAKEAWAYS

- The software business is attractive due to near-zero marginal costs and an opportunity to establish a standard—creating the competitive advantages of network effects and switching costs.
- New trends in the software industry, including open source software (OSS), hardware clouds, software as a service (SaaS), and virtualization are creating challenges and opportunity across tech markets. Understanding the impact of these developments can help a manager make better technology choices and investment decisions.

QUESTIONS AND EXERCISES

1. What major trends, outlined in the section above, are reshaping how we think about software? What industries and firms are potentially impacted by these changes? Why do managers, investors, and technology buyers care about these changes?
2. Which organizations might benefit from these trends? Which might be threatened? Why?
3. What are marginal costs? Are there other industries that have cost economics similar to the software industry?
4. Investigate the revenues and net income of major software players: Microsoft, Google, Oracle, Red Hat, and Salesforce.com. Which firms have higher revenues? Net income? Which have better margins? What do the trends in OSS, SaaS, and cloud computing suggest for these and similar firms?
5. How might the rise of OSS, SaaS, and cloud computing impact hardware sales? How might it impact entrepreneurship and smaller businesses?

2. OPEN SOURCE

LEARNING OBJECTIVES

1. **Define open source software and understand how it differs from conventional offerings.**
2. **Provide examples of open source software and how firms might leverage this technology.**

Who would have thought a twenty-one-year-old from Finland could start a revolution that continues to threaten the Microsoft Windows empire? But Linus Torvalds did just that. During a marathon six-month coding session, Torvalds created the first version of Linux[3] marshalling open source revolutionaries like no one before him. Instead of selling his operating system, Torvalds gave it away. Now morphed and modified into scores of versions by hundreds of programmers, **Linux** can be found just about everywhere, and most folks credit Linux as being the most significant product in the OSS arsenal. Today Linux powers everything from cell phones to stock exchanges, set top boxes to supercomputers. You'll find the OS on 16 to 30 percent of the servers in corporate America (depending on how you slice the numbers),[4] on about one in four smartphones,[5] and supporting most Web servers (including those at Google, Amazon, and Facebook). Linux forms the core of the TiVo operating system, it underpins Google's Android and Chrome OS offerings, and it has even gone interplanetary. Linux has been used to power the Phoenix Lander and to control the Spirit and Opportunity Mars rovers.[6] Yes, Linux is even on Mars!

Linux

An open source software operating system.

How Do You Pronounce Linux?

Most English speakers in the know pronounce Linux in a way that rhymes with *"cynics."* You can easily search online to hear video and audio clips of Linus (whose name is actually pronounced "Lean-us" in Finish) pronouncing the name of his OS. In deference to Linux, some geeks prefer something that sounds more like *"lean-ooks."*[7] Just don't call it *"line-ucks,"* or the tech-savvy will think you're an open source **n00b**! Oh yeah, and while we're on the topic of operating system pronunciation, the Macintosh operating system OS X is pronounced "oh es ten."

Tux, the Linux Mascot

n00b

Written with two zeros, pronounced "newb." Geek-slang (leet speak) derogatory term for an uninformed or unskilled person.

Open source software (OSS) is often described as free. While most OSS can be downloaded for free over the Internet, it's also "free" as in liberated (you may even see the acronym FLOSS for free/libre/open source software). The source code for OSS products is openly shared. Anyone can look at the source code, change it, and even redistribute it, provided the modified software continues to remain open and free.[8] This openness is in stark contrast to the practice of conventional software firms, who treat their intellectual property as closely guarded secrets and who almost never provide the source code for their commercial software products. At times, many software industry execs have been downright hostile toward OSS. The former President of SAP once referred to the open source movement as "socialism," while Microsoft's Steve Balmer has called Linux a "cancer."[9]

But while execs at some firms see OSS as a threat undermining the lifeblood of their economic model, other big-name technology companies are now solidly behind the open source movement. The old notion of open source being fueled on the contributions of loners tooling away for the glory of contributing to better code is now largely inaccurate. The vast majority of people who work on efforts like Linux are now paid to do so by commercially motivated employers.[10] Nearly every major hardware firm has paid staff contributing to open source projects, and most firms also work together to fund foundations that set standards and coordinate the release of product revisions and improvements. Such coordination is critical—helping, for example, to ensure that various versions of Linux work alike. Sun Microsystems claims to have eleven thousand engineers contributing to OSS.[11] Guido van Rossum, the inventor of the open source Python programming language, works for Google where he continues to coordinate development. IBM programmers work on several open source projects, including Linux. The firm has even deeded a commercially developed programming tool (including an IDE) to the Eclipse foundation, where it's now embraced and supported by dozens of firms.

LAMP

An acronym standing for **L**inux, the **A**pache Web server software, the **M**ySQL database, and any of several programming languages that start with **P** (e.g., Perl, Python, or PHP).

Turn on the LAMP—It's Free!

Open source is big on the Web. In fact, you'll often hear Web programmers and open source advocates refer to the LAMP stack. **LAMP** is an acronym that stands for the Linux operating system, the Apache Web server software, the MySQL database, and any of several programming languages that start with the letter "P"—Perl, Python, and PHP. From Facebook to YouTube, you'll find LAMP software powering many of the sites you visit each day.

KEY TAKEAWAYS

- OSS is not only available for free, but also makes source code available for review and modification (for the Open Source Initiatives list of the criteria that define an open source software product, see http://opensource.org/docs/osd).
- While open source alternatives are threatening to conventional software firms, some of the largest technology companies now support OSS initiatives and work to coordinate standards, product improvements, and official releases.
- The flagship OSS product is the Linux operating system, now available on all scales of computing devices from cell phones to supercomputers.
- The LAMP stack of open source products is used to power many of the Internet's most popular Web sites. Linux can be found on 30 percent of corporate servers, supports most Web servers, and is integral to TiVo and Android-based cell phones.
- The majority of persons who work on open source projects are paid by commercially motivated employers.

QUESTIONS AND EXERCISES

1. Who developed Linux?
2. Who develops it today?
3. List the components of the LAMP stack. Which commercial products do these components compete with (investigate online, if necessary)?
4. Why do commercial firms contribute to open source consortia and foundations?
5. Free doesn't always win. Why might a firm turn down free software in favor of a commercial alternative?

3. WHY OPEN SOURCE?

LEARNING OBJECTIVES

1. **Know the primary reasons firms choose to use OSS.**
2. **Understand how OSS can beneficially impact industry and government.**

There are many reasons why firms choose open source products over commercial alternatives:

Cost—Free alternatives to costly commercial code can be a tremendous motivator, particularly since conventional software often requires customers to pay for every copy used and to pay more for software that runs on increasingly powerful hardware. Big Lots stores lowered costs by as much as $10 million by finding viable OSS[12] to serve their system needs. Online broker E*TRADE estimates that its switch to open source helped save over $13 million a year.[13] And Amazon claimed in SEC filings that the switch to open source was a key contributor to nearly $20 million in tech savings.[14] Firms like TiVo, which use OSS in their own products, eliminate a cost spent either developing their own operating system or licensing similar software from a vendor like Microsoft.

Reliability—There's a saying in the open source community, "Given enough eyeballs, all bugs are shallow."[15] What this means is that the more people who look at a program's code, the greater the likelihood that an error will be caught and corrected. The open source community harnesses the power of legions of geeks who are constantly trawling OSS products, looking to squash bugs and improve product quality. And studies have shown that the quality of popular OSS products outperforms proprietary commercial competitors.[16] In one study, Carnegie Mellon University's Cylab estimated the quality of Linux code to be less buggy than commercial alternatives by a factor of two hundred![17]

Security—OSS advocates also argue that by allowing "many eyes" to examine the code, the security vulnerabilities of open source products come to light more quickly and can be addressed with greater speed and reliability.[18] High profile hacking contests have frequently demonstrated the strength of OSS products. In one well-publicized 2008 event, laptops running Windows and Macintosh were both hacked (the latter in just two minutes), while a laptop running Linux remained uncompromised.[19] Government agencies and the military often appreciate the opportunity to scrutinize open source efforts to verify system integrity (a particularly sensitive issue among foreign governments leery of legislation like the USA PATRIOT Act of 2001).[20] Many OSS vendors offer **security focused** (sometimes called *hardened*) versions of their products. These can include systems that monitor the integrity of an OSS distribution, checking file size and other indicators to be sure that code has not been modified and redistributed by bad guys who've added a back door, malicious routines, or other vulnerabilities.

security focused

Also known as "hardened." Term used to describe technology products that contain particularly strong security features.

Scalability—Many major OSS efforts can run on everything from cheap commodity hardware to high-end supercomputing. **Scalability** allows a firm to scale from start-up to blue chip without having to significantly rewrite their code, potentially saving big on software development costs. Not only can many forms of OSS be migrated to more powerful hardware, packages like Linux have also been optimized to balance a server's workload among a large number of machines working in tandem. Brokerage firm E*TRADE claims that usage spikes following 2008 U.S. Federal Reserve moves flooded the firm's systems, creating the highest utilization levels in five years. But E*TRADE credits its scalable open source systems for maintaining performance while competitors' systems struggled.[21]

scalability

Ability to either handle increasing workloads or to be easily expanded to manage workload increases. In a software context, systems that aren't scalable often require significant rewrites or the purchase or development of entirely new systems.

Agility and Time to Market—Vendors who use OSS as part of product offerings may be able to skip whole segments of the software development process, allowing new products to reach the market faster than if the entire software system had to be developed from scratch, in-house. Motorola has claimed that customizing products built on OSS has helped speed time-to-market for the firm's mobile phones, while the team behind the Zimbra e-mail and calendar effort built their first product in just a few months by using some forty blocks of free code.[22]

KEY TAKEAWAYS

- The most widely cited benefits of using OSS include low cost; increased reliability; improved security and auditing; system scalability; and helping a firm improve its time to market.
- Free OSS has resulted in cost savings for many large companies in several industries.
- OSS often has fewer bugs than its commercial counterparts due to the large number of persons who have looked at the code.
- The huge exposure to scrutiny by developers and other people helps to strengthen the security of OSS.
- "Hardened" versions of OSS products often include systems that monitor the integrity of an OSS distribution, checking file size and other indicators to be sure that code has not been modified and redistributed by bad guys who have added a back door, malicious routines, or other vulnerabilities.
- OSS can be easily migrated to more powerful computers as circumstances dictate, and also can balance workload by distributing work over a number of machines.
- Vendors who use OSS as part of product offerings may be able to skip whole segments of the software development process, allowing new products to reach the market faster.

QUESTIONS AND EXERCISES

1. What advantages does OSS offer TiVo? What alternatives to OSS might the firm consider and why do you suppose the firm decided on OSS?
2. What's meant by the phrase, "Given enough eyeballs, all bugs are shallow"? Provide evidence that the insight behind this phrase is an accurate one.
3. How has OSS benefited E*TRADE? Amazon? Motorola? Zimbra? What benefits were achieved in each of these examples?
4. Describe how OSS provides a firm with scalability. What does this mean, and why does this appeal to a firm? What issues might a firm face if chosen systems aren't scalable?
5. The Web site NetCraft (http://www.netcraft.com) is one of many that provide a tool to see the kind of operating system and Web server software that a given site is running. Visit NetCraft or a similar site and enter the address of some of your favorite Web sites. How many run open source products (e.g., the Linux OS or Apache Web server)? Do some sites show their software as "unknown"? Why might a site be reluctant to broadcast the kind of software that it uses?

4. EXAMPLES OF OPEN SOURCE SOFTWARE

LEARNING OBJECTIVES

1. **Recognize that just about every type of commercial product has an open source equivalent.**
2. **Be able to list commercial products and their open source competitors.**

Just about every type of commercial product has an open source equivalent. SourceForge.net lists over two hundred and thirty thousand such products![23] Many of these products come with the installation tools, support utilities, and full documentation that make them difficult to distinguish from traditional commercial efforts.[24] In addition to the LAMP products, some major examples include the following:

- Firefox—a Web browser that competes with Internet Explorer
- OpenOffice—a competitor to Microsoft Office
- Gimp—a graphic tool with features found in Photoshop
- Alfresco—collaboration software that competes with Microsoft Sharepoint and EMC's Documentum
- Marketcetera—an enterprise trading platform for hedge fund managers that competes with FlexTrade and Portware
- Zimbra—open source e-mail software that competes with Outlook server
- MySQL, Ingres, and PostgreSQL—open source relational database software packages that each go head-to-head with commercial products from Oracle, Microsoft, Sybase, and IBM

- HBase and Cassandra—nonrelational distributed databases used to power massive file systems (used to power key features on Facebook, Twitter, LinkedIn, and Amazon)
- SugarCRM—customer relationship management software that competes with Salesforce.com and Siebel
- Asterix—an open source implementation for running a PBX corporate telephony system that competes with offerings from Nortel and Cisco, among others
- Free BSD and Sun's OpenSolaris—open source versions of the Unix operating system

KEY TAKEAWAYS

- There are thousands of open source products available, covering nearly every software category. Many have a sophistication that rivals commercial software products.
- Not all open source products are contenders. Less popular open source products are not likely to attract the community of users and contributors necessary to help these products improve over time (again we see network effects are a key to success—this time in determining the quality of an OSS effort).
- Just about every type of commercial product has an open source equivalent.

QUESTIONS AND EXERCISES

1. Visit http://www.SourceForge.net. Make a brief list of commercial product categories that an individual or enterprise might use. Are there open source alternatives for these categories? Are well-known firms leveraging these OSS offerings? Which commercial firms do they compete with?
2. Are the OSS efforts you identified above provided by commercial firms, nonprofit organizations, or private individuals? Does this make a difference in your willingness to adopt a particular product? Why or why not? What other factors influence your adoption decision?
3. Download a popular, end-user version of an OSS tool that competes with a desktop application that you own, or that you've used (hint: choose something that's a smaller file or easy to install). What do you think of the OSS offering compared to the commercial product? Will you continue to use the OSS product? Why or why not?

5. WHY GIVE IT AWAY? THE BUSINESS OF OPEN SOURCE

LEARNING OBJECTIVES

1. **Understand the disproportional impact OSS has on the IT market.**
2. **Understand how vendors make money on open source.**
3. **Know what SQL and MySQL are.**

Open source is a sixty-billion-dollar industry,[25] but it has a disproportionate impact on the trillion-dollar IT market. By lowering the cost of computing, open source efforts make more computing options accessible to smaller firms. More reliable, secure computing also lowers costs for all users. OSS also diverts funds that firms would otherwise spend on fixed costs, like operating systems and databases, so that these funds can be spent on innovation or other more competitive initiatives. Think about Google, a firm that some estimate has over 1.4 million servers. Imagine the costs if it had to license software for each of those boxes!

Commercial interest in OSS has sparked an acquisition binge. Red Hat bought open source application server firm JBoss for $350 million. Novell snapped up SUSE Linux for $210 million (and was later bought by Attachmate for $2.2 billion). And Sun plunked down over $1 billion for open source database provider MySQL.[26] And with Oracle's acquisition of Sun, one of the world's largest commercial software firms has zeroed in on one of the deepest portfolios of open source products.

But how do *vendors* make money on open source? One way is by selling support and consulting services. While not exactly Microsoft money, Red Hat, the largest purely OSS firm, reported nearly a billion dollars in revenue from paying customers subscribing for access to software updates and support services.[27] Oracle, a firm that sells commercial ERP and database products, provides Linux for free, selling high-margin Linux support contracts for as much as five hundred thousand dollars.[28] The added benefit for Oracle? Weaning customers away from Microsoft—a firm that sells many products that compete head-to-head with Oracle's offerings. Service also represents the most important part of IBM's business. The firm now makes more from services than from selling hardware and software.[29] And every dollar saved on buying someone else's software product means more money IBM customers can spend on IBM computers and services. Sun Microsystems was a leader in OSS, even before the Oracle acquisition bid. The firm has used OSS to drive advanced hardware sales, but the firm also sells proprietary products that augment its open source efforts. These products include special optimization, configuration management and performance tools that can tweak OSS code to work its best.[30]

Here's where we also can relate the industry's evolution to what we've learned about standards competition in our earlier chapters. In the pre-Linux days, nearly every major hardware manufacturer made its own, incompatible version of the Unix operating system. These fractured, incompatible markets were each so small that they had difficulty attracting third-party vendors to write application software. Now, much to Microsoft's dismay, all major hardware firms run Linux. That means there's a large, unified market that attracts software developers who might otherwise write for Windows.

To keep standards unified, several Linux-supporting hardware and software firms also back the Linux Foundation, the nonprofit effort where Linus Torvalds serves as a fellow, helping to oversee Linux's evolution. Sharing development expenses in OSS has been likened to going in on a pizza together. Everyone wants a pizza with the same ingredients. The pizza doesn't make you smarter or better. So why not share the cost of a bigger pie instead of buying by the slice?[31] With OSS, hardware firms spend less money than they would in the brutal, head-to-head competition where each once offered a "me too" operating system that was incompatible with rivals but offered little differentiation. Hardware firms now find their technical talent can be deployed in other value-added services mentioned above: developing commercial software add-ons, offering consulting services, and enhancing hardware offerings.

total cost of ownership (TCO)

All of the costs associated with the design, development, testing, implementation, documentation, training and maintenance of a software system.

Linux on the Desktop?

While Linux is a major player in enterprise software, mobile phones, and consumer electronics, the Linux OS can only be found on a tiny fraction of desktop computers. There are several reasons for this. Some suggest Linux simply isn't as easy to install and use as Windows or the Mac OS. This complexity can raise the **total cost of ownership (TCO)** of Linux desktops, with additional end-user support offsetting any gains from free software. The small number of desktop users also dissuades third party firms from porting popular desktop applications over to Linux. For consumers in most industrialized nations, the added complexity and limited desktop application availability of desktop Linux just it isn't worth the one to two hundred dollars saved by giving up Windows.

But in developing nations where incomes are lower, the cost of Windows can be daunting. Consider the OLPC, Nicholas Negroponte's "one-hundred-dollar" laptop. An additional one hundred dollars for Windows would double the target cost for the nonprofit's machines. It is not surprising that the first OLPC laptops ran Linux. Microsoft recognizes that if a whole generation of first-time computer users grows up without Windows, they may favor open source alternatives years later when starting their own businesses. As a result, Microsoft has begun offering low-cost versions of Windows (in some cases for as little as seven dollars) in nations where populations have much lower incomes. Microsoft has even offered a version of Windows to the backers of the OLPC. While Microsoft won't make much money on these efforts, the low cost versions will serve to entrench Microsoft products as standards in emerging markets, staving off open source rivals and positioning the firm to raise prices years later when income levels rise.

structured query language

A language for creating and manipulating databases. SQL is by far the most common database standard in use today, and is supported by many commercial and open source products.

MySQL: Turning a Ten-Billion-Dollars-a-Year Business into a One-Billion-Dollar One

Finland is not the only Scandinavian country to spawn an open source powerhouse. Uppsala Sweden's MySQL (pronounced "my sequel") is the "M" in the LAMP stack, and is used by organizations as diverse as FedEx, Lufthansa, NASA, Sony, UPS, and YouTube.

The "SQL" in name stands for the **structured query language**, a standard method for organizing and accessing data. SQL is also employed by commercial database products from Oracle, Microsoft, and Sybase. Even Linux-loving IBM uses SQL in its own lucrative DB2 commercial database product. Since all of these databases are based on the same standard, switching costs are lower, so migrating from a commercial product to MySQL's open source alternative is relatively easy. And that spells trouble for commercial firms. Granted, the commercial efforts offer some bells and whistles that MySQL doesn't yet have, but those extras aren't necessary in a lot of standard database use. Some organizations, impressed with MySQL's capabilities, are mandating its use on all new development efforts, attempting to cordon off proprietary products in legacy code that is maintained but not expanded.

Savings from using MySQL can be huge. The Web site PriceGrabber pays less than ten thousand dollars in support for MySQL compared to one hundred thousand to two hundred thousand dollars for a comparable Oracle effort. Lycos Europe switched from Oracle to MySQL and slashed costs from one hundred twenty thousand dollars a year to seven thousand dollars. And the travel reservation firm Sabre used open source products such as MySQL to slash ticket purchase processing costs by 80 percent.[32]

MySQL does make money, just not as much as its commercial rivals. While you can download a version of MySQL over the Net, the flagship product also sells for four hundred ninety-five dollars per server computer compared to a list price for Oracle that can climb as high as one hundred sixty thousand dollars. Of the roughly eleven million copies of MySQL in use, the company only gets paid for about one in a thousand.[33] Firms pay for what's free for one of two reasons: (1) for MySQL service, and (2) for the right to incorporate MySQL's code into their own products.[34] Amazon, Facebook, Gap, NBC, and Sabre pay MySQL for support; Cisco, Ericsson, HP, and Symantec pay for the rights to the code.[35] Top-level round-the-clock support for MySQL for up to fifty servers is fifty thousand dollars a year, still a fraction of the cost for commercial alternatives. Founder Marten Mickos has stated an explicit goal of the firm is "turning the $10-billion-a-year database business into a $1 billion one."[36]

When Sun Microsystems spent over $1 billion to buy Mickos' MySQL in 2008, Sun CEO Jonathan Schwartz called the purchase the "most important acquisition in the company's history."[37] Sun hoped the cheap database software could make the firm's hardware offerings seem more attractive. And it looked like Sun was good for MySQL, with the product's revenues growing 55 percent in the year after the acquisition.[38]

But here's where it gets complicated. Sun also had a lucrative business selling hardware to support commercial ERP and database software from Oracle. That put Sun and partner Oracle in a relationship where they were both competitors and collaborators (the "coopetition" or "frenemies" phenomenon mentioned in Chapter 6). Then in spring 2009, Oracle announced it was buying Sun. Oracle CEO Larry Ellison mentioned acquiring the Java language was the crown jewel of the purchase, but industry watchers have raised several questions. Will the firm continue to nurture MySQL and other open source products, even as this software poses a threat to its bread-and-butter database products? Will the development community continue to back MySQL as the de facto standard for open source SQL databases, or will they migrate to an alternative? Or will Oracle find the right mix of free and fee-based products and services that allow MySQL to thrive while Oracle continues to grow? The implications are serious for investors, as well as firms that have made commitments to Sun, Oracle, and MySQL products. The complexity of this environment further demonstrates why technologists need business savvy and market monitoring skills and why business folks need to understand the implications of technology and tech-industry developments.

Legal Risks and Open Source Software: A Hidden and Complex Challenge

Open source software isn't without its risks. Competing reports cite certain open source products as being difficult to install and maintain (suggesting potentially higher total cost of ownership, or TCO). Adopters of OSS without support contracts may lament having to rely on an uncertain community of volunteers to support their problems and provide innovative upgrades. Another major concern is legal exposure. Firms adopting OSS may be at risk if they distribute code and aren't aware of the licensing implications. Some commercial software firms have pressed legal action against the users of open source products when there is a perceived violation of software patents or other unauthorized use of their proprietary code.

For example, in 2007 Microsoft suggested that Linux and other open source software efforts violated some two hundred thirty-five of its patents.[39] The firm then began collecting payments and gaining access to the patent portfolios of companies that use the open source Linux operating system in their products, including Fuji, Samsung, and Xerox. Microsoft also cut a deal with Linux vendor Novell in which both firms pledged not to sue each other's customers for potential patent infringements.

Also complicating issues are the varying open source license agreements (these go by various names, such as GPL and the Apache License), each with slightly different legal provisions—many of which have evolved over time. Keeping legal with so many licensing standards can be a challenge, especially for firms that want to bundle open source code into their own products.[40] An entire industry has sprouted up to help firms navigate the minefield of open source legal licenses. Chief among these are products, such as those offered by the firm Black Duck, which analyze the composition of software source code and report on any areas of concern so that firms can honor any legal obligations associated with their offerings. Keeping legal requires effort and attention, even in an environment where products are allegedly "free." This also shows that even corporate lawyers had best geek-up if they want to prove they're capable of navigating a twenty-first-century legal environment.

KEY TAKEAWAYS

- Business models for firms in the open source industry are varied, and can include selling services, licensing OSS for incorporation into commercial products, and using OSS to fuel hardware sales.
- Many firms are trying to use OSS markets to drive a wedge between competitors and their customers.
- Linux has been very successful on mobile devices and consumer electronics, as well as on high-end server class and above computers. But it has not been as successful on the desktop. The small user base for desktop Linux makes the platform less attractive for desktop software developers. Incompatibility with Windows applications, switching costs, and other network effects-related issues all suggest that Desktop Linux has an uphill climb in more mature markets.
- MySQL is the dominant open source database software product. Adoption of the SQL standard eases some issues with migrating from commercial products to MySQL.
- OSS also has several drawbacks and challenges that limit its appeal. These include complexity of some products and a higher total cost of ownership for some products, concern about the ability of a product's development community to provide support or product improvement, and legal and licensing concerns.

QUESTIONS AND EXERCISES

1. Describe the impact of OSS on the IT market.
2. Show your understanding of the commercial OSS market. How do Red Hat, Oracle, Oracle's Sun division, and IBM make money via open source?
3. Visit Mozilla.org. Which open source products does this organization develop? Investigate how development of these efforts is financed. How does this organization differ from the ones mentioned above?
4. What is the Linux Foundation? Why is it necessary? Which firms are members, underwriting foundation efforts?
5. List the reasons why Linux is installed on only a very small fraction of desktop computers. Are there particular categories of products or users who might see Linux as more appealing than conventional operating systems? Do you think Linux's share of the desktop market will increase? Why or why not?
6. How is Microsoft combating the threat of open source software and other free tools that compete with its commercial products?
7. What is the dominant open source database software product? Which firms use this product? Why?
8. Which firm developed the leading OSS database product? Do you think it's more or less likely that a firm would switch to an OSS database instead of an OSS office suite or desktop alternative? Why or why not?
9. How has stewardship of the leading OSS database effort changed in recent years? Who oversees the effort today? What questions does this raise for the product's future? Although this book is updated regularly, current events continue to change after publication of this chapter. Investigate the current status of this effort—reaction of the developer community, continued reception of the product—and be prepared to share your findings with class.
10. List some of the risks associated with using OSS. Give examples of firms that might pass on OSS software, and explain why.

6. CLOUD COMPUTING: HYPE OR HOPE?

LEARNING OBJECTIVES

1. **Understand the concept of cloud computing.**
2. **Identify the two major categories of cloud computing.**

Oracle Chairman Larry Ellison, lamenting the buzzword-chasing character of the tech sector, once complained that the computer industry is more fashion-focused than even the women's clothing business.[41] Ellison has a point: when a technology term becomes fashionable, the industry hype machine shifts into overdrive. The technology attracts press attention, customer interest, and vendor marketing teams scramble to label their products and services as part of that innovation. Recently, few tech trends have been more fashionable than *cloud computing*.

Like Web 2.0, trying to nail down an exact definition for cloud computing is tough. In fact, it's been quite a spectacle watching industry execs struggle to clarify the concept. HP's Chief Strategy Office "politely refused" when asked by *BusinessWeek* to define the term cloud computing.[42] Richard Stallman, founder of the Free Software Foundation said about cloud computing, "It's worse than stupidity. It's a marketing hype campaign."[43] And Larry Ellison, always ready with a sound bite, offered up this priceless quip, "Maybe I'm an idiot, but I have no idea what anyone is talking about. What is it? It's complete gibberish. It's insane."[44] Insane, maybe, but also big bucks. The various businesses that fall under the rubric of cloud computing had already grown from an estimated $36 billion market in 2008 to $68 billion in 2010, accounting for over 13 percent of global software sales![45]

When folks talk about cloud computing they're really talking about replacing computing resources—either an organization's or an individual's hardware or software—with *services* provided over the Internet. The name actually comes from the popular industry convention of drawing the Internet or other computer network as a big cloud.

Cloud computing encompasses a bunch of different efforts. We'll concentrate on describing, providing examples, and analyzing the managerial implications of two separate categories of cloud computing: (1) *software as a service (SaaS)*, where a firm subscribes to a third-party software-replacing service that is delivered online, and (2) models often referred to as **utility computing**, which can include variants such as platform as a service (PaaS) and infrastructure as a service (IaaS). Using these latter techniques, an organization develops its own systems, but runs them over the Internet on someone else's hardware. A later section on virtualization will discuss how some organizations are developing their own **private clouds**, pools of computing resources that reside inside an organization and that can be served up for specific tasks as need arrives.

The benefits and risks of SaaS and the utility computing-style efforts are very similar, but understanding the nuances of each effort can help you figure out if and when the cloud makes sense for your organization. The evolution of cloud computing also has huge implications across the industry: from the financial future of hardware and software firms, to cost structure and innovativeness of adopting organizations, to the skill sets likely to be most valued by employers.

utility computing

A form of cloud computing where a firm develops its own software, and then runs it over the Internet on a service provider's computers.

private clouds

Pools of computing resources that reside inside an organization and that can be served up for specific tasks as need arrives.

KEY TAKEAWAYS

- Cloud computing is difficult to define. Managers and techies use the term cloud computing to describe computing services provided over a network, most often commercial services provided over the Internet by a third party that can replace or offload tasks that would otherwise run on a user or organization's existing hardware or software.
- Software as a service (SaaS) refers to a third-party software-replacing service that is delivered online.
- Hardware cloud computing services replace hardware that a firm might otherwise purchase.
- Estimated to be a thirty-six-billion-dollar industry, cloud computing is reshaping software, hardware, and service markets, and is impacting competitive dynamics across industries.

QUESTIONS AND EXERCISES

1. Identify and contrast the two categories of cloud computing.
2. Define cloud computing.

7. THE SOFTWARE CLOUD: WHY BUY WHEN YOU CAN RENT?

LEARNING OBJECTIVES

1. **Know how firms using SaaS products can dramatically lower several costs associated with their information systems.**
2. **Know how SaaS vendors earn their money.**
3. **Be able to list the benefits to users that accrue from using SaaS.**
4. **Be able to list the benefits to vendors from deploying SaaS.**

If open source isn't enough of a threat to firms that sell packaged software, a new generation of products, collectively known as SaaS, claims that you can now get the bulk of your computing done through your Web browser. Don't install software—let someone else run it for you and deliver the results over the Internet.

Software as a service (SaaS) refers to software that is made available by a third party online. You might also see the terms ASP (application service provider) or HSV (hosted software vendor) used to identify this type of offering, but those are now used less frequently. SaaS is potentially a very big deal. Firms using SaaS products can dramatically lower several costs associated with the care and feeding of their information systems, including software licenses, server hardware, system maintenance, and IT staff. Most SaaS firms earn money via a usage-based pricing model akin to a monthly subscription. Others offer free services that are supported by advertising, while others promote the sale of upgraded or premium versions for additional fees.

Make no mistake, SaaS is yet another direct assault on traditional software firms. The most iconic SaaS firm is Salesforce.com, an enterprise customer relationship management (CRM) provider. This "un-software" company even sports a logo featuring the word "software" crossed out, *Ghostbusters*-style.[46]

FIGURE 10.3

The antisoftware message is evident in the logo of SaaS leader Salesforce.com.

Other enterprise-focused SaaS firms compete directly with the biggest names in software. Some of these upstarts are even backed by leading enterprise software executives. Examples include NetSuite (funded in part by Oracle's Larry Ellison—the guy's all over this chapter), which offers a comprehensive SaaS ERP suite; Workday (launched by founders of Peoplesoft), which has SaaS offerings for managing human resources; and Aravo, which offers supply chain management software as SaaS. Several traditional software firms have countered start-ups by offering SaaS efforts of their own. IBM offers a SaaS version of its Cognos business intelligence products, Oracle offers CRM On Demand, and SAP's Business ByDesign includes a full suite of enterprise SaaS offerings. Even Microsoft has gone SaaS, with a variety of Web-based services that include CRM, Web meeting tools, collaboration, e-mail, and calendaring.

SaaS is also taking on desktop applications. Intuit has online versions of its QuickBooks, TurboTax, and Quicken finance software. Adobe has an online version of Photoshop. Google and Zoho offer office suites that compete with desktop alternatives, prompting Microsoft's own introduction of an online version of Office, with Oracle following as well. And if you use a service like Dropbox or you store photos on Flickr or Picasa, instead of your PC's hard drive, then you're using SaaS, too.

FIGURE 10.4

A look at Zoho's home page shows the diversity of both desktop and enterprise offerings from this SaaS upstart. Note that the firm makes it services available through browsers, phones, and even Facebook.

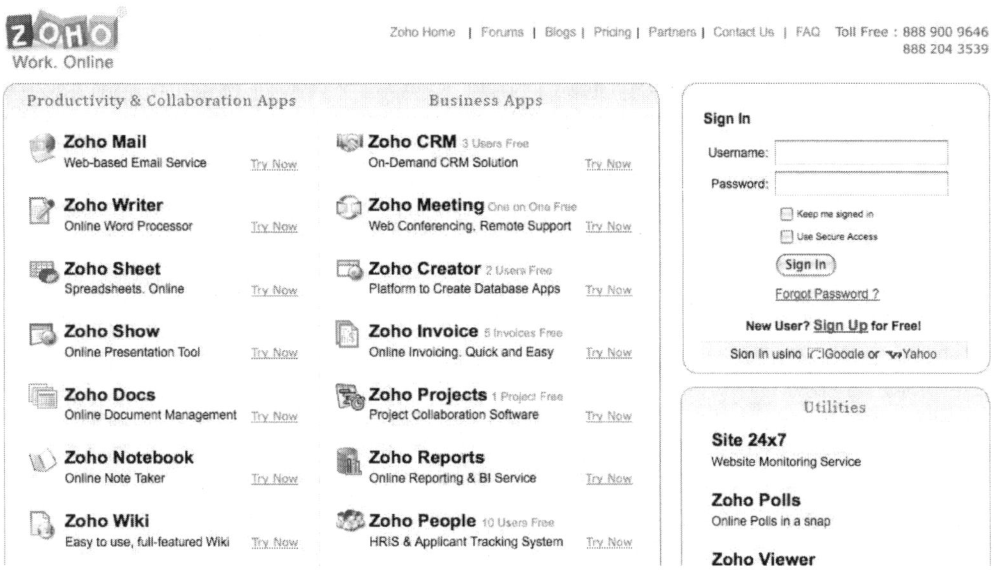

7.1 The Benefits of SaaS

Firms can potentially save big using SaaS. Organizations that adopt SaaS forgo the large upfront costs of buying and installing software packages. For large enterprises, the cost to license, install, and configure products like ERP and CRM systems can easily run into the hundreds of thousands or even millions of dollars. And these costs are rarely a one time fee. Additional costs like annual maintenance contracts have also been rising as rivals fail or get bought up. Less competition among traditional firms recently allowed Oracle and SAP to raise maintenance fees to as much as 20 percent.[47]

Firms that adopt SaaS don't just save on software and hardware, either. There's also the added cost for the IT staff needed to run these systems. Forrester Research estimates that SaaS can bring cost savings of 25 to 60 percent if all these costs are factored in.[48]

There are also accounting and corporate finance implications for SaaS. Firms that adopt software as a service never actually buy a system's software and hardware, so these systems become a variable operating expense. This flexibility helps mitigate the financial risks associated with making a large capital investment in information systems. For example, if a firm pays Salesforce.com sixty-five dollars per month per user for its CRM software, it can reduce payments during a slow season with a smaller staff, or pay more during heavy months when a firm might employ temporary workers. At these rates, SaaS not only looks good to large firms, it makes very sophisticated technology available to smaller firms that otherwise wouldn't be able to afford expensive systems, let alone the IT staff and hardware required to run them.

In addition to cost benefits, SaaS offerings also provide the advantage of being highly scalable. This feature is important because many organizations operate in environments prone to wide variance in usage. Some firms might expect systems to be particularly busy during tax time or the period around quarterly financial reporting deadlines, while others might have their heaviest system loads around a holiday season. A music label might see spikes when an artist drops a new album. Using conventional software, an organization would have to buy enough computing capacity to ensure that it could handle its heaviest anticipated workload. But sometimes these loads are difficult to predict, and if the difference between high workloads and average use is great, a lot of that expensive computer hardware will spend most of its time doing nothing. In SaaS, however, the vendor is responsible for ensuring that systems meet demand fluctuation. Vendors frequently sign a **service level agreement (SLA)** with their customers to ensure a guaranteed uptime and define their ability to meet demand spikes.

service level agreement (SLA)

A negotiated agreement between the customer and the vendor. The SLA may specify the levels of availability, serviceability, performance, operation, or other commitment requirements.

When looking at the benefits of SaaS, also consider the potential for higher quality and service levels. SaaS firms benefit from economies of scale that not only lower software and hardware costs, but also potentially boost quality. The volume of customers and diversity of their experiences means that an established SaaS vendor is most likely an expert in dealing with all sorts of critical computing issues. SaaS firms handle backups, instantly deploy upgrades and bug fixes, and deal with the continual burden of security maintenance—all costly tasks that must be performed regularly and with care, although each offers little strategic value to firms that perform these functions themselves in-house. The breadth of a SaaS vendor's customer base typically pushes the firm to evaluate and address new technologies as they emerge, like quickly offering accessibility from mobile platforms like the BlackBerry and iPhone. And many contend that cloud computing can actually be greener. SaaS and other cloud firms often have data centers that are better designed to pool and efficiently manage computing resources, and they are often located in warehouse-style buildings designed for computers, not people. Contrast that with corporate data centers that may have wasteful excess capacity to account for service spikes and may be crammed inside inefficiently cooled downtown high-rises. For all but the savviest of IT shops, an established SaaS vendor can likely leverage its scale and experience to provide better, cheaper, more reliable standard information systems than individual companies typically can.

Software developers who choose to operate as SaaS providers also realize benefits. While a packaged software company like SAP must support multiple versions of its software to accommodate operating systems like Windows, Linux, and various flavors of Unix, an SaaS provider develops, tests, deploys, and supports just one version of the software executing on its own servers.

An argument might also be made that SaaS vendors are more attuned to customer needs. Since SaaS firms run a customer's systems on their own hardware, they have a tighter feedback loop in understanding how products are used (and why they fail)—potentially accelerating their ability to enhance their offerings. And once made, enhancements or fixes are immediately available to customers the next time they log in.

vertical niches

Sometimes referred to as vertical markets. Products and services designed to target a specific industry (e.g., pharmaceutical, legal, apparel retail).

SaaS applications also impact distribution costs and capacity. As much as 30 percent of the price of traditional desktop software is tied to the cost of distribution—pressing CD-ROMs, packaging them in boxes, and shipping them to retail outlets.[49] Going direct to consumers can cut out the middleman, so vendors can charge less or capture profits that they might otherwise share with a store or other distributor. Going direct also means that SaaS applications are available anywhere someone has an Internet connection, making them truly global applications. This feature has allowed many SaaS firms to address highly specialized markets (sometimes called **vertical niches**). For example, the Internet allows a company writing specialized legal software, for example, or a custom package for the pharmaceutical industry, to have a national deployment footprint from day one. Vendors of desktop applications that go SaaS benefit from this kind of distribution, too.

Finally, SaaS allows a vendor to counter the vexing and costly problem of software piracy. It's just about impossible to make an executable, illegal copy of a subscription service that runs on a SaaS provider's hardware.

KEY TAKEAWAYS

- SaaS firms may offer their clients several benefits including the following:
  - *lower costs* by eliminating or reducing software, hardware, maintenance, and staff expenses
  - *financial risk mitigation* since start-up costs are so low
  - potentially *faster deployment times* compared with installed packaged software or systems developed in-house
  - costs that are a *variable operating expense* rather than a large, fixed capital expense
  - *scalable systems* that make it easier for firms to ramp up during periods of unexpectedly high system use
  - *higher quality and service levels* through instantly available upgrades, vendor scale economies, and expertise gained across its entire client base
  - *remote access and availability*—most SaaS offerings are accessed through any Web browser, and often even by phone or other mobile device
- Vendors of SaaS products benefit from the following:
  - *limiting development to a single platform*, instead of having to create versions for different operating systems
  - *tighter feedback loop* with clients, helping fuel innovation and responsiveness
  - ability to *instantly deploy bug fixes and product enhancements* to all users
  - *lower distribution costs*
  - *accessibility* to anyone with an Internet connection
  - greatly *reduced risk of software piracy*
- SaaS (and the other forms of cloud computing) are also thought to be better for the environment, since cloud firms more efficiently pool resources and often host their technologies in warehouses designed for cooling and energy efficiency.

QUESTIONS AND EXERCISES

1. Firms that buy conventional enterprise software spend money buying software and hardware. What additional and ongoing expenses are required as part of the "care and feeding" of enterprise applications?
2. In what ways can firms using SaaS products dramatically lower costs associated with their information systems?
3. How do SaaS vendors earn their money?
4. Give examples of enterprise-focused SaaS vendors and their products. Visit the Web sites of the firms that offer these services. Which firms are listed as clients? Does there appear to be a particular type of firm that uses its services, or are client firms broadly represented?
5. Give examples of desktop-focused SaaS vendors and their products. If some of these are free, try them out and compare them to desktop alternatives you may have used. Be prepared to share your experiences with your class.
6. List the cost-related benefits to users that accrue from using SaaS.
7. List the benefits other than cost-related that accrue to users from using SaaS.
8. List the benefits realized by vendors that offer SaaS services instead of conventional software.
9. Why might cloud computing be greener than conventional computing alternatives? Research online and share examples suggesting that cloud firms could be less environmentally taxing than if a firm built and ran its own corporate data center.

8. SAAS: NOT WITHOUT RISKS

LEARNING OBJECTIVE

1. **Be able to list and appreciate the risks associated with SaaS.**

Like any technology, we also recognize there is rarely a silver bullet that solves all problems. A successful manager is able to see through industry hype and weigh the benefits of a technology against its weaknesses and limitations. And there are still several major concerns surrounding SaaS.

The largest concerns involve the tremendous dependence a firm develops with its SaaS vendor. While some claim that the subscription-based SaaS model means that you can simply walk away from a vendor if you become dissatisfied, in fact there is quite a bit of lock-in with SaaS vendors, too. And in addition to the switching costs associated with switching on conventional software platforms, switching SaaS vendors may involve the slow and difficult task of transferring very large data files over the Internet. Having all of your eggs in one basket can leave a firm particularly vulnerable. If a traditional software company goes out of business, in most cases its customers can still go on using its products. But if your SaaS vendor goes under, you're hosed. They've got all your data, and even if firms could get their data out, most organizations don't have the hardware, software, staff, or expertise to quickly absorb an abandoned function.

Beware with whom you partner. Any hot technology is likely to attract a lot of start-ups, and most of these start-ups are unlikely to survive. In just a single year, the leading trade association found the number of SaaS vendors dropped from seven hundred members to four hundred fifty.[50] One of the early efforts to collapse was Pandesic, a joint venture between SAP and Intel—two large firms that might have otherwise instilled confidence among prospective customers. In another example, Danish SaaS firm "IT Factory" was declared "Denmark's Best IT Company" by *Computerworld*, only to follow the award one week later with a bankruptcy declaration.[51] Indeed, despite the benefits, the costs of operating as a SaaS vendor can be daunting. NetSuite's founder claimed it "takes ten years and $100 million to do right"[52] —maybe that's why the firm still wasn't profitable, even three and a half years after going public.

Firms that buy and install packaged software usually have the option of sticking with the old stuff as long as it works, but organizations adopting SaaS may find they are forced into adopting new versions. This fact is important because any radical changes in a SaaS system's user interface or system functionality might result in unforeseen training costs, or increase the chance that a user might make an error.

Keep in mind that SaaS systems are also reliant on a network connection. If a firm's link to the Internet goes down, its link to its SaaS vendor is also severed. Relying on an Internet connection also means that data is transferred to and from a SaaS firm at Internet speeds, rather than the potentially higher speeds of a firm's internal network. Solutions to many of these issues are evolving as Internet speeds become faster and Internet service providers become more reliable. There are also several programs that allow for offline use of data that is typically stored in SaaS systems, including Gears and Adobe AIR. With these products a user can download a subset of data to be offline (say on a plane flight or other inaccessible location) and then sync the data when the connection is restored. Ultimately, though, SaaS users have a much higher level of dependence on their Internet connections.

And although a SaaS firm may have more security expertise than your organization, that doesn't mean that security issues can be ignored. Any time a firm allows employees to access a corporation's systems and data assets from a remote location, a firm is potentially vulnerable to abuse and infiltration. Some firms may simply be unacceptably uncomfortable with critical data assets existing outside their own network. There may also be contractual or legal issues preventing data from being housed remotely, especially if a SaaS vendor's systems are in another country operating under different laws and regulations. "We're very bound by regulators in terms of client data and country-of-origin issues, so it's very difficult to use the cloud," says Rupert Brown, a chief architect at Merrill Lynch.[53]

SaaS systems are often accused of being less flexible than their installed software counterparts—mostly due to the more robust configuration and programming options available in traditional software packages. It is true that many SaaS vendors have improved system customization options and integration with standard software packages. And at times a lack of complexity can be a blessing—fewer choices can mean less training, faster start-up time, and lower costs associated with system use. But firms with unique needs may find SaaS restrictive.

SaaS offerings usually work well when the bulk of computing happens at the server end of a distributed system because the kind of user interface you can create in a browser isn't as sophisticated as what you can do with a separate, custom-developed desktop program. A comparison of the first few iterations of the Web-based Google Docs office suite, which offers word processing, presentation software, and a spreadsheet, reveals a much more limited feature set than Microsoft's Office desktop software. The bonus, of course, is that an online office suite is accessible anywhere and makes sharing documents a snap. Again, an understanding of trade-offs is key.

Here's another challenge for a firm and its IT staff: SaaS means a greater *consumerization* of technology. Employees, at their own initiative, can go to firms such as Socialtext or PBworks and set up a wiki, WordPress to start blogging, or subscribe to a SaaS offering like Salesforce.com, all without corporate oversight and approval. This work can result in employees operating outside established firm guidelines and procedures, potentially introducing operational inconsistencies or even legal and security concerns.

The consumerization of corporate technology isn't all bad. Employee creativity can blossom with increased access to new technologies, costs might be lower than home grown solutions, and staff could introduce the firm to new tools that might not otherwise be on the radar of the firm's IS Department. But all this creates an environment that requires a level of engagement between a firm's technical staff and the groups that it serves that is deeper than that employed by any prior generation of technology workers. Those working in an organization's information systems group must be sure to conduct regular meetings with representative groups of employees across the firm to understand their pain points and assess their changing technology needs. Non-IT managers should regularly reach out to IT to ensure that their needs are on the tech staff's agenda. Organizations with internal IT-staff R&D functions that scan new technologies and critically examine their relevance and potential impact on the firm can help guide an organization through the promise and peril of new technologies. Now more than ever, IT managers must be deeply knowledgeable about business areas, broadly aware of new technologies, and able to bridge the tech and business worlds. Similarly, any manager looking to advance his or her organization has to regularly consider the impact of new technologies.

KEY TAKEAWAYS

The risks associated with SaaS include the following:

- *dependence on a single vendor.*
- concern about the long-term *viability of partner firms.*
- users *may be forced to migrate to new versions*—possibly incurring unforeseen training costs and shifts in operating procedures.
- *reliance on a network connection*—which may be slower, less stable, and less secure.
- *data asset stored off-site*—with the potential for security and legal concerns.
- *limited configuration, customization, and system integration options* compared to packaged software or alternatives developed in-house.
- *the user interface of Web-based software is often less sophisticated and lacks the richness of most desktop alternatives.*
- ease of adoption *may lead to pockets of unauthorized IT* being used throughout an organization.

QUESTIONS AND EXERCISES

1. Consider the following two firms: a consulting start-up, and a defense contractor. Leverage what you know about SaaS and advise whether each might consider SaaS efforts for CRM or other enterprise functions? Why or why not?
2. Think of firms you've worked for, or firms you would like to work for. Do SaaS offerings make sense for these firms? Make a case for or against using certain categories of SaaS.
3. What factors would you consider when evaluating a SaaS vendor? Which firms are more appealing to you and why?
4. Discuss problems that may arise because SaaS solutions rely on Internet connections. Discuss the advantages of through-the-browser access.
5. Evaluate trial versions of desktop SaaS offerings (offered by Adobe, Google, Microsoft, Zoho, or others). Do you agree that the interfaces of Web-based versions are not as robust as desktop rivals? Are they good enough for you? For most users?

9. THE HARDWARE CLOUD: UTILITY COMPUTING AND ITS COUSINS

LEARNING OBJECTIVES

1. **Distinguish between SaaS and hardware clouds.**
2. **Provide examples of firms and uses of hardware clouds.**
3. **Understand the concepts of cloud computing, cloudbursting, and black swan events.**
4. **Understand the challenges and economics involved in shifting computing hardware to the cloud.**

While SaaS provides the software *and* hardware to replace an internal information system, sometimes a firm develops its own custom software but wants to pay someone else to run it for them. That's where hardware clouds, utility computing, and related technologies come in. In this model, a firm replaces computing hardware that it might otherwise run on-site with a service provided by a third party online. While the term utility computing was fashionable a few years back (and old timers claim it shares a lineage with terms like hosted computing or even time sharing), now most in the industry have begun referring to this as an aspect of cloud computing, often referred to as **hardware clouds**. Computing hardware used in this scenario exists "in the cloud," meaning somewhere on the Internet. The costs of systems operated in this manner look more like a utility bill—you only pay for the amount of processing, storage, and telecommunications used. Tech research firm Gartner has estimated that 80 percent of corporate tech spending goes toward data center maintenance.[54] Hardware-focused cloud computing provides a way for firms to chip away at these costs.

Major players are spending billions building out huge data centers to take all kinds of computing out of the corporate data center and place it in the cloud. While cloud vendors typically host your software on their systems, many of these vendors also offer additional tools to help in creating and hosting apps in the cloud. Salesforce.com offers Force.com, which includes not only a hardware cloud but also several cloud-supporting tools, such as a programming environment (IDE) to write applications specifically tailored for Web-based delivery. Google's App Engine offers developers several tools, including a database product called Big Table. And Microsoft offers a competing product—Windows Azure that runs the SQL Azure database. These efforts are often described by the phrase **platform as a service (PaaS)** since the cloud vendor provides a more complete platform (e.g., hosting hardware, operating system, database, and other software), which clients use to build their own applications.

hardware clouds

A cloud computing model in which a service provider makes computing resources such as hardware and storage, along with infrastructure management, available to a customer on an as-needed basis. The provider typically charges for specific resource usage rather than a flat rate. In the past, similar efforts have been described as utility computing, hosting, or even time sharing.

platform as a service (PaaS)

Where cloud providers offer services that include the hardware, operating system, tools, and hosting (i.e., the platform) that its customers use to *build their own applications* on the provider's infrastructure. In this scenario the cloud firm usually manages the platform (hosting, hardware, and supporting software), while the client has control over the creation and deployment of their appliation.

Another alternative is called **infrastructure as a service (IaaS)**. This is a good alternative for firms that want even more control. In IaaS, clients can select their own operating systems, development environments, underlying applications like databases, or other software packages (i.e., clients, and not cloud vendors, get to pick the platform), while the cloud firm usually manages the infrastructure (providing hardware and networking). IaaS services are offered by a wide variety of firms, including Amazon, Rackspace, Oracle, Dell, HP, and IBM.

Still other cloud computing efforts focus on providing a virtual replacement for operational hardware like storage and backup solutions. These include the cloud-based backup efforts like EMC's Mozy, and corporate storage services like Amazon's Simple Storage Solution (S3). Even efforts like Apple's iCloud that sync user data across devices (phone, multiple desktops) are considered part of the cloud craze. The common theme in all of this is leveraging computing delivered over the Internet to satisfy the computing needs of both users and organizations.

infrastructure as a service (IaaS)

Where cloud providers offer services that include running the remote hardware and networking (i.e., the infrastructure), but client firms can choose software used (which may include operating systems, programming languages, databases, and other software packages). In this scenario the cloud firm usually manages the infrastructure (keeping the hardware and networking running), while the client has control over most other things (operating systems, storage, deployed applications, and perhaps even security and networking features like firewalls and security systems).

cloudbursting

Describes the use of cloud computing to provide excess capacity during periods of spiking demand. Cloudbursting is a scalability solution that is usually provided as an overflow sservice, kicking in as needed.

black swans

Unpredicted, but highly impactful events. Scalable computing resources can help a firm deal with spiking impact from Black Swan events. The phrase entered the managerial lexicon from the 2007 book of the same name by Nassim Taleb.

Clouds in Action: A Snapshot of Diverse Efforts

Large, established organizations, small firms and start-ups are all embracing the cloud. The examples below illustrate the wide range of these efforts.

Journalists refer to the *New York Times* as, "The Old Gray Lady," but it turns out that the venerable paper is a cloud-pioneering whippersnapper. When the *Times* decided to make roughly one hundred fifty years of newspaper archives (over fifteen million articles) available over the Internet, it realized that the process of converting scans into searchable PDFs would require more computing power than the firm had available.[55] To solve the challenge, a *Times* IT staffer simply broke out a credit card and signed up for Amazon's EC2 cloud computing and S3 cloud storage services. The *Times* then started uploading terabytes of information to Amazon, along with a chunk of code to execute the conversion. While anyone can sign up for services online without speaking to a rep, someone from Amazon eventually contacted the *Times* to check in after noticing the massive volume of data coming into its systems. Using one hundred of Amazon's Linux servers, the *Times* job took just twenty-four hours to complete. In fact, a coding error in the initial batch forced the paper to rerun the job. Even the blunder was cheap—just two hundred forty dollars in extra processing costs. Says a member of the *Times* IT group: "It would have taken a month at our facilities, since we only had a few spare PCs.…It was cheap experimentation, and the learning curve isn't steep."[56]

NASDAQ also uses Amazon's cloud as part of its Market Replay system. The exchange uses Amazon to make terabytes of data available on demand, and uploads an additional thirty to eighty gigabytes every day. Market Reply allows access through an Adobe AIR interface to pull together historical market conditions in the ten-minute period surrounding a trade's execution. This allows NASDAQ to produce a snapshot of information for regulators or customers who question a trade. Says the exchange's VP of Product Development, "The fact that we're able to keep so much data online indefinitely means the brokers can quickly answer a question without having to pull data out of old tapes and CD backups."[57] NASDAQ isn't the only major financial organization leveraging someone else's cloud. Others include Merrill Lynch, which uses IBM's Blue Cloud servers to build and evaluate risk analysis programs; and Morgan Stanley, which relies on Force.com for recruiting applications.

IBM's cloud efforts, which count Elizabeth Arden and the U.S. Golf Association among their customers, offer several services, including so-called **cloudbursting**. In a cloudbursting scenario a firm's data center running at maximum capacity can seamlessly shift part of the workload to IBM's cloud, with any spikes in system use metered, utility style. Cloudbursting is appealing because forecasting demand is difficult and can't account for the ultrarare, high-impact events, sometimes called **black swans**. Planning to account for usage spikes explains why the servers at many conventional corporate IS shops run at only 10 to 20 percent capacity.[58] While Cloud Labs cloudbursting service is particularly appealing for firms that already have a heavy reliance on IBM hardware in-house, it is possible to build these systems using the hardware clouds of other vendors, too.

Salesforce.com's Force.com cloud is especially tuned to help firms create and deploy custom Web applications. The firm makes it possible to piece together projects using premade Web services that provide software building blocks for features like calendaring and scheduling. The integration with the firm's SaaS CRM effort, and with third-party products like Google Maps allows enterprise mash-ups that can combine services from different vendors into a single application that's run on Force.com hardware. The platform even includes tools to help deploy Facebook applications. Intuitive Surgical used Force.com to create and host a custom application to gather clinical trial data for the firm's surgical robots. An IS manager at Intuitive noted, "We could build it using just their tools, so in essence, there was no programming."[59] Other users include Jobscience, which used Force.com to launch its online recruiting site; and Harrah's Entertainment, which uses Force.com applications to manage room reservations, air travel programs, and player relations.

9.1 Challenges Remain

Hardware clouds and SaaS share similar benefits and risk, and as our discussion of SaaS showed, cloud efforts aren't for everyone. Some additional examples illustrate the challenges in shifting computing hardware to the cloud.

For all the hype about cloud computing, it doesn't work in all situations. From an architectural standpoint, most large organizations run a hodgepodge of systems that include both package applications and custom code written in-house. Installing a complex set of systems on someone else's hardware can be a brutal challenge and in many cases is just about impossible. For that reason we can expect most cloud computing efforts to focus on new software development projects rather than options for old software. Even for efforts that can be custom-built and cloud-deployed, other roadblocks remain. For example, some firms face stringent regulatory compliance issues. To quote one tech industry executive, "How do you demonstrate what you are doing is in compliance when it is done outside?"[60]

Firms considering cloud computing need to do a thorough financial analysis, comparing the capital and other costs of owning and operating their own systems over time against the variable costs over the same period for moving portions to the cloud. For high-volume, low-maintenance systems, the numbers may show that it makes sense to buy rather than rent. Cloud costs can seem super cheap at first. Sun's early cloud effort offered a flat fee of one dollar per CPU per hour. Amazon's cloud storage rates were twenty-five cents per gigabyte per month. But users often also pay for the number of accesses and the number of data transfers.[61] A quarter a gigabyte a month may seem like a small amount, but system maintenance costs often include the need to clean up old files or put them on tape. If unlimited data is stored in the cloud, these costs can add up.

Firms should enter the cloud cautiously, particularly where mission-critical systems are concerned. Amazon's spring 2011 cloud collapse impacted a number of firms, especially start-ups looking to leanly ramp up by avoiding buying and hosting their own hardware. HootSuite and Quora were down completely, Reddit was in "emergency read-only mode," and Foursquare, GroupMe, and SCVNGR experienced glitches. Along with downtime, a small percentage (roughly 0.07 percent) of data involved in the crash was lost.[62] If a cloud vendor fails you and all your eggs are in one basket, then you're down, too. Vendors with multiple data centers that are able to operate with fault-tolerant provisioning, keeping a firm's efforts at more than one location to account for any operating interruptions, will appeal to firms with stricter uptime requirements, but even this isn't a guarantee. A human configuration error hosed Amazon's clients, despite the fact that the firm had confirmed redundant facilities in multiple locations.[63] Cloud firms often argue that their expertise translates into less downtime and failure than conventional corporate data centers, but no method is without risks.

KEY TAKEAWAYS

- It's estimated that 80 percent of corporate tech spending goes toward data center maintenance. Hardware-focused cloud computing initiatives from third party firms help tackle this cost by allowing firms to run their own software on the hardware of the provider.
- Amazon, EMC, Google, IBM, Microsoft, Oracle/Sun, Rackspace, and Salesforce.com are among firms offering platforms to run custom software projects. Some offer additional tools and services, including additional support for cloud-based software development, hosting, application integration, and backup.
- Cloud computing varieties include platform as a service (PaaS), where vendors provide a platform (e.g., the operating system and supporting software like database management systems) but where client firms write their own code; and infrastructure as a service (IaaS), where cloud vendors provide and manage the underlying infrastructure (hardware and networking), while clients can create their own platform, choosing operating systems, applications, and configurations.
- Users of cloud computing run the gamut of industries, including publishing (the *New York Times*), finance (NASDAQ), and cosmetics and skin care (Elizabeth Arden).
- Benefits and risks are similar to those discussed in SaaS efforts. Benefits include the use of the cloud for handling large batch jobs or limited-time tasks, offloading expensive computing tasks, and cloudbursting efforts that handle system overflow when an organization needs more capacity.
- Most legacy systems can't be easily migrated to the cloud, meaning most efforts will be new efforts or those launched by younger firms.
- Cloud (utility) computing doesn't work in situations where complex legacy systems have to be ported or where there may be regulatory compliance issues.
- Some firms may still find TCO and pricing economics favor buying over renting—scale sometimes suggests an organization is better off keeping efforts in-house.

QUESTIONS AND EXERCISES

1. What are hardware clouds? What kinds of services are described by this terms? What are other names for this phenomenon? How does this differ from SaaS?
2. Which firms are the leading providers of hardware clouds? How are clients using these efforts?
3. List the circumstances where hardware clouds work best and where it works poorly. When would each alternative make more sense—SaaS, PaaS, and IaaS? What sorts of issues should firms consider, and what sorts of expertise would be necessary when adopting each alternative?
4. Research cloud-based alternatives for backing up your hard drive. Which are among the best reviewed product or services? Why? Do you or would you use such a service? Why or why not?
5. Can you think of "black swan" events that have caused computing services to become less reliable? Describe the events and its consequences for computing services. Suggest a method and vendor for helping firms overcome the sorts of events that you encountered.

10. CLOUDS AND TECH INDUSTRY IMPACT

LEARNING OBJECTIVES

1. **Understand how cloud computing's impact across industries is proving to be broad and significant.**
2. **Know the effects of cloud computing on high-end server sales and the influence on the trend shifting from hardware sales to service.**
3. **Know the effects of cloud computing on innovation and the influence on the changes in the desired skills mix and job outlook for IS workers.**
4. **Know that by lowering the cost to access powerful systems and software, cloud computing can decrease barriers to entry.**
5. **Understand the importance, size, and metrics of server farms.**

Although still a relatively recent phenomenon, cloud computing's impact across industries is already proving to be broad and significant.

Cloud computing is affecting the competitive dynamics of the hardware, software, and consulting industries. In the past, firms seeking to increase computing capacity invested heavily in expensive, high margin server hardware, creating a huge market for computer manufacturers. But now hardware firms find these markets may be threatened by the cloud. The trend shifting from hardware to services is evident in IBM's quarterly numbers. The firm recently reported its overall earnings were up 12 percent, even though hardware sales were off by 20 percent.[64] What made up the difference? The growth of Big Blue's services business. IBM is particularly well positioned to take advantage of the shift to services because it employs more technology consultants than any other firm in the world, while most of its competitors are forced to partner to offer something comparable. Consulting firm Capgemini's partnership to offer cloud services through Amazon is one such example.

The shift to cloud computing also alters the margin structure for many in the computing industry. While Moore's Law has made servers cheap, deploying SaaS and operating a commercial cloud is still very expensive—much more so than simply making additional copies of conventional, packaged software. Microsoft surprised Wall Street when it announced it would need to pour at least $2 billion more than analysts expected into the year's **server farm** capital spending. The firm's stock—among the world's most widely held—sank 11 percent in a day.[65] As a result, many portfolio managers started paying closer attention to the business implications of the cloud.

server farm

A massive network of computer servers running software to coordinate their collective use. Server farms provide the infrastructure backbone to SaaS and hardware cloud efforts, as well as many large-scale Internet services.

Cloud computing can accelerate innovation and therefore changes the desired skills mix and job outlook for IS workers. If cloud computing customers spend less on expensive infrastructure investments, they potentially have more money to reinvest in strategic efforts and innovation. IT careers may change, too. Demand for nonstrategic skills like hardware operations and maintenance are likely to decrease. Organizations will need more business-focused technologists who intimately understand a firm's competitive environment, and can create systems that add value and differentiate the firm from its competition.[66] While these tech jobs require more business training, they're also likely to be more durable and less likely to be outsourced to a third party with a limited understanding of the firm.

By lowering the cost to access powerful systems and software, barriers to entry also decrease. Firms need to think about the strategic advantages they can create, even as technology is easily duplicated. This trend means the potential for more new entrants across industries, and since start-ups can do more with less, it's also influencing entrepreneurship and venture capital. The CTO of SlideShare, a start-up that launched using Amazon's S3 storage cloud, offers a presentation on his firm's site labeled "Using S3 to Avoid VC." Similarly, the CEO of online payments start-up Zuora claims to have saved between half a million and $1 million by using cloud computing: "We have no servers, we run the entire business in the cloud."[67] And the sophistication of these tools lowers development time. Enterprise firm Apttus claims it was able to perform the equivalent of six months of development in a couple of weekends by using cloud services. The firm scored its first million-dollar deal in three months, and was break-even in nine months, a ramp-up time that would have been unheard of, had they needed to plan, purchase, and deploy their own data center, and create from scratch the Web services that were provided by its cloud vendor.[68]

So What's It Take to Run This Thing?

In the countryside surrounding the Columbia River in the Pacific Northwest, potato farms are yielding to server farms. Turns out the area is tailor made for creating the kinds of massive data installations that form the building blocks of cloud computing. The land is cheap, the region's hydroelectric power costs a fraction of Silicon Valley rates, and the area is served by ultrafast fiber-optic connections. Even the area's mild temperatures cut cooling costs.

Most major players in cloud computing have server farms in the region, each with thousands of processors humming away simultaneously. Microsoft's Quincy, Washington, facility is as big as ten American football fields and has nearly six hundred miles of wiring, 1.5 metric tons of battery backup, and three miles of chiller piping to keep things cool. Storage is big enough to store 6.75 trillion photos. Just a short drive away, Yahoo! has two facilities on fifty acres, including one that runs at a zero carbon footprint. Google has a thirty-acre site sprawled across former farmland in The Dalles, Oregon. The Google site includes two massive buildings, with a third on the way. And in Boardman, Oregon, Amazon has a three building petabyte palace that sports its own ten-megawatt electrical substation.[69]

While U.S. activity has been particularly intense in the Pacific Northwest, server farms that support cloud computing are popping up from Shanghai to São Paulo. Not only does a diverse infrastructure offer a degree of fault tolerance and disaster recovery (Oregon down? Shift to North Carolina), the myriad of national laws and industry-specific regulatory environments may require some firms to keep data within a specific country or region. To meet the challenge, cloud vendors are racing to deploy infrastructure worldwide and allowing customers to select regional availability zones for their cloud computing needs.

The build-out race has become so intense that many firms have developed rapid-deployment server farm modules that are preconfigured and packed inside shipping containers. Some of these units contain as many as three thousand servers each. Just drop the containers on-site, link to power, water, and telecom, and presto—you've got yourself a data center. More than two hundred containers can be used on a single site. One Microsoft VP claimed the configuration has cut the time to open a data center to just a few days, claiming Microsoft's San Antonio facility was operational in less time than it took a local western wear firm to deliver her custom-made cowboy boots![70] Microsoft's Dublin-based fourth generation data center will be built entirely of containers—no walls or roof—using the outside air for much of the cooling.[71]

This Sun server-packed container is designed for rapid data center deployment.

While firms are buying less hardware, cloud vendors have turned out to be the computing industry's best customers. Amazon has spent well over $2 billion on its cloud infrastructure. Google reportedly has 1.4 million servers operating across three dozen data centers.[72] Demonstrating it won't be outdone, Microsoft plans to build as many as twenty server farms, at costs of up to $1 billion each.[73] Look for the clouds to pop up in unexpected places. Microsoft has scouted locations in Siberia, while Google has applied to patent a method for floating data centers on an offshore platform powered by wave motions.[74]

KEY TAKEAWAYS

- Cloud computing's impact across industries is proving to be broad and significant.
- Clouds can lower barriers to entry in an industry, making it easier for start-ups to launch and smaller firms to leverage the backing of powerful technology.
- Clouds may also lower the amount of capital a firm needs to launch a business, shifting power away from venture firms in those industries that had previously needed more VC money.
- Clouds can shift resources out of capital spending and into profitability and innovation.
- Hardware and software sales may drop as cloud use increases, while service revenues will increase.
- Cloud computing can accelerate innovation and therefore changes the desired skills mix and job outlook for IS workers. Tech skills in data center operations, support, and maintenance may shrink as a smaller number of vendors consolidate these functions.
- Demand continues to spike for business-savvy technologists. Tech managers will need even stronger business skills and will focus an increasing percentage of their time on strategic efforts. These latter jobs are tougher to outsource, since they involve an intimate knowledge of the firm, its industry, and its operations.
- The market for expensive, high margin, sever hardware is threatened by companies moving applications to the cloud instead of investing in hardware.
- Server farms require plenty of cheap land, low cost power, ultrafast fiber-optic connections, and benefit from mild climates.
- Sun, Microsoft, IBM, and HP have all developed rapid-deployment server farm modules that are pre configured and packed inside shipping containers.

QUESTIONS AND EXERCISES

1. Describe the change in IBM's revenue stream resulting from the shift to the cloud.
2. Why is IBM particularly well positioned to take advantage of the shift to services?
3. Describe the shift in skill sets required for IT workers that is likely to result from the widespread adoption of cloud computing.
4. Why do certain entry barriers decrease as a result of cloud computing? What is the effect of lower entry barriers on new entrants, entrepreneurship, and venture capital? On existing competitors?
5. What factors make the Columbia River region of the Pacific Northwest an ideal location for server farms?
6. What is the estimated number of computers operated by Google?
7. Why did Microsoft's shift to cloud computing create an unexpected shock among stock analysts who cover the firm? What does this tell you about the importance of technology understanding among finance and investment professionals?
8. Why do cloud computing vendors build regional server farms instead of one mega site?
9. Why would a firm build a container-based data center?

11. VIRTUALIZATION: SOFTWARE THAT MAKES ONE COMPUTER ACT LIKE MANY

LEARNING OBJECTIVES

1. **Know what virtualization software is and its impact on cloud computing.**
2. **Be able to list the benefits to a firm from using virtualization.**

The reduced costs and increased power of commodity hardware are not the only contributors to the explosion of cloud computing. The availability of increasingly sophisticated software tools has also had an impact. Perhaps the most important software tool in the cloud computing toolbox is **virtualization**. Think of virtualization as being a kind of operating system for operating systems. A server running virtualization software can create smaller compartments in memory that each behave as a separate computer with its own operating system and resources. The most sophisticated of these tools also allow firms to combine servers into a huge pool of computing resources that can be allocated as needed.[75]

Virtualization can generate huge savings. Some studies have shown that on average, conventional data centers run at 15 percent or less of their maximum capacity. Data centers using virtualization software have increased utilization to 80 percent or more.[76] This increased efficiency means cost savings in hardware, staff, and real estate. Plus it reduces a firm's IT-based energy consumption, cutting costs, lowering its carbon footprint, and boosting "green cred."[77] Using virtualization, firms can buy and maintain fewer servers, each running at a greater capacity. It can also power down servers until demand increases require them to come online.

While virtualization is a key software building block that makes public cloud computing happen, it can also be used in-house to reduce an organization's hardware needs, and even to create a firm's own private cloud of scalable assets. Bechtel, BT, Merrill Lynch, and Morgan Stanley are among the firms with large private clouds enabled by virtualization.[78] Another kind of virtualization, **virtual desktops** allow a server to run what amounts to a copy of a PC—OS, applications, and all—and simply deliver an image of what's executing to a PC or other connected device. This allows firms to scale, back up, secure, and upgrade systems far more easily than if they had to maintain each individual PC. One game start-up hopes to remove the high-powered game console hardware attached to your television and instead put the console in the cloud, delivering games to your TV as they execute remotely on superfast server hardware. Virtualization can even live on your desktop. Anyone who's ever run Windows in a window on Mac OS X is using virtualization software; these tools inhabit a chunk of your Mac's memory for running Windows and actually fool this foreign OS into thinking that it's on a PC.

Interest in virtualization has exploded in recent years. VMware, the virtualization software division of storage firm EMC, was the biggest IPO of 2007. But its niche is getting crowded. Microsoft has entered the market, building virtualization into its server offerings. Dell bought a virtualization software firm for $1.54 billion. And there's even an open source virtualization product called Xen.[79]

virtualization

A type of software that allows a single computer (or cluster of connected computers) to function as if it were several different computers, each running its own operating system and software. Virtualization software underpins most cloud computing efforts, and can make computing more efficient, cost-effective, and scalable.

virtual desktop

When a firm runs an instance of a PC's software on another machine and simply delivers the image of what's executing to the remote device. Using virtualization, a single server can run dozens of PCs, simplifying backup, upgrade, security, and administration.

KEY TAKEAWAYS

- Virtualization software allows one computing device to function as many. The most sophisticated products also make it easy for organizations to scale computing requirements across several servers.
- Virtualization software can lower a firm's hardware needs, save energy, and boost scalability.
- Data center virtualization software is at the heart of many so-called private clouds and scalable corporate data centers, as well as the sorts of public efforts described earlier.
- Virtualization also works on the desktop, allowing multiple operating systems (Mac OS X, Linux, Windows) to run simultaneously on the same platform.
- Virtualization software can increase data center utilization to 80 percent or more.
- While virtualization is used to make public cloud computing happen, it can also be used in-house to create a firm's own private cloud.
- A number of companies, including Microsoft and Dell, have entered the growing virtualization market.

QUESTIONS AND EXERCISES

1. List the benefits to a firm from using virtualization.
2. What is the average utilization rate for conventional data centers?
3. List companies that have virtualization-enabled private clouds.
4. Give an example of desktop virtualization.
5. Name three companies that are players in the virtualization software industry.

12. MAKE, BUY, OR RENT

LEARNING OBJECTIVES

1. **Know the options managers have when determining how to satisfy the software needs of their companies.**
2. **Know the factors that must be considered when making the make, buy, or rent decision.**

So now you realize managers have a whole host of options when seeking to fulfill the software needs of their firms. An organization can purchase packaged software from a vendor, use open source offerings, leverage SaaS or other type of cloud computing, outsource development or other IT functions to another firm either domestically or abroad, or a firm can develop all or part of the effort themselves. When presented with all of these options, making decisions about technologies and systems can seem pretty daunting.

First, realize that that for most firms, technology decisions are not binary options for the whole organization in all situations. Few businesses will opt for an IT configuration that is 100 percent in-house, packaged, or SaaS. Being aware of the parameters to consider can help a firm make better, more informed decisions. It's also important to keep in mind that these decisions need to be continuously reevaluated as markets and business needs change. What follows is a summary of some of the key variables to consider.

Competitive Advantage—*Do we rely on unique processes, procedures, or technologies that create vital, differentiating competitive advantage?* If so, then these functions aren't a good candidate to outsource or replace with a package software offering. Amazon.com had originally used recommendation software provided by a third party, and Netflix and Dell both considered third-party software to manage inventory fulfillment. But in all three cases, these firms felt that mastery of these functions was too critical to competitive advantage, so each firm developed proprietary systems unique to the circumstances of each firm.

Security—*Are there unacceptable risks associated with using the packaged software, OSS, cloud solution, or an outsourcing vendor? Are we convinced that the prospective solution is sufficiently secure and reliable? Can we trust the prospective vendor with our code, our data, our procedures and our way of doing business? Are there noncompete provisions for vendor staff that may be privy to our secrets? For off-site work, are there sufficient policies in place for on-site auditing?* If the answers to any of these questions is no, outsourcing might not be a viable option.

Legal and Compliance—*Is our firm prohibited outright from using technologies? Are there specific legal and compliance requirements related to deploying our products or services?* Even a technology as innocuous as instant messaging may need to be deployed in such a way that it complies with laws requiring firms to record and reproduce the electronic equivalent of a paper trail. For example, SEC Rule 17a-4 requires broker dealers to retain client communications for a minimum of three years. HIPAA laws governing health care providers state that electronic communications must also be captured and stored.[80] While tech has gained a seat in the board room, legal also deserves a seat in systems planning meetings.

Skill, Expertise, and Available Labor—*Can we build it?* The firm may have skilled technologists, but they may not be sufficiently experienced with a new technology. Even if they are skilled, managers must consider the costs of allocating staff away from existing projects for this effort.

Cost—*Is this a cost-effective choice for our firm?* A host of factors must be considered when evaluating the cost of an IT decision. The costs to build, host, maintain, and support an ongoing effort involve labor (software development, quality assurance, ongoing support, training, and maintenance), consulting, security, operations, licensing, energy, and real estate. Any analysis of costs should consider not only the aggregate spending required over the lifetime of the effort but also whether these factors might vary over time.

Time—*Do we have time to build, test, and deploy the system?*

Vendor Issues—*Is the vendor reputable and in a sound financial position? Can the vendor guarantee the service levels and reliability we need? What provisions are in place in case the vendor fails or is acquired? Is the vendor certified via the Carnegie Mellon Software Institute or other standards organizations in a way that conveys quality, trust, and reliability?*

The list above is a starter. It should also be clear that these metrics are sometimes quite tough to estimate. Welcome to the challenges of being a manager! At times an environment in flux can make an executive feel like he or she is working on a surfboard, constantly being buffeted about by unexpected currents and waves. Hopefully the issues outlined in this chapter will give you the surfing skills you need for a safe ride that avoids the organizational equivalent of a wipeout.

KEY TAKEAWAYS

- The make, buy, or rent decision may apply on a case-by-case basis that might be evaluated by firm, division, project or project component. Firm and industry dynamics may change in a way that causes firms to reassess earlier decisions, or to alter the direction of new initiatives.
- Factors that managers should consider when making a make, buy, or rent decision include the following: competitive advantage, security, legal and compliance issues, the organization's skill and available labor, cost, time, and vendor issues.
- Factors must be evaluated over the lifetime of a project, not at a single point in time.
- Managers have numerous options available when determining how to satisfy the software needs of their companies: purchase packaged software from a vendor, use OSS, use SaaS or utility computing, outsourcing development, or developing all or part of the effort themselves.
- If a company relies on unique processes, procedures, or technologies that create vital, differentiating, competitive advantages, the functions probably aren't a good candidate to outsource.

QUESTIONS AND EXERCISES

1. What are the options available to managers when seeking to meet the software needs of their companies?
2. What are the factors that must be considered when making the make, buy, or rent decision?
3. What are some security-related questions that must be asked when making the make, buy, or rent decision?
4. What are some vendor-related questions that must be asked when making the make, buy, or rent decision?
5. What are some of the factors that must be considered when evaluating the cost of an IT decision?
6. Why must factors be evaluated over the lifetime of a project, not at a single point in time?

ENDNOTES

1. D. Kirkpatrick, "How the Open Source World Plans to Smack Down Microsoft and Oracle, and…," *Fortune*, February 23, 2004.
2. F. Vogelstein, "Rebuilding Microsoft," *Wired*, October 2006.
3. D. Diamond, "The Good-Hearted Wizard—Linus Torvalds," *Virtual Finland*, January 2008.
4. Sarah Lacy, "Open Warfare in Open Source," *BusinessWeek*, August 21, 2006; "Worldwide Server Market Revenues Increase 12.1% in First Quarter as Market Demand Continues to Improve, according to IDC," *IDC*, May 24, 2011.
5. "Gartner Says Worldwide Mobile Phone Sales Grew 35 Percent in Third Quarter 2010; Smartphone Sales Increased 96 Percent," *Gartner*, November 10, 2010.
6. J. Brockmeier, "NASA Using Linux," *Unix Review*, March 2004; and S. Barrett, "Linux on Mars," *Science News, Space News, Technology News*, June 6, 2008.
7. For examples, see http://mostlylinux.ca/pronounce/torvalds-says-linux.wav and http://suseroot.com/about-suse-linux/how-do-you-pronounce-linux.php.
8. A list of criteria defining open source software can be found at the Open Source Initiative at http://opensource.org/osr.
9. J. Fortt, "Why Larry Loves Linux (and He's Not Alone)," *Fortune*, December 19, 2007.
10. D. Woods, "The Commercial Bear Hug of Open Source," *Forbes*, August 18, 2008.
11. C. Preimesberger, "Sun's 'Open'-Door Policy," *eWeek*, April 21, 2008.
12. M. Castelluccio, "Enterprise Open Source Adoption," *Strategic Finance*, November 2008.
13. R. King, "Cost-Conscious Companies Turn to Open-Source Software," *BusinessWeek*, December 1, 2008.
14. S. Shankland, M. Kane, and R. Lemos, "How Linux Saved Amazon Millions," *CNET*, October 30, 2001.
15. E. Raymond, *The Cathedral and the Bazaar: Musings on Linux and Open Source by an Accidental Revolutionary* (Sebastopol, CA: O'Reilly, 1999).
16. J. Ljungberg, "Open Source Movements as a Model for Organizing," *European Journal of Information Systems* 9, no. 4 (December 2000): 208–16.
17. M. Castelluccio, "Enterprise Open Source Adoption," *Strategic Finance*, November 2008.
18. D. Wheeler, *Secure Programming for Linux and Unix*, 2003, http://www.dwheeler.com/secure-programs/Secure-Programs-HOWTO/index.html.
19. R. McMillan, "Gone in Two Minutes," *InfoWorld*, March 27, 2008.
20. S. Lohr, "Microsoft to Give Governments Access to Code," *New York Times*, January 15, 2003.
21. R. King, "Cost-Conscious Companies Turn to Open-Source Software," *BusinessWeek*, December 1, 2008.
22. R. Guth, "Virtual Piecework: Trolling the Web for Free Labor, Software Upstarts Are a New Force," *Wall Street Journal*, November 13, 2006.
23. See http://sourceforge.net.
24. D. Woods, "The Commercial Bear Hug of Open Source," *Forbes*, August 18, 2008.
25. M. Asay, "Open Source Is a $60 Billion Industry," *CNET*, May 15, 2008.
26. A. Greenberg, "Sun Snaps Up Database Firm, MySQL," *Forbes*, January 16, 2008; G. Huang, "Attachmate Buys Novell for $2.2B—The End of an Era," *Xconomy*, November 22, 2010.
27. A. Greenberg, "Sun Snaps Up Database Firm, MySQL," *Forbes*, January 16, 2008.
28. J. Fortt, "Why Larry Loves Linux (and He's Not Alone)," *Fortune*, December 19, 2007.
29. J. Robertson, "IBM Sees Better-Than-Expected 2009 Profit, Earns US$4.4 Billion in Q4," *Associated Press*, January 20, 2009, http://humantimes.com/finance/business/sanfrancis/54853.
30. C. Preimesberger, "Sun's 'Open'-Door Policy," *eWeek*, April 21, 2008.
31. S. Cohen, "Open Source: The Model Is Broken," *BusinessWeek*, December 1, 2008.
32. D. Lyons, "Cheapware," *Forbes*, September 6, 2004.
33. A. Ricadela, "The Worth of Open Source? Open Question," *BusinessWeek*, June 26, 2007.
34. D. Kirkpatrick, "How the Open Source World Plans to Smack Down Microsoft and Oracle, and…," *Fortune*, February 23, 2004.
35. A. Ricadela, "The Worth of Open Source? Open Question," *BusinessWeek*, June 26, 2007.
36. D. Kirkpatrick, "How the Open Source World Plans to Smack Down Microsoft and Oracle, and…," *Fortune*, February 23, 2004.
37. S. Shankland, "Google's Open-Source Android Now Actually Open," *CNET*, October 21, 2008, http://news.cnet.com/8301-1001_3-10071093-92.html.
38. M. Asay, "Open-Source Database Market Shows Muscles," *CNET*, February 3, 2009, http://news.cnet.com/8301-13505_3-10156188-16.html.
39. A. Ricadela, "Microsoft Wants to 'Kill' Open Source," *BusinessWeek*, May 15, 2007.
40. Sarah Lacy, "Open Warfare in Open Source," *BusinessWeek*, August 21, 2006.
41. D. Farber, "Oracle's Ellison Nails Cloud Computing," *CNET*, September 26, 2008, http://news.cnet.com/8301-13953_3-10052188-80.html?tag=mncol;txt.
42. S. Hamm, "Cloud Computing: Eyes on the Skies," *BusinessWeek*, April 24, 2008.
43. L. McKay, "30,000-Foot Views of the Cloud," *Customer Relationship Management*, January 2009.
44. D. Lyons, "A Mostly Cloudy Computing Forecast," *Washington Post*, November 4, 2008.
45. M. Liedtke, "Cloud Computing: Pie in the Sky Concept or the Next Big Breakthrough on Tech Horizon?" *Associated Press Newswires*, December 21, 2008; A. Gonsalves, "Cloud Services Top $68 Billion in 2010," *InformationWeek*, June 22, 2010.
46. J. Hempel, "Salesforce Hits Its Stride," *Fortune*, March 2, 2009.
47. Sarah Lacy, "On-Demand Computing: A Brutal Slog," *BusinessWeek*, July 18, 2008.
48. J. Quittner, "How SaaS Helps Cut Small Business Costs," *BusinessWeek*, December 5, 2008.
49. M. Drummond, "The End of Software as We Know It," *Fortune*, November 19, 2001.
50. M. Drummond, "The End of Software as We Know It," *Fortune*, November 19, 2001.
51. R. Wauters, "The Extraordinary Rise and Fall of Denmark's IT Factory," *TechCrunch*, December 2, 2008.
52. Sarah Lacy, "On-Demand Computing: A Brutal Slog," *BusinessWeek*, July 18, 2008.
53. G. Gruman, "Early Experiments in Cloud Computing," *InfoWorld*, April 7, 2008.
54. J. Rayport, "Cloud Computing Is No Pipe Dream," *BusinessWeek*, December 9, 2008.
55. J. Rayport, "Cloud Computing Is No Pipe Dream," *BusinessWeek*, December 9, 2008.
56. G. Gruman, "Early Experiments in Cloud Computing," *InfoWorld*, April 7, 2008.
57. P. Grossman, "Cloud Computing Begins to Gain Traction on Wall Street," *Wall Street and Technology*, January 6, 2009.
58. J. Parkinson, "Green Data Centers Tackle LEED Certification," *SearchDataCenter.com*, January 18, 2007.
59. G. Gruman, "Early Experiments in Cloud Computing," *InfoWorld*, April 7, 2008.
60. G. Gruman, "Early Experiments in Cloud Computing," *InfoWorld*, April 7, 2008.
61. C. Preimesberger, "Sun's 'Open'-Door Policy," *eWeek*, April 21, 2008.
62. A. Hesseldahl, "Amazon Details Last Week's Cloud Failure, and Apologizes," *AllThingsD*, April 29, 2011.
63. M. Rosoff, "Inside Amazon's Cloud Disaster," *BusinessInsider*, April 22, 2011.
64. J. Fortt, "Goodbye, PC (and Mac). Hello, Services," *Fortune*, February 4, 2009.
65. S. Mehta, "Behold the Server Farm," *Fortune*, July 28, 2006.
66. J. Fortt, "Tech Execs Get Sexy," *Fortune*, February 12, 2009.
67. E. Ackerman, "Forecast for Computing: Cloudy," *San Jose Mercury News*, December 23, 2008.
68. J. Rayport, "Cloud Computing Is No Pipe Dream," *BusinessWeek*, December 9, 2008.
69. R. Katz, "Tech Titans Building Boom," *IEEE Spectrum* 46, no. 2 (February 1, 2009): 40–43.
70. P. Burrows, "Microsoft to Google: Get Off of My Cloud," *BusinessWeek*, November 21, 2008.
71. T. Vanderbilt, "Data Center Overload," *New York Times*, June 8, 2009.
72. R. Katz, "Tech Titans Building Boom," *IEEE Spectrum* 46, no. 2 (February 1, 2009): 40–43.
73. P. Burrows, "Microsoft to Google: Get Off of My Cloud," *BusinessWeek*, November 21, 2008.
74. R. Katz, "Tech Titans Building Boom," *IEEE Spectrum* 46, no. 2 (February 1, 2009): 40–43.
75. D. Lyons, "A Mostly Cloudy Computing Forecast," *Washington Post*, November 4, 2008.
76. R. Katz, "Tech Titans Building Boom," *IEEE Spectrum* 46, no. 2 (February 1, 2009): 40–43.
77. K. Castro, "The Virtues of Virtualization," *BusinessWeek*, December 3, 2007.
78. J. Brodkin, "Private Clouds Bring IT Mgmt. Challenges," *NetworkWorld*, December 15, 2008.
79. K. Castro, "The Virtues of Virtualization," *BusinessWeek*, December 3, 2007.
80. D. Shapiro, "Instant Messaging and Compliance Issues: What You Need to Know," *SearchCIO*, May 17, 2004.

CHAPTER 11

The Data Asset: Databases, Business Intelligence, and Competitive Advantage

1. INTRODUCTION

LEARNING OBJECTIVES

1. **Understand how increasingly standardized data, access to third-party data sets, cheap, fast computing and easier-to-use software are collectively enabling a new age of decision making.**
2. **Be familiar with some of the enterprises that have benefited from data-driven, fact-based decision making.**

The planet is awash in data. Cash registers ring up transactions worldwide. Web browsers leave a trail of cookie crumbs nearly everywhere they go. And with radio frequency identification (RFID), inventory can literally announce its presence so that firms can precisely journal every hop their products make along the value chain: "I'm arriving in the warehouse," "I'm on the store shelf," "I'm leaving out the front door."

A study by Gartner Research claims that the amount of data on corporate hard drives doubles every six months,[1] while IDC states that the collective number of those bits already exceeds the number of stars in the universe.[2] Wal-Mart alone boasts a data volume well over *125 times* as large as the *entire* print collection of the U.S. Library of Congress, and rising.[3] You'll hear managers today broadly refer to this torrent of bits as "Big Data."

And with this flood of data comes a tidal wave of opportunity. Increasingly standardized corporate data, and access to rich, third-party data sets—all leveraged by cheap, fast computing and easier-to-use software—are collectively enabling a new age of data-driven, fact-based decision making. You're less likely to hear old-school terms like "decision support systems" used to describe what's going on here. The phrase of the day is business intelligence (BI), a catchall term combining aspects of reporting, data exploration and ad hoc queries, and sophisticated data modeling and analysis. Alongside business intelligence in the new managerial lexicon is the phrase analytics, a term describing the extensive use of data, statistical and quantitative analysis, explanatory and predictive models, and fact-based management to drive decisions and actions.[4]

The benefits of all this data and number crunching are very real, indeed. Data leverage lies at the center of competitive advantage we've studied in the Zara, Netflix, and Google cases. Data mastery has helped vault Wal-Mart to the top of the *Fortune* 500 list. It helped Harrah's Casino Hotels grow to be twice as profitable as similarly sized Caesars and rich enough to acquire this rival (Harrah's did decide that it liked the Caesars name better and is now known as Caesars Entertainment). And data helped Capital One find valuable customers that competitors were ignoring, delivering ten-year financial performance a full ten times greater than the S&P 500. Data-driven decision making is even credited with helping the Red Sox win their first World Series in eighty-three years and with helping the New England Patriots win three Super Bowls in four years. To quote from a *BusinessWeek* cover story on analytics, "Math Will Rock Your World!"[5]

Sounds great, but it can be a tough slog getting an organization to the point where it has a leveragable data asset. In many organizations data lies dormant, spread across inconsistent formats and incompatible systems, unable to be turned into anything of value. Many firms have been shocked at the

big data

A general term used to describe massive amount of data available to today's managers. Big data are often unstructured and are too big and costly to easily work through use of conventional databases, but new tools are making these massive datasets available for analysis and insight.

business intelligence (BI)

A term combining aspects of reporting, data exploration and ad hoc queries, and sophisticated data modeling and analysis.

analytics

A term describing the extensive use of data, statistical and quantitative analysis, explanatory and predictive models, and fact-based management to drive decisions and actions.

amount of work and complexity required to pull together an infrastructure that empowers its managers. But not only can this be done, it must be done. Firms that are basing decisions on hunches aren't managing; they're gambling. And today's markets have no tolerance for uninformed managerial dice rolling.

While we'll study technology in this chapter, our focus isn't as much on the technology itself as it is on what you can do with that technology. Consumer products giant P&G believes in this distinction so thoroughly that the firm renamed its IT function as "Information and Decision Solutions."[6] Solutions drive technology decisions, not the other way around.

In this chapter we'll study the data asset, how it's created, how it's stored, and how it's accessed and leveraged. We'll also study many of the firms mentioned above, and more; providing a context for understanding how managers are leveraging data to create winning models, and how those that have failed to realize the power of data have been left in the dust.

Data, Analytics, and Competitive Advantage

Anyone can acquire technology—but data is oftentimes considered a defensible source of competitive advantage. The data a firm can leverage is a true strategic asset when it's rare, valuable, imperfectly imitable, and lacking in substitutes (see Chapter 2).

If more data brings more accurate modeling, moving early to capture this rare asset can be the difference between a dominating firm and an also-ran. But be forewarned, there's no monopoly on math. Advantages based on capabilities and data that others can acquire will be short-lived. Those advances leveraged by the Red Sox were originally pioneered by the Oakland A's and are now used by nearly every team in the major leagues.

This doesn't mean that firms can ignore the importance data can play in lowering costs, increasing customer service, and other ways that boost performance. But differentiation will be key in distinguishing operationally effective data use from those efforts that can yield true strategic positioning.

KEY TAKEAWAYS

- The amount of data on corporate hard drives doubles every six months.
- In many organizations, available data is not exploited to advantage.
- Data is oftentimes considered a defensible source of competitive advantage; however, advantages based on capabilities and data that others can acquire will be short-lived.

QUESTIONS AND EXERCISES

1. Name and define the terms that are supplanting discussions of decision support systems in the modern IS lexicon.
2. Is data a source of competitive advantage? Describe situations in which data might be a source for sustainable competitive advantage. When might data not yield sustainable advantage?
3. Are advantages based on analytics and modeling potentially sustainable? Why or why not?
4. What role do technology and timing play in realizing advantages from the data asset?

2. DATA, INFORMATION, AND KNOWLEDGE

LEARNING OBJECTIVES

1. **Understand the difference between data and information.**
2. **Know the key terms and technologies associated with data organization and management.**

Data refers simply to raw facts and figures. Alone it tells you nothing. The real goal is to turn data into **information**. Data becomes information when it's presented in a context so that it can answer a question or support decision making. And it's when this information can be combined with a manager's **knowledge**—their insight from experience and expertise—that stronger decisions can be made.

data

Raw facts and figures.

information

Data presented in a context so that it can answer a question or support decision making.

knowledge

Insight derived from experience and expertise.

Trusting Your Data

The ability to look critically at data and assess its validity is a vital managerial skill. When decision makers are presented with wrong data, the results can be disastrous. And these problems can get amplified if bad data is fed to automated systems. As an example, look at the series of man-made and computer-triggered events that brought about a billion-dollar collapse in United Airlines stock.

In the wee hours one Sunday morning in September 2008, a single reader browsing back stories on the *Orlando Sentinel*'s Web site viewed a 2002 article on the bankruptcy of United Airlines (UAL went bankrupt in 2002, but emerged from bankruptcy four years later). That lone Web surfer's access of this story during such a low-traffic time was enough for the *Sentinel*'s Web server to briefly list the article as one of the paper's "most popular." Google crawled the site and picked up this "popular" news item, feeding it into Google News.

Early that morning, a worker in a Florida investment firm came across the Google-fed story, assumed United had yet again filed for bankruptcy, then posted a summary on Bloomberg. Investors scanning Bloomberg jumped on what looked like a reputable early warning of another United bankruptcy, dumping UAL stock. Blame the computers again—the rapid plunge from these early trades caused automatic sell systems to kick in (event-triggered, computer-automated trading is responsible for about 30 percent of all stock trades). Once the machines took over, UAL dropped like a rock, falling from twelve to three dollars. That drop represented the vanishing of $1 billion in wealth, and all this because no one checked the date on a news story. Welcome to the new world of paying attention![7]

2.1 Understanding How Data Is Organized: Key Terms and Technologies

A **database** is simply a list (or more likely, several related lists) of data. Most organizations have several databases—perhaps even hundreds or thousands. And these various databases might be focused on any combination of functional areas (sales, product returns, inventory, payroll), geographical regions, or business units. Firms often create specialized databases for recording transactions, as well as databases that aggregate data from multiple sources in order to support reporting and analysis.

database

A single table or a collection of related tables.

Databases are created, maintained, and manipulated using programs called **database management systems (DBMS)**, sometimes referred to as *database software*. DBMS products vary widely in scale and capabilities. They include the single-user, desktop versions of Microsoft Access or Filemaker Pro, Web-based offerings like Intuit QuickBase, and industrial strength products from Oracle, IBM (DB2), Sybase, Microsoft (SQL Server), and others. Oracle is the world's largest database software vendor, and database software has meant big bucks for Oracle cofounder and CEO Larry Ellison. Ellison perennially ranks in the Top 10 of the *Forbes* 400 list of wealthiest Americans.

database management systems (DBMS)

Sometimes called "databade software"; software for creating, maintaining, and manipulating data.

The acronym SQL (often pronounced *sequel*) also shows up a lot when talking about databases. **Structured query language (SQL)** is by far the most common language for creating and manipulating databases. You'll find variants of SQL inhabiting everything from lowly desktop software, to high-powered enterprise products. Microsoft's high-end database is even called SQL Server. And of course there's also the open source MySQL (whose stewardship now sits with Oracle as part of the firm's purchase of Sun Microsystems). Given this popularity, if you're going to learn one language for database use, SQL's a pretty good choice. And for a little inspiration, visit Monster.com or another job site and search for jobs mentioning SQL. You'll find page after page of listings, suggesting that while database systems have been good for Ellison, learning more about them might be pretty good for you, too.

structured query language (SQL)

A language used to create and manipulate databases.

database administrator (DBA)

Job title focused on directing, performing, or overseeing activities associated with a database or set of databases. These may include (but not necessarily be limited to): database design, creation, implementation, maintenance, backup and recovery, policy setting and enforcement, and security.

Even if you don't become a database programmer or **database administrator (DBA)**, you're almost surely going to be called upon to dive in and use a database. You may even be asked to help identify your firm's data requirements. It's quite common for nontech employees to work on development teams with technical staff, defining business problems, outlining processes, setting requirements, and determining the kinds of data the firm will need to leverage. Database systems are powerful stuff, and can't be avoided, so a bit of understanding will serve you well.

FIGURE 11.1 A Simplified Relational Database for a University Course Registration System

Students (1)

STUDENT_ID	FIRST_NAME	LAST_NAME	CAMPUS_ADDR	...
U11-00001	Phil	D'Basket	Weaver Hall 411	
U11-00002	Art	Major	101 Creative Commons	
U11-00003	Anne	Teak	Stickley 014	
U11-00004	Anita	Knapp	Highway View 303	
U11-00005	Easton	West	N. South Hall 123	
U11-00006	Jack	Hammer	Tule 543	
...				

Course Title (1)

COURSE_NUM	COURSE_NUM	...
MI101	IS for Managers	
MI201	Prog. for Mgmt.	
MI202	Database Sys. & Bus. Intell.	
EN101	Intro. to Lit.	
CJ101	Fighting Cyber-Crime	
...		

Enrollment (M)

STUDENT_ID	COURSE_INDX (M)	...
U11-00002	9301	
U11-00002	9303	
U11-00002	9306	
U11-00005	9305	
U11-00003	9301	
...		

Course List

COURSE_INDX (1)	...	COURSE_NUM (M)	TIME	LOCATION	FAC_ID (M)	...
9301		MI101	MWF 9	Fulton 250	F-100009	
9302		MI101	TTh 10	Fulton 250	F-100010	
9303		MI201	MWF 11	Fulton 150	F-100009	
9304		MI202	TTh 1:30	Fulton 130	F-100009	
9305		EN101	TTh 3	Gasson 205	F-100007	
9306		CJ101	MWF 3	Robsham 021	F-100005	
...						

Faculty (1)

FAC_ID	FIRST_NAME	LAST_NAME	DEPT.	CAMPUS_ADDR	...
F-100005	Marshall	Law	Criminal Justice	Warren 232	
F-100006	Bo	Ring	Sleep Studies	Giles B-12	
F-100007	Paige	Turner	English	Gasson 134	
F-100008	Penny	Wyse	Finance	Fulton 480A	
F-100009	Meg	Abe-Bight	Information Systems	Fulton 460C	
F-100010	Mike	Rowe	Information Systems	Fulton 460B	
...					

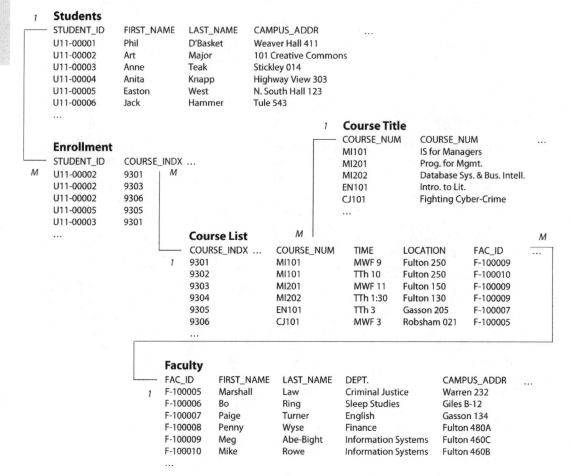

A complete discourse on technical concepts associated with database systems is beyond the scope of our managerial introduction, but here are some key concepts to help get you oriented, and that all managers should know.

- A **table or file** refers to a list of data.
- A *database* is either a single table or a collection of related tables. The course registration database above depicts five tables.
- A **column or field** defines the data that a table can hold. The "Students" table above shows columns for STUDENT_ID, FIRST_NAME, LAST_NAME, CAMPU.S._ADDR (the "..." symbols above are meant to indicate that in practice there may be more columns or rows than are shown in this simplified diagram).
- A **row or record** represents a single instance of whatever the table keeps track of. In the example above, each row of the "Students" table represents a student, each row of the "Enrollment" table represents the enrollment of a student in a particular course, and each row of the "Course List" represents a given section of each course offered by the University.
- A **key** is the field used to relate tables in a database. Look at how the STUDENT_ID key is used above. There is *one* unique STUDENT_ID for each student, but the STUDENT_ID may appear *many* times in the "Enrollment" table, indicating that each student may be enrolled in many classes. The "1" and "M" in the diagram above indicate the one to many relationships among the keys in these tables.

Databases organized like the one above, where multiple tables are related based on common keys, are referred to as **relational databases**. There are many other database formats (sporting names like *hierarchical*, and *object-oriented*), but relational databases are far and away the most popular. And all SQL databases are relational databases.

Even though SQL and the relational model are hugely popular and dominate many corporate environments, other systems exist. An increasingly popular set of technologies known as NoSQL avoid SQL and the rigid structure of relational databases. NoSQL technologies are especially popular with Internet firms that rely on massive, unwieldy, and disparately structured data.

We've just scratched the surface for a very basic introduction. Expect that a formal class in database systems will offer you far more detail and better design principles than are conveyed in the elementary example above. But you're already well on your way!

table or file

A list of data, arranged in columns (fields) and rows (records).

column or field

A column in a database table. Columns represent each category of data contained in a record (e.g., first name, last name, ID number, date of birth).

row or record

A row in a database table. Records represent a single instance of whatever the table keeps track of (e.g., student, faculty, course title).

key

Code that unlocks encryption.

relational database

The most common standard for expressing databases, whereby tables (files) are related based on common keys.

KEY TAKEAWAYS

- Data includes raw facts that must be turned into information in order to be useful and valuable.
- Databases are created, maintained, and manipulated using programs called database management systems (DBMS), sometimes referred to as database software.
- All data fields in the same database have unique names, several data fields make up a data record, multiple data records make up a table or data file, and one or more tables or data files make up a database.
- Relational databases are the most common database format.

QUESTIONS AND EXERCISES

1. Define the following terms: table, record, field. Provide another name for each term along with your definition.
2. Answer the following questions using the course registration database system, diagramed above:
    a. Imagine you also want to keep track of student majors. How would you do this? Would you modify an existing table? Would you add new tables? Why or why not?
    b. Why do you suppose the system needs a "Course Title" table?
    c. This database is simplified for our brief introduction. What additional data would you need to keep track of if this were a real course registration system? What changes would you make in the database above to account for these needs?
3. Research to find additional examples of organizations that made bad decisions based on bad data. Report your examples to your class. What was the end result of the examples you're citing (e.g., loss, damage, or other outcome)? What could managers have done to prevent problems in the cases that you cited? What role did technology play in the examples that you cite? What role did people or procedural issues play?
4. Why is an understanding of database terms and technologies important, even for nontechnical managers and staff? Consider factors associated with both system use and system development. What other skills, beyond technology, may be important when engaged in data-driven decision making?

3. WHERE DOES DATA COME FROM?

LEARNING OBJECTIVES

1. **Understand various internal and external sources for enterprise data.**
2. **Recognize the function and role of data aggregators, the potential for leveraging third-party data, the strategic implications of relying on externally purchased data, and key issues associated with aggregators and firms that leverage externally sourced data.**

Organizations can pull together data from a variety of sources. While the examples that follow aren't meant to be an encyclopedic listing of possibilities, they will give you a sense of the diversity of options available for data gathering.

3.1 Transaction Processing Systems

For most organizations that sell directly to their customers, **transaction processing systems (TPS)** represent a fountain of potentially insightful data. Every time a consumer uses a point-of-sale system, an ATM, or a service desk, there's a **transaction** (some kind of business exchange) occurring, representing an event that's likely worth tracking.

The cash register is the data generation workhorse of most physical retailers, and the primary source that feeds data to the TPS. But while TPS can generate a lot of bits, it's sometimes tough to match this data with a specific customer. For example, if you pay a retailer in cash, you're likely to remain a mystery to your merchant because your name isn't attached to your money. Grocers and retailers can tie you to cash transactions if they can convince you to use a **loyalty card**. Use one of these cards and you're in effect giving up information about yourself in exchange for some kind of financial incentive. The explosion in retailer cards is directly related to each firm's desire to learn more about you and to turn you into a more loyal and satisfied customer.

Some cards provide an instant discount (e.g., the CVS Pharmacy ExtraCare card), while others allow you to build up points over time (Best Buy's Reward Zone). The latter has the additional benefit of acting as a switching cost. A customer may think "I could get the same thing at Target, but at Best Buy, it'll increase my existing points balance and soon I'll get a cash back coupon."

transaction processing systems (TPS)

Systems that record a transaction (some form of business-related exchange), such as a cash register sale, ATM withdrawal, or product return.

transaction

Some kind of business exchange.

loyalty card

Systems that provide rewards and usage incentives, typically in exchange for a method that provides a more detailed tracking and recording of customer activity. In addition to enhancing data collection, loyalty cards can represent a significant switching cost.

Tesco: Tracked Transactions, Increased Insights, and Surging Sales

UK grocery giant Tesco, the planet's third-largest retailer, is envied worldwide for what analysts say is the firm's unrivaled ability to collect vast amounts of retail data and translate this into sales.[8]

Tesco's data collection relies heavily on its ClubCard loyalty program, an effort pioneered back in 1995. But Tesco isn't just a physical retailer. As the world's largest Internet grocer, the firm gains additional data from Web site visits, too. Remove products from your virtual shopping cart? Tesco can track this. Visited a product comparison page? Tesco watches which product you've chosen to go with and which you've passed over. Done your research online, then traveled to a store to make a purchase? Tesco sees this, too.

Tesco then mines all this data to understand how consumers respond to factors such as product mix, pricing, marketing campaigns, store layout, and Web design. Consumer-level targeting allows the firm to tailor its marketing messages to specific subgroups, promoting the right offer through the right channel at the right time and the right price. To get a sense of Tesco's laser-focused targeting possibilities, consider that the firm sends out close to ten million different, targeted offers each quarter.[9] Offer redemption rates are the best in the industry, with some coupons scoring an astronomical 90 percent usage![10]

The firm's data-driven management is clearly delivering results. Even while operating in the teeth of a global recession, Tesco repeatedly posted record corporate profits and the highest earnings ever for a British retailer.[11]

3.2 Enterprise Software (CRM, SCM, and ERP)

Firms increasingly set up systems to gather additional data beyond conventional purchase transactions or Web site monitoring. CRM or customer relationship management systems are often used to empower employees to track and record data at nearly every point of customer contact. Someone calls for a quote? Brings a return back to a store? Writes a complaint e-mail? A well-designed CRM system can capture all these events for subsequent analysis or for triggering follow-up events.

Enterprise software includes not just CRM systems but also categories that touch every aspect of the value chain, including supply chain management (SCM) and enterprise resource planning (ERP) systems. More importantly, enterprise software tends to be more integrated and standardized than the prior era of proprietary systems that many firms developed themselves. This integration helps in combining data across business units and functions, and in getting that data into a form where it can be turned into information (for more on enterprise systems, see Chapter 9).

3.3 Surveys

Sometimes firms supplement operational data with additional input from surveys and focus groups. Oftentimes, direct surveys can tell you what your cash register can't. Zara store managers informally survey customers in order to help shape designs and product mix. Online grocer FreshDirect (see Chapter 2) surveys customers weekly and has used this feedback to drive initiatives from reducing packaging size to including star ratings on produce.[12] Many CRM products also have survey capabilities that allow for additional data gathering at all points of customer contact.

artificial intelligence (AI)

Computer software that seeks to reproduce or mimic (perhaps with improvements) human thought, decision making, or brain functions.

Can Technology "Cure" U.S. Health Care?

The U.S. health care system is broken. It's costly, inefficient, and problems seem to be getting worse. Estimates suggest that health care spending makes up a whopping 18 percent of U.S. gross domestic product.[13] U.S. automakers spend more on health care than they do on steel.[14] Even more disturbing, it's believed that medical errors cause as many as ninety-eight thousand unnecessary deaths in the United States each year, more than motor vehicle accidents, breast cancer, or AIDS.[15]

For years it's been claimed that technology has the potential to reduce errors, improve health care quality, and save costs. Now pioneering hospital networks and technology companies are partnering to help tackle cost and quality issues. For a look at possibilities for leveraging data throughout the doctor-patient value chain, consider the "event-driven medicine" system built by Dr. John Halamka and his team at Boston's Beth Israel Deaconess Medical Center (part of the Harvard Medical School network).

When docs using Halamka's system encounter a patient with a chronic disease, they generate a decision support "screening sheet." Each event in the system: an office visit, a lab results report (think the medical equivalent of transactions and customer interactions), updates the patient database. Combine that electronic medical record information with **artificial intelligence** on best practice, and the system can offer recommendations for care, such as, "Patient is past due for an eye exam" or, "Patient should receive pneumovax [a vaccine against infection] this season."[16] The systems don't replace decision making by doctors and nurses, but they do help to ensure that key issues are on a provider's radar.

More efficiencies and error checks show up when prescribing drugs. Docs are presented with a list of medications covered by that patient's insurance, allowing them to choose quality options while controlling costs. Safety issues, guidelines, and best practices are also displayed. When correct, safe medication in the right dose is selected, the electronic prescription is routed to the patients' pharmacy of choice. As Halamka puts it, going from "doctor's brain to patients vein" without any of that messy physician handwriting, all while squeezing out layers where errors from human interpretation or data entry might occur.

President Obama believes technology initiatives can save health care as much as $120 billion a year, or roughly two thousand five hundred dollars per family.[17] An aggressive number, to be sure. But with such a large target to aim at, it's no wonder that nearly every major technology company now has a health solutions group. Microsoft and Google even offer competing systems for electronically storing and managing patient health records. If systems like Halamka's and others realize their promise, big benefits may be just around the corner.

3.4 External Sources

Sometimes it makes sense to combine a firm's data with bits brought in from the outside. Many firms, for example, don't sell directly to consumers (this includes most drug companies and packaged goods firms). If your firm has partners that sell products for you, then you'll likely rely heavily on data collected by others.

Data bought from sources available to all might not yield competitive advantage on its own, but it can provide key operational insight for increased efficiency and cost savings. And when combined with a firm's unique data assets, it may give firms a high-impact edge.

Consider restaurant chain Brinker, a firm that runs seventeen hundred eateries in twenty-seven countries under the Chili's, On The Border, and Maggiano's brands. Brinker (whose ticker symbol is EAT), supplements their own data with external feeds on weather, employment statistics, gas prices, and other factors, and uses this in predictive models that help the firm in everything from determining staffing levels to switching around menu items.[18]

In another example, Carnival Cruise Lines combines its own customer data with third-party information tracking household income and other key measures. This data plays a key role in a recession, since it helps the firm target limited marketing dollars on those past customers that are more likely to be able to afford to go on a cruise. So far it's been a winning approach. For three years in a row, the firm has experienced double-digit increases in bookings by repeat customers.[19]

data aggregators

Firms that collect and resell data.

Who's Collecting Data about You?

There's a thriving industry collecting data about you. Buy from a catalog, fill out a warranty card, or have a baby, and there's a very good chance that this event will be recorded in a database somewhere, added to a growing digital dossier that's made available for sale to others. If you've ever gotten catalogs, coupons, or special offers from firms you've never dealt with before, this was almost certainly a direct result of a behind-the-scenes trafficking in the "digital you."

Firms that trawl for data and package them up for resale are known as **data aggregators**. They include Acxiom, a $1.3 billion a year business that combines public source data on real estate, criminal records, and census reports, with private information from credit card applications, warranty card surveys, and magazine subscriptions. The firm holds data profiling some two hundred million Americans.[20]

Or maybe you've heard of Lexis-Nexis. Many large universities subscribe to the firm's electronic newspaper, journal, and magazine databases. But the firm's parent, Reed Elsevier, is a data sales giant, with divisions packaging criminal records, housing information, and additional data used to uncover corporate fraud and other risks. In February, 2008, the firm got even more data rich, acquiring Acxiom competitor ChoicePoint for $4.1 billion. With that kind of money involved, it's clear that data aggregation is very big business.[21]

The Internet also allows for easy access to data that had been public but otherwise difficult to access. For one example, consider home sale prices and home value assessments. While technically in the public record, someone wanting this information previously had to traipse down to their Town Hall and speak to a clerk, who would hand over a printed log book. Not exactly a Google-speed query. Contrast this with a visit to Zillow.com. The free site lets you pull up a map of your town and instantly peek at how much your neighbors paid for their homes. And it lets them see how much you paid for yours, too.

Computerworld's Robert Mitchell uncovered a more disturbing issue when public record information is made available online. His New Hampshire municipality had digitized and made available some of his old public documents without obscuring that holy grail for identity thieves, his Social Security number.[22]

Then there are accuracy concerns. A record incorrectly identifying you as a cat lover is one thing, but being incorrectly named to the terrorist watch list is quite another. During a five-week period airline agents tried to block a particularly high profile U.S. citizen from boarding airplanes on five separate occasions because his name resembled an alias used by a suspected terrorist. That citizen? The late Ted Kennedy, who at the time was the senior U.S. senator from Massachusetts.[23]

For the data trade to continue, firms will have to treat customer data as the sacred asset it is. Step over that "creep-out" line, and customers will push back, increasingly pressing for tighter privacy laws. Data aggregator Intellius used to track cell phone customers, but backed off in the face of customer outrage and threatened legislation.

Another concern—sometimes data aggregators are just plain sloppy, committing errors that can be costly for the firm and potentially devastating for victimized users. For example, in 2005, ChoicePoint accidentally sold records on 145,000 individuals to a cybercrime identity theft ring. The ChoicePoint case resulted in a $15 million fine from the Federal Trade Commission.[24] In 2011, hackers stole at least 60 million e-mail addresses from marketing firm Epsilon, prompting firms as diverse as Best Buy, Citi, Hilton, and the College Board to go through the time-consuming, costly, and potentially brand-damaging process of warning customers of the breach. Epsilon faces liabilities charges of almost a quarter of a billion dollars, but some estimate that the total price tag for the breach could top $4 billion.[25] Just because you can gather data and traffic in bits doesn't mean that you should. Any data-centric effort should involve input not only from business and technical staff, but from the firm's legal team as well (for more, see the box ""Privacy Regulation: A Moving Target"").

Privacy Regulation: A Moving Target

New methods for tracking and gathering user information appear daily, testing user comfort levels. For example, the firm Umbria uses software to analyze millions of blog and forum posts every day, using sentence structure, word choice, and quirks in punctuation to determine a blogger's gender, age, interests, and opinions. While Google refused to include facial recognition as an image search product ("too creepy," said its chairman),[26] Facebook, with great controversy, turned on facial recognition by default.[27] It's quite possible that in the future, someone will be able to upload a photo to a service and direct it to find all the accessible photos and video on the Internet that match that person's features. And while targeting is getting easier, a Carnegie Mellon study showed that it doesn't take much to find someone with a minimum of data. Simply by knowing gender, birth date, and postal zip code, 87 percent of people in the United States could be pinpointed by name.[28] Another study showed that publicly available data on state and date of birth could be used to predict U.S. Social Security numbers—a potential gateway to identity theft.[29]

Some feel that Moore's Law, the falling cost of storage, and the increasing reach of the Internet have us on the cusp of a privacy train wreck. And that may inevitably lead to more legislation that restricts data-use possibilities. Noting this, strategists and technologists need to be fully aware of the legal environment their systems face (see Chapter 14 for examples and discussion) and consider how such environments may change in the future. Many industries have strict guidelines on what kind of information can be collected and shared.

For example, HIPAA (the U.S. Health Insurance Portability and Accountability Act) includes provisions governing data use and privacy among health care providers, insurers, and employers. The financial industry has strict requirements for recording and sharing communications between firm and client (among many other restrictions). There are laws limiting the kinds of information that can be gathered on younger Web surfers. And there are several laws operating at the state level as well.

International laws also differ from those in the United States. Europe, in particular, has a strict European Privacy Directive. The directive includes governing provisions that limit data collection, require notice and approval of many types of data collection, and require firms to make data available to customers with mechanisms for stopping collection efforts and correcting inaccuracies at customer request. Data-dependent efforts plotted for one region may not fully translate in another effort if the law limits key components of technology use. The constantly changing legal landscape also means that what works today might not be allowed in the future.

Firms beware—the public will almost certainly demand tighter controls if the industry is perceived as behaving recklessly or inappropriately with customer data.

KEY TAKEAWAYS

- For organizations that sell directly to their customers, transaction processing systems (TPS) represent a source of potentially useful data.
- Grocers and retailers can link you to cash transactions if they can convince you to use a loyalty card which, in turn, requires you to give up information about yourself in exchange for some kind of financial incentive such as points or discounts.
- Enterprise software (CRM, SCM, and ERP) is a source for customer, supply chain, and enterprise data.
- Survey data can be used to supplement a firm's operational data.
- Data obtained from outside sources, when combined with a firm's internal data assets, can give the firm a competitive edge.
- Data aggregators are part of a multibillion-dollar industry that provides genuinely helpful data to a wide variety of organizations.
- Data that can be purchased from aggregators may not in and of itself yield sustainable competitive advantage since others may have access to this data, too. However, when combined with a firm's proprietary data or integrated with a firm's proprietary procedures or other assets, third-party data can be a key tool for enhancing organizational performance.
- Data aggregators can also be quite controversial. Among other things, they represent a big target for identity thieves, are a method for spreading potentially incorrect data, and raise privacy concerns.
- Firms that mismanage their customer data assets risk lawsuits, brand damage, lower sales, fleeing customers, and can prompt more restrictive legislation.
- Further raising privacy issues and identity theft concerns, recent studies have shown that in many cases it is possible to pinpoint users through allegedly anonymous data, and to guess Social Security numbers from public data.
- New methods for tracking and gathering user information are raising privacy issues which possibly will be addressed through legislation that restricts data use.

QUESTIONS AND EXERCISES

1. Why would a firm use a loyalty card? What is the incentive for the firm? What is the incentive for consumers to opt in and use loyalty cards? What kinds of strategic assets can these systems create?
2. In what ways does Tesco gather data? Can other firms match this effort? What other assets does Tesco leverage that helps the firm remain among top performing retailers worldwide?
3. Make a list of the kind of data you might give up when using a cash register, a Web site, or a loyalty card, or when calling a firm's customer support line. How might firms leverage this data to better serve you and improve their performance?
4. Are you concerned by any of the data-use possibilities that you outlined in prior questions, discussed in this chapter, or that you've otherwise read about or encountered? If you are concerned, why? If not, why not? What might firms, governments, and consumers do to better protect consumers?
5. What are some of the sources data aggregators tap to collect information?
6. Privacy laws are in a near constant state of flux. Conduct research to identify the current state of privacy law. Has major legislation recently been proposed or approved? What are the implications for firms operating in effected industries? What are the potential benefits to consumers? Do consumers lose anything from this legislation?
7. Self-regulation is often proposed as an alternative to legislative efforts. What kinds of efforts would provide "teeth" to self-regulation. Are there steps firms could do to make you believe in their ability to self-regulate? Why or why not?
8. What is HIPPA? What industry does it impact?
9. How do international privacy laws differ from U.S. privacy laws?

4. DATA RICH, INFORMATION POOR

LEARNING OBJECTIVES

1. **Know and be able to list the reasons why many organizations have data that can't be converted to actionable information.**
2. **Understand why transactional databases can't always be queried and what needs to be done to facilitate effective data use for analytics and business intelligence.**
3. **Recognize key issues surrounding data and privacy legislation.**

Despite being awash in data, many organizations are data rich but information poor. A survey by consulting firm Accenture found 57 percent of companies reporting that they didn't have a beneficial, consistently updated, companywide analytical capability. Among major decisions, only 60 percent were backed by analytics—40 percent were made by intuition and gut instinct.[30] The big culprit limiting BI initiatives is getting data into a form where it can be used, analyzed, and turned into information. Here's a look at some factors holding back information advantages.

4.1 Incompatible Systems

Just because data is collected doesn't mean it can be used. This limit is a big problem for large firms that have **legacy systems**, outdated information systems that were not designed to share data, aren't compatible with newer technologies, and aren't aligned with the firm's current business needs. The problem can be made worse by mergers and acquisitions, especially if a firm depends on operational systems that are incompatible with its partner. And the elimination of incompatible systems isn't just a technical issue. Firms might be under extended agreement with different vendors or outsourcers, and breaking a contract or invoking an escape clause may be costly. Folks working in M&A (the area of investment banking focused on valuing and facilitating mergers and acquisitions) beware—it's critical to uncover these hidden costs of technology integration before deciding if a deal makes financial sense.

legacy system

Older information systems that are often incompatible with other systems, technologies, and ways of conducting business. Incompatible legacy systems can be a major roadblock to turning data into information, and they can inhibit firm agility, holding back operational and strategic initiatives.

Legacy Systems: A Prison for Strategic Assets

The experience of one *Fortune* 100 firm that your author has worked with illustrates how incompatible information systems can actually hold back strategy. This firm was the largest in its category, and sold identical commodity products sourced from its many plants worldwide. Being the biggest should have given the firm scale advantages. But many of the firm's manufacturing facilities and international locations developed or purchased separate, incompatible systems. Still more plants were acquired through acquisition, each coming with its own legacy systems.

The plants with different information systems used *different* part numbers and naming conventions even though they sold *identical* products. As a result, the firm had no timely information on how much of a particular item was sold to which worldwide customers. The company was essentially operating as a collection of smaller, regional businesses, rather than as the worldwide behemoth that it was.

After the firm developed an information system that standardized data across these plants, it was, for the first time, able to get a single view of worldwide sales. The firm then used this data to approach their biggest customers, negotiating lower prices in exchange for increased commitments in worldwide purchasing. This trade let the firm take share from regional rivals. It also gave the firm the ability to shift manufacturing capacity globally, as currency prices, labor conditions, disaster, and other factors impacted sourcing. The new information system in effect liberated the latent strategic asset of scale, increasing sales by well over a billion and a half dollars in the four years following implementation.

4.2 Operational Data Can't Always Be Queried

Another problem when turning data into information is that most transactional databases aren't set up to be simultaneously accessed for reporting and analysis. When a customer buys something from a cash register, that action may post a sales record and deduct an item from the firm's inventory. In most TPS systems, requests made to the database can usually be performed pretty quickly—the system adds or modifies the few records involved and it's done—in and out in a flash.

But if a manager asks a database to analyze historic sales trends showing the most and least profitable products over time, they may be asking a computer to look at thousands of transaction records, comparing results, and neatly ordering findings. That's not a quick in-and-out task, and it may very well require significant processing to come up with the request. Do this against the very databases you're using to record your transactions, and you might grind your computers to a halt.

Getting data into systems that can support analytics is where data warehouses and data marts come in, the topic of our next section.

KEY TAKEAWAYS

- A major factor limiting business intelligence initiatives is getting data into a form where it can be used (i.e., analyzed and turned into information).
- Legacy systems often limit data utilization because they were not designed to share data, aren't compatible with newer technologies, and aren't aligned with the firm's current business needs.
- Most transactional databases aren't set up to be simultaneously accessed for reporting and analysis. In order to run analytics the data must first be ported to a data warehouse or data mart.

QUESTIONS AND EXERCISES

1. How might information systems impact mergers and acquisitions? What are the key issues to consider?
2. Discuss the possible consequences of a company having multiple plants, each with a different information system using different part numbers and naming conventions for identical products.
3. Why does it take longer, and require more processing power, to analyze sales trends by region and product, as opposed to posting a sales transaction?

5. DATA WAREHOUSES AND DATA MARTS

LEARNING OBJECTIVES

1. Understand what data warehouses and data marts are and the purpose they serve.
2. Know the issues that need to be addressed in order to design, develop, deploy, and maintain data warehouses and data marts.

Since running analytics against transactional data can bog down a system, and since most organizations need to combine and reformat data from multiple sources, firms typically need to create separate data repositories for their reporting and analytics work—a kind of staging area from which to turn that data into information.

Two terms you'll hear for these kinds of repositories are **data warehouse** and **data mart**. A data warehouse is a set of databases designed to support decision making in an organization. It is structured for fast online queries and exploration. Data warehouses may aggregate enormous amounts of data from many different operational systems.

data warehouse

A set of databases designed to support decision making in an organization.

data mart

A database or databases focused on addressing the concerns of a specific problem (e.g., increasing customer retention, improving product quality) or business unit (e.g., marketing, engineering).

A data mart is a database focused on addressing the concerns of a specific problem (e.g., increasing customer retention, improving product quality) or business unit (e.g., marketing, engineering).

Marts and warehouses may contain huge volumes of data. For example, a firm may not need to keep large amounts of historical point-of-sale or transaction data in its operational systems, but it might want past data in its data mart so that managers can hunt for patterns and trends that occur over time.

FIGURE 11.2

Information systems supporting operations (such as TPS) are typically separate, and "feed" information systems used for analytics (such as data warehouses and data marts).

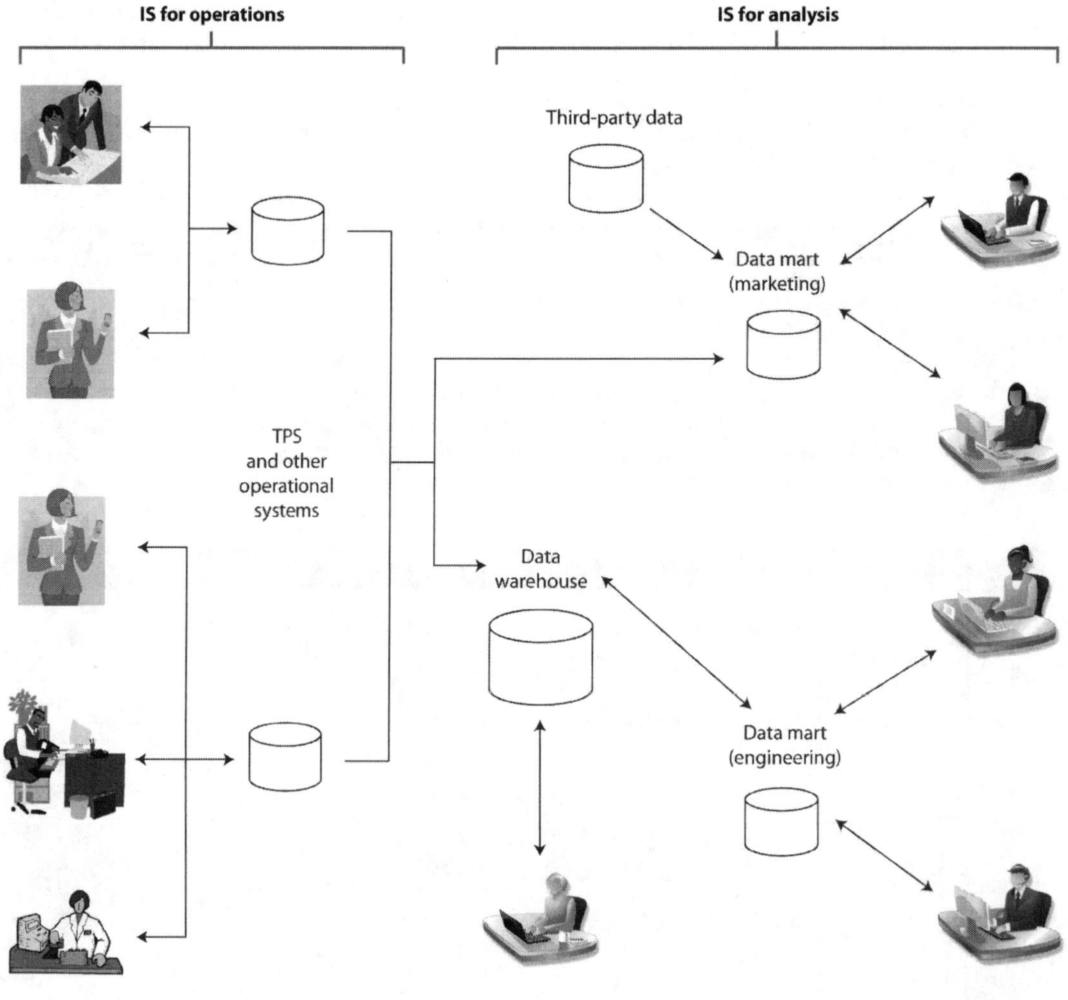

It's easy for firms to get seduced by a software vendor's demonstration showing data at your fingertips, presented in pretty graphs. But as mentioned earlier, getting data in a format that can be used for analytics is hard, complex, and challenging work. Large data warehouses can cost millions and take years to build. Every dollar spent on technology may lead to five to seven more dollars on consulting and other services.[31]

Most firms will face a trade-off—do we attempt a large-scale integration of the whole firm, or more targeted efforts with quicker payoffs? Firms in fast-moving industries or with particularly complex businesses may struggle to get sweeping projects completed in enough time to reap benefits before business conditions change. Most consultants now advise smaller projects with narrow scope driven by specific business goals.[32]

Firms can eventually get to a unified data warehouse but it may take time. Even analytics king Wal-Mart is just getting to that point. Retail giant Wal-Mart once reported having over seven hundred different data marts and hired Hewlett-Packard for help in bringing the systems together to form a more integrated data warehouse.[33]

The old saying from the movie *Field of Dreams*, "If you build it, they will come," doesn't hold up well for large-scale data analytics projects. This work should start with a clear vision with business-focused objectives. When senior executives can see objectives illustrated in potential payoff, they'll be able to champion the effort, and experts agree, having an executive champion is a key success factor. Focusing on business issues will also drive technology choice, with the firm better able to focus on products that best fit its needs.

Once a firm has business goals and hoped-for payoffs clearly defined, it can address the broader issues needed to design, develop, deploy, and maintain its system:[34]

- *Data relevance.* What data is needed to compete on analytics and to meet our current and future goals?
- *Data sourcing.* Can we even get the data we'll need? Where can this data be obtained from? Is it available via our internal systems? Via third-party data aggregators? Via suppliers or sales partners? Do we need to set up new systems, surveys, and other collection efforts to acquire the data we need?
- *Data quantity.* How much data is needed?
- *Data quality.* Can our data be trusted as accurate? Is it clean, complete, and reasonably free of errors? How can the data be made more accurate and valuable for analysis? Will we need to 'scrub,' calculate, and consolidate data so that it can be used?
- *Data hosting.* Where will the systems be housed? What are the hardware and networking requirements for the effort?
- *Data governance.* What rules and processes are needed to manage data from its creation through its retirement? Are there operational issues (backup, disaster recovery)? Legal issues? Privacy issues? How should the firm handle security and access?

For some perspective on how difficult this can be, consider that an executive from one of the largest U.S. banks once lamented at how difficult it was to get his systems to do something as simple as properly distinguishing between men and women. The company's customer-focused data warehouse drew data from thirty-six separate operational systems—bank teller systems, ATMs, student loan reporting systems, car loan systems, mortgage loan systems, and more. Collectively these legacy systems expressed gender in *seventeen* different ways: "M" or "F"; "m" or "f"; "Male" or "Female"; "MALE" or "FEMALE"; "1" for man, "0" for woman; "0" for man, "1" for woman and more, plus various codes for "unknown." The best math in the world is of no help if the values used aren't any good. There's a saying in the industry, "garbage in, garbage out."

5.1 Hadoop: Big Insights from Unstructured "Big Data"

Having neatly structured data warehouses and data-marts are great—the tools are reliable and can often be turned over to end-users or specialists who can rapidly produce reports and other analyses. But roughly 80 percent of corporate data is messy and unstructured, and it is not stored in conventional, relational formats—think of data stored in office productivity documents, e-mail, and social media.[35] Conventional tools often choke when trying to sift through the massive amounts of data collected by many of today's firms. The open-source project known as Hadoop was created to analyze massive amounts of raw information better than traditional, highly-structured databases.

Hadoop is made up of some half-dozen separate software pieces and requires the integration of these pieces to work. Hadoop-related projects have names such as Hive, Pig, and Zookeeper. Their use is catching on like wildfire, with some expecting that within five years, more than half of the world's data will be stored in Hadoop environments.[36] Expertise is in short supply, with Hadoop-savvy technologists having lots of career opportunities.

There are four primary advantages to Hadoop:[37]

- *Flexibility*: Hadoop can absorb any type of data, structured or not, from any type of source (geeks would say such a system is *schema-less*). But this disparate data can still be aggregated and analyzed.
- *Scalability*: Hadoop systems can start on a single PC, but thousands of machines can eventually be combined to work together for storage and analysis.
- *Cost effectiveness*: Since the system is open source and can be started with low-end hardware, the technology is cheap by data-warehousing standards. Many vendors also offer Hadoop as a cloud service, allowing firms to avoid hardware costs altogether.
- *Fault tolerance*: One of the servers running your Hadoop cluster just crashed? No big deal. Hadoop is designed in such a way so that there will be no single point of failure. The system will continue to work, relying on the remaining hardware.

Financial giant Morgan Stanley is a big believer in Hadoop. One senior technology manager at the firm contrasts Hadoop with highly structured systems, saying that in the past, "IT asked the business what they want, creates a data structure and writes structured query language, sources the data, conforms it to the table and writes a structured query. Then you give it to them and they often say that is not what they wanted." But with Hadoop overseeing a big pile of unstructured (or less structured) data, technical staff can now work with users to carve up and combine data in lots of different ways, or even set systems loose in the data to hunt for unexpected patterns (see the discussion of data mining later in this chapter). Morgan Stanley's initial Hadoop experiments started with a handful of old servers that were about to be retired, but the company has steadily ramped up its efforts. Now by using Hadoop, the firm sees that it is able to analyze data on a far larger scale ("petabytes of data, which is unheard of in the traditional database world") with potentially higher-impact results. The bank is looking at customers' financial objectives and trying to come up with investment insights to help them invest appropriately, and it is seeking "Big Data" insights to help the firm more effectively manage risk.[38]

FIGURE 11.3 The Hadoop Logo

The project was named after a toy elephant belonging to the son of Hadoop Developer Doug Cutting.

Other big name-firms using Hadoop for "Big Data" insights include Bank of America, Disney, GE, LinkedIn, Nokia, Twitter, and Wal-Mart. Hadoop is an open source project overseen by the Apache Software Foundation. It has an Internet pedigree and is based on ideas by Google and lots of software contributed by Yahoo! (two firms that regularly need to dive into massive and growing amounts of unstructured data—web pages, videos, images, social media, user account information, and more). IBM used Hadoop as the engine that helped power Watson to defeat human opponents on *Jeopardy*, further demonstrating the technology's ability to analyze wildly different data for accurate insight. Other tech firms embracing Hadoop and offering some degree of support for the technology include HP, EMC, and Microsoft.

e-discovery

The process of identifying and retrieving relevant electronic information to support litigation efforts.

E-discovery: Supporting Legal Inquiries

Data archiving isn't just for analytics. Sometimes the law requires organizations to dive into their electronic records. **E-discovery** refers to identifying and retrieving relevant electronic information to support litigation efforts. E-discovery is something a firm should account for in its archiving and data storage plans. Unlike analytics that promise a boost to the bottom line, there's no profit in complying with a judge's order—it's just a sunk cost. But organizations can be compelled by court order to scavenge their bits, and the cost to uncover difficult to access data can be significant, if not planned for in advance.

In one recent example, the Office of Federal Housing Enterprise Oversight (OFHEO) was subpoenaed for documents in litigation involving mortgage firms Fannie Mae and Freddie Mac. Even though the OFHEO wasn't a party in the lawsuit, the agency had to comply with the search—an effort that cost $6 million, a full 9 percent of its total yearly budget.[39]

KEY TAKEAWAYS

- Data warehouses and data marts are repositories for large amounts of transactional data awaiting analytics and reporting.
- Large data warehouses are complex, can cost millions, and take years to build.
- The open source Hadoop effort provides a collection of technologies for manipulating massive amounts of unstructured data. The system is flexible, saleable, cost-effective, and fault-tolerant. Hadoop grew from large Internet firms but is now being used across industries.

QUESTIONS AND EXERCISES

1. List the issues that need to be addressed in order to design, develop, deploy, and maintain data warehouses and data marts.
2. What is meant by "data relevance"?
3. What is meant by "data governance"?
4. What is the difference between a data mart and a data warehouse?
5. Why are data marts and data warehouses necessary? Why can't an organization simply query its transactional database?
6. How can something as simple as customer gender be difficult to for a large organization to establish in a data warehouse?
7. What is Hadoop? Why would a firm use Hadoop instead of conventional data warehousing and data mart technologies?
8. Research the current state of "Big Data" analysis. Identify major firms leveraging Hadoop or similar technologies and share high-impact examples with your classmates and professor.

6. THE BUSINESS INTELLIGENCE TOOLKIT

LEARNING OBJECTIVES

1. **Know the tools that are available to turn data into information.**
2. **Identify the key areas where businesses leverage data mining.**
3. **Understand some of the conditions under which analytical models can fail.**
4. **Recognize major categories of artificial intelligence and understand how organizations are leveraging this technology.**

So far we've discussed where data can come from, and how we can get data into a form where we can use it. But how, exactly, do firms turn that data into information? That's where the various software tools of business intelligence (BI) and analytics come in. Potential products in the business intelligence toolkit range from simple spreadsheets to ultrasophisticated data mining packages leveraged by teams employing "rocket-science" mathematics.

6.1 Query and Reporting Tools

The idea behind query and reporting tools is to present users with a subset of requested data, selected, sorted, ordered, calculated, and compared, as needed. Managers use these tools to see and explore what's happening inside their organizations.

canned reports

Reports that provide regular summaries of information in a predetermined format.

ad hoc reporting tools

Tools that put users in control so that they can create custom reports on an as-needed basis by selecting fields, ranges, summary conditions, and other parameters.

dashboards

A heads-up display of critical indicators that allow managers to get a graphical glance at key performance metrics.

Canned reports provide regular summaries of information in a predetermined format. They're often developed by information systems staff and formats can be difficult to alter. By contrast, **ad hoc reporting tools** allow users to dive in and create their own reports, selecting fields, ranges, and other parameters to build their own reports on the fly. **Dashboards** provide a sort of heads-up display of critical indicators, letting managers get a graphical glance at key performance metrics. Some tools may allow data to be exported into spreadsheets. Yes, even the lowly spreadsheet can be a powerful tool for modeling "what if" scenarios and creating additional reports (of course be careful: if data can be easily exported, then it can potentially leave the firm dangerously exposed, raising privacy, security, legal, and competitive concerns).

FIGURE 11.4 The Federal IT Dashboard

The Federal IT dashboard offers federal agencies, and the general public, information about the government's IT investments.

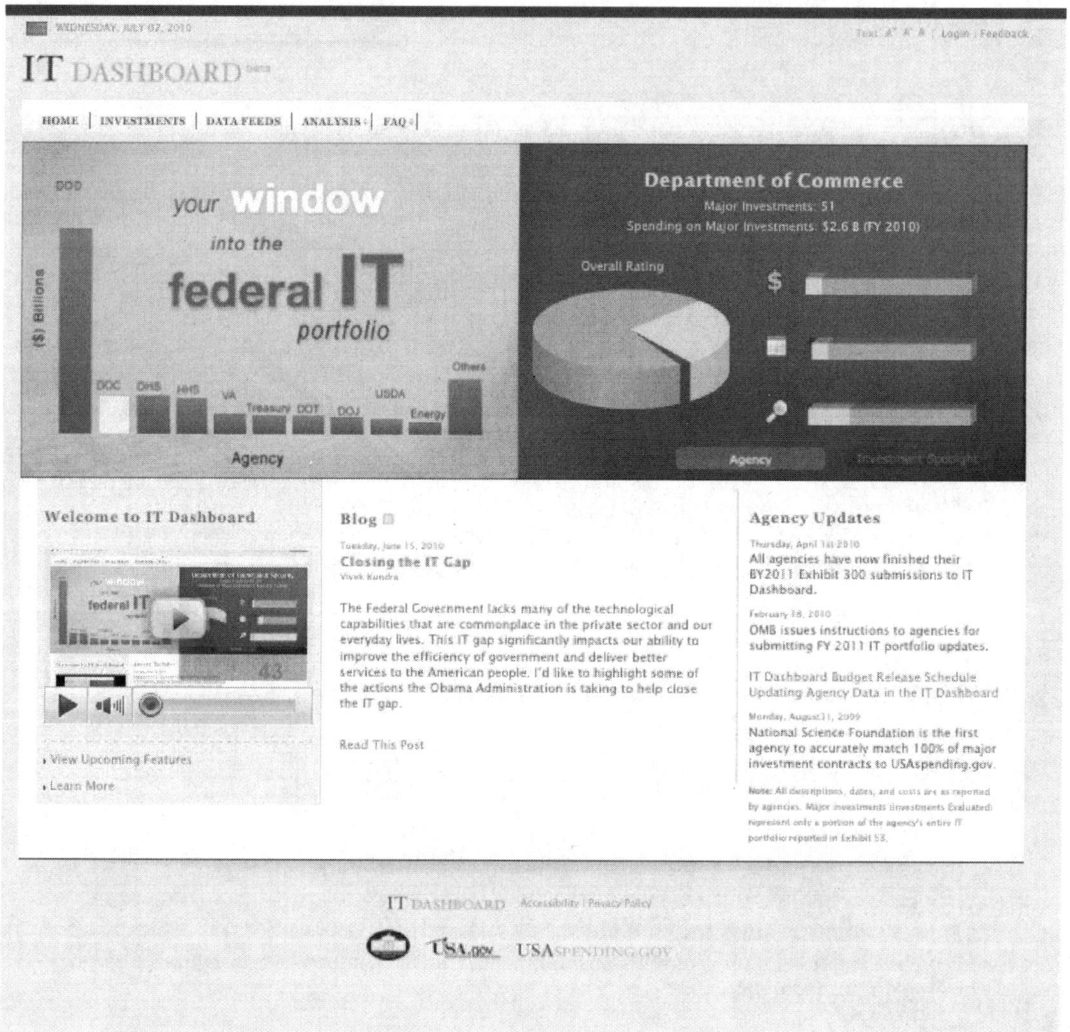

A subcategory of reporting tools is referred to as **online analytical processing (OLAP)** (pronounced "oh-lap"). Data used in OLAP reporting is usually sourced from standard relational databases, but it's calculated and summarized in advance, across multiple dimensions, with the data stored in a special database called a **data cube**. This extra setup step makes OLAP fast (sometimes one thousand times faster than performing comparable queries against conventional relational databases). Given this kind of speed boost, it's not surprising that data cubes for OLAP access are often part of a firm's data mart and data warehouse efforts.

A manager using an OLAP tool can quickly explore and compare data across multiple factors such as time, geography, product lines, and so on. In fact, OLAP users often talk about how they can "slice and dice" their data, "drilling down" inside the data to uncover new insights. And while conventional reports are usually presented as a summarized list of information, OLAP results look more like a spreadsheet, with the various dimensions of analysis in rows and columns, with summary values at the intersection.

online analytical processing (OLAP)

A method of querying and reporting that takes data from standard relational databases, calculates and summarizes the data, and then stores the data in a special database called a data cube.

data cube

A special database used to store data in OLAP reporting.

FIGURE 11.5

This OLAP report compares multiple dimensions. Company is along the vertical axis, and product is along the horizontal access. Many OLAP tools can also present graphs of multidimensional data.

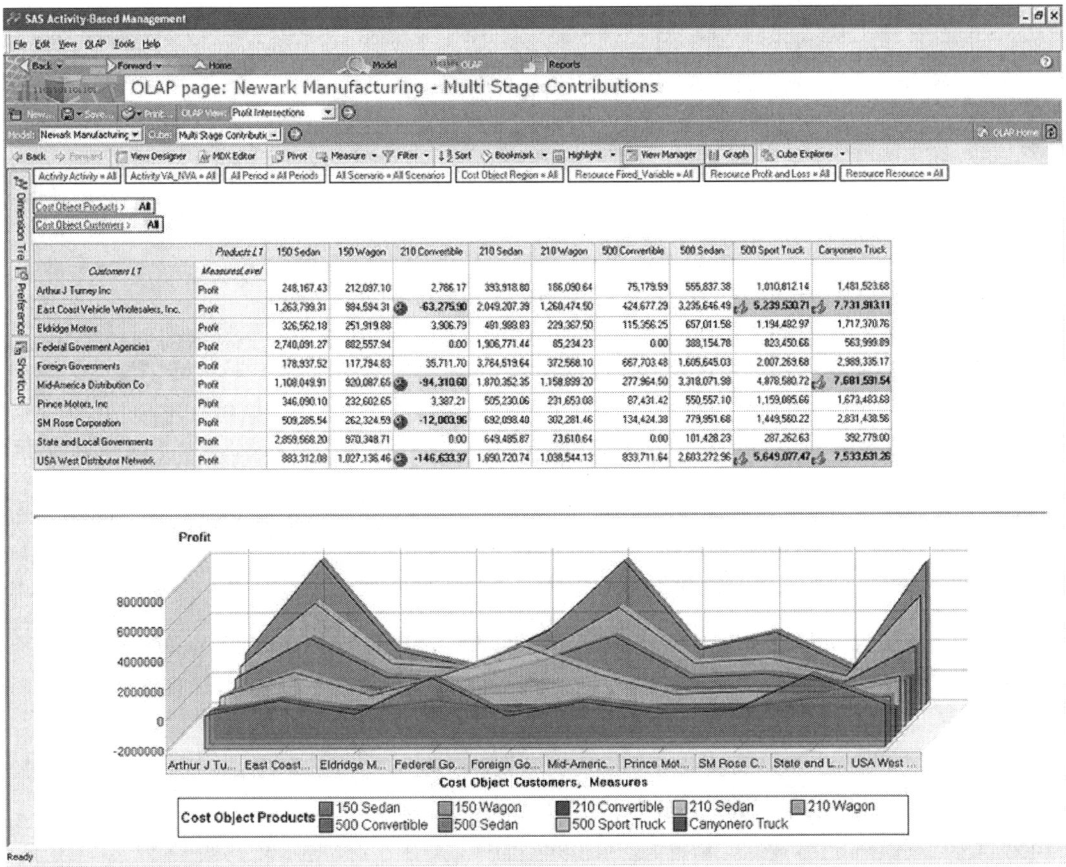

Public Sector Reporting Tools in Action: Fighting Crime and Fighting Waste

Access to ad hoc query and reporting tools can empower all sorts of workers. Consider what analytics tools have done for the police force in Richmond, Virginia. The city provides department investigators with access to data from internal sources such as 911 logs and police reports, and combines this with outside data including neighborhood demographics, payday schedules, weather reports, traffic patterns, sports events, and more.

Experienced officers dive into this data, exploring when and where crimes occur. These insights help the department decide how to allocate its limited policing assets to achieve the biggest impact. While IT staffers put the system together, the tools are actually used by officers with expertise in fighting street crime—the kinds of users with the knowledge to hunt down trends and interpret the causes behind the data. And it seems this data helps make smart cops even smarter—the system is credited with delivering a single-year crime-rate reduction of 20 percent.[40]

As it turns out, what works for cops also works for bureaucrats. When administrators for Albuquerque were given access to ad hoc reporting systems, they uncovered all sorts of anomalies, prompting excess spending cuts on everything from cell phone usage to unnecessarily scheduled overtime. And once again, BI performed for the public sector. The Albuquerque system delivered the equivalent of $2 million in savings in just the first three weeks it was used.[41]

6.2 Data Mining

data mining

The process of using computers to identify hidden patterns in, and to build models from, large data sets.

While reporting tools can help users explore data, modern data sets can be so large that it might be impossible for humans to spot underlying trends. That's where data mining can help. **Data mining** is the process of using computers to identify hidden patterns and to build models from large data sets.

Some of the key areas where businesses are leveraging data mining include the following:

- *Customer segmentation*—figuring out which customers are likely to be the most valuable to a firm.
- *Marketing and promotion targeting*—identifying which customers will respond to which offers at which price at what time.
- *Market basket analysis*—determining which products customers buy together, and how an organization can use this information to cross-sell more products or services.
- *Collaborative filtering*—personalizing an individual customer's experience based on the trends and preferences identified across similar customers.
- *Customer churn*—determining which customers are likely to leave, and what tactics can help the firm avoid unwanted defections.
- *Fraud detection*—uncovering patterns consistent with criminal activity.
- *Financial modeling*—building trading systems to capitalize on historical trends.
- *Hiring and promotion*—identifying characteristics consistent with employee success in the firm's various roles.

For data mining to work, two critical conditions need to be present: (1) the organization must have clean, consistent data, and (2) the events in that data should reflect current and future trends. The recent financial crisis provides lessons on what can happen when either of these conditions isn't met.

First lets look at problems with using bad data. A report in the *New York Times* has suggested that in the period leading up to the 2008 financial crisis, some banking executives deliberately deceived risk management systems in order to skew capital-on-hand requirements. This deception let firms load up on risky debt, while carrying less cash for covering losses.[42] Deceive your systems with bad data and your models are worthless. In this case, wrong estimates from bad data left firms grossly overexposed to risk. When debt defaults occurred; several banks failed, and we entered the worst financial crisis since the Great Depression.

Now consider the problem of historical consistency: Computer-driven investment models can be very effective when the market behaves as it has in the past. But models are blind when faced with the equivalent of the "hundred-year flood" (sometimes called *black swans*); events so extreme and unusual that they never showed up in the data used to build the model.

We saw this in the late 1990s with the collapse of the investment firm Long Term Capital Management. LTCM was started by Nobel Prize–winning economists, but when an unexpected Russian debt crisis caused the markets to move in ways not anticipated by its models, the firm lost 90 percent of its value in less than two months. The problem was so bad that the Fed had to step in to supervise the firm's multibillion-dollar bailout. Fast forward a decade to the banking collapse of 2008, and we again see computer-driven trading funds plummet in the face of another unexpected event—the burst of the housing bubble.[43]

over-engineer

Build a model with so many variables that the solution arrived at might only work on the subset of data you've used to create it.

Data mining presents a host of other perils, as well. It's possible to **over-engineer** a model, building it with so many variables that the solution arrived at might only work on the subset of data you've used to create it. You might also be looking at a random but meaningless statistical fluke. In demonstrating how flukes occur, one quantitative investment manager uncovered a correlation that at first glance appeared statistically to be a particularly strong predictor for historical prices in the S&P 500 stock index. That predictor? Butter production in Bangladesh.[44] Sometimes durable and useful patterns just aren't in your data.

One way to test to see if you're looking at a random occurrence in the numbers is to divide your data, building your model with one portion of the data, and using another portion to verify your results. This is the approach Netflix has used to test results achieved by teams in the Netflix Prize, the firm's million-dollar contest for improving the predictive accuracy of its movie recommendation engine (see Chapter 4).

Finally, sometimes a pattern is uncovered but determining the best choice for a response is less clear. As an example, let's return to the data-mining wizards at Tesco. An analysis of product sales data showed several money-losing products, including a type of bread known as "milk loaf." Drop those products, right? Not so fast. Further analysis showed milk loaf was a "destination product" for a loyal group of high-value customers, and that these customers would shop elsewhere if milk loaf disappeared from Tesco shelves. The firm kept the bread as a loss-leader and retained those valuable milk loaf fans.[45] Data miner, beware—first findings don't always reveal an optimal course of action.

This last example underscores the importance of recruiting a data mining and business analytics team that possesses three critical skills: information technology (for understanding how to pull together data, and for selecting analysis tools), statistics (for building models and interpreting the strength and validity of results), and business knowledge (for helping set system goals, requirements, and offering deeper insight into what the data really says about the firm's operating environment). Miss one of these key functions and your team could make some major mistakes.

While we've focused on tools in our discussion above, many experts suggest that business intelligence is really an organizational process as much as it is a set of technologies. Having the right team is critical in moving the firm from goal setting through execution and results.

Artificial Intelligence

Data mining has its roots in a branch of computer science known as artificial intelligence (or AI). The goal of AI is create computer programs that are able to mimic or improve upon functions of the human brain. Data mining can leverage **neural networks** or other advanced algorithms and statistical techniques to hunt down and expose patterns, and build models to exploit findings.

Expert systems are AI systems that leverage rules or examples to perform a task in a way that mimics applied human expertise. Expert systems are used in tasks ranging from medical diagnoses to product configuration.

Genetic algorithms are model building techniques where computers examine many potential solutions to a problem, iteratively modifying (mutating) various mathematical models, and comparing the mutated models to search for a best alternative. Genetic algorithms have been used to build everything from financial trading models to handling complex airport scheduling, to designing parts for the international space station.[46]

While AI is not a single technology, and not directly related to data creation, various forms of AI can show up as part of analytics products, CRM tools, transaction processing systems, and other information systems.

neural network

An AI system that examines data and hunts down and exposes patterns, in order to build models to exploit findings.

expert systems

AI systems that leverages rules or examples to perform a task in a way that mimics applied human expertise.

genetic algorithms

Model building techniques where computers examine many potential solutions to a problem, iteratively modifying (mutating) various mathematical models, and comparing the mutated models to search for a best alternative.

KEY TAKEAWAYS

- Canned and ad hoc reports, digital dashboards, and OLAP are all used to transform data into information.
- OLAP reporting leverage data cubes, which take data from standard relational databases, calculating and summarizing data for superfast reporting access. OLAP tools can present results through multidimensional graphs, or via spreadsheet-style cross-tab reports.
- Modern data sets can be so large that it might be impossible for humans to spot underlying trends without the use of data mining tools.
- Businesses are using data mining to address issues in several key areas including customer segmentation, marketing and promotion targeting, collaborative filtering, and so on.
- Models influenced by bad data, missing or incomplete historical data, and over-engineering are prone to yield bad results.
- One way to test to see if you're looking at a random occurrence in your data is to divide your data, building your model with one portion of the data, and using another portion to verify your results.
- Analytics may not always provide the total solution for a problem. Sometimes a pattern is uncovered, but determining the best choice for a response is less clear.
- A competent business analytics team should possess three critical skills: information technology, statistics, and business knowledge.

QUESTIONS AND EXERCISES

1. What are some of the tools used to convert data into information?
2. What is the difference between a canned reports and an ad hoc reporting?
3. How do reports created by OLAP differ from most conventional reports?
4. List the key areas where businesses are leveraging data mining.
5. What is market basket analysis?
6. What is customer churn?
7. For data mining to work, what two critical data-related conditions must be present?
8. Discus occurrences of model failure caused by missing or incomplete historical data.
9. Discuss Tesco's response to their discovery that "milk loaf" was a money-losing product.
10. List the three critical skills a competent business analytics team should possess.
11. Do any of the products that you use leverage artificial intelligence? What kinds of AI might be used in Netflix's movie recommendation system, Apple's iTunes Genius playlist builder, or Amazon's Web site personalization? What kind of AI might help a physician make a diagnosis or help an engineer configure a complicated product in the field?

7. DATA ASSET IN ACTION: TECHNOLOGY AND THE RISE OF WAL-MART

LEARNING OBJECTIVES

1. **Understand how Wal-Mart has leveraged information technology to become the world's largest retailer.**
2. **Be aware of the challenges that face Wal-Mart in the years ahead.**

Wal-Mart demonstrates how a physical product retailer can create and leverage a data asset to achieve world-class supply chain efficiencies targeted primarily at driving down costs.

Wal-Mart isn't just the largest retailer in the world, over the past several years it has popped in and out of the top spot on the *Fortune* 500 list—meaning that the firm has had revenues greater than *any* firm in the United States. Wal-Mart is so big that in three months it sells more than a whole year's worth of sales at number two U.S. retailer, Home Depot.[47]

At that size, it's clear that Wal-Mart's key source of competitive advantage is scale. But firms don't turn into giants overnight. Wal-Mart grew in large part by leveraging information systems to an extent never before seen in the retail industry. Technology tightly coordinates the Wal-Mart value chain from tip to tail, while these systems also deliver a mineable data asset that's unmatched in U.S. retail. To get a sense of the firm's overall efficiencies, at the end of the prior decade a McKinsey study found that Wal-Mart was responsible for some 12 percent of the productivity gains in the *entire* U.S. economy.[48] The firm's capacity as a systems innovator is so respected that many senior Wal-Mart IT executives have been snatched up for top roles at Dell, HP, Amazon, and Microsoft. And lest one think that innovation is the province of only those located in the technology hubs of Silicon Valley, Boston, and Seattle, remember that Wal-Mart is headquartered in Bentonville, Arkansas.

7.1 A Data-Driven Value Chain

inventory turnover ratio

The ratio of a company's annual sales to its inventory.

The Wal-Mart efficiency dance starts with a proprietary system called Retail Link, a system originally developed in 1991 and continually refined ever since. Each time an item is scanned by a Wal-Mart cash register, Retail Link not only records the sale, it also automatically triggers inventory reordering, scheduling, and delivery. This process keeps shelves stocked, while keeping inventories at a minimum. An AMR report ranked Wal-Mart as having the seventh best supply chain in the country (the only other retailer in the top twenty was Tesco, at number fifteen).[49] The firm's annual **inventory turnover ratio** of 8.5 means that Wal-Mart sells the equivalent of its entire inventory roughly every six weeks (by comparison, Target's turnover ratio is 6.4, Sears' is 3.4, and the average for U.S. retail is less than 2).[50]

Back-office scanners keep track of inventory as supplier shipments come in. Suppliers are rated based on timeliness of deliveries, and you've got to be quick to work with Wal-Mart. In order to avoid a tractor-trailer traffic jam in store parking lots, deliveries are choreographed to arrive at intervals less than ten minutes apart. When Levi's joined Wal-Mart, the firm had to guarantee it could replenish shelves every two days—no prior retailer had required a shorter than five day window from Levi's.[51]

Wal-Mart has been a catalyst for technology adoption among its suppliers. The firm is currently leading an adoption effort that requires partners to leverage RFID technology to track and coordinate inventories. While the rollout has been slow, a recent P&G trial showed RFID boosted sales nearly 20 percent by ensuring that inventory was on shelves and located where it should be.[52]

7.2 Data Mining Prowess

Wal-Mart also mines its mother lode of data to get its product mix right under all sorts of varying environmental conditions, protecting the firm from "a retailer's twin nightmares: too much inventory, or not enough."[53] For example, the firm's data mining efforts informed buyers that customers stock up on certain products in the days leading up to predicted hurricanes. Bumping up prestorm supplies of batteries and bottled water was a no brainer, but the firm also learned that Pop-Tarts sales spike sevenfold before storms hit, and that beer is the top prestorm seller. This insight has lead to truckloads full of six packs and toaster pastries streaming into gulf states whenever word of a big storm surfaces.[54]

Data mining also helps the firm tighten operational forecasts, helping to predict things like how many cashiers are needed at a given store at various times of day throughout the year. Data drives the organization, with mined reports forming the basis of weekly sales meetings, as well as executive strategy sessions.

Wal-Mart leverages its huge Hadoop-based data trove to support some of its data mining efforts, sifting through massive amounts of social media—Twitter posts, Facebook updates, and other so-called unstructured data—to gain insights on product offerings, sales leads, pricing, and more. The firm purchased social startup Kosmix for $300 million to deepen social and Big Data expertise in the company's @WalmartLabs.[55] Says Kosmix founder Anand Rajaraman (who previously sold a firm to Amazon and was an early investor in Facebook), "The first generation of e-commerce was about bringing the store to the Web. The next generation will be about building integrated experiences that leverage the store, the Web and mobile, with social identity being the glue that binds the experience."[56]

7.3 Sharing Data, Keeping Secrets

While Wal-Mart is demanding of its suppliers, it also shares data with them, too. Data can help firms become more efficient so that Wal-Mart can keep dropping prices, and data can help firms uncover patterns that help suppliers sell more. P&G's Gillette unit, for example, claims to have mined Wal-Mart data to develop promotions that increased sales as much as 19 percent. More than seventeen thousand suppliers are given access to their products' Wal-Mart performance across metrics that include daily sales, shipments, returns, purchase orders, invoices, claims and forecasts. And these suppliers collectively interrogate Wal-Mart data warehouses to the tune of twenty-one million queries a year.[57]

While Wal-Mart shares sales data with relevant suppliers, the firm otherwise fiercely guards this asset. Many retailers pool their data by sharing it with information brokers like Information Resources and ACNielsen. This sharing allows smaller firms to pool their data to provide more comprehensive insight on market behavior. But Wal-Mart stopped sharing data with these agencies years ago. The firm's scale is so big, the additional data provided by brokers wasn't adding much value, and it no longer made sense to allow competitors access to what was happening in its own huge chunk of retail sales.

Other aspects of the firm's technology remain under wraps, too. Wal-Mart custom builds large portions of its information systems to keep competitors off its trail. As for infrastructure secrets, the Wal-Mart Data Center in McDonald County, Missouri, was considered so off limits that the county assessor was required to sign a nondisclosure statement before being allowed on-site to estimate property value.[58]

7.4 Challenges Abound

But despite success, challenges continue. While Wal-Mart grew dramatically throughout the 1990s, the firm's U.S. business has largely matured. And as a mature business it faces a problem not unlike the example of Microsoft discussed at the end of Chapter 14; Wal-Mart needs to find huge markets or dramatic cost savings in order to boost profits and continue to move its stock price higher.

The firm's aggressiveness and sheer size also increasingly make Wal-Mart a target for criticism. Those low prices come at a price, and the firm has faced accusations of subpar wages and remains a magnet for union activists. Others had identified poor labor conditions at some of the firm's contract manufacturers. Suppliers that compete for Wal-Mart's business are often faced with a catch-22. If they bypass Wal-Mart they miss out on the largest single chunk of world retail sales. But if they sell to Wal-Mart, the firm may demand prices so aggressively low that suppliers end up cannibalizing their own sales at other retailers. Still more criticism comes from local citizen groups that have accused Wal-Mart of ruining the market for mom-and-pop stores.[59]

While some might see Wal-Mart as invincibly standing at the summit of world retail, it's important to note that other megaretailers have fallen from grace. In the 1920s and 1930s, the A&P grocery chain once controlled 80 percent of U.S. grocery sales, at its peak operating five times the number of stores that Wal-Mart has today. But market conditions changed, and the government stepped in to draft antipredatory pricing laws when it felt A&Ps parent was too aggressive.

For all of Wal-Mart's data brilliance, historical data offers little insight on how to adapt to more radical changes in the retail landscape. The firm's data warehouse wasn't able to foretell the rise of Target and other up-market discounters. And yet another major battle is brewing, as Tesco methodically attempts to take its globally honed expertise to U.S. shores. Savvy managers recognize that data use is a vital tool, but not the only tool in management's strategic arsenal.

KEY TAKEAWAYS

- Wal-Mart demonstrates how a physical product retailer can create and leverage a data asset to achieve world-class value chain efficiencies.
- Wal-Mart uses data mining in numerous ways, from demand forecasting to predicting the number of cashiers needed at a store at a particular time.
- To help suppliers become more efficient, and as a result lower prices, Wal-Mart shares data with them.
- Despite its success, Wal-Mart is a mature business that needs to find huge markets or dramatic cost savings in order to boost profits and continue to move its stock price higher. The firm's success also makes it a high impact target for criticism and activism. And the firm's data assets could not predict impactful industry trends such as the rise of Target and other upscale discounters.

QUESTIONS AND EXERCISES

1. List the functions performed by Retail Link. What is its benefit to Wal-Mart?
2. Which supplier metrics does Retail Link gather and report? How is this valuable to Wal-Mart and suppliers?
3. Name the technology does Wal-Mart require partners to use to track and coordinate inventory. Do you know of other uses for this technology?
4. What steps has Wal-Mart taken to protect its data from competitors?
5. List the criticisms leveled at Wal-Mart. Do you think these critiques are valid or not? What can Wal-Mart do to counteract this criticism? Should it take these steps? Why or why not?

8. DATA ASSET IN ACTION: CAESARS' SOLID GOLD CRM FOR THE SERVICE SECTOR

LEARNING OBJECTIVES

1. **Understand how Caesars has used IT to move from an also-ran chain of casinos to become the largest gaming company based on revenue.**
2. **Name some of the technology innovations that Caesars is using to help it gather more data, and help push service quality and marketing program success.**

Caesars Entertainment (formerly known by the name of its acquirerer, Harrah's) provides an example of exceptional data asset leverage in the service sector, focusing on how this technology enables world-class service through customer relationship management. And as you read this case, keep in mind that the firm's CEO, Gary Loveman, claims that what he did at Caesars he could have done at most firms in most other industries.[60]

Gary Loveman is a sort of management major trifecta. The CEO of Caesars Entertainment is a former *operations* professor who has leveraged *information technology* to create what may be the most effective *marketing* organization in the service industry. If you ever needed an incentive to motivate you for cross-disciplinary thinking, Loveman provides it.

Caesars has leveraged its data-powered prowess to move from an also-ran chain of casinos to become the largest gaming company by revenue. The firm operates some fifty-three casinos, employing more than eighty-five thousand workers on five continents. Brands include Harrah's, Caesars Palace, Bally's, Horseshoe, and Paris Las Vegas. Under Loveman's leadership, the firm formerly known as Harrah's aggressively swallowed competitors, with the firm's $9.4 billion buyout of Caesars Entertainment being its largest deal to date (while as separate firms, Harrah's under Loveman trounced Caesars in financial performance, the Caesars name was seen as a stronger brand).

8.1 Collecting Data

Data drives the firm. Caesars collects customer data on just about everything you might do at their properties—gamble, eat, grab a drink, attend a show, stay in a room. The data's then used to track your preferences and to size up whether you're the kind of customer that's worth pursuing. Prove your worth, and the firm will surround you with top-tier service and develop a targeted marketing campaign to keep wooing you back.[61]

The ace in the firm's data collection hole is its Total Rewards loyalty card system. Launched over a decade ago, the system is constantly being enhanced by an IT staff of seven hundred, with an annual budget in excess of $100 million.[62] Total Rewards is an **opt-in** loyalty program, but customers consider the incentives to be so good that the card is used by some 80 percent of patrons, collecting data on over forty-four million customers.[63]

opt-in

Program (typically a marketing effort) that requires customer consent. This program is contrasted with opt-out programs, which enroll all customers by default.

Customers signing up for the card provide Caesars with demographic information such as gender, age, and address. Visitors then present the card for various transactions. Slide it into a slot machine, show it to the restaurant hostess, present it to the parking valet, share your account number with a telephone reservation specialist—every contact point is an opportunity to collect data. Between three hundred thousand and one million customers come through Caesars' doors daily, adding to the firm's data stash and keeping that asset fresh.[64]

8.2 Who Are the Most Valuable Customers?

All that data is heavily and relentlessly mined. Customer relationship management should include an assessment to determine which customers are worth having a relationship with. And because Caesars has so much detailed historical data, the firm can make fairly accurate projections of **customer lifetime value (CLV)**. CLV represents the present value of the likely future income stream generated by an individual purchaser.[65] Once you know this, you can get a sense of how much you should spend to keep that customer coming back. You can size them up next to their peer group, and if they fall below expectations, you can develop strategies to improve their spending.

customer lifetime value (CLV)

The present value of the likely future income stream generated by an individual purchaser.

The firm tracks over ninety demographic segments, and each responds differently to different marketing approaches. Identifying segments and figuring out how to deal with each involves an iterative model of mining the data to identify patterns, creating a hypothesis (customers in group X will respond to a free steak dinner; group Y will want ten dollars in casino chips), then testing that hypothesis against a control group, turning again to analytics to statistically verify the outcome.

The firm runs hundreds of these small, controlled experiments each year. Loveman says that when marketers suggest new initiatives, "I ask, did we test it first? And if I find out that we just whole-hogged, went after something without testing it, I'll kill 'em. No matter how clever they think it is, we test it."[66] The former ops professor is known to often quote quality guru W. Edwards Deming, saying, "In God we trust; all others must bring data."

When Caesars began diving into the data, they uncovered patterns that defied the conventional wisdom in the gaming industry. Big money didn't come from European princes, Hong Kong shipping heirs, or the *Ocean's 11* crowd—it came from locals. The less than 30 percent of customers who spent between one hundred and five hundred dollars per visit accounted for over 80 percent of revenues and nearly 100 percent of profits.[67]

The data also showed that the firm's most important customers weren't the families that many Vegas competitors were trying to woo with Disneyland-style theme casinos—it was Grandma! The firm focuses on customers forty-five years and older: twenty-somethings have no money, while thirty-somethings have kids and are too busy. To the premiddle-aged crowd, Loveman says, "God bless you, but we don't need you."[68]

8.3 Data-Driven Service: Get Close (but Not Too Close) to Your Customers

The names for reward levels on the Total Rewards card convey increasing customer value—Gold, Diamond, and Platinum. Spend more money at Caesars and you'll enjoy shorter lines, discounts, free items, and more. And if Caesars' systems determine you're a high-value customer, expect white-glove treatment. The firm will lavish you with attention, using technology to try to anticipate your every need. Customers notice the extra treatment that top-tier Total Rewards members receive and actively work to improve their status.

To illustrate this, Loveman points to the obituary of an Ashville, North Carolina, woman who frequented a casino his firm operates on a nearby Cherokee reservation. "Her obituary was published in the Asheville paper and indicated that at the time of her death, she had several grandchildren, she sang in the Baptist choir and she was *a holder of the [the firm's] Diamond Total Rewards card.*" Quipped Loveman, "When your loyalty card is listed in someone's obituary, I would maintain *you have traction.*"[69]

The degree of customer service pushed through the system is astonishing. Upon check-in, a Caesars customer who enjoys fine dining may find his or her table is reserved, along with tickets for a show afterward. Others may get suggestions or special offers throughout their stay, pushed via text message to their mobile device.[70] The firm even tracks gamblers to see if they're suffering unusual losses, and Caesars will dispatch service people to intervene with a feel-good offer: "Having a bad day? Here's a free buffet coupon."[71]

The firm's CRM effort monitors any customer behavior changes. If a customer who usually spends a few hundred a month hasn't shown up in a while, the firm's systems trigger follow-up contact methods such as sending a letter with a promotion offer, or having a rep make a phone call inviting them back.[72]

Customers come back to Caesars because they feel that those casinos treat them better than the competition. And Caesars' laser-like focus on service quality and customer satisfaction are embedded into its information systems and operational procedures. Employees are measured on metrics that include speed and friendliness and are compensated based on guest satisfaction ratings. Hourly workers are notoriously difficult to motivate: they tend to be high-turnover, low-wage earners. But at Caesars, incentive bonuses depend on an entire location's ratings. That encourages strong performers to share tips to bring the new guy up to speed. The process effectively changed the corporate culture at Caesars from an every-property-for-itself mentality to a collaborative, customer-focused enterprise.[73]

While Caesars is committed to learning how to make your customer experience better, the firm is also keenly sensitive to respecting consumer data. The firm has never sold or given away any of its bits to third parties. And the firm admits that some of its efforts to track customers have misfired, requiring special attention to find the sometimes subtitle line between helpful and "too helpful." For example, the firm's CIO has mentioned that customers found it "creepy and Big Brother-ish" when employees tried to greet them by name and talk with them about their past business history with the firm, so it backed off.[74]

8.4 Innovation

Caesars is constantly tinkering with new innovations that help it gather more data and help push service quality and marketing program success. When the introduction of gaming in Pennsylvania threatened to divert lucrative New York City gamblers from Caesars' Atlantic City properties, the firm launched an interactive billboard in New York's Times Square, allowing passersby to operate a virtual slot machine using text messages from their cell phones. Players dialing into the video billboard not only control the display, they receive text message offers promoting Caesars' sites in Atlantic City.[75]

At Caesars, tech experiments abound. RFID-enabled poker chips and under-table RFID readers allow pit bosses to track and rate game play far better than they could before. The firm is experimenting with using RFID-embedded bracelets for poolside purchases and Total Rewards tracking for when customers aren't carrying their wallets. The firm has also incorporated drink ordering into gaming machines—why make customers get up to quench their thirst? A break in gambling is a halt in revenue.

The firm was also one of the first to sign on to use Microsoft's Surface technology—a sort of touch-screen and sensor-equipped tabletop. Customers at these tables can play bowling and group pinball games and even pay for drinks using cards that the tables will automatically identify. Tech even helps Caesars fight card counters and crooks, with facial recognition software scanning casino patrons to spot the bad guys.[76]

And Total Rewards is going social, too. Caesars has partnered with Silicon Valley—based TopGuest to tie social media to its loyalty program. Caesars customers who register with TopGuest (which also works with clients Virgin America, Holiday Inn, and Avis, among others) can receive fifty

Total Rewards bonus credits for each geolocation check-in, tweet, or Instagram photo taken at participating venues.[77]

8.5 Strategy

A walk around Vegas during Caesars' ascendency would find rivals with bigger, fancier casinos. Says Loveman, "We had to compete with the kind of place that God would build if he had the money....The only thing we had was data."[78]

That data advantage creates intelligence for a high-quality and highly personal customer experience. Data gives the firm a service differentiation edge. The loyalty program also represents a switching cost. And these assets combined to be leveraged across a firm that has gained so much scale that it's now the largest player in its industry, gaining the ability to cross-sell customers on a variety of properties—Vegas vacations, riverboat gambling, locally focused reservation properties, and more.

The firm's chief marketing officer points out that when the Total Rewards effort started, the firm was earning about thirty-six cents on every dollar customers spent gaming—the rest went to competitors. A climb to forty cents would be considered monstrous. But within a few short years that number had climbed to forty-five cents, making Caesars the biggest monster in the industry.[79] Some of the firm's technology investments have paid back tenfold in just two years—bringing in hundreds of millions of dollars.[80]

The firm's technology has been pretty tough for others to match, too. Caesars holds several patents covering key business methods and technologies used in its systems. After being acquired by Harrah's, employees of the old Caesars properties lamented that they had, for years, unsuccessfully attempted to replicate Harrah's systems without violating the firm's intellectual property.[81]

8.6 Challenges

Caesars' efforts to gather data, extract information, and turn this into real profits is unparalleled, but it's not a cure-all. Broader events can often derail even the best strategy. Gaming is a discretionary spending item, and when the economy tanks, gambling is one of the first things consumers will cut. Caesars has not been immune to the world financial crisis and experienced a loss in 2008.

Also note that if you look up Caesars' stock symbol you won't find it. The firm was **taken private** in January 2008, when buyout firms Apollo Management and TPG Capital paid $30.7 billion for all of the firm's shares. At that time Loveman signed a five-year deal to remain on as CEO, and he's spoken positively about the benefits of being private—primarily that with the distraction of quarterly earnings off the table, he's been able to focus on the long-term viability and health of the business.[82] Plans for a late 2010 IPO were put on hold as the economy continued to sour.[83]

taken private

The process by which a publicly held company has its outstanding shares purchased by an individual or by a small group of individuals who wish to obtain complete ownership and control.

But the firm also holds $24 billion in debt from expansion projects and the buyout, all at a time when economic conditions have not been favorable to leveraged firms.[84] A brilliantly successful firm that developed best-in-class customer relationship management is now in a position many consider risky due to debt assumed as part of an overly optimistic buyout occurring at precisely the time when the economy went into a terrible funk. Caesars' awesome risk-reducing, profit-pushing analytics failed to offer any insight on the wisdom (or risk) in the debt and private equity deals.

KEY TAKEAWAYS

- Caesars Entertainment provides an example of exceptional data asset leverage in the service sector, focusing on how this technology enables world-class service through customer relationship management.
- Caesars uses its Total Rewards loyalty card system to collect customer data on just about everything you might do at their properties—gamble, eat, drink, see a show, stay in a room, and so on.
- Individual customers signing up for the Total Rewards loyalty card provide Caesars with demographic information such as gender, age, and address, which is combined with transactional data as the card is used.
- Data mining also provides information about ninety-plus customer demographic segments, each of which responds differently to different marketing approaches.
- If Caesars' systems determine you're a high-value customer, you can expect a higher level of perks and service.
- Caesars' CRM effort monitors any customer behavior changes.
- Caesars uses its information systems and operating procedures to measure employees based on metrics that include speed and friendliness and compensates them based on guest satisfaction ratings.

QUESTIONS AND EXERCISES

1. What types of customer data does Caesars gather?
2. How is the data that Caesars collects used?
3. Describe Caesars' most valuable customers. Approximately what percentage of profits does this broad group deliver to the firm?
4. List the services a Rewards Card cardholder might expect.
5. What happens when a good, regular customer stops showing up?
6. Describe how Caesars treats customer data.
7. List some of the technology innovations that Caesars is using to help it gather more data and help push service quality and marketing program success.
8. How does Caesars' Total Rewards loyalty card system represent a switching cost?
9. What is customer lifetime value? Do you think this is an easier metric to calculate at Caesars or Wal-Mart? Why?
10. How did intellectual property protection benefit Caesars?
11. Discuss the challenges Caesars may have to confront in the near future.
12. Describe the role that testing plays in initiatives? What advantage does testing provide the firm? What's the CEO's attitude to testing? Do you agree with this level of commitment? Why or why not?
13. Do you think the firm's described foray into social media is a good idea or a bad one? Why? Discuss any potential upsides and downsides that you see coming from the effort.

ENDNOTES

1. C. Babcock, "Data, Data, Everywhere", *InformationWeek*, January 9, 2006.
2. L. Mearian, "Digital Universe and Its Impact Bigger Than We Thought," *Computerworld*, March 18, 2008.
3. Derived by comparing Wal-Mart's 2.5 petabytes (E. Lai, "Teradata Creates Elite Club for Petabyte-Plus Data Warehouse Customers," *Computerworld*, October 18, 2008) to the Library of Congress estimate of 20 TB (D. Gewirtz, "What If Someone Stole the Library of Congress?" *CNN.com/AC360*, May 25, 2009). It's further noted that the Wal-Mart figure is just for data stored on systems provided by the vendor Teradata. Wal-Mart has many systems outside its Teradata-sourced warehouses, too.
4. T. Davenport and J. Harris, *Competing on Analytics: The New Science of Winning* (Boston: Harvard Business School Press, 2007).
5. S. Baker, "Math Will Rock Your World," *BusinessWeek*, January 23, 2006, http://www.businessweek.com/magazine/content/06_04/b3968001.htm.htm.
6. J. Soat, "P&G's CIO Puts IT at Users' Service," *InformationWeek*, December 15, 2007.
7. M. Harvey, "Probe into How Google Mix-Up Caused $1 Billion Run on United," *Times Online*, September 12, 2008, http://technology.timesonline.co.uk/tol/news/tech_and_web/article4742147.ece.
8. K. Capell, "Tesco: 'Wal-Mart's Worst Nightmare,'" *BusinessWeek*, December 29, 2008.
9. T. Davenport and J. Harris, "Competing with Multichannel Marketing Analytics," *Advertising Age*, April 2, 2007.
10. M. Lowenstein, "Tesco: A Retail Customer Divisibility Champion," *CustomerThink*, October 20, 2002.
11. K. Capell, "Tesco Hits Record Profit, but Lags in U.S.," *BusinessWeek*, April 21, 2009; A. Hawkes, "Tesco Reports Record Profits of £3.8bn," *Guardian*, April. 19, 2011.
12. R. Braddock, "Lessons of Internet Marketing from FreshDirect," *Wall Street Journal*, May 11, 2009.
13. J. Zhang, "Recession Likely to Boost Government Outlays on Health Care," *Wall Street Journal*, February 24, 2009.
14. S. Milligan, "Business Warms to Democratic Leaders," *Boston Globe*, May 28, 2009.
15. R. Appleton, "Less Independent Doctors Could Mean More Medical Mistakes," *InjuryBoard.com*, June 14, 2009; and B. Obama, President's Speech to the American Medical Association, Chicago, IL, June 15, 2009, http://www.whitehouse.gov/the_press_office/Remarks-by-the-President-to-the-Annual-Conference-of-the-American-Medical-Association.
16. J. Halamka, "IT Spending: When Less Is More," *BusinessWeek*, March 2, 2009.
17. D. McCullagh, "Q&A: Electronic Health Records and You," *CNET/CBSNews.com*, May 19, 2009.
18. R. King, "Intelligence Software for Business," *BusinessWeek* podcast, February 27, 2009.
19. R. King, "Intelligence Software for Business," *BusinessWeek* podcast, February 27, 2009.
20. A. Gefter and T. Simonite, "What the Data Miners Are Digging Up about You," *CNET*, December 1, 2008.
21. A. Greenberg, "Companies That Profit from Your Data," *Forbes*, May 14, 2008.
22. R. Mithchell, "Why You Should Be Worried about Your Privacy on the Web," *Computerworld*, May 11, 2009.
23. R. Swarns, "Senator? Terrorist? A Watch List Stops Kennedy at Airport," *New York Times*, August 20, 2004.
24. A. Greenberg, "Companies That Profit from Your Data," *Forbes*, May 14, 2008.
25. F. Rashid, "Epsilon Data Breach to Cost Billions in Worst-Case Scenario," *eWeek*, May 3, 2011.
26. M. Warman, "Google Warns against Facial Recognition Database," *Telegraph*, May 16, 2011.
27. N. Bilton, "Facebook Changes Privacy Settings to Enable Facial Recognition," *New York Times*, June 7, 2011.
28. A. Gefter and T. Simonite, "What the Data Miners Are Digging Up about You," *CNET*, December 1, 2008.
29. E. Mills, "Report: Social Security Numbers Can Be Predicted," *CNET*, July 6, 2009, http://news.cnet.com/8301-1009_3-10280614-83.html.
30. R. King, "Business Intelligence Software's Time Is Now," *BusinessWeek*, March 2, 2009.
31. R. King, "Intelligence Software for Business," *BusinessWeek* podcast, February 27, 2009.
32. D. Rigby and D. Ledingham, "CRM Done Right," *Harvard Business Review*, November 2004; and R. King, "Intelligence Software for Business," *BusinessWeek* podcast, February 27, 2009.
33. H. Havenstein, "HP Nabs Wal-Mart as Data Warehousing Customer," *Computerworld*, August 1, 2007.
34. Key points adapted from Davenport and J. Harris, *Competing on Analytics: The New Science of Winning* (Boston: Harvard Business School Press, 2007).
35. R. King, "Getting a Handle on Big Data with Hadoop," *BusinessWeek*, September 7, 2011.
36. R. King, "Getting a Handle on Big Data with Hadoop," *BusinessWeek*, September 7, 2011.
37. IBM Big Data, "What is Hadoop?" YouTube video, 3:12 May 22, 2012, http://www.youtube.com/watch?v=RQr0qd8gxW8.
38. T. Groenfeldt, "Morgan Stanley takes on Big Data with Hadoop," *Forbes*, May 30, 2012.
39. A. Conry-Murray, "The Pain of E-discovery," *InformationWeek*, June 1, 2009.
40. S. Lohr, "Reaping Results: Data-Mining Goes Mainstream," *New York Times*, May 20, 2007.
41. R. Mulcahy, "ABC: An Introduction to Business Intelligence," *CIO*, March 6, 2007.
42. S. Hansell, "How Wall Street Lied to Its Computers," *New York Times*, September 18, 2008.
43. P. Wahba, "Buffeted 'Quants' Are Still in Demand," *Reuters*, December 22, 2008.
44. P. Coy, "He Who Mines Data May Strike Fool's Gold," *BusinessWeek*, June 16, 1997.
45. B. Helm, "Getting Inside the Customer's Mind," *BusinessWeek*, September 11, 2008.
46. Adapted from J. Kahn, "It's Alive," *Wired*, March 2002; O. Port, "Thinking Machines," *BusinessWeek*, August 7, 2000; and L. McKay, "Decisions, Decisions," *CRM Magazine*, May 1, 2009.
47. From 2006 through 2009, Wal-Mart has appeared as either number one or number two in the *Fortune* 100 rankings.
48. C. Fishman, "The Wal-Mart You Don't Know," *Fast Company*, December 19, 2007.
49. T. Friscia, K. O'Marah, D. Hofman, and J. Souza, "The AMR Research Supply Chain Top 25 for 2009," *AMR Research*, May 28, 2009, http://www.amrresearch.com/Content/View.aspx?compURI=tcm:7-43469.
50. Twelve-month figures from midyear 2009, via *Forbes* and Reuters.
51. C. Fishman, "The Wal-Mart You Don't Know," *Fast Company*, December 19, 2007.
52. D. Joseph, "Supermarket Strategies: What's New at the Grocer," *BusinessWeek*, June 8, 2009.
53. C. Hays, "What Wal-Mart Knows about Customer Habits," *New York Times*, November 14, 2004.
54. C. Hays, "What Wal-Mart Knows about Customer Habits," *New York Times*, November 14, 2004.
55. R. King, "Getting a Handle on Big Data with Hadoop," *BusinessWeek*, September 7, 2011.
56. C. Nicholson, "Wal-Mart Buys Social Media Firm Kosmix," *New York Times*, April 19, 2011.
57. K. Evans-Correia, "Dillman Replaced as Wal-Mart CIO," *SearchCIO*, April 6, 2006.
58. M. McCoy, "Wal-Mart's Data Center Remains Mystery," *Joplin Globe*, May 28, 2006.
59. C. Fishman, "The Wal-Mart You Don't Know," *Fast Company*, December 19, 2007.
60. D. Talbot, "Using IT to Drive Innovation," *Technology Review*, February 16, 2011.
61. V. Magnini, E. Honeycutt, and S. Hodge, "Data Mining for Hotel Firms: Use and Limitations," *Cornell Hotel and Restaurant Administration Quarterly*, April 2003, http://www.entrepreneur.com/tradejournals/article/101938457.html.
62. P. Swabey, "Nothing Left to Chance," *Information Age*, January 18, 2007.
63. M. Wagner, "Harrah's Places Its Bet On IT," *InformationWeek*, September 16, 2008; and L. Haugsted, "Better Take Care of Big Spenders; Harrah's Chief Offers Advice to Cablers," *Multichannel News*, July 30, 2007.
64. N. Hoover, "Chief of the Year: Harrah's CIO Tim Stanley," *Information Week Research and Reports*, 2007.
65. "Which Customers Are Worth Keeping and Which Ones Aren't? Managerial Uses of CLV," *Knowledge@Wharton*, July 30, 2003, http://knowledge.wharton.upenn.edu/article.cfm?articleid=820.
66. J. Nickell, "Welcome to Harrah's," *Business 2.0*, April 2002.
67. P. Swabey, "Nothing Left to Chance," *Information Age*, January 18, 2007.
68. L. Haugsted, "Better Take Care of Big Spenders; Harrah's Chief Offers Advice to Cablers," *Multichannel News*, July 30, 2007.
69. G. Loveman, Speech and Comments, Chief Executive Club of Boston College, January 2005; emphasis added.
70. M. Wagner, "Harrah's Places Its Bet On IT," *InformationWeek*, September 16, 2008.
71. T. Davenport and J. Harris, *Competing on Analytics: The New Science of Winning* (Boston: Harvard Business School Press, 2007).
72. G. Loveman, Speech and Comments, Chief Executive Club of Boston College, January 2005.
73. V. Magnini, E. Honeycutt, and S. Hodge, "Data Mining for Hotel Firms: Use and Limitations," *Cornell Hotel and Restaurant Administration Quarterly*, April 2003, http://www.entrepreneur.com/tradejournals/article/101938457.html.
74. M. Wagner, "Harrah's Places Its Bet On IT," *InformationWeek*, September 16, 2008.
75. "Future Tense: The Global CMO," *Economist Intelligence Unit*, September 2008.
76. S. Lohr, "Reaping Results: Data-Mining Goes Mainstream," *New York Times*, May 20, 2007.
77. "Topguest Rewards Vegas Visitors for Social Check-Ins," *Pulse of Vegas Blog* (hosted at Harrahs.com), April 22, 2011.
78. P. Swabey, "Nothing Left to Chance," *Information Age*, January 18, 2007.
79. E. Lundquist, "Harrah's Bets Big on IT," *eWeek*, July 20, 2005.

80. P. Swabey, "Nothing Left to Chance," *Information Age*, January 18, 2007.

81. N. Hoover, "Chief of the Year: Harrah's CIO Tim Stanley," *Information Week Research and Reports*, 2007.

82. A. Knightly, "Harrah's Boss Speaks," *Las Vegas Review-Journal*, June 14, 2009.

83. C. Vannucci and L. Spears, "Harrah's Pulls $531 Million Private Equity-Backed IPO," *BusinessWeek*, November 19, 2011.

84. P. Lattman, "A Buyout-Shop Breather," *Wall Street Journal*, May 30, 2009.

CHAPTER 12

A Manager's Guide to the Internet and Telecommunications

1. INTRODUCTION

There's all sorts of hidden magic happening whenever you connect to the Internet. But what really makes it possible for you to reach servers halfway around the world in just a fraction of a second? Knowing this is not only flat-out fascinating stuff; it's also critically important for today's manager to have at least a working knowledge of how the Internet functions.

That's because the Internet is a platform of possibilities and a business enabler. Understanding how the Internet and networking works can help you brainstorm new products and services and understand roadblocks that might limit turning your ideas into reality. Marketing professionals who know how the Internet reaches consumers have a better understanding of how technologies can be used to find and target customers. Finance firms that rely on trading speed to move billions in the blink of an eye need to master Internet infrastructure to avoid being swept aside by more nimble market movers. And knowing how the Internet works helps all managers understand where their firms are vulnerable. In most industries today, if your network goes down then you might as well shut your doors and go home; it's nearly impossible to get anything done if you can't get online. Managers who know the Net are prepared to take the appropriate steps to secure their firms and keep their organization constantly connected.

2. INTERNET 101: UNDERSTANDING HOW THE INTERNET WORKS

LEARNING OBJECTIVES

1. **Describe how the technologies of the Internet combine to answer these questions: What are you looking for? Where is it? And how do we get there?**
2. **Interpret a URL, understand what hosts and domains are, describe how domain registration works, describe cybersquatting, and give examples of conditions that constitute a valid and invalid domain-related trademark dispute.**
3. **Describe certain aspects of the Internet infrastructure that are fault-tolerant and support load balancing.**
4. **Discuss the role of hosts, domains, IP addresses, and the DNS in making the Internet work.**

The Internet is a network of networks—millions of them, actually. If the network at your university, your employer, or in your home has Internet access, it connects to an **Internet service provider (ISP)**. Many (but not all) ISPs are big telecommunications companies like Verizon, Comcast, and AT&T. These providers connect to one another, exchanging traffic, and ensuring your messages can get to any other computer that's online and willing to communicate with you.

Internet service provider (ISP)

An organization or firm that provides access to the Internet.

The Internet has no center and no one owns it. That's a good thing. The Internet was designed to be redundant and fault-tolerant—meaning that if one network, connecting wire, or server stops working, everything else should keep on running. Rising from military research and work at educational institutions dating as far back as the 1960s, the Internet really took off in the 1990s, when graphical Web browsing was invented, and much of the Internet's operating infrastructure was transitioned to be supported by private firms rather than government grants.

FIGURE 12.1

The Internet is a network of networks, and these networks are connected together. In the diagram above, the "state.edu" campus network is connected to other networks of the Internet via two ISPs: Cogent and Verizon.

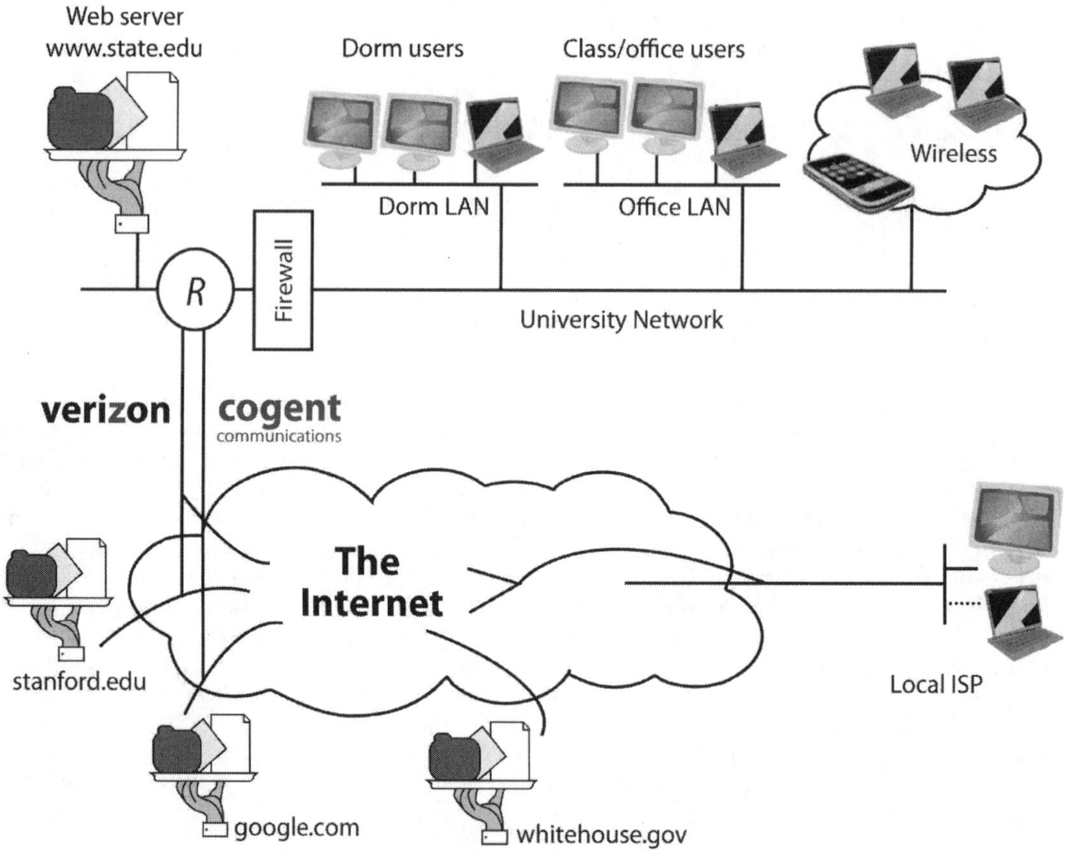

Enough history—let's see how it all works! If you want to communicate with another computer on the Internet then your computer needs to know the answer to three questions: What are you looking for? Where is it? And how do we get there? The computers and software that make up Internet infrastructure can help provide the answers. Let's look at how it all comes together.

2.1 The URL: "What Are You Looking For?"

When you type an address into a Web browser (sometimes called a **URL** for *uniform resource locator*), you're telling your browser what you're looking for. Figure 12.2 describes how to read a typical URL.

URL (uniform resource locator)

Often used interchangeably with "Web address," URLs identify resources on the Internet along with the application protocol need to retrieve it.

FIGURE 12.2 Anatomy of a Web Address

The URL displayed really says, "Use the Web (http://) to find a host server named 'www' in the 'nytimes.com' network, look in the 'tech' directory, and access the 'index.html' file."

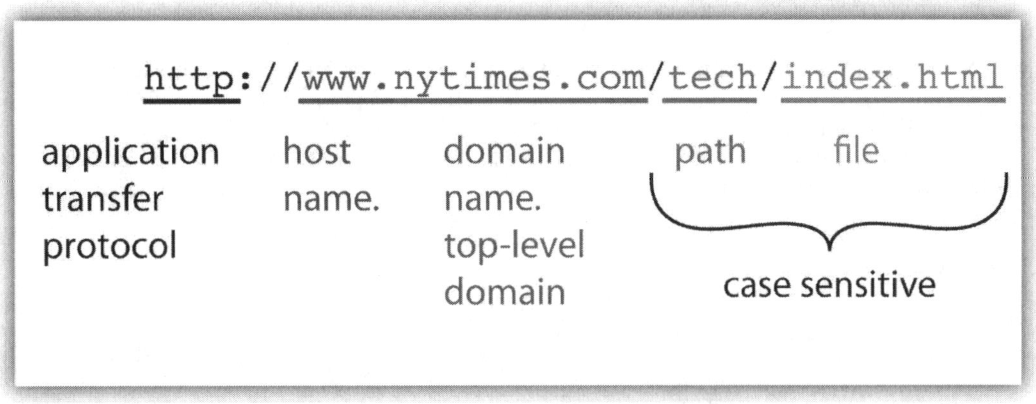

The http:// you see at the start of most Web addresses stands for **hypertext transfer protocol**. A **protocol** is a set of rules for communication—sort of like grammar and vocabulary in a language like English. The http protocol defines how Web browser and Web servers communicate and is designed to be independent from the computer's hardware and operating system. It doesn't matter if messages come from a PC, a Mac, a huge mainframe, or a pocket-sized smartphone; if a device speaks to another using a common protocol, then it will be heard and understood.

The Internet supports lots of different applications, and many of these applications use their own application transfer protocol to communicate with each other. The server that holds your e-mail uses something called *SMTP*, or simple mail transfer protocol, to exchange mail with other e-mail servers throughout the world. FTP, or file transfer protocol, is used for—you guessed it—file transfer. FTP is how most Web developers upload the Web pages, graphics, and other files for their Web sites. Even the Web uses different protocols. When you surf to an online bank or when you're ready to enter your payment information at the Web site of an Internet retailer, the http at the beginning of your URL will probably change to https (the "s" is for secure). That means that communications between your browser and server will be encrypted for safe transmission. The beauty of the Internet infrastructure is that any savvy entrepreneur can create a new application that rides on top of the Internet.

hypertext transfer protocol (http)

Application transfer protocol that allows Web browsers and Web servers to communicate with each other.

protocol

Enables communication by defining the format of data and rules for exchange.

file transfer protocol (FTP)

Application transfer protocol that is used to copy files from one computer to another.

Hosts and Domain Names

The next part of the URL in our diagram holds the host and domain name. Think of the domain name as the name of the network you're trying to connect to, and think of the host as the computer you're looking for on that network.

Many domains have lots of different hosts. For example, Yahoo!'s main Web site is served from the host named "www" (at the address http://www.yahoo.com), but Yahoo! also runs other hosts including those named "finance" (finance.yahoo.com), "sports" (sports.yahoo.com), and "games" (games.yahoo.com).

Host and Domain Names: A Bit More Complex Than That

While it's useful to think of a host as a single computer, popular Web sites often have several computers that work together to share the load for incoming requests. Assigning several computers to a host name offers **load balancing** and **fault tolerance**, helping ensure that all visits to a popular site like http://www.google.com won't overload a single computer, or that Google doesn't go down if one computer fails.

It's also possible for a single computer to have several host names. This might be the case if a firm were hosting several Web sites on a single piece of computing hardware.

Some domains are also further broken down into subdomains—many times to represent smaller networks or subgroups within a larger organization. For example, the address http://www.rhsmith.umd.edu is a University of Maryland address with a host "www" located in the subdomain "rhsmith" for the Robert H. Smith School of Business. International URLs might also include a second-level domain classification scheme. British URLs use

load balancing

Distributing a computing or networking workload across multiple systems to avoid congestion and slow performance.

fault tolerance

The ability of a system to continue operation even if a component fails.

this scheme, for example, with the BBC carrying the commercial (.co) designation—http://www.bbc.co.uk—and the University of Oxford carrying the academic (.ac) designation—http://www.ox.ac.uk. You can actually go 127 levels deep in assigning subdomains, but that wouldn't make it easy on those who have to type in a URL that long.

Most Web sites are configured to load a default host, so you can often eliminate the host name if you want to go to the most popular host on a site (the default host is almost always named "www"). Another tip: most browsers will automatically add the "http://" for you, too.

Host and domain names are not case sensitive, so you can use a combination of upper and lower case letters and you'll still get to your destination.

Web hosting service

A firm that provides hardware and services to run the Web sites of others.

ICANN (Internet Corporation for Assigned Names and Numbers)

Nonprofit organization responsible for managing the Internet's domain and numbering systems.

cybersquatting

Acquiring a domain name that refers to a firm, individual, product, or trademark, with the goal of exploiting it for financial gain. The practice is illegal in many nations, and ICANN has a dispute resolution mechanism that in some circumstances can strip cybersquatters of registered domains.

I Want My Own Domain

You can stake your domain name claim in cyberspace by going through a firm called a *domain name registrar*. You don't really buy a domain name; you simply pay a registrar for the right to use that name, with the right renewable over time. While some registrars simply register domain names, others act as **Web hosting services** that are able to run your Web site on their Internet-connected servers for a fee.

Registrars throughout the world are accredited by **ICANN (Internet Corporation for Assigning Names and Numbers)**, a nonprofit governance and standards-setting body. Each registrar may be granted the ability to register domain names in one or more of the Net's generic top-level domains (gTLDs), such as ".com," ".net," or ".org." There are dozens of registrars that can register ".com" domain names, the most popular gTLD.

Some generic top-level domain names, like ".com," have no restrictions on use, while others limit registration. For example, ".edu" is restricted to U.S.-accredited, postsecondary institutions. ICANN has also announced plans to allow organizations to sponsor their own top-level domains (e.g., ".berlin," or ".coke").

There are also separate agencies that handle over 250 different two-character country code top-level domains, or ccTLDs (e.g., ".uk" for the United Kingdom and ".jp" for Japan). Servers or organizations generally don't need to be housed within a country to use a country code as part of their domain names, leading to a number of creatively named Web sites. The URL-shortening site "bit.ly" uses Libya's ".ly" top-level domain; many physicians are partial to Moldova's code (".md"); and the tiny Pacific island nation of Tuvulu might not have a single broadcast television station, but that doesn't stop it from licensing its country code to firms that want a ".tv" domain name.[1] Recent standards also allow domain names in languages that use non-Latin alphabets such as Arabic and Russian.

Domain name registration is handled on a first-come, first-served basis and all registrars share registration data to ensure that no two firms gain rights to the same name. Start-ups often sport wacky names, partly because so many domains with common words and phrases are already registered to others. While some domain names are held by legitimate businesses, others are registered by investors hoping to resell a name's rights.

Trade in domain names can be lucrative. For example, the "Insure.com" domain was sold to QuinStreet for $16 million in fall 2009.[2] But knowingly registering a domain name to profit from someone else's firm name or trademark is known as **cybersquatting** and that's illegal. The United States has passed the Anticybersquatting Consumer Protection Act (ACPA), and ICANN has the Domain Name Dispute Resolution Policy that can reach across boarders. Try to extort money by holding a domain name that's identical to (or in some cases, even similar to) a well-known trademark holder and you could be stripped of your domain name and even fined.

Courts and dispute resolution authorities will sometimes allow a domain that uses the trademark of another organization if it is perceived to have legitimate, nonexploitive reasons for doing so. For example, the now defunct site Verizonreallysucks.com was registered as a protest against the networking giant and was considered fair use since owners didn't try to extort money from the telecom giant.[3] However, the courts allowed the owner of the PETA trademark (the organization People for the Ethical Treatment of Animals) to claim the domain name peta.org from original registrant, who had been using that domain to host a site called "People Eating Tasty Animals."[4]

Trying to predict how authorities will rule can be difficult. The musician Sting's name was thought to be too generic to deserve the rights to Sting.com, but Madonna was able to take back her domain name (for the record, Sting now owns Sting.com).[5] Apple executive Jonathan Ive was denied the right to reclaim domain names incorporating his own name, but that had been registered by another party and without his consent. The publicity-shy design guru wasn't considered enough of a public figure to warrant protection.[6] And sometimes disputing parties can come to an agreement outside of court or ICANN's dispute resolution mechanisms. When Canadian teenager Michael Rowe registered a site for his part-time Web design business, a firm south of the border took notice of his domain name—Mikerowesoft.com. The two parties eventually settled in a deal that swapped the domain for an Xbox and a trip to the Microsoft Research Tech Fest.[7]

Path Name and File Name

Look to the right of the top-level domain and you might see a slash followed by either a path name, a file name, or both. If a Web address has a path and file name, the path maps to a folder location where the file is stored on the server; the file is the name of the file you're looking for.

Most Web pages end in ".html," indicating they are in **hypertext markup language**. While http helps browsers and servers communicate, html is the language used to create and format (render) Web pages. A file, however, doesn't need to be .html; Web servers can deliver just about any type of file: Acrobat documents (.pdf), PowerPoint documents (.ppt or .pptx), Word docs (.doc or .docx), JPEG graphic images (.jpg), and—as we'll see in Chapter 13—even malware programs that attack your PC. At some Web addresses, the file displays content for every visitor, and at others (like amazon.com), a file will contain programs that run on the Web server to generate custom content just for you.

hypertext markup language (HTML)

Language used to compose Web pages.

You don't always type a path or file name as part of a Web address, but there's always a file lurking behind the scenes. A Web address without a file name will load content from a default page. For example, when you visit "google.com," Google automatically pulls up a page called "index.html," a file that contains the Web page that displays the Google logo, the text entry field, the "Google Search" button, and so on. You might not see it, but it's there.

Butterfingers, beware! Path and file names are case sensitive—amazon.com/books is considered to be different from amazon.com/BOOKS. Mistype your capital letters after the domain name and you might get a 404 error (the very unfriendly Web server error code that means the document was not found).

2.2 IP Addresses and the Domain Name System: "Where Is It? And How Do We Get There?"

The IP Address

If you want to communicate, then you need to have a way for people to find and reach you. Houses and businesses have street addresses, and telephones have phone numbers. Every device connected to the Internet has an identifying address, too—it's called an *IP (Internet protocol) address.*

A device gets its **IP address** from whichever organization is currently connecting it to the Internet. Connect using a laptop at your university and your school will assign the laptop's IP address. Connect at a hotel, and the hotel's Internet service provider lends your laptop an IP address. Laptops and other end-user machines might get a different IP address each time they connect, but the IP addresses of servers rarely change. It's OK if you use different IP addresses during different online sessions because services like e-mail and Facebook identify you by your username and password. The IP address simply tells the computers that you're communicating with where they can find you right now. IP addresses can also be used to identify a user's physical location, to tailor search results, and to customize advertising. See Chapter 14 to learn more.

IP address

A value used to identify a device that is connected to the Internet. IP addresses are usually expressed as four numbers (from 0 to 255), separated by periods.

The original and still widely used format for IP addresses is known as IPv4. Under IPv4, IP addresses are expressed as a string of four numbers between 0 and 255, separated by three periods. Want to know which IP address your smartphone or computer is using? Visit a Web site like ip-adress.com (one "d"), whatismyipaddress.com, or ipchicken.com.

NAT (network address translation)

A technique often used to conserve IP addresses by maps devices on a private network to single Internet-connected device that acts on their behalf.

The Internet Is Full—We've Run Out of IP Addresses

If you do the math, four combinations of 0 to 255 gives you a little over four billion possible IP addresses. Four billion sounds like a lot, but the number of devices connecting to the Internet is exploding! Internet access is now baked into smartphones, tablets, televisions, DVD players, video game consoles, utility meters, thermostats, appliances, picture frames, and more. Another problem is a big chunk of existing addresses weren't allocated efficiently, and these can't be easily reclaimed from the corporations, universities, and other organizations that initially received them. All of this means that we've run out of IP addresses. In February 2011 the last batches were made available to regional Internet registries.[8]

There are some schemes to help delay the impact of this IP address drought. For example, a technique known as **NAT (network address translation)** uses a gateway that allows multiple devices to share a single IP address. But NAT slows down Internet access and is complex, cumbersome, and expensive to administer.[9]

The only long-term solution is to shift to a new IP scheme. Fortunately, one was developed more than a decade ago. IPv6 increases the possible address space from the 2^{32} (4,294,967,296) addresses used in the current system (called IPv4) to a new theoretical limit of 2^{128} addresses, which is a really big number—bigger than 34 with 37 zeros after it. That's more IPv6 addresses than there are gains of sand on the earth.[10]

But not all the news is good. Unfortunately, IPv6 isn't backward compatible with IPv4, and the transition to the new standard has been painfully slow. This gives us the equivalent of many islands of IPv6 in a sea of IPv4, with translation between the two schemes happening when these networks come together. Others consider it the equivalent of two Internets with a translation bridge between IPv4 and IPv6 (and that bridge introduces a delay).[11] While most modern hardware and operating systems providers now support IPv6, converting a network to IPv6 currently involves a lot of cost with little short-term benefit.[12] Upgrading may take years.[13]

Some organizations have stepped up to try to hasten the transition. Facebook, Google, Microsoft, Yahoo!, and some of the Internet's largest networks have made most of its services IPv6 accessible, the U.S. government has mandated IPv6 support for most agencies, China has spurred conversion within its borders, and Comcast and Verizon have major IPv6 rollouts under way. While the transition will be slow, when wide scale deployment does arrive, IPv6 will offer other benefits, including potentially improving the speed, reliability, and security of the Internet.

The DNS: The Internet's Phonebook

You can actually type an IP address of a Web site into a Web browser and that page will show up. But that doesn't help users much because four sets of numbers are really hard to remember.

domain name service (DNS)

Internet directory service that allows devices and services to be named and discoverable. The DNS, for example, helps your browser locate the appropriate computers when entering an address like http://finance.google.com.

This is where the **domain name service (DNS)** comes in. The domain name service is a distributed database that looks up the host and domain names that you enter and returns the actual IP address for the computer that you want to communicate with. It's like a big, hierarchical set of phone books capable of finding Web servers, e-mail servers, and more. These "phone books" are called *nameservers*—and when they work together to create the DNS, they can get you anywhere you need to go online.

FIGURE 12.3

When your computer needs to find the IP address for a host or domain name, it sends a message to a DNS resolver, which looks up the IP address starting at the root nameserver. Once the lookup has taken place, that IP address can be saved in a holding space called a cache, to speed future lookups.

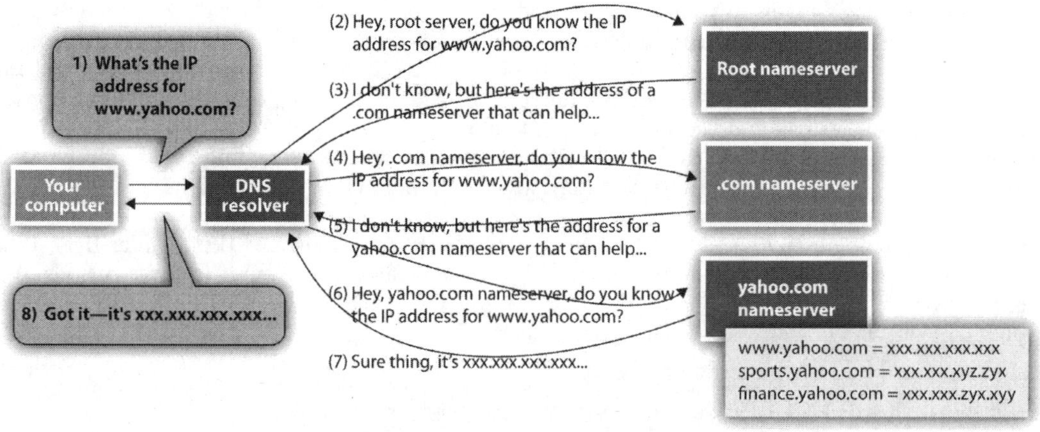

To get a sense of how the DNS works, let's imagine that you type www.yahoo.com into a Web browser. Your computer doesn't know where to find that address, but when your computer connected to the network, it learned where to find a service on the network called a DNS resolver. The DNS resolver can look up host/domain name combinations to find the matching IP address using the "phone book" that is the DNS. The resolver doesn't know everything, but it does know where to start a lookup that will eventually give you the address you're looking for. If this is the first time anyone on that network has tried to find "www.yahoo.com," the resolver will contact one of thirteen identical root nameservers. The root acts as a lookup starting place. It doesn't have one big list, but it can point you to a nameserver for the next level, which would be one of the ".com" nameservers in our example. The ".com" nameserver can then find one of the yahoo.com nameservers. The yahoo.com nameserver can respond to the resolver with the IP address for www.yahoo.com, and the resolver passes that information back to your computer. Once your computer knows Yahoo!'s IP address, it's then ready to communicate directly with www.yahoo.com. The yahoo.com nameserver includes IP addresses for all Yahoo!'s public sites: www.yahoo.com, games.yahoo.com, sports.yahoo.com, finance.yahoo.com, and so on.

The system also remembers what it's done so the next time you need the IP address of a host you've already looked up, your computer can pull this out of a storage space called a **cache**, avoiding all those nameserver visits. Caches are periodically cleared and refreshed to ensure that data referenced via the DNS stays accurate.

cache

A temporary storage space used to speed computing tasks.

Distributing IP address lookups this way makes sense. It avoids having one huge, hard-to-maintain, and ever-changing list. Firms add and remove hosts on their own networks just by updating entries in their nameserver. And it allows host IP addresses to change easily, too. Moving your Web server off-site to a hosting provider? Just update your nameserver with the new IP address at the hosting provider, and the world will invisibly find that new IP address on the new network by using the same old, familiar host/domain name combination. The DNS is also fault-tolerant—meaning that if one nameserver goes down, the rest of the service can function. There are exact copies at each level, and the system is smart enough to move on to another nameserver if its first choice isn't responding.

But What If the DNS Gets Hacked?

A hacked DNS would be a disaster! Think about it. If bad guys could change which Web sites load when you type in a host and domain name, they could redirect you to impostor Web sites that look like a bank or e-commerce retailer but are really set up to harvest passwords and credit card data.

This exact scenario played out when the DNS of NET Virtua, a Brazilian Internet service provider, was hacked via a technique called *DNS cache poisoning*. Cache poisoning exploits a hole in DNS software, redirecting users to sites they didn't request. The Brazilian DNS hack redirected NET Virtua users wishing to visit the Brazilian bank Bradesco to fraudulent Web sites that attempted to steal passwords and install malware. The hack impacted about 1 percent of the bank's customers before the attack was discovered.[14]

The exploit showed the importance of paying attention to security updates. A few months earlier, a group that *Wired* magazine referred to as "A Secret Geek A-Team"[15] had developed a software update that would have prevented the DNS poisoning exploit used against NET Virtua, but administrators at the Brazilian Internet service provider failed to update their software so the hackers got in. An additional upgrade to a DNS system, known as DNSSEC (domain name service security extensions), promises to further limit the likelihood of cache poisoning, but it may take years for the new standards to be rolled out everywhere.[16]

KEY TAKEAWAYS

- The Internet is a network of networks. Internet service providers connect with one another to share traffic, enabling any Internet-connected device to communicate with any other.
- URLs may list the application protocol, host name, domain name, path name, and file name, in that order. Path and file names are case sensitive.
- A domain name represents an organization. Hosts are public services offered by that organization. Hosts are often thought of as a single computer, although many computers can operate under a single host name and many hosts can also be run off a single computer.
- You don't buy a domain name but can register it, paying for a renewable right to use that domain name. Domains need to be registered within a generic top-level domain such as ".com" or ".org" or within a two-character country code top-level domain such as ".uk," ".ly," or ".md."
- Registering a domain that uses someone else's trademark in an attempt to extract financial gain is considered cybersquatting. The United States and other nations have anticybersquatting laws, and ICANN has a dispute resolution system that can overturn domain name claims if a registrant is considered to be cybersquatting.
- Every device connected to the Internet has an IP address. These addresses are assigned by the organization that connects the user to the Internet. An IP address may be assigned temporarily, for use only during that online session.
- We're running out of IP addresses. The current scheme (IPv4) is being replaced by IPv6, a scheme that will give us many more addresses and additional feature benefits but is not backward compatible with the IPv4 standard. Transitioning to IPv6 will be costly, take time, and introduce delay when traffic transfers between IPv4 and IPv6 networks.
- The domain name system is a distributed, fault-tolerant system that uses nameservers to map host/domain name combinations to IP addresses.

QUESTIONS AND EXERCISES

1. Find the Web page for your school's information systems department. What is the URL that gets you to this page? Label the host name, domain name, path, and file for this URL. Are there additional subdomains? If so, indicate them, as well.
2. Go to a registrar and see if someone has registered your first or last name as a domain name. If so, what's hosted at that domain? If not, would you consider registering your name as a domain name? Why or why not?
3. Investigate cases of domain name disputes. Examine a case that you find especially interesting. Who were the parties involved? How was the issue resolved? Do you agree with the decision?
4. Describe how the DNS is fault-tolerant and promotes load balancing. Give examples of other types of information systems that might need to be fault-tolerant and offer load balancing. Why?
5. Research DNS poisoning online. List a case, other than the one mentioned in this chapter, where DNS poisoning took place. Which network was poisoned, who were the victims, and how did hackers exploit the poisoned system? Could this exploit have been stopped? How? Whose responsibility is it to stop these kinds of attacks?
6. Why is the switch from IPv4 to IPv6 so difficult? What key principles, discussed in prior chapters, are slowing migration to the new standard?
7. Test to see if networks that you frequently use (home, school, work, mobile) are ready for IPv6 by visiting http://test-ipv6.com/ (or a similar site). Search online to see if your service provider has posted details outlining their IPv6 transition strategy and be prepared to share your results with the class. Do you use other products not tested by the Web site mentioned above (e.g., network-enabled video games or other software)? Search online to see if your favorite products and services are IPv6 ready.

3. GETTING WHERE YOU'RE GOING

LEARNING OBJECTIVES

1. Understand the layers that make up the Internet—application protocol, transmission control protocol, and Internet protocol—and describe why each is important.
2. Discuss the benefits of Internet architecture in general and TCP/IP in particular.
3. Name applications that should use TCP and others that might use UDP.
4. Understand what a router does and the role these devices play in networking.
5. Conduct a traceroute and discuss the output, demonstrating how Internet interconnections work in getting messages from point to point.
6. Understand why mastery of Internet infrastructure is critical to modern finance and be able to discuss the risks in automated trading systems.
7. Describe VoIP, and contrast circuit versus packet switching, along with organizational benefits and limitations of each.

3.1 TCP/IP: The Internet's Secret Sauce

OK, we know how to read a Web address, we know that every device connected to the Net needs an IP address, and we know that the DNS can look at a Web address and find the IP address of the machine that you want to communicate with. But how does a Web page, an e-mail, or an iTunes download actually get from a remote computer to your desktop?

For our next part of the Internet journey, we'll learn about two additional protocols: TCP and IP. These protocols are often written as TCP/IP and pronounced by reading all five letters in a row, "T-C-P-I-P" (sometimes they're also referred to as the *Internet protocol suite*). TCP and IP are built into any device that a user would use to connect to the Internet—from handhelds to desktops to supercomputers—and together TCP/IP make Internet working happen.

FIGURE 12.4 TCP/IP in Action

In this example, a server on the left sends a Web page to the user on the right. The application (the Web server) passes the contents of the page to TCP (which is built into the server's operating system). TCP slices the Web page into packets. Then IP takes over, forwarding packets from router to router across the Internet until it arrives at the user's PC. Packets sometimes take different routes, and occasionally arrive out of order. TCP running on the receiving system on the right checks that all packets have arrived, requests that damaged or lost packets be resent, puts them in the right order, and sends a perfect, exact copy of the Web page to your browser.

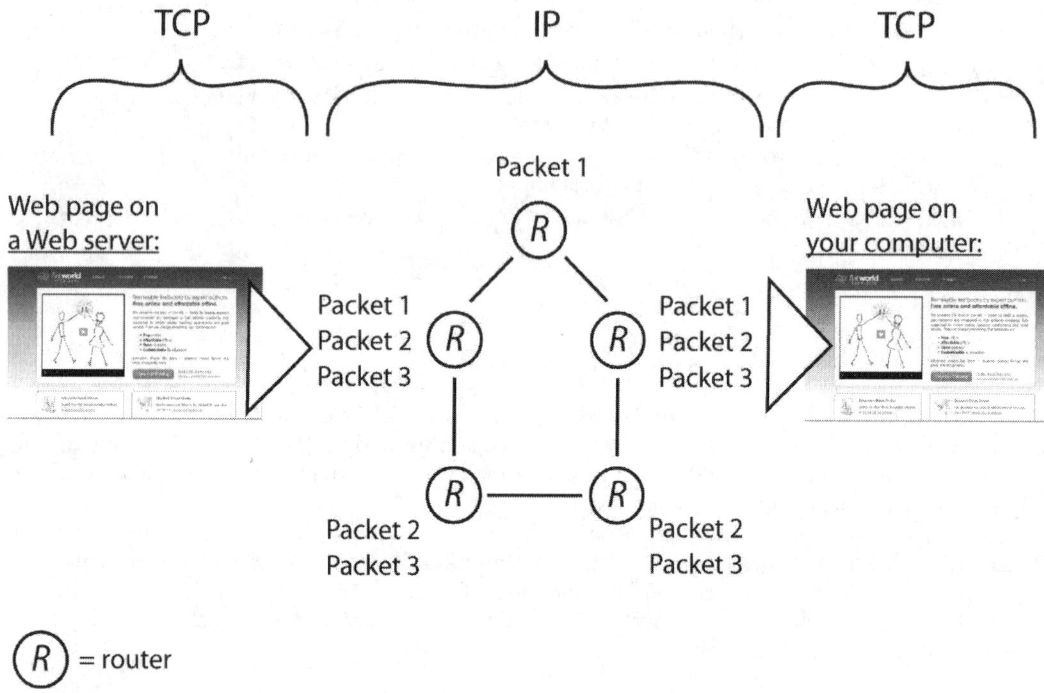

TCP (transmission control protocol)

Works at both ends of most Internet communication to ensure a perfect copy of a message is sent.

packet (or datagram)

A unit of data forwarded by a network. All Internet transmissions—URLs, Web pages, e-mails—are divided into one or more packets.

IP (Internet protocol)

Routing protocol that is in charge of forwarding packets on the Internet.

router

A computing device that connects networks and exchanges data between them.

TCP and IP operate below http and the other application transfer protocols mentioned earlier. **TCP (transmission control protocol)** works its magic at the start and endpoint of the trip—on both your computer and on the destination computer you're communicating with. Let's say a Web server wants to send you a large Web page. The Web server application hands the Web page it wants to send to its own version of TCP. TCP then slices up the Web page into smaller chunks of data called **packets (or datagrams)**. The packets are like little envelopes containing part of the entire transmission—they're labeled with a destination address (where it's going) and a source address (where it came from). Now we'll leave TCP for a second, because TCP on the Web server then hands those packets off to the second half of our dynamic duo, IP.

It's the job of **IP (Internet protocol)** to route the packets to their final destination, and those packets might have to travel over several networks to get to where they're going. The relay work is done via special computers called **routers**, and these routers speak to each other and to other computers using IP (since routers are connected to the Internet, they have IP addresses, too. Some are even named). Every computer on the Internet is connected to a router, and all routers are connected to at least one (and usually more than one) other router, linking up the networks that make up the Internet.

Routers don't have perfect, end-to-end information on all points in the Internet, but they do talk to each other all the time, so a router has a pretty good idea of where to send a packet to get it closer to where it needs to end up. This chatter between the routers also keeps the Internet decentralized and fault-tolerant. Even if one path out of a router goes down (a networking cable gets cut, a router breaks, the power to a router goes out), as long as there's another connection out of that router, then your packet will get forwarded. Networks fail, so good, fault-tolerant network design involves having alternate paths into and out of a network.

Once packets are received by the destination computer (your computer in our example), that machine's version of TCP kicks in. TCP checks that it has all the packets, makes sure that no packets were damaged or corrupted, requests replacement packets (if needed), and then puts the packets in the correct order, passing a perfect copy of your transmission to the program you're communicating with (an e-mail server, Web server, etc.).

This progression—application at the source to TCP at the source (slice up the data being sent), to IP (for forwarding among routers), to TCP at the destination (put the transmission back together and make sure it's perfect), to application at the destination—takes place in both directions, starting at the server for messages coming to you, and starting on your computer when you're sending messages to another computer.

UDP (user datagram protocol)

Protocol that operates instead of TCP in applications where delivery speed is important and quality can be sacrificed.

UDP: TCP's Faster, Less Reliable Sibling

TCP is a perfectionist and that's what you want for Web transmissions, e-mail, and application downloads. But sometimes we're willing to sacrifice perfection for speed. You'd make this sacrifice for streaming media applications like Windows Media Player, Real Player, Internet voice chat, and video conferencing. Having to wait to make sure each packet is perfectly sent would otherwise lead to awkward pauses that interrupt real-time listening. It'd be better to just grab the packets as they come and play them, even if they have minor errors. Packets are small enough that if one packet doesn't arrive, you can ignore it and move on to the next without too much quality disruption. A protocol called **UDP (user datagram protocol)** does exactly this, working as a TCP stand-in when you've got the need for speed, and are willing to sacrifice quality. If you've ever watched a Web video or had a Web-based phone call and the quality got sketchy, it's probably because there were packet problems, but UDP kept on chugging, making the "get it fast" instead of "get it perfect" trade-off.

voice over Internet protocol (VoIP)

Transmission technologies that enable voice communications (phone calls) to take place over the Internet as well as private packet-switched networks.

VoIP: When Phone Calls Are Just Another Internet Application

The increasing speed and reliability of the Internet means that applications such as Internet phone calls (referred to as *VoIP*, or **voice over Internet protocol**) are becoming more reliable. That doesn't just mean that Skype becomes a more viable alternative for consumer landline and mobile phone calls; it's also good news for many businesses, governments, and nonprofits.

Many large organizations maintain two networks—one for data and another for *POTS* (plain old telephone service). Maintaining two networks is expensive, and while conventional phone calls are usually of a higher quality than their Internet counterparts, POTS equipment is also inefficient. Old phone systems use a technology called *circuit switching*. A "circuit" is a dedicated connection between two entities. When you have a POTS phone call, a circuit is open, dedicating a specific amount of capacity between you and the party on the other end. You're using that "circuit" regardless of whether you're talking. Pause between words or put someone on hold, and the circuit is still in use. Anyone who has ever tried to make a phone call at a busy time (say, early morning on Mother's Day or at midnight on New Year's Eve) and received an "all circuits are busy" recording has experienced congestion on an inefficient circuit-switched phone network.

But unlike circuit-switched counterparts, Internet networks are packet-switched networks, which can be more efficient. Since we can slice conversations up into packets, we can squeeze them into smaller spaces. If there are pauses in a conversation or someone's on hold, applications don't hold up the network. And that creates an opportunity to use the network's available capacity for other users. The trade-off is one that swaps circuit switching's quality of service (QoS) with packet switching's efficiency and cost savings. Try to have a VoIP call when there's too much traffic on a portion of the network and your call quality will drop. But packet switching quality is getting much better. Networking standards are now offering special features, such as "packet prioritization," that can allow voice packets to gain delivery priority over packets for applications like e-mail, where a slight delay is OK.

When voice is digitized, "telephone service" simply becomes another application that sits on top of the Internet, like the Web, e-mail, or FTP. VoIP calls between remote offices can save long distance charges. And when the phone system becomes a computer application, you can do a lot more. Well-implemented VoIP systems allow users' browsers access to their voice mail inbox, one-click video conferencing and call forwarding, point-and-click conference call setup, and other features, but you'll still have a phone number, just like with POTS.

What Connects the Routers and Computers?

Routers are connected together, either via cables or wirelessly. A cable connecting a computer in a home or office is probably copper (likely what's usually called an Ethernet cable), with transmissions sent through the copper via electricity. Long-haul cables, those that carry lots of data over long distances, are usually fiber-optic lines—glass lined cables that transmit light (light is faster and travels farther distances than electricity, but fiber-optic networking equipment is more expensive than the copper-electricity kind). Wireless transmission can happen via Wi-Fi (for shorter distances), or cell phone tower or satellite over longer distances. But the beauty of the Internet protocol suite (TCP/IP) is that it doesn't matter what the actual transmission media are. As long as your routing equipment can connect any two networks, and as long as that equipment "speaks" IP, then you can be part of the Internet.

In reality, your messages likely transfer via lots of different transmission media to get to their final destination. If you use a laptop connected via Wi-Fi, then that wireless connection finds a base station, usually within about three hundred feet. That base station is probably connected to a local area network (LAN) via a copper cable. And your firm or college may connect to fast, long-haul portions of the Internet via fiber-optic cables provided by that firm's Internet service provider (ISP).

Most big organizations have multiple ISPs for redundancy, providing multiple paths in and out of a network. This is so that if a network connection provided by one firm goes down, say an errant backhoe cuts a cable, other connections can route around the problem (see Figure 12.1).

peering

When separate ISPs link their networks to swap traffic on the Internet.

In the United States (and in most deregulated telecommunications markets), Internet service providers come in all sizes, from smaller regional players to sprawling international firms. When different ISPs connect their networking equipment together to share traffic, it's called **peering**. Peering usually takes place at neutral sites called *Internet exchange points* (IXPs), although some firms also have private peering points. Carriers usually don't charge one another for peering. Instead, "the money is made" in the ISP business by charging the end-points in a network—the customer organizations and end users that an ISP connects to the Internet. Competition among carriers helps keep prices down, quality high, and innovation moving forward.

colocation facility

Sometimes called a "colo," or carrier hotel; provides a place where the gear from multiple firms can come together and where the peering of Internet traffic can take place. Equipment connecting in colos could be high-speed lines from ISPs, telecom lines from large private data centers, or even servers hosted in a colo to be closer to high-speed Internet connections.

Finance Has a Need for Speed

When many folks think of Wall Street trading, they think of the open outcry pit at the New York Stock Exchange (NYSE). But human traders are just too slow for many of the most active trading firms. Over half of all U.S. stock trades and a quarter of worldwide currency trades now happen via programs that make trading decisions without any human intervention.[17] There are many names for this automated, data-driven frontier of finance—algorithmic trading, black-box trading, or high-frequency trading. And while firms specializing in automated, high-frequency trading represent only about 2 percent of the trading firms operating in the United States, they account for about three quarters of all U.S. equity trading volume.[18]

Programmers lie at the heart of modern finance. "A geek who writes code—those guys are now the valuable guys" says the former head of markets systems at Fidelity Investments, and that rare breed of top programmer can make "tens of millions of dollars" developing these systems.[19] Such systems leverage data mining and other model-building techniques to crunch massive volumes of data and discover exploitable market patterns. Models are then run against real-time data and executed the instant a trading opportunity is detected. (For more details on how data is gathered and models are built, see Chapter 11.)

Winning with these systems means being quick—very quick. Suffer delay (what techies call *latency*) and you may have missed your opportunity to pounce on a signal or market imperfection. To cut latency, many trading firms are moving their servers out of their own data centers and into **colocation facility**. These facilities act as storage places where a firm's servers get superfast connections as close to the action as possible. And by renting space in a "*colo*," a firm gets someone else to manage the electrical and cooling issues, often providing more robust power backup and lower energy costs than a firm might get on its own.

Equinix, a major publicly traded IXP and colocation firm with facilities worldwide, has added a growing number of high-frequency trading firms to a roster of customers that includes e-commerce, Internet, software, and telecom companies. In northern New Jersey alone (the location of many of the servers where "Wall Street" trading takes place), Equinix hosts some eighteen exchanges and trading platforms as well as the NYSE Secure Financial Transaction Infrastructure (SFTI) access node.

Less than a decade ago, eighty milliseconds was acceptably low latency, but now trading firms are pushing below one millisecond into microseconds.[20] So it's pretty clear that understanding how the Internet works, and how to best exploit it, is of fundamental and strategic importance to those in finance. But also recognize that this kind of automated trading comes with risks. Systems that run on their own can move many billions in the blink of an eye, and the actions of one system may cascade, triggering actions by others.

The spring 2010 "Flash Crash" resulted in a nearly 1,000-point freefall in the Dow Jones Industrial Index, it's biggest intraday drop ever. Those black boxes can be mysterious—months after the May 6th event, experts were still parsing through trading records, trying to unearth how the flash crash happened.[21] Regulators and lawmakers recognize they now need to understand technology, telecommunications, and its broader impact on society so that they can create platforms that fuel growth without putting the economy at risk.

Watching the Packet Path via Traceroute

Want to see how packets bounce from router to router as they travel around the Internet? Check out a tool called *traceroute*. Traceroute repeatedly sends a cluster of three packets starting at the first router connected to a computer, then the next, and so on, building out the path that packets take to their destination.

Traceroute is built into all major desktop operating systems (Windows, Macs, Linux), and several Web sites will run traceroute between locations (traceroute.org and visualroute.visualware.com are great places to explore).

The message below shows a traceroute performed between Irish firm VistaTEC and Boston College. At first, it looks like a bunch of gibberish, but if we look closely, we can decipher what's going on.

```
Traceroute to www.bc.edu (136.167.2.220), 30 hops max, 38 byte packets
 1  vlan120.switch.deg.vistatec.ie (85.159.16.65)  0.758 ms  1.141 ms  2.189 ms
 2  ge0-1.router.deg.vistatec.ie (85.159.16.25)  4.109 ms  0.561 ms  0.485 ms
 3  xe-0-1-0-119.dub20.ip4.tinet.net (77.67.66.213)  0.698 ms  0.734 ms  0.691 ms
 4  xe-10-1-0.lon11.ip4.tinet.net (89.149.186.197)  11.290 ms  11.335 ms  11.300 ms
 5  te7-6.mpd02.lon01.atlas.cogentco.com (130.117.15.49)  11.496 ms  11.197 ms  11.454 ms
 6  te0-2-0-1.mpd21.jfk02.atlas.cogentco.com (66.28.4.189)  85.687 ms  85.627 ms  85.685 ms
 7  te2-2.mpd01.bos01.atlas.cogentco.com (154.54.6.1)  233.730 ms  91.406 ms  91.368 ms
 8  te4-2.ccr01.orh01.atlas.cogentco.com (66.28.4.222)  92.498 ms  92.615 ms  92.457 ms
 9  38.104.218.10 (38.104.218.10)  94.491 ms  94.458 ms  94.253 ms
10  136.167.9.226 (136.167.9.226)  94.816 ms  94.475 ms  94.586 ms
```

The table above shows ten hops, starting at a domain in vistatec.ie and ending in 136.167.9.226 (the table doesn't say this, but all IP addresses starting with 136.167 are Boston College addresses). The three groups of numbers at the end of three lines shows the time (in milliseconds) of three packets sent out to test that hop of our journey. These numbers might be interesting for network administrators trying to diagnose speed issues, but we'll ignore them and focus on how packets get from point to point.

At the start of each line is the name of the computer or router that is relaying packets for that leg of the journey. Sometimes routers are named, and sometimes they're just IP addresses. When routers are named, we can tell what network a packet is on by looking at the domain name. By looking at the router names to the left of each line in the traceroute above, we see that the first two hops are within the vistatec.ie network. Hop 3 shows the first router outside the vistatec.ie network. It's at a domain named tinet.net, so this must be the name of VistaTEC's Internet service provider since it's the first connection outside the vistatec.ie network.

Sometimes routers names suggest their locations (oftentimes they use the same three character abbreviations you'd see in airports). Look closely at the hosts in hops 3 through 7. The subdomains dub20, lon11, lon01, jfk02, and bos01 suggest the packets are going from Dublin, then east to London, then west to New York City (John F. Kennedy International Airport), then north to Boston. That's a long way to travel in a fraction of a second!

Hop 4 is at tinet.net, but hop 5 is at cogentco.com (look them up online and you'll find out that cogentco.com, like tinet.net, is also an ISP). That suggests that between those hops peering is taking place and traffic is handed off from carrier to carrier.

Hop 8 is still cogentco.com, but it's not clear who the unnamed router in hop 9, 38.104.218.10, belongs to. We can use the Internet to sleuth that out, too. Search the Internet for the phrase "IP address lookup" and you'll find a bunch of tools to track down the organization that "owns" an IP address. Using the tool at whatismyip.com, I found that this number is registered to PSI Net, which is now part of cogentco.com.

Routing paths, ISPs, and peering all revealed via traceroute. You've just performed a sort of network "CAT scan" and looked into the veins and arteries that make up a portion of the Internet. Pretty cool!

If you try out traceroute on your own, be aware that not all routers and networks are traceroute friendly. It's possible that as your trace hits some hops along the way (particularly at the start or end of your journey), three "*" characters will show up at the end of each line instead of the numbers indicating packet speed. This indicates that traceroute has timed out on that hop. Some networks block traceroute because hackers have used the tool to probe a network to figure out how to attack an organization. Most of the time, though, the hops between the source and destination of the traceroute (the steps involving all the ISPs and their routers) are visible.

Traceroute can be a neat way to explore how the Internet works and reinforce the topics we've just learned. Search for traceroute tools online or browse the Internet for details on how to use the traceroute command built into your computer.

There's Another Internet?

If you're a student at a large research university, there's a good chance that your school is part of Internet2. Internet2 is a research network created by a consortium of research, academic, industry, and government firms. These organizations have collectively set up a high-performance network running at speeds of up to one hundred gigabits per second to support and experiment with demanding applications. Examples include high-quality video conferencing; high-reliability, high-bandwidth imaging for the medical field; and applications that share huge data sets among researchers.

If your university is an Internet2 member and you're communicating with another computer that's part of the Internet2 consortium, then your organization's routers are smart enough to route traffic through the superfast Internet2 backbone. If that's the case, you're likely already using Internet2 without even knowing it!

KEY TAKEAWAYS

- TCP/IP, or the Internet protocol suite, helps get perfect copies of Internet transmissions from one location to another. TCP works on the ends of transmission, breaking up transmissions up into manageable packets at the start and putting them back together while checking quality at the end. IP works in the middle, routing packets to their destination.
- Routers are special computing devices that forward packets from one location to the next. Routers are typically connected with more than one outbound path, so in case one path becomes unavailable, an alternate path can be used.
- UDP is a replacement for TCP, used when it makes sense to sacrifice packet quality for delivery speed. It's often used for media streaming.
- TCP/IP doesn't care about the transition media. This allows networks of different types—copper, fiber, and wireless—to connect to and participate in the Internet.
- The ability to swap in new applications, protocols, and media files gives the network tremendous flexibility.
- Decentralization, fault tolerance, and redundancy help keep the network open and reliable.
- VoIP allows voice and phone systems to become an application traveling over the Internet. This is allowing many firms to save money on phone calls and through the elimination of old, inefficient circuit-switched networks. As Internet applications, VoIP phone systems can also have additional features that circuit-switched networks lack. The primary limitation of many VoIP systems is quality of service.
- Many firms in the finance industry have developed automated trading models that analyze data and execute trades without human intervention. Speeds substantially less than one second may be vital to capitalizing on market opportunities, so firms are increasingly moving equipment into collocation facilities that provide high-speed connectivity to other trading systems.

QUESTIONS AND EXERCISES

1. How can the Internet consist of networks of such physically different transmission media—cable, fiber, and wireless?
2. What is the difference between TCP and UDP? Why would you use one over the other?
3. Would you recommend a VoIP phone system to your firm or University? Why or why not? What are the advantages? What are the disadvantages? Can you think of possible concerns or benefits not mentioned in this section? Research these concerns online and share your finding with your instructor.
4. What are the risks in the kinds of automated trading systems described in this section? Conduct research and find an example of where these systems have caused problems for firms and/or the broader market. What can be done to prevent such problems? Whose responsibility is this?
5. Search the Internet for a traceroute tool, or look online to figure out how to use the traceroute command built into your PC. Run three or more traceroutes to different firms at different locations around the world. List the number of ISPs that show up in the trace. Circle the areas where peering occurs. Do some of the "hops" time out with "*" values returned? If so, why do you think that happened?
6. Find out if your school or employer is an Internet2 member. If it is, run traceroutes to schools that are and are not members of Internet2. What differences do you see in the results?

4. LAST MILE: FASTER SPEED, BROADER ACCESS

LEARNING OBJECTIVES

1. **Understand the last-mile problem and be able to discuss the pros and cons of various broadband technologies, including DSL, cable, fiber, and various wireless offerings.**
2. **Describe 3G and 4G systems, listing major technologies and their backers.**
3. **Understand the issue of Net neutrality and put forth arguments supporting or criticizing the concept.**

The **Internet backbone** is made of fiber-optic lines that carry data traffic over long distances. Those lines are pretty speedy. In fact, several backbone providers, including AT&T and Verizon, are rolling out infrastructure with 100 Gbps transmission speeds (that's enough to transmit a two-hour high-definition [HD] movie in about eight seconds).[22] But when considering overall network speed, remember **Amdahl's Law**: a system's speed is determined by its slowest component.[23] More often than not, the bottleneck isn't the backbone but the so-called **last mile**, or the connections that customers use to get online.

High-speed last-mile technologies are often referred to as *broadband Internet access* (or just **broadband**). What qualifies as broadband varies. In 2009, the Federal Communications Commission (FCC) redefined broadband as having a minimum speed of 768 Kbps (roughly fourteen times the speed of those old 56 Kbps modems). Other agencies worldwide may have different definitions. But one thing is clear: a new generation of bandwidth-demanding services requires more capacity. As we increasingly consume Internet services like HD streaming, real-time gaming, video conferencing, and music downloads, we are in fact becoming a bunch of voracious, bit-craving gluttons.

With the pivotal role the United States has played in the creation of the Internet, and in pioneering software, hardware, and telecommunications industries, you might expect the United States to lead the world in last-mile broadband access. Not even close. A recent study ranked the United States twenty-sixth in download speeds,[24] while others have ranked the United States far behind in speed, availability, and price.[25]

Sounds grim, but help is on the way. A range of technologies and firms are upgrading infrastructure and developing new systems that will increase capacity not just in the United States but also worldwide. Here's an overview of some of the major technologies that can be used to speed the Internet's last mile.

Internet backbone

High-speed data lines provided by many firms all across the world that interconnect and collectively form the core of the Internet.

Amdahl's Law

A system's speed is determined by its slowest component.

last-mile technologies

Technologies that connect end users to the Internet. The last-mile problem refers to the fact that these connections are usually the slowest part of the network.

broadband (broadband Internet access)

Broadly refers to high-speed Internet connections and is often applied to "last-mile" technologies.

bandwidth

Network transmission speeds, typically expressed in some form of bits per second (bps).

Understanding Bandwidth

When folks talk about **bandwidth**, they're referring to data transmission speeds. Bandwidth is often expressed in bits per second, or bps. Prefix letters associated with multiples of bps are the same as the prefixes we mentioned in Chapter 5 when discussing storage capacity in bytes: Kbps = thousand bits (or kilobits) per second, Mbps = million bits (or megabits) per second, Gbps = billion bits (or gigabits) per second (or terabit), and Tbps = trillion bits (or terabits) per second.

Remember, there are eight bits in a byte, and one byte is a single character. One megabyte is roughly equivalent to one digital book, forty-five seconds of music, or twenty seconds of medium-quality video.[26] But you can't just divide the amount of bytes by eight to estimate how many bits you'll need to transfer. When a file or other transmission is sliced into packets (usually of no more than about 1,500 bytes), there's some overhead added. Those packets "wrap" data chunks in an envelope surrounded by source and destination addressing and other important information.

Here are some rough demand requirements for streaming media. For streaming audio like Pandora, you'd need at least 150 Kbps for acceptable regular quality, and at least 300 Kbps for high quality.[27] For streaming video (via Netflix), at a minimum you'd need 1.5 Mbps, but 3.0 Mbps will ensure decent video and audio. For what Netflix calls HD streaming, you'll need a minimum of 5 Mbps, but would likely want 8 Mbps or more to ensure the highest quality video and audio.[28]

4.1 Cable Broadband

coaxial cable (or coax)

Insulated copper cable commonly used by cable television providers.

Roughly 90 percent of U.S. homes are serviced by a cable provider, each capable of using a thick copper wire to offer broadband access. That wire (called a **coaxial cable** or *coax*) has shielding that reduces electrical interference, allowing cable signals to travel longer distances without degrading and with less chance of interference than conventional telephone equipment.

One potential weakness of cable technology lies in the fact that most residential providers use a system that requires customers to share bandwidth with neighbors. If the guy next door is a BitTorrent-using bandwidth hog, your traffic could suffer.[29]

Cable is fast and it's getting faster. Many cable firms are rolling out a new technology called DOCSIS 3.0 that offers speeds up to and exceeding 50 Mbps (previous high-end speeds were about 16 Mbps and often much less than that). Cable firms are also creating so-called *fiber-copper hybrids* that run higher-speed fiber-optic lines into neighborhoods, then use lower-cost, but still relatively high-speed, copper infrastructure over short distances to homes.[30] Those are fast networks, but they are also very expensive to build, since cable firms are laying entirely new lines into neighborhoods instead of leveraging the infrastructure that they've already got in place.

4.2 DSL: Phone Company Copper

digital subscriber line (DSL)

Broadband technology that uses the wires of a local telephone network.

Digital subscriber line (DSL) technology uses the copper wire the phone company has already run into most homes. Even as customers worldwide are dropping their landline phone numbers, the wires used to provide this infrastructure can still be used for broadband.

DSL speeds vary depending on the technology deployed. Worldwide speeds may range from 7 Mbps to as much as 100 Mbps (albeit over very short distances).[31] The Achilles heel of the technology lies in the fact that DSL uses standard copper telephone wiring. These lines lack the shielding used by cable, so signals begin to degrade the further you are from the connecting equipment in telephone company offices. Speeds drop off significantly at less than two miles from a central office or DSL hub. If you go four miles out, the technology becomes unusable. Some DSL providers are also using a hybrid fiber-copper system, but as with cable's copper hybrids, this is expensive to build.

The superspeedy DSL implementations that are popular in Europe and Asia work because foreign cities are densely populated and so many high-value customers can be accessed over short distances. In South Korea, for example, half the population lives in apartments, and most of those customers live in and around Seoul. This density also impacts costs—since so many people live in apartments, foreign carriers run fewer lines to reach customers, digging up less ground or stringing wires across fewer telephone poles. Their U.S. counterparts by contrast need to reach a customer base sprawled across the suburbs, so U.S. firms have much higher infrastructure costs. [32]

There's another company with copper, electricity-carrying cables coming into your home—the electrical utility. BPL, or broadband over power line, technology has been available for years. However, there are few deployments because it is considered to be pricier and less practical than alternatives.[33]

4.3 Fiber: A Light-Filled Glass Pipe to Your Doorstep

fiber to the home (FTTH)

Broadband service provided via light-transmitting fiber-optic cables.

Fiber to the home (FTTH) is the fastest last-mile technology around. It also works over long distances. Verizon's FiOS technology boasts 50 Mbps download speeds but has tested network upgrades that increase speeds by over six times that.[34] The problem with fiber is that unlike cable or DSL copper, fiber to the home networks weren't already in place. That means firms had to build their own fiber networks from scratch.

The cost of this build out can be enormous. Verizon, for example, has spent over $23 billion on its FTTH infrastructure. However, most experts think the upgrade was critical. Verizon has copper into millions of homes, but U.S. DSL is uncompetitive. Verizon's residential landline business was dying as users switch to mobile phone numbers, and while mobile is growing, Verizon Wireless is a joint venture with the United Kingdom's Vodaphone, not a wholly owned firm. This means it shares wireless unit profits with its partner. With FiOS, Verizon now offers pay television, competing with cable's core product. It also offers some of the fastest home broadband services anywhere, and it gets to keep everything it earns.

Google is also in the process of bringing high-speed fiber to the home in several U.S. communities, including Kansas City, Kansas, and Kansas City, Missouri. Google deems its effort an experiment—it's more interested in learning how developers and users take advantage of ultrahigh-speed fiber to the home (e.g., what kinds of apps are created and used, how do usage and time spent online change), rather than becoming a nationwide ISP itself. Google says it will investigate ways to build and operate networks less expensively and plans to share findings with others. The Google network will be "open," allowing other service providers to use Google's infrastructure to resell services to consumers. The firm has pledged to bring speeds of 1 Gbps at competitive prices to at least 50,000 and potentially as many as 500,000 homes. Over 1,100 U.S. communities applied to be part of the Google experimental fiber network.[35]

4.4 Wireless

Mobile wireless service from cell phone access providers is delivered via cell towers. While these providers don't need to build a residential wired infrastructure, they still need to secure space for cell towers, build the towers, connect the towers to a backbone network, and license the **wireless spectrum** (or airwave frequency space) for transmission.

wireless spectrum

Frequencies used for communication. Most mobile cell phone services have to license spectrum. Some technologies (such as Wi-Fi) use unlicensed public spectrum.

We need more bandwidth for mobile devices, too. AT&T now finds that the top 3 percent of its mobile network users gulp up 40 percent of the network's capacity (thanks, iPhone users), and network strain will only increase as more people adopt smartphones. These users are streaming Major League Baseball games, exploring the planet with Google Earth, watching YouTube and Netflix, streaming music through Pandora, and more. Get a bunch of iPhone users in a crowded space, like in a college football stadium on game day, and the result is a network-choking data traffic jam. AT&T estimates that it's not uncommon for 80 percent of game-day iPhone users to take out their phones and surf the Web for stats, snap and upload photos, and more. But cell towers often can't handle the load.[36] If you've ever lost coverage in a crowd, you've witnessed mobile network congestion firsthand. Trying to have enough capacity to avoid congestion traffic jams will cost some serious coin. In the midst of customer complaints, AT&T committed to spending $18 billion on network upgrades to address its wireless capacity problem.[37]

TABLE 12.1 Average Demand Usage by Function

Usage	Demand
Voice Calls	4 MB/hr.
iPhone Browsing	40–60 MB/hr.
Net Radio	60 MB/hr.
YouTube	200–400 MB/hr.
Conventional mobile phones use an estimated 100 MB/month, iPhones 560 MB/month, and iPads almost 1 GB/month.	

Source: R. Farzad, "The Truth about Bandwidth," BusinessWeek, February 3, 2010.

We're in the midst of transitioning from third generation (*3G*) to fourth generation (*4G*) wireless networks. 3G systems offer access speeds usually less than 2 Mbps (often a lot less).[38] While variants of 3G wireless might employ an alphabet soup of technologies—EV-DO (evolution data optimized), UMTS (universal mobile telecommunications systems), and HSDPA (high-speed downlink packet link access) among them—3G standards can be narrowed down to two camps: those based on the dominant worldwide standard called *GSM* (global system for mobile communications) and the runner-up standards based on *CDMA* (code division multiple access). Most of Europe and a good chunk of the rest of the world use GSM. In the United States, AT&T and T-Mobile use GSM-based 3G. Verizon Wireless and Sprint use the CDMA 3G standard. Typically, handsets designed for one network can't be used on networks supporting the other standard. CDMA has an additional limitation in not being able to use voice and data at the same time.

But 3G is being replaced by high-bandwidth 4G (fourth-generation) mobile networks. 4G technologies also fall into two standards camps: LTE (Long Term Evolution) and WiMAX (Worldwide Interoperability for Microwave Access).

LTE looks like the global winner. In the United States, every major wireless firm, except for Sprint, is betting on LTE victory. Bandwidth for the service rivals what we'd consider fast cable a few years back. Average speeds range from 5 to 12 Mbps for downloads and 2 to 5 Mbps for upload, although Verizon tests in Boston and Seattle showed download speeds as high as 50 Mbps and upload speeds reaching 25 Mbps.[39]

Competing with LTE is WiMAX; don't confuse it with Wi-Fi. As with other 3G and 4G technologies, WiMAX needs cell towers and operators need to have licensed spectrum from their respective governments (often paying multibillion-dollar fees to do so). Average download and upload speeds should start out at 3–6 Mbps and 1 Mbps, respectively, although this may go much higher.[40]

WiMAX looks like a particularly attractive option for cable firms, offering them an opportunity to get into the mobile phone business and offer a "quadruple play" of services: pay television, broadband Internet, home phone, and mobile. Comcast and Time Warner have both partnered with Clearwire (a firm majority-owned by Sprint), to gain access to WiMAX-based 4G mobile.

4G could also rewrite the landscape for home broadband competition. If speeds increase, it may be possible for PCs, laptops, and set-top boxes (STB) to connect to the Internet wirelessly via 4G, cutting into DSL, cable, and fiber markets.

4.5 Satellite Wireless

Wireless systems provided by earth-bound base stations like cell phone towers are referred to as *terrestrial wireless*, but it is possible to provide telecommunications services via satellite. Early services struggled due to a number of problems. For example, the first residential satellite services were only used for downloads, which still needed a modem or some other connection to send any messages from the computer to the Internet. Many early systems also required large antennas and were quite expensive. Finally, some services were based on satellites in geosynchronous earth orbit (GEO). GEO satellites circle the earth in a fixed, or stationary, orbit above a given spot on the globe, but to do so they must be positioned at a distance that is roughly equivalent to the planet's circumference. That means signals travel the equivalent of an around-the-world trip to reach the satellite and then the same distance to get to the user. The "last mile" became the last 44,000 miles at best. And if you used a service that also provided satellite upload as well as download, double that to about 88,000 miles. All that distance means higher latency (more delay).[41]

A firm named O3b Networks thinks it might have solved the challenges that plagued early pioneers. O3b has an impressive list of big-name backers that include HSBC bank, cable magnate John Malone, European aerospace firm SES, and Google.

The name O3b stands for the "Other 3 Billion," of the world's population who lack broadband Internet access, and the firm hopes to provide "fiber-quality" wireless service to more than 150 countries, specifically targeting underserved portions of the developing world. These "middle earth orbit" satellites will circle closer to the earth to reduce latency (only about 5,000 miles up, less than one-fourth the distance of GEO systems). To maintain the lower orbit, O3b's satellites orbit faster than the planet spins, but with plans to launch as many as twenty satellites, the system will constantly blanket regions served. If one satellite circles to the other side of the globe, another one will circle around to take its place, ensuring there's always an O3b "bird" overhead.

Only about 3 percent of the sub-Saharan African population uses the Internet, compared to about 70 percent in the United States. But data rates in the few places served can cost as much as one hundred times the rates of comparable systems in the industrialized world.[42] O3b hopes to change that equation and significantly lower access rates. O3b customers will be local telecommunication firms, not end users. The plan is for local firms to buy O3b's services wholesale and then resell it to customers alongside rivals who can do the same thing, collectively providing more consumer access, higher quality, and lower prices through competition. O3b is a big, bold, and admittedly risky plan, but if it works, its impact could be tremendous.

4.6 Wi-Fi and Other Hotspots

Wi-Fi

A term used to brand wireless local-area networking devices. Devices typically connect to an antenna-equipped base station or hotspot, which is then connected to the Internet. Wi-Fi devices use standards known as IEEE 802.11, and various version of this standard (e.g., b, g, n) may operate in different frequency bands and have access ranges.

Many users access the Internet via **Wi-Fi** (which stands for *wireless fidelity*). Computer and mobile devices have Wi-Fi antennas built into their chipsets, but to connect to the Internet, a device needs to be within range of a *base station* or *hotspot*. The base station range is usually around three hundred feet (you might get a longer range outdoors and with special equipment; and less range indoors when signals need to pass through solid objects like walls, ceilings, and floors). Wi-Fi base stations used in the home are usually bought by end users, then connected to a cable, DSL, or fiber provider.

And now a sort of mobile phone hotspot is being used to overcome limitations in those services, as well. Mobile providers can also be susceptible to poor coverage indoors. That's because the spectrum used by most mobile phone firms doesn't travel well through solid objects. Cell coverage is also often limited in the United States because of a lack of towers, which is a result of the *NIMBY problem* (not in my backyard). People don't want an eighty-foot to four-hundred-foot unsightly tower clouding their local landscape, even if it will give their neighborhood better cell phone coverage.[43] To overcome reception and availability problems, mobile telecom services firms have begun offering femtocells. These devices are usually smaller than a box of cereal and can sell for $150 or less (some are free with specific service contracts). Plug a femtocell into a high-speed Internet connection like an in-home cable or fiber service and you can get "five-bar" coverage in a roughly 5,000-square-foot footprint.[44] That can be a great solution for someone who has an in-home, high-speed Internet connection, but wants to get phone and mobile data service indoors, too.

4.7 Net Neutrality: What's Fair?

Across the world, battle lines are being drawn regarding the topic of Net neutrality. Net neutrality is the principle that all Internet traffic should be treated equally.[45] Sometimes access providers have wanted to offer varying (some say "discriminatory") coverage, depending on the service used and bandwidth consumed. But where regulation stands is currently in flux. In a pivotal U.S. case, the FCC ordered Comcast to stop throttling (blocking or slowing down) subscriber access to the peer-to-peer file sharing service BitTorrent. BitTorrent users can consume a huge amount of bandwidth—the service is often used to transfer large files, both legitimate (like version of the Linux operating system) and pirated (HD movies). Then in spring 2010, a federal appeals court moved against the FCC's position, unanimously ruling that the agency did not have the legal authority to dictate terms to Comcast.[46]

On one side of the debate are Internet service firms, with Google being one of the strongest Net neutrality supporters. In an advocacy paper, Google states, "Just as telephone companies are not permitted to tell consumers who they can call or what they can say, broadband carriers should not be allowed to use their market power to control activity online."[47] Many Internet firms also worry that if network providers move away from flat-rate pricing toward usage-based (or metered) schemes, this may limit innovation. Says Google's Vint Cerf (who is considered one of the "fathers of the Internet" for his work on the original Internet protocol suite) "You are less likely to try things out. No one wants a surprise bill at the end of the month."[48] Metered billing may limit the use of everything from iTunes to Netflix; after all, if you have to pay for per-bit bandwidth consumption as well as for the download service, then it's as if you're paying twice.

The counterargument is that if firms are restricted from charging more for their investment in infrastructure and services, then they'll have little incentive to continue to make the kinds of multibillion-dollar investments that innovations like 4G and fiber networks require. Telecom industry executives have railed against Google, Microsoft, Yahoo! and others, calling them free riders who earn huge profits by piggybacking off ISP networks, all while funneling no profits back to the firms that provide the infrastructure. One Verizon vice president said, "The network builders are spending a fortune constructing and maintaining the networks that Google intends to ride on with nothing but cheap servers....It is enjoying a free lunch that should, by any rational account, be the lunch of the facilities providers."[49] AT&T's previous CEO has suggested that Google, Yahoo! and other services firms should pay for "preferred access" to the firm's customers. The CEO of Spain's Telefonica has also said the firm is considering charging Google and other Internet service firms for network use.[50]

ISPs also lament the relentlessly increasingly bandwidth demands placed on their networks. Back in 2007, YouTube streamed as much data in three months as the world's radio, cable, and broadcast television channels combined stream in one year,[51] and YouTube has only continued to grow since then. Should ISPs be required to support the strain of this kind of bandwidth hog? And what if this one application clogs network use for other traffic, such as e-mail or Web surfing? Similarly, shouldn't firms have the right to prioritize some services to better serve customers? Some network providers argue that services like video chat and streaming audio should get priority over, say, e-mail which can afford slight delay without major impact. In that case, there's a pretty good argument that providers should be able to discriminate against services. But improving efficiency and throttling usage are two different things.

Internet service firms say they create demand for broadband business, broadband firms say Google and allies are ungrateful parasites that aren't sharing the wealth. The battle lines on the Net neutrality frontier continue to be drawn, and the eventual outcome will impact consumers, investors, and will likely influence the continued expansion and innovation of the Internet.

4.8 Summing Up

Hopefully, this chapter helped reveal the mysteries of the Internet. It's interesting to know how "the cloud" works but it can also be vital. As we've seen, the executive office in financial services firms considers mastery of the Internet infrastructure to be critically important to their competitive advantage. Media firms find the Internet both threatening and empowering. The advancement of last-mile technologies and issues of Net neutrality will expose threats and create opportunity. And a manager who knows how the Internet works will be in a better position to make decisions about how to keep the firm and its customers safe and secure, and be better prepared to brainstorm ideas for winning in a world where access is faster and cheaper, and firms, rivals, partners, and customers are more connected.

KEY TAKEAWAYS

- The slowest part of the Internet is typically the last mile, not the backbone. While several technologies can offer broadband service over the last mile, the United States continues to rank below many other nations in terms of access speed, availability, and price.
- Cable firms and phone companies can leverage existing wiring for cable broadband and DSL service, respectively. Cable services are often criticized for shared bandwidth. DSL's primary limitation is that it only works within a short distance of telephone office equipment.
- Fiber to the home can be very fast but very expensive to build.
- An explosion of high-bandwidth mobile applications is straining 3G networks. 4G systems may alleviate congestion by increasing capacities to near-cable speeds. Fentocells are another technology that can improve service by providing a personal mobile phone hotspot that can plug into in-home broadband access.
- The two major 3G standards (popularly referred to as GSM and CDMA) will be replaced by two unrelated 4G standards (LTE and WiMAX). GSM has been the dominant 3G technology worldwide. LTE looks like it will be the leading 4G technology.
- Satellite systems show promise in providing high-speed access to underserved parts of the world, but few satellite broadband providers have been successful so far.
- Net neutrality is the principle that all Internet traffic should be treated equally. Google and other firms say it is vital to maintain the openness of the Internet. Telecommunications firms say they should be able to limit access to services that overtax their networks, and some have suggested charging Google and other Internet firms for providing access to their customers.

QUESTIONS AND EXERCISES

1. Research online for the latest country rankings for broadband service. Where does the United States currently rank? Why?
2. Which broadband providers can service your home? Which would you choose? Why?
3. Research the status of Google's experimental fiber network. Report updated findings to your class. Why do you suppose Google would run this "experiment"? What other Internet access experiments has the firm been involved in?
4. Show your understanding of the economics and competitive forces of the telecom industry. Discuss why Verizon chose to go with fiber. Do you think this was a wise decision or not? Why? Feel free to do additional research to back up your argument.
5. Why have other nations enjoyed faster broadband speeds, greater availability, and lower prices?
6. The iPhone has been called both a blessing and a curse for AT&T. Why do you suppose this is so?
7. Investigate the status of mobile wireless offerings (3G and 4G). Which firm would you choose? Why? Which factors are most important in your decision?
8. Name the two dominant 3G standards. What are the differences between the two? Which firms in your nation support each standard?
9. Name the two dominant 4G standards. Which firms in your nation will support the respective standards?
10. Have you ever lost communication access—wirelessly or via wired connection? What caused the loss or outage?
11. What factors shape the profitability of the mobile wireless provider industry? How do these economics compare with the cable and wire line industry? Who are the major players and which would you invest in? Why?
12. Last-mile providers often advertise very fast speeds, but users rarely see speeds as high as advertised rates. Search online to find a network speed test and try it from your home, office, mobile device, or dorm. How fast is the network? If you're able to test from home, what bandwidth rates does your ISP advertise? Does this differ from what you experienced? What could account for this discrepancy?
13. How can 4G technology help cable firms? Why might it hurt them?
14. What's the difference between LEO satellite systems and the type of system used by O3b? What are the pros and cons of these efforts? Conduct some additional research. What is the status of O3b and other satellite broadband efforts?
15. What advantages could broadband offer to underserved areas of the world? Is Internet access important for economic development? Why or why not?
16. Does your carrier offer a fentocell? Would you use one? Why or why not?
17. Be prepared to debate the issue of Net neutrality in class. Prepare positions both supporting and opposing Net neutrality. Which do you support and why?
18. Investigate the status of Net neutrality laws in your nation and report your findings to your instructor. Do you agree with the stance currently taken by your government? Why or why not?

ENDNOTES

1. K. Maney, "Tuvalu's Sinking, But Its Domain Is on Solid Ground," *USA Today*, April 27, 2004.
2. B. Bosker, "The 11 Most Expensive Domain Names Ever," *The Huffington Post*, March 10, 2010.
3. D. Streitfeld, "Web Site Feuding Enters Constitutional Domain," *The Washington Post*, September 11, 2000.
4. D. McCullagh, "Ethical Treatment of PETA Domain," *Wired*, August 25, 2001.
5. R. Konrad and E. Hansen, "Madonna.com Embroiled in Domain Ownership Spat," *CNET*, August 21, 2000.
6. D. Morson, "Apple VP Ive Loses Domain Name Bid," *MacWorld*, May 12, 2009.
7. M. Kotadia, "MikeRoweSoft Settles for an Xbox," *CNET*, January 26, 2004.
8. J. Biggs, "Everybody Panic: Why We're Running Out of IP Addresses and What's Going to Happen Now," *CrunchGear*, February 2, 2011.
9. S. Shankland, "Google Tries to Break IPv6 Logjam by Own Example," *CNET*, March 27, 2009.
10. V. Kopytoff, "Happy IPv6 Day," *New York Times*, June 8, 2011.
11. M. Peckham, "World IPv6 Launch: Only The Biggest Change to the Internet Since Inception," *Time*, June 6, 2012.
12. S. Shankland, "Google Tries to Break IPv6 Logjam by Own Example," *CNET*, March 27, 2009.
13. B. Arnoldy, "IP Address Shortage to Limit Internet Access," *USA Today*, August 3, 2007.
14. D. Godin, "Cache-Poisoning Attack Snares Top Brazilian Bank," *The Register*, April 22, 2009.
15. J. Davis, "Secret Geek A-Team Hacks Back, Defends Worldwide Web," *Wired*, Nov. 24, 2008.
16. J. Hutchinson, "ICANN, Verisign Place Last Puzzle Pieces in DNSSEC Saga," *NetworkWorld*, May 2, 2010.
17. H. Timmons, "A London Hedge Fund that Opts for Engineers, Not M.B.A.'s," *New York Times*, August 18, 2006.
18. R. Iati, "The Real Story of Trading Software Espionage," *Advanced Trading*, July 10, 2009.
19. A. Berenson, "Arrest Over Software Illuminates Wall St. Secret," *New York Times*, August 23, 2009.
20. I. Schmerken, "High-Frequency Trading Shops Play the Colocation Game," *Advanced Trading*, October 5, 2009.
21. E. Daimler and G. Davis, "'Flash Crash' Proves Diversity Needed in Market Mechanisms," *Pittsburgh Post-Gazette*, May 29, 2010; H. Moore, "'Flash Crash' Anniversary Leaves Unanswered Questions," *Marketplace Radio*, May 5, 2011.
22. T. Spangler, "Cisco Clarifies 100-Gig AT&T Backbone Claim," *Multichannel News*, March 9, 2010; Zacks.com, "AT&T Tests 100 Gb Ethernet in Move toward Faster Internet," *SeekingAlpha*, March 10, 2010.
23. G. Gilder, *Telecosm: How Infinite Bandwidth Will Revolutionize Our World* (New York: Free Press, 2000).
24. S. Lawson, "US Ranks 26th in New Broadband Index," *Computerworld*, May 25, 2010.
25. S. Hansell, "The Broadband Gap: Why Is Theirs Faster?" *New York Times*, March 10, 2009.
26. R. Farzad, "The Truth about Bandwidth," *BusinessWeek*, February 3, 2010.
27. Pandora, "Frequently Asked Questions," http://blog.pandora.com/faq.
28. LG Knowledge Base, "Bandwidth Needed for Instant Streaming," http://lgknowledgebase.com/kb/index.php?View=entry&EntryID=6241.
29. R. Thompson, "DSL Internet vs. Cable Internet," *High Speed Internet Access Guide*, March 23, 2010.
30. S. Hansell, "The Broadband Gap: Why Is Theirs Faster?" *New York Times*, March 10, 2009.
31. S. Hansell, "The Broadband Gap: Why Is Theirs Faster?" *New York Times*, March 10, 2009.
32. S. Hansell, "The Broadband Gap: Why Is Theirs Faster?" *New York Times*, March 10, 2009.
33. R. King, "Telecom Companies Scramble for Funding," *BusinessWeek*, August 3, 2009.
34. S. Higginbotham, "Verizon Tests 10 Gbps to the Home. Yeah, You'll Have to Share," *GigaOM*, December 17, 2009.
35. M. Ingersoll and J. Kelly, "Think Big with a Gig: Our Experimental Fiber Network," The Google Blog, February 2, 2010; L. Rao, "The Final Tally: More Than 1100 Cities Apply for Google's Fiber Network," *TechCrunch*, March 27, 2010.
36. R. Farzad, "AT&T's iPhone Mess," *BusinessWeek*, February 3, 2010.
37. C. Edwards and O. Kharif, "Sprint's Bold Play on a 4G Network," *BusinessWeek*, March 30, 2010.
38. K. German, "On Call: Welcome to 4G," *CNET*, March 9, 2010.
39. K. German, "On Call: Welcome to 4G," *CNET*, March 9, 2010.
40. N. Lee, "Sprint's 4G Plans Explained," *CNET*, May 19, 2010.
41. G. Ou, "Why Satellite Service Is So Slow," *ZDNet*, February 23, 2008.
42. G. Lamb, "O3b Networks: A Far-Out Plan to Deliver the Web," *Christian Science Monitor*, September 24, 2008.
43. G. Dechter and O. Kharif, "How Craig McCaw Built a 4G Network on the Cheap," *BusinessWeek*, May 24, 2010.
44. C. Mims, "A Personal Cell Phone Tower," *Technology Review*, April 7, 2010.
45. M. Honan, "Inside Net Neutrality," *MacWorld*, February 12, 2008.
46. "What Is Net Neutrality?" *The Week*, April 7, 2010.
47. Google, "A Guide to Net Neutrality for Google Users," 2008, http://www.docstoc.com/docs/1064274/A-Guide-to-Net-Neutrality-for-Google-Users.
48. M. Jesdanun, "As the Internet Turns 40, Barriers Threaten Growth," *Technology Review*, August 31, 2009.
49. A. Mohammed, "Verizon Executive Calls for End to Google's 'Free Lunch,'" *Washington Post*, February 7, 2006.
50. I. Lunden, "Broadband Content Bits: Web Drama Investment, PPL Video Store, Telefonica to Charge?" *paidContent:UK*, February 11, 2010.
51. B. Swanson, "The Coming Exaflood," *Wall Street Journal*, January 20, 2007.

CHAPTER 13

Information Security: Barbarians at the Gateway (and Just About Everywhere Else)

1. INTRODUCTION

LEARNING OBJECTIVES

1. Recognize that information security breaches are on the rise.
2. Understand the potentially damaging impact of security breaches.
3. Recognize that information security must be made a top organizational priority.

Sitting in the parking lot of a Minneapolis Marshalls, a hacker armed with a laptop and a telescope-shaped antenna infiltrated the store's network via an insecure Wi-Fi base station.[1] The attack launched what would become a billion-dollar-plus nightmare scenario for TJX, the parent of retail chains that include Marshalls, Home Goods, and T. J. Maxx. Over a period of several months, the hacker and his gang stole at least 45.7 million credit and debit card numbers and pilfered driver's licenses and other private information from an additional 450,000 customers.[2]

TJX, at the time a $17.5 billion *Fortune* 500 firm, was left reeling from the incident. The attack deeply damaged the firm's reputation. It burdened customers and banking partners with the time and cost of reissuing credit cards. And TJX suffered under settlement costs, payouts from court-imposed restitution, legal fees, and more. The firm estimated that it spent more than $150 million to correct security problems and settle with consumers affected by the breach, and that was just the tip of the iceberg. Estimates peg TJX's overall losses from this incident at between $1.35 billion and $4.5 billion.[3]

A number of factors led to and amplified the severity of the TJX breach. There was a personnel betrayal: the mastermind was an alleged FBI informant who previously helped bring down a massive credit card theft scheme but then double-crossed the Feds and used insider information to help his gang outsmart the law and carry out subsequent hacks.[4] There was a technology lapse: TJX made itself an easy mark by using WEP, a wireless security technology less secure than the stuff many consumers use in their homes—one known for years to be trivially compromised by the kind of "drive-by" hacking initiated by the perpetrators. And there was a procedural gaffe: retailers were in the process of rolling out a security rubric known as the Payment Card Industry Data Security Standard. Despite an industry deadline, however, TJX had requested and received an extension, delaying the rollout of mechanisms that might have discovered and plugged the hole before the hackers got in.[5]

The massive impact of the TJX breach should make it clear that security must be a top organizational priority. Attacks are on the rise. Security firm Symantec reported that in 2010, Web-based security attacks increased 93 percent over the prior year,[6] and the first few months of 2011 saw shocking, high-profile attacks hit at several firms, including Sony, data provider Epsilon, Google, and even security software firm RSA.[7] While the examples and scenarios presented here are shocking, the good news is that the vast majority of security breaches can be prevented. Let's be clear from the start: no text can provide an approach that will guarantee that you'll be 100 percent secure. And that's not the goal of this chapter. The issues raised in this brief introduction can, however, help make you aware of vulnerabilities; improve your critical thinking regarding current and future security issues; and help you consider whether a firm has technologies, training, policies, and procedures in place to assess risks, lessen the likelihood of damage, and respond in the event of a breach. A constant vigilance regarding security needs to be part of your individual skill set and a key component in your organization's culture. An awareness of the threats and approaches discussed in this chapter should help reduce your chance of becoming a victim.

As we examine security issues, we'll first need to understand what's happening, who's doing it, and what their motivation is. We'll then examine how these breaches are happening with a focus on technologies and procedures. Finally, we'll sum up with what can be done to minimize the risks of being victimized and quell potential damage of a breach for both the individual and the organization.

KEY TAKEAWAYS

- Information security is everyone's business and needs to be made a top organizational priority.
- Firms suffering a security breach can experience direct financial loss, exposed proprietary information, fines, legal payouts, court costs, damaged reputations, plummeting stock prices, and more.
- Information security isn't just a technology problem; a host of personnel and procedural factors can create and amplify a firm's vulnerability.

QUESTIONS AND EXERCISES

1. The 2011 data theft at database firm Epsilon impacted a number of the firm's clients, including Best Buy, Capital One, Citi, the Home Shopping Network, JP Morgan Chase, Kroger, Walgreens, and the College Board. Were you impacted by this breach (or any other)? How did you find out about the breach? Did you take action as a result? Research and report the estimated costs associated with this breach. Has the theft resulted in additional security issues for the individuals who had their data stolen?
2. As individuals or in groups assigned by your instructor, search online for recent reports on information security breaches. Come to class prepared to discuss the breach, its potential impact, and how it might have been avoided. What should the key takeaways be for managers studying your example?
3. Think of firms that you've done business with online. Search to see if these firms have experienced security breaches in the past. What have you found out? Does this change your attitude about dealing with the firm? Why or why not?
4. What factors were responsible for the TJX breach? Who was responsible for the breach? How do you think the firm should have responded?

2. WHY IS THIS HAPPENING? WHO IS DOING IT? AND WHAT'S THEIR MOTIVATION?

LEARNING OBJECTIVES

1. **Understand the source and motivation of those initiating information security attacks.**
2. **Relate examples of various infiltrations in a way that helps raise organizational awareness of threats.**

Thieves, vandals, and other bad guys have always existed, but the environment has changed. Today, nearly every organization is online, making any Internet-connected network a potential entry point for the growing worldwide community of computer criminals. Software and hardware solutions are also more complex than ever. Different vendors, each with their own potential weaknesses, provide technology components that may be compromised by misuse, misconfiguration, or mismanagement. Corporations have become data packrats, hoarding information in hopes of turning bits into bucks by licensing databases, targeting advertisements, or cross-selling products. And flatter organizations also mean that lower-level employees may be able to use technology to reach deep into corporate assets—amplifying threats from operator error, a renegade employee, or one compromised by external forces.

There are a lot of bad guys out there, and motivations vary widely, including the following:

- Account theft and illegal funds transfer
- Stealing personal or financial data
- Compromising computing assets for use in other crimes
- Extortion
- Espionage
- Cyberwarfare
- Terrorism
- Pranksters
- Protest hacking (hacktivism)
- Revenge (disgruntled employees)

Criminals stole more than $560 million from U.S. firms in 2009, and they did it "without drawing a gun or passing a note to a teller."[8] While some steal cash for their own use, others resell their hacking take to others. There is a thriving cybercrime underworld market in which **data harvesters** sell to **cash-out fraudsters**: criminals who might purchase data from the harvesters in order to buy (then resell) goods using stolen credit cards or create false accounts via identity theft. These collection and resale operations are efficient and sophisticated. Law enforcement has taken down sites like DarkMarket and ShadowCrew, in which card thieves and hacking tool peddlers received eBay-style seller ratings vouching for the "quality" of their wares.[9]

Hackers might also infiltrate computer systems to enlist hardware for subsequent illegal acts. A cybercrook might deliberately hop through several systems to make his path difficult to follow, slowing cross-border legal pursuit or even thwarting prosecution if launched from nations without extradition agreements.

In fact, your computer may be up for rent by cyber thieves right now. **Botnets** of zombie computers (networks of infiltrated and compromised machines controlled by a central command) are used for all sorts of nefarious activity. This includes sending spam from thousands of difficult-to-shut-down accounts, launching tough-to-track click fraud efforts or staging what's known as **distributed denial of service (DDoS)** attacks (effectively shutting down Web sites by overwhelming them with a crushing load of seemingly legitimate requests sent simultaneously by thousands of machines). Botnets have been discovered that are capable of sending out 100 billion spam messages a day,[10] and botnets as large as 10 million zombies have been identified. Such systems theoretically control more computing power than the world's fastest supercomputers.[11]

Extortionists might leverage botnets or hacked data to demand payment to avoid retribution. Three eastern European gangsters used a botnet and threatened DDoS to extort $4 million from UK sports bookmakers,[12] while an extortion plot against the state of Virginia threatened to reveal names, Social Security numbers, and prescription information stolen from a medical records database.[13] Competition has also lowered the price to inflict such pain. *BusinessWeek* reports that the cost of renting out ten thousand machines, enough to cripple a site like Twitter, has tumbled to just $200 a day.[14]

Corporate espionage might be performed by insiders, rivals, or even foreign governments. Gary Min, a scientist working for DuPont, was busted when he tried to sell information valued at some $400 million, including R&D documents and secret data on proprietary products.[15] Spies also breached the $300 billion U.S. Joint Strike Fighter project, siphoning off terabytes of data on navigation and other electronics systems.[16] Hackers infiltrated security firm RSA, stealing data keys used in the firm's commercial authentication devices. The hackers then apparently leveraged the heist to enter the systems of RSA customers, U.S. Defense contractors L-3, Lockheed Martin, and Northrop Grumman.[17] Google has identified China as the nation of origin for a series of hacks targeting the Google accounts of diplomats and activists.[18] And the government of Tunisia even attempted a whole-scale hacking of local users' Facebook accounts during protests that eventually led to the ouster of the regime. The so-called man-in-the-middle style attack intercepted Facebook traffic at the state-affiliated ISP as it traveled between Tunisian Web surfers and Facebook's servers, enabling the government to steal passwords and delete posts and photos that criticized the regime.[19]

Cyberwarfare has also become a legitimate threat, with several attacks demonstrating how devastating technology disruptions by terrorists or a foreign power might be (see sidebar on Stuxnet). Brazil has seen hacks that cut off power to millions, and the *60 Minutes* news program showed a demonstration by "white hat" hackers that could compromise a key component in an oil refinery, force it to overheat, and cause an explosion. Taking out key components of the vulnerable U.S. power grid may be particularly devastating, as the equipment is expensive, much of it is no longer made in the United States, and some components may take three to four months to replace.[20]

data harvesters

Cybercriminals who infiltrate systems and collect data for illegal resale.

cash-out fraudsters

Firms that purchase assets from data harvesters. Actions may include using stolen credit card numbers to purchase goods, creating fake accounts via identity fraud, and more.

botnets

Hordes of surreptitiously infiltrated computers, linked and controlled remotely, also known as zombie networks

distributed denial of service (DDoS)

An attack where a firm's computer systems are flooded with thousands of seemingly legitimate requests, the sheer volume of which will slow or shut down the site's use. DDoS attacks are often performed via botnets.

Stuxnet: A New Era of Cyberwarfare

Stuxnet may be the most notorious known act of cyberwarfare effort to date (one expert called it "the most sophisticated worm ever created").[21] Suspected to have been launched by either U.S. or Israeli intelligence (or both), Stuxnet infiltrated Iranian nuclear facilities and reprogramed the industrial control software operating hundreds of uranium-enriching centrifuges. The worm made the devices spin so fast that the centrifuges effectively destroyed themselves, in the process setting back any Iranian nuclear ambitions. The attack was so sophisticated that it even altered equipment readings to report normal activity so that operators didn't even know something was wrong until it was too late.

Some might fear Stuxnet in the wild—what happens if the code spread to systems operated by peaceful nations or systems controlling critical infrastructure that could threaten lives if infected? All important questions, but in Stuxnet's case the worm appears to have been designed to target very specific systems. If it got onto a nontarget machine, it would become inert. Propagation was also limited, with each copy designed to infect only three additional machines. And the virus was also designed to self-destruct at a future date.[22]

Stuxnet showed that with computers at the heart of so many systems, it's now possible to destroy critical infrastructure without firing a shot.[23] While few want to see Iran get the bomb, what does the rise of cyberwarfare mean for future combat and for citizen vulnerability, and what might this mean for businesses whose products, services, or organizations may become targets?

hacktivist

A protester seeking to make a political point by leveraging technology tools, often through system infiltration, defacement, or damage.

Other threats come from malicious pranksters (sometimes called *griefers* or *trolls*), like the group that posted seizure-inducing images on Web sites frequented by epilepsy sufferers.[24] Others are **hacktivists**, targeting firms, Web sites, or even users as a protest measure. In 2009, Twitter was brought down and Facebook and LiveJournal were hobbled as Russian-sympathizing hacktivists targeted the social networking and blog accounts of the Georgian blogger known as Cyxymu. The silencing of millions of accounts was simply collateral damage in a massive DDoS attack meant to mute this single critic of the Russian government.[25]

And as power and responsibility is concentrated in the hands of a few revenge-seeking employees can do great damage. The San Francisco city government lost control of a large portion of its own computer network over a ten-day period when a single disgruntled employee refused to divulge critical passwords.[26]

The bad guys are legion and the good guys often seem outmatched and underresourced. Law enforcement agencies dealing with computer crime are increasingly outnumbered, outskilled, and underfunded. Many agencies are staffed with technically weak personnel who were trained in a prior era's crime fighting techniques. Governments can rarely match the pay scale and stock bonuses offered by private industry. Organized crime networks now have their own R&D labs and are engaged in sophisticated development efforts to piece together methods to thwart current security measures.

hacker

A term that, depending on the context, may be applied to either 1) someone who breaks into computer systems, or 2) to a particularly clever programmer.

hack

A term that may, depending on the context, refer to either 1) breaking into a computer system, or 2) a particularly clever solution.

white hat hacker

Someone who uncovers computer weaknesses without exploiting them. The goal of the white hat hacker is to improve system security.

black hat hacker

A computer criminal.

"Hacker": Good or Bad?

The terms **hacker** and **hack** are widely used, but their meaning is often based on context. When referring to security issues, the media widely refers to hackers as bad guys who try to break into (hack) computer systems. Some geezer geeks object to this use, as the term *hack* in computer circles originally referred to a clever (often technical) solution and the term *hacker* referred to a particularly skilled programmer. Expect to see the terms used both positively and negatively.

You might also encounter the terms **white hat hackers** and **black hat hackers**. The white hats are the good guys who probe for weaknesses, but don't exploit them. Instead, they share their knowledge in hopes that the holes they've found will be plugged and security will be improved. Many firms hire consultants to conduct "white hat" hacking expeditions on their own assets as part of their auditing and security process. "Black hats" are the bad guys. Some call them "crackers." There's even a well-known series of hacker conventions known as the Black Hat conference.

KEY TAKEAWAYS

- Computer security threats have moved beyond the curious teen with a PC and are now sourced from a number of motivations, including theft, leveraging compromised computing assets, extortion, espionage, warfare, terrorism, pranks, protest, and revenge.
- Threats can come from both within the firm as well as from the outside.
- Cybercriminals operate in an increasingly sophisticated ecosystem where data harvesters and tool peddlers leverage sophisticated online markets to sell to cash-out fraudsters and other crooks.
- Technical and legal complexity make pursuit and prosecution difficult.
- Many law enforcement agencies are underfunded, underresourced, and underskilled to deal with the growing hacker threat.

QUESTIONS AND EXERCISES

1. What is a botnet? What sorts of exploits would use a botnet? Why would a botnet be useful to cybercriminals?
2. Why are threats to the power grid potentially so concerning? What are the implications of power-grid failure and of property damage? Who might execute these kinds of attacks? What are the implications for firms and governments planning for the possibility of cyberwarfare and cyberterror?
3. Scan the trade press for examples of hacking that apply to the various motivations mentioned in this chapter. What happened to the hacker? Were they caught? What penalties do they face?
4. Why do cybercriminals execute attacks across national borders? What are the implications for pursuit, prosecution, and law enforcement?
5. Why do law enforcement agencies struggle to cope with computer crime?
6. A single rogue employee effectively held the city of San Francisco's network hostage for ten days. What processes or controls might the city have created that could have prevented this kind of situation from taking place?
7. The Geneva Conventions are a set of international treaties that in part set standards for protecting citizens in and around a war zone. Should we have similar rules that set the limits of cyberwarfare? Would such limits even be effective? Why or why not?
8. What does the rise of cyberwarfare suggest for businesses and organizations? What sorts of contingencies should firms consider and possibly prepare for? How might considerations also impact a firm's partners, customers, and suppliers?

3. WHERE ARE VULNERABILITIES? UNDERSTANDING THE WEAKNESSES

LEARNING OBJECTIVES

1. Recognize the potential entry points for security compromise.
2. Understand infiltration techniques such as social engineering, phishing, malware, Web site compromises (such as SQL injection), and more.
3. Identify various methods and techniques to thwart infiltration.

FIGURE 13.1

This diagram shows only some of the potential weaknesses that can compromise the security of an organization's information systems. Every physical or network "touch point" is a potential vulnerability. Understanding where weaknesses may exist is a vital step toward improved security.

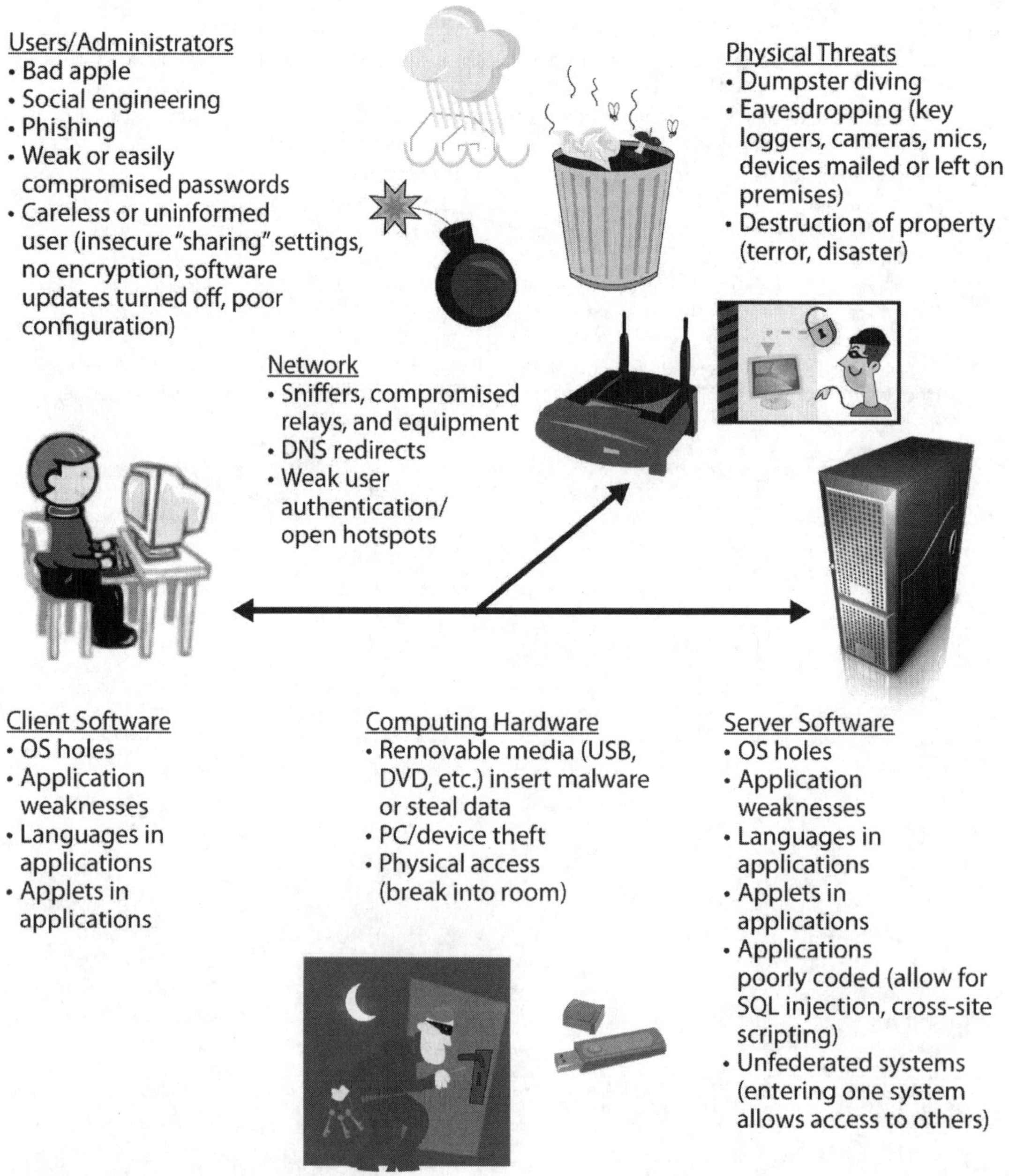

Source: http://office.microsoft.com/en-us/clipart/default.aspx

Modern information systems have lots of interrelated components and if one of these components fails, there might be a way in to the goodies. This creates a large attack surface for potential infiltration and compromise, as well as one that is simply vulnerable to unintentional damage and disruption.

3.1 User and Administrator Threats

Bad Apples

While some of the more sensational exploits involve criminal gangs, research firm Gartner estimates that 70 percent of loss-causing security incidents involve insiders.[27] Rogue employees can steal secrets, install malware, or hold a firm hostage. Check processing firm Fidelity National Information Services was betrayed when one of its database administrators lifted personal records on 2.3 million of the firm's customers and illegally sold them to direct marketers.

And it's not just firm employees. Many firms hire temporary staffers, contract employees, or outsource key components of their infrastructure. Other firms have been compromised by members of their cleaning or security staff. A contract employee working at Sentry Insurance stole information on 110,000 of the firm's clients.[28]

Social Engineering

As P. T. Barnum is reported to have said, "There's a sucker born every minute." Con games that trick employees into revealing information or performing other tasks that compromise a firm are known as *social engineering* in security circles. In some ways, crooks have never had easier access to background information that might be used to craft a scam. It's likely that a directory of a firm's employees, their titles, and other personal details is online right now via social networks like LinkedIn and Facebook. With just a few moments of searching, a skilled con artist can piece together a convincing and compelling story.

A Sampling of Methods Employed in Social Engineering

- Impersonating senior management, a current or new end user needing help with access to systems, investigators, or staff (fake uniforms, badges)
- Identifying a key individual by name or title as a supposed friend or acquaintance
- Making claims with confidence and authority ("Of course I belong at this White House dinner.")
- Baiting someone to add, deny, or clarify information that can help an attacker
- Using harassment, guilt, or intimidation
- Using an attractive individual to charm others into gaining information, favors, or access
- Setting off a series of false alarms that cause the victim to disable alarm systems
- Answering bogus surveys (e.g., "Win a free trip to Hawaii—just answer three questions about your network.")

Data aggregator ChoicePoint sold private information to criminals who posed as legitimate clients, compromising the names, addresses, and Social Security numbers of some 145,000 individuals. In this breach, not a single computer was compromised. Employees were simply duped into turning data over to crooks. Gaffes like that can be painful. ChoicePoint paid $15 million in a settlement with the Federal Trade Commission, suffered customer loss, and ended up abandoning once lucrative businesses.[29]

Phishing

Phishing refers to cons executed through technology. The goal of phishing is to leverage the reputation of a trusted firm or friend to trick the victim into performing an action or revealing information. The cons are crafty. Many have masqueraded as a security alert from a bank or e-commerce site ("Our Web site has been compromised, click to log in and reset your password."), a message from an employer, or even a notice from the government ("Click here to update needed information to receive your tax refund transfer."). Sophisticated con artists will lift logos, mimic standard layouts, and copy official language from legitimate Web sites or prior e-mails. Gartner estimates that these sorts phishing attacks cost consumers $3.2 billion in 2007.[30]

> **phishing**
> A con executed using technology, typically targeted at acquiring sensitive information or tricking someone into installing malicious software.

Other phishing attempts might dupe a user into unwittingly downloading dangerous software (malware) that can do things like record passwords and keystrokes, provide hackers with deeper access to your corporate network, or enlist your PC as part of a botnet. One attempt masqueraded as a message from a Facebook friend, inviting the recipient to view a video. Victims clicking the link were then told they need to install an updated version of the Adobe Flash plug-in to view the clip. The plug in was really a malware program that gave phishers control of the infected user's computer.[31] Other attempts have populated P2P networks (peer-to-peer file distribution systems such as BitTorrent) with malware-installing files masquerading as video games or other software, movies, songs, and pornography.

So-called spear phishing attacks specifically target a given organization or group of users. In one incident, employees of a medical center received e-mails purportedly from the center itself, indicating that the recipient was being laid off and offering a link to job counseling resources. The link really offered a software payload that recorded and forwarded any keystrokes on the victim's PC.[32] And with this type of phishing, the more you know about a user, the more convincing it is to con them. Phishers using pilfered résumé information from Monster.com crafted targeted and personalized e-mails. The request, seemingly from the job site, advised users to download the "Monster Job Seeker Tool"; this "tool" installed malware that encrypted files on the victim's PC, leaving a ransom note demanding payment to liberate a victim's hard disk.[33]

spoof

Term used in security to refer to forging or disguising the origin or identity. E-mail transmissions and packets that have been altered to seem as if they came from another source are referred to as being "spoofed."

Don't Take the Bait: Recognizing the "Phish Hooks"

Web browser developers, e-mail providers, search engines, and other firms are actively working to curtail phishing attempts. Many firms create blacklists that block access to harmful Web sites and increasingly robust tools screen for common phishing tactics. But it's still important to have your guard up. Some exploits may be so new that they haven't made it into screening systems (so-called zero-day exploits).

Never click on a link or download a suspicious, unexpected enclosure without verifying the authenticity of the sender. If something looks suspicious, don't implicitly trust the "from" link in an e-mail. It's possible that the e-mail address has been **spoofed** (faked) or that it was sent via a colleague's compromised account. If unsure, contact the sender or your security staff.

Also know how to read the complete URL to look for tricks. Some firms misspell Web address names (http://wwwyourbank.com—note the missing period), set up subdomains to trick the eye (http://yourbank.com.sneakysite.com—which is hosted at sneakysite.com even though a quick glance looks like yourbank.com), or hijack brands by registering a legitimate firm's name via foreign top-level domains (http://yourbank.cn).

A legitimate URL might also appear in a phishing message, but an HTML coding trick might make something that looks like http://yourbank.com/login actually link to http://sneakysite.com. Hovering your cursor over the URL or an image connected to a link should reveal the actual URL as a tool tip (just don't click it, or you'll go to that site).

This e-mail message looks like it's from Bank of America. However, hovering the cursor above the "Continue to Log In" button reveals the URL without clicking through to the site. Note how the actual URL associated with the link is not associated with Bank of America.

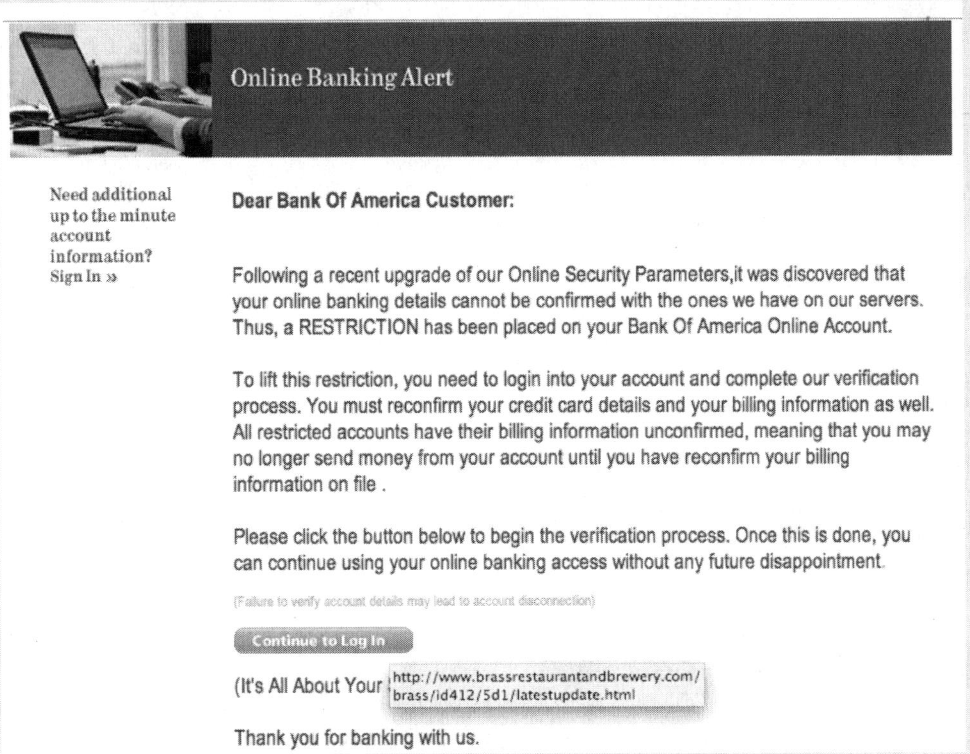
Online Banking Alert
Need additional up to the minute account information? Sign In »
Dear Bank Of America Customer:
Following a recent upgrade of our Online Security Parameters,it was discovered that your online banking details cannot be confirmed with the ones we have on our servers. Thus, a RESTRICTION has been placed on your Bank Of America Online Account.
To lift this restriction, you need to login into your account and complete our verification process. You must reconfirm your credit card details and your billing information as well. All restricted accounts have their billing information unconfirmed, meaning that you may no longer send money from your account until you have reconfirm your billing information on file .
Please click the button below to begin the verification process. Once this is done, you can continue using your online banking access without any future disappointment.
(Failure to verify account details may lead to account disconnection)
Continue to Log In
(It's All About Your
http://www.brassrestaurantandbrewery.com/brass/id412/5d1/latestupdate.html
Thank you for banking with us.

This image is from a phishing scheme masquerading as an eBay message. The real destination is a compromised .org domain unassociated with eBay, but the phishers have created a directory at this domain named "signin.ebay.com" in hopes that users will focus on that part of the URL and not recognize they're really headed to a non-eBay site.

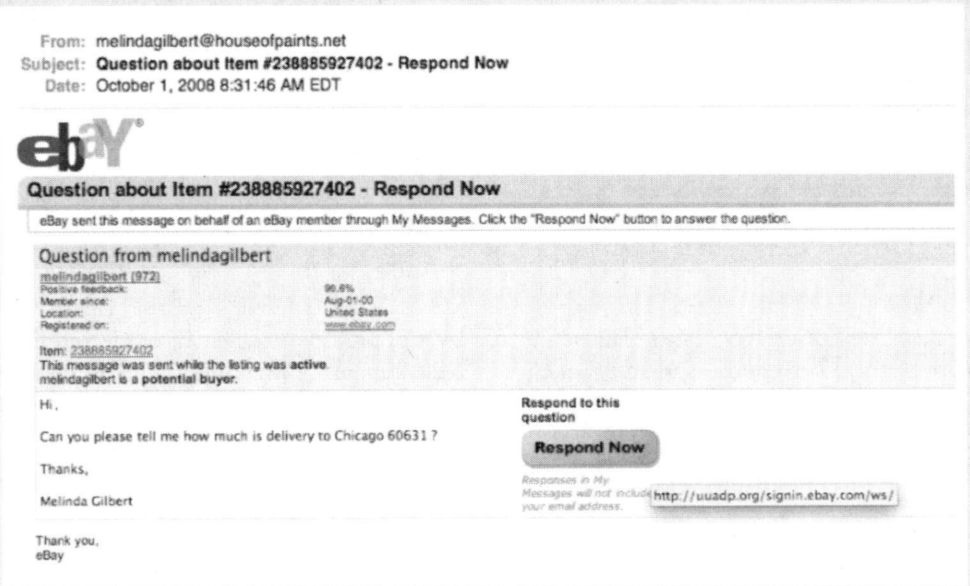
From: melindagilbert@houseofpaints.net
Subject: Question about Item #238885927402 - Respond Now
Date: October 1, 2008 8:31:46 AM EDT
Question about Item #238885927402 - Respond Now
eBay sent this message on behalf of an eBay member through My Messages. Click the "Respond Now" button to answer the question.
Question from melindagilbert
melindagilbert (972)
Member since: Aug-01-00
Location: United States
Registered on: www.ebay.com
Item: 238885927402
This message was sent while the listing was active.
melindagilbert is a potential buyer.
Hi ,
Can you please tell me how much is delivery to Chicago 60631 ?
Thanks,
Melinda Gilbert
Respond to this question
Respond Now
http://uuadp.org/signin.ebay.com/ws/
your email address.
Thank you,
eBay

zero-day exploits

Attacks that are so new that they haven't been clearly identified, and so they haven't made it into security screening systems.

Web 2.0: The Rising Security Threat

Social networks and other Web 2.0 tools are a potential gold mine for crooks seeking to pull off phishing scams. Malware can send messages that seem to come from trusted "friends." Messages such as status updates and tweets are short, and with limited background information, there are fewer contexts to question a post's validity. Many users leverage bit.ly or other URL-shortening services that don't reveal the Web site they link to in their URL, making it easier to hide a malicious link. While the most popular URL-shortening services maintain a blacklist, early victims are threatened by **zero-day exploits**. Criminals have also been using a variety of techniques to spread malware across sites or otherwise make them difficult to track and catch.

The technical openness of many Web 2.0 efforts can also create problems if schemes aren't implemented properly. For example, Mark Zuckerberg's Facebook page fell victim to hackers who used a hole in a Facebook API that allowed unauthorized status update posts to public Facebook fan pages.[34] APIs can allow firms to share services, collaborate, and enable mash-ups, but if code is poorly implemented it can also be an open back door where the bad guys can sneak in.

Some botnets have even used Twitter to communicate by sending out coded tweets to instruct compromised machines.[35] Social media can also be a megaphone for loose lips, enabling a careless user to broadcast proprietary information to the public domain. A 2009 Congressional delegation to Iraq was supposed to have been secret. But Rep. Peter Hoekstra tweeted his final arrival into Baghdad for all to see, apparently unable to contain his excitement at receiving BlackBerry service in Iraq. Hoekstra tweeted, "Just landed in Baghdad. I believe it may be first time I've had bb service in Iraq. 11th trip here." You'd think he would have known better. At the time, Hoekstra was a ranking member of the House Intelligence Committee!

A member of the House Intelligence Committee uses Twitter and reveals his locale on a secret trip.

Passwords

Many valuable assets are kept secure via just one thin layer of protection—the password. And if you're like most users, your password system is a mess.[36] With so many destinations asking for passwords, chances are you're using the same password (or easily guessed variants) in a way that means getting just one "key" would open many "doors." The typical Web user has 6.5 passwords, each of which is used at four sites, on average.[37] Some sites force users to change passwords regularly, but this often results in insecure compromises. Users make only minor tweaks (e.g., appending the month or year); they write passwords down (in an unlocked drawer or Post-it note attached to the monitor); or they save passwords in personal e-mail accounts or on unencrypted hard drives.

The challenge questions offered by many sites to automate password distribution and reset are often pitifully insecure. What's your mother's maiden name? What elementary school did you attend? Where were you born? All are pretty easy to guess. One IEEE study found acquaintances could correctly answer colleagues' secret questions 28 percent of the time, and those who did not know the person still guessed right at a rate of 17 percent. Plus, within three to six months, 16 percent of study participants forgot answers to *their own* security questions.[38] In many cases, answers to these questions can be easily uncovered online. Chances are, if you've got an account at a site like Ancestry.com, classmates.com, or Facebook, then some of your secret answers have already been exposed—by you! A Tennessee teen hacked into Sarah Palin's personal Yahoo! account (gov.palin@yahoo.com) in part by correctly guessing where she met her husband. A similar attack hit staffers at Twitter, resulting in the theft of hundreds of internal documents, including strategy memos, e-mails, and financial forecasts, many of which ended up embarrassingly posted online.[39]

Related to the password problem are issues with system setup and configuration. Many vendors sell software with a common default password. For example, for years, leading database products came with the default account and password combination "scott/tiger." Any firm not changing default accounts and passwords risks having an open door. Other firms are left vulnerable if users set systems for open access—say turning on file sharing permission for their PC. Programmers, take note: well-designed products come with secure default settings, require users to reset passwords at setup, and also offer strong warnings when security settings are made weaker. But unfortunately, there are a lot of legacy products out there, and not all vendors have the insight to design for out-of-the-box security.

biometrics

Technologies that measure and analyze human body characteristics for identification or authentication. These might include fingerprint readers, retina scanners, voice and face recognition, and more.

Building a Better Password

There's no simple answer for the password problem. **Biometrics** are often thought of as a solution, but technologies that replace conventionally typed passwords with things like fingerprint readers, facial recognition, or iris scans are still rarely used, and PCs that include such technologies are widely viewed as novelties. Says Carnegie Mellon University CyLab fellow Richard Power, "Biometrics never caught on and it never will."[40]

Other approaches leverage technology that distributes single use passwords. These might arrive via external devices like an electronic wallet card, key chain fob, or cell phone. Security firm RSA has even built the technology into BlackBerrys. Enter a user name and receive a phone message with a temporary password. Even if a system was compromised by keystroke capture malware, the password is only good for one session. Lost device? A central command can disable it. This may be a good solution for situations that demand a high level of security, and Wells Fargo and PayPal are among the firms offering these types of services as an option. However, for most consumer applications, slowing down users with a two-tier authentication system would be an impractical mandate.

While you await technical fixes, you can at least work to be part of the solution rather than part of the problem. It's unlikely you've got the memory or discipline to create separate unique passwords for all of your sites, but at least make it a priority to create separate, hard-to-guess passwords for each of your highest priority accounts (e.g., e-mail, financial Web sites, corporate network, and PC). Remember, the integrity of a password shared across Web sites isn't just up to you. That hot start-up Web service may not have the security resources or experience to protect your special code, and if that Web site's account is hacked, your user name and password are now in the hands of hackers that can try out those "keys" across the Web's most popular destinations.

Web sites are increasingly demanding more "secure" passwords, requiring users to create passwords at least eight characters in length and that include at least one number and other nonalphabet character. Beware of using seemingly clever techniques to disguise common words. Many commonly available brute-force password cracking tools run through dictionary guesses of common words or phrases, substituting symbols or numbers for common characters (e.g., "@" for "a," "+" for "t"). For stronger security, experts often advise basing passwords on a phrase, where each letter makes up a letter in an acronym. For example, the phrase "My first Cadillac was a real lemon so I bought a Toyota" becomes "M1stCwarlslbaT."[41] Be careful to choose an original phrase that's known only by you and that's easy for you to remember. Studies have shown that acronym-based passwords using song lyrics, common quotes, or movie lines are still susceptible to dictionary-style hacks that build passwords from pop-culture references (in one test, two of 144 participants made password phrases from an acronym of the Oscar Meyer wiener jingle).[42] Finding that balance between something tough for others to guess yet easy for you to remember will require some thought—but it will make you more secure. Do it now!

3.2 Technology Threats (Client and Server Software, Hardware, and Networking)

Malware

Any accessible computing device is a potential target for infiltration by malware. *Malware* (for malicious software) seeks to compromise a computing system without permission. Client PCs and a firm's servers are primary targets, but as computing has spread, malware now threatens nearly any connected system running software, including mobile phones, embedded devices, and a firm's networking equipment.

Some hackers will try to sneak malware onto a system via techniques like phishing. In another high-profile hacking example, infected USB drives were purposely left lying around government offices.

Those seemingly abandoned office supplies really contained code that attempted to infiltrate government PCs when inserted by unwitting employees.

Machines are constantly under attack. Microsoft's Internet Safety Enforcement Team claims that the mean time to infection for an unprotected PC is less than five minutes.[43] Oftentimes malware attempts to compromise weaknesses in software—either bugs, poor design, or poor configuration.

Years ago, most attacks centered on weaknesses in the operating system, but now malware exploits have expanded to other targets, including browsers, plug-ins, and scripting languages used by software. *BusinessWeek* reports that Adobe has replaced Microsoft as the primary means by which hackers try to infect or take control of PCs. Even trusted Web sites have become a conduit to deliver malware payloads. More than a dozen sites, including those of the *New York Times*, *USA Today*, and *Nature*, were compromised when seemingly honest advertising clients switched on fake ads that exploit Adobe software.[44] Some attacks were delivered through Flash animations that direct computers to sites that scan PCs, installing malware payloads through whatever vulnerabilities are discovered. Others circulated via e-mail through PDF triggered payloads deployed when a file was loaded via Acrobat Reader. Adobe is a particularly tempting target, as Flash and Acrobat Reader are now installed on nearly every PC, including Mac and Linux machines.

Malware goes by many names. Here are a few of the more common terms you're likely to encounter.[45]

Methods of infection are as follows:

- *Viruses.* Programs that infect other software or files. They require an executable (a running program) to spread, attaching to other executables. Viruses can spread via operating systems, programs, or the boot sector or auto-run feature of media such as DVDs or USB drives. Some applications have executable languages (macros) that can also host viruses that run and spread when a file is open.
- *Worms.* Programs that take advantage of security vulnerability to automatically spread, but unlike viruses, worms do not require an executable. Some worms scan for and install themselves on vulnerable systems with stunning speed (in an extreme example, the SQL Slammer worm infected 90 percent of vulnerable software worldwide within just ten minutes).[46]
- *Trojans.* Exploits that, like the mythical Trojan horse, try to sneak in by masquerading as something they're not. The payload is released when the user is duped into downloading and installing the malware cargo, oftentimes via phishing exploits.

While the terms above cover methods for infection, the terms below address the goal of the malware:

- *Botnets or zombie networks.* Hordes of surreptitiously infected computers linked and controlled remotely by a central command. Botnets are used in crimes where controlling many difficult-to-identify PCs is useful, such as when perpetrating click fraud, sending spam, registering accounts that use **CAPTCHAs**[47] (those scrambled character images meant to thwart things like automated account setup or ticket buying), executing "dictionary" password cracking attempts, or launching denial-of-service attacks.
- *Malicious adware.* Programs installed without full user consent or knowledge that later serve unwanted advertisements.
- *Spyware.* Software that surreptitiously monitors user actions, network traffic, or scans for files.
- *Keylogger.* Type of spyware that records user keystrokes. Keyloggers can be either software-based or hardware, such as a recording "dongle" that is plugged in between a keyboard and a PC.
- *Screen capture.* Variant of the keylogger approach. This category of software records the pixels that appear on a user's screen for later playback in hopes of identifying proprietary information.
- *Blended threats.* Attacks combining multiple malware or hacking exploits.

CAPTCHA

An acronym for Completely Automated Public Turing Test to Tell Computers and Humans Apart. CAPTCHAs are those scrambled character images that many sites require to submit some sort of entry (account setup, ticket buying). CAPTCHAs were developed because computers have difficulty discerning letters that are distorted or mixed inside a jumbled graphic. CAPTCHAs are meant to be a *Turing Test*—a test to distinguish if a task is being performed by a computer or a human.

All the News Fit to Print (Brought to You by Scam Artists)

In fall 2009, bad guys posing as the telecom firm Vonage signed up to distribute ads through the *New York Times* Web site. Many firms that display online ads on their Web sites simply create placeholders on their Web pages, with the actual ad content served by the advertisers themselves (see Chapter 14 for details). In this particular case, the scam artists posing as Vonage switched off the legitimate-looking ads and switched on code that, according to the *New York Times*, "took over the browsers of many people visiting the site, as their screens filled with an image that seemed to show a scan for computer viruses. The visitors were then told that they needed to buy antivirus software to fix a problem, but the software was more snake oil than a useful program."[48] Sites ranging from Fox News, the *San Francisco Chronicle*, and British tech site The Register have also been hit with ad scams in the past. In the *Times* case, malware wasn't distributed directly to user PCs, but by passing through ads from third parties to consumers, the *Times* became a conduit for a scam. In the same way that manufacturers need to audit their supply chain to ensure that partners aren't engaged in sweatshop labor or disgraceful pollution, sites that host ads need to audit their partners to ensure they are legitimate and behaving with integrity.

The Virus in Your Pocket

Most mobile phones are really pocket computers, so it's not surprising that these devices have become malware targets. And there are a lot of pathways to exploit. Malware might infiltrate a smartphone via e-mail, Internet surfing, MMS attachments, or even Bluetooth. The "commwarrior" mobile virus spread to at least eight countries, propagating from a combination of MMS messages and Bluetooth.[49]

Most smartphones have layers of security to block the spread of malware, so hackers typically hunt for the weakest victims. Easy marks include "jail-broken" iPhones, devices with warranty-voiding modifications in which security restrictions are overridden to allow phones to be used off network, and for the installation of unsanctioned applications. Estimates suggest some 10 percent of iPhones are jail-broken, and early viruses exploiting the compromised devices ranged from a "Rick roll" that replaced the home screen image with a photo of 1980s crooner Rick Astley[50] to the more nefarious Ikee.B, which scanned text messages and hunted out banking codes, forwarding the nabbed data to a server in Lithuania.[51]

The upside? Those smart devices are sometimes crime fighters themselves. A Pittsburgh mugging victim turned on Apple's "Find My iPhone" feature within its MobileMe service, mapping the perpetrator's path, then sending the law to bust the bad guys while they ate at a local restaurant.[52]

A "jail-broken" iPhone gets "Rick rolled" by malware.

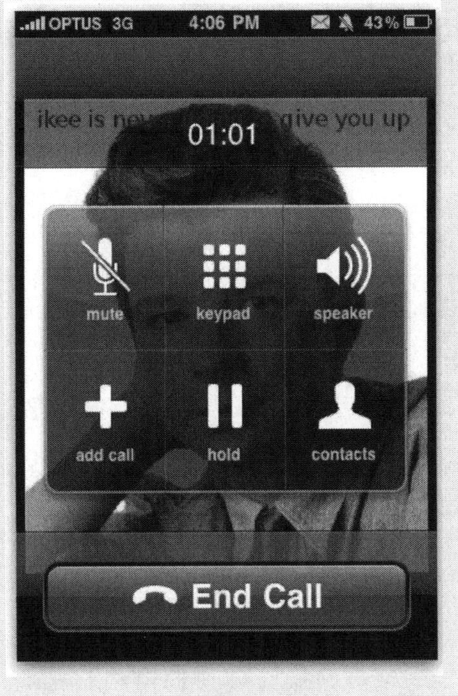

Compromising Web Sites

Some exploits directly target poorly designed and programmed Web sites. Consider the SQL injection technique. It zeros in on a sloppy programming practice where software developers don't validate user input.

It works like this. Imagine that you visit a Web site and are asked to enter your user ID in a field on a Web page (say your user ID is smith). A Web site may be programmed to take the data you enter from the Web page's user ID field (smith), then add it to a database command (creating the equivalent of a command that says "find the account for 'smith'"). The database then executes that command.

But Web sites that don't verify user entries and instead just blindly pass along entered data are vulnerable to attack. Hackers with just a rudimentary knowledge of SQL could type actual code fragments into the user ID field, appending this code to statements executed by the site (see sidebar for a more detailed description). Such modified instructions could instruct the Web site's database software to drop (delete) tables, insert additional data, return all records in a database, or even redirect users to another Web site that will scan clients for weaknesses, then launch further attacks. Security expert Ben Schneier noted a particularly ghastly SQL injection vulnerability in the publicly facing database for the Oklahoma Department of Corrections, where "anyone with basic SQL knowledge could have registered anyone he wanted as a sex offender."[53]

Not trusting user input is a cardinal rule of programming, and most well-trained programmers know to validate user input. But there's a lot of sloppy code out there, which hackers are all too eager to exploit. IBM identifies SQL injection as the fastest growing security threat, with over half a million attack attempts recorded each day.[54] Some vulnerable systems started life as quickly developed proofs of concepts, and programmers never went back to add the needed code to validate input and block these exploits. Other Web sites may have been designed by poorly trained developers who have moved on to other projects, by staff that have since left the firm, or where development was outsourced to another firm. As such, many firms don't even know if they suffer from this vulnerability.

SQL injection and other application weaknesses are particularly problematic because there's not a commercial software patch or easily deployed piece of security software that can protect a firm. Instead, firms have to meticulously examine the integrity of their Web sites to see if they are vulnerable.[55]

How SQL Injection Works

For those who want to get into some of the geekier details of a SQL injection attack, consider a Web site that executes the code below to verify that an entered user ID is in a database table of usernames. The code executed by the Web site might look something like this:

*"SELECT * FROM users WHERE userName = '" + userID + "';"*

The statement above tells the database to SELECT (find and return) all columns (that's what the "*" means) from a table named users where the database's userName field equals the text you just entered in the userID field. If the Web site's visitor entered smith, that text is added to the statement above, and it's executed as:

*"SELECT * FROM users WHERE userName = 'smith';"*

No problem. But now imagine a hacker gets sneaky and instead of just typing smith, into the Web site's userID field, they also add some *additional* SQL code like this:

*smith'; DROP TABLE users; DELETE * FROM users WHERE 't' = 't*

If the programming statement above is entered into the user ID, the Web site adds this code to its own programming to create a statement that is executed as:

*SELECT * FROM users WHERE userName = 'smith'; DELETE * FROM users WHERE 't' = 't';*

The semicolons separate SQL statements. That second statement says delete all data in the users table for records where 't' = 't' (this last part, 't' = 't,' is always true, so all records will be deleted). Yikes! In this case, someone entering the kind of code you'd learn in the first chapter of *SQL for Dummies* could annihilate a site's entire user ID file using one of the site's own Web pages as the attack vehicle.[56]

Related programming exploits go by names such as cross-site scripting attacks and HTTP header injection. We'll spare you the technical details, but what this means for both the manager and the programmer is that all systems must be designed and tested with security in mind. This includes testing new applications, existing and legacy applications, partner offerings, and SaaS (software as a service) applications—everything. Visa and MasterCard are among the firms requiring partners to rigorously apply testing standards. Firms that aren't testing their applications will find they're locked out of business; if caught with unacceptable breaches, such firms may be forced to pay big fines and absorb any costs associated with their weak practices.[57]

3.3 Push-Button Hacking

Not only are the list of technical vulnerabilities well known, hackers have created tools to make it easy for the criminally inclined to automate attacks. Chapter 14 outlines how Web sites can interrogate a system to find out more about the software and hardware used by visitors. Hacking toolkits can do the same thing. While you won't find this sort of software for sale on Amazon, a casual surfing of the online underworld (not recommended or advocated) will surface scores of tools that probe systems for the latest vulnerabilities then launch appropriate attacks. In one example, a $700 toolkit (MPack v. 86) was used to infiltrate a host of Italian Web sites, launching Trojans that infested 15,000 users in just a six-day period.[58] As an industry executive in *BusinessWeek* has stated, "The barrier of entry is becoming so low that literally anyone can carry out these attacks."[59]

Network Threats

The network itself may also be a source of compromise. Recall that the TJX hack happened when a Wi-Fi access point was left open and undetected. A hacker just drove up and performed the digital equivalent of crawling through an open window. The problem is made more challenging since wireless access points are so inexpensive and easy to install. For less than $100, a user (well intentioned or not) could plug in to an access point that could provide entry for anyone. If a firm doesn't regularly monitor its premises, its network, and its network traffic, it may fall victim.

Other troubling exploits have targeted the very underpinning of the Internet itself. This is the case with so-called DNS cache poisoning. The DNS, or domain name service, is a collection of software that maps an Internet address, such as (http://www.bc.edu), to an IP address, such as 136.167.2.220. 220 (see Chapter 12 for more detail). DNS cache poisoning exploits can redirect this mapping and the consequences are huge. Imagine thinking that you're visiting your bank's Web site, but instead your network's DNS server has been poisoned so that you really visit a carefully crafted replica that hackers use to steal your log-in credentials and drain your bank account. A DNS cache poisoning attack launched against one of China's largest ISPs redirected users to sites that launched malware exploits, targeting weaknesses in RealPlayer, Adobe Flash, and Microsoft's ActiveX technology, commonly used in browsers.[60]

Physical Threats

A firm doesn't just have to watch out for insiders or compromised software and hardware; a host of other physical threats can grease the skids to fraud, theft, and damage. Most large firms have disaster-recovery plans in place. These often include provisions to backup systems and data to off-site locales, to protect operations and provide a fall back in the case of disaster. Such plans increasingly take into account the potential impact of physical security threats such as terrorism, or vandalism, as well.

Anything valuable that reaches the trash in a recoverable state is also a potential security breach. Hackers and spies sometimes practice **dumpster diving**, sifting through trash in an effort to uncover valuable data or insights that can be stolen or used to launch a security attack. This might include hunting for discarded passwords written on Post-it notes, recovering unshredded printed user account listings, scanning e-mails or program printouts for system clues, recovering tape backups, resurrecting files from discarded hard drives, and more.

dumpster diving

Combing through trash to identify valuable assets.

Other compromises might take place via **shoulder surfing**, simply looking over someone's shoulder to glean a password or see other proprietary information that might be displayed on a worker's screen.

shoulder surfing

Gaining compromising information through observation (as in looking over someone's shoulder).

Firms might also fall victim to various forms of eavesdropping, such as efforts to listen into or record conversations, transmissions, or keystrokes. A device hidden inside a package might sit inside a mailroom or a worker's physical inbox, scanning for open wireless connections, or recording and forwarding conversations.[61] Other forms of eavesdropping can be accomplished via compromised wireless or other network connections, malware keylogger or screen capture programs, as well as hardware devices such as replacement keyboards with keyloggers embedded inside, microphones to capture the slightly unique and identifiable sound of each key being pressed, programs that turn on built-in microphone or cameras that are now standard on many PCs, or even James Bond-style devices using Van Eck techniques that attempt to read monitors from afar by detecting their electromagnetic emissions.

encryption

Scrambling data using a code or formula, known as a cipher, such that it is hidden from those who do not have the unlocking key.

key

Code that unlocks encryption.

brute-force attack

An attack that exhausts all possible password combinations in order to break into an account. The larger and more complicated a password or key, the longer a brute-force attack will take.

The Encryption Prescription

During a routine physical transfer of backup media, Bank of America lost tapes containing the private information—including Social Security and credit card numbers—of hundreds of thousands of customers.[62] This was potentially devastating fodder for identity thieves. But who cares if someone steals your files if they still can't read the data? That's the goal of encryption!

Encryption scrambles data, making it essentially unreadable to any program that doesn't have the descrambling password, known as a **key**. Simply put, the larger the key, the more difficult it is for a brute-force attack to exhaust all available combinations and crack the code. When well implemented, encryption can be the equivalent of a rock solid vault. To date, the largest known **brute-force attacks**, demonstration hacks launched by grids of simultaneous code-cracking computers working in unison, haven't come close to breaking the type of encryption used to scramble transmissions that most browsers use when communicating with banks and shopping sites. The problem occurs when data is nabbed before encryption or after decrypting, or in rare cases, if the encrypting key itself is compromised.

Extremely sensitive data—trade secrets, passwords, credit card numbers, and employee and customer information—should be encrypted before being sent or stored.[63] Deploying encryption dramatically lowers the potential damage from lost or stolen laptops, or from hardware recovered from dumpster diving. It is vital for any laptops carrying sensitive information.

Encryption is also employed in virtual private network (VPN) technology, which scrambles data passed across a network. Public wireless connections pose significant security threats—they may be set up by hackers that pose as service providers, while really launching attacks on or monitoring the transmissions of unwitting users. The use of VPN software can make any passed-through packets unreadable. Contact your firm or school to find out how to set up VPN software.

In the Bank of America example above, the bank was burned. It couldn't verify that the lost tapes were encrypted, so it had to notify customers and incur the cost associated with assuming data had been breached.[64]

Encryption is not without its downsides. Key management is a potentially costly procedural challenge for most firms. If your keys aren't secure, it's the equivalent of leaving the keys to a safe out in public. Encryption also requires additional processing to scramble and descramble data—drawing more power and slowing computing tasks. Moore's Law will speed things along, but it also puts more computing power in the hands of attackers. With hacking threats on the rise, expect to see laws and compliance requirements that mandate encrypted data, standardize encryption regimes, and simplify management.

public key encryption

A two key system used for securing electronic transmissions. One key distributed publicly is used to encrypt (lock) data, but it cannot unlock data. Unlocking can only be performed with the private key. The private key also cannot be reverse engineered from the public key. By distributing public keys, but keeping the private key, Internet services can ensure transmissions to their site are secure.

certificate authority

A trusted third party that provides authentication services in public key encryption schemes.

How Do Web Sites Encrypt Transmissions?

Most Web sites that deal with financial transactions (e.g., banks, online stores) secure transmissions using a method called **public key encryption**. The system works with two keys—a public key and a private key. The public key can "lock" or encrypt data, but it can't unlock it: that can only be performed by the private key. So a Web site that wants you to transmit secure information will send you a public key—you use this to lock the data, and no one that intercepts that transmission can break in unless they've got the private key. If the Web site does its job, it will keep the private key out of reach of all potentially prying eyes.

Wondering if a Web site's transmissions are encrypted? Look at the Web address. If it begins with "https" instead of "http", it should be secure. Also, look for the padlock icon in the corner of your Web browser to be closed (locked). Finally, you can double click the padlock to bring up a verification of the Web site's identity (verified by a trusted third party firm, known as a **certificate authority**). If this matches your URL and indicates the firm you're doing business with, then you can be pretty sure verified encryption is being used by the firm that you intend to do business with.

In this screenshot, a Firefox browser is visiting Bank of America. The padlock icon was clicked to bring up digital certificate information. Note how the Web site's name matches the URL. The verifying certificate authority is the firm VeriSign.

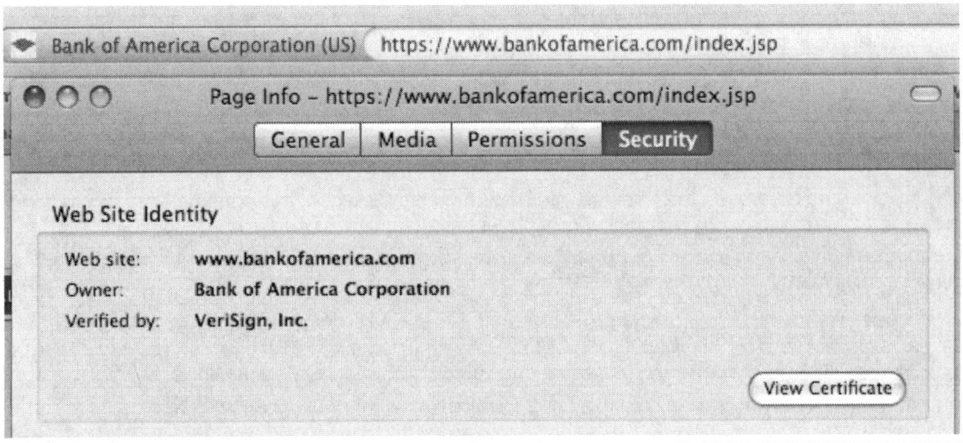

KEY TAKEAWAYS

- An organization's information assets are vulnerable to attack from several points of weakness, including users and administrators, its hardware and software, its networking systems, and various physical threats.
- Social engineering attempts to trick or con individuals into providing information, while phishing techniques are cons conducted through technology.
- While dangerous, a number of tools and techniques can be used to identify phishing scams, limiting their likelihood of success.
- Social media sites may assist hackers in crafting phishing or social engineering threats, provide information to password crackers, and act as conduits for unwanted dissemination of proprietary information.
- Most users employ inefficient and insecure password systems; however, techniques were offered to improve one's individual password regime.
- Viruses, worms, and Trojans are types of infecting malware. Other types of malware might spy on users, enlist the use of computing assets for committing crimes, steal assets, destroy property, serve unwanted ads, and more.
- Examples of attacks and scams launched through advertising on legitimate Web pages highlight the need for end-user caution, as well as for firms to ensure the integrity of their participating online partners.
- SQL injection and related techniques show the perils of poor programming. Software developers must design for security from the start—considering potential security weaknesses, and methods that improve end-user security (e.g., in areas such as installation and configuration).
- Encryption can render a firm's data assets unreadable, even if copied or stolen. While potentially complex to administer and resource intensive, encryption is a critical tool for securing an organization's electronic assets.

QUESTIONS AND EXERCISES

1. Consider your own personal password regime and correct any weaknesses. Share any additional password management tips and techniques with your class.
2. Why is it a bad idea to use variants of existing passwords when registering for new Web sites?
3. Relate an example of social engineering that you've experienced or heard of. How might the victim have avoided being compromised?
4. Have you ever seen phishing exploits? Have you fallen for one? Why did you take the bait, or what alerted you to the scam? How can you identify phishing scams?
5. Have you or has anyone you know fallen victim to malware? Relate the experience—how do you suppose it happened? What damage was done? What, if anything, could be done to recover from the situation?
6. Why are social media sites such a threat to information security? Give various potential scenarios where social media use might create personal or organizational security compromises.
7. Some users regularly update their passwords by adding a number (say month or year) to their code. Why is this bad practice?
8. What kind of features should a programmer build into systems in order to design for security? Think about the products that you use. Are there products that you feel did a good job of ensuring security during setup? Are there products you use that have demonstrated bad security design? How?
9. Why are SQL injection attacks more difficult to address than the latest virus threat?
10. How should individuals and firms leverage encryption?
11. Investigate how you might use a VPN if traveling with your laptop. Be prepared to share your findings with your class and your instructor.

4. TAKING ACTION

LEARNING OBJECTIVES

1. **Identify critical steps to improve your individual and organizational information security.**
2. **Be a tips, tricks, and techniques advocate, helping make your friends, family, colleagues, and organization more secure.**
3. **Recognize the major information security issues that organizations face, as well as the resources, methods, and approaches that can help make firms more secure.**

4.1 Taking Action as a User

The weakest link in security is often a careless user, so don't make yourself an easy mark. Once you get a sense of threats, you understand the kinds of precautions you need to take. Security considerations then become more common sense than high tech. Here's a brief list of major issues to consider:

- *Surf smart.* Think before you click—question links, enclosures, download request, and the integrity of Web sites that you visit. Avoid suspicious e-mail attachments and Internet downloads. Be on guard for phishing, and other attempts to con you into letting in malware. Verify anything that looks suspicious before acting. Avoid using public machines (libraries, coffee shops) when accessing sites that contain your financial data or other confidential information.
- *Stay vigilant.* Social engineering con artists and rogue insiders are out there. An appropriate level of questioning applies not only to computer use, but also to personal interactions, be it in person, on the phone, or electronically.
- *Stay updated.* Turn on software update features for your operating system and any application you use (browsers, applications, plug-ins, and applets), and manually check for updates when needed. Malware toolkits specifically scan for older, vulnerable systems, so working with updated programs that address prior concerns lowers your vulnerable attack surface.
- *Stay armed.* Install a full suite of security software. Many vendors offer a combination of products that provide antivirus software that blocks infection, personal firewalls that repel unwanted intrusion, malware scanners that seek out bad code that might already be nesting on your PC, antiphishing software that identifies if you're visiting questionable Web sites, and more. Such tools are increasingly being built into operating systems, browsers, and are deployed at the ISP or service provider (e-mail firm, social network) level. But every consumer should make it a priority

to understand the state of the art for personal protection. In the way that you regularly balance your investment portfolio to account for economic shifts, or take your car in for an oil change to keep it in top running condition, make it a priority to periodically scan the major trade press or end-user computing sites for reviews and commentary on the latest tools and techniques for protecting yourself (and your firm).

- *Be settings smart.* Don't turn on risky settings like unrestricted folder sharing that may act as an invitation for hackers to drop off malware payloads. Secure home networks with password protection and a firewall. Encrypt hard drives—especially on laptops or other devices that might be lost or stolen. Register mobile devices for location identification or remote wiping. Don't click the "Remember me" or "Save password" settings on public machines, or any device that might be shared or accessed by others. Similarly, if your machine might be used by others, turn off browser settings that auto-fill fields with prior entries—otherwise you make it easy for someone to use that machine to track your entries and impersonate you. And when using public hotspots, be sure to turn on your VPN software to encrypt transmission and hide from network eavesdroppers.
- *Be password savvy.* Change the default password on any new products that you install. Update your passwords regularly. Using guidelines outlined earlier, choose passwords that are tough to guess, but easy for you (and only you) to remember. Federate your passwords so that you're not using the same access codes for your most secure sites. Never save passwords in nonsecured files, e-mail, or written down in easily accessed locations.
- *Be disposal smart.* Shred personal documents. Wipe hard drives with an industrial strength software tool before recycling, donating, or throwing away—remember in many cases "deleted" files can still be recovered. Destroy media such as CDs and DVDs that may contain sensitive information. Erase USB drives when they are no longer needed.
- *Back up.* The most likely threat to your data doesn't come from hackers; it comes from hardware failure.[65] Yet most users still don't regularly back up their systems. This is another do-it-now priority. Cheap, plug-in hard drives work with most modern operating systems to provide continual backups, allowing for quick rollback to earlier versions if you've accidentally ruined some vital work. And services like EMC's Mozy provide monthly, unlimited backup over the Internet for less than what you probably spent on your last lunch (a fire, theft, or similar event could also result in the loss of any backups stored on-site, but Internet backup services can provide off-site storage and access if disaster strikes).
- *Check with your administrator.* All organizations that help you connect to the Internet—your ISP, firm, or school—should have security pages. Many provide free security software tools. Use them as resources. Remember—it's in their interest to keep you safe, too!

4.2 Taking Action as an Organization

Frameworks, Standards, and Compliance

Developing organizational security is a daunting task. You're in an arms race with adversaries that are tenacious and constantly on the lookout for new exploits. Fortunately, no firm is starting from scratch—others have gone before you and many have worked together to create published best practices.

There are several frameworks, but perhaps the best known of these efforts comes from the International Organization for Standards (ISO), and is broadly referred to as ISO27k or the ISO 27000 series. According to ISO.org, this evolving set of standards provides "a model for establishing, implementing, operating, monitoring, reviewing, maintaining, and improving an Information Security Management System."

Firms may also face compliance requirements—legal or professionally binding steps that must be taken. Failure to do so could result in fine, sanction, and other punitive measures. At the federal level, examples include HIPAA (the Health Insurance Portability and Accountability Act), which regulates health data; the Graham-Leach-Bliley Act, which regulates financial data; and the Children's Online Privacy Protection Act, which regulates data collection on minors. U.S. government agencies must also comply with FISMA (the Federal Information Security Management Act), and there are several initiatives at the other government levels. By 2009, some level of state data breach laws had been passed by over thirty states, while multinationals face a growing number of statues throughout the world. Your legal team and trade associations can help you understand your domestic and international obligations. Fortunately, there are often frameworks and guidelines to assist in compliance. For example, the ISO standards include subsets targeted at the telecommunications and health care industries, and major credit card firms have created the PCI (payment card industry) standards. And there are skilled consulting professionals who can help bring firms up to speed in these areas, and help expand their organizational radar as new issues develop.

Here is a word of warning on frameworks and standards: compliance does not equal security. Outsourcing portions security efforts without a complete, organizational commitment to being secure can also be dangerous. Some organizations simply approach compliance as a necessary evil: a sort of checklist that can reduce the likelihood of a lawsuit or other punitive measure.[66] While you want to make sure you're doing everything in your power not to get sued, this isn't the goal. The goal is taking all appropriate measures to ensure that your firm is secure for your customers, employees, shareholders, and others. Frameworks help shape your thinking and expose things you should do, but security doesn't stop there—this is a constant, evolving process that needs to pervade the organization from the CEO suite and board, down to front line workers and potentially out to customers and partners. And be aware of the security issues associated with any mergers and acquisitions. Bringing in new firms, employees, technologies, and procedures means reassessing the security environment for all players involved.

The Heartland Breach

On inauguration day 2009, credit card processor Heartland announced that it had experienced what was one of the largest security breaches in history. The Princeton, New Jersey, based firm was, at the time, the nation's fifth largest payments processor. Its business was responsible for handling the transfer of funds and information between retailers and cardholders' financial institutions. That means infiltrating Heartland was like breaking into Fort Knox.

It's been estimated that as many as 100 million cards issued by more than 650 financial services companies may have been compromised during the Heartland breach. Said the firm's CEO, this was "the worst thing that can happen to a payments company and it happened to us."[67] Wall Street noticed. The firm's stock tanked—within a month, its market capitalization had plummeted over 75 percent, dropping over half a billion dollars in value.[68]

The Heartland case provides a cautionary warning against thinking that security ends with compliance. Heartland had in fact passed multiple audits, including one conducted the month before the infiltration began. Still, at least thirteen pieces of malware were uncovered on the firm's servers. Compliance does not equal security. Heartland was complaint, but a firm can be compliant and not be secure. Compliance is not the goal, security is.

Since the breach, the firm's executives have championed industry efforts to expand security practices, including encrypting card information at the point it is swiped and keeping it secure through settlement. Such "cradle-to-grave" encryption can help create an environment where even compromised networking equipment or intercepting relay systems wouldn't be able to grab codes.[69] Recognize that security is a continual process, it is never done, and firms need to pursue security with tenacity and commitment.

Education, Audit, and Enforcement

Security is as much about people, process, and policy, as it is about technology.

From a people perspective, the security function requires multiple levels of expertise. Operations employees are involved in the day-to-day monitoring of existing systems. A group's R&D function is involved in understanding emerging threats and reviewing, selecting, and implementing updated security techniques. A team must also work on broader governance issues. These efforts should include representatives from specialized security and broader technology and infrastructure functions. It should also include representatives from general counsel, audit, public relations, and human resources. What this means is that even if you're a nontechnical staffer, you may be brought in to help a firm deal with security issues.

Processes and policies will include education and awareness—this is also everyone's business. As the Vice President of Product Development at security firm Symantec puts it, "We do products really well, but the next step is education. We can't keep the Internet safe with antivirus software alone."[70] Companies should approach information security as a part of their "collective corporate responsibility...regardless of whether regulation requires them to do so."[71]

For a lesson in how important education is, look no further than the head of the CIA. Former U.S. Director of Intelligence John Deutch engaged in shockingly loose behavior with digital secrets, including keeping a daily journal of classified information—some 1,000+ pages—on memory cards he'd transport in his shirt pocket. He also downloaded and stored Pentagon information, including details of covert operations, at home on computers that his family used for routine Internet access.[72]

Employees need to know a firm's policies, be regularly trained, and understand that they will face strict penalties if they fail to meet their obligations. Policies without eyes (audit) and teeth (enforcement) won't be taken seriously. Audits include real-time monitoring of usage (e.g., who's accessing what, from where, how, and why; sound the alarm if an anomaly is detected), announced audits, and surprise spot checks. This function might also stage white hat demonstration attacks—attempts to hunt for and expose weaknesses, hopefully before hackers find them. Frameworks offer guidelines on auditing, but a recent survey found most organizations don't document enforcement procedures in their information security policies, that more than one-third do not audit or monitor user compliance with security policies, and that only 48 percent annually measure and review the effectiveness of security policies.[73]

A firm's technology development and deployment processes must also integrate with the security team to ensure that from the start, applications, databases, and other systems are implemented with security in mind. The team will have specialized skills and monitor the latest threats and are able to advise on precautions necessary to be sure systems aren't compromised during installation, development, testing, and deployment.

What Needs to Be Protected and How Much Is Enough?

A worldwide study by PricewaterhouseCoopers and *Chief Security Officer* magazine revealed that most firms don't even know what they need to protect. Only 33 percent of executives responded that their organizations kept accurate inventory of the locations and jurisdictions where data was stored, and only 24 percent kept inventory of all third parties using their customer data.[74] What this means is that most firms don't even have an accurate read on where their valuables are kept, let alone how to protect them.

So information security should start with an inventory-style auditing and risk assessment. Technologies map back to specific business risks. What do we need to protect? What are we afraid might happen? And how do we protect it? Security is an economic problem, involving attack likelihood, costs, and prevention benefits. These are complex trade-offs that must consider losses from theft or resources, systems damage, data loss, disclosure of proprietary information, recovery, downtime, stock price declines, legal fees, government and compliance penalties, and intangibles such as damaged firm reputation, loss of customer and partner confidence, industry damage, promotion of adversary, and encouragement of future attacks.

While many firms skimp on security, firms also don't want to misspend, targeting exploits that aren't likely, while underinvesting in easily prevented methods to thwart common infiltration techniques. Hacker conventions like DefCon can show some really wild exploits. But it's up to the firm to assess how vulnerable it is to these various risks. The local donut shop has far different needs than a military installation, law enforcement agency, financial institution, or firm housing other high-value electronic assets. A skilled risk assessment team will consider these vulnerabilities and what sort of countermeasure investments should take place.

Economic decisions usually drive hacker behavior, too. While in some cases attacks are based on vendetta or personal reasons, in most cases exploit economics largely boils down to

$$\text{Adversary ROI} = \text{Asset value to adversary} - \text{Adversary cost.}$$

An adversary's costs include not only the resources, knowledge, and technology required for the exploit, but also the risk of getting caught. Make things tough to get at, and lobbying for legislation that imposes severe penalties on crooks can help raise adversary costs and lower your likelihood of becoming a victim.

Technology's Role

Technical solutions often involve industrial strength variants of the previously discussed issues individuals can employ, so your awareness is already high. Additionally, an organization's approach will often leverage multiple layers of protection and incorporate a wide variety of protective measures.

Patch. Firms must be especially vigilant to pay attention to security bulletins and install software updates that plug existing holes, (often referred to as *patches*). Firms that don't plug known problems will be vulnerable to trivial and automated attacks. Unfortunately, many firms aren't updating all components of their systems with consistent attention. With operating systems automating security update installations, hackers have moved on to application targets. But a major study recently found that organizations took at least twice as long to patch application vulnerabilities as they take to patch operating system holes.[75] And remember, software isn't limited to conventional PCs and servers. Embedded systems abound, and connected, yet unpatched devices are vulnerable. Malware has infected everything from unprotected ATM machines[76] to restaurant point-of-sale systems[77] to fighter plane navigation systems.[78]

As an example of unpatched vulnerabilities, consider the DNS cache poisoning exploit described earlier in this chapter. The discovery of this weakness was one of the biggest security stories the year it was discovered, and security experts saw this as a major threat. Teams of programmers worldwide raced to provide fixes for the most widely used versions of DNS software. Yet several months after patches were available, roughly one quarter of all DNS servers were still unpatched and exposed.[79]

To be fair, not all firms delay patches out of negligence. Some organizations have legitimate concerns about testing whether the patch will break their system or whether the new technology contains a change that will cause problems down the road.[80] And there have been cases where patches themselves have caused problems. Finally, many software updates require that systems be taken down. Firms may have uptime requirements that make immediate patching difficult. But ultimately, unpatched systems are an open door for infiltration.

Lock down hardware. Firms range widely in the security regimes used to govern purchase through disposal system use. While some large firms such as Kraft are allowing employees to select their own hardware (Mac or PC, desktop or notebook, iPhone or BlackBerry),[81] others issue standard systems that prevent all unapproved software installation and force file saving to hardened, backed-up, scanned, and monitored servers. Firms in especially sensitive industries such as financial services may regularly reimage the hard drive of end-user PCs, completely replacing all the bits on a user's hard drive with a pristine, current version—effectively wiping out malware that might have previously sneaked onto a user's PC. Other lock-down methods might disable the boot capability of removable media (a common method for spreading viruses via inserted discs or USBs), prevent Wi-Fi use or require VPN encryption before allowing any network transmissions, and more. The cloud helps here, too. (See Chapter 10.) Employers can also require workers to run all of their corporate applications inside a remote desktop where the actual executing hardware and software is elsewhere (likely hosted as a virtual machine session on the organization's servers), and the user is simply served an image of what is executing remotely. This seals the virtual PC off in a way that can be thoroughly monitored, updated, backed up, and locked down by the firm.

In the case of Kraft, executives worried that the firm's previously restrictive technology policies prevented employees from staying in step with trends. Employees opting into the system must sign an agreement promising they'll follow mandated security procedures. Still, financial services firms, law offices, health care providers, and others may need to maintain stricter control, for legal and industry compliance reasons.

Lock down the network. Network monitoring is a critical part of security, and a host of technical tools can help.

Firms employ **firewalls** to examine traffic as it enters and leaves the network, potentially blocking certain types of access, while permitting approved communication. **Intrusion detection systems** specifically look for unauthorized behavior, sounding the alarm and potentially taking action if something seems amiss. Some firms deploy **honeypots**—bogus offerings meant to distract attackers. If attackers take honeypot bait, firms may gain an opportunity to recognize the hacker's exploits, identify the IP address of intrusion, and take action to block further attacks and alert authorities.

firewall

A system that acts as a control for network traffic, blocking unauthorized traffic while permitting acceptable use.

intrusion detection system

A system that monitors network use for potential hacking attempts. Such a system may take preventative action to block, isolate, or identify attempted infiltration, and raise further alarms to warn security personnel.

honeypot

A seemingly tempting, but bogus target meant to draw hacking attempts. By monitoring infiltration attempts against a honeypot, organizations may gain insight into the identity of hackers and their techniques, and they can share this with partners and law enforcement.

Many firms also deploy **blacklists**—denying the entry or exit of specific IP addresses, products, Internet domains, and other communication restrictions. While blacklists block known bad guys, **whitelists** are even more restrictive—permitting communication only with approved entities or in an approved manner.

These technologies can be applied to network technology, specific applications, screening for certain kinds of apps, malware signatures, and hunting for anomalous patterns. The latter is important, as recent malware has become polymorphic, meaning different versions are created and deployed in a way that their signature, a sort of electronic fingerprint often used to recognize malicious code, is slightly altered. This also helps with zero-day exploits, and in situations where whitelisted Web sites themselves become compromised.

Many technical solutions, ranging from network monitoring and response to e-mail screening, are migrating to "the cloud." This can be a good thing—if network monitoring software immediately shares news of a certain type of attack, defenses might be pushed out to all clients of a firm (the more users, the "smarter" the system can potentially become—again we see the power of network effects in action).

Lock down partners. Insist partner firms are compliant, and audit them to ensure this is the case. This includes technology providers and contract firms, as well as value chain participants such as suppliers and distributors. Anyone who touches your network is a potential point of weakness. Many firms will build security expectations and commitments into performance guarantees known as service level agreements (SLAs).

Lock down systems. Audit for SQL injection and other application exploits. The security team must constantly scan exploits and then probe its systems to see if it's susceptible, advising and enforcing action if problems are uncovered. This kind of auditing should occur with all of a firm's partners.

Access controls can also compartmentalize data access on a need-to-know basis. Such tools can not only enforce access privileges, they can help create and monitor audit trails to help verify that systems are not being accessed by the unauthorized, or in suspicious ways.

Audit trails are used for deterring, identifying, and investigating these cases. Recording, monitoring, and auditing access allows firms to hunt for patterns of abuse. Logs can detail who, when, and from where assets are accessed. Giveaways of nefarious activity may include access from unfamiliar IP addresses, from nonstandard times, accesses that occur at higher than usual volumes, and so on. Automated alerts can put an account on hold or call in a response team for further observation of the anomaly.

Single-sign-on tools can help firms offer employees one very strong password that works across applications, is changed frequently (or managed via hardware cards or mobile phone log-in), and can be altered by password management staff.

Multiple administrators should jointly control key systems. Major configuration changes might require approval of multiple staffers, as well as the automatic notification of concerned personnel. And firms should employ a recovery mechanism to regain control in the event that key administrators are incapacitated or uncooperative. This balances security needs with an ability to respond in the event of a crisis. Such a system was not in place in the earlier described case of the rogue IT staffer who held the city of San Francisco's networks hostage by refusing to give up vital passwords.

Have failure and recovery plans. While firms work to prevent infiltration attempts, they should also have provisions in place that plan for the worst. If a compromise has taken place, what needs to be done? Do stolen assets need to be devalued (e.g., accounts terminated, new accounts issued)? What should be done to notify customers and partners, educate them, and advise them through any necessary responses? Who should work with law enforcement and with the media? Do off-site backups or redundant systems need to be activated? Can systems be reliably restored without risking further damage?

Best practices are beginning to emerge. While postevent triage is beyond the scope of our introduction, the good news is that firms are now sharing data on breaches. Given the potential negative consequences of a breach, organizations once rarely admitted they'd been compromised. But now many are obligated to do so. And the broad awareness of infiltration both reduces organizational stigma in coming forward, and allows firms and technology providers to share knowledge on the techniques used by cybercrooks.

Information security is a complex, continually changing, and vitally important domain. The exploits covered in this chapter seem daunting, and new exploits constantly emerge. But your thinking on key issues should now be broader. Hopefully you've now embedded security thinking in your managerial DNA, and you are better prepared to be a savvy system user and a proactive participant working for your firm's security. Stay safe!

blacklists

Programs that deny the entry or exit of specific IP addresses, products, Internet domains, and other communication restrictions.

whitelists

Highly restrictive programs that permit communication only with approved entities and/or in an approved manner.

KEY TAKEAWAYS

- End users can engage in several steps to improve the information security of themselves and their organizations. These include surfing smart, staying vigilant, updating software and products, using a comprehensive security suite, managing settings and passwords responsibly, backing up, properly disposing of sensitive assets, and seeking education.
- Frameworks such as ISO27k can provide a road map to help organizations plan and implement an effective security regime.
- Many organizations are bound by security compliance commitments and will face fines and retribution if they fail to meet these commitments.
- The use of frameworks and being compliant is not equal to security. Security is a continued process that must be constantly addressed and deeply ingrained in an organization's culture.
- Security is about trade-offs—economic and intangible. Firms need to understand their assets and risks in order to best allocate resources and address needs.
- Information security is not simply a technical fix. Education, audit, and enforcement regarding firm policies are critical. The security team is broadly skilled and constantly working to identify and incorporate new technologies and methods into their organizations. Involvement and commitment is essential from the boardroom to frontline workers, and out to customers and partners.

QUESTIONS AND EXERCISES

1. Visit the security page for your ISP, school, or employer. What techniques do they advocate that we've discussed here? Are there any additional techniques mentioned and discussed? What additional provisions do they offer (tools, services) to help keep you informed and secure?
2. What sorts of security regimes are in use at your university, and at firms you've worked or interned for? If you don't have experience with this, ask a friend or relative for their professional experiences. Do you consider these measures to be too restrictive, too lax, or about right?
3. While we've discussed the risks in having security that is too lax, what risk does a firm run if its security mechanisms are especially strict? What might a firm give up? What are the consequences of strict end-user security provisions?
4. What risks does a firm face by leaving software unpatched? What risks does it face if it deploys patches as soon as they emerge? How should a firm reconcile these risks?
5. What methods do firms use to ensure the integrity of their software, their hardware, their networks, and their partners?
6. An organization's password management system represents "the keys to the city." Describe personnel issues that a firm should be concerned with regarding password administration. How might it address these concerns?

ENDNOTES

1. Particular thanks goes to my Boston College colleague, Professor Sam Ransbotham, whose advice, guidance, and suggestions were invaluable in creating this chapter. Any errors or omissions are entirely my own.
2. E. Mills, "Attacks on Sony, Others, Show It's Open Hacking Season," *CNET*, June 8, 2011.
3. A. Matwyshyn, *Harboring Data: Information Security, Law, and the Corporation* (Palo Alto, CA: Stanford University Press, 2009).
4. D. Goldman, "Cybercrime: A Secret Underground Economy," *CNNMoney*, September 17, 2009.
5. K. Voigt, "Analysis: The Hidden Cost of Cybercrime," *CNN*, June 6, 2011.
6. *Synamtec Internet Security Threat Report*, Symantec Corporation, April 2011.
7. R. King, "Lessons from the Data Breach at Heartland," *BusinessWeek*, July 6, 2009.
8. S. Kroft, "Cyberwar: Sabotaging the System," *60 Minutes*, November 8, 2009; J. Leyden, "Cybercrime Losses Almost Double," *Register*, March 15, 2010.
9. R. Singel, "Underground Crime Economy Health, Security Group Finds," *Wired*, November 24, 2008.
10. K. J. Higgins, "SecureWorks Unveils Research on Spamming Botnets," *DarkReading*, April 9, 2008.
11. B. Krebs, "Storm Worm Dwarfs World's Top Supercomputer," *Washington Post*, August 31, 2007.
12. Trend Micro, "Web Threats Whitepaper," March 2008.
13. S. Kroft, "Cyberwar: Sabotaging the System," *60 Minutes*, November 8, 2009.
14. J. Schectman, "Computer Hacking Made Easy," *BusinessWeek*, August 13, 2009.
15. J. Vijayan, "Software Consultant Who Stole Data on 110,000 People Gets Five-Year Sentence," *Computerworld*, July 10, 2007.
16. S. Gorman, A. Cole, and Y. Dreazen. "Computer Spies Breach Fighter-Jet Project," *Wall Street Journal*, April 21, 2009.
17. E. Mills, "China Linked to New Breaches Tied to RSA," *CNET*, June 6, 2011.
18. P. Eckert, "Analysis: Can Naming, Shaming Curb Cyber Attacks from China?" *Reuters*, June 3, 2011.
19. A. Madrigal, "The Inside Story of How Facebook Responded to Tunisian Hacks," *Atlantic*, January 24, 2011.
20. S. Kroft, "Cyberwar: Sabotaging the System," *60 Minutes*, November 8, 2009.
21. N. Firth, "Computer Super-Virus 'Targeted Iranian Nuclear Power Station' but Who Made It?" *Daily Mail*, September 24, 2010.
22. M. Gross, "A Declaration of Cyber-War," *Vanity Fair*, April 2011.
23. T. Butterworth, "The War against Iran Has Already Started," *Forbes*. September 21, 2010.
24. M. Schwartz, "The Trolls among Us," *New York Times*, August 3, 2008.
25. J. Schectman, "Computer Hacking Made Easy," *BusinessWeek*, August 13, 2009.
26. J. Vijayan, "After Verdict, Debate Rages in Terry Childs Case," *Computerworld*, April 28, 2010.
27. J. Mardesich, "Ensuring the Security of Stored Data," CIO Strategy Center, 2009.
28. J. Vijayan, "Software Consultant Who Stole Data on 110,000 People Gets Five-Year Sentence," *Computerworld*, July 10, 2007.
29. G. Anthes, "The Grill: Security Guru Ira Winkler Takes the Hot Seat," *Computerworld*, July 28, 2008.
30. L. Avivah, "Phishing Attacks Escalate, Morph, and Cause Considerable Damage," *Gartner*, December 12, 2007.
31. B. Krebs, "'Koobface' Worm Resurfaces on Facebook, MySpace," *Washington Post*, March 2, 2009.
32. C. Garretson, "Spam that Delivers a Pink Slip," *NetworkWorld*, November 1, 2006.
33. T. Wilson, "Trojan On Monster.com Steals Personal Data," *Forbes*, August 20, 2007.
34. G. Cluley, "Mark Zuckerberg Fan Page Hacked on Facebook: What Really Happened?" *NakedSecurity*, January 27, 2011.
35. UnsafeBits, "Botnets Go Public by Tweeting on Twitter," *Technology Review*, August 17, 2009.
36. F. Manjoo, "Fix Your Terrible, Insecure Passwords in Five Minutes," *Slate*, November 12, 2009.
37. N. Summers, "Building a Better Password," *Newsweek*, October 19, 2009.
38. R. Lemos, "Are Your 'Secret Questions' Too Easily Answered?" *Technology Review*, May 18, 2009.
39. N. Summers, "Building a Better Password," *Newsweek*, October 19, 2009.
40. N. Summers, "Building a Better Password," *Newsweek*, October 19, 2009.
41. F. Manjoo, "Fix Your Terrible, Insecure Passwords in Five Minutes," *Slate*, November 12, 2009.
42. N. Summers, "Building a Better Password," *Newsweek*, October 19, 2009.
43. J. Markoff, "A Robot Network Seeks to Enlist Your Computer," *New York Times*, October 20, 2008.
44. A. Ricadela, "Can Adobe Beat Back the Hackers?" *BusinessWeek*, November 19, 2009.
45. Portions adapted from G. Perera, "Your Guide to Understanding Malware," *LaptopLogic.com*, May 17, 2009.
46. M. Broersma, "Slammer—the First 'Warhol' Worm?" *CNET*, February 3, 2003.
47. G. Keizer, "Botnet Busts Newest Hotmail CAPTCHA," *Computerworld*, February 19, 2009.
48. A. Vance, "Times Web Ads Show Security Breach," *New York Times*, September 14, 2009.
49. J. Charney, "Commwarrior Cell Phone Virus Marches On," *CNET*, June 5, 2005.
50. S. Steade, "It's Shameless How They Flirt," *Good Morning Silicon Valley*, November 9, 2009.
51. R. Lemos, "Nasty iPhone Worm Hints at the Future," *Technology Review*, November 29, 2009.
52. J. Murrell, "The iWitness News Roundup: Crime-fighting iPhone," *Good Morning Silicon Valley*, August 31, 2009.
53. B. Schneier, "Oklahoma Data Leak," *Schneier on Security*, April 18, 2008.
54. A. Wittmann, "The Fastest-Growing Security Threat," *InformationWeek*, November 9, 2009.
55. While some tools exist to automate testing, this is by no means as easy a fix as installing a commercial software patch or virus protection software.
56. B. Schneier, "Oklahoma Data Leak," *Schneier on Security*, April 18, 2008.
57. "Information Security: Why Cybercriminals Are Smiling," *Knowledge@Wharton*, August 19, 2009.
58. "Web Threats Whitepaper," *Trend Micro*, March 2008.
59. J. Schectman, "Computer Hacking Made Easy," *BusinessWeek*, August 13, 2009.
60. J. London, "China Netcom Falls Prey to DNS Cache Poisoning," *Computerworld*, August 22, 2008.
61. J. Robertson, "Hackers Mull Physical Attacks on a Networked World," *San Francisco Chronicle*, August 8, 2008.
62. J. Mardesich, "Ensuring the Security of Stored Data," CIO Strategy Center, 2009.
63. J. Mardesich, "Ensuring the Security of Stored Data," CIO Strategy Center, 2009.
64. J. Mardesich, "Ensuring the Security of Stored Data," CIO Strategy Center, 2009.
65. C. Taylor, "The Tech Catastrophe You're Ignoring," *Fortune*, October 26, 2009.
66. M. Davis, "What Will It Take?" *InformationWeek*, November 23, 2009.
67. R. King, "Lessons from the Data Breach at Heartland," *BusinessWeek*, July 6, 2009.
68. T. Claburn, "Payment Card Industry Gets Encryption Religion," *InformationWeek*, November 13, 2009.
69. T. Claburn, "Payment Card Industry Gets Encryption Religion," *InformationWeek*, November 13, 2009; R. King, "Lessons from the Data Breach at Heartland," *BusinessWeek*, July 6, 2009.
70. D. Goldman, "Cybercrime: A Secret Underground Economy," *CNNMoney*, September 17, 2009.
71. Knowledge@Wharton, "Information Security: Why Cybercriminals Are Smiling," August 19, 2009.
72. N. Lewis, "Investigation Of Ex-Chief Of the C.I.A. Is Broadened," *New York Times*, September 17, 2000.
73. A. Matwyshyn, *Harboring Data: Information Security, Law, and The Corporation* (Palo Alto, CA: Stanford University Press, 2009).
74. A. Matwyshyn, *Harboring Data: Information Security, Law, and The Corporation* (Palo Alto, CA: Stanford University Press, 2009).
75. S. Wildstrom, "Massive Study of Net Vulnerabilities: They're Not Where You Think They Are," *BusinessWeek*, September 14, 2009.
76. P. Lilly, "Hackers Targeting Windows XP-Based ATM Machines," *Maximum PC*, June 4, 2009.
77. R. McMillan, "Restaurants Sue Vendors after Point-of-Sale Hack," *CIO*, December 1, 2009.
78. C. Matyszczyk, "French Planes Grounded by Windows Worm," *CNET*, February 8, 2009.
79. IBM, *X-Force Threat Report: 2008 Year in Review*, January 2009.
80. For example, the DNS security patch mentioned was incompatible with the firewall software deployed at some firms.
81. N. Wingfield, "It's a Free Country…So Why Can't I Pick the Technology I Use in the Office?" *Wall Street Journal*, November 15, 2009.

CHAPTER 14

Google in Three Parts: Search, Online Advertising, and Beyond

1. INTRODUCTION

LEARNING OBJECTIVES

1. **Understand the extent of Google's rapid rise and its size and influence when compared with others in the media industry.**
2. **Recognize the shift away from traditional advertising media to Internet advertising.**
3. **Gain insight into the uniqueness and appeal of Google's corporate culture.**

Google has been called a one-trick pony,[1] but as tricks go, it's got an exquisite one. Google's "trick" is matchmaking—pairing Internet surfers with advertisers and taking a cut along the way. This cut is substantial—about $38 billion in 2011. In fact, as *Wired*'s Steve Levy puts it, Google's matchmaking capabilities may represent "the most successful business idea in history."[2] For perspective, consider that as a ten-year-old firm, and one that had been public for less than five years, Google had already grown to earn more annual advertising dollars than *any* U.S. media company. No television network, no magazine group, no newspaper chain brings in more ad bucks than Google. And none is more profitable. While Google's stated mission is "to organize the world's information and make it universally accessible and useful," advertising drives profits and lets the firm offer most of its services for free.

FIGURE 14.1 U.S. Advertising Spending (by selected media)

Online advertising represents the only advertising category trending with positive growth. Figures for 2012 (and 2011 figures for Yellow Pages) are estimates.

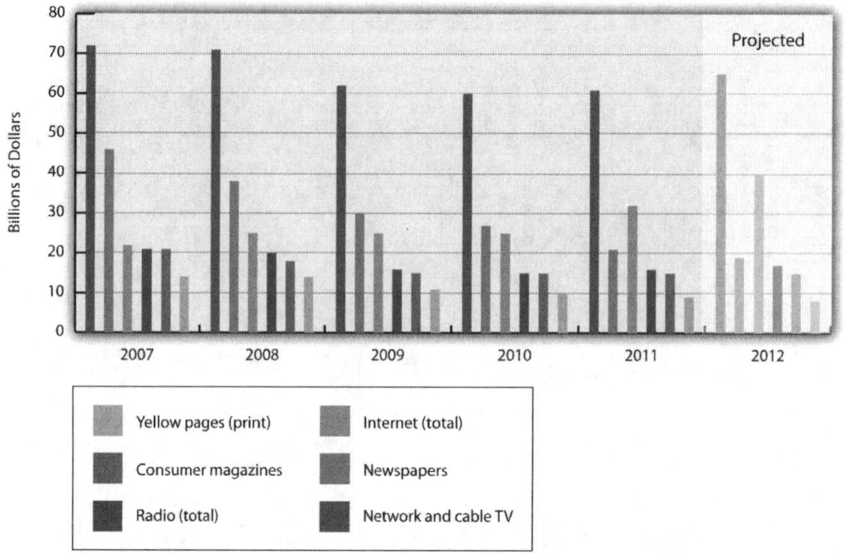

Source: Data retrieved via eMarketer.com.

FIGURE 14.2 U.S. Online Ad Spending (by format)

Search captures the most online ad dollars, and Google dominates search advertising. Figures for 2011 and beyond are estimates.

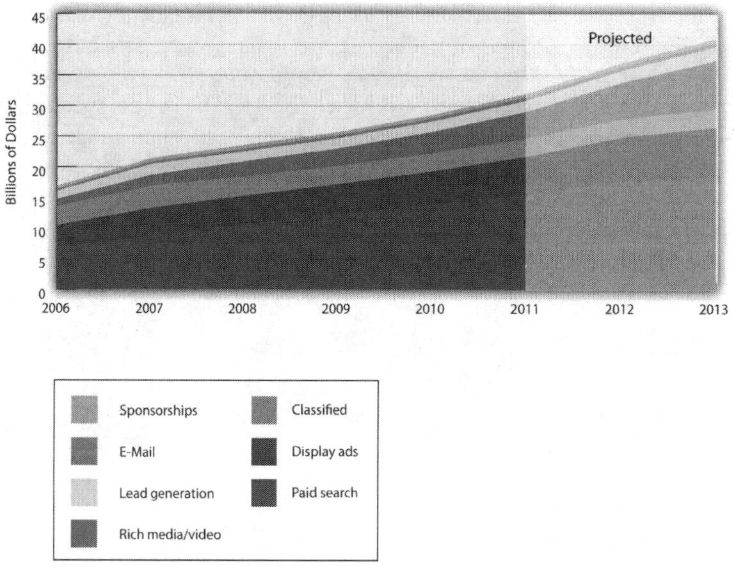

Source: Data retrieved via eMarketer.com.

As more people spend more time online, advertisers are shifting spending away from old channels to the Internet; and Google is swallowing the lion's share of this funds transfer.[3] By some estimates Google has 76 percent of the search advertising business.[4] Add to that Google's lucrative AdSense network that serves ads to sites ranging from small time bloggers to the *New York Times*, plus markets served by Google's acquisition of display ad leader DoubleClick, and the firm controls the majority of *all* online advertising dollars.[5] Facebook, Bing, Yahoo!, AOL, all the ads sold directly by media sites—add up *all* their advertising and together they're *still* less than Google's take. Google has one of the world's strongest brands[6] (its name is a verb—*just Google it*). It is regularly voted among the best firms to work for in America (topping *Fortune*'s list three times). While rivals continue to innovate (see the box "Search: Google Rules, but It Ain't Over" in Section 10), Google continues to dominate the search market.

FIGURE 14.3 U.S. Search Market Share (Volume of Searches, June 2012)[7]

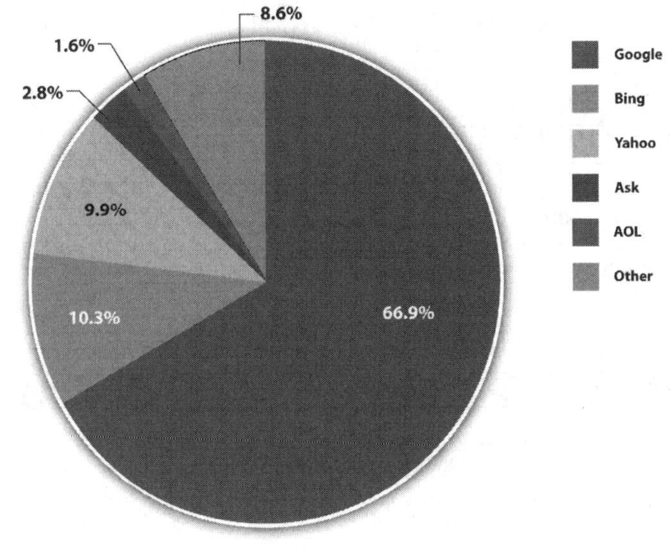

Wall Street has rewarded this success. The firm's **market capitalization (market cap)**, the value of the firm calculated by multiplying its share price by the number of shares, makes Google the most valuable media company on the planet. By 2007 the firm's founding duo, Sergey Brin and Larry Page, were billionaires, tying for fifth on the *Forbes* 400 list of wealthiest Americans. By early 2009, Google's market cap was greater than that of News Corp (which includes all of the Fox Networks, and the *Wall Street Journal*), Disney (including ABC, ESPN, theme parks, and Pixar), Time Warner (*Fortune*, *Time*, *Sports Illustrated*, CNN, and Warner Bros.), Viacom (MTV, VH1, and Nickelodeon), CBS, and the *New York Times*—combined! And by 2010 Google had become one of the twenty most profitable firms in the United States and was the youngest firm on the list—by far. Not bad for a business started by two twenty-something computer science graduate students.

market capitalization (market cap)

The value of a firm calculated by multiplying its share price by the number of shares.

While the bulk of the firm's revenues come from advertising, the firm is now clearly engaged in a wide-ranging multi-front war that includes mobile, browsers, cloud infrastructure, email, office apps, social media, maps, tablets, television, video, and more. And while the firm's performance in each space varies, the success of its existing businesses provides a massive cash horde that allows the firm to fuel experimentation, constantly innovate, tolerate failure, acquire aggressively, and patiently build new markets.

Genius Geeks and Plum Perks

Brin and Page have built a talent magnet. At the Googleplex, the firm's Mountain View, California headquarters, geeks are lavished with perks that include on-site laundry, massage, carwash, bicycle repair, free haircuts, state of the art gyms, and **Wi-Fi** equipped shuttles that ferry employees around Silicon Valley and the San Francisco Bay area. The Googleplex is also pretty green. The facility gets 30 percent of its energy from solar cells, representing the largest corporate installation of its kind.[8]

Wi-Fi

A term used to brand wireless local-area networking devices. Devices typically connect to an antenna-equipped base station or hotspot, which is then connected to the Internet. Wi-Fi devices use standards known as IEEE 802.11, and various version of this standard (e.g., b, g, n) may operate in different frequency bands and have access ranges.

The firm's quirky tech-centric culture is evident everywhere. A T-Rex skeleton looms near the volleyball court. Hanging from the lobby ceiling is a replica of SpaceShipOne, the first commercial space vehicle. And visitors to the bathroom will find "testing on the toilet," coding problems or other brainteasers to keep gray matter humming while seated on one of the firm's $800 remote-controlled Japanese commodes. Staff also enjoy an A-list lecture series attracting luminaries ranging from celebrities to heads of state.

And of course there's the food—all of it free. The firm's founders felt that no employee should be more than 100 feet away from nourishment, and a tour around Google offices will find espresso bars, snack nooks, and fully stocked beverage refrigerators galore. There are eleven gourmet cafeterias on-site, the most famous being "Charlie's Place," first run by the former executive chef for the Grateful Dead.

Chairman and former CEO Eric Schmidt said the goal of all this is "to strip away everything that gets in our employees' way."[9] And the perks, culture, and sense of mission have allowed the firm to assemble one of the most impressive rosters of technical talent anywhere. The Googleplex is like a well-fed Manhattan project, and employee ranks have included a gaggle of geniuses that helped invent critical technologies such as the Macintosh user interface, the python programming language, the XML standard, and even the protocols that underlie the Internet itself.

Engineers find Google a particularly attractive place to work, in part due to a corporate policy of offering "20 percent time," the ability to work the equivalent of one day a week on new projects that interest them. It's a policy that has fueled innovation. Roughly half of Google products got their start in 20 percent time.[10]

Studying Google gives us an idea of how quickly technology-fueled market disruptions can happen, and how deeply these disruptions penetrate various industries. You can consider this chapter as consisting of three extended sections. The first part (Section 2) covers Google Search, the firm's core product. The second part (Section 3 through Section 9) covers how the firm makes most of its money—advertising. By reading this section you'll get a solid introduction to various types of online advertising, how customer profiling works, and issues of online privacy and fraud. The last section (Section 10) covers the firm's evolving strategy, its competition with disparate rivals, and the opportunities and challenges the firm faces going forward.

KEY TAKEAWAYS

- Online advertising represents the only advertising category that, over the last several years, has been consistently trending with positive growth.
- Google dominates Internet search volume and controls the lion's share of the Internet search advertising business and online advertising dollars. The firm also earns more total advertising revenue than any other firm, online or off.
- Google's market cap makes it the most valuable media company in the world; it has been rated as having one of the world's strongest brands, and it ranks among the most profitable firms in the United States.

QUESTIONS AND EXERCISES

1. List the reasons why Google has been considered a particularly attractive firm to work for. Are all of these associated with perks?
2. Market capitalization and market share change frequently. Investigate Google's current market cap and compare it with other media companies. Do patterns suggested in this case continue to hold? Why or why not?
3. Search industry numbers presented are through mid-2012. Research online to find out the most current Google versus Bing versus Yahoo! market share. Are there any credible newcomers to the field? Does Google's position seem secure to you? Why or why not?

2. UNDERSTANDING SEARCH

LEARNING OBJECTIVES

1. **Understand the mechanics of search, including how Google indexes the Web and ranks its organic search results.**
2. **Examine the infrastructure that powers Google and how its scale and complexity offer key competitive advantages.**

Before diving into how the firm makes money, let's first understand how Google's core service, search, works.

Perform a search (or **query**) on Google or another search engine, and the results you'll see are referred to by industry professionals as **organic or natural search**. Search engines use different algorithms for determining the order of organic search results, but at Google the method is called **PageRank** (a bit of a play on words, it ranks Web pages, and was initially developed by Google cofounder Larry Page). Google does not accept money for placement of links in organic search results. Instead, PageRank results are a kind of popularity contest. Web pages that have more pages *linking to them* are ranked higher (while organic search results can't be bought, firms do pay for preferred placement in some Google products, including Google Shopping, Hotels, and Flight Search, and in financial products listed in Google Advisor).[11]

query

Search.

organic or natural search

Search engine results returned and ranked according to relevance.

PageRank

Algorithm developed by Google cofounder Larry Page to rank Web sites.

FIGURE 14.4

The query for "Toyota Prius" triggers organic search results, flanked top and right by advertisements.

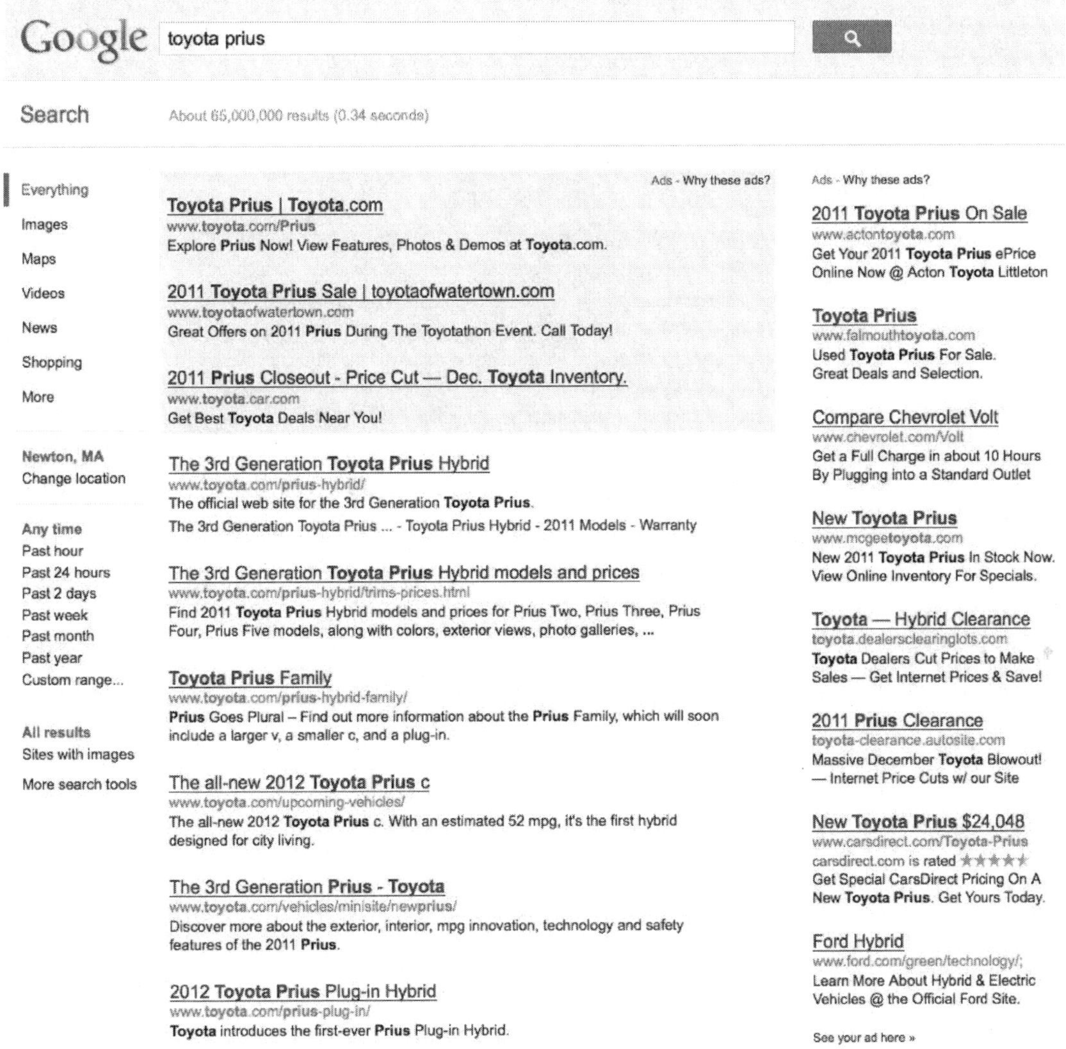

The process of improving a page's organic search results is often referred to as **search engine optimization (SEO)**. SEO has become a critical function for many marketing organizations since if a firm's pages aren't near the top of search results, customers may never discover its site.

Google is a bit vague about the specifics of precisely how PageRank has been refined, in part because many have tried to game the system. In addition to in-bound links, Google's organic search results also consider some two hundred other signals, and the firm's search quality team is relentlessly analyzing user behavior for clues on how to tweak the system to improve accuracy.[12] The less scrupulous have tried creating a series of bogus Web sites, all linking back to the pages they're trying to promote (this is called **link fraud**, and Google actively works to uncover and shut down such efforts—see the "Link Fraudsters" sidebar).

search engine optimization (SEO)

The process of improving a page's organic search results.

link fraud

Also called "spamdexing" or "link farming." The process of creating a series of bogus Web sites, all linking back to the pages one is trying to promote.

Link Fraudsters, Be Prepared to Experience Google's "Death Penalty"

JCPenney is a big retailer, for sure, but not necessarily the first firm to come to mind when you think of most retail categories. So the *New York Times* suspected that something fishy was up when the retailer's site came out tops for dozens of Google searches, including the phrases "skinny jeans," "dresses," "bedding," "area rugs," "home decor," "comforter sets," "furniture," and "table cloths". The phrase "Samsonite carry on luggage" even placed Penney ahead of Samsonite's own site!

The *Times* reported that "someone paid to have thousands of links placed on hundreds of sites scattered around the Web, all of which lead directly to JCPenney.com." And there was little question it was blatant link fraud. Phrases related to dresses and linking back to the retailer were coming from such nondress sites as nuclear.engineeringaddict.com, casino-focus.com, and bulgariapropertyportal.com. One SEO expert called the effort the most ambitious link farming attempt he'd ever seen.

Link fraud undercuts the credibility of Google's core search product, so when the search giant discovers a firm engaged in link farming they drop the hammer. In this case Google both manually demoted Penney rankings and launched tweaks to its ranking algorithm. Within two hours JCPenney organic results plummeted, in some cases from first to seventy-first (the *Times* calls this the organic search equivalent of the "death penalty"). Getting a top spot in Google search results is a big deal. On average, 34 percent of clicks go to the top result, about twice the percentage that goes to number two. Google's punishment was administered despite the fact that Penney was also a large online ad customer, at times paying Google some $2.5 million a month for ads.[13]

Google is constantly playing defense against firms gaming organic search results. In another example a Brooklyn-based eyewear firm allegedly mistreated customers in order to get more ranking-influencing links (albeit from negative mentions) from service review sites. For a time these associated with bad ratings actually pushed the eyewear firm's search results *ahead* of rivals, and since users typically focus on the top ranking, many customers went to the firm without seeing the bad reviews (Google has since changed search results to make it difficult to benefit from cultivating negative reviews). The owner of the busted eyewear retailer has also pled guilty to multiple counts, including sending threatening communications, one count of mail fraud, and one count of wire fraud.[14]

JCPenney isn't the first firm busted. When Google discovered so-called black hat SEO was being used to push BMW up in organic search rankings, Google made certain BMW sites virtually unfindable in its organic search results. JCPenney claims that they were the victim of rogue behavior by an SEO consultant (who was promptly fired) and that the retailer was otherwise unaware of the unethical behavior. But it is surprising that the retailer's internal team didn't see their unbelievably successful organic search results as a red flag that something was amiss, and this case highlights the types of things managers need to watch for in the digital age. Penney outsourced SEO, and the fraud uncovered in this story underscores the critical importance of vetting and regularly auditing the performance of partners throughout a firm's supply chain.[15]

While Google doesn't divulge specifics on the weighting of inbound links from a given Web site, we do know that links from some Web sites carry more weight than others. For example, links from Web sites that Google deems "influential" have greater weight in PageRank calculations than links from run-of-the-mill sites. Additionally, different users might not see identical results in organic search. Google defaults to a mix of rankings that includes individual user behavior and, for those users searching while logged into Google accounts, social connections (although displaying generic results remains an option).[16]

Spiders and Bots and Crawlers—Oh My!

When performing a search via Google or another search engine, you're not actually searching the Web. What really happens is that you're searching something that amounts to a *copy* of the Web that major search engines make by storing and indexing the text of online documents on their own computers. Google's index considers over one trillion URLs.[17] Google starts to retrieve results as soon as you begin to type, and the upper right-hand corner of a Google query shows you just how fast a search can take place.

To create these massive indexes, search firms use software to crawl the Web and uncover as much information as they can find. This software is referred to by several different names—**spiders, Web crawlers, software robots**—but they all pretty much work the same way. The spiders ask each public computer network for a list of its public Web sites (for more on this see DNS in Chapter 12). Then the spiders go through this list ("crawling" a site), following every available link until all pages are uncovered.

Google will crawl frequently updated sites, like those run by news organizations, as often as several times an hour. Rarely updated, less popular sites might only be reindexed every few days. The method used to crawl the Web also means that if a Web site isn't the first page on a public server, or isn't linked to from another public page, then it'll never be found.[18] Also note that each search engine also offers a page where you can submit your Web site for indexing.

While search engines show you what they've found on their *copy* of the Web's contents; clicking a search result will direct you to the actual Web site, not the copy. But sometimes you'll click a result only to find that the Web site doesn't match what the search engine found. This happens if a Web site was updated before your search engine had a chance to reindex the changes. In most cases you can still pull up the search engine's copy of the page. Just click the "Cached" link below the result (the term **cache**, which is pronounced "cash," refers to a temporary storage space used to speed computing tasks).

But what if you want the content on your Web site to remain off limits to search engine indexing and caching? Organizations have created a set of standards to stop the spider crawl, and all commercial search engines have agreed to respect these standards. One way is to put a line of *HTML code* invisibly embedded in a Web page that tells all software robots to stop indexing a page, stop following links on the page, or stop offering old page archives in a cache. Users don't see this code, but commercial Web crawlers do. For those familiar with HTML code (the language used to describe a Web site), the command to stop Web crawlers from indexing a page, following links, and listing archives of cached pages looks like this:

⟨META NAME="ROBOTS" CONTENT="NOINDEX, NOFOLLOW, NOARCHIVE"⟩

There are other techniques to keep the spiders out, too. Web site administrators can add a special file (called robots.txt) that provides similar instructions on how indexing software should treat the Web site. And a lot of content lies inside the "**dark Web**," either behind corporate firewalls or inaccessible to those without a user account—think of private Facebook updates no one can see unless they're your friend—all of that is out of Google's reach.

spiders, Web crawlers, software robots

Software that traverses available Web links in an attempt to perform a given task. Search engines use spiders to discover documents for indexing and retrieval.

cache

A temporary storage space used to speed computing tasks.

dark Web

Internet content that can't be indexed by Google and other search engines.

What's It Take to Run This Thing?

Sergey Brin and Larry Page started Google with just four scavenged computers.[19] But in a decade, the infrastructure used to power the search sovereign has ballooned to the point where it is now the largest of its kind in the world.[20] Google doesn't disclose the number of servers it uses, but by some estimates, it runs over 1.4 million servers in over a dozen so-called **server farms** worldwide.[21] In the first three months of 2011 alone, the firm spent $890 million on data centers.[22] Building massive server farms to index the ever-growing Web is now the cost of admission for any firm wanting to compete in the search market. This is clearly no longer a game for two graduate students working out of a garage.

server farm

A massive network of computer servers running software to coordinate their collective use. Server farms provide the infrastructure backbone to SaaS and hardware cloud efforts, as well as many large-scale Internet services.

fault-tolerant

Capable of continuing operation even if a component fails.

Google's Container Data Center

Take a virtual tour of one of Google's data centers.

View the video online at: http://www.youtube.com/v/zRwPSFpLX8I

The size of this investment not only creates a barrier to entry, it influences industry profitability, with market-leader Google enjoying huge economies of scale. Firms may spend the same amount to build server farms, but if Google has roughly two-thirds of this market while Microsoft's search draws just a fraction of this traffic, which do you think enjoys the better return on investment?

The hardware components that power Google aren't particularly special. In most cases the firm uses the kind of Intel or AMD processors, low-end hard drives, and RAM chips that you'd find in a desktop PC. These components are housed in rack-mounted servers about 3.5 inches thick, with each server containing two processors, eight memory slots, and two hard drives.

In some cases, Google mounts racks of these servers inside standard-sized shipping containers, each with as many as 1,160 servers per box.[23] A given data center may have dozens of these server-filled containers all linked together. Redundancy is the name of the game. Google assumes individual components will regularly fail, but no single failure should interrupt the firm's operations (making the setup what geeks call **fault-tolerant**). If something breaks, a technician can easily swap it out with a replacement.

Each server farm layout has also been carefully designed with an emphasis on lowering power consumption and cooling requirements. And the firm's custom software (much of it built upon open source products) allows all this equipment to operate as the world's largest grid computer.

Web search is a task particularly well suited for the massively parallel architecture used by Google and its rivals. For an analogy of how this works, imagine that working alone (the human equivalent of a single-server effort), you need try to find a particular phrase in a hundred-page document. That'd take a while. Next, imagine that you can distribute the task across five thousand people, giving each of them a separate sentence to scan (that's the human equivalent of a multi-server grid). The speed difference between a single searching entity and a search involving many entities simultaneously focused on a subset of the same task gives you a sense of how search firms use massive numbers of servers and the divide-and-conquer approach of grid computing to quickly find the needles you're searching for within the Web's haystack. (For more on grid computing, see Chapter 5, and for more on server farms, see Chapter 10.)

The Google Search Appliance is a hardware product that firms can purchase in order to run Google search technology within the privacy and security of an organization's firewall.

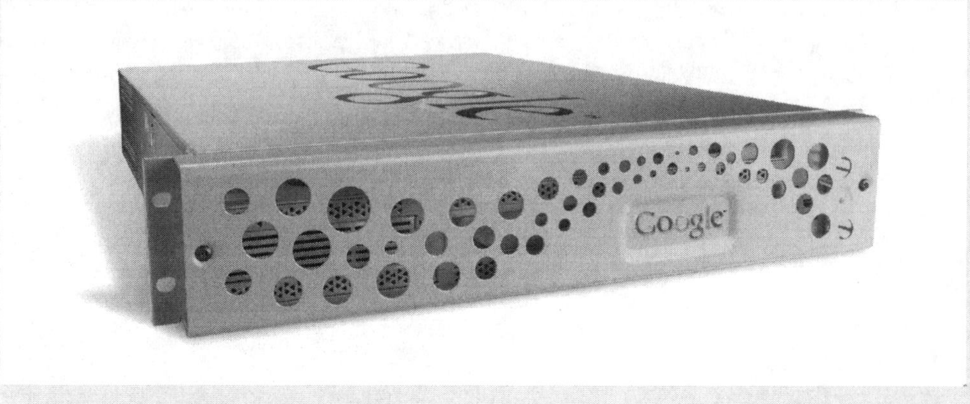

Google will even sell you a bit of its technology so that you can run your own little Google in-house without sharing documents with the rest of the world. Google's line of search appliances are rack-mounted servers that can index documents within the servers on a corporation's own network, even managing user password and security access on a per-document basis. Selling hardware isn't a large business for Google, and other vendors offer similar solutions, but search appliances can be vital tools for law firms, investment banks, and other document-rich organizations.

Trendspotting with Google

Google not only gives you search results, it lets you see aggregate trends in what its users are searching for, and this can yield powerful insights. For example, by tracking search trends for flu symptoms, Google's Flu Trends Web site can pinpoint outbreaks one to two weeks faster than the Centers for Disease Control and Prevention.[24] Want to go beyond the flu? Google's Trends, and Insights for Search services allow anyone to explore search trends, breaking out the analysis by region, category (image, news, product), date, and other criteria. Savvy managers can leverage these and similar tools for competitive analysis, comparing a firm, its brands, and its rivals.

Google Insights for Search can be a useful tool for competitive analysis and trend discovery. This chart shows a comparison (over a twelve-month period, and geographically) of search interest in the terms Wii, Playstation, and Xbox.

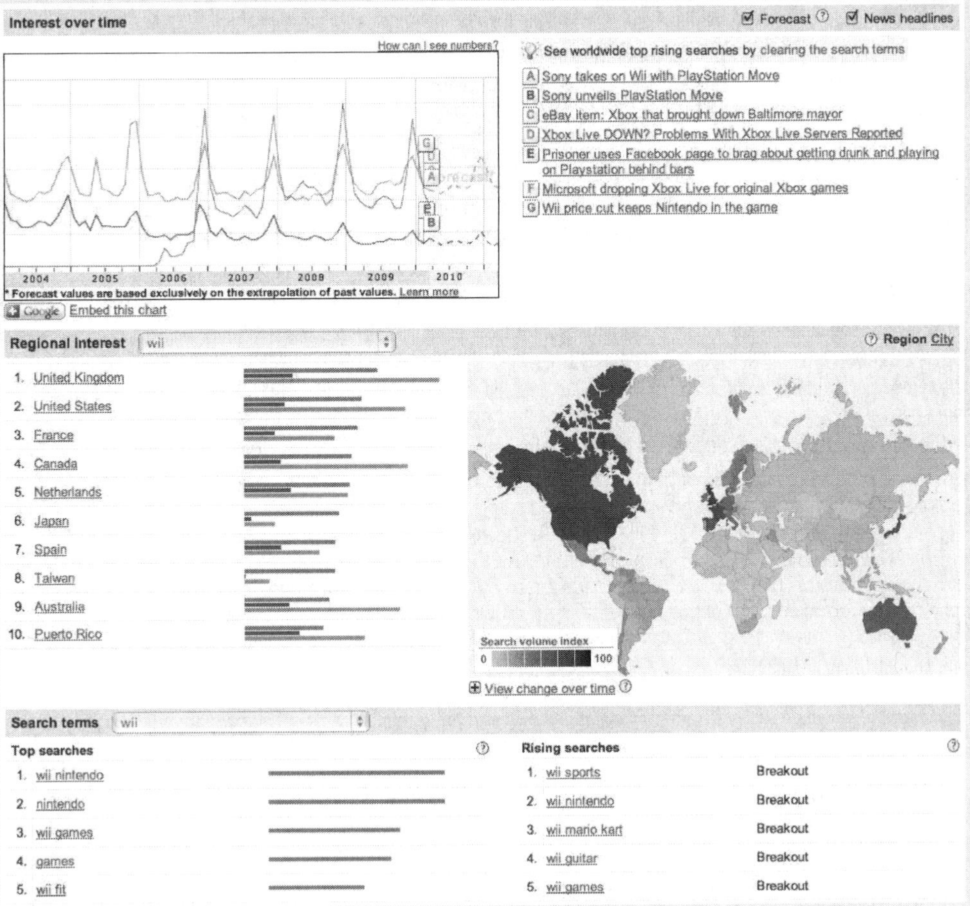

KEY TAKEAWAYS

- Ranked search results are often referred to as organic or natural search. PageRank is Google's algorithm for ranking search results. PageRank orders organic search results based largely on the number of Web sites linking to them, and the "weight" of each page as measured by its "influence."
- Search engine optimization (SEO) is the process of using natural or organic search to increase a Web site's traffic volume and visitor quality. The scope and influence of search has made SEO an increasingly vital marketing function.
- Users don't really search the Web; they search an archived copy stored on a search firm's computers. A firm creates such a copy by crawling and indexing discoverable documents.
- Google operates from a massive network of server farms containing hundreds of thousands of servers built from standard, off-the-shelf parts. The cost of the operation is a significant barrier to entry for competitors. Google's share of search suggests the firm can realize economies of scales over rivals required to make similar investments while delivering fewer results (and hence ads).
- Web site owners can hide pages from popular search engine Web crawlers using a number of methods, including HTML tags, a no-index file, or ensuring that Web sites aren't linked to other pages and haven't been submitted to Web sites for indexing.

QUESTIONS AND EXERCISES

1. How do search engines discover pages on the Internet? What kind of capital commitment is necessary to go about doing this? How does this impact competitive dynamics in the industry?
2. How does Google rank search results? Investigate and list some methods that an organization might use to improve its rank in Google's organic search results. Are there techniques Google might not approve of? What risk does a firm run if Google or another search firm determines that it has used unscrupulous SEO techniques to try to unfairly influence ranking algorithms?
3. Sometimes Web sites returned by major search engines don't contain the words or phrases that initially brought you to the site. Why might this happen?
4. What's a cache? What other products or services have a cache?
5. What can be done if you want the content on your Web site to remain off limits to search engine indexing and caching?
6. What is a "search appliance"? Why might an organization choose such a product?
7. Become a better searcher: Look at the advanced options for your favorite search engine. Are there options you hadn't used previously? Be prepared to share what you learn during class discussion.
8. Visit Google Trends and Google Insights for Search. Explore the tool as if you were comparing a firm with its competitors. What sorts of useful insights can you uncover? How might businesses use these tools?
9. Some Web sites are accused of being "content farms," offering low-quality content designed to attract searchers that include popular query terms and using this content to generate ad revenue. Demand Media, which went public at $1.5 billion, and Associated Content, which Yahoo! purchased for $100 million, have been accused of being content farms. Investigate the claims and visit these sites. Do you find the content useful? Do you think these sites are or are not content farms? Research how Google changed its ranking algorithm to penalize content farms. What has been the impact on these sites? Make a list of categories of firms and individuals that would likely be impacted by such moves. What does this tell you about Google's influence?

3. UNDERSTANDING THE INCREASE IN ONLINE AD SPENDING

LEARNING OBJECTIVES

1. **Understand how media consumption habits are shifting.**
2. **Be able to explain the factors behind the growth and appeal of online advertising.**

For several years, Internet advertising has been the only major media ad category to show significant growth. There are three factors driving online ad growth trends: (1) increased user time online, (2) improved measurement and accountability, and (3) targeting.

American teenagers (as well as the average British, Australian, and New Zealander Web surfer) now spend more time on the Internet than watching television.[25] They're reading fewer print publications, and radio listening among the iPod generation is down 30 percent.[26] So advertisers are simply following the market. Online channels also provide advertisers with a way to reach consumers at work—something that was previously much more difficult to do.

Many advertisers have also been frustrated by how difficult it's been to gauge the effectiveness of traditional ad channels such as TV, print, and radio. This frustration is reflected in the old industry saying, "I know that half of my advertising is working—I just don't know which half." Well, with the Internet, now you know. While measurement technologies aren't perfect, advertisers can now count ad **impressions** (the number of times an ad is shown on a Web site), whether a user clicks on an ad, and the product purchases or other Web site activity that comes from those clicks.[27] And as we'll see, many online ad payment schemes are directly linked to ad performance.

impression

Each time an ad is served to a user for viewing.

Various technologies and techniques also make it easier for firms to target users based on how likely a person is to respond to an ad. In theory a firm can use targeting to spend marketing dollars only on those users deemed to be its best prospects. Let's look at a few of these approaches in action.

KEY TAKEAWAYS

- There are three reasons driving online ad growth trends: (1) increasing user time online, (2) improved measurement and accountability, and (3) targeting.
- Digital media is decreasing time spent through traditional media consumption channels (e.g., radio, TV, newspapers), potentially lowering the audience reach of these old channels and making them less attractive for advertisers.
- Measurement techniques allow advertisers to track the performance of their ads—indicating things such as how often an ad is displayed, how often an ad is clicked, where an ad was displayed when it was clicked, and more. Measurement metrics can be linked to payment schemes, improving return on investment (ROI) and accountability compared to many types of conventional advertising.
- Advertising ROI can be improved through targeting. Targeting allows a firm to serve ads to specific categories of users, so firms can send ads to groups it is most interested in reaching, and those that are most likely to respond to an effort.

QUESTIONS AND EXERCISES

1. How does your media time differ from your parents? Does it differ among your older or younger siblings, or other relatives? Which media are you spending more time with? Less time with?
2. Put yourself in the role of a traditional media firm that is seeing its market decline. What might you do to address decline concerns? Have these techniques been attempted by other firms? Do you think they've worked well? Why or why not?
3. Put yourself in the role of an advertiser for a product or service that you're interested in. Is the Internet an attractive channel for you? How might you use the Internet to reach customers you are most interested in? Where might you run ads? Who might you target? Who might you avoid? How might the approach you use differ from traditional campaigns you'd run in print, TV, or radio? How might the size (money spent, attempted audience reach) and timing (length of time run, time between campaigns) of ad campaigns online differ from offline campaigns?
4. List ways in which you or someone you know has been targeted in an Internet ad campaign. Was it successful? How do you feel about targeting?

4. SEARCH ADVERTISING

LEARNING OBJECTIVES

1. Understand Google's search advertising revenue model.
2. Know the factors that determine the display and ranking of advertisements appearing on Google's search results pages.
3. Be able to describe the uses and technologies behind geotargeting.

search engine marketing (SEM)

The practice of designing, running and optimizing search engine ad campaigns.

The practice of running and optimizing search engine ad campaigns is referred to as **search engine marketing (SEM)**.[28] SEM is a hot topic in an increasingly influential field, so it's worth spending some time learning how search advertising works on the Internet's largest search engine.

Over two-thirds of Google's revenues come from ads served on its own sites, and the vast majority of this revenue comes from search engine ads.[29] During Google's early years, the firm actually resisted making money through ads. In fact, while at Stanford, Brin and Page even coauthored a paper titled "The Evils of Advertising."[30] But when Yahoo! and others balked at buying Google's search technology (offered for as little as $500,000), Google needed to explore additional revenue streams. It wasn't until two years after incorporation that Google ran ads alongside organic search results. That first ad, one for "Live Mail Order Lobsters," appeared just minutes after the firm posted a link reading "See Your Ad Here".[31]

keyword advertising

Advertisements that are targeted based on a user's query.

Google has only recently experimented with incorporating video and image ads into search, but for the most part, the ads you'll see to the right (and sometimes top) of Google's organic search results are text ads. These ads are **keyword advertising**, meaning they're targeted based on the words in a user's search query. Advertisers bid on the keywords and phrases that they'd like to use to trigger the display of their ad. Linking ads to search was a brilliant move, since the user's search term indicates an overt interest in a given topic. Want to sell hotel stays in Tahiti? Link your ads to the search term "Tahiti Vacation." Google ads show up when many users have some sort of *purchasing intent*. This makes Google search ads far more effective than standard display ads like those on Facebook (see Chapter 8 for a more detailed comparison of the two firms). Google's ability to tie advertising to purchasing intent (or to some other action that advertisers are willing to pay for) is the main reason the firm's ads are so valuable.

pay-per-click (PPC)

A concept where advertisers don't pay unless someone clicks on their ad.

cost-per-click (CPC)

The maximum amount of money an advertiser is willing to pay for each click on their ad.

Not only are search ads highly targeted, advertisers only pay for results. Text ads appearing on Google search pages are billed on a **pay-per-click (PPC)** basis, meaning that advertisers don't spend a penny unless someone actually clicks on their ad. Note that the term pay-per-click is sometimes used interchangeably with the term **cost-per-click (CPC)**.

Not Entirely Google's Idea

Google didn't invent pay-for-performance search advertising. A firm named GoTo.com (later renamed Overture) pioneered pay-per-click ads and bidding systems and held several key patents governing the technology. Overture provided pay-per-click ad services to both Yahoo! and Microsoft, but it failed to refine and match the killer combination of ad auctions and search technology that made Google a star. Yahoo! eventually bought Overture and sued Google for patent infringement. In 2004, the two firms settled, with Google giving Yahoo! 2.7 million shares in exchange for a "fully paid, perpetual license" to over sixty Overture patents.[32]

If an advertiser wants to display an ad on Google search, they can set up a Google AdWords advertising account in minutes, specifying just a single ad, or multiple ad campaigns that trigger different ads for different keywords. Advertisers also specify what they're willing to pay each time an ad is clicked, how much their overall ad budget is, and they can control additional parameters, such as the timing and duration of an ad campaign.

If no one clicks on an ad, Google doesn't make money, advertisers don't attract customers, and searchers aren't seeing ads they're interested in. So in order to create a winning scenario for everyone, Google has developed a precise ad ranking formula that rewards top performing ads by considering two metrics: the maximum CPC that an advertiser is willing to pay, and the advertisement's quality score—a broad measure of ad performance. Create high quality ads and your advertisements might appear ahead of competition, even if your competitors bid more than you. But if ads perform poorly they'll fall in rankings or even drop from display consideration.

Below is the formula used by Google to determine the rank order of sponsored links appearing on search results pages.

$$\text{Ad Rank} = \text{Maximum CPC} \times \text{Quality Score}$$

One factor that goes into determining an ad's quality score is the **click-through rate (CTR)** for the ad, the number of users who clicked an ad divided by the number of times the ad was delivered (the impressions). The CTR measures the percentage of people who clicked on an ad to arrive at a destination-site. Also included in a quality score are the overall history of click performance for the keywords linked to the ad, the relevance of an ad's text to the user's query, and Google's automated assessment of the user experience on the **landing page**—the Web page displayed when a user clicks on the ad. Ads that don't get many clicks, ad descriptions that have nothing to do with query terms, and ads that direct users to generic pages that load slowly or aren't strongly related to the keywords and descriptions used in an ad will all lower an ad's chance of being displayed.[33]

When an ad is clicked, advertisers don't actually pay their maximum CPC; Google discounts ads to just one cent more than the minimum necessary to maintain an ad's position on the page. So if you bid one dollar per click, but the ad ranked below you bids ninety cents, you'll pay just ninety-one cents if the ad is clicked. Discounting was a brilliant move. No one wants to get caught excessively overbidding rivals, so discounting helps reduce the possibility of this so-called bidder's remorse. And with this risk minimized, the system actually encouraged higher bids![34]

Ad ranking and cost-per-click calculations take place as part of an automated auction that occurs *every time* a user conducts a search. Advertisers get a running total of ad performance statistics so that they can monitor the return on their investment and tweak promotional efforts for better results. And this whole system is automated for self-service—all it takes is a credit card, an ad idea, and you're ready to go.

click-through rate (CTR)

The number of users who clicked an ad divided by the number of times the ad was delivered (the impressions). The CTR measures the percentage of people who clicked on an ad to arrive at a destination-site.

landing page

The Web page displayed when a user clicks on an advertisement.

4.1 How Much Do Advertisers Pay per Click?

Google rakes in billions on what amounts to pocket change earned one click at a time. Most clicks bring in between thirty cents and one dollar. However, costs can vary widely depending on industry and current competition. Table 14.1 shows some of the highest reported CPC rates. But remember, any values fluctuate in real time based on auction participants.

TABLE 14.1 10 Most Expensive Industries for Keyword Ads

Business/Industry	Keywords in the Top 100	Average CPC
Asbestos Lawyers	12	$68.03
Mesothelioma Lawyers	65	$67.18
Structured Settlements	8	$63.48
DUI Lawyers	14	$62.64
Criminal Defense Lawyers	1	$59.69

Source: Consolidated from SpyFu.com, June 2011.

Since rates are based on auctions, top rates reflect what the market is willing to bear. As an example, law firms, which bring in big bucks from legal fees, decisions, and settlement payments, often justify higher customer acquisition costs. And firms that see results will keep spending. Los Angeles–based Chase Law Group has said that it brings in roughly 60 percent of its clients through Internet advertising.[35]

4.2 IP Addresses and Geotargeting

Geotargeting occurs when computer systems identify a user's physical location (sometimes called the *geolocation*) for the purpose of delivering tailored ads or other content. On Google AdWords, for example, advertisers can specify that their ads only appear for Web surfers located in a particular country, state, metropolitan region, or a given distance around a precise locale. They can even draw a custom ad-targeting region on a map and tell Google to only show ads to users detected inside that space.

geotargeting

Identifying a user's physical location (sometimes called geolocation) for the purpose of delivering tailored ads or other content.

IP address

A value used to identify a device that is connected to the Internet. IP addresses are usually expressed as four numbers (from 0 to 255), separated by periods.

Ads in Google Search are geotargeted based on **IP address**. Every device connected to the Internet has a unique IP address assigned by the organization connecting the device to the network. Normally you don't see your IP address. It's likely a set of four numbers, from 0 to 255, separated by periods (e.g., 136.167.2.220), but this standard (known as IPv4) is gradually being replaced by the IPv6 standard, which offers far more potential addresses. IP addresses are used in targeting because the range of IP addresses "owned" by major organizations and Internet service providers (ISPs) is public knowledge. In many cases it's possible to make an accurate guess as to where a computer, laptop, or mobile phone is located simply by cross-referencing a device's current IP address with this public list.

For example, it's known that all devices connected to the Boston College network contain IP addresses starting with the numbers 136.167. If a search engine detects a query coming from an IP address that begins with those two numbers, it can be fairly certain that the person using that device is in the greater Boston area.

FIGURE 14.7

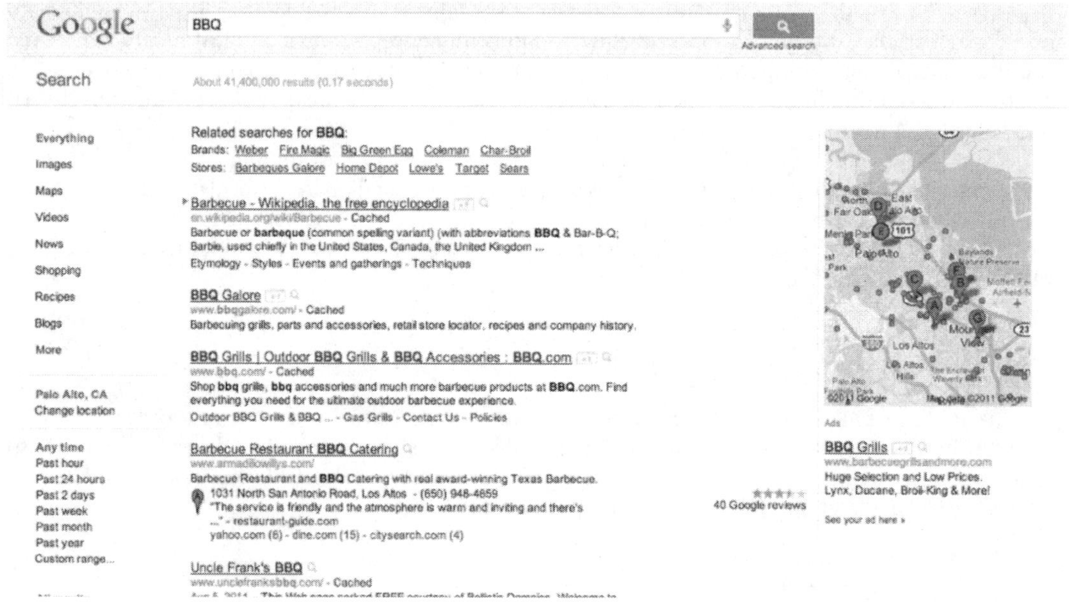

FIGURE 14.8

In this geotargeting example, the same search term is used at roughly the same time on separate computers located in Silicon Valley area (first image) and Boston (second image). Note how geotargeting impacts the search results and that the Boston-based search includes a geotargeted ad that does not show up in the Palo Alto search.

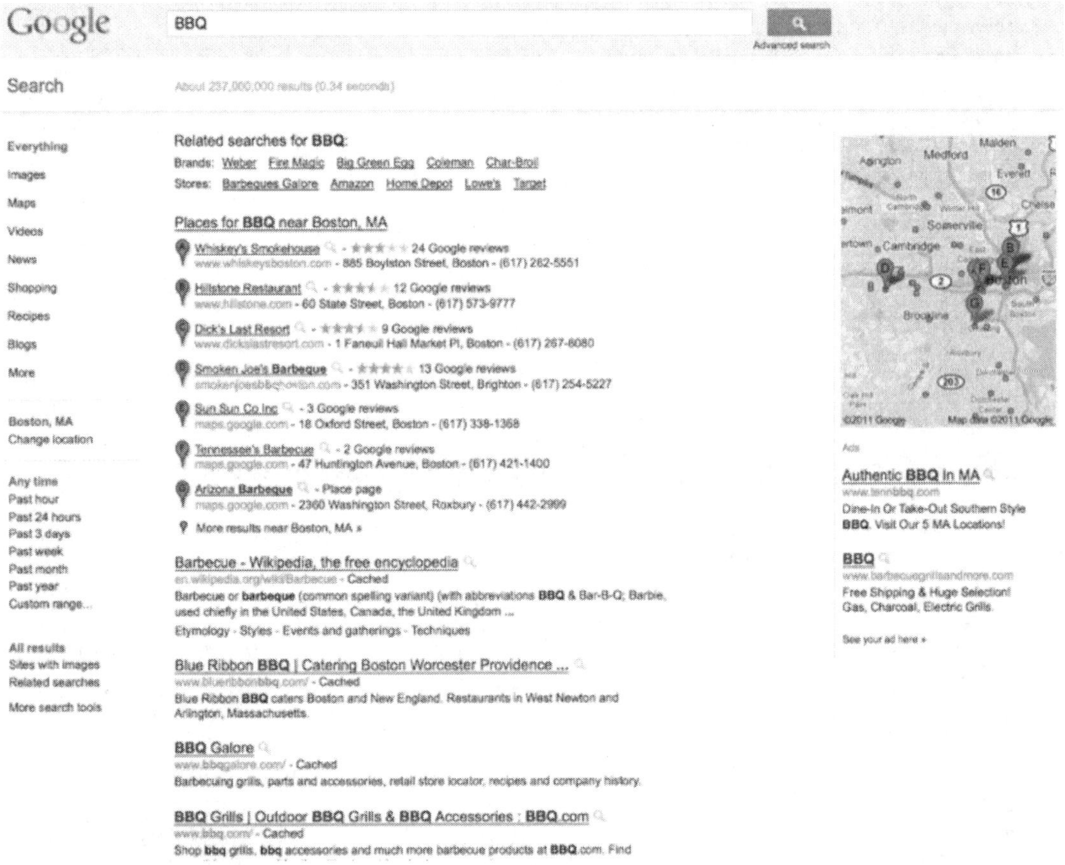

IP addresses will change depending on how and where you connect to the Internet. Connect your laptop to a hotel's Wi-Fi when visiting a new city, and you're likely to see ads specific to that location. That's because your Internet service provider has changed, and the firm serving your ads has detected that you are using an IP address known to be associated with your new location.

Geotargeting via IP address is fairly accurate, but it's not perfect. For example, some Internet service providers may provide imprecise or inaccurate information on the location of their networks. Others might be so vague that it's difficult to make a best guess at the geography behind a set of numbers (values assigned by a multinational corporation with many locations, for example). And there are other ways locations are hidden, such as when Internet users connect to **proxy servers**, third-party computers that pass traffic to and from a specific address without revealing the address of the connected users.

proxy servers

A third-party computer that passes traffic to and from a specific address without revealing the address of the connected user.

What's My IP Address?

While every operating system has a control panel or command that you can use to find your current IP address, there are also several Web sites that will quickly return this value (and a best guess at your current location). One such site is http://ip-adress.com (note the spelling has only one "d"). Visit this or a similar site with a desktop, laptop, and mobile phone. Do the results differ and are they accurate? Why?

Wi-Fi

A term used to brand wireless local-area networking devices. Devices typically connect to an antenna-equipped base station or hotspot, which is then connected to the Internet. Wi-Fi devices use standards known as IEEE 802.11, and various version of this standard (e.g., b, g, n) may operate in different frequency bands and have access ranges.

global positioning system (GPS)

A network of satellites and supporting technologies used to identify a device's physical location.

Geotargeting Evolves Beyond the IP Address

There are several other methods of geotargeting. Firms like Skyhook Wireless, Apple, and Google can identify a location based on mapping **Wi-Fi** hotspots and nearby cell towers. Many mobile devices come equipped with **global positioning system (GPS)** chips (identifying location via the GPS satellite network). And if a user provides location values such as a home address or zip code to a Web site, then that value might be stored and used again to make a future guess at a user's location.

Many firms build and maintain accurate location databases by regularly collecting location information from smartphones and using this data to refine maps. Phones submit data anonymously; however, this process can be controversial.

KEY TAKEAWAYS

- More than two-thirds of Google's revenues come from ads served on its own sites, and the vast majority of this revenue comes from search engine ads.
- Search ads on Google are both more effective (in terms of click-through rate) and more sought after by advertisers, because they are often associated with a user's purchasing intent.
- Advertisers choose and bid on the keywords and phrases that they'd like to use to trigger the display of their ad.
- Advertisers pay for cost-per-click advertising only if an ad is clicked on. Google makes no money on CPC ads that are displayed but not clicked.
- Google determines ad rank by multiplying CPC by Quality Score. Ads with low ranks might not display at all.
- Advertisers usually don't pay their maximum CPC. Instead, Google discounts ads to just one cent more than the minimum necessary to maintain an ad's position on the page—a practice that encourages higher bids.
- Geotargeting occurs when computer systems identify a user's physical location (sometimes called geolocation) for the purpose of delivering tailored ads or other content.
- Google uses IP addresses to target ads.
- Geotargeting can also be enabled by the satellite-based global positioning system (GPS) or based on estimating location from cell phone towers or Wi-Fi hotspots.

QUESTIONS AND EXERCISES

1. Which firm invented pay-per-click advertising? Why does Google dominate today and not this firm?
2. How are ads sold via Google search superior to conventional advertising media such as TV, radio, billboard, print, and yellow pages? Consider factors like the available inventory of space to run ads, the cost to run ads, the cost to acquire new advertisers, and the appeal among advertisers.
3. Are there certain kinds of advertising campaigns and goals where search advertising wouldn't be a good fit? Give examples and explain why.
4. Can a firm buy a top ad ranking? Why or why not?
5. List the four factors that determine an ad's quality score.
6. How much do firms typically pay for a single click?
7. Sites like SpyFu.com and KeywordSpy.com provide a list of the keywords with the highest cost per click. Visit the Top Lists page at SpyFu, KeywordSpy, or a comparable site, to find estimates of the current highest paying cost per click. Which keywords pay the most? Why do you think firms are willing to spend so much?
8. What is bidder's remorse? How does Google's ad discounting impact this phenomenon?
9. Visit http://www.ip-adress.com/ (or a similar Web site that displays a device's IP address) using a desktop, laptop, and mobile phone (work with a classmate or friend if you don't have access to one of these devices). How do results differ? Why? Are they accurate? What factors go into determining the accuracy of IP-based geolocation?
10. List and briefly describe other methods of geotargeting besides IP address, and indicate the situations and devices where these methods would be more and less effective.
11. The field of search engine marketing (SEM) is relatively new and rising in importance. And since the field is so new and constantly changing, there are plenty of opportunities for young, knowledgeable professionals. Which organizations, professional certification, and other resources are available to SEM professionals? Spend some time searching for these resources online and be prepared to share your findings with your class.

5. AD NETWORKS—DISTRIBUTION BEYOND SEARCH

LEARNING OBJECTIVES

1. **Understand ad networks, and how ads are distributed and served based on Web site content.**
2. **Recognize how ad networks provide advertiser reach and support niche content providers.**
3. **Be aware of content adjacency problems and their implications.**
4. **Know the strategic factors behind ad network appeal and success.**

Google runs ads not just in search, but also across a host of Google-owned sites like Gmail, Google News, and Blogger. It will even tailor ads for its map products and for mobile devices. But about 30 percent of Google's revenues come from running ads on Web sites that the firm doesn't even own.[36]

Next time you're surfing online, look around the different Web sites that you visit and see how many sport boxes labeled "Ads by Google." Those Web sites are participating in Google's AdSense ad network, which means they're running ads for Google in exchange for a cut of the take. Participants range from small-time bloggers to some of the world's most highly trafficked sites. Google lines up the advertisers, provides the targeting technology, serves the ads, and handles advertiser payment collection. To participate, content providers just sign up online, put a bit of Google-supplied HTML code on their pages, and wait for Google to send them cash (Web sites typically get about seventy to eighty cents for every AdSense dollar that Google collects).[37]

Google originally developed AdSense to target ads based on keywords automatically detected inside the content of a Web site. A blog post on your favorite sports team, for example, might be accompanied by ads from ticket sellers or sports memorabilia vendors. AdSense and similar online ad networks provide advertisers with access to the long tail of niche Web sites by offering both increased opportunities for ad exposure as well as more-refined targeting opportunities.

FIGURE 14.9

The images show advertising embedded around a story on the *New York Times* Web site. The page runs several ads provided by different ad networks. For example, the WebEx banner ad above the article's headline was served by the AOL Advertising network. The "Ads by Google" box appeared at the end of the article. Note how the Google ads are related to the content of the *Times* article.

Running ads on your Web site is by no means a guaranteed path to profits. The Internet graveyard is full of firms that thought they'd be able to sustain their businesses on ads alone. But for many Web sites, ad networks can be like oxygen, sustaining them with revenue opportunities they'd never be able to achieve on their own.

For example, AdSense provided early revenue for the multimillion-dollar *TechCrunch* media empire. It supports Disaboom, a site run by physician and quadriplegic Dr. Glen House. And it continues to be the primary revenue generator for AskTheBuilder.com. That site's founder, former builder Tim Carter, had been writing a handyman's column syndicated to some thirty newspapers. The newspaper columns didn't bring in enough to pay the bills, but with AdSense he hit pay dirt, pulling in over $350,000 in ad revenue in just his first year![38]

FIGURE 14.10

Tim Carter's Ask the Builder Web site runs ads from Google and other ad networks. Note different ad formats surrounding the content. Video ads are also integrated into many of the site's video tutorials.

contextual advertising

Advertising based on a Web site's content.

content adjacency problem

A situation where ads appear alongside text the advertiser would like to avoid.

BEWARE THE CONTENT ADJACENCY PROBLEM

Contextual advertising based on keywords is lucrative, but like all technology solutions it has its limitations. Vendors sometimes suffer from **content adjacency problems** when ads appear alongside text they'd prefer to avoid. In one particularly embarrassing example, a *New York Post* article detailed a gruesome murder where hacked up body parts were stowed in suitcases. The online version of the article included contextual advertising and was accompanied by...luggage ads.[39]

To combat embarrassment, ad networks provide opportunities for both advertisers and content providers to screen out potentially undesirable pairings based on factors like vendor, Web site, and category. Advertisers can also use negative keywords, which tell networks to avoid showing ads when specific words appear (e.g., setting negative keywords to "murder" or "killer" could have spared luggage advertisers from the embarrassing problem mentioned above). Ad networks also refine ad-placement software based on feedback from prior incidents (for more on content adjacency problems, see Chapter 8).

Google launched AdSense in 2003, but Google is by no means the only company to run an ad network nor was it the first to come up with the idea. Rivals include the Yahoo! Publisher Network, Microsoft's adCenter, AdBrite, and AOL Advertising. Advertisers also aren't limited to choosing just one ad network. In fact, many content provider Web sites will serve ads from several ad networks (as well as exclusive space sold by their own sales force), oftentimes mixing several different offerings on the same page.

5.1 Ad Networks and Competitive Advantage

While advertisers can use multiple ad networks, there are several key strategic factors driving the industry. For Google, its ad network is a distribution play. The ability to reach more potential customers across more Web sites attracts more advertisers to Google. And content providers (the Web sites that distribute these ads) want there to be as many advertisers as possible in the ad networks that they join, since this should increase the price of advertising, the number of ads served, and the accuracy of user targeting. If advertisers attract content providers, which in turn attract more advertisers, then we've just described network effects! More participants bringing in more revenue also help the firm benefit from scale economies—offering a better return on investment from its ad technology and infrastructure. No wonder Google's been on such a tear—the firm's loaded with assets for competitive advantage!

Google's Ad Reach Gets Bigger

While Google has the largest network specializing in distributing text ads, it had been a laggard in graphical display ads (sometimes called image ads). That changed with the firm's $3.1 billion acquisition of display ad network and targeting company DoubleClick. Now in terms of the number of users reached, Google controls both the largest text ad network and the largest display ad network.[40]

KEY TAKEAWAYS

- Google also serves ads through non-Google partner sites that join its ad network. These partners distribute ads for Google in exchange for a percentage of the take.
- AdSense ads are targeted based on keywords that Google detects inside the content of a Web site.
- AdSense and similar online ad networks provide advertisers with access to the long tail of niche Web sites.
- Ad networks handle advertiser recruitment, ad serving, and revenue collection, opening up revenue earning possibilities to even the smallest publishers.

QUESTIONS AND EXERCISES

1. On a percentage basis, how important is AdSense to Google's revenues?
2. Why do ad networks appeal to advertisers? Why do they appeal to content providers? What functions are assumed by the firm overseeing the ad network?
3. What factors determine the appeal of an ad network to advertisers and content providers? Which of these factors are potentially sources of competitive advantage?
4. Do dominant ad networks enjoy strong network effects? Are there also strong network effects that drive consumers to search? Why or why not?
5. How difficult is it for a Web site to join an ad network? What does this imply about ad network switching costs? Does it have to exclusively choose one network over another? Does ad network membership prevent a firm from selling its own online advertising, too?
6. What is the content adjacency problem? Why does it occur? What classifications of Web sites might be particularly susceptible to the content adjacency problem? What can advertisers do to minimize the likelihood that a content adjacency problem will occur?

6. MORE AD FORMATS AND PAYMENT SCHEMES

LEARNING OBJECTIVES

1. **Know the different formats and media types that Web ads can be displayed in.**
2. **Know the different ways ads are sold.**
3. **Know that games can be an ad channel under the correct conditions.**

Online ads aren't just about text ads billed in CPC. Ads running through Google AdSense, through its DoubleClick subsidiary, or on most competitor networks can be displayed in several formats and media types, and can be billed in different ways. The specific ad formats supported depend on the ad network but can include the following: **image (or display) ads** (such as horizontally oriented banners, smaller rectangular buttons, and vertically oriented "skyscraper" ads); **rich media ads** (which can include animation or video); and **interstitials** (ads that run before a user arrives at a Web site's contents). The industry trade group, the **Internet Advertising Bureau (IAB)** sets common standards for display ads so that a single creative (the design and content of the advertisement) can run unmodified across multiple ad networks and Web sites.[41]

And there are lots of other ways ads are sold besides cost-per-click. Most graphical display ads are sold according to the number of times the ad appears (the **impression**). Ad rates are quoted in **CPM**, meaning cost per thousand impressions (the M representing the roman numeral for one thousand). Display ads sold on a CPM basis are often used as part of branding campaigns targeted more at creating awareness than generating click-throughs. Such techniques often work best for promoting products like soft drinks, toothpaste, or movies.

image (or display) ads

Graphical advertising (as opposed to text ads).

rich media ads

Online ads that include animation, audio, or video.

interstitials

Ads that run before a user arrives at a Web site's contents.

Internet Advertising Bureau (IAB)

A nonprofit industry trade group for the interactive advertising industry. The IAB evaluates and recommends interactive advertising standards and practices and also conducts research, education, and legislative lobbying.

impression

Each time an advertisement is displayed.

CPM

Cost per thousand impressions (the M representing the roman numeral for one thousand).

cost-per-action (CPA)

A method of charging for advertising whenever a user performs a specified action such as signing up for a service, requesting material, or making a purchase.

affiliate program

A cost-per-action program, where program sponsors (e.g., Amazon.com, iTunes) pay referring Web sites a percentage of revenue earned from the referral.

Cost-per-action (CPA) ads pay whenever a user clicks through and performs a specified action such as signing up for a service, requesting material, or making a purchase. **Affiliate programs** are a form of cost-per-action, where vendors share a percentage of revenue with Web sites that direct purchasing customers to their online storefronts. Amazon runs the world's largest affiliate program, and referring sites can earn 4 percent to 15 percent of sales generated from these click-throughs. Purists might not consider affiliate programs as advertising (rather than text or banner ads, Amazon's affiliates offer links and product descriptions that point back to Amazon's Web site), but these programs can be important tools in a firm's promotional arsenal.

And rather than buying targeted ads, a firm might sometimes opt to become an exclusive advertiser on a site. For example, a firm could buy access to all ads served on a site's main page; it could secure exclusive access to a region of the page (such as the topmost banner ad); or it may pay to sponsor a particular portion or activity on a Web site (say a parenting forum, or a "click-to-print" button). Such deals can be billed based on a flat rate, CPM, CPC, or any combination of metrics.

Ads in Games?

As consumers spend more time in video games, it's only natural that these products become ad channels, too. Finding a way to introduce ads without eroding the game experience can be a challenge. Advertising can work in racing or other sports games (the Obama campaign famously ran virtual billboards in EA's Burnout Paradise), but ads make less sense for games set in the past, future, or on other worlds. Branding ads often work best since click-throughs are typically not something you want disrupting your gaming experience.

Advertisers have also explored sponsorships of Web-based and mobile games. Sponsorships often work best with casual games, such as those offered on Yahoo! Games or EA's Pogo. Firms have also created online mini games (so-called *advergames*) for longer term, immersive brand engagement (e.g., Mini Cooper's Slide Parking and Stride Gum's Chew Challenge). Others have tried a sort of virtual product placement integrated into experiences. A version of The Sims, for example, included virtual replicas of real-world inventory from IKEA and H&M. And Zynga has done a variety of in-game promotions that include work with Lady Gaga in Farmville and CityVille promotions of Kung Fu Panda 2.

Obama Campaign's Virtual Billboard in EA's Burnout Paradise

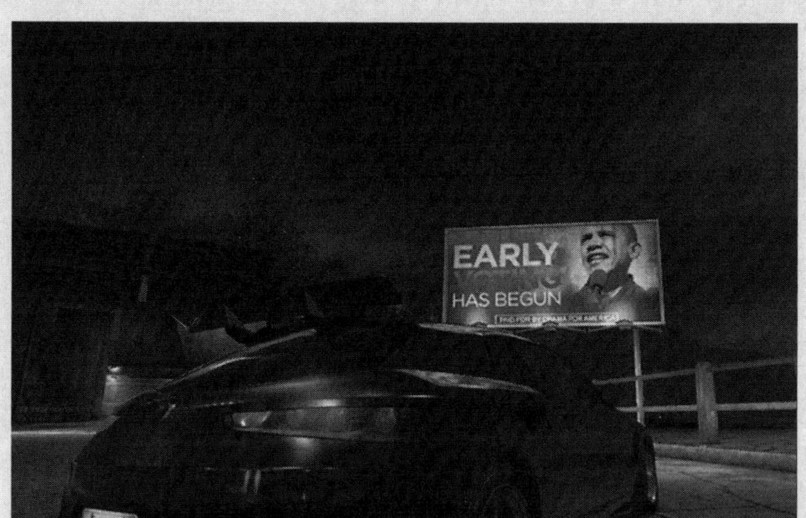

Source: Barack Obama U.S. Presidential Campaign Team, 2008.

In-game ad-serving technology also lacks the widely accepted standards of Web-based ads, so it's unlikely that ads designed for a Wii sports game could translate into a PS3 first-person shooter.

In-game advertising shows promise, but the medium is considerably more complicated than conventional Web site ads. That complexity lowers relative ROI and will likely continue to constrain growth. As a sign of the difficulty in the space, consider that Microsoft shuttered its in-game advertising unit, Massive, just four years after acquiring the firm for an estimated $200 million to $400 million.[42]

KEY TAKEAWAYS

- Web ad formats include, but are not limited to, the following: *image* (or *display*) *ads* (such as horizontally oriented *banners*, smaller rectangular *buttons*, and vertically oriented *skyscraper ads*), *rich media ads* (which can include animation or video), and *interstitials* (ads that run before a user arrives at a Web site's contents).
- In addition to cost-per-click, ads can be sold based on the number of times the ad appears (impressions), whenever a user performs a specified action such as signing up for a service, requesting material, or making a purchase (cost-per-action), or on an exclusive basis which may be billed at a flat rate.
- In-game advertising shows promise, with successful branding campaigns run as part of sports games, through in-game product placement, or via sponsorship of casual games, or in brand-focused advergames.
- A lack of standards, concerns regarding compatibility with gameplay, and the cost of developing and distributing games are all stifling the growth of in-game ads.

QUESTIONS AND EXERCISES

1. What is the IAB and why is it necessary?
2. What are the major ad format categories?
3. What's an interstitial? What's a rich media ad? Have you seen these? Do you think they are effective? Why or why not?
4. List four major methods for billing online advertising.
5. Which method is used to bill most graphical advertising? What's the term used for this method and what does it stand for?
6. How many impressions are recorded if a single user is served the same ad one thousand times? How many if one thousand users are served the same ad once?
7. Imagine the two scenarios below. Decide which type of campaign would be best for each: text-based CPC advertising or image ads paid for on a CPM basis. Explain your reasoning.
    a. Netflix is looking to attract new customers by driving traffic to its Web site in hopes that this will increase subscriptions.
    b. A movie studio would like to promote the upcoming theatrical release of a new major motion picture.
8. Which firm runs the world's largest affiliate program? Why is this form of advertising particularly advantageous to the firm (think about the ROI for this sort of effort)?
9. Given examples where in-game advertising might work and those where it might be less desirable. List key reasons why in-game advertising has not be as successful as other forms Internet-distributed ads.

7. CUSTOMER PROFILING AND BEHAVIORAL TARGETING

LEARNING OBJECTIVES

1. **Be familiar with various tracking technologies and how they are used for customer profiling and ad targeting.**
2. **Understand why customer profiling is both valuable and controversial.**
3. **Recognize steps that organizations can take to help ease consumer and governmental concerns.**

Advertisers are willing to pay more for ads that have a greater chance of reaching their target audience, and online firms have a number of targeting tools at their disposal. Much of this targeting occurs whenever you visit a Web site, where a behind-the-scenes software dialogue takes place between Web browser and Web server that can reveal a number of pieces of information, including IP address, the type of browser used, the computer type, its operating system, and unique identifiers, called cookies.

cookie

A line of identifying text, assigned and retrieved by a given Web server and stored by your browser.

And remember, *any* server that serves you content can leverage these profiling technologies. You might be profiled not just by the Web site that you're visiting (e.g., nytimes.com), but also by any ad networks that serve ads on that site (e.g., Platform-A, DoubleClick, Google AdSense, Microsoft adCenter).

IP addresses are leveraged extensively in customer profiling. An IP address not only helps with geolocation, it can also indicate a browser's employer or university, which can be further matched with information such as firm size or industry. IBM has used IP targeting to tailor its college recruiting banner ads to specific schools, for example, "There Is Life After Boston College, Click Here to See Why." That campaign garnered click-through rates ranging from 5 to 30 percent[43] compared to average rates that are currently well below 1 percent for untargeted banner ads. DoubleClick once even served a banner that included a personal message for an executive at then-client Modem Media. The ad, reading "Congratulations on the twins, John Nardone," was served across hundreds of sites, but was only visible from computers that accessed the Internet from the Modem Media corporate network.[44]

The ability to identify a surfer's computer, browser, or operating system can also be used to target tech ads. For example, Google might pitch its Chrome browser to users detected running Internet Explorer, Firefox, or Safari; while Apple could target Mac ads just to Windows users.

But perhaps the greatest degree of personalization and targeting comes from cookies. Visit a Web site for the first time, and in most cases, a dialogue between server and browser takes place that goes something like this:

Server: *Have I seen you before?*

Browser: *No.*

Server: *Then take this unique string of numbers and letters (called a cookie). I'll use it to recognize you from now on.*

The cookie is just a line of identifying text assigned and retrieved by a given Web server and stored on your computer by your browser. Upon accepting this cookie your browser has been tagged, like an animal. As you surf around the firm's Web site, that cookie can be used to build a profile associated with your activities. If you're on a portal like Yahoo! you might type in your zip code, enter stocks that you'd like to track, and identify the sports teams you'd like to see scores for. The next time you return to the Web site, your browser responds to the server's "*Have I see you before?*" question with the equivalent of "*Yes, you know me*;," and it presents the cookie that the site gave you earlier. The site can then match this cookie against your browsing profile, showing you the weather, stock quotes, sports scores, and other info that it thinks you're interested in.

Cookies are used for lots of purposes. Retail Web sites like Amazon use cookies to pay attention to what you've shopped for and bought, tailoring Web sites to display products that the firm suspects you'll be most interested in. Sites also use cookies to keep track of what you put in an online "shopping cart," so if you quit browsing before making a purchase, these items will reappear the next time you visit. And many Web sites also use cookies as part of a "remember me" feature, storing user IDs and passwords. Beware this last one! If you check the "remember me" box on a public Web browser, the next person who uses that browser is potentially using *your* cookie, and can log in as you!

third-party cookies

Sometimes called "tracking cookies" and are served by ad networks or other customer profiling firms. Tracking cookies are used to identify users and record behavior across multiple Web sites.

An organization can't read cookies that it did not give you. So businessweek.com can't tell if you've also got cookies from forbes.com. But you can see all of the cookies in your browser. Take a look and you'll almost certainly see cookies from dozens of Web sites that you've never visited before. These are **third-party cookies** (sometimes called *tracking cookies*), and they are usually served by ad networks or other customer profiling firms.

FIGURE 14.12

The Preferences setting in most Web browsers allows you to see its cookies. This browser has received cookies from several ad networks, media sites, and the University of Minnesota Carlson School of Management.

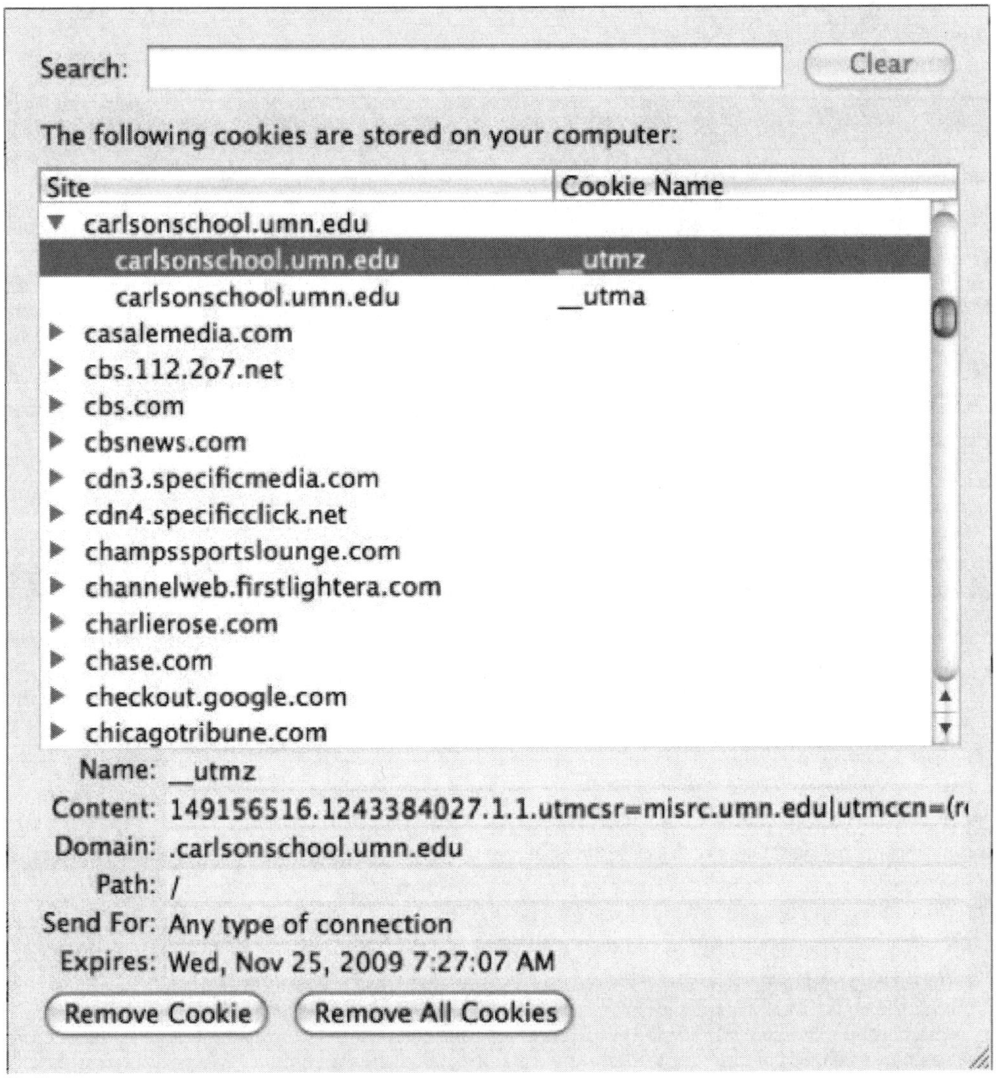

By serving and tracking cookies in ads shown across partner sites, ad networks can build detailed browsing profiles that include sites visited, specific pages viewed, duration of visit, and the types of ads you've seen and responded to. And that surfing might give an advertising network a better guess at demographics like gender, age, marital status, and more. Visit a new parent site and expect to see diaper ads in the future, even when you're surfing for news or sports scores!

But What If I Don't Want a Cookie!

If all of this creeps you out, remember that you're in control. The most popular Web browsers allow you to block all cookies, block just third-party cookies, purge your cookie file, or even ask for your approval before accepting a cookie. Of course, if you block cookies, you block any benefits that come along with them, and some Web site features may require cookies to work properly. Also note that while deleting a cookie breaks a link between your browser and that Web site, if you supply identifying information in the future (say by logging into an old profile), the site might be able to assign your old profile data to the new cookie.

While the Internet offers targeting technologies that go way beyond traditional television, print, and radio offerings, none of these techniques is perfect. Since users are regularly assigned different IP addresses as they connect and disconnect from various physical and Wi-Fi networks, IP targeting can't reliably identify individual users. Cookies also have their weaknesses. They're assigned by browsers and associated with a given user's account on that computer. That means that if several people use the same browser on the same computer without logging on to that machine as separate users, then all their Web surfing activity may be mixed into the same cookie profile. (One solution is to create different log-in accounts on that computer. Your PC will then keep separate cookies for each account.) Some users might also use different browsers on the same machine or use different computers. Unless a firm has a way to match up these different cookies assigned across browsers (say by linking cookies on separate machines to a single log-in used at multiple locations), then a site may be working with multiple, incomplete profiles.

KEY TAKEAWAYS

- The communication between Web browser and Web server can identify IP address, the type of browser used, the computer type, its operating system, time and date of access, and duration of Web page visit, and can read and assign unique identifiers, called cookies—all of which can be used in customer profiling and ad targeting.
- An IP address not only helps with geolocation; it can also be matched against other databases to identify the organization providing the user with Internet access (such as a firm or university), that organization's industry, size, and related statistics.
- A cookie is a unique line of identifying text, assigned and retrieved by a given Web server and stored on a computer by the browser, that can be used to build a profile associated with your Web activities.
- The most popular Web browsers allow you to block all cookies, block just third-party cookies, purge your cookie file, or even ask for your approval before accepting a cookie.

QUESTIONS AND EXERCISES

1. Give examples of how the ability to identify a surfer's computer, browser, or operating system can be used to target tech ads.
2. Describe how IBM targeted ad delivery for its college recruiting efforts. What technologies were used? What was the impact on click-through rates?
3. What is a cookie? How are cookies used? Is a cookie a computer program? Which firms can read the cookies in your Web browser?
4. Does a cookie accurately identify a user? Why or why not?
5. What is the danger of checking the "remember me" box when logging in to a Web site using a public computer?
6. What's a third-party cookie? What kinds of firms might use these? How are they used?
7. How can users restrict cookie use on their Web browsers? What is the downside of blocking cookies?
8. Work with a faculty member and join the Google Online Marketing Challenge (held in the spring of every year—see http://www.google.com/onlinechallenge). Google offers ad credits for student teams to develop and run online ad campaigns for real clients and offers prizes for winning teams. Some of the experiences earned in the Google Challenge can translate to other ad networks as well; and first-hand client experience has helped many students secure jobs, internships, and even start their own businesses.

8. PROFILING AND PRIVACY

LEARNING OBJECTIVES

1. **Understand the privacy concerns that arise as a result of using third-party or tracking cookies to build user profiles.**
2. **Be aware of the negative consequences that could result from the misuse of third-party or tracking cookies.**
3. **Know the steps Google has taken to demonstrate its sensitivity to privacy issues.**
4. **Know the kinds of user information that Google stores, and the steps Google takes to protect the privacy of that information.**

While AdSense has been wildly successful, contextual advertising has its limits. For example, what kind of useful targeting can firms really do based on the text of a news item on North Korean nuclear testing?[45] For more accurate targeting, Google offers what it calls "interest-based ads," which is based on a third-party cookie that tracks browsing activity across Google properties and AdSense partner sites.

AdSense builds a profile, identifying users within dozens of broad categories and over six hundred subcategories.[46] Of course, there's a financial incentive to do this too. Ads deemed more interesting should garner more clicks, meaning more potential customer leads for advertisers, more revenue for Web sites that run AdSense, and more money for Google.

But while targeting can benefit Web surfers, users will resist if they feel that they are being mistreated, exploited, or put at risk. Negative backlash might also result in a change in legislation. The U.S. Federal Trade Commission has already called for more transparency and user control in online advertising and for requesting user consent (**opt-in**) when collecting sensitive data.[47] Mishandled user privacy could curtail targeting opportunities, limiting growth across the online advertising field. And with less ad support, many of the Internet's free services could suffer.

opt-in

Program (typically a marketing effort) that requires customer consent. This program is contrasted with opt-out programs, which enroll all customers by default.

FIGURE 14.13

Here's an example of one user's interests, as tracked by Google's "Interest-based Ads" and displayed in the firm's "Ad Preferences Manager."

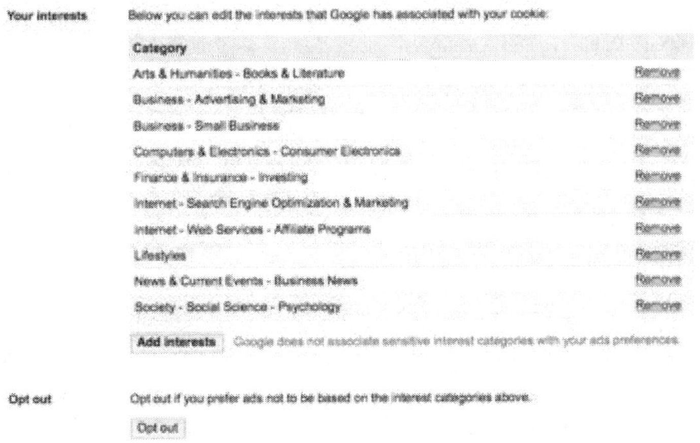

Google's roll-out of interest-based ads shows the firm's sensitivity to these issues. The firm has also placed significant control in the hands of users, with options at program launch that were notably more robust than those of its competitors.[48] Each interest-based ad is accompanied by an "Ads by Google" link that will bring users to a page describing Google advertising and which provides access to the company's "Ads Preferences Manager." This tool allows surfers to see any of the hundreds of potential categorizations that Google has assigned to that browser's tracking cookie. Users can remove categorizations, and even add interests if they want to improve ad targeting. Some topics are too sensitive to track, and the technology avoids profiling race, religion, sexual orientation, health, political or trade union affiliation, and certain financial categories.[49]

Google also allows users to install a cookie that opts them out of interest-based tracking. And since browser cookies can expire or be deleted, the firm has gone a step further, offering a browser **plug-in** that will remain permanent, even if a user's **opt-out** cookie is purged.

plug-in

A small computer program that extends the feature set or capabilities of another application.

opt-out

Programs that enroll all customers by default, but that allow consumers to discontinue participation if they want to.

Google, Privacy Advocates, and the Law

Google's moves are meant to demonstrate transparency in its ad targeting technology, and the firm's policies may help raise the collective privacy bar for the industry. While privacy advocates have praised Google's efforts to put more control in the hands of users, many continue to voice concern over what they see as the increasing amount of information that the firm houses.[50] For an avid user, Google could conceivably be holding e-mail (Gmail), photos (Picasa), social media activity (Google+), a Web surfing profile (AdSense and DoubleClick), location (Google Latitude), appointments (Google Calendar), music and other media (Google Play), files stored in the cloud (Google Drive), transcripts of phone messages (Google Voice), work files (Google Docs), and more.

Google insists that reports portraying it as a data-hoarding Big Brother are inaccurate. Data is not sold to third parties. Any targeting is fully disclosed, with users empowered to opt out at all levels.[51] Google has introduced several tools, including Google Dashboard and Google Ad Preferences Manager, that allow users to see information Google stores about them, clear their browsing history, and selectively delete collected data.[52] But critics counter that corporate intentions and data use policies (articulated in a Web site's Terms of Service) can change over time, and that a firm's good behavior today is no guarantee of good behavior in the future.[53] Google has modified its policy several times in the past, including changes that now allow the firm to link search history to ad targeting. It has also unified its privacy policy in a way that allows for greater profiling, sharing, and tailored services across Google offerings.[54]

Google does enjoy a lot of user goodwill, and it is widely recognized for its unofficial motto "Don't Be Evil." However, some worry that even though Google might not be evil, it could still make a mistake, and that despite its best intentions, a security breach or employee error could leave data dangerously or embarrassingly exposed.

Gaffes have repeatedly occurred. A system flaw inadvertently shared some Google Docs with contacts who were never granted access to them.[55] When the firm introduced its Google Buzz social networking service, many users were horrified that their most frequently used Gmail contacts were automatically added to Buzz, allowing others to see who you're communicating with. As one report explained, "Suddenly, journalists' clandestine contacts were exposed, secret affairs became dramatically less secret, and stalkers obtained a new tool to harass their victims. Oops."[56] Eleven congressmen subsequently asked the U.S. Federal Trade Commission to investigate the Google Buzz for possible breaches of consumer privacy.[57] Google admitted that some of its "Street View" cars, while driving through neighborhoods and taking photos for Google maps, had inadvertently collected personal data, including e-mails and passwords.[58] And in May 2011, Google scrambled to plug a hole that could potentially allow hackers to access the contacts, calendars, and photos on Android phones connecting to the Internet over open Wi-Fi networks.[59] A rogue employee was fired for violating the firm's strict guidelines and procedures on information access.[60] The firm has also been accused of bypassing privacy settings in Apple's Safari web browser in order to better track users.[61]

Privacy advocates also worry that the amount of data stored by Google serves as one-stop shopping for litigators and government investigators. The counter argument points to the fact that Google has continually reflected an aggressive defense of data privacy in court cases. When Viacom sued Google over copyright violations in YouTube, the search giant successfully fought the original subpoena, which had requested user-identifying information.[62] Google has also resisted Justice Department subpoenas for search queries, while rivals have complied.[63]

Google has also claimed that it has been targeted by some foreign governments that are deliberately hacking or interfering with the firm's services in order to quash some information sharing and to uncover dissident activity.[64]

Google is increasingly finding itself in precedent-setting cases where the law is vague. Google's Street View, for example, has been the target of legal action in the United States, Canada, Japan, Greece, and the United Kingdom. Varying legal environments create a challenge to the global rollout of any data-driven initiative.[65]

Ad targeting brings to a head issues of opportunity, privacy, security, risk, and legislation. Google is now taking a more active public relations and lobbying role to prevent misperceptions and to be sure its positions are understood. While the field continues to evolve, Google's experience will lay the groundwork for the future of personalized technology and provide a case study for other firms that need to strike the right balance between utility and privacy. Despite differences, it seems clear to Google, its advocates, and its detractors that with great power comes great responsibility.

KEY TAKEAWAYS

- Possible consequences resulting from the misuse of customer tracking and profiling technologies include user resistance and legislation. Mishandled user privacy could curtail targeting opportunities and limit growth in online advertising. With less ad support, many of the Internet's free services could suffer.
- Google has taken several steps to protect user privacy. The firm offers several tools that enable users not only to see information that Google collects but also to delete, pause, or modify data collection and profiling terms.
- Google's "Ads Preferences Manager" allows surfers to see, remove, and add to, any of the categorizations that Google has assigned to that browser's tracking cookie. The technology also avoids targeting certain sensitive topics. The firm's Privacy Dashboard provides additional access to and user control over Google's profiling and data collection.
- Google allows users to install a cookie or plug-in that opts them out of interest-based tracking.
- Some privacy advocates have voiced concern over what they see as the increasing amount of information that Google and other firms collect.
- Even the best-intentioned and most competent firms can have a security breach that compromises stored information. Google has suffered privacy breaches from product flaws and poorly planned feature rollouts, as well as deliberate hacks and attacks. The firm has also changed policies regarding data collection and privacy as its services have evolved. Such issues may lead to further investigation, legislation, and regulation.

QUESTIONS AND EXERCISES

1. Gmail uses contextual advertising. The service will scan the contents of e-mail messages and display ads off to the side. Test the "creep out" factor in Gmail—create an account (if you don't already have one), and send messages to yourself with controversial terms in them. Which ones showed ads? Which ones didn't?
2. Google has never built user profiles based on Gmail messages. Ads are served based on a real-time scanning of keywords. Is this enough to make you comfortable with Google's protection of your own privacy? Why or why not?
3. List the negative consequences that could result from the misuse of tracking cookies.
4. What steps does Google take to protect the privacy of user information? What steps has Google taken to give users control over the user data that the firm collects and the ads the users wish to see?
5. Which topics does "Ads Preferences Manager" avoid in its targeting system?
6. Visit Google's Ad Preferences page. Is Google tracking your interests? Do you think the list of interests is accurate? Browse the categories under the "Ad Interest" button. Would you add any of these categories to your profile? Why or why not? What do you gain or lose by taking advantage of Google's "Opt Out" option? Visit rival ad networks. Do you have a similar degree of control? More or less?
7. Visit Google Dashboard. What information is Google collecting about you? Does any of this surprise you? How do you suppose the firm uses this to benefit you? After seeing this information, did you make any changes to the settings in the privacy center? Why or why not?
8. List the types of information that Google might store for an individual. Do you feel that Google is a fair and reliable steward for this information? Are there Google services or other online efforts that you won't use due to privacy concerns? Why?
9. Google's "interest-based advertising" was launched as an opt-out effort. What are the pros and cons for Google, users, advertisers, and AdSense partner sites if Google were to switch to an opt-in system? How would these various constituencies be impacted if the government mandated that users explicitly opt in to third-party cookies and other behavior-tracking techniques?
10. What is Google's unofficial motto?
11. What is "Street View"? Where and on what grounds is it being challenged?
12. Cite two court cases where Google has mounted a vigorous defense of data privacy.
13. *Wired News* quoted a representative of privacy watchdog group, The Center for Digital Democracy, who offered a criticism of online advertising. The representative suggested that online firms were trying to learn "everything about individuals and manipulate their weaknesses" and that the federal government should "investigate the role [that online ads] played in convincing people to take out mortgages they should not have."[66] Do you think online advertising played a significant role in the mortgage crisis? What role do advertisers, ad networks, and content providers have in online advertising oversight? Should this responsibility be any different from oversight in traditional media (television, print, radio)? What guidelines would you suggest?
14. Even well-intentioned firms can compromise user privacy. How have Google's missteps compromised user privacy? As a manager, what steps would you take in developing and deploying information systems that might prevent these kinds of problems from occurring?

9. SEARCH ENGINES, AD NETWORKS, AND FRAUD

LEARNING OBJECTIVES

1. **Be able to identify various types of online fraud, as well as the techniques and technologies used to perpetrate these crimes.**
2. **Understand how firms can detect, prevent, and prosecute fraudsters.**

There's a lot of money to be made online, and this has drawn the attention of criminals and the nefarious. Online fraudsters may attempt to steal from advertisers, harm rivals, or otherwise dishonestly game the system. But bad guys beware—such attempts violate terms-of-service agreements and may lead to prosecution and jail time.

Studying ad-related fraud helps marketers, managers, and technologists understand potential vulnerabilities, as well as the methods used to combat them. This process also builds tech-centric critical thinking, valuation, and risk assessment skills.

Some of the more common types of fraud that are attempted in online advertising include the following:

click fraud

Generating bogus clicks, either for financial gain (enriching fraud), or to attack rivals by draining their online ad budget (depleting fraud).

- *Enriching* **click fraud**—when site operators generate bogus ad clicks to earn PPC income.
- *Enriching impression fraud*—when site operators generate false page views (and hence ad impressions) in order to boost their site's CPM earnings.
- *Depleting click fraud*—clicking a rival's ads to exhaust their PPC advertising budget.
- *Depleting impression fraud*—generating bogus impressions to exhaust a rival's CPM ad budget.
- *Rank-based impression fraud*—on-sites where ad rank is based on click performance, fraudsters repeatedly search keywords linked to rival ads or access pages where rival ads appear. The goal is to generate impressions without clicks. This process lowers the performance rank (quality score) of a rival's ads, possibly dropping ads from rank results, and allowing fraudsters to subsequently bid less for the advertising slots previously occupied by rivals.
- *Disbarring fraud*—attempting to frame a rival by generating bogus clicks or impressions that appear to be associated with the rival, in hopes that this rival will be banned from an ad network or punished in search engine listings.
- *Link fraud (also known as spamdexing or link farming)*—creating a series of bogus Web sites, all linking back to a page, in hopes of increasing that page's results in organic search.
- *Keyword stuffing*—packing a Web site with unrelated keywords (sometimes hidden in fonts that are the same color as a Web site's background) in hopes of either luring users who wouldn't normally visit a Web site, or attracting higher-value contextual ads.

Disturbing stuff, but firms are after the bad guys and they've put their best geeks on the case. Widespread fraud would tank advertiser ROI and crater the online advertising market, so Google and rivals are diligently working to uncover and prosecute the crooks.

9.1 Busting the Bad Guys

On the surface, enriching click fraud seems the easiest to exploit. Just set up a Web site, run PPC ads on the page, and click like crazy. Each click should ring the ad network cash register, and a portion of those funds will be passed on to the perpetrating site owner—*ka ching*! But remember, each visitor is identified by an IP address, so lots of clicks from a single IP make the bad guys easy to spot.

click farms

Recruiting a network of users to engage in click fraud with the goal of spreading IP addresses across several systems and make a fraud effort more difficult to detect.

So organized crime tried to raise the bar, running so-called **click farms** to spread fraud across dozens of IP addresses. *The Times of India* uncovered one such effort where Indian housewives were receiving up to twenty-five cents for each ad click made on fraudster-run Web sites.[67] But an unusually large number of clicks detected as coming from Indian IP addresses foiled these schemes as well.

Fraudsters then moved on to use **botnets or zombie networks**—hordes of surreptitiously infiltrated computers, linked and controlled by rogue software.[68] To create botnets, hackers exploit security holes, spread viruses, or use so-called phishing techniques to trick users into installing software that will lie dormant, awaiting commands from a central location. The controlling machine then sends out tasks for each bot (or zombie), instructing them to visit Web sites and click on ads in a way that mimics real traffic. Botnets can be massive. Dutch authorities once took down a gang that controlled some 1.5 million machines.[69]

botnets or zombie networks

Hordes of surreptitiously infiltrated computers, linked and controlled remotely. This technique is used to perpetrate click fraud, as well as a variety of other computer security crimes.

Scary, but this is where scale, expertise, and experience come in. The more activity an ad network can monitor, the greater the chance that it can uncover patterns that are anomalous. Higher click-through rates than comparable sites? Caught. Too many visits to a new or obscure site? Caught. Clicks that don't fit standard surfing patterns for geography, time, and day? Caught.

Sometimes the goal isn't theft, but sabotage. Google's Ad Traffic Quality Team backtracked through unusual patterns to uncover a protest effort targeted at Japanese credit card firms. Ad clicks were eventually traced to an incendiary blogger who incited readers to search for the Japanese word *kiyashinku* (meaning cashing credit, or credit cards), and to click the credit card firm ads that show up, depleting firm search marketing budgets. Sneaky, but uncovered and shut down, without harm to the advertisers.[70]

Search firm and ad network software can use data patterns and other signals to ferret out most other types of fraud, too, including rank-based impression fraud, spamdexing, and keyword stuffing. While many have tried to up the stakes with increasingly sophisticated attacks, large ad networks have worked to match them, increasing their anomaly detection capabilities across all types of fraud.[71] Here we see another scale and data-based advantage for Google. Since the firm serves more search results and advertisements than its rivals do, it has vastly more information on online activity. And if it knows more about what's happening online than any other firm, it's likely to be first to shut down anyone who tries to take advantage of the system.

Click Fraud: How Bad Is It?

Accounts on the actual rate of click fraud vary widely. Some third-party firms contend that nearly one in five clicks is fraudulent.[72] But Google adamantly disputes these headline-grabbing numbers, claiming that many such reports are based on-site logs that reflect false data from conditions that Google doesn't charge for (e.g., double counting a double click, or adding up repeated use of the browser back button in a way that looks like multiple clicks have occurred). The firm also offers monitoring, analytics, and reporting tools that can uncover this kind of misperceived discrepancy.

Google contends that all invalid clicks (mistakes and fraud) represent less than 10 percent of all clicks, that the vast majority of these clicks are filtered out, and that Google doesn't charge advertisers for clicks flagged as mistakes or suspicious.[73] In fact, Google says their screening bar is so high and so accurate that less than 0.02 percent of clicks are reactively classified as invalid and credited back to advertisers.[74]

So who's right? While it's impossible to identify the intention behind every click, the market ultimately pays for performance. And advertisers are continuing to flock to PPC ad networks (and to Google in particular). While that doesn't mean that firms can stop being vigilant, it does suggest that for most firms, Google seems to have the problem under control.

KEY TAKEAWAYS

- Fraud can undermine the revenue model behind search engines, ad networks, and the ad-based Internet. It also threatens honest competition among rivals that advertise online.
- There are many forms of online fraud, including enriching fraud (meant to line the pockets of the perpetrators), depleting fraud (meant to waste the ad budgets of rivals), disbarring fraud (meant to frame the innocent as fraudsters), and methods to lower rival ad rank performance, or gain search engine ranking algorithms.
- While fraudsters have devised ingenious ways to exploit the system (including click farms and botnets), IP addresses and detailed usage pattern monitoring increasingly reveal bogus activity.
- Fraud rates are widely disputed. However, it is clear that if widespread fraud were allowed to occur, advertisers would see lower ROI from online ad efforts, and Internet business models would suffer. The continued strength of the online advertising market suggests that while fraud may be impossible to stop completely, most fraud is under control.

QUESTIONS AND EXERCISES

1. Why is it difficult for an unscrupulous individual to pull off enriching click fraud simply by setting up a Web site, running ad network ads, and clicking?
2. Why did hackers develop botnets? What advantage do they offer the criminals? How are they detected? Why do larger ad networks have an advantage in click fraud detection?
3. How can you prevent botnet software from inhabiting your computers? Are you reasonably confident that your computer is free from a botnet infection? Why or why not?
4. What are spamdexing and keyword stuffing? What risks does a legitimate business run if it engages in these practices, and if they are discovered by search engines? What would this mean for the career of the manager who thought he could game the system?
5. Which types of fraud can be attempted against search advertising? Which are perpetrated over its ad network?
6. What are the consequences if click fraud were allowed to continue? Does this ultimately help or hurt firms that run ad networks? Why?

10. THE BATTLE UNFOLDS

LEARNING OBJECTIVES

1. **Understand the challenges of maintaining growth as a business and industry mature.**
2. **Recognize how the businesses of many firms in a variety of industries are beginning to converge.**
3. **Critically evaluate the risks and challenges of businesses that Google, Microsoft, and other firms are entering.**
4. **Appreciate the magnitude of this impending competition, and recognize the competitive forces that will help distinguish winners from losers.**

Google has been growing like gangbusters, but the firm's twin engines of revenue growth—ads served on search and through its ad networks—will inevitably mature. And it will likely be difficult for Google to find new growth markets that are as lucrative as these. Emerging advertising outlets such as social networks have lower click-through rates than conventional advertising, and Google has struggled to develop a presence in social media—trends suggesting that Google will have to work harder for less money.

To understand what can happen when maturity hits, look at Microsoft. The House that Gates Built is more profitable than Google, and continues to dominate the incredibly lucrative markets served by Windows and Office. But these markets haven't grown much for over a decade. In industrialized nations, most Windows and Office purchases come not from growth, but when existing users upgrade or buy new machines. And without substantial year-on-year growth, the stock price doesn't move.

FIGURE 14.14 A Comparison of Stock Price Change—Google (GOOG) versus Microsoft (MSFT)

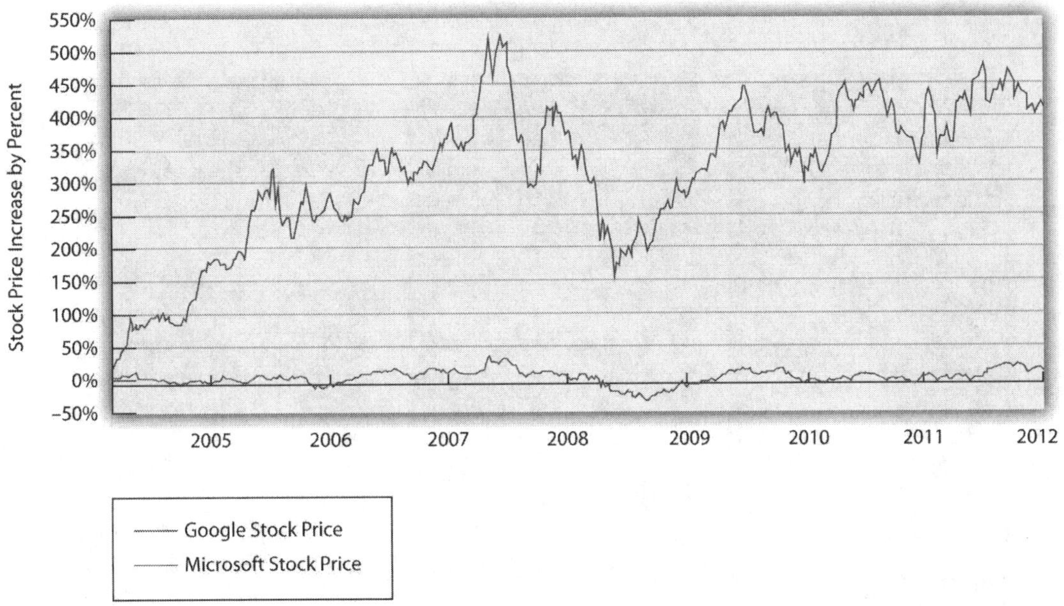

For big firms like Microsoft and Google, pushing stock price north requires not just new markets, but *billion-dollar* ones. Adding even $100 million in new revenues doesn't do much for firms bringing in nearly $70 billion and $38 billion a year, respectively. That's why you see Microsoft swinging for the fences, investing in the uncertain but potentially gargantuan markets of video games, mobile phone software, cloud computing (see Chapter 10), music and video, and of course, search and everything else that fuels online ad revenue. Finding new billion-dollar markets is wonderful, but rare. Apple seems to have done it with the iPad. But trying to unseat a dominant leader possessing strategic resources can be ferociously expensive, with unclear prospects for success. Microsoft's Bing group lost over $2 billion over just nine months, winning almost no share from Google despite the lavish spend.[75]

Search: Google Rules, but It Ain't Over

PageRank is by no means the last word in search, and offerings from Google and its rivals continue to evolve. Google supplements PageRank results with news, photos, video, and other categories. Yahoo! is continually refining its search algorithms and presentation. And Microsoft's third entry into the search market, the "decision engine" Bing, sports nifty tweaks for specific kinds of queries. Restaurant searches in Bing are bundled with ratings stars, product searches show up with reviews and price comparisons, and airline flight searches not only list flight schedules and fares, but also a projection on whether those fares are likely go up or down. The Bing sidebar will surface additional data alongside search results, including (if logged into Facebook) friends that might have input on your query and public social media posts you might be interested in.[76] Bing also comes with a one-hundred-million-dollar marketing budget, showing that Microsoft is serious about search.

New tools like the Wolfram Alpha "knowledge engine" move beyond Web page rankings and instead aggregate data for comparison, formatting findings in tables and graphs. Web sites are also starting to wrap data in invisible tags that can be recognized by search engines, analysis tools, and other services. If a search engine can tell that a number on a restaurant's Web site is, for example, either a street address, an average entrée price, or the seating capacity, it will be much easier for computer programs to accurately categorize, compare, and present this information. This is what geeks are talking about when they refer to the **semantic Web**. Google has begun to draw from several resources on the Web to build its own semantic Web classifications. If you search for "Taj Mahal" on the Web, it presents a summary of the famous Indian landmark, but it also asks if you'd like to see results regarding the Grammy Award–winning musician or the New Jersey casino that also share that same name.[77]

semantic Web

Sites that wrap data in invisible tags that can be recognized by search engines, analysis tools, and other services to make it easier for computer programs to accurately categorize, compare, and present this information.

Google Goggles returns search results by photographing objects. It can even translate foreign language text.

Source: Google.

And who says you need to use words to conduct a search? Google Goggles uses the camera in your mobile phone to "enter" search criteria. Snap a picture of a landmark, book, or piece of artwork, for example, and Google will use that image to retrieve search results. The product can even return translations of foreign text. All signs point to more innovation, more competition, and an increasingly more useful Internet!

Both Google and Microsoft are on a collision course. But there's also an impressive roster of additional firms circling this space, each with the potential to be competitors, collaborators, merger partners, or all of the above. While wounded and shrinking, Yahoo! is still a powerhouse, ranking ahead of Google in some overall traffic statistics. Google's competition with Apple in the mobile phone business prompted Google's then CEO Eric Schmidt to resign from Apple's board of directors. Meanwhile, Google's three-quarters-of-a-billion-dollar purchase of the leading mobile advertiser AdMob was quickly followed by Apple snapping up number two mobile ad firm Quattro Wireless for $275 million. Add in Amazon, Facebook, eBay, Twitter, Salesforce.com, Netflix, the video game industry, telecom and mobile carriers, cable firms, and the major media companies and the next few years have the makings of a big, brutal fight.

10.1 Strategic Issues

As outlined earlier, Google enjoys major scale advantages in search, and network effects in advertising. The firm's dominance helps grow a data asset that can be used in service improvement, all while its expertise in core markets continues to grow over time. But the strength of Google's other competitive resources is less clear.

Within Google's ad network, there are *switching costs* for advertisers and for content providers. Google partners have set up accounts and are familiar with the firm's tools and analytics. Content providers would also need to modify Web sites to replace AdSense or DoubleClick ads with rivals. But choosing Google doesn't cut out the competition. Many advertisers and content providers participate in multiple ad networks, making it easier to shift business from one firm to another. This likely means that Google will have to keep advertisers by offering superior value rather than relying on lock-in.

Another vulnerability may exist with search consumers. While Google's brand is strong, switching costs for search users are incredibly low. Move from Google.com to Bing.com and you actually save two letters of typing!

Still, there are no signs that Google's search leadership is in jeopardy. So far users have been creatures of habit; no rival has offered technology compelling enough to woo away the Googling masses. Defeating Google with some sort of technical advantage will be difficult since Web-based innovation can often be quickly imitated. Google now rolls out over 550 tweaks to its search algorithm annually, with many features mimicking or outdoing innovations from rivals.[78]

The Google Toolbar helps reinforce search habits among those who have it installed, and Google has paid the Mozilla foundation (the folks behind the Firefox browser) upwards of $66 million a year to serve as its default search option for the open source browser.[79] But Google's track record in expanding reach through distribution deals is mixed. The firm spent nearly $1 billion to run ads on MySpace, later stating the deal had not been as lucrative as it had hoped (see Chapter 8). The firm has also spent nearly $1 billion to have Dell preinstall its computers with the Google browser toolbar and Google desktop search products. But Microsoft later inked deals that displaced Google on Dell machines, and it also edged Google out in a five-year search contract with Verizon Wireless.[80] Google has shown that if it can't buy its way into a distribution channel, it can create one. The firm's Web browser, Chrome, has beaten out Internet Explorer to become the number one product used by Web surfers worldwide.[81]

How Big Is Too Big?

Microsoft could benefit from embedding its Bing search engine into its most popular products (imagine putting Bing in the right-mouseclick menu alongside *cut*, *copy*, and *paste*). But with Office above 80 percent and Windows at roughly 90 percent,[82] this seems unlikely.

European antitrust officials have already taken action against Redmond's bundling Windows Media Player and Internet Explorer with Windows. Add in a less favorable antitrust climate in the United States, and tying any of these products to Bing is almost certainly out of bounds. What's not clear is whether regulators would allow Bing to be bundled with less dominant Microsoft offerings, such as mobile phone software, Xbox, and MSN.

Being big isn't enough to violate U.S. antitrust law. Harvard Law's Andrew Gavil says, "You've got to be big, and you have to be bad. You have to be both."[83] This may be a difficult case to make against Google, a firm that has a history of being a relentless supporter of open computing standards. And as mentioned earlier, there can be no forcing users to stick with Google—the firm must continue to win this market on its own merits.

That said, a big firm is a big target for attracting serious scrutiny. Google was forced to abandon a search advertising partnership with Yahoo! after the Justice Department indicated its intention to block the agreement (Yahoo! and Microsoft have since inked a deal to share search technology and ad sales). The Justice Department is also investigating a Google settlement with the Authors' Guild, a deal in which critics have suggested that Google scored a near monopoly on certain book scanning, searching, and data serving rights.[84]

Some suggest regulators may see Google's search dominance as an unfair advantage in promoting its own properties such as YouTube, Google Maps, Google-owned Zagat, and Google+ over those offered by rivals.[85] The toolbar that appears across the top of most Google websites also provides preferred access to Google properties but not rivals—some may argue that these advantages are not unlike Microsoft's use of Windows to promote Media Player and Internet Explorer. While Google may escape all of these investigations, increased antitrust scrutiny is a downside that comes along with the advantages of market-dominating scale.

10.2 More Ads, More Places, More Formats

Google has been a champion of increased Internet access. But altruism aside, more net access also means a greater likelihood of ad revenue.

Google's effort to catalyze Internet use worldwide comes through on multiple fronts. In the United States, Google has supported (with varying degrees of success) efforts to offer free Wi-Fi. Google announced it would offer high-speed, fiber-optic net access to homes in select U.S. cities, with Kansas City, Kansas, and Kansas City, Missouri, chosen for the first rollouts.[86] The experimental network would offer competitively priced Internet access of up to 1GB per second—that's a speed some one hundred times faster than many Americans have access to today. The networks are meant to be open to other service providers and Google hopes to learn and share insights on how to build high-speed networks more efficiently. Google will also be watching to see how access to ultrahigh-speed networks impacts user behavior and fuels innovation. Globally, Google is also a major backer (along with Liberty Global and HSBC) of the O3b satellite network. O3b stands for "the other three billion" of the world's population who currently lack Internet access. O3b plans to have multiple satellites circling the globe, blanketing underserved regions with **low latency** (low delay), high-speed Internet access.[87] With Moore's Law dropping computing costs as world income levels rise, Google hopes to empower the currently disenfranchised masses to start surfing. Good for global economies, good for living standards, and good for Google.

low latency

Low delay.

walled garden

A closed network or single set of services controlled by one dominant firm. Term is often applied to mobile carriers that act as gatekeepers, screening out hardware providers and software services from their networks.

Google has also successfully lobbied the U.S. government to force wireless telecom carriers to be more open, dismantling what are known in the industry as **walled gardens**. Before Google's lobbying efforts, mobile carriers could act as gatekeepers, screening out hardware providers and software services from their networks. Now, paying customers of carriers that operate over the recently allocated U.S. wireless spectrum will have access to a choice of hardware and less restrictive access to Web sites and services. And Google hopes this expands its ability to compete without obstruction.

Another way Google can lower the cost of surfing is by giving away mobile phone and tablet software. That's the thinking behind the firm's Android offering. With Android, Google provides mobile phone vendors with a Linux-based operating system, supporting tools, standards, and an application marketplace akin to Apple's App Store. Android itself isn't ad-supported—there aren't Google ads embedded in the OS. But the hope is that if manufacturers don't have to write their own software, the cost of wireless mobile devices will go down. And cheaper devices mean that more users will have access to the mobile Internet, adding more ad-serving opportunities for Google and its partner sites. Google already controls 97 percent of fast-growing paid search on mobile devices.[88] One analyst estimates that Android should bring in $10 per handset in search advertising by 2012, goosing advertising revenue by about $1.3 billion.[89] If this prediction holds, this would mean Android has helped Google deliver that rare, new billion-dollar opportunity that so many large firms seek.

Developers are now leveraging tailored versions of Android on a wide range of devices, including e-book readers, tablets, televisions, set-top boxes, robots, and automobiles. Google has dabbled in selling ads for television (as well as radio and print), and there may be considerable potential in bringing variants of ad targeting technology, search, and a host of other services across these devices. Google also offers a platform for creating what the firm calls "Chromebooks"—a direct challenge to Windows in the netbook PC market. Powered by a combination of open source Linux and Google's open source Chrome browser, the Chrome OS is specifically designed to provide a lightweight but consistent user interface for applications that otherwise live in the cloud, preferably residing on Google's server farms (see Chapter 10).

10.3 Motorola Mobility

Google's massive, multi-billion dollar cash horde is also allowing the firm to go on a buying spree—gobbling up 57 firms in just the first three quarters of 2011.[90] Google's biggest deal to date was the purchase of Motorola Mobility. This makes Google a mobile phone handset manufacturer. While Google CEO Larry Page has said that Android will remain open and that Motorola Mobility will be run as a separate business,[91] Google's entry into the low-margin handset business may also alienate other potential Android partners.

The deal also gives Google ownership of the leading set-top box manufacturer, with products that sit in roughly 65 percent of US homes with cable TV sets.[92] While Google's plans for the set-top box business are unclear, possibilities could include opening up new markets for existing Internet advertising, and creating new businesses serving targeted video ads. Adding Google TV software into cable set-top boxes might also bring a Google app store to your television. Executing on these possibilities will be challenging, as most cable firms (the customers for Motorola's set-top boxes) have fiercely defended their walled gardens from running apps from Netflix or other potentially threatening services.[93] But Google may find neutral ground for a subset of services that can keep cable providers and television networks happy by sharing in new revenue opportunities.

The $12.5 billion for Motorola also brings in 17,000 patents—a potentially vital resource as big firms sue one another to protect their markets. Apple has leveraged its patents to shut down Samsung tablet sales in Germany and Australia,[94] and Google fears that Cupertino may come knocking, claiming Android is a copy of the heavily patented iPhone. Motorola's patents give Google an intellectual property counterpunch. (A brief side note, IP means *Internet protocol*, but is also often used to refer to *intellectual property*. When see the term IP, be sure to consider the context so you know which IP is being talked about).

10.4 YouTube

It's tough to imagine any peer-produced video site displacing YouTube. Users go to YouTube because there's more content, while amateur content providers go there seeking more users (classic two-sided network effects). This critical advantage was the main reason why, in 2006, Google paid $1.65 billion for what was then just a twenty-month-old start-up. But Google isn't content to let YouTube be simply the home for online amateur hour. The site now "rents" hundreds of TV shows and movies at prices ranging from $.99 to $3.99 It's also been offering seed grants of several million dollars to producers of original content for YouTube.[95] And it even poached a senior Netflix executive to help grow the premium content business.[96]

YouTube's popularity comes at a price. Even with falling bandwidth and storage costs, at forty-eight hours of video uploaded to YouTube *every minute*, the cost to store and serve this content is cripplingly large.[97] Analysts estimate that for YouTube to break even, it would need to achieve an ad CPM of $9.48 on each of the roughly seventy-five billion streams it'll serve up this year. A tough task. Most user-generated content sports CPM rates south of a buck.[98] The specifics of YouTube's financials aren't broken out. Even as a public company, Google can keep mum about YouTube specifics. Says the firm's CFO, "We know our cost position, but nobody else does."[99] It may be in Google's interest to allow others to think of YouTube as more of a money pit than it really is. That perception might keep rivals away longer, allowing the firm to solidify its dominant position while getting the revenue model right.

The explosion of video uploading is also adding to costs as more cell phones become Net-equipped video cameras. YouTube's mobile uploads were up 400 percent in just the first week following the launch of the first video-capturing iPhone.[100] Viewing will also skyrocket as mobile devices and television sets ship with YouTube access (the YouTube division is now home to the Google TV consumer electronics platform), adding to revenue potential. The firm is still experimenting with ad models—these include traditional banner and text ads, plus ads transparently layered across the bottom 20 percent of the screen, *preroll* commercials that appear before the selected video, and more. Google has both the money and time to invest in nurturing this market, and it continues to be hesitant in saturating the media with ads that may annoy users and constrain adoption.

10.5 Google Wallet

Google Wallet is another example of how the search giant is looking to deliver value through mobile devices. Google Wallet allows phones to replace much of the "stuff" inside your wallet. It can be used to pay for goods, store gift cards, collect and redeem coupons and special offers, and manage loyalty programs. To use the service, users simply wave phones at an NFC (near field communication)-equipped payment terminal (with transaction confirmed and secured by typing in a PIN). Fifteen retailers (including Macy's, Subway, Walgreens, Toys "R" Us, Peet's Coffee and Tea, and Footlocker) were announced as payment-accepting partners, and Wallet has the capability to work with some 300,000 retail registers that are already using MasterCard's PayPass contactless payment terminals.[101] Phones will have to be equipped with an NFC chip, and only one model from one carrier was available at announcement, although a limited version of Wallet will be available by using an NFC sticker that can be attached to the back of non-NFC mobile devices. Google also envisions billboards and storefronts that can communicate with Wallet and distribute offers, Web links, and more—just wave your phone at a sign to get a deal. The product is less about becoming the "Bank of Google"—Wallet links to existing credit cards (although Google offers a prepaid card, too), and at rollout Google said there would be no payment fees for the service. But Google hopes payment and other services will be a way to promote new revenue channels, such as growing its Google Offers coupon service, allowing it to compete with daily deal sites like Groupon and LivingSocial.[102] . Google could sell advertisers couponing services distributed via search, online ads, NFC-equipped signs, and geolocation; have the deals and promotions delivered to a Google Wallet account; and allow deals to be quickly redeemed via NFC swipe at a retailer. Could this grow to be a billion-dollar market, too? Emerging technologies like NFC are sure to attract competitors and innovation.

NFC

Near field communication; a short-range, wireless communication standard. NFC is being used to support contactless payment and transactions over NFC-equipped mobile devices.

FIGURE 14.16 Google Wallet

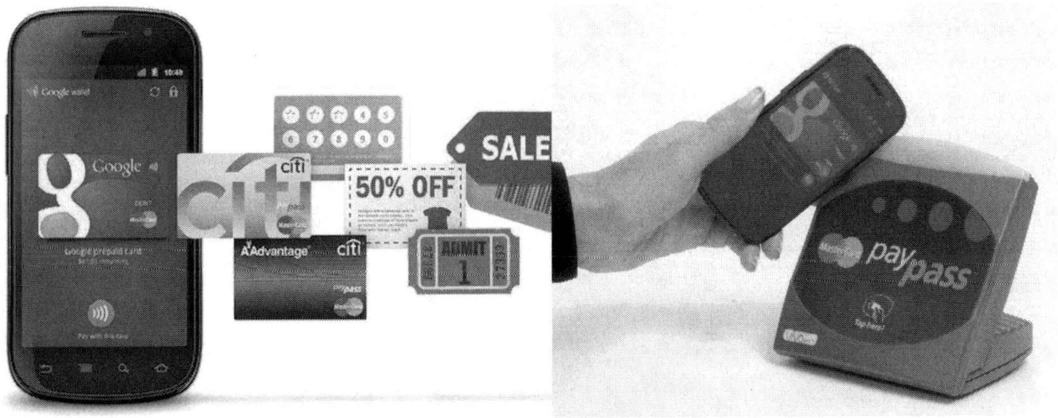

Source: Google.

10.6 Social: Google+

Google's success in social media has been mixed. Its two biggest successes—YouTube and Blogger—were both acquired from other firms. Internally-developed Orkut has for years ranked as the top social network in Brazil but has limited success in only a few other nations; and Google-hatched Buzz and Wave were both dismal failures. But with Google+ the firm may have finally created a service with staying power.

Google+ rolled out in summer 2011 as an integrated collection of social products associated with a user's Google profile. Stream is a newsfeed. Sparks is a recommendation engine. Hangouts is a video chat service that can support groups, and enables screen sharing and group document editing. Huddle offers group texting. Circles helps manage sharing contacts (so you can share a given item with just 'friends,' 'business contacts,' or any other sharing circles you want to create). And Photos is an image sharing service that leverages the firm's Picasa offering. This allows Google to offer up a set of features similar to those found in Facebook, Twitter, Tumblr, Skype, and Group.me. And initial Google+ features were just a start—the firm has been hard at work adding Games, Zagat reviews, Questions, services that allow businesses to get in on the socializing, and more.

Learning from earlier failure, Google+ got a lot of things right. The interface design was praised (Andy Hertzfeld, a member of the original Macintosh design team, was behind design efforts), and the new features were tightly integrated with other Google products. A toolbar that runs on top of most Google services means that Google+ is just a click away. Circles were easily built from Gmail contacts, but offered a degree of sharing control, customization, and privacy that distinguished it as a solid alternative to Facebook and other offerings. Despite being launched only in invitation-only beta, Google+ attracted some 10 million members in just its first two weeks, making it the fastest growing social network of all time.[103] While growing faster than Facebook and Twitter did at this stage, the Google+ user base is still very far behind both. If Google+ is a hit, the firm could gain an opportunity to serve more ads, grow additional revenue lines (e.g. a game currency to rival Facebook Credits), and gain additional data and insight that can be used to help in search, content recommendations, and ad targeting. Competing in winner-take-most markets where network effects dominate will be tough, but Google brings a number of assets to the table and seems committed to growing the effort. CEO Larry Page has event stated Google will tie employee bonuses to the success of the firm's social efforts.

What's Google Up To?

With all this innovation, it's tough to stay current with Google's cutting edge product portfolio. But the company does offer "beta" releases of some projects, and invites the public to try out and comment on its many experiments. To see a current list of many of the firm's offerings, check out http://www.google.com/options.

Experimentation and innovation are deeply ingrained in Google's tech-centric culture, and this can produce both hits and misses. While Google introduces scores of products each year,[104] it has also cancelled several along the way, including Jaiku (which couldn't beat Twitter), Google Video (which was superseded by the YouTube acquisition), Google Buzz (a social networking flop), Google Wave (despite its splashy launch), and a bunch more you've likely not heard of, like Dodgeball, Notebook, Catalog Search, and Mashup Editor.[105] But the firm's relentless commitment to developing new products and services, coupled with wildly profitable core businesses, allows Google to survive the flops and push the edge of what's possible. The firm's secretive lab, Google X, is working on all sorts of gee-whiz offerings, including self-driving cars, space elevators, and refrigerators that can order your groceries when they run low.[106] As another example, consider the firm's Project Glass, which looks to introduce a new screen for information—one that you wear like a pair of glasses, providing a heads-up display for queries and information.

Project Glass One Day

View the video online at: http://www.youtube.com/v/9c6W4CCU9M4

10.7 Apps and Innovation

Google's "apps" are mostly Web-based software-as-a-service offerings. Apps include an Office-style suite that sports a word processor, presentation tool, and spreadsheet, all served through a browser. While initially clunky, the products are constantly being refined. The spreadsheet product, for example, has been seeing new releases every two weeks, with features such as graphing and pivot tables inching it closer in capabilities to desktop alternatives.[107] And new browser standards, such as HTML 5, will make it even easier for what lives in the browser to mimic what you're currently using on your desktop, even allowing apps to be used offline when net access isn't available. That'll be critical as long as Internet access is less reliable than your hard drive, but online collaboration is where these products can really excel (no pun intended). Most Google apps allow not only group viewing, but also collaborative editing, common storage, and version control. And it seems Google isn't stopping at Office files, video, and photos—Google's cloud will hold your music and other media, too. Google's Play service allows you to upload thousands of the tracks that you already own to what some have called a sort of "locker in the sky." Users can stream the tracks over the Internet, sync frequently played songs and albums for offline play, and even share tracks with friends via Google+ (friends usually get one full listen for free).[108] And Google Drive offers several gigs of free cloud-based storage that can be shared and synced across computers.

Unknown is how much money Google will make off all of this. Consumers and small businesses have free access to these products, with usage for up to fifty users funded by in-app ads. But is there much of a market serving ads to people working on spreadsheets? Enterprises can gain additional, ad-free licenses for a fee. While users have been reluctant to give up Microsoft Office, many have individually migrated to Google's Web-based e-mail and calendar tools. Google's enterprise apps group will now do the same thing for organizations, acting as a sort of outsourcer by running e-mail, calendar, and other services for a firm and all while handling upgrades, spam screening, virus protection, backup, and other administrative burdens. Virgin America, Jaguar, National Geographic, and Genentech are among the Google partners that have signed on to make the firm's app offerings available to thousands. Google Play doesn't just hold your music; it's also an iTunes-like marketplace where you can buy all sorts of media: movies, TV shows, books, and apps. Google Drive is free for the first 5 GB, but if you want more, you'll have to pay.

And of course, Microsoft won't let Google take this market without a fight. Microsoft has experimented with offering a simplified, free, ad-supported, Web-based, online options for Word, Excel, PowerPoint, and OneNote; Office 365 offers more robust online tools, ad free, for a low monthly subscription cost; and Microsoft can also migrate an organization's applications like e-mail and calendaring off corporate computers and onto Microsoft's server farms.

Google's Global Reach and the Censorship Challenge

In the spring of 2010, Google clashed publicly with the government of China, a nation that many consider to be the world's most potentially lucrative market. For the previous four years and at the request of the Chinese government, Google had censored results returned from the firm's google.cn domain (e.g., an image search on the term "Tiananmen" showed kite flying on google.cn, but protestors confronting tanks on google.com).

However, when reports surfaced of Chinese involvement in hacking attempts against Google and at least twenty other U.S. companies and human rights dissidents, the firm began routing google.cn traffic outside the country. The days that followed saw access to a variety of Google services blocked within China, restricted by what many call the government's "Great Firewall of China."

Speaking for Google, the firm's deputy counsel Nicole Wong states, "We are fundamentally guided by the belief that more information for our users is ultimately better." But even outside of China, Google continues to be challenged by its interest in providing unfettered access to information on one hand, and the radically divergent laws, regulations, and cultural expectations of host nations on the other. Google has been prompted to block access to its services at some point in at least twenty-five of one hundred countries the firm operates in.

The kind of restriction varies widely. French, German, and Polish law requires Google to prohibit access to Nazi content. Turkish law requires Google to block access to material critical of the nation's founder. Access in Thailand is similarly blocked from content mocking that nation's king. In India, Google has been prompted to edit forums or remove comments flagged by the government as violating restrictions against speech that threatens public order or is otherwise considered indecent or immoral. At the extreme end of the spectrum, Vietnam, Saudi Arabia, and Iran, have aggressively moved to restrict access to wide swaths of Internet content.

Google usually waits for governments to notify it that offensive content must be blocked. This moves the firm from actively to reactively censoring access. Still, this doesn't isolate the company from legal issues. Italian courts went after YouTube executives after a video showing local teenagers tormenting an autistic child remained online long enough to garner thousands of views.

In the United States, Google's organic results often reveal content that would widely be viewed as offensive. In the most extreme cases, the firm has run ads alongside these results with the text, "Offensive Search Results: We're disturbed about these results as well. Please read our note here."

Other Internet providers have come under similar scrutiny, and technology managers will continue to confront similar ethically charged issues as they consider whether to operate in new markets. But Google's dominant position puts it at the center of censorship concerns. The threat is ultimately that the world's chief information gateway might also become "the Web's main muzzle."

It's not until considered in its entirety that one gets a sense of what Google has the potential to achieve. It's possible that increasing numbers of users worldwide will adopt light, cheap netbooks and other devices powered by free Google software (Android, Google's Chrome browser, Google TV, and Chrome OS). Productivity apps, e-mail, calendaring, and collaboration tools will all exist in the cloud, accessible through any browser, with files stored on Google's servers in a way that minimizes hard drive needs. Google will entertain you, help you find the information you need, help you shop, handle payment, and more. And the firms you engage online may increasingly turn to Google to replace their existing hardware and software infrastructure with corporate computing platforms like Google Apps Engine (see Chapter 10). All of this would be based on open standards, but switching costs, scale, and increasing returns from expertise across these efforts could yield enormous advantages.

Studying Google allowed us to learn about search and the infrastructure that powers this critical technology. We've studied the business of ads, covering search advertising, ad networks, and ad targeting in a way that blends strategic and technology issues. And we've covered the ethical, legal, growth, and competitive challenges that Google and its rivals face. Studying Google in this context should not only help you understand what's happening today, it should also help you develop critical thinking skills for assessing the opportunities and threats that will emerge across industries as technologies continue to evolve.

KEY TAKEAWAYS

- For over a decade, Google's business has been growing rapidly, but that business is maturing.
- Slower growth will put pressure on the firm's stock price, so a firm Google's size will need to pursue very large, risky, new markets—markets that are also attractive to well-financed rivals, smaller partners, and entrepreneurs.
- Rivals continue to innovate in search. Competing with technology is extremely difficult since it is often easy for a firm to mimic the innovations of a pioneer with a substitute offering. Microsoft, with profits to invest in infrastructure, advertising, and technology, may pose Google's most significant, conventional threat.
- Although Microsoft has many distribution channels (Windows, Internet Explorer, Office) for its search and other services, European and U.S. regulators will likely continue to prevent the firm from aggressive product and service bundling.
- Google is investing heavily in methods that promote wider Internet access. These include offering free software to device manufacturers and several telecommunications and lobbying initiatives meant to lower the cost of getting online. The firm hopes that more users spending more time online will allow it to generate more revenue through ads and perhaps other services.
- Google Wallet uses NFC communications to allow mobile phones to make credit and debit card payments, manage loyalty programs, redeem coupons, and more. Payments are linked to existing credit cards. Google will not charge for transaction fees but plans to use Wallet as a way to sell other services such as those offered by its Google Offers coupon and deal program.
- YouTube demonstrates how a firm can create a large and vastly influential business in a short period of time but also that businesses that host and serve large files of end-user content can be costly.
- Google, Microsoft, and smaller rivals are also migrating applications to the Web, allowing Office-style software to execute within a browser, with portions of this computing experience and storage happening off a user's computer, "in the cloud" of the Internet. Revenue models for this business are also uncertain.
- With scale and influence comes increased governmental scrutiny. Google has increasingly become a target of antitrust regulators. The extent of this threat is unclear. Google's extreme influence is clear. However, the firm's software is based on open standards; competitors have a choice in ad networks, search engines, and other services; switching costs are relatively low; users and advertisers aren't locked into exclusive contracts for the firm's key products and services; and there is little evidence of deliberate, predatory pricing or other "red-flag" activity that usually brings government regulation.

QUESTIONS AND EXERCISES

1. Perform identical queries on both Google and on rival search engines (Bing, Yahoo!, Blekko, and DuckDuckGo are all possibilities). Try different categories (research for school projects, health, business, sports, entertainment, local information). Which sites do you think give you the better results? Why? Would any of these results cause you to switch to one search engine versus the other?
2. Investigate new services that attempt to extend the possibilities for leveraging online content. Visit Wolfram Alpha and any other such efforts that intrigue you. Assume the role of a manager and use these engines to uncover useful information. Assume your role as a student and see if these tools provide valuable information for this or other classes. Are you likely to use these tools in the future? Why or why not? Under what circumstances are they useful and when do they fall short?
3. Assume the role of an industry analyst: Consider the variety of firms mentioned in this section that may become competitors or partners. Create a chart listing your thoughts on which firms are likely to collaborate and work together and which firms are likely to compete. What are the advantages or risks in these collaborations for the partners involved? Do you think any of these firms are "acquisition bait?" Defend your predictions and be prepared to discuss them with your class.
4. Assume the role of an IT manager: To the extent that you can, evaluate online application offerings by Google, Microsoft, and rivals. In your opinion, are these efforts ready for prime time? Why or why not? Would you recommend that a firm choose these applications? Are there particular firms or users that would find these alternatives particularly appealing? Would you ever completely replace desktop offerings with online ones? Why or why not?
5. Does it make sense for organizations to move their e-mail and calendaring services off their own machines and pay Google, Microsoft, or someone else to run them? Why or why not?
6. What are Chrome, the Chrome OS, and Android? Are these software products successful in their respective categories? Investigate the state of the market for products that leverage any of these software offerings. Would you say that they are successful? Why or why not? What do you think the outlook is for Chrome, the Chrome OS, and Android? As an IT manager, would you recommend products based on this software? As an investor, do you think it continues to make sense for Google to develop these efforts? Why or why not?
7. What will it take for Google Wallet to be successful? What challenges must the effort overcome?
8. Research the current state of Google Wallet's competitors. What competing efforts exist? Which firms are best positioned to dominate this market? How large could this market become?
9. Google's unofficial motto is "Don't be evil." But sometimes it's challenging for managers to tell what path is "most right" or "least wrong." Google operates in countries that require the firm to screen and censor results. Short term, this is clearly a limitation on freedom of speech. But long-term, access to the Internet could catalyze economic development and spread information in a way that leads to more democratization. Investigate and consider both of these arguments and be prepared to argue the case either for limiting work in speech-limiting countries or working within them as a potential agent of change. What other pressures is a publicly traded firm under to choose one path or the other? Which path would you choose and why?
10. Investigate Google+. Are you a Google+ user? Why or why not? What will it take for Google+ to attract users and usage? Compared with rivals, how has the service performed? What advantages does Google have that it can leverage with Google+? What competitive advantages do rivals have over Google?
11. Why did Google acquire Motorola Mobility? What benefits does the firm gain through the acquisition? What risks does the acquisition present?
12. Investigate how Google TV has performed on the market. Why does Google offer a TV product? How might the firm make money from this effort? What obstacles does the firm have to overcome in order for Google TV to grow?

ENDNOTES

1. C. Li, "Why Google's One-Trick Pony Struggles to Learn New Tricks," *Harvard Business Publishing*, May 2009.
2. S. Levy, "The Secrets of Googlenomics," *Wired*, June 2009.
3. J. Pontin, "But Who's Counting?" *Technology Review*, March/April 2009.
4. C. Sherman, "Report: Google Leads U.S. Search Advertising Market With 76% Market Share," *Search Engine Land*, January 20, 2009.
5. L. Baker, "Google Now Controls 69% of Online Advertising Market," *Search Engine Journal*, March 31, 2008. Another study says in 2011 Google controlled 54 percent—significant given the rise of Facebook and other online ad outlets. See J. Edwards, "How Google Takes 54 Cents of Every Dollar Spent on Web Advertising," *BNET*, May 27, 2011.
6. L. Rao, "Guess Which Brand Is Now Worth $100 Billion?" *TechCrunch*, April 30, 2009.
7. Adapted from Experian Hitwise, "Top Search Engine Volume, All Categories, 4 Weeks Ending June 2, 2012."
8. D. Weldon, "Google's Power Play," *EnergyDigital*, August 30, 2007.
9. L. Wolgemuth, "Forget the Recession, I Want a Better Chair," *U.S. News and World Report*, April 28, 2008.
10. B. Casnocha, "Success on the Side," *The American: The Journal of the American Enterprise Institute*, April 24, 2009.
11. G. Duncan, "Pay Your Way to the Top of Search Results with Google Shopping," *Digital Trends*, June 1, 2012.
12. S. Levy, "Inside the Box," *Wired*, March 2010.
13. D. Segal, "The Dirty Little Secrets of Search," *New York Times*, February 12, 2011.
14. D. Segal, "Online Seller Who Bullied Customers Pleads Guilty," *New York Times*, May 12, 2011.
15. D. Segal, "The Dirty Little Secrets of Search," *New York Times*, February 12, 2011.
16. D. Sullivan, "Google's Results Get More Personal with 'Search Plus Your World,'" *Search Engine Land*, January 10, 2012.
17. A. Wright, "Exploring a 'Deep Web' That Google Can't Grasp," *New York Times*, February 23, 2009.
18. Most Web sites do have a link where you can submit a Web site for indexing, and doing so can help promote the discovery of your content.
19. M. Liedtke, "Google Reigns as World's Most Powerful 10-Year-Old," *Associated Press*, September 5, 2008.
20. David F. Carr, "How Google Works," *Baseline*, July 6, 2006.
21. R. Katz, "Tech Titans Building Boom," *IEEE Spectrum* 46, no. 2 (February 1, 2009).
22. R. Miller, "Google Invests $890 Million in Data Centers," *Data Center Knowledge*, April 15, 2011.
23. S. Shankland, "Google Unlocks Once-Secret Server," *CNET*, April 1, 2009.
24. S. Bruce, "Google Says User Data Aids Flu Detection," *eHealthInsider*, May 25, 2009.
25. "American Teenagers Spend More Time Online Than Watching Television," *MediaWeek*, June 19, 2008; A. Hendry, "Connected Aussies Spend More Time Online Than Watching TV," *Computerworld Australia*, May 21, 2008; and "Brits Spend More Time Online Than Watching TV," *BigMouthMedia*, July 12, 2007.
26. M. Tobias, "Newspapers under Siege," *Philstar*, May 18, 2009.
27. For a more detailed overview of the limitations in online ad measurement, see L. Rao, "Guess Which Brand Is Now Worth $100 Billion?" *TechCrunch*, April 30, 2009.
28. S. Elliott, "More Agencies Investing in Marketing with a Click," *New York Times*, March 14, 2006.
29. Google, "Google Announces Fourth Quarter and Fiscal Year 2008 Results," press release, January 22, 2009.
30. D. Vise, "Google's Decade," *Technology Review*, September 12, 2008.
31. S. Levy, "The Secrets of Googlenomics," *Wired*, June 2009.
32. S. Olsen, "Google, Yahoo Bury the Legal Hatchet," *CNET*, August 9, 2004.
33. Google, *Marketing and Advertising Using Google: Targeting Your Advertising to the Right Audience* (Boston: Cengage Learning, 2007).
34. S. Levy, "The Secrets of Googlenomics," *Wired*, June 2009.
35. C. Mann, "How Click Fraud Could Swallow the Internet," *Wired*, January 2006.
36. Google, "Google Announces Fourth Quarter and Fiscal Year 2008 Results," press release, January 22, 2009.
37. B. Tedeschi, "Google's Shadow Payroll Is Not Such a Secret Anymore," *New York Times*, January 16, 2006.
38. R. Rothenberg, "The Internet Runs on Ad Billions," *BusinessWeek*, April 10, 2008.
39. A. Overholt, "Search for Tomorrow," *Fast Company*, December 19, 2007.
40. L. Baker, "Google Now Controls 69% of Online Advertising Market," *Search Engine Journal*, March 31, 2008.
41. See Interactive Advertising Bureau Ad Unit Guidelines for details at http://www.iab.net/iab_products_and_industry_services/1421/1443/1452.
42. M. Shields, "Exclusive: Microsoft to Shutter Massive," *AdWeek*, October 8, 2010.
43. M. Moss, "These Web Sites Know Who You Are," *ZDNet UK*, October 13, 1999.
44. M. Moss, "These Web Sites Know Who You Are," *ZDNet UK*, October 13, 1999.
45. R. Singel, "Online Behavioral Targeting Targeted by Feds, Critics," *Wired News*, June 3, 2009.
46. R. Hof, "Behavioral Targeting: Google Pulls Out the Stops," *BusinessWeek*, March 11, 2009.
47. R. Singel, "Online Behavioral Targeting Targeted by Feds, Critics," *Wired News*, June 3, 2009.
48. S. Hansell, "A Guide to Google's New Privacy Controls," *New York Times*, March 12, 2009.
49. R. Mitchell, "What Google Knows about You," *Computerworld*, May 11, 2009.
50. M. Helft, "BITS; Google Lets Users See a Bit of Selves" *New York Times*, November 9, 2009.
51. R. Mitchell, "What Google Knows about You," *Computerworld*, May 11, 2009.
52. "Policies and Principles," *Google*, http://www.google.com/policies/privacy/ (accessed June 11, 2012).
53. R. Mitchell, "What Google Knows about You," *Computerworld*, May 11, 2009.
54. C. Boulton, "Google Privacy Policy Changes are Live: Here are Your Options," *eWeek*, March 1, 2012.
55. J. Kincaid, "Google Privacy Blunder Shares Your Docs without Permission," *TechCrunch*, March 7, 2009.
56. A. Gold, "Keep Your Buzz to Yourself: Google Misjudged Its Users' Right to Privacy," *The Harvard Crimson*, February 22, 2010.
57. G. Gross, "Lawmakers Ask for FTC Investigation of Google Buzz," *PCWorld*, March 29, 2010.
58. A. Oreskovic, "Google Admits to Broader Collection of Personal Data," *Washington Post*, October 23, 2010.
59. D. Goldman, "Major Security Flaw Found in Android Phones," *CNN*, May 18, 2011.
60. T. Kranzit, "Google Fired Engineer for Privacy Breach," *CNet*, September 14, 2010.
61. D. Basulto, "Google, Safari, and Our Final Privacy Wake-Up Call," *The Washington Post*, February 22, 2012.
62. R. Mitchell, "What Google Knows about You," *Computerworld*, May 11, 2009.
63. A. Broache, "Judge: Google Must Give Feds Limited Access to Records," *CNET*, March 17, 2006.
64. D. Rushe, "Google Accuses China of Interfering with Gmail E-mail System," *Guardian*, March 20, 2011.
65. L. Sumagaysay, "Not Everyone Likes the (Google Street) View," *Good Morning Silicon Valley*, May 20, 2009.
66. R. Singel, "Online Behavioral Targeting Targeted by Feds, Critics," *Wired News*, June 3, 2009.
67. N. Vidyasagar, "India's Secret Army of Online Ad 'Clickers,'" *Times of India*, May 3, 2004.
68. C. Mann, "How Click Fraud Could Swallow the Internet," *Wired*, January 2006.
69. T. Sanders, "Dutch Botnet Gang Facing Jail," *IT News Australia*, January 18, 2007; and N. Daswani and M. Stoppleman, "The Anatomy of Clickbot" (paper, Proceedings of the First Conference on First Workshop on Hot Topics in Understanding Botnets, Cambridge, MA, April 11–13, 2007).
70. M. Jakobsson and Z. Ramzan, *Crimeware: Understanding New Attacks and Defenses* (Cupertino, CA: Symantec Press, 2008).
71. M. Jakobsson and Z. Ramzan, *Crimeware: Understanding New Attacks and Defenses* (Cupertino, CA: Symantec Press, 2008).
72. S. Hamner, "Pay-per-Click Advertisers Combat Costly Fraud," *New York Times*, May 12, 2009.
73. M. Lafsky, "Google and Click Fraud: Behind the Numbers," *New York Times*, February 27, 2008.
74. M. Jakobsson and Z. Ramzan, *Crimeware: Understanding New Attacks and Defenses* (Cupertino, CA: Symantec Press, 2008).
75. D. Goldman, "Microsoft Profits Soars 31% on Strong Office and Kinect Sales," CNNMoney, April 28, 2011.
76. R. Metz, "With New Look, Bing Gets More Organized, Social," *Technology Review*, May 10, 2012.
77. D. Pogue, "Going Beyond Search, Into Fetch," *New York Times*, May 23, 2012.
78. S. Levy, "Inside the Box," *Wired*, March 2010.
79. S. Shankland, "Thanks, Google: Mozilla Revenue Hits $75 Million," *CNET*, November 19, 2008.
80. N. Wingfield, "Microsoft Wins Key Search Deals," *Wall Street Journal*, January 8, 2009.
81. D. Ionescu, "Google Chrome Overtakes Internet Explorer," *PCWorld*, May 21, 2012.
82. Data source: http://marketshare.hitslink.com; and E. Montalbano, "Forrester: Micosoft Office in No Danger from Competitors," *InfoWorld*, June 4, 2009.

83. S. Lohr and M. Helft, "New Mood in Antitrust May Target Google," *New York Times*, May 18, 2009.
84. S. Wildstrom, "Google Book Search and the Dog in the Manger," *BusinessWeek*, April 18, 2009.
85. F. Vogelstein, "Why Is Obama's Top Antitrust Cop Gunning for Google?" *Wired*, July 20, 2009.
86. L. Horsley, "KC Council Unanimously Approves Deal with Google," *Kansas City Star*, May 19, 2011.
87. O. Malik, "Google Invests in Satellite Broadband Startup," *GigaOM*, September 9, 2008.
88. "Google Manages 97 Percent of Paid Mobile Search, 40 Pct of Google Maps Usage Is Mobile," *Mobile Marketing Watch*, March 14, 2011.
89. G. Sterling, "Google Will Make $10 Per Android User in 2012: Report," *SearchEngineLand*, February 9, 2011.
90. E. Rusli, "For Google, A New High in Deal-Making," The New York Times, Oct. 27, 2011.
91. J. Cox, "CEO Larry Page Blogs On Why Google's Buying Motorola Mobility," ComputerWorld, Aug. 15, 2011.
92. T. Spangler, "Does Google Actually Have a Plan for Motorola's Cable Business?", Multichannel News, Aug. 15, 2011.
93. R. Lawler and R. Kim, "With Motorola, Google TV Just Got a Huge Shot in the Arm," GigaOm, Aug. 15, 2011.
94. M. Ricknäs, "Motorola Gets Injunction Against Apple in Germany," PC World, Nov. 7, 2011.
95. M. Learmonth, "YouTube's Premium-Content Strategy Starts to Take Shape," AdAge, March 14, 2011.
96. D. Chmielewski, "YouTube counting on former Netflix exec to help it turn a profit." Los Angeles Times. May 31, 2011.
97. J. Roettgers, "YouTube Users Upload 48 Hours of Video Every Minute," GigaOm, May 25, 2011.
98. B. Wayne, "YouTube Is Doomed," Silicon Alley Insider, April 9, 2009.
99. "How Can YouTube Survive?" Independent, July 7, 2009.
100. J. Kincaid, "YouTube Mobile Uploads Up 400% Since iPhone 3GS Launch," TechCrunch, June 25, 2009.
101. D. Melanson, "Google Wallet Mobile Payment Service, Google Offers Announced," *Engadget*, May 26, 2011; E. Hamburger, "Google Introduces Wallet, Google Wallet Works at Over 300,000 MasterCard PayPass Merchants," *BusinessInsider*, May 26, 2011.
102. H. Tsukayama, "Google Wallet: Search Giant Introduces Automatic Cellphone Payment System," The Washington Past, May 26, 2011.
103. D. Goldman, "Google+ Grows to 10 Million Users," Fortune, July 14, 2011. M. Schuster, M. Schuster, "Report: Google+ the Fastest-Growing Social Network Ever," Minyanville, July 12, 2011.
104. M. Shiels, "Google Unveils 'Smarter Search,'" BBC News, May 13, 2009.
105. R. Needleman, "Google Killing Jaiku, Dodgeball, Notebook, Other Projects," CNET, January 14, 2009.
106. C. C. Miller and N. Bolton, "Google's Lab of Wildest Dreams," The New York Times, Nov. 13, 2011.
107. D. Girouard, "Google Inc. Presentation" (Bank of America and Merrill Lynch 2009 Technology Conference, New York, June 4, 2009).
108. D. Murph, "Google Music Beta Walkthrough: What It Is and How It Works (Video)," *Engadget*, May 11, 2011.

Index